T0345114

Applications of Machine Learning in UAV Networks

Jahan Hassan
Central Queensland University, Australia

Saeed Alsamhi
Insight Centre for Data Analytics, University of Galway, Ireland

A volume in the Advances in Computational
Intelligence and Robotics (ACIR) Book Series

Published in the United States of America by
    IGI Global
    Engineering Science Reference (an imprint of IGI Global)
    701 E. Chocolate Avenue
    Hershey PA, USA 17033
    Tel: 717-533-8845
    Fax: 717-533-8661
    E-mail: cust@igi-global.com
    Web site: http://www.igi-global.com

Library of Congress Cataloging-in-Publication Data

Names: Hassan, Jahan, 1973- editor. | Alsamhi, Saeed, 1985- editor.
Title: Applications of machine learning in UAV networks / edited by Jahan
   Hassan, Saeed Alsamhi.
Description: Hershey, PA : Engineering Science Reference, [2024] | Includes
   bibliographical references and index. | Summary: "This book provides
   readers with a comprehensive understanding of the various application
   possibilities for machine learning in UAV networks"-- Provided by
   publisher.
Identifiers: LCCN 2023041801 (print) | LCCN 2023041802 (ebook) | ISBN
   9798369305782 (h/c) | ISBN 9798369305799 (s/c) | ISBN 9798369305805
   (ebook)
Subjects: LCSH: Drone aircraft--Industrial applications. | Drone aircraft
   in remote sensing--Data processing. | Machine learning.
Classification: LCC TL685.35 .A67 2024 (print) | LCC TL685.35 (ebook) |
   DDC 006.3/1--dc23/eng/20240216
LC record available at https://lccn.loc.gov/2023041801
LC ebook record available at https://lccn.loc.gov/2023041802

This book is published in the IGI Global book series Advances in Computational Intelligence and Robotics (ACIR) (ISSN: 2327-0411; eISSN: 2327-042X)

British Cataloguing in Publication Data
A Cataloguing in Publication record for this book is available from the British Library.

All work contributed to this book is new, previously-unpublished material. The views expressed in this book are those of the authors, but not necessarily of the publisher.

For electronic access to this publication, please contact: eresources@igi-global.com.

Advances in Computational Intelligence and Robotics (ACIR) Book Series

Ivan Giannoccaro
University of Salento, Italy

ISSN:2327-0411
EISSN:2327-042X

MISSION

While intelligence is traditionally a term applied to humans and human cognition, technology has progressed in such a way to allow for the development of intelligent systems able to simulate many human traits. With this new era of simulated and artificial intelligence, much research is needed in order to continue to advance the field and also to evaluate the ethical and societal concerns of the existence of artificial life and machine learning.

The **Advances in Computational Intelligence and Robotics (ACIR) Book Series** encourages scholarly discourse on all topics pertaining to evolutionary computing, artificial life, computational intelligence, machine learning, and robotics. ACIR presents the latest research being conducted on diverse topics in intelligence technologies with the goal of advancing knowledge and applications in this rapidly evolving field.

COVERAGE

- Computational Intelligence
- Heuristics
- Robotics
- Adaptive and Complex Systems
- Artificial Life
- Algorithmic Learning
- Intelligent Control
- Neural Networks
- Cognitive Informatics
- Synthetic Emotions

IGI Global is currently accepting manuscripts for publication within this series. To submit a proposal for a volume in this series, please contact our Acquisition Editors at Acquisitions@igi-global.com or visit: http://www.igi-global.com/publish/.

Titles in this Series

For a list of additional titles in this series, please visit: http://www.igi-global.com/book-series/advances-computational-intelligence-robotics/73674

Handbook of Research on AI and ML for Intelligent Machines and Systems

Brij B. Gupta (Asia University, Taichung, Taiwan & Lebanese American University, Beirut, Lebanon) and Francesco Colace (University of Salerno, Italy)

Engineering Science Reference • © 2024 • 503pp • H/C (ISBN: 9781668499993) • US $380.00

Advances in Explainable AI Applications for Smart Cities

Mangesh M. Ghonge (Sandip Institute of Technology and Research Centre, India) Nijalingappa Pradeep (Bapuji Institute of Engineering and Technology, India) Noor Zaman Jhanjhi (School of Computer Science and Engineering, Faculty of Innovation and Technology, Taylor's University, Malaysia) and Praveen M Kulkarni (KLS Gogte Institute of Technology, India)

Engineering Science Reference • © 2024 • 300pp • H/C (ISBN: 9781668463611) • US $270.00

Perspectives on Artificial Intelligence in Times of Turbulence Theoretical Background to Applications

Nuno Geada (ISCTE, University Institute of Lisboa, Portugal) and George Leal Jamil (Informações em Rede C e T Ltda., Brazil)

Engineering Science Reference • © 2024 • 232pp • H/C (ISBN: 9781668498149) • US $300.00

Artificial Intelligence in the Age of Nanotechnology

Wassim Jaber (ESPCI Paris - PSL, France)

Engineering Science Reference • © 2024 • 330pp • H/C (ISBN: 9798369303689) • US $300.00

Application and Adoption of Robotic Process Automation for Smart Cities

R.K. Tailor (Manipal University Jaipur, India)

Engineering Science Reference • © 2023 • 226pp • H/C (ISBN: 9781668471937) • US $270.00

Deterministic and Stochastic Approaches in Computer Modeling and Simulation

Radi Petrov Romansky (Technical University of Sofia, Bulgaria) and Nikolay Lyuboslavov Hinov (Technical University of Sofia, Bulgaria)

Engineering Science Reference • © 2023 • 513pp • H/C (ISBN: 9781668489475) • US $265.00

Technological Tools for Predicting Pregnancy Complications

D. Satishkumar (Nehru Institute of Technology, India) and P. Maniiarasan (Nehru Institute of Engineering and Technology, India)

Engineering Science Reference • © 2023 • 392pp • H/C (ISBN: 9798369317181) • US $365.00

701 East Chocolate Avenue, Hershey, PA 17033, USA
Tel: 717-533-8845 x100 • Fax: 717-533-8661
E-Mail: cust@igi-global.com • www.igi-global.com

Editorial Advisory Board

Table of Contents

Detailed Table of Contents

Chapter 1

    Sadaf Javed, National University of Sciences and Technology (NUST), Pakistan
    Ali Hassan, National University of Sciences and Technology (NUST), Pakistan
    Rizwan Ahmad, National University of Sciences and Technology (NUST), Pakistan
    Shams Qazi, National University of Sciences and Technology (NUST), Pakistan
    Ahsan Saadat, National University of Sciences and Technology (NUST), Pakistan
    Waqas Ahmed, Pakistan Institute of Engineering and Applied Sciences, Pakistan

An unmanned aerial vehicle (UAV) is a pilotless aircraft that is capable of flying and maintaining altitude without the need for a human operator, offers more cost-efficient solutions, and can carry out even important tasks cost-effectively. UAVs can provide several benefits and a wide range of uses because of their mobility, versatility, and flexibility at different altitudes. Over recent years, UAV technology has gained significant attention in various fields, such as traffic management, surveillance, agriculture, wireless communication, delivering medicine, border monitoring, photography, infrastructure inspection, post-disaster operations, etc. Despite the many benefits of UAVs, there are also many challenges related to UAVs, such as path planning, mission planning, optimal deployment, decision-making, collision avoidance, security, energy management, etc. The main aim of this proposed book chapter is to exploit algorithms that can provide optimal deployment and path-planning solutions for UAVs based on machine learning (ML) techniques.

Chapter 2

    Santiago García Gil, University of Extremadura, Spain
    José A. Gómez de la Hiz, University of Extremadura, Spain
    Diego Ramos Ramos, University of Extremadura, Spain
    Juan Manuel Murillo, Cénits-COMPUTAEX, Spain
    Jaime Galán-Jimenez, University of Extremadura, Spain

UAV networks have become a promising approach to provide wireless coverage to regions with limited connectivity. The combination of UAV networks and technologies such as the internet of things (IoT), have resulted in an enhancement in the quality of life of people living in rural areas. Therefore, it is crucial to implement fast, low-complexity, and effective strategies for UAV placement and resource allocation. In this chapter, a deep reinforcement learning (DRL) solution, based on the proximal policy optimization

(PPO) algorithm, is proposed to maximize the coverage provided to users requesting microservice-based IoT applications. In order to maximize the coverage and autonomously adapt to the environment in real time, the algorithm aims to find optimal flight paths for the set of UAVs, considering the location of the users and flight restrictions. Simulation results over a realistic scenario show that the proposed solution is able to maximize the percentage of covered users.

Chapter 3

Ramya R., SRM Institute of Science and Technology, India
padmapriya R., SRM Institute of Science and Technology, India
Anand M., SRM Institute of Science and Technology, India

UAVs are aircrafts that operate without a human pilot and are equipped with sensors to collect data from the environment. They offer advantages over manned aircraft, such as cost-effectiveness, accessibility, flexibility, and the ability to access remote or hazardous areas. This chapter provides the detailed analysis of machine learning in UANs based detecting and tracking objects and people with different use cases, existing technologies with methodologies, future methodologies, challenges, and finally methodologies to overcome challenges. Through this chapter anyone can understand all the details regarding machine learning in UAVs based detecting and tracking objects and people and this will provide future research scope and idea for the researchers.

Chapter 4

Rashid A. Saeed, Department of Computer Engineering, College of Computers and
Information Technology, Taif University, Saudi Arabia
Nahla A. Nur Elmadina, Department of electrical engineering, Alzaiem Alazhari University,
Sudan

This chapter provides an overview of the diverse applications of ML in UAVs for object and people detection and tracking. It begins by examining the current landscape of ML-driven UAV technologies and their potential. The related work section discusses the advancements in object and people detection and tracking. The subsequent sections delve into the technical aspects, focusing on the next generation of UAV convolutional neural network (CNN) backbones, including the contextual multi-scale region-based CNN (CMSRCNN), single shot multibox detector (SSD), and you only look once (YOLO), highlighting their significance in enhancing detection capabilities. Furthermore, it explores practical applications of ML in UAVs, encompassing object and people detection and tracking, path planning, navigation, and image and video analysis. Challenges and complexities in vision-based UAV navigation are addressed. Additionally, it showcases the potential for UAV networks to locate objects in real time.

    Zeinab E. Ahmed, Department of Computer Engineering, University of Gezira, Sudan &
        Department of Electrical and Computer Engineering, International Islamic University
        Malaysia, Malaysia
    Aisha H. A. Hashim, Department of Electrical and Computer Engineering, International
        Islamic University Malaysia, Malaysia
    Rashid A. Saeed, Department of Computer Engineering, College of Computers and
        Information Technology, Taif University, Saudi Arabia
    Mamoon M. Saeed, Department of Communications and Electronics Engineering, Faculty of
        Engineering, University of Modern Sciences (UMS), Yemen

Wildlife monitoring is critical for ecological study, conservation, and wildlife management, but traditional approaches have drawbacks. The combination of unmanned aerial vehicles (UAVs) with machine learning (ML) offers a viable approach to overcoming the limits of traditional wildlife monitoring methods and improving wildlife management and conservation tactics. The combination of UAVs and ML provides efficient and effective solutions for wildlife monitoring. UAVs with high-resolution cameras record airborne footage, while machine learning algorithms automate animal detection, tracking, and behavior analysis. The chapter discusses challenges, limitations, and future directions in using UAVs and ML for wildlife monitoring, addressing regulatory, technical, and ethical considerations, and emphasizing the need for ongoing research and technological advancements. Overall, the integration of UAVs and ML provides a promising solution to overcome the limitations of traditional wildlife monitoring methods and enhance wildlife management and conservation strategies.

    R. Raffik, Kumaraguru College of Technology, India
    M. Mahima Swetha, Kumaraguru College of Technology, India
    Rithish Ramamoorthy Sathya, Kumaraguru College of Technology, India
    V. Vaishali, Kumaraguru College of Technology, India
    B. Madhana Adithya, Kumaraguru College of Technology, India
    S. Balavedhaa, Kumaraguru College of Technology, India

Two cutting-edge technologies, unmanned aerial vehicle (UAV) systems and deep learning algorithms, have the potential to completely change how wildlife is monitored and conserved. Data collection across wide areas, in challenging locations, and in real time are all possible with UAVs. Data collection via UAVs is possible in locations that are difficult or impossible to reach using conventional human approaches. Along with spotting strange behavior by wild creatures, the UAV can also spot it in human activity. Deep learning algorithms can be used to recognize certain animals, follow their motions, and categorize their behavior. The ecology of wildlife populations may be better understood using this knowledge, which can also be utilized to create more successful conservation plans. A novel technique that has promise for wildlife monitoring and conservation is the fusion of UAV systems and deep learning algorithms. The anticipation is even more creative and successful methods to use UAVs and deep learning to protect animals as technology progresses.

Chapter 7

Rishi Chhabra, Madhav Institute of Technology and Science, Gwalior, India
Aditya Bhagat, G.H. Raisoni College of Engineering, Nagpur, India
Gaurav Mishra, Visvesvaraya National Institute of Technology, Nagpur, India
Ashish Tiwari, Visvesvaraya National Institute of Technology, Nagpur, India
M. M. Dhabu, Visvesvaraya National Institute of Technology, Nagpur, India

Wildfires, also referred to as forest fires, pose serious risks to heavily vegetated forested areas, demanding the development of sophisticated techniques for accurate forecasting and early detection. Unmanned aerial vehicles (UAV) and machine learning integration has been identified as a possible strategy to improve forest fire prediction systems. This thorough study seeks to provide an overview of the research that has been done in the field of machine learning-based UAV-based forest fire prediction. It discusses the benefits of using UAVs for data collection, the use of machine learning techniques, current difficulties, and potential future developments in this area. The main goal of this research is to clearly explain the state-of-the-art UAV-based forest fire prediction in order to facilitate future research projects and practical applications. Drones with sensors and imaging equipment make it possible to collect vital information on vegetation, weather, and fire behavior in real-time, which aids in more efficient wildfire management.

Chapter 8

Sanoufar Abdul Azeez, Kerala University of Digital Sciences, Innovation, and Technology, India
Sumedha Arora, Kerala University of Digital Sciences, Innovation, and Technology, India

Wildfires pose a significant threat to ecosystems and human lives, underscoring the necessity of early detection and rapid response to mitigate the devastating effects of these fires. In recent times, advancements in unmanned aerial vehicle (UAV) technology have provided new avenues for enhancing wildfire monitoring and response. This chapter explores the potential of an innovative framework for UAV swarms that can be controlled and coordinated autonomously for managing wildfires. The comprehensive framework also integrates other technologies such as computer vision, sensor networks, swarm intelligence, and reinforcement learning algorithms to enable collaborative and autonomous UAV swarm operation. The framework addresses navigation challenges in dense forest environments, facilitates swarm coordination, and enables data-driven decision-making for wildfires and diverse real-world applications. This chapter also provides insights into the method of implementation in a simulated 100X100 2D grid environment, showcasing its potential and effectiveness in realistic scenarios.

   Simeon Okechukwu Ajakwe, Hanyang University, Seoul, South Korea
   Nkechi Faustina Esomonu, Federal University of Technology, Owerri, Nigeria
   Opeyemi Deji-Oloruntoba, Inje University, Gimhae, South Korea
   Ihunanya Udodiri Ajakwe, Federal University of Technology, Owerri, Nigeria
   Jae-Min Lee, Kumoh National Institute of Technology, Gumi, South Korea
   Dong Seong Kim, Kumoh National Institute of Technology, Gumi, South Korea

Over the years, economic loss in the agricultural sector has been attributed to the late detection of varying plant diseases due to incongruent detection technologies. With the advent of disruptive technologies and their deployment, such as incorporating artificial intelligence (AI) models into unmanned autonomous vehicles for real-time monitoring, the curtailment of losses and inadvertent waste of agricultural produce can be significantly addressed. This study examines the role of deploying AI models in improving the early and accurate detection of crop lesions for prompt, intuitive, and decisive action to forestall recurrence and guarantee a return on investment to farmers. Furthermore, the chapter established scientific basis for the acceleration of crop yields through allied mechano-biosynthesis in a quest to cushion the effect of the contemporary global food crisis. Connected intelligence in smart farming can be achieved through convergence technology for cost effective agro-allied production by improving the limitations of UAVs and AI-models.

   Tej Bahadur Shahi, Central Queensland University, Australia
   Ram Bahadur Khadka, Nepal Agricultural Research Council, Nepal
   Arjun Neupane, Central Queensland University, Australia

Food demands are increasing globally. Various issues such as urbanization, climate change, and desertification increasingly favour crop pests and diseases that limit crop productivity. Elaborating and discussing the pragmatic knowledge and information on recent advances in tools and techniques for crop monitoring developed in recent decades might help agronomists make more informed decisions. This chapter discusses the progress and development of new techniques equipped with recent sensors and platforms such as drones that have revolutionized the way of understanding plant physiology and stresses. It begins with the introduction to various tools available for crop stress estimation, mainly based on optical imaging such as multispectral, thermal, and hyperspectral imaging. An overview of unmanned aerial vehicle (UAV) -based image processing pipeline is presented and shed light on the possible avenues of UAV-based remote sensing for crop health monitoring using machine learning approaches.

This chapter aims to investigate the applications of reinforcement learning (RL) and Multi-Agent RL (MARL) in UAV networks in warehouse management. Different applications of UAVs in warehousing and different applications of RL in UAV networks are reviewed. Currently, most research in this area relies on single-agent RL approaches. Transitioning from single-agent RL to MARL offers the opportunity can potentially achieve higher levels of optimization, scalability, and adaptability in warehouse management using UAV networks. However, the application of multi-agent approaches in UAV-based warehouse management is still in its early stages, and may introduce new challenges. Thus, this chapter specifically focuses on the challenges and solutions associated with adopting MARL in the context of UAV-based warehouse management tasks. This includes addressing challenges such as non-stationary, partial observability, credit assignment, scalability, and task allocation. The authors highlight challenges and present some of the widely-used approaches to address these challenges.

This chapter focuses on the enhancement of medical services through the integration of unmanned aerial vehicle (UAV) technology and machine learning algorithms. It explores the broad spectrum of applications and benefits that arise from combining these two technologies. By employing UAVs for automated delivery, medical supplies can be efficiently transported to remote or inaccessible regions, thereby improving access to vital items. Remote patient monitoring, facilitated through UAVs and machine learning, enables real-time data collection and analysis, enabling the early identification of health issues. UAVs equipped with medical equipment and machine learning capabilities enhance emergency medical response by providing immediate assistance during critical situations. Disease surveillance and outbreak management can benefit from the use of UAVs and machine-learning algorithms to identify disease hotspots and predict the spread of illnesses.

Preface

In the ever-evolving landscape of unmanned aerial vehicles (UAVs), the intersection with machine learning has forged a path of innovation that transcends traditional boundaries. This edited reference book, *Applications of Machine Learning in UAV Networks*, delves into the dynamic synergy between machine learning and UAVs, spotlighting its transformative impact across an array of domains.

Jahan Hassan and Saeed Alsamhi, our esteemed editors affiliated with the Central Queensland University, Australia, and the Insight Centre for Data Analytics at the University of Galway, Ireland, respectively, have orchestrated a compilation that captures the essence of this profound convergence.

As UAVs become increasingly pervasive in applications ranging from precision agriculture to disaster response, the integration of machine learning emerges as a catalyst for heightened efficiency and effectiveness. This collection of original research is a response to the burgeoning need for an expansive exploration of the potential applications of machine learning in UAV networks. The diverse fields covered include engineering, robotics, computer science, agriculture, environmental studies, and disaster management, offering a panoramic view of the possibilities.

OBJECTIVES OF THE BOOK

This book is more than a mere compilation; it serves as a beacon for readers seeking a comprehensive understanding of the multifaceted applications of machine learning in UAV networks. Each chapter meticulously dissects a specific application area, offering in-depth insights into how machine learning amplifies UAV network operations in diverse contexts. The breadth of topics covered spans precision agriculture, environmental monitoring, surveillance and security, disaster response, and beyond.

TARGET AUDIENCE

Designed for a diverse readership, this book caters to researchers and practitioners in machine learning, UAVs, robotics, and IoT networks. Professionals engaged in any of the application areas explored will find invaluable insights within these pages. Moreover, students and academics with an interest in the intersection of machine learning and UAVs will discover a rich repository of knowledge.

ORGANIZATION OF THE BOOK

Chapter 1: The opening chapter of our edited reference book sets the stage by delving into the multi-faceted world of Unmanned Aerial Vehicles (UAVs). From their cost-efficient solutions to their diverse applications in traffic management, surveillance, agriculture, and more, UAVs have garnered significant attention. However, challenges such as path planning, and optimal deployment persist. This chapter aims to address these challenges by exploring algorithms rooted in Machine Learning (ML) techniques. The objective is to provide readers with insights into achieving optimal deployment and path-planning solutions for UAVs, paving the way for a comprehensive understanding of this evolving field.

Chapter 2: Chapter 2 unfolds the promising landscape of UAV networks, particularly in providing wireless coverage to regions with limited connectivity. The integration of UAV networks with technologies like the Internet of Things (IoT) holds the potential to enhance the quality of life in rural areas. This chapter introduces a Deep Reinforcement Learning (DRL) solution, based on the Proximal Policy Optimization (PPO) algorithm, to maximize coverage for microservice-based IoT applications. The proposed algorithm autonomously adapts to the environment in real time, seeking optimal flight paths for UAVs to maximize coverage. Simulation results demonstrate the efficacy of the proposed solution in maximizing the percentage of covered users.

Chapter 3: This chapter provides an in-depth analysis of the application of Machine Learning (ML) in Unmanned Aerial Networks (UANs) for detecting and tracking objects and people. Offering insights into existing technologies, methodologies, and future research scopes, this chapter is a comprehensive guide for researchers and practitioners. By addressing challenges and proposing methodologies to overcome them, the chapter serves as a valuable resource for anyone seeking a nuanced understanding of ML in UAVs for object and people detection, setting the stage for future research endeavors.

Chapter 4: Chapter 4 builds on the foundation laid by its predecessor, offering an overview of diverse applications of ML in UAVs for object and people detection and tracking. Delving into the current landscape of ML-driven UAV technologies, the chapter explores advancements in detection capabilities through next-generation Convolutional Neural Network (CNN) backbones. It examines technologies like CMSRCNN, SSD, and YOLO, showcasing their significance. The chapter also navigates practical applications of ML in UAVs, addressing challenges in vision-based UAV navigation and highlighting the potential for real-time object location in UAV networks.

Chapter 5: Wildlife monitoring takes center stage in Chapter 5, emphasizing the critical role UAVs and machine learning (ML) play in overcoming traditional limitations. By combining high-resolution cameras on UAVs with ML algorithms, efficient solutions for wildlife monitoring, detection, and behavior analysis are presented. The chapter explores challenges, limitations, and future directions in this dynamic collaboration, addressing regulatory, technical, and ethical considerations. It underscores the potential of integrating UAVs and ML to revolutionize wildlife management and conservation strategies, marking a significant advancement in ecological studies.

Chapter 6: Chapter 6 introduces a transformative fusion of two cutting-edge technologies: unmanned aerial vehicle (UAV) systems and deep learning algorithms. With the capability to collect real-time data across wide areas, even in challenging locations, UAVs equipped with deep learning algorithms offer a novel approach to wildlife monitoring and conservation. This chapter anticipates creative and successful methods as technology progresses, showcasing the potential of this fusion to revolutionize how wildlife is monitored and conserved.

Chapter 7: The threat of wildfires to heavily vegetated forested areas is addressed in Chapter 7. Recognizing the need for accurate forecasting and early detection, the chapter explores the integration of Unmanned Aerial Vehicles (UAVs) and machine learning (ML) to improve forest fire prediction systems. Offering an overview of research in ML-based UAV-based forest fire prediction, the chapter discusses the benefits of using UAVs for data collection, machine learning techniques, current challenges, and potential future developments. It aims to elucidate the state-of-the-art in UAV-based forest fire prediction, facilitating future research projects and practical applications.

Chapter 8: Building on the wildfire theme, Chapter 8 introduces an innovative framework for autonomous UAV swarms in managing wildfires. This comprehensive framework integrates UAV technology with computer vision, sensor networks, swarm intelligence, and reinforcement learning algorithms. It addresses challenges in navigation, facilitates swarm coordination, and enables data-driven decision-making for wildfires and diverse real-world applications. The chapter provides insights into the method of implementation, showcasing its potential and effectiveness in realistic scenarios.

Chapter 9: In Chapter 9, the focus shifts to the agricultural sector, addressing economic losses attributed to late detection of plant diseases. The chapter examines the role of deploying artificial intelligence (AI) models in unmanned autonomous vehicles for real-time monitoring. By improving early and accurate detection of crop lesions, the chapter aims to curtail losses and enhance agricultural productivity. It establishes a scientific basis for accelerating crop yields through allied mechano-biosynthesis, offering insights into connected intelligence in smart farming.

Chapter 10: Chapter 10 delves into the increasing global demands for food and the challenges posed by issues such as urbanization and climate change. Highlighting recent advances in tools and techniques for crop monitoring, the chapter introduces UAV-based remote sensing equipped with sensors and platforms like drones. It provides an overview of the image processing pipeline and explores the potential of UAV-based remote sensing for crop health monitoring using machine learning approaches. This chapter serves as a guide for agronomists seeking to make informed decisions in the evolving landscape of crop monitoring.

Chapter 11: Chapter 11 explores the applications of reinforcement learning (RL) and Multi-Agent RL (MARL) in UAV networks for warehouse management. Reviewing different applications of UAVs and RL in warehousing, the chapter emphasizes the transition from single-agent RL to MARL for optimization, scalability, and adaptability. While acknowledging the early stages of multi-agent approaches in UAV-based warehouse management, the chapter focuses on challenges and solutions associated with adopting MARL, providing a roadmap for researchers and practitioners in this emerging field.

Chapter 12: The final chapter of our edited reference book delves into the broad spectrum of applications and benefits arising from the integration of Unmanned Aerial Vehicle (UAV) technology and machine learning algorithms in the realm of medical services. From automated delivery of medical supplies to remote patient monitoring and disease surveillance, this chapter showcases the potential of UAVs and machine learning to enhance healthcare services. Providing a comprehensive overview, the chapter serves as a crucial read for those interested in the evolving landscape of UAV-assisted healthcare.

The book's chapters encapsulate a wide spectrum of applications, including:

- Applications of machine learning in plant recognition, crop monitoring, and yield prediction using UAVs.
- Precision agriculture and sustainable farming practices empowered by machine learning.
- Real-time monitoring of natural habitats and ecosystems using UAVs.

- Automated security systems and intelligent monitoring using UAVs.
- Applications of machine learning in UAVs assisted warehouse management.
- Enhanced medical services using UAVs equipped with machine learning algorithms.
- Intelligent forest fire management using UAVs.

These chapters exemplify the book's commitment to exploring the far-reaching impact of machine learning in UAV networks across various industries.

CONCLUSION

In embracing the symbiosis of machine learning and UAVs, this reference book stands as a testament to the transformative power of interdisciplinary collaboration. As technology continues its rapid evolution, the insights within these pages will guide and inspire the next generation of researchers, practitioners, and innovators. We extend our deepest appreciation to the contributors who, through their collective efforts, have enriched this volume with their expertise. Their contributions, including those of the writers, reviewers, and editorial board members, have transformed it into a valuable resource for anyone seeking to navigate the exciting frontier of machine learning in UAV networks.

Editors,

Jahan Hassan
School of Engineering and Technology, Central Queensland University, Australia

Saeed Alsamhi
Insight Centre for Data Analytics, University of Galway, Ireland

Chapter 1
The Role of Machine Learning in UAV–Assisted Communication

Sadaf Javed

National University of Sciences and Technology (NUST), Pakistan

Shams Qazi

National University of Sciences and Technology (NUST), Pakistan

Ali Hassan

National University of Sciences and Technology (NUST), Pakistan

Ahsan Saadat

National University of Sciences and Technology (NUST), Pakistan

Rizwan Ahmad

iD https://orcid.org/0000-0002-4758-7895

National University of Sciences and Technology (NUST), Pakistan

Waqas Ahmed

Pakistan Institute of Engineering and Applied Sciences, Pakistan

ABSTRACT

An unmanned aerial vehicle (UAV) is a pilotless aircraft that is capable of flying and maintaining altitude without the need for a human operator, offers more cost-efficient solutions, and can carry out even important tasks cost-effectively. UAVs can provide several benefits and a wide range of uses because of their mobility, versatility, and flexibility at different altitudes. Over recent years, UAV technology has gained significant attention in various fields, such as traffic management, surveillance, agriculture, wireless communication, delivering medicine, border monitoring, photography, infrastructure inspection, post-disaster operations, etc. Despite the many benefits of UAVs, there are also many challenges related to UAVs, such as path planning, mission planning, optimal deployment, decision-making, collision avoidance, security, energy management, etc. The main aim of this proposed book chapter is to exploit algorithms that can provide optimal deployment and path-planning solutions for UAVs based on machine learning (ML) techniques.

DOI: 10.4018/979-8-3693-0578-2.ch001

1. INTRODUCTION

The research on Unmanned Aerial Vehicles (UAVs) is significantly growing due to their integral features such as flying and maintaining altitude without the need for any operator, offering promising solutions, and carrying out important tasks cost-effectively without putting human life at risk. UAVs can provide several benefits and a wide range of uses because of their mobility, versatility, and flexibility at different altitudes. As technology develops, the scope of UAV use cases grows (Aslan et al., 2022; Daud et al., 2022). UAVs have widespread uses in military operations, enemy identification, anti-poaching initiatives, border control, and marine surveillance (Hassija et al., 2020). Due to their portability, speed, and ability to operate in hazardous environments, UAVs play an important role in disaster management. With their help, rescue personnel are better equipped to do recovery operations and evaluate harm more quickly. UAVs also play a significant role in disaster preparation by aiding in the dissemination of vital supplies, easing speedy rescue operations, and delivering early warning signals. The role of UAVs in precision agriculture is transformative. By collecting data from ground sensors, spraying pesticides, detecting diseases, scheduling irrigation, and monitoring crop health, UAVs enhance productivity, crop yields, and overall profitability in farming systems. This technology optimizes agricultural practices and provides data-driven insights for smart decision-making (Macrina et al., 2020). Moreover, UAVs are actively integrated into road traffic monitoring systems. They play a crucial role in automating transportation operations, monitoring road conditions, and providing real-time assistance during accidents or traffic management scenarios. Law enforcement agencies utilize UAVs to track suspect vehicles, enforce traffic rules, and enhance road safety. UAV research is rapidly growing, driven by technological advancements and an expanding range of applications.

The use of UAVs to support conventional communication networks is the subject of cutting-edge study. UAVs equipped with communication interfaces, provide promising solutions for monitoring, inspecting, and delivering goods. UAVs can be used in 5G and beyond communication. More specifically, UAVs have been found highly beneficial in remote areas that are unreachable by humans due to their mobility and ease of deployment (Elnabty et al., 2022). The integration of UAV technology into next-generation communication highly depends on various emerging technologies such as Computer Vision (CV), Machine Learning (ML), Deep Learning (DL) (Mandloi et al.), Artificial Intelligence (AI), and Mobile-Edge Computing (MEC) (Khan et al., 2022b; Yagnasree & Jain, 2022). UAVs can be used as Aerial Base Stations (ABS) to significantly enhance communication coverage because of their flexible deployment, low cost, and high chance of line-of-sight (LoS) communication with ground users to improve wireless connectivity and coverage (Hoseini et al., 2021; Rolly et al., 2022). UAVs can also be used for data collection purposes from Internet-of-Things (IoT) nodes without installing costly infrastructures for data collection to enable a smart decision-making process (Lyu & Zhang, 2019). However, certain challenges are associated with UAVs, such as path planning, mission planning, optimal deployment, decision-making, collision avoidance, security, energy management, etc (Mozaffari et al., 2019; Shakhatreh et al., 2019). For instance, in path planning, if the trajectories of UAVs are not optimized, longer flight time may be required to reach a given target position. If proper mission planning is not done, more resources may be consumed. Energy management is one of the important issues of UAVs because they have limited power resources which can limit flight time. Traditionally, UAVs were operated manually through a high-level controller, and human resources were required. Recently, intelligence has been added to UAVs, such as preplanned or built-in controlled algorithms used for decision-making or autonomously completing the mission and making decisions based on environmental changes like reinforcement learning. In autonomous UAVs, decision-making is one of the major issues in different scenarios such as environmental conditions, bad weather, and rain situations. UAVs have security issues as well because they can be subject to attack by malicious UAVs or GPS spoofing. However, in this work, our main focus is to explore path planning and optimal deployment of UAVs.

The main aim of this proposed chapter is to exploit existing work and algorithms that can provide path planning and optimal deployment solutions for UAVs based on ML techniques. We will examine how these algorithms may assess real-time data, improve resource allocation, and adapt to changing situations, ultimately improving the performance and capabilities of the UAVs. Overall, the goal of this chapter is to show how ML methods aid UAV operations and will shape the future of autonomous aerial systems.

For the reader's convenience, the detail of upcoming sections are provided as follows: Section 2 provides the classification and description of ML techniques. Section 3 discusses the path planning of UAVs and role of ML techniques in planning single UAV and multiple UAVs paths. Section 4 provides the optimal deployment of UAVs using ML algorithms. Section 5 concludes this chapter.

2. MACHINE LEARNING TECHNIQUES

ML techniques play a significant role in UAV technology to enable them to accomplish complex missions in dynamic environments. These ML techniques can be classified into supervised, unsupervised, semi-supervised, deep learning, and reinforcement learning as shown in Figure 1.

Figure 1. Machine learning techniques classification

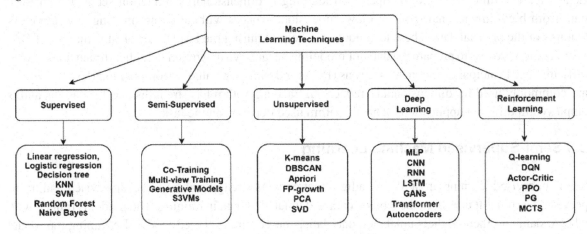

2.1 Supervised Machine Learning

Supervised learning is a category of ML that trains a model based on a labeled dataset. This learning method is used in diverse applications to make accurate predictions based on the labeled dataset training. It can be broadly sub-categorized into classification and regression problem based on the output type. The classification problem aims to predict the class of an object by predicting certain value belonging to a particular class. Classification problems can be binary or multiclass. The binary is for two categories.

For example, whether mail is spam or not. Multiclass analysis predicts which of many classes, such as classifying an image of fruit as an orange, apple, or pear. The regression aims to predict a continuous outcome variable. For example, prediction of house price based on its available certain features. Different supervised algorithms like linear regression, random forest, logistic regression, K-Nearest Neighbors (KNN), decision trees, Support Vector Machines (SVM), and naive Bayes have been developed for specific tasks in literature (Greco et al., 2021; Hong et al., 2022; Pang et al., 2022). Each technique has advantages and limitations, making them suitable for different situations based on data type and nature.

2.2 Unsupervised Machine Learning

Unsupervised learning refers to a category of ML where the objective is to identify hidden patterns inside a dataset. It cannot be applied directly to any regression problem or classification problem. Unlike supervised learning, which relies on human-labeled data, unsupervised learning involves modeling probability densities of inputs without human intervention. The unsupervised learning techniques include clustering, association rules, and dimensionality reduction. The most common approach employed in unsupervised learning for exploratory data analysis includes identifying hidden patterns within a dataset through grouping. The clusters algorithms are used to group data points into clusters of items represented by a similarity measure determined based on metrics such as Euclidean or probabilistic distance. Clustering can be useful in several applications where data is unknown. K-means, hierarchical clustering, and DBSCAN are all examples of clustering methods. This second unsupervised learning approach is discovering interesting relationships between features in a given dataset. It uses a measure of interest to identify strong rules within a dataset. Association rule learning techniques includes Apriori, FP-growth, Eclat, etc. The third approach in supervised learning is dimensionality reduction seeks to transform data from high-dimensional spaces to low-dimensional spaces without compromising any important features of the original data. These techniques are helpful during the Exploratory Data Analysis (EDA) visualization process to prepare the data for modeling because visualization in higher dimensions is very difficult. The Principal Component Analysis (PCA) and Singular Value Decomposition (SVD) methods are commonly used for dimensionality reduction. Each algorithm has strengths and limitations and is employed in different applications. The algorithm used depends on the task.

2.3 Semi-Supervised Machine Learning

Semi-supervised learning are a ML paradigm that couples strengths of both the supervised and unsupervised learning. It uses both the labeled data and unlabeled data in training. The model is trained with labeled data and then predicts unlabeled data labels based on developed model. Retraining the model adds the most confident predictions to the training set with their expected labels and continues until a stop condition is reached. This method requires that multiple data views may provide different insights. Semi-supervised learning techniques are co-training, multi-view training, generative models, S3VMs, and graph-based approaches. The objective and data frequently determine the algorithm to choose, as each has advantages and disadvantages.

2.4 Deep Learning

DL is a subfield within the broader domain of ML. It involves utilizing neural networks that consist of three or more layers. Traditional ML algorithms require knowledge and expertise relevant field of the data for effective feature selection. In contrast, DL algorithms learn these features directly from the data, but models require a huge amount of data and preprocessing on data to learn effectively. The deep learning model is developed by figuring out the appropriate number of layers, nodes within each layer, and the activation function for each layer. The model is learned by running the data through the network and changing the weights and biases based on the performance matrix errors. The training process is continued until the error is minimized. After training, the model is tested on the unseen data. If performance is unsatisfactory, then it requires a model tuning where changes in the network architecture by increasing or decreasing the layers or number of neurons change the activation function, collect more data, or preprocessing is required. After the performance is satisfactory, it is deployed in real-time application on hardware. There exist several known DL models, which include the Multilayer Perceptron (MLP), Long Short-Term Memory (LSTM), Convolutional Neural Networks (CNN), Recurrent Neural Networks (RNN), Generative Adversarial Networks (GANs), transformer models, and autoencoders. Each of these models possesses specific features and is employed for various tasks. The selection of the appropriate model depends upon the task's specific requirements.

2.5 Reinforcement Learning

Reinforcement Learning (RL) is a type learning that focuses on agent learning for decisions making by interacting with an environment by providing rewards for desired behaviors and penalties for undesired behaviors. The key elements for designing the RL model are the agent, the environment, actions, states, and rewards. The agent is the AI algorithm that learns from the environment. The environment is the world where the agent moves and interacts. Action is all the things the agent can do in the environment, and all possible actions are called the action space. The state is the policy's input, affecting the agent's actions, and the set of all available states that an agent can be in is called the state space. The state space's size and complexity can vary depending on the problem. Rewards can be defined as immediate outcomes provided by the environment for evaluating the previous action. The main goal of the agent is to maximize the overall reward based on actions performed.

There are certain elements in the reinforcement model including value, policy, and discount factors. The value is the long-term expected outcome compared to the instant reward obtained as a consequence of actions. The policy is the strategic way that agents adopt to find the next action based on the present state. Discount factor is the constant term used that shows the importance of reward over time. It is important for getting the future reward value. RL is used in diverse applications. There are various RL-based algorithms such as Q-learning and its variants, Monte Carlo Tree Search (MCTS), Policy Gradients (PG), etc. Each algorithm has advantages and some limitations. These algorithms are used based on application requirements such as the magnitude and complexity of the state and action spaces, objectives, the presence of an environment model, and available computational resources.

3. UAV PATH PLANNING

Path planning is a critical component of UAV autonomy and efficiency. Path planning entails determining the best or most feasible path for a UAV to reach its destination or complete a certain mission without collision with obstacles, adhering to constraints, and adapting to changing environments. Path planning algorithms ensure that UAVs can navigate safely, conserve energy, and achieve their objectives with remarkable effectiveness. Path planning is the foundation of UAV operations, allowing for the calculation of the most efficient route while expertly avoiding obstacles. It not only optimizes the UAV's flight path, but also increases battery life, range, and overall safety during missions. Geo-referenced data is critical in route planning because it provides precise information about the UAV's surroundings. The UAV's intelligent navigation system allows it to avoid potential hazards and obstacles in its path. The key to energy conservation is a well-optimized route, which leads to longer flight duration and improved battery life, maximizing the UAV's operational capabilities. The continuous refinement of obstacle avoidance strategies is central to path planning which enables UAV to respond quickly to changes in its environment.

The operations such as surveillance, communication, remote sensing, and monitoring depend on the optimal path planning of UAVs. Particularly, in case of disaster scenarios where traditional communication infrastructures get completely damaged, the optimal path planning of UAVs provides a wide range of communication coverage to enable communication services over the whole targeted area (Khan et al., 2022a). The path planning algorithms are designed based on certain factors such as terrain, obstacles, UAV's energy, users' coverage, etc. The selection of path-planning algorithms mainly depends on available computational resources, environmental complexity, and real-time requirements. The path planning can be performed in three ways: offline path planning, online path planning, and cooperative path planning. The offline path planning is performed when global information about the target environment is available. Using this information, the optimal waypoints of UAV can be obtained and then these waypoints can be used for UAV navigation in order to accomplish the targeted mission. The online path planning is performed when the information about the target environment is partially available. The cooperative path planning is performed to accomplish complex missions using multiple UAVs (Yang et al., 2015). Generally, path planning enables UAVs to navigate through the targeted environment and accomplish their mission. The path planning process can significantly vary depending on the number of UAVs which are involved in the operation. This chapter focuses on machine learning-based solutions in the context of single UAV path planning and multiple UAVs path planning.

3.1 Path Planning of a Single UAV

Single UAV plays a significant role in small-scale missions such as small-scale surveillance, public safety networks for small-scale disaster scenarios, network extension, and enabling communication in a remote area. The path planning of a single UAV involves the process of finding the optimal path from the starting point to a target point for a single UAV that is involved in a mission. The main purpose of single UAV path planning is to find a collision-free optimal route that enables UAV to achieve mission goals with minimum flight time, efficient energy use, and avoid collisions with static or known obstacles in the surroundings. Figure 2 depicts the illustration of single UAV path planning where a single UAV has to cover a whole area to accomplish a particular mission. The conventional algorithms for single UAV include A-star, Dijkstra, and their variants used for offline path planning. The A-star algorithm is based on function which is the sum of path cost and defined heuristic function. The heuristic function represents the approximated distance from every point to the desire point. Its aim is to find a path between the initial point and the target point with the smallest distance based on a defined function (Mandloi et al., 2021). Dijkstra algorithm is based on the cumulative cost which is the sum of the cost from the initial point to each point in a graph-based environment. To find the shortest path, at each point, the UAV selects the point with minimum cumulative cost until the target point is reached (Dhulkefl et al., 2020). These conventional algorithms mainly depend on the heuristic calculation and graph-based model of the environment and can work well in a static environment. However, dynamic environment conditions such as changing weather, and moving obstacles, can significantly affect the performance of offline path planning algorithms.

Figure 2. Illustration of single UAV path planning

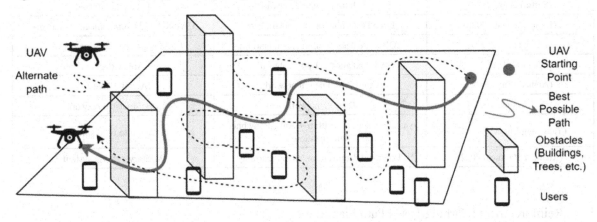

The integration of ML in UAV path planning can overcome the limitations of offline path planning and enhance adaptability by enabling UAV to navigate through dynamic environments. In recent years, ML has received significant attention for UAV path planning due to its ability to enable UAV for adoptability. Various ML-based algorithms have been used for the path planning of a single UAV. The summary of latest literature on single UAV path planning is summarized in Table 1. However, other research works which are significant, are discussed in the subsections.

Table 1. Summary of recent literature on single UAV path planning

References	Techniques	Application Area
(Wu et al., 2023)	Adaptive Q-learning	Search and rescue operations
(Souto et al., 2023)	Q-learning	Urban infrastructure inspection,
(Huang et al., 2023; Nithya et al., 2023)	Deep Q-learning	Crops surveying & spraying
(Dai et al., 2023)	Genetic algorithm	Power lines inspection
(Guo et al., 2023)	Deep Q-network	Wireless sensor network
(Tu & Juang, 2023)	Q-learning	Aquaculture cage detection
(Javed et al., 2023)	RSAND + K-means	UAV trajectory planning for disaster scenarios
(Sartori et al., 2023)	Convolutional neural network	Urban monitoring
(Khurshid et al., 2023)	Deep Deterministic Policy Gradient	UAV-assisted Communication Network
(Peng et al., 2022)	AOI-aware deep-reinforcement learning	UAV-assisted computing network
(Yuan et al., 2022)	GA-based good-set-point algorithm	Area Coverage
(Arshad et al., 2022)	Convolution neural network	Aerial deliveries
(Y. Lu et al., 2022)	Deep Q-network	UAV-assisted network
(Yangyang Liu et al., 2022)	Dynamic genetic algorithm + Ant colony binary optimization	Agriculture field spraying
(Khalil & Rahman, 2022)	Federated deep-reinforcement learning	Military defense system

i.   Reinforcement Learning-based Path Planning

Reinforcement learning is a type of ML in which agents/UAVs interact with the environment to learn from the environment so that decisions can be made effectively (Tu & Juang, 2023). Reinforcement learning-based path planning enables UAVs to take action, learn from the environment, and improve actions based on learning over time. The key aspect of reinforcement learning-based algorithms is that these algorithms can enable UAVs to learn complex

environments and adapt well to the environment changes (Kiran et al., 2021). Many researches have been proposed for single UAV path planning based on reinforcement learning-based algorithms. A Q-learning based adaptive exploration technique is proposed for single UAV path planning to navigate it while avoiding obstacles. Q-learning is a type of reinforcement learning that works based on a model-free environment to find the optimal value of an action in a particular state in the environment. The main idea of this approach is to allow UAVs to explore the target environment and make decisions according to that environment exploration (Souto et al., 2023; Yijing et al., 2017). A path planning approach based on improved Q-learning is developed for a single UAV in an hostile environment which significantly improved the learning efficiency and planning's success rate (Yan & Xiang, 2018). A hybrid path planning approach based on Q-learning and A-star algorithms is proposed for optimal collision-free path planning of a single UAV. That approach improves the search strategy and cost function based on the A-star algorithm which results in a short path and adapts to the dynamic environment based on Q-learning (Li et al., 2021). Wu et al. (2023) proposed an adaptive conversion speed algorithm based on Q-learning to obtain a secure and energy-efficient path for UAV for search and rescue operations in an unknown environment. Another RL-based approach based on deep Q-Learning Networks (DQN) is proposed for addressing coverage path planning. DQN is the variant of Q-learning that integrates the deep neural network to represent the Q-function of Q-learning to manage a large number of the environment's states and actions (Li et al., 2022). Authors in (Y. Lu et al., 2022) investigated the UAV trajectory planning based on the DQN in order to prolong the UAV energy and enhance the network throughput in UAV-assisted networks.

ii.   DL-based path planning

DL is inspired by the intelligent behavior of the human brain that uses a multi-layered neural network to find features and patterns based on large available data. DL plays a significant role in complex UAV path planning. Generally, DL-based models for path planning require significantly large amounts of data for training models such as terrain information, obstacle information, and weather conditions. The model learns patterns from this information and develops the decision-making capability to design the path for UAVs. In this context, a CNN is a commonly used DL model that has the ability to process and analyze imaginary data (Sartori et al., 2023). A CNN model can be developed based on imaginary data of the target environment to recognize the safe and secure path for UAVs in order to navigate UAVs through complex environments (Arshad et al., 2022). Many other research used CNN to design collision-free paths for UAVs by processing UAV's camera images (Yang Liu et al., 2022; Wu et al., 2020). A real-time path planning model is proposed based on a deep neural network for 3D UAV path planning and it is tested in Gazebo to validate its performance in real applications (de Castro et al., 2023). A neural network-based model has the capability of capturing both global and local structural details of environments and creating spatially structured output (Terasawa et al., 2020). Other DL models include RNN and LSTM which are more significant in real-path planning where environmental conditions change over time. RNN and LSTM enable UAVs to adapt well to these changes (Wang et al., 2021; Yao et al., 2020).

iii.   Genetic algorithm approaches for path planning

The genetic algorithm approach has been widely used for the path planning of UAV to find the optimal path between two points while optimizing some predefined criteria such as path length, obstacle avoidance, etc (Liu, 2023). In a genetic algorithm, each possible path between two points is considered as an individual and then evaluated based on fitness function which is defined on some predefined criteria such as path length, time, obstacle avoidance, energy, etc. Then best path is selected iteratively for reproduction purposes in order to create offspring by combining segments of two parents' paths. This process is repeated until a particular level of fitness is met. This process is significant in enabling the genetic algorithm to explore the search space of possible paths and produce efficient paths for UAVs (Lamini et al., 2018). The genetic algorithm with distance and energy optimization is proposed for UAV path planning to address the coverage problem (Shivgan & Dong, 2020). Different approaches can be used to generate the initial population in order to improve the efficiency of the genetic algorithm (Pehlivanoglu & Pehlivanoglu, 2021). The authors in (Yuan et al., 2022), used good-set-point algorithms to generate the initial population in order to improve the conventional genetic algorithms for coverage path planning.

3.2 Path Planning of Multiple UAVs

Multiple UAVs have been used in various use cases such as large-scale communication coverage, border monitoring, surveillance, terrain mapping, crop monitoring, etc. Multiple UAVs offer benefits in terms of cost-efficiency, reduced mission completion time, increased redundancy, and increased flexibility. Multiple UAVs perform missions through coordinated action which significantly reduces mission completion time. Multiple UAVs involve strong coordination among each other to accomplish coordinated actions. Path planning of multiple UAVs involves the process of finding optimal paths for each UAV. Path planning of multiple UAVs is a bit more challenging compared to single UAVs because, in the case of multiple UAVs, each UAV not only has to avoid collision with obstacles in the environment but also has to avoid collision with other UAVs involved in the mission. Figure 3 shows the multi-UAV path planning where multiple UAVs have to cover a whole area to accomplish a particular mission while avoiding collision with obstacles and other UAVs as well. The primary goal of multiple UAVs path planning is to enable communication between UAVs so that they can coordinate and collaborate with each other. Based on this coordination collision-free paths can be developed for each UAV.

Figure 3. Illustration of multiple UAVs path planning

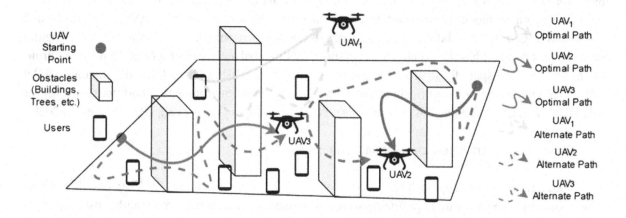

ML has emerged as a powerful approach for addressing the challenges related with the path planning of multiple UAVs. The integration of ML techniques in the path planning process of multiple UAVs not only develops efficient paths for each UAV but also enables each UAV for adaptability and improved decision-making in unknown dynamic environments. There are several machine learning-based approaches that have been used for path planning of multiple UAVs such as multi-agent RL (Khan et al.), Decentralized Multi-agent RL (D-MARL), and swarm intelligence algorithms. Table 2 summarizes the latest research work on multiple UAV path planning and other significant research work is provided in the below subsections.

Table 2. Summary of recent literature on multiple UAV path planning

References	Techniques	Application Area
(Qin et al., 2023)	Multi-agent deep RL	UAV-assisted IoT network
(Chen et al., 2023)	Multi-agent deep deterministic policy gradient	Target searching
(Marwah et al., 2023)	Multi-agent RL	Agriculture field coverage
(Ergunsah et al., 2023)	Multi-agent Q-learning	Wireless sensor network
(Y. Chen et al., 2022)	Multi-reinforcement learning	Reconnaissance missions
(Wu et al., 2022)	Distributed reinforcement learning	Emergency network
(X. Wang et al., 2022)	Dueling double deep Q-network	IoT network
(Y. Wang et al., 2022)	Particle Swarm Optimization + genetic algorithm	Forest monitoring
(Cao et al., 2023)	Particle Swarm Optimization	Emergency network
(Tianle et al., 2022)	Deep reinforcement learning + Particle Swarm Optimization	Wireless sensor network
(Manullang et al., 2023)	Ant colony optimization + 2-opt Algorithm.	Agriculture fields
(Zheng, 2022)	Ant colony optimization	Agriculture Spraying
(Minhas et al., 2021)	Reinforcement learning	Public safety networks

i.   Multi-agent reinforcement learning

Multi-agent RL is the extension of reinforcement learning for multiple agents. Here agents refer to the UAVs. MARL involves the process and analysis of multiple learning UAVs that are sharing the environment to accomplish a common mission (Xue & Chen, 2023). In MARL, each UAV interacts with the environment and other UAVs to maximize cumulative reward. The actions of one UAV in MARL have a significant on the learning and rewards of other UAVs, making the learning process dynamic and more complex (Zhang et al., 2021b). Various MARL-based approaches have been proposed for the path planning of multiple UAVs. Authors in (Wang et al., 2020) proposed the multi-UAV assisted framework for mobile edge computing where the multi-agent deep deterministic policy gradient (MDPG) approach based on MARL is used to manage paths of UAVs for jointly optimizing fairness and energy consumption of devices. The MDPG approach is also used for simultaneously task allocation and path planning of UAVs to effectively deal with the complex environment (Qie et al., 2019). Another work proposed the Multi-Agent Deep RL (MADRL) to develop UAVs' trajectories for improving the freshness of information collected from Internet-of-Things (IoTs) in terms of Age-of-Information (AOI) (Chi et al., 2022; Hu et al., 2020). In another work, a proximal policy optimization-based deep RL approach is proposed to develop the optimal paths of UAVs for enhancing UAV-to-ground users' association. Proximal Policy Optimization (PPO) is the policy gradient method for RL (Hassan et al., 2022). A feature fusion PPO approach based on deep reinforcement learning is proposed to realize path planning of multiple UAVs without having an exact target location by fusing original image information with image recognition information. This fusion-based PPO approach is based on independent policy which enables multiple UAVs to accomplish cooperative path planning through distributed control (Y. Xu et al., 2023). Authors in (Sun et al., 2020), investigated the multi-UAV that enables communication for emergency scenarios and optimized the trajectories of the multiple UAVs by coupling the mean-field theory with Q-learning to meet the Quality of Service (QoS) requirement of ground users.

ii.   Decentralized multi-agent reinforcement learning

Decentralized multi-agent RL is an emerging technique that enables multiple UAVs involved in a common environment to interact with the environment and learn to plan paths without depending on each other learnings and experiences (Zhang et al., 2021a). The main benefit of D-MARL based path planning is that it enables flexibility and scalability through decentralized learning-based actions. Based on D-MARL UAVs can plan sub-optimal or optimal paths, avoid collisions with each other and obstacles, and reduce path costs. It can also enable UAVs to coordinate with each other for collision avoidance even when each UAV is independently interacting and learning from the environment. Lin et al. (2021) proposed a decentralized path planning approach for UAVs-enabled communication networks so that UAVs can accomplish their goals effectively. The work of Zhao et al. (2021) used the decentralized RL approach for developing multiple UAV trajectories to effectively provide energy-efficient long-term coverage. Hu et al. (2020) proposed the distributed trajectory approach for the internet of UAVs to improve UAVs' cooperative sensing and transmission. Hu et al. (2020) stated that trajectory optimization strongly impacts UAVs coordinated sensing and transmission.

iii.   Swarm intelligence algorithms

Swarm intelligence algorithms are biological-inspired algorithms that are developed inspired by the interaction of living organisms who fly and work in groups such as flocks of birds, colonies of bees, schools of fish, etc. The key idea of swarm intelligence algorithms is to employ a number of UAVs with such properties that enable them to emerge as a team to show global behavior (Aljalaud et al., 2023; Chakraborty & Kar, 2017). These algorithms have strong potential for the path planning of multiple UAVs by using the principle of decentralization and self-organization to mimic the coordinating behavior of living organisms. These algorithms help in developing multiple UAVs' path with more efficient, scalable, and robust strategies. There are various swarm intelligence algorithms that have been used for path planning of multiple UAVs such as Particle Swarm Optimization (PSO), ant Colony Optimization (ACO), Bee Colony Optimization (BCO), etc (Kumar et al., 2023; Shafiq et al., 2022; Tan et al., 2023; Yu et al., 2022). In the case of optimal path planning of multiple UAVs, the PSO algorithm considers each UAV as a particle and optimally plans its path based on its experience and other UAVs while maintaining distance between UAVs, their velocities, etc. The work in L. Xu et al. (2023) proposed a dynamic multi-swarm PSO-based model for planning paths of multiple UAVs cooperatively with the consideration of collision avoidance, obstacle avoidance, and quality communication factors. Ahmed et al. (2021) proposed distributed path planning with priority coverage of the area based on the PSO algorithm for optimal planning and the Bresenham algorithm for ensuring complete coverage of the area under operation. The work in (K. Lu et al., 2022) proposed a distributed path planning framework using knowledge-based PSO for optimal cooperative path planning of UAVs and Monte Carlo Tree Search (MCTS) for assigning tasks to UAVs in different areas to avoid collisions. K. Lu et al. (2022) have verified this framework for scalability and adaptability by considering different numbers of UAVs. ACO is introduced based on the ants' behavior that enables them to seek a path between source food and their colony. The work in (Shafiq et al., 2022) couples the ACO algorithm with Cauchy Mutant (CM) operators for collision-free and cooperative path planning of UAVs in a dynamic environment. A comprehensive study on the investigation of ACO-based approaches is presented for planning paths for multiple UAVs (Ntakolia & Lyridis, 2022). The work of J. Chen et al. (2022) considered the coverage path planning of heterogeneous UAVs, using the ACO-based approach to get the optimal paths of UAVs and full coverage of all regions. BCO is developed based on the cooperative behavior of bees. The work of H. Liu et al. (2021) used the BCO-based approach and adaptive genetic algorithm to plan the mission and paths of multiple UAVs for performing rescue operations in disaster scenarios. Q. Liu et al. (2021) proposed a path planning method based on a neural network and sparrow search algorithm to design short distance paths for multiple UAVs in an environment with mountains.

4. UAV OPTIMAL DEPLOYMENT

The optimal deployment involves the strategic positioning of UAVs based on various factors such as operational constraints, mission requirements, and available resources (Zhao et al., 2018). The optimal deployment enables UAVs to use their fullest potential for accomplishing mission goals with minimum utilization of available resources. There are various factors that are important to consider for UAV optimal deployment problems such as a particular nature of the mission, reliable communication between UAVs and ground-users, and the optimal number of UAVs to provide coverage over the targeted area, etc. For UAV optimal deployment, these factors can vary from mission to mission. For instance, in the case of communication networks, UAVs offer promising solutions to overcome network coverage issues when a conventional network is congested or unavailable due to some emergency. Figure 4 shows the optimal deployment of UAVs in the context of coverage extension. In such cases, the optimal position of UAVs can give benefits in terms of enhanced coverage and communication capacity. Moreover, their position can be intelligently changed to provide on-demand communication services to overcome coverage issues. The main objective of optimal deployment is to maximize spectral efficiency and maintain the QoS requirement of users in order to ensure a satisfactory user experience (Liu et al., 2023). UAVs' use-cases can be divided into two categories based on area: small-scale use-cases and large-scale use-cases. Small-scale use-cases involve small areas of operation such as event monitoring, crowd sensing, aerial photography, man-made disasters, relaying, etc. In these use-cases, a single UAV is enough to accomplish mission goals which are relatively simple and require fewer resources. For instance, authors in (Hassan et al., 2020b) proposed a k-mean based approach to optimally deploy a single UAV to enable wireless connectivity in a disaster scenario. They also implement this approach on real man-made disaster scenarios to check the proper functioning of the proposed approach. Zhou et al. (2022) proposed an energy-efficient 3D single UAV deployment algorithm based on model-based learning to ensure maximum coverage to the ground users. In their work, different altitude of UAVs are considered for dataset construction and channel parameters are estimated based on that data, and the optimal position of the UAV is obtained using gradient descent. Large-scale use-cases such as natural disasters, UAV-enable communication network, surveying, environment monitoring, and many more involves a large area of operation. In such cases, more resources and more than one UAV are required to accomplish the mission while covering the whole area. In the case of large-scale applications, the optimal number of UAVs are required to efficiently use the resource and manage the mission. Thus, the optimal number of UAVs is important to consider for optimal deployment of UAVs.

Figure 4. Illustration of UAV optimal deployment

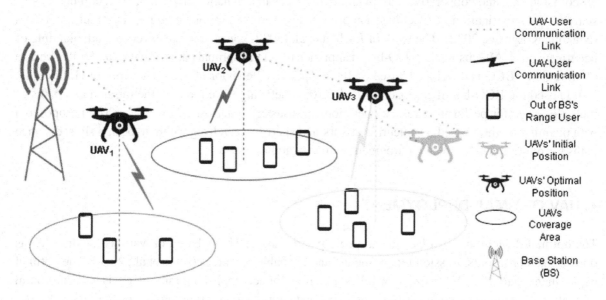

However, optimal UAV deployment requires prior information of hotspot points and congestion events. To this end, ML can be used to predict and analyze demand patterns. ML has the potential to leverage big data analytics that enable the accurate prediction of network traffic and data distribution. These predictions can be used to optimally deploy UAVs as an ABS on the target area to provide delay-free, on-demand, and energy-efficient wireless services to users. UAVs as an ABS have been addressed in (Mozaffari et al., 2016; Zhang et al., 2023) to provide energy-efficient wireless services to users. There are various machine learning-based approaches that have been used for UAV optimal deployment. In Table 3, some of recent research work based on ML approaches for deploying UAVs are investigated in different application areas.

Table 3. Summary of recent literature on machine learning approaches for UAV deployment

References	Techniques	Application Area
(Ma et al., 2023)	KNN	UAV-enabled sensor network
(Tariq et al., 2023)	PSO + Genetic algorithm	Border surveillance
(Tran et al., 2022)	K-means	UAV-enabled IoT Network
(Liu et al., 2019)	Q-learning + K-means	Multi-UAV network
(Hassan et al., 2020a)	Modified K-means	UAV-assisted disaster networks
(Shakhatreh et al., 2023)	K-means and PSO	Future wireless network
(Lim & Lee, 2023)	Decentralized Q-learning	UAVs-enabled 6G communication
(Park et al., 2023)	Multi-agent Q-learning	UAV-enabled network
(Mandloi & Arya, 2023)	Q learning technique	UAV-enabled emergency network
(L. Wang et al., 2022)	Multi-agent Q-learning	UAV-assisted cellular network
(Tarekegn et al., 2022)	CNN and deep Q-learning	UAV-assisted wireless communication
(Pasandideh et al., 2023)	PSO-based algorithm	Cellular network
(Misbah et al., 2023)	Conjugate Gradient PSO approach	RIS-enabled UAV network
(Mao et al., 2023)	PSO algorithm	Multi UAV-enabled network
(Waheed et al., 2023)	Reinforcement Learning	UAV-assisted Emergency networks
(Mahmood et al., 2022)	PSO-based location algorithm	UAV-assisted MIMO systems
(Abdel-Razeq et al., 2021)	PSO algorithm	UAV-enabled NOMA network
(Tan 2022)	K-means based artificial bee colony	UAV-aided emergency network

4.1 Multi-Agent Learning Based UAV Deployment Approaches

Multi-agent learning involves the studying of the behavior of multiple UAVs that are involved in a certain mission in a shared environment. In the learning-based approach, UAVs take actions based on learning experiences gained from the environment and they improve their performance based on rewards obtained by performing actions. Multi-agent learning-based approaches include reinforcement learning, deep reinforcement learning, Q-learning, deep Q-learning, etc. Reinforcement learning is about learning dynamically based on trial and error techniques in real time to improve performance. Deep reinforcement learning uses the neural network which is trained based on existing datasets to obtain states and then a trained model is used for a particular model. Q-learning is a model-free approach that is used to determine the optimal set of actions to be taken based on a given state. It develops and maintains a Q-table for all possible states and actions. Deep Q-learning uses a neural network for approximating the Q-value for each action based on all the possible states in the environment. There are many of research that used learning-based methods to optimally deploy UAVs. The work (Lim & Lee, 2023) in proposed the decentralized Q-learning based optimal deployment and transmit power control approach for the optimal deployment of UAVs in 6G communication networks so that the high line-of-sight probability and 3D connectivity can be achieved. This approach is helpful in the joint optimization of UAVs' deployment and transmit power in order to achieve high individual users' data rates. Multi-agent Q-learning based approach is used in joint communication and radar networks to obtain the optimal power allocation strategy and achieve optimal deployment of UAVs so that UAVs can efficiently relay data from base stations to user equipment to get high throughput for user equipment (Park et al., 2023). Optimal deployment of UAVs helps in enabling wireless communication services in disaster scenarios. The work in (Mandloi & Arya, 2023) proposed the Q-learning based optimization along with a 3D range-based localization technique to determine the optimal position of UAVs based on users' position in a disaster environment. Mostafa et al. (2023) proposed the auto-aggressive integrated moving average estimation approach to determine the traffic patterns in conventional cellular networks and based on those traffic patterns they developed the reinforcement learning-based approach for optimally deploying UAVs as temporary aerial base stations so that UAVs can be used for traffic offloading in case of excess traffic loads. L. Wang et al. (2022) designed the centralized multi-agent Q-learning approach for deploying multiple UAVs based on statistical location information of users in order to minimize transmit power in UAV-assisted cellular networks. (Tarekegn et al., 2022) addressed the communication coverage and network connectivity problem in UAV-aided wireless networks. They designed the CNN and deep Q-learning based approach for providing enhanced communication coverage and service. The CNN model is used for estimating communication link quality whereas Q-learning is used for deploying UAVs at optimal positions based on link quality estimation.

4.2 Supervised UAV Deployment Approaches

Supervised UAV deployment approaches include KNN, random forest, and SVM algorithms which are based on labeled datasets. KNN makes prediction about the partitioning of data points based on similarity or proximity principle. (Ma et al., 2023) designed the KNN-based algorithm to address the UAV deployment and user association problem. They used the KNN to manage the deployment of UAVs.

4.3 Unsupervised UAV Deployment Approaches

K-means unsupervised clustering is commonly used for UAVs optimal deployment. K-means involves the partitioning of the whole target area into k clusters and deploys UAV at the position of centroid in each cluster to optimally cover the whole area. This approach is particularly advantageous in surveillance and communication network use-cases of UAVs where it optimally places UAVs according to the geographical position of users. For instance, K-means based algorithm is designed to optimally place multi-antenna UAVs as an IoT relay in order to improve outage probability and energy efficiency of UAV-enable IoT networks (Tran et al., 2022). The work in (Hassan et al., 2020a) proposed the modified K-mean clustering to deploy UAVs for disaster scenarios for managing critical nodes. The work in (Liu et al., 2019) proposed the Q-learning approach along with K-mean to deploy multiple UAVs in multiple-UAV networks. Another work in (Kaleem et al., 2022) took advantage of K-means and Q-learning by combining both K-means and Q-learning algorithms for optimal placement of UAVs as an aerial base station to support emergence network. (Ozturk et al., 2020) use the K-means clustering for 3D UAVs placement as an additional base station to improve network capacity in order to meet load demands. They compared the proposed approach with two benchmark approaches: symmetric and random deployment of UAVs and found that the proposed K-mean clustering approach is more robust for optimal deployment of UAVs. The work in (Luo et al., 2022) performed the user-centric deployment of UAVs based on the K-means algorithm. This work used the weighted K-means for deployment by considering the users' location. (Shakhatreh et al., 2023) designed the hybrid approach based on K-means and PSO algorithms to determine the efficient 3D position of UAVs in order to improve network capacity and coverage.

4.4 Bio-Inspired UAV Deployment Approaches

Bio-inspired optimization is an emerging approach that is developed based on the inspiration of principles and behaviors of biological living things to solve optimization problems efficiently in a diverse range of applications. Over recent years, bio-inspired approaches have been used in the science and engineering field to obtain optimal solutions to complex problems. More specifically, many works have been proposed on optimal deployment of UAVs based on bio-inspired approaches. Bio-inspired algorithms include particle swarm optimization, bee colony algorithms, ant colony algorithms, etc. Among these PSO is the most commonly used algorithm for UAVs optimal deployment. PSO algorithm is developed based on the movement and the behaviors of flocking birds. It considers each agent in an environment as a particle and then assigns a random position to each particle. Then position of each particle is updated based on velocity which is calculated based on the PSO equation. PSO algorithm converges faster and it has high computational efficiency. The work in (Pasandideh et al., 2023) addressed the connectivity problem of cellular networks in disaster scenarios. To overcome the connectivity problem, they proposed the PSO-based algorithm for optimal deployment of UAVs as cellular base stations to enable reliable communication services. Authors in (Misbah et al., 2023) proposed the conjugate gradient PSO approach for optimal 3D deployment of RIS (reconfigurable intelligent surface) UAV in RIS-enable UAV network to increase the system's sum rate performance. (Mao et al., 2023) jointly optimized the UAVs position and resource allocation using successive convex optimization and PSO algorithm. PSO algorithm is also used in UAV-enable massive MIMO (Multi-Input-Multi-Output) systems. The work in (Mahmood et al., 2022) proposed the PSO-based location algorithm to optimally place UAVs in order to maximize sum-rate in a massive MIMO system. (Abdel-Razeq et al., 2021) develop a PSO-based algorithm to deploy UAVs optimally in 3D space in order to minimize path loss in UAV-enabled Non-Orthogonal Multiple Access (NOMA) networks. (Tan, 2022) proposed the K-means based artificial bee colony approach to optimally deploy UAVs in order to enable communication services in large-scale disaster areas.

5. CONCLUSION

In this book chapter, we have investigated the vast potential of UAVs, highlighting their advantages and challenges. Specifically, we have emphasized on the role of ML approaches in the context of UAVs' path planning and deployment. A broad classification of the ML approaches is provided, namely supervised learning, semi-supervised learning, unsupervised learning, DL, and RL. The integration of UAV technology with these ML techniques offers a promising solution for the optimization and efficiency of UAVs' path planning and deployment. These approaches play a key role in extending the capabilities of UAVs by enabling intelligence in UAV systems. A detailed investigation of UAV path planning and deployment for both single and multiple UAV systems is provided based on ML approaches. Considering the diversity of techniques and the scenarios, it is not fair to conclude which technique is better or optimal because one technique that is optimal in one scenario cannot be optimal in other scenarios with different settings and considerations. This book chapter will help in the subject domain by providing ways for optimizing UAV-based systems and new roads for future research and applications.

REFERENCES

Abdel-Razeq, S., Shakhatreh, H., Alenezi, A., Sawalmeh, A., Anan, M., & Almutiry, M. (2021). PSO-based UAV deployment and dynamic power allocation for UAV-enabled uplink NOMA network. *Wireless Communications and Mobile Computing*, *2021*, 1–17. doi:10.1155/2021/2722887

Ahmed, N., Pawase, C. J., & Chang, K. (2021). Distributed 3-D path planning for multi-UAVs with full area surveillance based on particle swarm optimization. *Applied Sciences (Basel, Switzerland)*, *11*(8), 3417. doi:10.3390/app11083417

Aljalaud, F., Kurdi, H., & Youcef-Toumi, K. (2023). Bio-Inspired Multi-UAV Path Planning Heuristics: A Review. *Mathematics*, *11*(10), 2356. doi:10.3390/math11102356

Arshad, M. A., Khan, S. H., Qamar, S., Khan, M. W., Murtza, I., Gwak, J., & Khan, A. (2022). Drone Navigation Using Region and Edge Exploitation-Based Deep CNN. *IEEE Access : Practical Innovations, Open Solutions*, *10*, 95441–95450. doi:10.1109/ACCESS.2022.3204876

Aslan, M. F., Durdu, A., Sabanci, K., Ropelewska, E., & Gültekin, S. S. (2022). A comprehensive survey of the recent studies with UAV for precision agriculture in open fields and greenhouses. *Applied Sciences (Basel, Switzerland)*, *12*(3), 1047. doi:10.3390/app12031047

Cao, Z., Li, D., Zhang, B., & Gou, K. (2023). Multi-UAV collaborative trajectory planning for emergency response mapping based on PSO. *International Conference on Geographic Information and Remote Sensing Technology (GIRST 2022)*. Spie. 10.1117/12.2667401

Chen, J., Ling, F., Zhang, Y., You, T., Liu, Y., & Du, X. (2022). Coverage path planning of heterogeneous unmanned aerial vehicles based on ant colony system. *Swarm and Evolutionary Computation*, *69*, 101005. doi:10.1016/j.swevo.2021.101005

Chen, J., Ma, R., & Oyekan, J. (2023). A deep multi-agent reinforcement learning framework for autonomous aerial navigation to grasping points on loads. *Robotics and Autonomous Systems*, *167*, 104489. doi:10.1016/j.robot.2023.104489

Chen, Y., Dong, Q., Shang, X., Wu, Z., & Wang, J. (2022). Multi-UAV autonomous path planning in reconnaissance missions considering incomplete information: A reinforcement learning method. *Drones (Basel)*, *7*(1), 10. doi:10.3390/drones7010010

Chi, K., Li, F., Zhang, F., Wu, M., & Xu, C. (2022). AoI Optimal Trajectory Planning for Cooperative UAVs: A Multi-Agent Deep Reinforcement Learning Approach. *2022 IEEE 5th International Conference on Electronic Information and Communication Technology (ICEICT)*. IEEE. PMID:35033326

De Castro, G. G., Pinto, M. F., Biundini, I. Z., Melo, A. G., Marcato, A. L., & Haddad, D. B. (2023). Dynamic Path Planning Based on Neural Networks for Aerial Inspection. *Journal of Control. Automation and Electrical Systems*, *34*(1), 85–105.

Dhulkefl, E., Durdu, A., & Terzioğlu, H. (2020). Dijkstra algorithm using UAV path planning. *Konya Journal of Engineering Sciences*, *8*, 92–105. doi:10.36306/konjes.822225

Elnabty, I. A., Fahmy, Y., & Kafafy, M. (2022). A survey on UAV placement optimization for UAV-assisted communication in 5G and beyond networks. *Physical Communication*, *51*, 101564. doi:10.1016/j. phycom.2021.101564

Ergunsah, S., Tümen, V., Kosunalp, S., & Demir, K. (2023). Energy-efficient animal tracking with multi-unmanned aerial vehicle path planning using reinforcement learning and wireless sensor networks. *Concurrency and Computation*, *35*(4), e7527. doi:10.1002/cpe.7527

Greco, C., Pace, P., Basagni, S., & Fortino, G. (2021). Jamming detection at the edge of drone networks using multi-layer perceptrons and decision trees. *Applied Soft Computing*, *111*, 107806. doi:10.1016/j. asoc.2021.107806

Guo, Z., Chen, H., & Li, S. (2023). Deep Reinforcement Learning-Based UAV Path Planning for Energy-Efficient Multitier Cooperative Computing in Wireless Sensor Networks. *Journal of Sensors*, *2023*, 2023. doi:10.1155/2023/2804943

Hassan, A., Ahmad, R., Ahmed, W., Magarini, M., & Alam, M. M. (2020a). UAV and SWIPT assisted disaster aware clustering and association. *IEEE Access : Practical Innovations, Open Solutions*, *8*, 204791–204803. doi:10.1109/ACCESS.2020.3035959

Hassan, S. S., Park, Y. M., Tun, Y. K., Saad, W., Han, Z., & Hong, C. S. (2022). 3TO: THz-enabled throughput and trajectory optimization of UAVs in 6G networks by proximal policy optimization deep reinforcement learning. *ICC 2022-IEEE International Conference on Communications*. IEEE.

Hong, T., Zhou, C., Kadoch, M., Tang, T., & Zuo, Z. (2022). Improvement of UAV tracking technology in future 6G complex environment based on GM-PHD filter. *Electronics*, *11*(24), 4140. doi:10.3390/ electronics11244140

Hoseini, S. A., Bokani, A., Hassan, J., Salehi, S., & Kanhere, S. S. (2021). Energy and service-priority aware trajectory design for UAV-BSs using double Q-learning. *2021 IEEE 18th Annual Consumer Communications & Networking Conference (CCNC)*.

Hu, J., Zhang, H., Song, L., Schober, R., & Poor, H. V. (2020). Cooperative internet of UAVs: Distributed trajectory design by multi-agent deep reinforcement learning. *IEEE Transactions on Communications*, *68*(11), 6807–6821. doi:10.1109/TCOMM.2020.3013599

Huang, Y.-Y., Li, Z.-W., Yang, C.-H., & Huang, Y.-M. (2023). Automatic Path Planning for Spraying Drones Based on Deep Q-Learning. *Wangji Wanglu Jishu Xuekan*, *24*(3), 565–575. doi:10.53106/160 792642023052403001

Javed, S., Hassan, A., Ahmad, R., Ahmed, W., Alam, M. M., & Rodrigues, J. J. (2023). UAV trajectory planning for disaster scenarios. *Vehicular Communications*, *39*, 100568. doi:10.1016/j.vehcom.2022.100568

Kaleem, Z., Khalid, W., Muqaibel, A., Nasir, A. A., Yuen, C., & Karagiannidis, G. K. (2022). Learning-aided UAV 3D placement and power allocation for sum-capacity enhancement under varying altitudes. *IEEE Communications Letters*, *26*(7), 1633–1637. doi:10.1109/LCOMM.2022.3172171

Khan, I., Schommer-Aikins, M., & Saeed, N. (2021). Cognitive Flexibility, Procrastination, and Need for Closure Predict Online Self-Directed Learning Among Pakistani Virtual University Students. *International Journal of Distance Education and E-Learning*, 6(2), 31–41. doi:10.36261/ijdeel.v6i2.1860

Khurshid, T., Ahmed, W., Rehan, M., Ahmad, R., Alam, M. M., & Radwan, A. (2023). A DRL Strategy for Optimal Resource Allocation along with 3D Trajectory Dynamics in UAV-MEC Network. *IEEE Access*. IEEE.

Kiran, B. R., Sobh, I., Talpaert, V., Mannion, P., Al Sallab, A. A., Yogamani, S., & Pérez, P. (2021). Deep reinforcement learning for autonomous driving: A survey. *IEEE Transactions on Intelligent Transportation Systems*, 23(6), 4909–4926. doi:10.1109/TITS.2021.3054625

Kumar, R., Singh, L., & Tiwari, R. (2023). Novel Reinforcement Learning Guided Enhanced Variable Weight Grey Wolf Optimization (RLV-GWO) Algorithm for Multi-UAV Path Planning. *Wireless Personal Communications*, 131(3), 1–31. doi:10.100711277-023-10534-w

Lamini, C., Benhlima, S., & Elbekri, A. (2018). Genetic algorithm based approach for autonomous mobile robot path planning. *Procedia Computer Science*, 127, 180–189. doi:10.1016/j.procs.2018.01.113

Li, D., Yin, W., Wong, W. E., Jian, M., & Chau, M. (2021). Quality-oriented hybrid path planning based on a* and q-learning for unmanned aerial vehicle. *IEEE Access : Practical Innovations, Open Solutions*, 10, 7664–7674. doi:10.1109/ACCESS.2021.3139534

Li, S., Chen, X., Zhang, M., Jin, Q., Guo, Y., & Xing, S. (2022). A UAV coverage path planning algorithm based on double deep q-network. *Journal of Physics: Conference Series*. IEEE.

Lim, S., & Lee, H. (2023). *Decentralized Q-learning based Optimal Placement and Transmit Power Control in Multi-TUAV Networks. 2023 IEEE 20th Consumer Communications & Networking Conference (CCNC)*. IEEE.

Lin, J.-S., Chiu, H.-T., & Gau, R.-H. (2021). Decentralized planning-assisted deep reinforcement learning for collision and obstacle avoidance in uav networks. *2021 IEEE 93rd Vehicular Technology Conference (VTC2021-Spring)*. IEEE.

Liu, H. (2023). A Novel Path Planning Method for Aerial UAV based on Improved Genetic Algorithm. *2023 Third International Conference on Artificial Intelligence and Smart Energy (ICAIS)*. IEEE.

Liu, H., Ge, J., Wang, Y., Li, J., Ding, K., Zhang, Z., Guo, Z., Li, W., & Lan, J. (2021). Multi-UAV optimal mission assignment and path planning for disaster rescue using adaptive genetic algorithm and improved artificial bee colony method. *Actuators*.

Liu, Q., Zhang, Y., Li, M., Zhang, Z., Cao, N., & Shang, J. (2021). Multi-UAV path planning based on fusion of sparrow search algorithm and improved bioinspired neural network. *IEEE Access : Practical Innovations, Open Solutions*, 9, 124670–124681.

Liu, X., Liu, Y., & Chen, Y. (2019). Reinforcement learning in multiple-UAV networks: Deployment and movement design. *IEEE Transactions on Vehicular Technology*, 68(8), 8036–8049. doi:10.1109/TVT.2019.2922849

Liu, X., Wang, X., Huang, M., Jia, J., Bartolini, N., Li, Q., & Zhao, D. (2023). Deployment of UAV-BSs for on-demand full communication coverage. *Ad Hoc Networks*, *140*, 103047. doi:10.1016/j.adhoc.2022.103047

Liu, Y., Zhang, P., Ru, Y., Wu, D., Wang, S., Yin, N., Meng, F., & Liu, Z. (2022). A scheduling route planning algorithm based on the dynamic genetic algorithm with ant colony binary iterative optimization for unmanned aerial vehicle spraying in multiple tea fields. *Frontiers in Plant Science*, *13*, 998962. doi:10.3389/fpls.2022.998962 PMID:36186015

Liu, Y., Zheng, Z., Qin, F., Zhang, X., & Yao, H. (2022). A residual convolutional neural network based approach for real-time path planning. *Knowledge-Based Systems*, *242*, 108400. doi:10.1016/j.knosys.2022.108400

Lu, K., Hu, R., Yao, Z., & Wang, H. (2022). Onboard Distributed Trajectory Planning through Intelligent Search for Multi-UAV Cooperative Flight. *Drones (Basel)*, *7*(1), 16. doi:10.3390/drones7010016

Lu, Y., Xiong, G., Zhang, X., Zhang, Z., Jia, T., & Xiong, K. (2022). Uplink Throughput Maximization in UAV-Aided Mobile Networks: A DQN-Based Trajectory Planning Method. *Drones (Basel)*, *6*(12), 378. doi:10.3390/drones6120378

Luo, J., Song, J., Zheng, F.-C., Gao, L., & Wang, T. (2022). User-centric UAV deployment and content placement in cache-enabled multi-UAV networks. *IEEE Transactions on Vehicular Technology*, *71*(5), 5656–5660. doi:10.1109/TVT.2022.3152246

Lyu, J., & Zhang, R. (2019). Network-connected UAV: 3-D system modeling and coverage performance analysis. *IEEE Internet of Things Journal*, *6*(4), 7048–7060. doi:10.1109/JIOT.2019.2913887

Ma, B., Zhang, J., Zhang, Z., & Zhang, J. (2023). Time efficient joint UAV-BS deployment and user association based on machine learning. *IEEE Internet of Things Journal*, *10*(14), 13077–13094. doi:10.1109/JIOT.2023.3263208

Macrina, G., Pugliese, L. D. P., Guerriero, F., & Laporte, G. (2020). Drone-aided routing: A literature review. *Transportation Research Part C, Emerging Technologies*, *120*, 102762. doi:10.1016/j.trc.2020.102762

Mahmood, M., Koc, A., & Le-Ngoc, T. (2022). PSO-Based Joint UAV Positioning and Hybrid Precoding in UAV-Assisted Massive MIMO Systems. *2022 IEEE 96th Vehicular Technology Conference (VTC2022-Fall)*. IEEE.

Mandloi, D., & Arya, R. (2023). Q-learning-based UAV-mounted base station positioning in a disaster scenario for connectivity to the users located at unknown positions. *The Journal of Supercomputing*, 1–32.

Mandloi, D., Arya, R., & Verma, A. K. (2021). Unmanned aerial vehicle path planning based on A* algorithm and its variants in 3d environment. *International Journal of System Assurance Engineering and Management*, *12*(5), 990–1000. doi:10.100713198-021-01186-9

Manullang, M. J. C., Priandana, K., & Hardhienata, M. K. D. (2023). Optimum trajectory of multi-UAV for fertilization of paddy fields using ant colony optimization (ACO) and 2-opt algorithms. AIP Conference Proceedings.

Mao, H., Liu, Y., Xiao, Z., Han, Z., & Xia, X.-G. (2023). Joint Resource Allocation and 3D Deployment for Multi-UAV Covert Communications. *IEEE Internet of Things Journal*. IEEE.

Marwah, N., Singh, V. K., Kashyap, G. S., & Wazir, S. (2023). An analysis of the robustness of UAV agriculture field coverage using multi-agent reinforcement learning. *International Journal of Information Technology : an Official Journal of Bharati Vidyapeeth's Institute of Computer Applications and Management, 15*(4), 1–11. doi:10.100741870-023-01264-0

Minhas, H. I., Ahmad, R., Ahmed, W., Waheed, M., Alam, M. M., & Gul, S. T. (2021). A reinforcement learning routing protocol for UAV aided public safety networks. *Sensors (Basel), 21*(12), 4121. doi:10.339021124121 PMID:34203912

Misbah, M., Kaleem, Z., Khalid, W., Yuen, C., & Jamalipour, A. (2023). Phase and 3D Placement Optimization for Rate Enhancement in RIS-Assisted UAV Networks. *IEEE Wireless Communications Letters*. IEEE.

Mostafa, A. F., Abdel-Kader, M., Gadallah, Y., & Elayat, O. (2023). Machine Learning-Based Multi-UAVs Deployment for Uplink Traffic Sizing and Offloading in Cellular Networks. *IEEE Access : Practical Innovations, Open Solutions, 11*, 71314–71325. doi:10.1109/ACCESS.2023.3293148

Mozaffari, M., Saad, W., Bennis, M., & Debbah, M. (2016). Optimal transport theory for power-efficient deployment of unmanned aerial vehicles. *2016 IEEE international conference on communications (ICC). IEEE*.

Mozaffari, M., Saad, W., Bennis, M., Nam, Y.-H., & Debbah, M. (2019). A tutorial on UAVs for wireless networks: Applications, challenges, and open problems. IEEE Communications Surveys and Tutorials, 21(3), 2334–2360. doi:10.1109/COMST.2019.2902862

Nithya, P., Annamani, T., Kamble, V. S., Kumar, C. M. S., Karthikeyan, T., & Sujaritha, M. (2023). An Effective Transportation System Method for Optimal Path Planning Using Logistics UAVs Using Deep Q Networks. *International Journal of Intelligent Systems and Applications in Engineering, 11*(9s), 424–428.

Ntakolia, C., & Lyridis, D. V. (2022). A comparative study on Ant Colony Optimization algorithm approaches for solving multi-objective path planning problems in case of unmanned surface vehicles. *Ocean Engineering, 255*, 111418. doi:10.1016/j.oceaneng.2022.111418

Ozturk, M., Nadas, J. P., Klaine, P. H., Hussain, S., & Imran, M. A. (2020). Clustering based UAV base station positioning for enhanced network capacity. *2019 International Conference on Advances in the Emerging Computing Technologies (AECT)*.

Pang, M., Zhu, Q., Lin, Z., Bai, F., Tian, Y., Li, Z., & Chen, X. (2022). Machine learning based altitude-dependent empirical LoS probability model for air-to-ground communications. *Frontiers of Information Technology & Electronic Engineering, 23*(9), 1378–1389.

Park, J. M., Lee, H., & Yu, H. (2023). *Optimal Power and Position Control for UAV-assisted JCR Networks: Multi-Agent Q-Learning Approach. 2023 IEEE 20th Consumer Communications & Networking Conference (CCNC)*. IEEE.

Pasandideh, F., & Rodriguez Cesen, E., F., Henrique Morgan Pereira, P., Esteve Rothenberg, C., & Pignaton de Freitas, E. (2023). An Improved Particle Swarm Optimization Algorithm for UAV Base Station Placement. *Wireless Personal Communications, 130*(2), 1343–1370. doi:10.100711277-023-10334-2

Pehlivanoglu, Y. V., & Pehlivanoglu, P. (2021). An enhanced genetic algorithm for path planning of autonomous UAV in target coverage problems. *Applied Soft Computing, 112*, 107796. doi:10.1016/j.asoc.2021.107796

Peng, Y., Liu, Y., Li, D., & Zhang, H. (2022). Deep reinforcement learning based freshness-aware path planning for UAV-assisted edge computing networks with device mobility. *Remote Sensing (Basel), 14*(16), 4016. doi:10.3390/rs14164016

Qie, H., Shi, D., Shen, T., Xu, X., Li, Y., & Wang, L. (2019). Joint optimization of multi-UAV target assignment and path planning based on multi-agent reinforcement learning. *IEEE Access : Practical Innovations, Open Solutions, 7*, 146264–146272. doi:10.1109/ACCESS.2019.2943253

Qin, P., Fu, Y., Xie, Y., Wu, K., Zhang, X., & Zhao, X. (2023). Multi-Agent Learning-Based Optimal Task Offloading and UAV Trajectory Planning for AGIN-Power IoT. *IEEE Transactions on Communications, 71*(7), 4005–4017. doi:10.1109/TCOMM.2023.3274165

Rolly, R. M., Malarvezhi, P., & Lagkas, T. D. (2022). Unmanned aerial vehicles: Applications, techniques, and challenges as aerial base stations. International Journal of Distributed Sensor Networks, 18(9).

Sartori, D., Zou, D., Pei, L., & Yu, W. (2023). Near-optimal 3D trajectory design in presence of obstacles: A convolutional neural network approach. *Robotics and Autonomous Systems, 167*, 104483. doi:10.1016/j.robot.2023.104483

Shafiq, M., Ali, Z. A., Israr, A., Alkhammash, E. H., Hadjouni, M., & Jussila, J. J. (2022). Convergence analysis of path planning of multi-UAVs using max-min ant colony optimization approach. *Sensors (Basel), 22*(14), 5395. doi:10.339022145395 PMID:35891074

Shakhatreh, H., Sawalmeh, A. H., Al-Fuqaha, A., Dou, Z., Almaita, E., Khalil, I., Othman, N. S., Khreishah, A., & Guizani, M. (2019). Unmanned aerial vehicles (UAVs): A survey on civil applications and key research challenges. *IEEE Access : Practical Innovations, Open Solutions, 7*, 48572–48634. doi:10.1109/ACCESS.2019.2909530

Shakhatreh, M., Shakhatreh, H., & Ababneh, A. (2023). Efficient 3D Positioning of UAVs and User Association Based on Hybrid PSO-K-Means Clustering Algorithm in Future Wireless Networks. *Mobile Information Systems, 2023*, 2023. doi:10.1155/2023/6567897

Shivgan, R., & Dong, Z. (2020). Energy-efficient drone coverage path planning using genetic algorithm. *2020 IEEE 21st International Conference on High Performance Switching and Routing (HPSR)*. IEEE.

Souto, A., Alfaia, R., Cardoso, E., Araújo, J., & Francês, C. (2023). UAV Path Planning Optimization Strategy: Considerations of Urban Morphology, Microclimate, and Energy Efficiency Using Q-Learning Algorithm. *Drones (Basel), 7*(2), 123.

Sun, Y., Li, L., Cheng, Q., Wang, D., Liang, W., Li, X., & Han, Z. (2020). Joint trajectory and power optimization in multi-type UAVs network with mean field Q-learning. *2020 IEEE International Conference on Communications Workshops (ICC Workshops)*. IEEE.

Tan, Y. (2022). Artificial Bee Colony-Aided UAV Deployment and Relay Communications for Geological Disasters. *2022 8th Annual International Conference on Network and Information Systems for Computers (ICNISC)*. IEEE.

Tarekegn, G. B., Juang, R.-T., Lin, H.-P., Munaye, Y. Y., Wang, L.-C., & Bitew, M. A. (2022). Deep-reinforcement-learning-based drone base station deployment for wireless communication services. *IEEE Internet of Things Journal, 9*(21), 21899–21915.

Tariq, M., Sadaat, A., Ahmad, R., Abaid, Z., & Rodrigues, J. J. P. C. (2023). Enhanced Border Surveillance through a Hybrid Swarm Optimization Algorithm. *IEEE Sensors Journal, 23*(22), 28172–28181. doi:10.1109/JSEN.2023.3317531

Terasawa, R., Ariki, Y., Narihira, T., Tsuboi, T., & Nagasaka, K. (2020). 3d-cnn based heuristic guided task-space planner for faster motion planning. *2020 IEEE International Conference on Robotics and Automation (ICRA)*. IEEE. 10.1109/ICRA40945.2020.9196883

Tianle, S., Wang, Y., Zhao, C., Li, Y., Zhang, G., & Zhu, Q. (2022). *Multi-Uav Wrsn Charging Path Planning Based on Improved Heed and Ia-Drl*. IEEE. doi:10.1109/ICRA40945.2020.9196883

Tran, T.-N., Nguyen, T.-L., & Voznak, M. (2022). Approaching K-Means for Multiantenna UAV Positioning in Combination With a Max-SIC-Min-Rate Framework to Enable Aerial IoT Networks. *IEEE Access: Practical Innovations, Open Solutions, 10*, 115157–115178. doi:10.1109/ACCESS.2022.3218799

Tu, G.-T., & Juang, J.-G. (2023). UAV Path Planning and Obstacle Avoidance Based on Reinforcement Learning in 3D Environments. *Actuators*.

Waheed, M., Ahmad, R., Ahmed, W., Mahtab Alam, M., & Magarini, M. (2023). On coverage of critical nodes in UAV-assisted emergency networks. *Sensors (Basel), 23*(3), 1586. doi:10.339023031586 PMID:36772624

Wang, H., Lu, B., Li, J., Liu, T., Xing, Y., Lv, C., Cao, D., Li, J., Zhang, J., & Hashemi, E. (2021). Risk assessment and mitigation in local path planning for autonomous vehicles with LSTM based predictive model. *IEEE Transactions on Automation Science and Engineering, 19*(4), 2738–2749. doi:10.1109/TASE.2021.3075773

Wang, L., Wang, K., Pan, C., Xu, W., Aslam, N., & Hanzo, L. (2020). Multi-agent deep reinforcement learning-based trajectory planning for multi-UAV assisted mobile edge computing. *IEEE Transactions on Cognitive Communications and Networking, 7*(1), 73–84. doi:10.1109/TCCN.2020.3027695

Wang, L., Zhang, H., Guo, S., & Yuan, D. (2022). Deployment and association of multiple UAVs in UAV-assisted cellular networks with the knowledge of statistical user position. *IEEE Transactions on Wireless Communications, 21*(8), 6553–6567. doi:10.1109/TWC.2022.3150429

Wang, X., Gursoy, M. C., Erpek, T., & Sagduyu, Y. E. (2022). Learning-based UAV path planning for data collection with integrated collision avoidance. *IEEE Internet of Things Journal, 9*(17), 16663–16676. doi:10.1109/JIOT.2022.3153585

Wang, Y., Jiang, R., & Li, W. (2022). A Novel Hybrid Algorithm Based on Improved Particle Swarm Optimization Algorithm and Genetic Algorithm for Multi-UAV Path Planning with Time Windows. *2022 IEEE 5th Advanced Information Management, Communicates, Electronic and Automation Control Conference (IMCEC).* IEEE.

Wu, J., Li, D., Shi, J., Li, X., Gao, L., Yu, L., Han, G., & Wu, J. (2023). *An Adaptive Conversion Speed Q-Learning Algorithm for Search and Rescue UAV Path Planning in Unknown Environments. IEEE Transactions on Vehicular Technology.* IEEE.

Wu, K., Wang, H., Esfahani, M. A., & Yuan, S. (2020). Achieving real-time path planning in unknown environments through deep neural networks. *IEEE Transactions on Intelligent Transportation Systems, 23*(3), 2093–2102. doi:10.1109/TITS.2020.3031962

Wu, S., Xu, W., Wang, F., Li, G., & Pan, M. (2022). Distributed federated deep reinforcement learning based trajectory optimization for air-ground cooperative emergency networks. *IEEE Transactions on Vehicular Technology, 71*(8), 9107–9112. doi:10.1109/TVT.2022.3175592

Xu, L., Cao, X., Du, W., & Li, Y. (2023). Cooperative path planning optimization for multiple UAVs with communication constraints. *Knowledge-Based Systems, 260*, 110164. doi:10.1016/j.knosys.2022.110164

Xu, Y., Wei, Y., Wang, D., Jiang, K., & Deng, H. (2023). Multi-UAV Path Planning in GPS and Communication Denial Environment. *Sensors (Basel), 23*(6), 2997. doi:10.339023062997 PMID:36991708

Xue, Y., & Chen, W. (2023). Multi-Agent Deep Reinforcement Learning for UAVs Navigation in Unknown Complex Environment. *IEEE Transactions on Intelligent Vehicles*, 1–14. doi:10.1109/TIV.2023.3298292

Yagnasree, S., & Jain, A. (2022). A Comprehensive Review of Emerging Technologies: Machine Learning and UAV in Crop Management. *Journal of Physics: Conference Series.*

Yan, C., & Xiang, X. (2018). A path planning algorithm for uav based on improved q-learning. *2018 2nd international conference on robotics and automation sciences (ICRAS).* IEEE.

Yang, P., Tang, K., Lozano, J. A., & Cao, X. (2015). *Path Planning for Single Unmanned Aerial Vehicle by Separately Evolving Waypoints. IEEE Transactions on Robotics.* IEEE.

Yao, H., Liu, Y., & Zhang, X. (2020). Developing deep LSTM model for real-time path planning in unknown environments. *2020 7th International Conference on Dependable Systems and Their Applications (DSA).* IEEE.

Yijing, Z., Zheng, Z., Xiaoyi, Z., & Yang, L. (2017). Q learning algorithm based UAV path learning and obstacle avoidance approach. *2017 36th Chinese control conference (CCC).* IEEE.

Yu, Z., Si, Z., Li, X., Wang, D., & Song, H. (2022). A novel hybrid particle swarm optimization algorithm for path planning of UAVs. *IEEE Internet of Things Journal, 9*(22), 22547–22558.

Yuan, J., Liu, Z., Lian, Y., Chen, L., An, Q., Wang, L., & Ma, B. (2022). Global optimization of UAV area coverage path planning based on good point set and genetic algorithm. *Aerospace (Basel, Switzerland)*, *9*(2), 86. doi:10.3390/aerospace9020086

Zhang, K., Yang, Z., & Başar, T. (2021a). Decentralized multi-agent reinforcement learning with networked agents: Recent advances. *Frontiers of Information Technology & Electronic Engineering*, *22*(6), 802–814. doi:10.1631/FITEE.1900661

Zhang, K., Yang, Z., & Başar, T. (2021b). Multi-agent reinforcement learning: A selective overview of theories and algorithms. Handbook of reinforcement learning and control, (pp. 321-384). University of Illnois.

Zhang, M., Xiong, Y., Ng, S. X., & El-Hajjar, M. (2023). Deployment of Energy-Efficient Aerial Communication Platforms With Low-Complexity Detection. *IEEE Transactions on Vehicular Technology*, *72*(9), 12016–12030. doi:10.1109/TVT.2023.3263275

Zhao, C., Liu, J., Sheng, M., Teng, W., Zheng, Y., & Li, J. (2021). Multi-UAV trajectory planning for energy-efficient content coverage: A decentralized learning-based approach. *IEEE Journal on Selected Areas in Communications*, *39*(10), 3193–3207. doi:10.1109/JSAC.2021.3088669

Zhao, H., Wang, H., Wu, W., & Wei, J. (2018). Deployment algorithms for UAV airborne networks toward on-demand coverage. *IEEE Journal on Selected Areas in Communications*, *36*(9), 2015–2031. doi:10.1109/JSAC.2018.2864376

Zheng, H. (2022). Ant Colony Optimization Based UAV Path Planning for Autonomous Agricultural Spraying. *2022 IEEE 5th International Conference on Automation, Electronics and Electrical Engineering (AUTEEE)*. IEEE.

Zhou, S., Cheng, Y., & Lei, X. (2022). Model-Based Machine Learning for Energy-Efficient UAV Placement. *2022 7th International Conference on Computer and Communication Systems (ICCCS)*. IEEE.

Chapter 2
DRL–Based Coverage Optimization in UAV Networks for Microservice–Based IoT Applications

Santiago García Gil
https://orcid.org/0009-0004-0537-5714
University of Extremadura, Spain

José A. Gómez de la Hiz
University of Extremadura, Spain

Diego Ramos Ramos
https://orcid.org/0009-0004-6989-3879
University of Extremadura, Spain

Juan Manuel Murillo
Cénits-COMPUTAEX, Spain

Jaime Galán-Jimenez
University of Extremadura, Spain

ABSTRACT

UAV networks have become a promising approach to provide wireless coverage to regions with limited connectivity. The combination of UAV networks and technologies such as the internet of things (IoT), have resulted in an enhancement in the quality of life of people living in rural areas. Therefore, it is crucial to implement fast, low-complexity, and effective strategies for UAV placement and resource allocation. In this chapter, a deep reinforcement learning (DRL) solution, based on the proximal policy optimization (PPO) algorithm, is proposed to maximize the coverage provided to users requesting microservice-based IoT applications. In order to maximize the coverage and autonomously adapt to the environment in real time, the algorithm aims to find optimal flight paths for the set of UAVs, considering the location of the users and flight restrictions. Simulation results over a realistic scenario show that the proposed solution is able to maximize the percentage of covered users.

DOI: 10.4018/979-8-3693-0578-2.ch002

1. INTRODUCTION

In recent years, Unmanned Aerial Vehicles (UAVs) have gained popularity in a wide range of applications, from package delivery to surveillance and infrastructure inspection (So, 2023). These devices have been such a revolution that they are now even being applied to activities in the primary sector, including crop monitoring (Radoglou-Grammatikis et al., 2020) and livestock breeding (Boursianis et al., 2020). All this thanks to the agility, ease and tools offered by these devices, such as measuring lasers, cameras, drums and even robotic arms.

Recently, taking advantage of these benefits, these devices are being applied to the mobile network sector, as it would not be a problem to mount WiFi/LTE antennas on UAVs to create swarms of UAVs that are responsible for providing coverage in the areas where they are deployed (Fotouhi et al., 2019), (Galán-Jiménez et al., 2021). Also, these networks have the capacity to be employed during crucial scenarios like disasters, where they can furnish communication services to terrestrial nodes. These nodes might encompass individuals who are in possession of portable devices and are in need of assistance (Erdelj et al., 2017). Similarly, they can also be used to relieve congestion in densely populated scenarios such as sporting events or concerts. These situations often involve a high number of devices attempting to access the cellular telecommunications infrastructure simultaneously (Zema et al., 2017). These swarms are innovative infrastructures made up of a multitude of interconnected UAVs, that enable the provisioning of connectivity in areas where traditional network architectures do not exist, due to their high cost and Low Return of Investment (ROI) (Cruz & Touchard, 2018). But it is not all advantages. These types of networks introduce a multitude of problems that did not appear in traditional networks and that must be addressed by the research community so that this proposal can be applied to reality.

If a little research is done on each of the techniques that could be applied to this problem, among others such as heuristics or mathematical programming, the characteristics offered by the different Machine Learning techniques stand out, which allow a quick and real-time response to different situations in changing environments, so it can be inferred that it could be a good solution to this problem.

The main goal of this work is to propose a solution that is able to maximize the coverage provided to users requesting IoT applications, as well as to react to their movement along the target area. For this purpose, a Deep Reinforcement Learning (DRL) based algorithm (machine learning sub-area), which exploits the ability of the Proximal Policy Optimization (PPO) algorithm to solve problems in dynamic environments, has been proposed. In order to maximize the coverage and autonomously adapt to the environment in real time, the algorithm aims to find near optimal flight paths for the set of UAVs, considering factors such as the location of points of interest, obstacles in the environment, as well as flight restrictions. Due to the limited capabilities of UAVs in terms of computation and battery, IoT applications requested by users are decomposed into microservices and each UAV is able to deploy and run a specific subset of them. Thus, depending on the type of microservice that users request, the algorithm aims at finding the best network configuration to maximize the coverage and satisfy users requirements. Simulation results over a realistic scenario with an area of 1 km² and a limited coverage radius of 100 m show that the proposed solution is able to maximize the percentage of users to which it provides coverage reaching values above 80% and an average of 65%, while minimizing the movement of UAVs deployed at 50% of their power.

The rest of the article is organized as follows: first, a review of related works is provided in Section Related Work. The system model is described in Section System Model, where the architecture of the UAV-based network, the UAVs coverage and path loss models are defined. The description of the DRL-based algorithm proposed to maximize the coverage to users requesting IoT applications is provided in Section <u>Deep Reinforcement Learning Model</u>. In particular, the specific DRL technique used in the work, PPO, is discussed, emphasizing the functions that allow achieving good results. Section <u>Experimental Results</u> discusses the experimental results. Finally, Section <u>Conclusion and Future Work</u> reviews the conclusions that are drawn.

2. RELATED WORK

In this section, an analysis of existing research related to the topic at hand is provided. The aim is to position our work within the framework of existing contributions, identifying the strengths and limitations of previous approaches. Additionally, the originality and relevance of our proposal w.r.t. the state of the art in the research area is highlighted.

In recent years, several studies have been conducted to address the optimization and coverage challenges for UAVs in various applications. (Bor-Yaliniz et al., 2016) investigate the coverage area, considering the altitude of the UAV and the horizontal positions of both the UAV and users. Results indicate that the size of the coverage area is influenced by the surrounding environment. Although they define a nonlinear mixed-integer problem that can be solved by commercially available solvers, computation times are not mentioned. Thus, it is expected to have a high computational cost prohibitive for real-time applications. In contrast, our model is based on DRL and adapts well to rapidly changing environments, delivering solutions in fractions of a second.

Zeng et al. (2018) address the problem of designing UAV trajectories to optimize mission completion time and reduce energy consumption in a multicasting system. To solve this problem, the authors simplify the trajectory constraint by using a formulation based on the analytical lower bound derived from the file retrieval probability. They discover that the UAVs optimal trajectory consists of connected line segments and propose two efficient schemes to design reference points and find the optimal speed along the route. Numerical tests are conducted to evaluate the performance of the proposed trajectory designs. Results demonstrate significant improvements compared to other reference schemes, highlighting the effectiveness of the proposed solutions. However, although the proposal is well thought out, a consequence of being designed as a Travel Salesman Problem is that the objective is to pass through all points of interest in such a way that energy consumption is minimized. On the other hand, our goal is to maximize the ratio of users that can be covered over time. This implies that the UAV must remain quasi-stationary over certain clusters of users on certain occasions, which is not contemplated in the proposed solution.

Valente et al. (2013) tackle the optimization problem of aerial coverage in precision agriculture management. They propose a unique approach to solving the coverage path planning problem using a music-inspired algorithm called Harmony Search. The Harmony Search algorithm operates by preserving a record of previous harmonies and leveraging them to formulate novel solutions. In the context of aerial coverage optimization, this algorithm employs a group of potential solutions. Each solution is depicted as a vector of candidates, where each candidate symbolizes a musical note. The fitness of these solutions is assessed by determining the number of turns necessary to cover the designated area. The study concludes that their approach successfully improved coverage paths, offering a viable alternative for optimizing agricultural management tasks. Authors find their proposals computation time acceptable since it is intended for offline execution, given the stable nature of the agricultural land. However, this system is not responsive to the dynamic nature of modern rural areas, where user mobility and patterns change rapidly. Our solution aims to function online, addressing this challenge and allowing for potential integration of collision avoidance capabilities.

Yan et al. (2019) address the trajectory planning for UAVs in dynamic and complex environments. The authors propose a DRL approach using a dueling double deep Q-network algorithm for action-prediction and an action-selection policy that combines ε-greedy strategies with heuristic search rules to avoid potential threats. They also propose a rapid situation evaluation model to represent dynamic enemy threats.

Results show their approach is effective, surpassing other methods in cumulative rewards and success rates. It also generalizes well in static and dynamic tasks. However, global data availability is challenging in practice, and experiments were limited to simulations. Using a DQN variant, they discretize UAV movement into eight actions (north, north-east, etc.), without considering variable speeds. Their proposal prioritizes risk and a single objective, while ours aims to connect numerous targets. To prevent discretization, we employ a different algorithm, PPO.

Zhang and Huang (2021) focus on enhancing trajectory planning for UAVs in surveillance and reconnaissance missions by considering occlusion. They propose two algorithms to address this problem in complex environments, such as mountains and urban areas. The first algorithm employs regular triangular patterns and the alternate clustered spiral method to achieve complete coverage of the area of interest. The second algorithm utilizes unsupervised learning and Bézier curves to tackle surveillance in geometrically complex environments.

Simulations demonstrate that these algorithms can provide full coverage of the area of interest with minimal waypoints, enhancing efficiency and surveillance quality. Moreover, by considering UAV limitations and obstacle occlusion, they ensure smooth and safe trajectories for the UAVs. Together, these algorithms have the potential to significantly improve the effectiveness of UAVs in complex surveillance and reconnaissance missions.

Even though this article proposes a novel algorithm to maximize coverage in an area under surveillance it does not fit well the problem of maximizing the connectivity provided to mobile users. This is because, as they state in their conclusion, the algorithms designed are not meant to work in a real time changing environment with moving users. In contrast, our solution learns to track users in real time.

Puente-Castro et al. (2022) present a reinforcement learning-based approach to solve the problem of route planning for multiple UAVs in a swarm. Their system can calculate optimal flight paths to achieve complete coverage in flying areas, particularly in field exploration tasks. Results indicate that using a global artificial neural network to control all UAVs in the swarm yields similar outcomes to using an individual artificial neural network for each UAV. As it has been stated, the authors of the paper focus on field prospection tasks rather than providing connectivity to users. Therefore, their model is meant to cover a designated area completely rather than searching and tracking the users inside the said area which means that the solution is not well suited to the problem that is being tackled in the current proposal.

Liu et al. (2020) present an innovative approach using DRL to dynamically plan the trajectory of an UAV and its association with mobile terminal users in mobile edge computing networks mounted on UAVs. By employing a Quality of Service (QoS)-based action selection policy, the algorithm achieves higher average reward and faster convergence, especially with lower UAV altitude or fewer mobile terminal users. Simulation results demonstrate the success of the proposed approach in enhancing the quality of service for users in mobile edge computing networks mounted on UAVs. Although this work serves as a basis of our proposal, we aim to avoid the use of DQN variants because they are incompatible with continuous action spaces and lead to a discretization of the environment and the actions that the agent can take. This translates into the hindering of the free movement of the UAV.

Chen et al. (2022) present an innovative solution for trajectory planning in heterogeneous autonomous UAVs coverage. By using an exact formulation based on mixed-integer linear programming and a clustering algorithm, they achieve optimal and approximately optimal trajectories for the UAVs. They propose two approaches: one fully explores the solution space to obtain optimal trajectories, while the other utilizes clustering to obtain approximately optimal point-to-point trajectories.

However, the first approach based on MILP is expected to have high execution times, making this model not appropriate for online computing in a real time environment. On top of that, the second approach inspired by density-based clustering is not well suited for rural scenarios where the points of interest are sparse and distant from each other.

As a summary, the works reviewed in this section highlight the diversity of approaches and techniques used in the field of trajectory planning for autonomous UAVs to maximize coverage. Although these studies have made important contributions, there are still challenges in the efficiency and accuracy of solutions for autonomous UAV trajectory planning. Thus, the authors of this chapter have developed a model that aims to cover the weaknesses of such works and that is adapted to the features of rural environments.

Table 1. Summary of the literature reviewed in conjunction with our work

Authors	Solution	Technique	Metrics	Tools
Bor-Yaliniz et al., (2016)	Area coverage	Mixed-integer non linear programming (MINLP)	Number of users covered and coverage area	X
Zeng et al. (2018)	Optimization UAV trajectories	Linear Programming (LP)	Packet retrieval probability, distance and mission completion time	MATLAB and CVX
Valente et al. (2013)	Optimization of aerial coverage	Harmony Search algorithm (HS)	Amplitude of turns and UAV movement	X
Yan et al. (2019)	Path planning	Deep Reinforcement Learning (DRL)	Success rate and computational efficiency	STAGE scenario tool, C++ and Python
Zhang & Huang (2021)	Optimization of aerial coverage	Unsupervised Learning and Bezier curves	Trajectory smoothness, trajectory length and uncovered area	X
Puente-Castro et al. (2022)	Path planning optimization	Reinforcement Learning (RL) and Evolutionary Computing	Execution time and area coverage	X
Liu et al. (2020)	Optimizing the trajectory	Deep Reinforcement Learning (DRL) and Double Deep Q-Network (DDQN)	Quality of Service (QoS), system usability and system reward	X
Chen et al. (2022)	Path planning optimization	Mixed Integer Linear Programming (MILP) and clustering-based algorithm	Task completion time and deviation ratio	X
This work	Optimization of aerial coverage and path planning optimization	Deep Reinforcement Learning (DRL)	Users covered ratio and distance of flight	Unity (ML-Agents) and Python

3. SYSTEM MODEL

In this section, the description of the system model for the optimal placement of the UAVs on the UAV-based network architecture is provided. Two fundamental aspects are taken in account: first, the considerations about the network architecture are described and then, the application of DRL techniques to achieve the optimal positioning of UAVs to cover the widest possible range of users.

For the development of the proposed model, it is necessary to introduce that we rely on an application model that follows the Service Oriented Architecture (SOA), i.e., IoT applications are decomposed into a set of microservices that execute a specific functionality (Waseem et al., 2020).

3.1 UAV-Based Network Architecture

The proposed network architecture based on UAVs with clusters and microservices is an approach in which UAVs are grouped into clusters, and each cluster is assigned to perform a specific type of task or service. This architecture takes advantage of the capacity of UAVs to perform coordinated missions.

The main components (concepts) that are part of the network architecture are listed below:

1. **UAVs**: each UAV has its own sensors, such as GPS, camera and proximity sensor, to perform the actions. UAVs are divided into clusters, which means that UAVs within the same cluster share similar characteristics and functionalities.
2. **Clusters:** UAVs are grouped into clusters based on specific criteria, such as geographic location or type of mission. Each cluster is assigned to a particular microservice, meaning that UAVs within the same cluster have the same type of software or capability deployed to perform a specific task.
3. **Microservices**: microservices are independent and autonomous software units that are deployed in UAVs. Each microservice is responsible for performing a specific task, such as object detection, packet delivery, surveillance, or image capture. UAVs within a cluster are equipped with instances of the same microservice in order to carry out their assigned task.
4. **Base station**: the base station is the control element of the UAV network. The DRL model is deployed at this station and is used to communicate with the UAVs, indicating their

Figure 1. Proposed network architecture

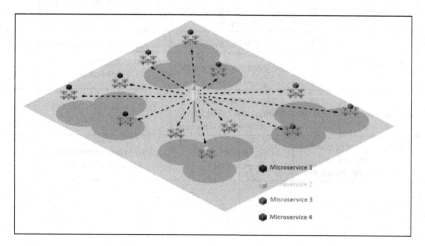

5. path to follow to reach their optimal position. Therefore, the DRL model uses information from the UAVs' sensors and other data to generate actions and guide the UAVs to their targets.

Communication among UAVs, clusters and the base station is done via a wireless network, such as an ad hoc communication network or a cellular network. The UAVs send data to and receive instructions from the base station, allowing them to coordinate their movements and execute their assigned tasks efficiently. Fig. 1 exemplifies the architecture described. Four clusters of UAVs can be observed, where each one provides one type of microservice.

3.2 UAVs Coverage and Path Loss Model

Based on the study in Galán-Jiménez et al. (2021), the coverage and path loss models considered for this work are described below.

The conical antenna mounted on the UAVs exhibits a specific propagation pattern characterized by an angle of θ. This pattern results in the projection of a circular area on the ground, as depicted in Figure 2. The radius of this circular area, denoted as r, is directly proportional to the altitude of the UAV, h, as described by Equation 1.

$$r = h \cdot \tan(\theta)$$

The angle θ represents the conical antenna's orientation on the UAV, while h corresponds to the current altitude of the UAV. Although we assume circular coverage from the UAV, the scenario is divided into discrete areas using a grid system. This division may result in slight overlapping of coverage between adjacent UAVs. Now, shifting our attention to the path loss model being considered, it is based on the aforementioned model. It defines the probabilistic mean path loss between an UAV positioned at altitude h and a specific location z=(x,y) according to Equation 2.

$$X\left(h,r\right) = \frac{A}{1 + d \cdot exp\left[-e \cdot \left(\frac{180}{\pi}\right) tan^{-1}\left(\frac{h}{r}\right) - d\right]} + 10\ log\left(h^2 +\ r^2\right) + B$$

Where $A = \eta L_{oS,}$ and $B = 20 \cdot log\left(\frac{4\pi f_c}{c}\right) + \eta_{NLoS}$. The average additional losses for Line of Sight (LoS) and No Line of Sight (NLoS) conditions are represented by $\eta L_{oS,}$ and $\eta NL_{oS,}$ respectively. Moreover, d and e are the S-curve parameters that depend on the environment, fc is the carrier frequency and k is the distance between the center of the UAV and the user that is served, as in Equation 3.

$$r = \sqrt{\left(x_k - x\right)^2 + \left(y_k - y\right)^2}$$

We emphasize that the considered path loss model is specifically tailored for the type of scenario in which the proposed solution is designed to operate. This scenario pertains to open areas where there is minimal interference caused by existing infrastructure or neighboring UAVs.

4. DEEP REINFORCEMENT LEARNING MODEL

Reinforcement Learning (RL) is a subfield of the Machine Learning (ML) techniques characterized by proposing a learning process similar to that of human beings, i.e., trial and error (Kaelbling et al., 1996). Through rewards, behaviors that are desired can be reinforced, while non-desired ones are discouraged. These rewards take the form of numerical values, and, by convention, positive ones are assigned to the behaviors that are deemed good, while the negatives are assigned to the bad outcomes.

RL is divided into another two categories, Q-Learning and Deep Reinforcement Learning (DRL). The first one is broadly characterized by the fact that it stores, for each state-action pair, the expected reward to be obtained. The data structure that holds the state-action pairs is called Q-table. Thus, it is able to choose, in real-time, the action that provides the best reward given a specific environmental state. However, this algorithm is not well suited for the problem that is being tackled in this chapter. The problem arises given the continuous nature of $\mathbb{R}3$, since the number of state-actions pairs to explore and to store in the Q-table would be very high.

On the other hand, this problem is not present if DRL is considered, which replaces the Q-table by the most powerful function approximation technique known to date, Deep Neural Networks (DNN). DRL is an algorithm that aims for an agent to learn to make decisions about what action to take in each state of an environment, with the goal of maximizing rewards. The rewards obtained after each decision of the algorithm cause a readjustment of the DNN weights (backpropagation), which will reinforce taking that action in that state (positive reward), or simply the opposite (negative reward).

In the following enumeration the architecture and the main concepts of the DRL technique applied to the problem at hand are described. Five key components can be distinguished in the proposed DRL-based solution:

Figure 2. Example of coverage range achieved by an UAV as a function of the altitude

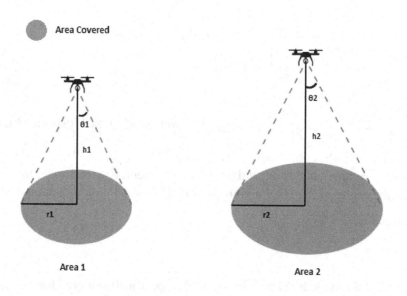

1. **Environment**: it refers to everything that surrounds the DRL agent. In the case of this model, the environment consists of the set of UAVs, the set of users and terminal devices, as well as possible obstacles that may prevent establishing LoS between UAVs and users.
2. **Agent**: this component of DRL refers to the entity that interacts with the environment based on the observations it can make. Observations are the pieces of information

Figure 3. UAV-based network scenario

about the state of the environment that are available to the agent. The interactions between the agent and the environment are the actions, which, in turn, lead to rewards (or penalties, if it is a negative reward). Based on the rewards, the agent is able to decide the action to be taken at any moment. This is possible thanks to the adjustment of the weights of the subjacent DNN. In the proposed model, the agent must choose the best action at each observation of the environment (state), to finally make the UAV move through the previously defined environment.

3. **State**: it is a representation of the environment in each moment, i.e., a snapshot. This representation is introduced to the DNN and, depending on its value, the best action to be carried out is estimated. In our proposal, the size of the state is associated with the following formula: $S=(U+P)*2$, where P, is the number of users requiring coverage in the environment, and U, the number of UAVs deployed in the scenario. P and U are multiplied by two because the DNN receives the coordinates x and z of each element in the environment. Since users and UAVs are not expected to move along the Y axis (the vertical movement of UAVs is left for future work), their y component is ignored. For example, Figure 3 shows an environment that produces an observation space (state) of 44 elements. This scenario is composed of 21 users that require coverage and each one produces two continuous values to the state, their x and z coordinates. In the environment of Figure 3, we can observe only

one UAV providing coverage and producing two additional continuous values, which are the x and z coordinates of the proper UAV. Thus, the state architecture of the proposed DRL algorithm varies according to the mobility of both users and UAVs.

4. **Actions**: they refer to the decisions made by the agent (run at the base station), so that the DNN will have as many output values as actions. In this case, three continuous variables per UAV are set as output. They represent a vector, $\vec{v} = (x, z)$, to indicate the direction of UAV motion in the XZ plane, and a third value specifying the magnitude of that motion. In the proposed algorithm, the DNN is not in charge of choosing the best action for each state, as they normally do, but sets a value for each DNN output, and these three values are used to act. In the example of Figure 3, having a single UAV deployed, the DNN will only have three outputs or actions.

5. **Rewards**: they are numerical values that feed back to the agent's DNN, indicating how good the agent's decision has been. The rewards cause the agent to regulate the weights of its DNN, thus learning from this agent-environment interaction. It is recommended to establish a rewards range between -1 and 1; due to the fact that by minimizing the range of rewards helps the neural network to converge when having to compare results across a small range of values. In our model, the agent can receive three types of rewards, which are listed below:

   ○ Episodic Reward. This reward is given to the agent at the end of each episode during the training process. The reward is based on the number of users that have been provided with connectivity by UAVs during the episode. In order to calculate this reward, in each step right after the execution of the actions, the percentage of users that have been covered, *stepCoverage*, is evaluated. At the end of the episode, the coverage obtained, *episodeCoverage*, is calculated by averaging the coverage of each step, *episodeReward= episodeCoverage=* $\dfrac{\sum_{i=0}^{MaxSteps} stepCoverage_i}{MaxSteps}$, where *MaxSteps* is a constant that holds the maximum number of steps per episode. In the case of our model, this value is equal to 5,000. The purpose of this function is to indicate the agent how well (or poorly) it has performed during the episode.

   ○ Step Reward. This second type of rewards are used to reduce the sparsity of feedback the agent receives. If only episodic rewards were to be used, the agent would take *MaxSteps* actions blindfolded. This situation hinders the learning process, and, through experimentation, it has been found that using small rewards during the episode helps the DNN to converge faster due to the fact that the agent has more feedback. The reward is calculated with the following formula: $stepReward = \begin{cases} \dfrac{stepCoverage}{MaxSteps}, & stepCoverage > 0 \\ \dfrac{-1}{MaxSteps}, & stepCoverage \leq 0 \end{cases}$. One can understand the step reward as short-term feedback, whereas episodic reward is longer-term oriented. The range of the episodic reward, [0, 1], with respect to the range of the step reward, $\left[\dfrac{-1}{MaxSteps}, \dfrac{1}{MaxSteps}\right]$ reinforces this intuitive perspective. The former can provide the agent with substantially higher rewards commensurate with its greater importance during the training process.

   ○ Out of Boundaries Reward. The third and last kind of (negative) reward is a penalty that is applied when the action of the agents leads to the UAV leaving the designated area. This situation is considered a major failure because the fact of trespassing the established boundaries can involve the UAV entering an air exclusion zone or jeopardizing its return to the BS. The occurrence of such an event implies the premature end of the episode and a negative reward calculated with the following formula: *outOfBoundariesReward= outOfBoundariesPenalty+* $\frac{\sum_{i=0}^{currentStep} stepCoverage_i}{MaxSteps}$, where *outOfBoundariesPenalty* is a constant that holds the value -1. The second part of the equation, $\frac{\sum_{i=0}^{currentStep} stepCoverage_i}{MaxSteps}$, plays an important role. Leaving the designated area is a bad action, but leaving as the episode begins is much worse than if the UAV leaves near the end of the episode and has also managed to cover a large percentage of users. This term takes this fact into account, softening the penalty in case the UAV leaves the designated zone at the end of the episode. On top of that, it helps the agent's learning in the early stages of the training process, where this event is much more likely to happen.

Once the five essential concepts of the DRL model are described, it is possible to define how they communicate with each other and in which order, to ultimately achieve its objective, i.e., maximizing rewards. For this purpose, we base our explanation on Figure 4, where each iteration (step) performed by our agent starts with an observation of the environment in which the relevant data for decision-making is obtained, i.e. the state is formed. The agent will pass this state through its DNN, which sets continuous values for each of the actions on its output. These values will define the movement of each UAV, as we described in the previous sections, thus producing a change in the environment and the generation of a new state, which is provided back to the agent for further decision-making. Moreover, this change in the environment produces a reward, which feeds back to the agent to adjust the weights of its DNN, reinforcing the decision taken in that state if the rewards are positive and weakening in the opposite case. The specific algorithm of DRL used in this model is the Proximal Policy Optimization (PPO), which is explained in the following subsection.

To conclude this subsection, the architecture of the DNN used in our model this algorithm is defined, which can be seen in simplified form in Figure 4. It consists of 10 layers: the input layer, the output layer and 8 hidden layers in between. The input layer is composed of as many neurons as there are elements in the observation space of the algorithm *((U * P) * 2)*, the eight hidden layers are composed of 512 neurons each, ending in the output layer of *U * 3* neurons, which provide to each UAV the 3 continuous values needed for its movement. The layers used in this model are of the General Matrix Multiplication (GEMM) type, based on matrix multiplications to obtain a result, which will be the input for the next layer. Finally, an activation function is applied to the values produced by each of the layers. In particular, the sigmoid activation function is applied, which limits the received values in the range [0,1]. This function eliminates the gradient through a saturation, thus producing a slow convergence but with good results in the last layer.

Figure 4. DRL system model diagram

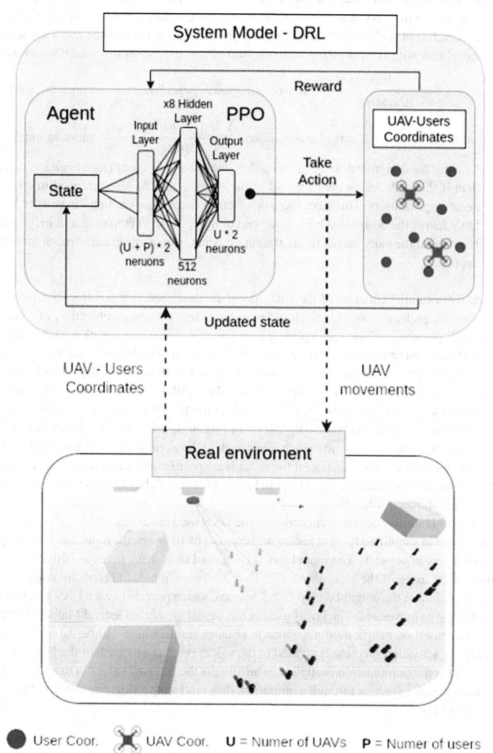

4.1 Proximal Policy Optimization (PPO)

As introduced in the previous section, the specific algorithm of DRL used in our proposed model is the Proximal Policy Optimization (PPO) method, proposed by Schulman et al. (2017) is one of the most advanced DRL methods developed to date. It outperforms other models in problems with continuous control environments in a wide variety of experiments of the MuJoCo physics engine (Todorov et al., 2012).

The main idea behind PPO is the introduction of a surrogate objective (Equation 4) with the aim of avoiding performance collapse. Such avoidance is carried out by guaranteeing monotonic performance improvement during optimization. In this way, the training process is stabilized. However, this does not guarantee that the model converges to the global maximum.

There exist two main variants of the PPO algorithm: PPO with adaptive Kullback-Leibler divergence penalty and PPO with clipped surrogate objective (Schulman et al., 2017). The second one is preferred because it is simpler, has lower computational cost and yields better performance. On top of that, it is the variant implemented by the Ml-Agents DRL framework (Juliani et al., 2020) and, therefore, the one used for the creation of the model proposed in this chapter. Equation 4 shows the surrogate function that is used by the variant of the algorithm.

$$L^{CLIP}(\theta) = \hat{E}_t \left[min \left(r_t(\theta) \hat{A}_t, clip \left(r_t(\theta), 1 - \varepsilon, 1 + \varepsilon \right) \hat{A}_t \right) \right]$$

Where LCLIP(θ) is the expectancy of the minimum value between $r_t(\theta) \hat{A}_t$ and $clip \left(r_t(\theta), 1 - \varepsilon, 1 + \varepsilon \right) \hat{A}_t$ known as clipped surrogate objective. θ is the vector of parameters that defines the policy, i.e., the weights of the underlying neural network in charge of taking actions given a state. rt(θ) is the probability ratio between the previous policy and the current one, $r_t(\theta) = \dfrac{\pi_\theta(a_t \mid s_t)}{\pi_{\theta_{old}}(a_t \mid s_t)}$. $\hat{A}_t$ is the advantage function, $\hat{A}_t = Q\grave{A}(s,a) - V\grave{A}(s)$, which serves the purpose of evaluating the impact of an specific action while taking into account the current state of the environment. The last term to be known is ε, which is a value that defines the clipping neighborhood and is a hyperparameter that must be tuned. When rt(θ) is within the interval [1-ε, 1+ε], both terms of the min() *expression are equal.

Once the reader has become familiar with the terms in the equation, it can be stated that it helps to solve the performance degradation problem to which gradient descent algorithms are exposed. This is achieved by preventing updates of the policy parameters from being too large, i.e., by limiting rt$(\theta_{,}$ to the interval [1-ε, 1+ε].

On the other hand, PPO falls into the on-policy group of DRL algorithms, which are characterized by being less sample-efficient. However, since in the current proposal the environment is being simulated, there is an unlimited number of samples to train that can be generated on the fly with low computational cost.

Compared to other state-of-the-art algorithms, such as Deep Q Network (DQN) and all its variants (Double DQN, Dueling DQN), PPO is better suited for the problem of coverage optimization. The reason behind this is that DQN cannot handle continuous action spaces. This limitation surely would lead to a discretization of the movement of the UAV which would reduce the inherent freedom they provide.

After explaining the characteristics of this algorithm, its suitability to the problem to be addressed and the low impact of the fact that it belongs to the on-policy method category given that the environment is simulated, the selection of this algorithm is justified. The next section shows the performance evaluation of the proposed DRL-based solution to maximize the coverage of users.

5. EXPERIMENTAL RESULTS

In this section, the proposed model is evaluated over a simulated scenario. First, the simulation set-up is described, including the considered scenario and the parameter setting. Then a brief introduction to the development environment used is presented. Finally, the performance analysis of the model is carried out, considering the impact of the distribution of users.

5.1 Simulation Set-Up

The possibility of simulating the scenario, creating a digital twin, makes this research economically viable, given the fact that DRL-based models are known to be sample-inefficient requiring a lot of trial-and-error to reach acceptable policies. This also eliminates the risks posed to the population and infrastructure where the experiment would be conducted. It should be noted that the source code is published in an open repository to facilitate access to it (coverageOptimization – GitHub Repository., 2023).

An example of the environment simulated using Unity is provided in Figure 5. It consists of a 1 km² rural area similar to the scenario exposed in Figure 3. The simulation contains the following elements:

In the simulation environment, users are depicted as dark red stick figures placed randomly around a selected center point, with their positions following a normal distribution relative to this point. These user positions remain static throughout each episode, changing only randomly at the episode's end. In Figure 5, line segments are drawn between users and UAVs to indicate line-of-sight (LoS); green lines denote LoS availability, while red lines indicate obstacles blocking LoS. However, this feature is currently unused during training as it hampers learning progress. Future work aims to incorporate this feature for a more realistic simulation. The UAVs, represented as purple cylinders, operate at a fixed low altitude of 50 meters and can move freely within the designated area but will restart at the area's center if they leave it prematurely. The conical volume beneath the UAVs helps identify users within their coverage area. Obstacles, depicted as translucent greyish rectangular cuboids, simulate two-story buildings commonly found in rural areas of Spain and are randomly placed within the designated area to block up LoS between users and UAVs.

Figure 5. Environment set-up in unity

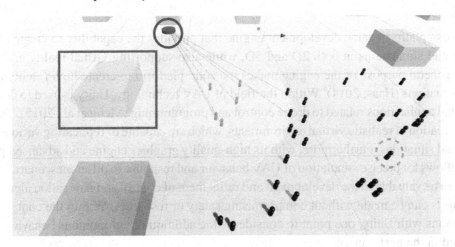

It should be noted that at the beginning of each episode, the position of users and obstacles is randomly initialized. However, the position of the UAV is left unmodified. These decisions are intended to introduce randomness to the training, to simulate the movement of the users to which the UAV must adapt and to avoid overfitting, a problem to which DNN models are exposed. Another relevant aspect that is worth mentioning is that the maximum episode length used during training is 5,000 steps. In that way, the UAV has enough time to roam across the map to reach the optimal position.

To conclude this section, the hardware and software specifications used for the development and testing of the proposed model are collected in Table 2 and Table 3.

Once the simulation set-up has been introduced, the development platform used for the implementation and testing of the model is detailed below.

Table 2. Hardware specifications of the conducted experiment

Component	Model Name
Processor	Intel Core i7-1260P, 2.10 GHz, 12 cores
GPU	Intel(R) Iris(R) Xe Graphics
RAM	16 GB
Storage	NVMe SAMSUNG MZVL21T0HCLR-00B00
Operating system	Ubuntu Linux 20.04 LTS

Table 3. Relevant software packages along with the versions used

Software Application	Version Name
Unity	202.3.4f1
ML-Agents	2.0.1
Torch	1.11.0
Tensor Flow	2.11.1

5.2 Unity

Unity is a cross-platform game development engine that provides the capability to create applications, experiences and simulations in both 2D and 3D, while also supporting virtual reality and augmented reality. The general purpose of the engine makes it a solid platform to create high fidelity simulations of real-life situations (Haas, 2014). Within the field of UAV technology, Unity is used to develop flight simulators and applications related to drone control and programming (Meng et al., 2015). This platform enables the creation of realistic virtual environments, which are capable of replicating various real-world conditions and situations. Furthermore, with its high-quality graphics engine and advanced physics system, Unity allows for precise simulation of UAV behavior and response to different scenarios and events. This proves to be valuable in the development and refinement of control and navigation algorithms since exhaustive tests can be made without compromising safety or resources. Within the context of interactive applications with Unity, one point to consider is the addition of autonomous behavior, which will be introduced in the next section.

5.3 ML-Agents

Unity ML-Agents is an open-source machine learning toolkit that provides developers with the ability to create environments for training intelligent agents (Juliani et al., 2020). In the area of autonomous control, Unity ML-Agents can be used to train agents that manage autonomous devices, such as UAVs and robots.

ML-Agents and Unity are relevant to the experiment being conducted because they provide the tools to create a simulation of the problem of maximizing the connectivity in rural areas through an ad-hoc ultra-fast and reliable UAV-aided MEC network. Despite being a popular software being used in recent studies (Zhan et al., 2022) (Gan et al., 2022) (Wang et al., 2021), we consider our proposal to be novel in that, to the best of the authors knowledge, there exists with no publications related with the enhancement of internet connectivity via UAVs that uses Unity as the environmental simulation framework. ML-Agents framework can be interpreted as a bridge between applications developed in Unity, i.e., digital twins of real-life problems, and well known libraries in the field of DRL research, such as Pytorch (Paszke et al., 2019), gym (Brockman et al., 2016) and PettingZoo (Terry, 2023). Through a set of wrappers, it is possible to create agents that observe the environment and communicate the state information to the model implemented in Pytorch through a low-level Python API. When the time of taking actions comes, the same process is carried out reversely, the model communicates to the agent the action that it must carry out and it is executed inside the environment.

Table 4. Relevant training parameters

Training Parameters	Parameter values
Environment dimensions	1,000 x 1,000 m^2
UAV height	50 m
UAV coverage radius	100 m
UAV speed	60 km/h (16.6 m/s)
People cluster radius	50m-200m
Number of users	40

5.4 Performance Evaluation

In this subsection different metrics are analyzed with the aim of better understanding the performance of the model. The metrics about the training process are discussed and, later on, the resulting model is compared to a baseline approach to measure its improvements over it.

The parameters used during training are specified in Table 4. In order to measure of the performance of the proposed model, a parametrized benchmark is used. It lasts for five whole episodes, or 25.000 steps, which corresponds to a execution of a duration of 7 minutes. The position of the users is updated in each episode so that the UAV has to actively find the optimal section of the scenario where it can serve the most users. The baseline approach has been measured under the same conditions.

5.4.1 Reward

The reward is a relevant metric during the process of training, it does indicates how well is the model performing in the task of covering as much users as possible during the length of each of the episodes. An increase of this metric during training indicates that the agent is in fact learning how to solve the problem.

Figure 6 contains the progress of the mean reward obtained during the 30.000.000 steps of the training process. The red dotted line clearly shows the improvement of this metric towards the end of the training. However, some details must be clearly explained to interpret this graph. First of all, the range of the reward obtained during an episode depends on the value of the rewards given to the agent. Given the possible values of the three types of rewards that the agent can receive (see Section <u>Deep Reinforcement Learning model</u>) the range of the reward is [-2, 2]. Since the location of the users is, to some extent, random, this implies that in most episodes the maximum obtainable reward falls below 2,

Figure 6. Reward progression during training

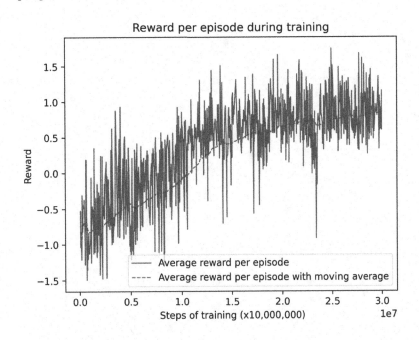

because the UAV has to reach the area where the users are located before obtaining positive rewards and even when it reaches that area, it is very likely that not all users will fit within the coverage radius of the UAV. The proposed model reaches reward values of 0.837 at the end of the training phase.

5.4.2 Episode Length

The duration of the episodes is another way of measuring the improvement of the agent during the training process. It is used to detect a pathologic behavior that must be avoided, the UAV trespassing the boundaries of the scenario. The occurrence of this event leads to the premature termination of the episode along with a negative reward.

From Figure 7 it can be clearly seen that the aforementioned event is quite frequent during the first 10.000.000 steps of training. This correlates to the negative rewards obtained during this part of the training process (see red solid line in Figure 6). However, from that point to, approximately 22.000.000 steps it only happens sporadically. At the same time, in that interval, the rewards obtained start tending to be positive. Finally, during the last 7.000.000 steps the UAV does not leave the designated area and, thus, has learned to avoid that behavior which leads to obtaining positive rewards. At the end of the training process, the proposed model consistently produces full-length episodes (5000 steps).

5.4.3 Loss Function

Figure 7. Episode length progression during training

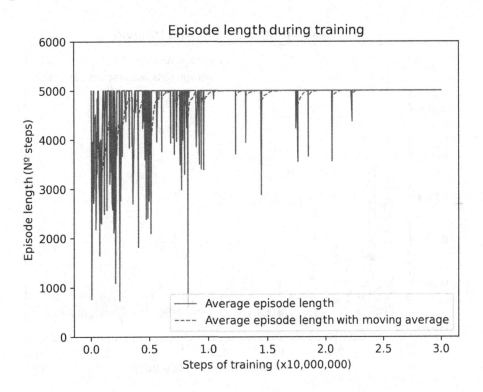

The last aspect that is going to be analyzed about the training process is the progression of the loss function. It represents the deviation between the expectancy of the reward to be obtained given the action selected to be applied in a particular state with respect to the reward obtained. Figure 8 represents this progression, and it shows that the loss does decrease as the training process progresses. However, as PPO follows a stochastic action selection process to promote curiosity-driven exploration, it sometimes leads the agent to take poorly rewarded actions which explains the spontaneous increases in the loss function. This effect is somewhat supported by comparing Figure 7 and Figure 8. The negative peaks of the former correspond to the positive peaks of the latter, but as training progresses, both functions stabilize. The non-smoothness of the loss function is an unavoidable consequence of the usage of minibatches in the PPO algorithm.

5.4.4 Percentage of Users Covered

Figure 8. Loss function progression during training

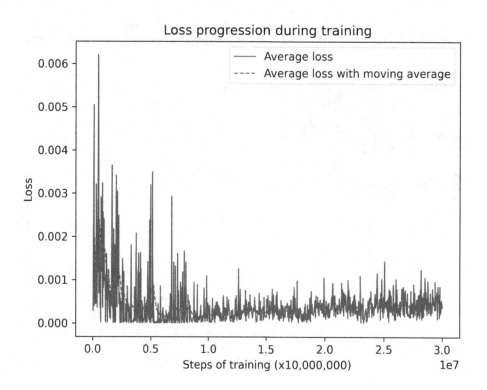

This metric and the following are the ones used to evaluate the trained model. They are compared to the baseline approach which is based on the UAV performing an across tracking scanning movement based on the work of Li and Xing (2019).

Figure 9 is proposed to show the percentages of users to whom the UAV can cover during the benchmark. It can be clearly seen that the proposed DRL approach is much more consistent than the reference method, obtaining coverage values above 60% of users for more than 65% of the experiment duration. In contrast, the heuristic method only exceeds 60% of users covered during 13% of the experiment duration. This means that the DRL approach quickly finds the area where connectivity can be provided to the largest number of users. Values of 80% are reached occasionally which is a really good value given the limited radius of the UAV and the dispersion of the users in the scenario. It is worth noting that the sudden drops of coverage of the DRL approach are induced because of the update of the user placement.

In addition, Figure 10 illustrates the relative cumulative coverage during the benchmark. The heuristic baseline method is clearly outperformed by the DRL model. At the start of the benchmark both

Figure 9. Instantaneous coverage obtained in each step of the benchmark

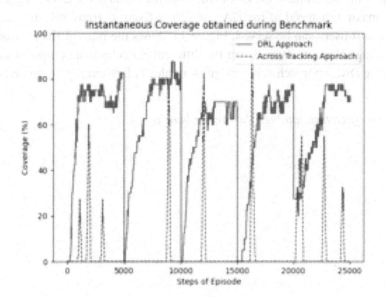

start at 0% of coverage and both approaches improve and eventually stabilize. However, the DRL approach peaks at 64,5% meanwhile the heuristic peaks at 7%.

5.4.5 Movement Efficiency

At the same time that the model significantly improves the number of users covered, it also reduces the distance the UAV travels. This makes more efficient use of the heavily constrained battery of the aircraft. This is a secondary objective of the proposal, given that battery life is perhaps the most limiting factor in the design of UAV-aided MEC.

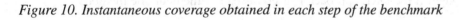

Figure 10. Instantaneous coverage obtained in each step of the benchmark

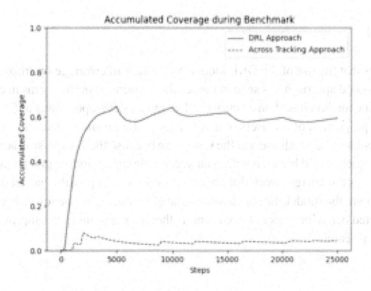

In each timestep of the benchmark, the model must decide to move the UAV with a speed comprised between 0 and the maximum speed of the UAV, which is fixed to 16.67 m/s in order to move to the location where the most users can be served. Figure 11 shows the ratio of the normalized speed with respect to the percentage of users covered over the different episodes that composes said benchmark. It is clearly seen that the DRL approach achieves greater values of efficiency compared to

Figure 11. Movement efficiency obtained during the benchmark

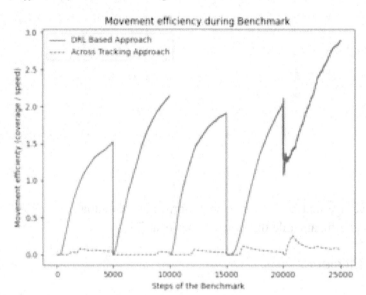

the baseline method. This is because the baseline method is constantly performing an across tracking movement at full speed to cover the map as fast as possible meanwhile the DRL approach modulates the speed to reach where the users are located according to the actual position of the AUV. Therefore, the battery of the UAVs last longer if the DRL approach is used instead of the heuristic method.

6. DISCUSSION

The results indicates that the use of the DRL models in the task of coverage optimization in UAV-aided MECs is, actually a good approach. As seen in the results sections, it outperforms in every single aspect measured the baseline method based on a heuristic. The model developed tends to find suboptimal positions where a large proportion of the users of a scenario can be given connectivity which is good news given that is not possible to serve all users at the same time because their dispersion across the designated area. In addition, it reaches said location within an acceptable time window given that the UAV's speed is limited. However, as the current work does not take into account possible aerial obstacles that force the UAV to avoid them, the model should choose to travel in a straight line towards where the users are located. This expected behavior does not occur and is therefore a point to be improved in future extensions of this line of research.

Figure 12. Multi UAV simulation setup using the resulting DRL Model

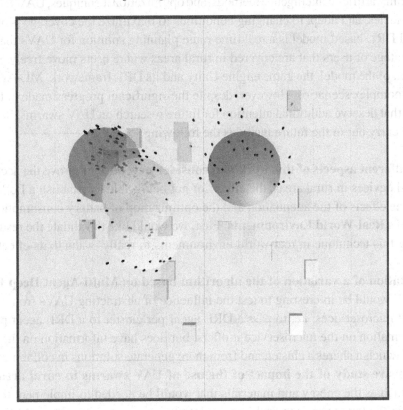

Although the DRL Model has shown exceptional performance when trained with 40 users, it is not possible to use it with a different number of users because the architecture of the subjacent neural network depends on this parameter. Therefore, another line of work would be designing a mechanism to homogenize the input for the neural network in such a way that one can be used with any number of users.

Figure 12 is proposed as a materialization of Figure 1, which is shown at the beginning of the chapter to illustrate the structure that this line of work is intended to achieve. In this, there are multiple users distributed in an area of interest, each one with particular needs. There are also UAVs that can serve these users, but in order to minimize the number of unattended users, the positioning of the UAVs is crucial. With the DRL model developed, each one is able to move towards areas that allow them to optimize this factor. Although multiple UAV are supported, the limitation of not allowing multiple UAVs to serve the same service must be overcome in future publications.

7. CONCLUSION AND FUTURE WORK

The use of UAVs has revolutionized numerous industries and sectors, offering unprecedented potential in various applications. Throughout this chapter, we have explored how UAVs have transformed areas such as agriculture, farming, infrastructure inspection, and packet delivery, among others. Path planning is a critical aspect to ensure optimal performance and safety of UAVs in these diverse tasks. By using advanced algorithms, artificial intelligence methods, and optimization techniques, UAVs can plan efficient routes, avoid obstacles, and adapt to changing conditions to maximize the coverage provided to users.

The proposed DRL-based model is a real time route planning solution for UAVs that aims at maximizing the percentage of users that are covered in rural areas where users move freely. For the training and the evaluation of the model, the game engine Unity and its DRL framework, ML-Agents, have been used to simulate complex scenarios. However, despite the significant progress made in this study, there are several areas that deserve additional attention for future research on UAV swarms. Some of the work we would like to carry out in the future includes the following:

- **Improve different aspects of this work and consider new ones**: improve the accurate modeling of users and devices in rural areas, the effects of not being able to establish a LoS between them, as well as the effects of the attenuation and the optimization of battery consumption.
- **Validation in Real-World Environments**: First, we would like to validate the results of this work by applying this technique in real-world environments to really evaluate its effectiveness in real conditions.
- **Implementation of a variation of the algorithm based on Multi-Agent Deep Reinforcement Learning**: It would be interesting to test the influence of abstracting UAVs from the existence of clusters and microservices, i.e. to pass a DRL agent per cluster to a DRL agent per UAV, which has no information on the microservice it offers, but does have information on the position of the UAVs with which it shares a cluster, and from there generate solutions in collaboration with them.
- **Comprehensive study of the impact of the use of UAV swarms in rural areas**: Retrieve information such as the energy and materials that would be needed to implement this solution and compare it in the long term with traditional solutions. Assess the impact on the ecosystem of the area, etc.
- **Long-term maintenance**: Researching techniques that allow for the long-term maintenance of these swarms while reducing costs, such as the ability to use renewable energy sources, researching the manufacturing of UAVs for long-term durable, recyclable and environmentally responsible materials.

REFERENCES

Al-Hourani, A., Kandeepan, S., & Lardner, S. (2014). Optimal LAP Altitude for Maximum Coverage. *IEEE Wireless Communications Letters*, *3*(6), 569–572. doi:10.1109/LWC.2014.2342736

Amorosi, L., Chiaraviglio, L., & Galan-Jimenez, J. (2019). Optimal Energy Management of UAV-Based Cellular Networks Powered by Solar Panels and Batteries: Formulation and Solutions. *IEEE Access : Practical Innovations, Open Solutions*, *7*, 53698–53717. doi:10.1109/ACCESS.2019.2913448

Bithas, P. S., Michailidis, E. T., Nomikos, N., Vouyioukas, D., & Kanatas, A. G. (2019). A Survey on Machine-Learning Techniques for UAV-Based Communications. *Sensors (Basel)*, *19*(23), 5170. doi:10.339019235170 PMID:31779133

Bor-Yaliniz, R. I., El-Keyi, A., & Yanikomeroglu, H. (2016, May 1). *Efficient 3-D placement of an aerial base station in next generation cellular networks.* IEEE Xplore. https://doi.org/ doi:10.1109/ ICC.2016.7510820

Boursianis, A. D., Papadopoulou, M. S., Diamantoulakis, P., Liopa-Tsakalidi, A., Barouchas, P., Salahas, G., Karagiannidis, G., Wan, S., & Goudos, S. K. (2020). Internet of Things (IoT) and Agricultural Unmanned Aerial Vehicles (UAVs) in smart farming: A comprehensive review. *Internet of Things : Engineering Cyber Physical Human Systems, 100187.* doi:10.1016/j.iot.2020.100187

Brockman, G., Cheung, V., Pettersson, L., Schneider, J., Schulman, J., Tang, J., & Zaremba, W. (2016). *OpenAI Gym.* ArXiv.org. https://arxiv.org/abs/1606.01540

Chen, J., Du, C., Zhang, Y., Han, P., & Wei, W. (2022). A Clustering-Based Coverage Path Planning Method for Autonomous Heterogeneous UAVs. *IEEE Transactions on Intelligent Transportation Systems, 23*(12), 25546–25556. doi:10.1109/TITS.2021.3066240

Cruz, G., & Touchard, G. (2018). *Enabling Rural Coverage - Regulatory and policy recommendations to foster mobile broadband coverage in developing countries.* GSMA. https://www.gsma.com/mobilefordevelopment/wp-content/uploads/2018/02/Enabling_Rural_Coverage_English_February_2018.pdf

Erdelj, M., Natalizio, E., Chowdhury, K. R., & Akyildiz, I. F. (2017). Help from the Sky: Leveraging UAVs for Disaster Management. *IEEE Pervasive Computing, 16*(1), 24–32. doi:10.1109/MPRV.2017.11

Fakhreddine, A., Raffelsberger, C., Sende, M., & Bettstetter, C. (2022, December 1). *Experiments on Drone-to-Drone Communication with Wi-Fi, LTE-A, and 5G.* IEEE Xplore. https://doi.org/ doi:10.1109/ GCWkshps56602.2022.10008743

Fotouhi, A., Qiang, H., Ding, M., Hassan, M., Giordano, L. G., Garcia-Rodriguez, A., & Yuan, J. (2019). Survey on UAV Cellular Communications: Practical Aspects, Standardization Advancements, Regulation, and Security Challenges. *IEEE Communications Surveys and Tutorials, 21*(4), 3417–3442. doi:10.1109/COMST.2019.2906228

Galán-Jiménez, J., Moguel, E., García-Alonso, J., & Berrocal, J. (2021). Energy-efficient and solar powered mission planning of UAV swarms to reduce the coverage gap in rural areas: The 3D case. *Ad Hoc Networks, 118*, 102517. doi:10.1016/j.adhoc.2021.102517

Galán-Jiménez, J., Vegas, A. G., & Berrocal, J. (2022, October 1). *Energy-efficient deployment of IoT applications in remote rural areas using UAV networks.* IEEE Xplore. doi:10.23919/WMNC56391.2022.9954292

Gan, W., Qu, X., Song, D., Sun, H., Guo, T., & Bao, W. (2022, October 1). *Research on Key Technology of Unmanned Surface Vehicle Motion Simulation Based on Unity3D.* IEEE Xplore. doi:10.1109/ OCEANS47191.2022.9977285

García Gil, S., Gómez de la Hiz, J. A., & Ramos Ramos, D. (2023, June 15). *sgarciatz/coverageOptimization.* GitHub. https://github.com/sgarciatz/coverageOptimization

Gupta, L., Jain, R., & Vaszkun, G. (2016). Survey of Important Issues in UAV Communication Networks. *IEEE Communications Surveys and Tutorials, 18*(2), 1123–1152. doi:10.1109/COMST.2015.2495297

Haas, J. K. (2014). *A History of the Unity Game Engine*. Www.semanticscholar.org. https://www.semanticscholar.org/paper/A-History-of-the-Unity-Game-Engine-Haas/5e6b2255d5b7565d11e71e980b1ca141aeb3391d

Jensen-Nau, K. R., Hermans, T., & Leang, K. K. (2021). Near-Optimal Area-Coverage Path Planning of Energy-Constrained Aerial Robots With Application in Autonomous Environmental Monitoring. *IEEE Transactions on Automation Science and Engineering, 18*(3), 1453–1468. doi:10.1109/TASE.2020.3016276

Juliani A. Berges V.-P. Teng E. Cohen A. Harper J. Elion C. Goy C. Gao Y. Henry H. Mattar M. Lange D. (2020). Unity: A General Platform for Intelligent Agents. *ArXiv:1809.02627 [Cs, Stat]*. https://arxiv.org/abs/1809.02627

Kaelbling, L. P., Littman, M. L., & Moore, A. W. (1996). Reinforcement Learning: A Survey. *Journal of Artificial Intelligence Research, 4*, 237–285. doi:10.1613/jair.301

Lee, W., Jeon, Y., Kim, T., & Kim, Y.-I. (2021). Deep Reinforcement Learning for UAV Trajectory Design Considering Mobile Ground Users. *Sensors (Basel), 21*(24), 8239. doi:10.339021248239 PMID:34960332

Li, X., & Xing, L. (2019). Use of Unmanned Aerial Vehicles for Livestock Monitoring based on Streaming K-Means Clustering. *IFAC-PapersOnLine, 52*(30), 324–329. doi:10.1016/j.ifacol.2019.12.560

Liu, Q., Shi, L., Sun, L., Li, J., Ding, M., & Shu, F. S. (2020). Path Planning for UAV-Mounted Mobile Edge Computing With Deep Reinforcement Learning. *IEEE Transactions on Vehicular Technology, 69*(5), 5723–5728. doi:10.1109/TVT.2020.2982508

Liu, X., Liu, Y., & Chen, Y. (2019). Reinforcement Learning in Multiple-UAV Networks: Deployment and Movement Design. *IEEE Transactions on Vehicular Technology, 68*(8), 8036–8049. doi:10.1109/TVT.2019.2922849

Meng, W., Hu, Y., Lin, J., Lin, F., & Teo, R. (2015). ROS+unity: An efficient high-fidelity 3D multi-UAV navigation and control simulator in GPS-denied environments. *IECON 2015 - 41st Annual Conference of the IEEE Industrial Electronics Society*. IEEE. 10.1109/IECON.2015.7392488

Miao, Y., Hwang, K., Wu, D., Hao, Y., & Chen, M. (2023). Drone Swarm Path Planning for Mobile Edge Computing in Industrial Internet of Things. *IEEE Transactions on Industrial Informatics, 19*(5), 6836–6848. doi:10.1109/TII.2022.3196392

Paszke, A., Gross, S., Massa, F., Lerer, A., Bradbury, J., Chanan, G., Killeen, T., Lin, Z., Gimelshein, N., Antiga, L., Desmaison, A., Köpf, A., Yang, E., DeVito, Z., Raison, M., Tejani, A., Chilamkurthy, S., Steiner, B., Fang, L., & Bai, J. (2019). *PyTorch: An Imperative Style, High-Performance Deep Learning Library*. ArXiv.org. https://arxiv.org/abs/1912.01703

Puente-Castro, A., Rivero, D., Pazos, A., & Fernandez-Blanco, E. (2022). UAV swarm path planning with reinforcement learning for field prospecting. *Applied Intelligence, 52*(12), 14101–14118. doi:10.100710489-022-03254-4

Qureshi, H. N., & Imran, A. (2019). On the Tradeoffs Between Coverage Radius, Altitude, and Beamwidth for Practical UAV Deployments. *IEEE Transactions on Aerospace and Electronic Systems, 55*(6), 2805–2821. doi:10.1109/TAES.2019.2893082

Radoglou-Grammatikis, P., Sarigiannidis, P., Lagkas, T., & Moscholios, I. (2020). A Compilation of UAV Applications for Precision Agriculture. *Computer Networks, 107148*, 107148. doi:10.1016/j.comnet.2020.107148

Rogers, K., Karaosmanoglu, S., Altmeyer, M., Suarez, A., & Nacke, L. E. (2022). Much Realistic, Such Wow! A Systematic Literature Review of Realism in Digital Games. *CHI Conference on Human Factors in Computing Systems*. ACM. 10.1145/3491102.3501875

Sami Oubbati, O., Atiquzzaman, M., Ahamed Ahanger, T., & Ibrahim, A. (2020). Softwarization of UAV Networks: A Survey of Applications and Future Trends. *IEEE Access : Practical Innovations, Open Solutions, 8*, 98073–98125. doi:10.1109/ACCESS.2020.2994494

Schulman, J., Wolski, F., Dhariwal, P., Radford, A., & Openai, O. (2017). *Proximal Policy Optimization Algorithms*. arXiv. https://arxiv.org/pdf/1707.06347.pdf

Shan, T., Wang, Y., Zhao, C., Li, Y., Zhang, G., & Zhu, Q. (2023). Multi-UAV WRSN charging path planning based on improved heed and IA-DRL. *Computer Communications, 203*, 77–88. doi:10.1016/j.comcom.2023.02.021

So, H. (2023). Migratory Unmanned Aerial Vehicle System (MiUAV) for Automated Infrastructure Inspection. *IEEE Access : Practical Innovations, Open Solutions, 11*, 56392–56399. doi:10.1109/AC-CESS.2023.3282995

Tang, C., Zhu, C., & Guizani, M. (2023). Coverage Optimization Based on Airborne Fog Computing for Internet of Medical Things. *IEEE Systems Journal, 17*(3), 1–12. doi:10.1109/JSYST.2023.3244923

Terry, J. K., Black, B., Grammel, N., Jayakumar, M., Hari, A., Sullivan, R., Santos, L., Perez, R., Horsch, C., Dieffendahl, C., Williams, N. L., Lokesh, Y., & Ravi, P. (2021, October 26). *PettingZoo: Gym for Multi-Agent Reinforcement Learning*. ArXiv.org. https://doi.org//arXiv.2009.14471 doi:10.48550

Todorov, E., Erez, T., & Tassa, Y. (2012, October 1). *MuJoCo: A physics engine for model-based control*. IEEE Xplore. doi:10.1109/IROS.2012.6386109

Valente, J., Del Cerro, J., Barrientos, A., & Sanz, D. (2013). Aerial coverage optimization in precision agriculture management: A musical harmony inspired approach. *Computers and Electronics in Agriculture, 99*, 153–159. doi:10.1016/j.compag.2013.09.008

Wang, Z., Han, K., & Tiwari, P. (2021). Digital Twin Simulation of Connected and Automated Vehicles with the Unity Game Engine. *2021 IEEE 1st International Conference on Digital Twins and Parallel Intelligence (DTPI)*. IEEE. 10.1109/DTPI52967.2021.9540074

Waseem, M., Liang, P., & Shahin, M. (2020). A Systematic Mapping Study on Microservices Architecture in DevOps. *Journal of Systems and Software, 170*, 110798. doi:10.1016/j.jss.2020.110798

Yan, C., Xiang, X., & Wang, C. (2019). Towards Real-Time Path Planning through Deep Reinforcement Learning for a UAV in Dynamic Environments. *Journal of Intelligent & Robotic Systems*. doi:10.100710846-019-01073-3

Zema, N., Natalizio, E., & Yanmaz, E. (2017). *An Unmanned Aerial Vehicle Network for Sport Event Filming with Communication Constraints* (p. 1731379). https://hal.science/hal-01731379/document

Zeng, Y., Xu, X., & Zhang, R. (2018). Trajectory Design for Completion Time Minimization in UAV-Enabled Multicasting. *IEEE Transactions on Wireless Communications*, *17*(4), 2233–2246. doi:10.1109/TWC.2018.2790401

Zhan, G., Zhang, X., Li, Z., Xu, L., Zhou, D., & Yang, Z. (2022). Multiple-UAV Reinforcement Learning Algorithm Based on Improved PPO in Ray Framework. *Drones (Basel)*, *6*(7), 166. doi:10.3390/drones6070166

Zhang, J., & Huang, H. (2021). Occlusion-Aware UAV Path Planning for Reconnaissance and Surveillance. *Drones (Basel)*, *5*(3), 98. doi:10.3390/drones5030098

KEY TERMS AND DEFINITIONS

Coverage: This refers to the extent or range of an area that is being monitored, mapped, explored, or inspected by a system, sensor, or vehicle, such as UAVs. It is the measure of how much of a specific region is being covered or explored by a particular operation or device.

Digital Twin: A real-time virtual representation of a physical object, system, or process. It uses data and models to simulate its behavior and state, enabling monitoring, analysis, and optimization of its performance in the real world.

DRL: (Deep Reinforcement Learning): A branch of machine learning that combines deep learning algorithms with the reinforcement learning approach, where an agent learns to make optimal decisions through interaction with an environment and receiving rewards or penalties for its actions.

LoS (Line of Sight): An imaginary line that connects the viewpoint of an observer with the object or point of interest being observed. In the context of UAVs, maintaining Line of Sight is important to retain a direct visual connection between the pilot or control system and the UAV during its operation, ensuring effective communication and control.

MEC (Mobile Edge Computing): A distributed computing architecture that allows processing and data storage to be carried out in proximity to the user or device, instead of relying solely on centralized cloud resources. MEC aims to reduce latency, improve network efficiency, and provide faster and more responsive services for mobile applications and devices.

Path Planning: The process of determining an optimal or safe route for a vehicle or mobile agent from its current position to a specific destination, taking into account obstacles, constraints, and other relevant environmental factors.

PPO (Proximal Policy Optimization): A reinforcement learning algorithm used to train artificial intelligence models in environments with rewards to improve decision-making and achieve better performance in specific tasks. PPO is known for its ability to enhance policies in a more stable and efficient manner compared to other policy optimization algorithms.

UAV: (Unmanned Aerial Vehicle): Commonly known as a drone. It is a type of aircraft that can fly autonomously or be remotely controlled without a pilot onboard.

Chapter 3
Applications of Machine Learning in UAV–Based Detecting and Tracking Objects:
Analysis and Overview

Ramya R.
 https://orcid.org/0000-0002-8071-9343
SRM Institute of Science and Technology, India

padmapriya R.
SRM Institute of Science and Technology, India

Anand M.
 https://orcid.org/0000-0001-5205-9678
SRM Institute of Science and Technology, India

ABSTRACT

UAVs are aircrafts that operate without a human pilot and are equipped with sensors to collect data from the environment. They offer advantages over manned aircraft, such as cost-effectiveness, accessibility, flexibility, and the ability to access remote or hazardous areas. This chapter provides the detailed analysis of machine learning in UANs based detecting and tracking objects and people with different use cases, existing technologies with methodologies, future methodologies, challenges, and finally methodologies to overcome challenges. Through this chapter anyone can understand all the details regarding machine learning in UAVs based detecting and tracking objects and people and this will provide future research scope and idea for the researchers.

DOI: 10.4018/979-8-3693-0578-2.ch003

1. INTRODUCTION

Machine learning has advanced the capabilities of unmanned aerial vehicles (UAVs) in detecting and tracking objects and people. These applications include surveillance and security, search and rescue, traffic monitoring and management, and crowd monitoring. Machine learning models can be trained to identify specific objects and raise alerts when anomalies are detected. Machine learning models can be used to identify potential overcrowding, suspicious behaviour, and safety hazards. They can also be used for infrastructure inspection, sports and event coverage, and border and coastline surveillance. This combination of machine learning and UAV technology provides valuable insights and support for a wide range of sectors, such as security, public safety, infrastructure management, and event monitoring.

1.1. Introduction to UAV

Unmanned Aerial Vehicles (UAVs), commonly known as drones, are aircraft that operate without an onboard human pilot. They are remotely controlled or can be programmed to operate autonomously using pre-defined flight plans. UAVs have gained significant popularity and become more accessible in recent years due to advancements in technology and their wide range of applications. The design of UAVs can vary greatly depending on their purpose. They can be small, handheld devices weighing only a few grammes or large, sophisticated systems with wingspans measuring several metres. UAVs can be equipped with various sensors, cameras, and other payloads to perform specific tasks(Cerro J, 2021).

Here are some key components and features of UAVs: Airframe: The airframe is the physical structure of the UAV, including the wings, body, and propulsion system. It can be fixed-wing (similar to traditional aeroplanes), rotary-wing (like helicopters), or multirotor (with multiple propellers). Flight Control System: UAVs use flight control systems that include electronic components, such as flight controllers and gyroscopes, to maintain stability and control the aircraft during flight. These systems can adjust motor speeds, control surfaces, or rotor positions to manoeuvre the UAV. Navigation and Guidance: UAVs employ various navigation and guidance systems to determine their position, altitude, and orientation. This can include GPS (Global Positioning System), inertial measurement units (IMUs), altimeters, and magnetometers. Communication Systems: UAVs rely on communication systems to receive commands from ground-based operators or transmit data, such as video feeds or telemetry, back to the operators. This communication can occur through radio frequency (RF) links or even satellite connections. Sensors and Payloads: UAVs can carry a wide range of sensors and payloads, depending on their intended applications. These can include high-resolution cameras, thermal imaging cameras, LiDAR (Light Detection and Ranging) scanners, multispectral or hyperspectral sensors, gas or chemical detectors, and more. Autonomous Capabilities: Many modern UAVs are equipped with autonomous features that allow them to perform tasks without constant human control. This can involve waypoint navigation, obstacle avoidance, automated takeoff and landing, and even advanced AI algorithms for decision-making.

UAVs have diverse applications across various industries. They are used in aerial photography and videography, agriculture for crop monitoring and spraying, infrastructure inspection of buildings, bridges, and power lines, environmental monitoring, disaster response and search and rescue operations, delivery services, and even recreational purposes. The capabilities of UAVs continue to evolve, driven by ongoing advancements in technology, regulations, and safety measures. They offer unique perspectives and data collection capabilities, making them increasingly valuable tools in many fields.

1.2. How Can UAV Work With and Without AI/ML

UAVs can operate both with and without AI or ML (Artificial intelligence or machine learning), depending on the specific requirements and objectives of their missions. Here's an overview of how UAVs work in both scenarios:

1. UAVs without AI or ML: UAVs can be flown manually by human operators without the need for AI or ML algorithms. In this case, the operator directly controls the UAV's flight path, altitude, and manoeuvres using remote controllers or ground control stations. The operator relies on their own judgement and experience to navigate the UAV and perform the desired tasks. For example, in aerial photography or videography, the operator manually controls the UAV to capture specific shots or angles. Similarly, in surveillance missions, the operator manually directs the UAV's camera to monitor areas of interest. In these scenarios, the UAV's onboard systems may still include basic automation and stabilisation features to assist the pilot, but they do not involve complex AI or ML algorithms.
2. UAVs with AI and ML: UAVs can also leverage AI and ML technologies to enhance their capabilities and perform advanced tasks autonomously or with minimal human intervention. AI and ML algorithms enable UAVs to process sensor data, make decisions, and adapt to changing situations in real-time.

Here are some examples of how UAVs work with AI and ML: Object Detection and Tracking: UAVs equipped with AI or ML algorithms can automatically detect and track objects of interest, such as vehicles, people, or wildlife, in real-time. This enables applications like surveillance, search and rescue, or wildlife monitoring. Autonomous Navigation: AI and ML algorithms can help UAVs navigate autonomously by analysing sensor data and making decisions based on predefined rules or learned patterns. This allows the UAV to avoid obstacles, follow pre-defined flight paths, or explore unknown environments. Anomaly Detection: AI and ML algorithms can be trained to recognise abnormal or suspicious behaviour. In surveillance or security applications, UAVs can detect unusual activities or objects and alert operators for further investigation. Payload Optimisation: UAVs can utilise AI or ML algorithms to optimise the use of their payloads. For example, in agriculture, AI algorithms can analyse crop health data collected by the UAV's sensors and provide recommendations for targeted spraying or irrigation. Path Planning and Mission Optimisation: AI and ML algorithms can optimise UAV flight paths and mission plans based on factors like weather conditions, fuel efficiency, or data collection requirements. This helps improve mission effectiveness and resource allocation.

In summary, UAVs can function without AI or ML, relying on human control for navigation and decision-making. However, integrating AI and ML technologies enables UAVs to operate autonomously, perform complex tasks, and make intelligent decisions based on real-time data analysis.

2. OVERVIEW OF UAV BASED OBJECT AND PEOPLE DETECTION AND TRACKING

UAV-based object and person detection and tracking refers to the use of unmanned aerial vehicles (UAVs), commonly known as drones, for the purpose of identifying and monitoring objects and individuals from an aerial perspective. This technology combines the capabilities of UAVs with computer vision and machine learning algorithms to enable real-time detection and tracking of objects and people (Cerro J, 2021).

The process typically involves the following steps: Image Acquisition: The UAV captures images or video footage using onboard cameras or sensors. These cameras can be RGB (colour) cameras, thermal cameras, or even LiDAR systems, depending on the application requirements. Object Detection: Computer vision algorithms analyse the acquired images to identify objects of interest, such as vehicles, buildings, or individuals. This is achieved through techniques like image segmentation, feature extraction, and pattern recognition. People Detection: Specifically for people detection, algorithms are designed to identify human-like shapes or patterns within the captured images. This can involve methods like Haar cascades, histograms of Oriented Gradients (HOG), or more advanced deep learning techniques such as convolutional neural networks (CNNs). Object and People Tracking: Once the objects or people are detected, tracking algorithms come into play to continuously monitor their movements across frames or video sequences. Multiple object tracking techniques, such as Kalman filters, particle filters, or data association algorithms, are commonly used to track the identified targets. Data Fusion and Analysis: The collected data from the detection and tracking processes is fused and analysed to extract meaningful information. This can include calculating trajectories, estimating speed or direction, monitoring crowd density, or detecting unusual behaviour or anomalies. Application-specific Actions: The information gathered through UAV-based object and person detection and tracking can be utilised for various purposes, depending on the application. Examples include surveillance, search and rescue operations, traffic monitoring, crowd management, or border security.

Advancements in computer vision, machine learning, and UAV technologies have made object and person detection and tracking increasingly efficient and accurate. These systems find applications in a wide range of industries, including public safety, agriculture, infrastructure inspection, environmental monitoring, and more.

2.1. What Are the Challenges Will Come in UAV To Work With AI/ML

Integrating AI and ML into UAV systems presents several challenges that need to be addressed for successful implementation. Some of the key challenges include: Computational Power and Resources: UAVs typically have limited computational power and resources due to their size, weight, and power constraints. AI and ML algorithms often require significant computing resources to process complex data and perform real-time analysis. Ensuring that the UAV's onboard processing capabilities are sufficient to handle the computational demands of AI and ML algorithms is a challenge.

Power Consumption: AI and ML algorithms can be computationally intensive and may consume more power, leading to reduced flight times for UAVs. Balancing the power consumption of AI and ML algorithms with the overall energy efficiency of the UAV system is crucial to maximising flight duration and operational efficiency. Power consumption is a critical concern for UAVs, as it directly impacts flight endurance and mission capabilities. Balancing computational complexity and power efficiency is essential for developing AI/ML-powered UAV systems that can operate efficiently and autonomously.

Computational Complexity vs. Power Efficiency:Computational complexity refers to the amount of processing power required to execute an algorithm or task. AI/ML algorithms, by their nature, can be computationally demanding, requiring significant processing power to analyze sensor data and make decisions. However, this increased processing power comes at the cost of increased power consumption.

Power efficiency, on the other hand, refers to the ability of a system to perform a given task with minimal power consumption. Achieving power efficiency is crucial for UAVs, as it directly translates to longer flight durations.:Balancing Trade-offs for Optimal Flight Endurance Balancing the trade-offs between computational complexity and power efficiency is essential for designing AI/ML-powered UAV systems that can achieve both computational performance and extended flight endurance. This balance can be achieved through several approaches: Algorithm design: Choosing algorithms that are inherently more power-efficient, such as lightweight neural networks or specialized AI architectures designed for low-power applications. Algorithm optimization: Optimizing algorithms to reduce their computational complexity without compromising their performance. This may involve techniques such as pruning redundant connections in neural networks or employing approximation methods. Hardware-software co-design: Carefully matching the hardware architecture to the chosen algorithms, ensuring that the hardware can efficiently execute the algorithms without excessive power consumption. Dynamic power management: Adapting the processing power requirements based on the task at hand, dynamically allocating resources to maximize efficiency while maintaining performance. Energy Harvesting: Incorporating energy harvesting technologies, such as solar panels or kinetic energy harvesting, to supplement the UAV's power supply, reducing reliance on onboard batteries.By carefully considering these trade-offs and employing appropriate optimization techniques, it is possible to develop AI/ML-powered UAV systems that can achieve both high computational performance and extended flight endurance, enabling them to operate effectively in a wide range of applications.

1. Data Processing and Storage: AI and ML algorithms require substantial amounts of data for training, inference, and decision-making. Collecting, processing, and storing data from UAV sensors can be challenging, especially when considering the limited onboard storage capacity and bandwidth constraints for transmitting data in real-time.
2. Real-time Performance and Latency: UAVs often require real-time decision-making to respond quickly to changing situations or dynamically adjust flight paths. AI and ML algorithms must be designed and optimised to meet the stringent latency requirements of UAV operations. Ensuring real-time performance without compromising accuracy is a significant challenge.
3. Algorithm Development and Training: Developing and training AI and ML algorithms for UAV applications requires access to relevant and high-quality training datasets. Collecting and annotating data for specific UAV tasks can be time-consuming and costly. Additionally, designing algorithms that generalise well across different environmental conditions, weather scenarios, or target types adds complexity to the development process.
4. Safety and Reliability: UAVs operate in various environments and may encounter unpredictable situations. Ensuring the safety and reliability of AI and ML-based UAV systems is crucial. Robust algorithms, redundant systems, fail-safe mechanisms, and comprehensive testing and validation procedures are necessary to minimise risks and ensure safe operations.
5. Regulatory and Legal Considerations: Integrating AI and ML into UAV systems may raise regulatory and legal challenges. UAV operations must comply with airspace regulations, privacy laws, and data protection requirements. Addressing these legal and regulatory aspects while leveraging AI and ML technologies can be complex.
6. Interpretability and Explainability: AI and ML algorithms often operate as black boxes, making it challenging to interpret their decision-making processes. Ensuring transparency, interpretability,

and explainability of AI and ML algorithms used in UAV systems is important, particularly in critical applications where human oversight and accountability are essential.

Addressing these challenges requires interdisciplinary collaboration between experts in UAV technology, AI/ML, computer vision, robotics, and regulatory frameworks. Overcoming these hurdles will pave the way for safer, more efficient, and intelligent UAV systems that leverage the power of AI and ML to accomplish complex tasks.

2.2. What Are the Challenges Will Come in UAV To Work With AI/ML For Object and People Detection and Tracking

Integrating AI and ML for object and person detection and tracking in UAVs introduces specific challenges that are unique to this application. Some of the key challenges include (Chandra A L, 2020):

1. Limited Training Data: Developing accurate and robust AI and ML models for object and person detection and tracking requires large and diverse training datasets. However, acquiring annotated training data specifically tailored to UAV scenarios can be challenging. Annotating aerial data with ground truth labels is time-consuming and may require expert knowledge. Obtaining a representative dataset that covers various environmental conditions, object sizes, orientations, and motion patterns is crucial for training effective models.

2. Real-time Performance: UAVs often operate in real-time scenarios where timely detection and tracking are essential. AI and ML algorithms need to process incoming sensor data, perform object detection and tracking, and make decisions within strict time constraints. Optimising the algorithms and their implementation to achieve real-time performance on limited onboard computing resources is a significant challenge.

3. Varying Environmental Conditions: UAVs encounter diverse environmental conditions, such as changes in lighting, weather, or cluttered backgrounds, which can affect the performance of object and person detection algorithms. Ensuring that the AI and ML models generalise well across different environments and can adapt to variations is crucial. Robustness to lighting conditions, occlusions, shadows, and complex backgrounds is essential for reliable detection and tracking.

4. Scale and Perspective Changes: UAVs capture imagery from an elevated perspective, resulting in variations in object scales and perspectives. Objects of interest may appear significantly smaller or larger than expected, making accurate detection and tracking challenging. Adapting the AI and ML algorithms to handle scale and perspective changes is necessary to maintain accurate object and person tracking.

5. Motion and Dynamics: Objects and people in UAV imagery often exhibit complex motion patterns, including fast movement, occlusions, or rapid changes in direction. Tracking such dynamic targets accurately and consistently poses a challenge. AI and ML algorithms need to handle object motion, predict trajectories, and account for uncertainties to ensure reliable tracking results.

6. Power and Energy Efficiency: Implementing AI and ML algorithms for object and person detection and tracking on UAVs needs to consider power and energy efficiency. Power consumption affects flight endurance, so optimising the algorithms to reduce computational requirements while maintaining performance is crucial for maximising the UAV's operational time.

7. Integration with Sensor Technologies: UAVs utilise various sensors, such as cameras, thermal imaging, or LiDAR, to capture data for object and person detection. Integrating these sensors with AI and ML algorithms, ensuring sensor synchronisation, and leveraging their complementary information pose technical challenges. The fusion of data from different sensors and modalities requires careful calibration, synchronisation, and processing techniques.

8. Interpretability and Explainability: AI and ML models used for object and person detection and tracking in UAVs need to provide interpretability and explainability. Understanding the reasons behind the algorithm's decisions is important for trust, accountability, and human oversight. Ensuring the algorithms are transparent and provide explanations for their detections and tracking results is crucial, particularly in critical applications.

Addressing these challenges requires a combination of data collection and annotation efforts, algorithm development and optimisation, sensor integration, testing and validation, and close collaboration between experts in UAV technology, computer vision, machine learning, and robotics. Overcoming these challenges will lead to improved object and person detection and tracking capabilities in UAV applications.

3. METHODOLOGIES OF ML IN UAVs FOR DETECTING AND TRACKING

Machine learning can be used in UAVs for object and people detection and tracking by leveraging image processing and computer vision techniques(Hii M S Y, 2019). Here's a general approach to using machine learning in UAVs for this purpose: 1. Data Collection: Collect a diverse dataset of images or videos that contain the objects or people you want to detect and track. This dataset should include a variety of backgrounds, lighting conditions, poses, and scales to ensure robust learning. 2. Data Preprocessing: Preprocess the collected data to enhance its quality and facilitate machine learning algorithms' effectiveness. This may involve resizing the images, normalizing the lighting conditions, and removing any noise or irrelevant elements. 3. Labeling and Annotation: Annotate the collected data by manually labeling the objects or people of interest in each image or video frame. This annotation provides ground truth information that the machine learning algorithm can learn from during training. 4. Training Data Preparation: Split the annotated dataset into training and validation sets. The training set will be used to train the machine learning model, while the validation set helps evaluate its performance during training and tune hyperparameters. 5. Feature Extraction: Extract meaningful features from the images or video frames to represent the objects or people. Common approaches include using handcrafted features (e.g., histograms of oriented gradients, Haar-like features) or employing convolutional neural networks (CNNs) to automatically learn features directly from the data. 6. Model Training: Train a machine learning model, such as a support vector machine (SVM), random forest, or deep neural network, using the labeled training data. The model learns to associate the extracted features with the corresponding object or person labels. 7. Model Evaluation: Evaluate the trained model's performance using the validation set. Metrics such as precision, recall, and accuracy can be used to assess the model's ability to detect and track objects or people accurately. 8. Deployment on UAV: Once the model has been trained and validated, it can be deployed on a UAV. The UAV captures real-time images or videos, and the machine learning model processes this data to detect and track objects or people of interest. 9. Real-time Object/ People Detection and Tracking: During operation, the UAV continuously captures images or video frames. The machine learning model processes these frames in real-time, identifying and tracking the objects or people based on their learned features and patterns. 10. Performance Monitoring and Improvement: Continuously monitor the performance of the object and people detection and tracking system. Gather feedback on the model's accuracy and refine it if necessary by iteratively updating the training data, retraining the model, and deploying improved versions.

It's important to note that the specific machine learning techniques and algorithms used can vary depending on the complexity of the task, available computational resources, and the size and quality of the dataset. Additionally, more advanced techniques like object tracking algorithms (e.g., Kalman filters, particle filters) can be integrated to track the detected objects or people over time. By combining machine learning with UAV technology, real-time object and people detection and tracking capabilities can be achieved, enabling a wide range of applications in surveillance, security, search and rescue, and more.

3.1. Existing Technologies of ML In UAVs Detecting and Tracking

There are several existing technologies in machine learning that have been successfully applied to UAVs for detecting and tracking objects and people. Here are some notable technologies(Ramya R,2022):

1. Convolutional Neural Networks (CNNs): CNNs have revolutionized computer vision tasks, including object detection and recognition. These deep learning models are capable of learning hierarchical representations of visual data and have been widely used in UAVs for detecting and tracking objects and people in real-time.
2. Region-based Convolutional Neural Networks (R-CNN): R-CNN is an object detection framework that combines CNNs with region proposal methods. It first generates region proposals in an image and then uses CNNs to classify and refine these proposals. This approach has been employed in UAVs for accurate object detection and tracking.
3. Single Shot MultiBox Detector (SSD): SSD is an object detection algorithm that combines high detection accuracy with real-time processing speed. It uses a series of convolutional layers with different scales to detect objects at various sizes. SSD has been used in UAVs to achieve efficient and accurate object detection and tracking.
4. You Only Look Once (YOLO): YOLO is an object detection algorithm that focuses on real-time processing by predicting bounding boxes and class probabilities directly from the input image in a single pass. YOLO has been applied to UAVs for real-time object detection and tracking tasks.
5. Tracking-by-Detection: Tracking-by-Detection is a popular approach for object tracking in UAVs. It combines object detection algorithms with tracking algorithms to track objects over time. Techniques such as correlation filters, Kalman filters, and particle filters are often used for object tracking in UAVs.
6. DeepSORT: DeepSORT is a deep learning-based object tracking algorithm that combines object detection with deep appearance feature embeddings. It enables robust multi-object tracking by associating detected objects across frames. DeepSORT has been applied to UAVs for accurate and persistent tracking of multiple objects or people.
7. Feature-Based Tracking: Feature-based tracking methods, such as the Kanade-Lucas-Tomasi (KLT) tracker, track objects by identifying and matching key features between consecutive frames. These methods are computationally efficient and have been used in UAVs for real-time tracking applications.

8. Transfer Learning: Transfer learning allows pre-trained models on large-scale datasets (e.g., ImageNet) to be fine-tuned for specific object detection and tracking tasks in UAVs. By leveraging pre-trained models, transfer learning can overcome data limitations and improve the performance of object detection and tracking algorithms.

9. Unsupervised Learning: Unsupervised learning techniques, such as clustering algorithms (e.g., k-means, DBSCAN) and self-organizing maps, can be used to discover patterns and group similar objects or people without the need for labeled training data. These methods have potential applications in UAV-based object clustering or anomaly detection.

10. Reinforcement Learning: Reinforcement learning algorithms can be utilized in UAVs to learn optimal tracking policies through interaction with the environment. This approach enables UAVs to adapt their tracking strategies based on feedback and maximize tracking performance in dynamic scenarios.

These are just a few examples of existing technologies in machine learning applied to UAVs for object and people detection and tracking. The field of UAV-based machine learning is rapidly evolving, and researchers are continuously developing and refining algorithms and techniques to improve detection accuracy, real-time performance, and robustness in various operational conditions.

3.2. Limitations of Existing Technologies of ML In UAVs Detecting and Tracking

While machine learning (ML) has shown promising results in UAV object detection and tracking, there are some limitations and challenges that exist with the existing technologies. These limitations include: Computational Resources: ML algorithms often require significant computational resources for training and inference. UAVs, especially smaller or lighter ones, have limited onboard computing capabilities. This constraint makes it challenging to deploy computationally intensive ML models directly on UAVs, which may affect the real-time performance and responsiveness of object detection and tracking systems. Data Annotation and Collection: Training ML models for object detection and tracking in UAVs requires large annotated datasets. However, manually annotating aerial data can be time-consuming and expensive. Obtaining diverse and representative datasets that cover different environmental conditions, object types, and motion patterns can be challenging, leading to potential limitations in the performance and generalisation of ML models.

1. Limited Training in UAV-Specific Scenarios: Most ML models for object detection and tracking are trained on datasets that primarily consist of ground-level images. Aerial imagery captured by UAVs has different perspectives, scales, and challenges (such as motion blur or occlusions). Training ML models with a focus on UAV-specific scenarios can help improve their performance in detecting and tracking objects accurately from an aerial viewpoint.

2. Generalisation to Diverse Environments: ML models trained on specific datasets may not generalise well to the diverse environments encountered by UAVs. Changes in lighting conditions, weather, or cluttered backgrounds can impact the performance of object detection and tracking algorithms. Ensuring robustness and adaptability to different environmental conditions remains a challenge for existing ML technologies.

3. Real-time Performance: Achieving real-time performance is critical for UAV applications. ML models with complex architectures or large computational requirements may not meet the strict

time constraints for real-time object detection and tracking. Optimising ML algorithms to reduce computational complexity, leveraging hardware acceleration, or using lightweight architectures can help improve real-time performance but can also introduce trade-offs in detection accuracy.

4. Power and Energy Efficiency: Implementing ML algorithms on UAVs requires careful consideration of power and energy efficiency. ML algorithms, particularly deep learning models, can be computationally intensive and power-hungry, impacting the UAV's flight endurance. Balancing the computational demands of ML algorithms with power constraints is crucial for extended UAV operations.

5. Interpretability and Explainability: ML models often operate as black boxes, making it challenging to interpret their decision-making processes. Understanding the reasons behind the ML model's detections and tracking outputs is important for trust, explainability, and accountability, especially in critical applications. Ensuring the interpretability and explainability of ML-based object detection and tracking systems is still an ongoing research area.

Addressing these limitations requires ongoing research and development efforts to design lightweight and efficient ML models, collect and annotate UAV-specific datasets, optimise algorithms for real-time performance, enhance generalisation to diverse environments, and improve the interpretability and explainability of ML-based object detection and tracking systems.

4. METHODOLOGIES OF ML IN UAVs BASED DETECTING AND TRACTING

Machine learning methodologies for object detection and tracking in Unmanned Aerial Vehicles (UAVs) typically involve a combination of techniques from computer vision, deep learning, and robotics. Here is a high-level methodology for implementing object detection and tracking in UAVs:

Data Collection and Preprocessing: Gather labeled training data consisting of images or videos captured by UAVs. This data should include examples of the objects you want to detect and track. Preprocess the data, including resizing, normalization, and augmentation, to ensure consistency and improve model robustness(Carrio A, 2017). Object Detection: Train or fine-tune an object detection model using deep learning techniques. You can use pre-trained models (e.g., Faster R-CNN, YOLO, or SSD) and adapt them to your specific dataset. Annotate the training data by bounding boxes around the objects of interest. Fine-tune the model on UAV-specific data to account for environmental conditions, altitudes, and camera characteristics. Optimize the model for real-time inference on the UAV's onboard hardware or edge AI accelerators. Object Tracking: After object detection, initialize trackers for detected objects. Various methods can be used for tracking, including Kalman filters, Particle filters, and deep learning-based trackers like DeepSORT. Continuously update the tracking results based on the movement of objects in subsequent frames. Implement logic to handle object occlusion, appearance changes, and tracking failures.

Data preprocessing is a crucial step in machine learning, as it involves preparing the raw data to make it suitable for training and evaluating machine learning models. The specific preprocessing steps involved vary depending on the type of data and the machine learning task, but some common techniques include:

Data Cleaning: Data cleaning involves identifying and correcting errors or inconsistencies in the data. This may include tasks such as: Handling missing values: Missing values can be replaced with estimated values, removed altogether, or imputed using techniques like mean or median imputation.

Detecting and removing outliers: Outliers are data points that deviate significantly from the rest of the data. They can be identified using statistical methods or visual inspection and removed or modified to prevent them from skewing the data. Correcting data entry errors: Data entry errors can introduce noise into the data. These errors can be detected and corrected using techniques like spell checking, pattern recognition, and data validation.

Data Transformation: Data transformation involves modifying the format or structure of the data to make it more suitable for machine learning algorithms. This may include tasks such as: Feature normalization: Feature normalization involves scaling the values of different features to a common range. This is important because some machine learning algorithms are sensitive to the scale of the input data. Data encoding: Categorical data, such as text or labels, needs to be encoded into numerical values before it can be used by machine learning algorithms. This can be done using techniques like one-hot encoding or label encoding. Feature engineering: Feature engineering involves creating new features from existing features or combining features to improve the performance of the machine learning model.

Noise Reduction: Noise reduction involves removing unwanted or irrelevant information from the data. This can be done using techniques such as: Filtering: Filtering involves applying a smoothing function to the data to remove high-frequency noise. Denoising: Denoising involves identifying and removing specific types of noise from the data. Outlier detection: Outlier detection involves identifying and removing data points that deviate significantly from the rest of the data.

Image Enhancement: Image enhancement involves improving the quality of images to make them more suitable for machine learning tasks. This may include tasks such as: Contrast adjustment: Adjusting the contrast of images to improve the visibility of details. Noise reduction: Removing noise from images to improve the clarity and sharpness of the image. Image segmentation: Segmenting images into meaningful regions to extract relevant features.

Data Augmentation: Data augmentation involves artificially increasing the size of the training dataset by creating new data samples from existing ones. This can be done using techniques such as: Geometric transformations: Applying geometric transformations, such as rotation, translation, and scaling, to images. Color space transformations: Modifying the color space of images to create variations in the appearance of objects. Adding noise: Adding noise to images to simulate real-world conditions.

Data preprocessing is an iterative process that may require multiple passes over the data to achieve the desired quality and format. The specific preprocessing steps involved depend on the characteristics of the data and the machine learning task, and it is often necessary to experiment with different techniques to find the optimal approach for each application. The availability of high-quality training data is crucial for developing effective machine learning models for UAV applications. However, collecting and annotating large amounts of real-world data can be challenging, time-consuming, and expensive. This limited training data can lead to several challenges, including: Overfitting: Overfitting occurs when the machine learning model learns the training data too well and fails to generalize to new data. This can result in poor performance on unseen data, making the model unreliable for real-world applications. Underfitting: Underfitting occurs when the machine learning model is too simple to capture the complex patterns in the training data. This can result in poor performance on both the training data and unseen data. Biased models: Biased models can reflect biases present in the training data, leading to unfair or discriminatory decisions. This is particularly concerning in UAV applications where decisions may have significant consequences, such as in search and rescue operations or infrastructure inspection.

To address the challenge of limited training data, several strategies can be employed: Data Augmentation: Data augmentation involves artificially increasing the size of the training dataset by creating new data samples from existing ones. This can be done using techniques such as: Geometric transformations: Applying geometric transformations, such as rotation, translation, and scaling, to images or sensor data. Color space transformations: Modifying the color space of images or sensor data to create variations in the appearance of objects. Adding noise: Adding noise to images or sensor data to simulate real-world conditions.

Data augmentation can help to improve the generalization ability of machine learning models by exposing them to a wider range of variations in the data. Transfer Learning: Transfer learning involves utilizing a pre-trained machine learning model on a related task to initialize the model for the UAV application. This can help to overcome the data scarcity problem by leveraging the knowledge learned from the larger dataset. For instance, a model trained on a massive dataset of natural images can be transferred to an image classification task for UAV applications, providing a strong starting point for learning despite the limited UAV-specific data.

Synthetic Data Generation: Synthetic data generation involves creating artificial data samples that mimic the characteristics of real-world data. This can be done using simulation techniques or generative models. Synthetic data can be particularly useful for generating rare or difficult-to-collect data, such as scenarios involving specific object interactions or extreme environmental conditions.

Data Collection Strategies: Careful planning and strategic data collection can also help to mitigate the data scarcity problem. This may involve: Targeted data collection: Focusing on collecting data that is most relevant to the specific UAV application. Active learning: Prioritizing the collection of data points that are most informative for the machine learning model. Data collaboration: Collaborating with other researchers or organizations to share data and resources.

By employing these strategies, researchers and developers can effectively address the challenge of limited training data in UAV applications, leading to the development of more robust, reliable, and unbiased machine learning models.

Sensor Fusion: If available, integrate data from multiple sensors, such as cameras, LiDAR, GPS, and IMU, to improve object detection and tracking accuracy. Sensor fusion helps compensate for the limitations of individual sensors and enhances situational awareness.

Trajectory Prediction: Implement trajectory prediction models that estimate the future positions of tracked objects based on historical tracking data. Use these predictions to improve the UAV's ability to maintain tracking even when objects change direction or speed.

Communication and Control Integration: Integrate the object detection and tracking results into the UAV's control system. This may involve sending commands to the UAV to follow, avoid, or interact with detected objects. Implement collision avoidance algorithms to ensure the UAV maintains a safe distance from obstacles.

Real-time Processing and Optimization: Ensure that the entire object detection and tracking pipeline is optimized for real-time or near-real-time processing on the UAV's hardware. Optimize the code and algorithms to minimize latency, as real-time tracking is crucial for many UAV applications.

Real-time performance is a crucial aspect of UAV operations, as many applications demand instantaneous decision-making and execution. Latency, the time lag between an event occurring and the corresponding response, plays a critical role in ensuring the effectiveness of UAV systems. Excessive latency can lead to delayed reactions, missed opportunities, and even safety hazards.

In UAV applications, latency can arise from various sources, including: Sensor data acquisition and transmission: The time it takes for sensors to collect data and transmit it to the processing unit can introduce latency. Data processing and analysis: The processing of sensor data, including image and video analysis, can be computationally demanding, contributing to latency. Decision-making and command generation: The time it takes to make decisions based on processed data and generate control commands can further add to latency. Command transmission and actuator response: The time it takes for control commands to be transmitted to the actuators and for the UAV to respond can introduce additional latency.

Minimizing latency is essential for several reasons in UAV operations: Time-critical tasks: Many UAV applications involve time-sensitive tasks, such as search and rescue, where timely decisions can save lives. Dynamic environments: UAVs often operate in dynamic environments where immediate re-actions to changing conditions are crucial for maintaining stability and avoiding collisions. Autonomy and responsiveness: Autonomous UAVs rely on real-time processing and decision-making to navigate autonomously and respond to unexpected situations.

AI/ML algorithms play a significant role in UAV operations, and their optimization is crucial for achieving real-time performance. To address latency challenges, several approaches can be employed: Hardware optimization: Utilizing hardware accelerators, such as GPUs or specialized AI chips, can significantly reduce the time required for data processing and analysis. Algorithm optimization: Optimizing AI/ML algorithms to reduce computational complexity and improve efficiency can minimize the time required for decision-making and command generation. Edge computing: Moving AI/ML computations closer to the data source, such as on-board the UAV, can reduce latency by minimizing data transmission times. Real-time operating systems: Employing real-time operating systems that prioritize real-time tasks and minimize scheduling overhead can ensure timely execution of critical processes. Predictive modeling: Incorporating predictive modeling techniques can anticipate future events and allow the UAV to make proactive decisions, reducing the need for real-time reactions and minimizing latency.

By addressing latency challenges and optimizing AI/ML algorithms, UAV systems can achieve the real-time performance required for effective and safe operation in various applications. Testing and Validation: Conduct extensive testing and validation in various real-world scenarios, including different lighting conditions, weather, altitudes, and object types. Continuously collect data and refine the models to improve detection and tracking performance. Deployment and Monitoring: Deploy the object detection and tracking system on the UAV. Continuously monitor the system's performance and update models as needed to adapt to changing conditions or requirements. Safety Measures: Implement fail-safe mechanisms and safety measures to handle unexpected situations or tracking failures, especially in autonomous UAV applications.

The methodology for object detection and tracking in UAVs is an iterative process that involves data collection, model development, testing, and refinement. It requires a multidisciplinary approach that combines expertise in machine learning, computer vision, robotics, and UAV operations. Additionally, adherence to safety and regulatory guidelines is crucial when deploying UAVs for object detection and tracking in real-world scenarios.

Figure 1. Detection-and-tracking-algorithm-flowchart shows the basic flow of process in object detection and tracking with algorithms.

Figure 1. Detection-and-tracking-algorithm-flowchart

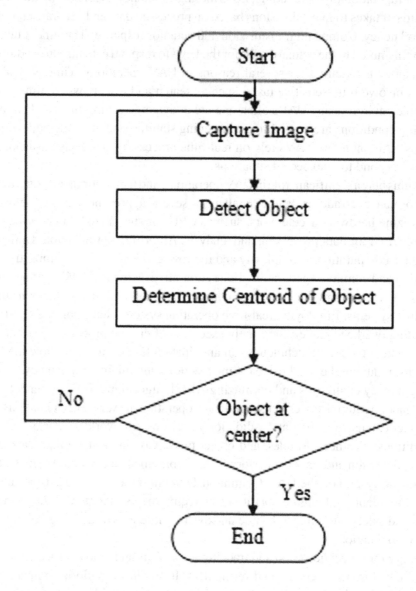

Table 1. Some machine learning algorithms used for object detection show the list of machine learning algorithms used for object detection with the details of the framework and year of invention.

Table 1. Some machine learning algorithms used for object detection

Algorithm	Framework	Year
YOLO (You Only Look Once)	Darknet, PyTorch	2016
SSD (Single Shot Detector)	TensorFlow, PyTorch	2016
Faster R-CNN	TensorFlow, PyTorch	2015
RetinaNet	TensorFlow, PyTorch	2017
Mask R-CNN	TensorFlow, PyTorch	2017
R-FCN (Region-based Fully Convolutional Networks)	Caffe	2016
FPN (Feature Pyramid Network)	TensorFlow, PyTorch	2017

4.1. Machine Learning Technology for Object Detection In UAV

Object detection in Unmanned Aerial Vehicles (UAVs) presents unique challenges and requirements compared to traditional object detection in static images or videos. UAVs often have limited computational resources, power constraints, and the need for real-time or near-real-time processing. Here are some machine learning technologies and considerations specifically tailored for object detection in UAVs(D Hong, 2021):

Deep Learning Models: Many of the deep learning models mentioned earlier (Faster R-CNN, YOLO, SSD, RetinaNet) can be adapted for object detection in UAVs. However, model selection should consider the trade-off between accuracy and computational efficiency due to the limited resources on UAVs.

Lightweight Models: UAVs typically have less powerful hardware compared to data centers. Therefore, lightweight deep learning models such as MobileNet, SqueezeNet, or TinyYOLO may be more suitable. These models have fewer parameters and are optimized for efficiency.

Real-time Inference: Real-time or near-real-time object detection is often essential for UAV applications, especially for tasks like tracking or collision avoidance. Optimizing the model and inference pipeline for speed is crucial.

On-Device Inference: To minimize latency and reduce communication overhead, consider deploying object detection models directly on the UAV's onboard processing unit or specialized hardware like edge AI accelerators.

Data Augmentation: UAVs capture images from different altitudes, angles, and lighting conditions. Data augmentation techniques should be used to increase the robustness of the model to various environmental conditions.

Transfer Learning: Transfer learning from pre-trained models on large datasets can be particularly valuable when you have limited labeled data for UAV-specific tasks.

Object Tracking: In many UAV applications, continuous tracking of detected objects is necessary. You can integrate object tracking algorithms (e.g., Kalman filters, Hungarian algorithm, or deep learning-based trackers like GOTURN) with your object detection system.

Geospatial Information: UAVs often provide geospatial information, such as GPS coordinates and altitude. This information can be used to improve object detection accuracy and context awareness.

Obstacle Avoidance: In UAV applications like autonomous drones, object detection is essential for obstacle avoidance. The system should be capable of detecting and reacting to obstacles in real-time to ensure safe navigation.

Custom Hardware: Depending on the UAV platform, you might consider custom hardware solutions, such as specialized vision sensors or hardware accelerators, to improve the efficiency of object detection tasks.

Energy Efficiency: Given the limited battery life of UAVs, energy-efficient inference is critical. Techniques like model quantization and pruning can reduce power consumption during inference.

Robustness to Environmental Conditions: Object detection models for UAVs should be trained and tested under various weather conditions (e.g., rain, fog, snow) and lighting conditions (e.g., day and night) to ensure robust performance.

When developing object detection solutions for UAVs, it's essential to consider the specific requirements of your application, hardware constraints, and the environmental conditions in which the UAV will operate. Additionally, rigorous testing and validation are crucial to ensure the safety and reliability of the system, especially when used in mission-critical scenarios.

4.2. Machine Learning Technology for Object Tracking in UAV

Object tracking in Unmanned Aerial Vehicles (UAVs) is a critical task that involves following and monitoring objects of interest as they move within the UAV's field of view. Several machine-learning technologies and techniques can be employed for object tracking in UAVs(Hossain S, 2019):

Deep Learning-based Tracking: Siamese Networks: Siamese networks are deep learning architectures designed for one-shot object tracking. They learn to distinguish between a target object and the background and can be used for real-time tracking tasks. DeepSORT: DeepSORT combines deep learning (CNN-based object detection) with the SORT (Simple Online and Realtime Tracking) algorithm to achieve robust and real-time object tracking. It's well-suited for multi-object tracking in UAVs. MOT (Multiple Object Tracking) with Deep Learning: MOT algorithms that incorporate deep learning techniques like deep appearance feature embeddings can enhance the accuracy of tracking, especially in complex scenarios.

Online Learning Algorithms: Online Boosting: Online boosting algorithms, such as AdaBoost, can be used to update the object tracker's appearance model over time. This helps adapt to changing lighting conditions and object appearances. Online Learning with SVM: Support Vector Machines (SVMs) can be trained online to improve object tracking robustness and adaptability. Reinforcement Learning (RL): Deep Reinforcement Learning for Tracking: RL can be used to train UAVs to perform tracking tasks more intelligently. Agents learn how to control the UAV's movements to keep objects in the field of view effectively. Kalman Filters and Variations: Extended Kalman Filters (EKF) and Unscented Kalman Filters (UKF): These are classic state estimation techniques used for object tracking. They can be combined with object detection to provide robust tracking. Particle Filters: Particle Filters (PF): PF is a probabilistic framework used for object tracking. It can handle non-linear and non-Gaussian state estimation problems, making it suitable for challenging tracking scenarios. Optical Flow: Optical Flow Algorithms: Optical flow methods estimate the motion of objects by analyzing the changes in pixel intensity over time. They can be used in conjunction with object detection to predict object movement. Custom Tracking Algorithms: Depending on the specific requirements of your UAV tracking application, you may need to develop custom tracking algorithms tailored to the types of objects you are tracking and the environment in which the UAV operates. Real-time Hardware Acceleration: To ensure real-time tracking performance on UAVs, consider optimizing your tracking algorithms for deployment on specialized hardware like GPUs or FPGAs. Sensor Fusion: Combine data from multiple sensors on the UAV, such as cameras, LiDAR, and GPS, to improve tracking accuracy and robustness. Trajectory Prediction:

Incorporate trajectory prediction models to anticipate the future positions of tracked objects, enhancing the UAV's ability to maintain tracking. Communication and Control Integration: Integrate tracking results with the UAV's control system to enable actions such as object following or collision avoidance. Evaluation and Benchmarking: Continuously evaluate and benchmark your tracking algorithms to ensure they meet the performance criteria required for your UAV application.

Object tracking in UAVs is a challenging task that demands a combination of computer vision, machine learning, and robotics expertise. The choice of technology and algorithm depends on the specific tracking requirements and constraints of your UAV system.

The integration of artificial intelligence (AI) and machine learning (ML) into unmanned aerial vehicles (UAVs) has revolutionized their capabilities, opening up new possibilities for their application in various industries. AI/ML-powered UAVs can now perceive their surroundings, make intelligent decisions, and adapt to dynamic environments in ways that were not possible with traditional UAVs.

Enhanced Accuracy and Precision: AI/ML algorithms can analyze data from UAV sensors, such as cameras and lidar, in real-time to extract precise information about the environment. This enables UAVs to perform tasks with greater accuracy and precision, such as: Mapping and 3D modeling: UAVs equipped with AI/ML can generate highly detailed maps and 3D models of complex environments, such as disaster zones or infrastructure projects. This information is crucial for planning and decision-making in various applications.

Object detection and classification: AI/ML algorithms can identify and classify objects in real-time, enabling UAVs to perform tasks such as counting wildlife populations, inspecting infrastructure for defects, or monitoring crops for pests and diseases.

Real-time Decision-making: AI/ML-powered UAVs can process data in real-time and make autonomous decisions based on their surroundings. This allows them to adapt to changing conditions and perform tasks without the need for constant human intervention. For example: Autonomous navigation: UAVs with AI/ML can navigate complex environments without predefined routes, avoiding obstacles and adapting to changing conditions. This is particularly useful in search and rescue operations or infrastructure inspections.

Real-time threat detection: AI/ML algorithms can analyze sensor data to identify potential threats, such as fire hazards or structural defects, and alert operators in real-time. This enables timely intervention and prevents potential disasters.

Handling Complex Environments: AI/ML can enable UAVs to operate in complex and dynamic environments that were previously inaccessible or too dangerous for human pilots. This includes environments with:Limited visibility: AI/ML algorithms can process data from lidar and thermal imaging sensors to navigate in low-light or foggy conditions.

Unstructured environments: AI/ML-powered UAVs can adapt to changing terrain and obstacles in real-time, making them suitable for tasks such as disaster relief or infrastructure inspection in remote areas.

Hazardous environments: AI/ML can enable UAVs to operate in hazardous environments, such as nuclear power plants or chemical spill sites, without exposing human pilots to risk.

Specific Examples of AI/ML-powered UAV Applications: Precision agriculture: AI/ML algorithms can analyze crop data to optimize irrigation, fertilization, and pesticide application, reducing waste and improving yields. Autonomous delivery: AI/ML-powered drones can deliver goods to remote locations, improving logistics and access to essential services. Wildlife monitoring: AI/ML can identify and track individual animals, enabling researchers to study animal behavior and conservation efforts. Infrastructure inspection: AI/ML can detect defects and damage in bridges, pipelines, and other infrastructure, reducing downtime and improving safety. Disaster response: AI/ML can map disaster zones, identify survivors, and assess damage, aiding emergency response teams. The integration of AI/ML into UAVs is still in its early stages, but the potential applications are vast. As AI/ML algorithms become more sophisticated and UAV technology continues to advance, we can expect to see even more innovative and transformative applications emerge in the years to come.

Model explainability refers to the ability to understand how an AI/ML model arrives at its decisions. This is particularly important for critical applications where the model's decisions may have significant consequences, such as in UAVs performing tasks like search and rescue, infrastructure inspection, or autonomous delivery.

In UAV applications, model explainability is crucial for several reasons: Trust and transparency: Users need to trust the decisions made by AI/ML-powered UAVs, especially in critical situations. Explainable models can help build trust by providing insights into the reasoning behind their decisions. Debugging and improvement: Understanding how a model works can help identify potential biases or errors in the model's decision-making process, allowing for improvements and refinements. Regulatory compliance: In some industries, regulations may require explainability for AI/ML systems used in decision-making processes.

Techniques for Model Explainability: Several techniques can be employed to enhance the explainability of AI/ML models for UAV applications:

Feature visualization: This technique involves visualizing the importance of different features in the model's decision-making process. For instance, in an image classification task, feature visualization can highlight the regions of an image that contribute most to the model's classification decision. Feature visualization in AI/ML.

Saliency maps: Saliency maps create visual representations of the parts of an input that most influence the model's output. This can help users understand which aspects of the input are most relevant to the model's decision. Saliency maps in AI/ML.

Interpretable models: Certain types of AI/ML models are inherently more interpretable than others. For example, decision trees and rule-based models can be more easily understood by humans compared to complex neural networks.

Counterfactual explanations: Counterfactual explanations involve generating alternative scenarios that would have resulted in a different model output. This can help users understand the boundaries of the model's decision-making process.

Human-in-the-loop explanations: In some cases, human experts may be involved in interpreting and explaining the model's decisions. This can be particularly useful for complex or nuanced applications where automated explanations may not be sufficient.

By employing these techniques, developers and users can gain a deeper understanding of how AI/ML models work, building trust, enabling debugging and improvement, and facilitating regulatory compliance.

5. THE FUTURE METHODOLOGIES OF ML IN UAVs BASED DETECTING AND TRACTING

The future of machine learning in UAVs-based detecting and tracking objects and people holds great potential for advancements in methodology. Here are some future methodologies that could shape this field(Yuan W, 2021):

1. Deep Reinforcement Learning: Combining deep learning with reinforcement learning can enable UAVs to learn complex policies for object detection and tracking. By interacting with the environment and receiving feedback, UAVs can adapt their tracking strategies and make intelligent decisions in real-time.

2. Online Learning: Online learning approaches allow UAVs to continuously update their models and adapt to changing environments. By incorporating new data and dynamically adjusting the model parameters, UAVs can improve their object detection and tracking capabilities over time.

3. Generative Adversarial Networks (GANs): GANs have the potential to enhance the quality and diversity of training data for object detection and tracking. UAVs can use GANs to generate synthetic data that resembles real-world scenarios, which can be combined with real data for improved training and generalization.

4. Multi-Sensor Fusion: Integrating data from multiple sensors, such as visual cameras, thermal sensors, LiDAR, or radar, can enhance object detection and tracking performance. Machine learning algorithms can be developed to effectively fuse data from different sensors, leveraging complementary information for better accuracy and robustness.

5. Active Learning: Active learning techniques can enable UAVs to intelligently select the most informative data for annotation, reducing the need for extensive manual labeling. By actively querying labels for uncertain or challenging instances, UAVs can improve their detection and tracking performance with minimal human supervision.

6. Few-Shot and Zero-Shot Learning: Few-shot and zero-shot learning approaches aim to address the challenge of limited annotated data for rare or novel objects or people. These methodologies enable UAVs to generalize their knowledge from a few labeled examples or learn from textual or semantic descriptions of objects, allowing for improved detection and tracking in diverse scenarios.

7. Explainable AI: Developing explainable machine learning models in UAVs is crucial for building trust and understanding their decision-making processes. Future methodologies may focus on interpretable deep learning models that can provide insights into the features or cues influencing object detection and tracking decisions made by UAVs.

8. Edge Computing and Onboard Processing: With the increasing computational capabilities of UAVs, future methodologies may explore onboard processing and edge computing for real-time object detection and tracking. This reduces the reliance on remote servers or cloud infrastructure, enabling faster response times and enhanced privacy.

9. Federated Learning: Federated learning allows UAVs in a network to collaboratively train a shared model while keeping the training data decentralized and private. This methodology can enable UAVs to learn from a collective dataset without compromising individual privacy, facilitating knowledge sharing and improved detection and tracking performance.

10. Continual Learning: Continual learning techniques focus on maintaining and updating machine learning models over an extended period, allowing UAVs to adapt to new object classes, environmental conditions, or tracking scenarios without catastrophic forgetting. Continual learning enables lifelong learning capabilities in UAVs-based object detection and tracking.

These future methodologies hold the potential to enhance the performance, adaptability, and efficiency of machine learning in UAVs-based detecting and tracking objects and people. As technology advances and research progresses, these methodologies are likely to shape the future of this field, enabling UAVs to achieve even higher levels of accuracy, autonomy, and intelligence in object detection and tracking tasks.

5.1. UAV Applications With Specific Examples

The UAV applications with specific examples or case study are listed in the Table 2.

Table 2. UAV applications with specific examples or case study

UAV Application	Specific Example or Case Study
Agriculture	Precision agriculture: Monitoring crop health, identifying pest and disease outbreaks, and optimizing irrigation and fertilizer application. Example: A drone equipped with multispectral sensors can be used to map a farmer's field, providing detailed information about crop health and identifying areas of stress or disease. This information can then be used to target specific areas of the field with treatment, saving time, money, and resources.
Inspection	Infrastructure inspection: Inspecting power lines, bridges, pipelines, and other infrastructure for damage or defects. Example: A drone can be used to inspect a high-voltage power line, flying along the line and taking high-resolution images of the wires and towers. These images can then be analyzed by engineers to identify any potential problems.
Public Safety	Search and rescue: Locating missing persons or survivors of natural disasters. Example: A drone with a thermal imaging camera can be used to search for survivors of a wildfire, flying over the affected area and identifying heat signatures that may indicate human presence.
Environmental Monitoring	Wildlife monitoring: Tracking animal populations, monitoring deforestation, and assessing environmental damage. Example: A drone can be used to monitor a population of endangered elephants, flying over the herd and taking photos to count individual elephants. This data can then be used to track the population's growth or decline.
Delivery and Logistics	Last-mile delivery: Delivering goods to remote or inaccessible locations. Example: A drone can be used to deliver medical supplies to a remote village in a developing country.

6. CONCLUSION

This proposed chapter aims to provide a comprehensive overview of the applications of machine learning in UAV-based object and people detection and tracking. It will cover the fundamentals of UAV systems and their relevance in surveillance, as well as the limitations of traditional detection methods. The chapter will delve into various machine learning techniques, including object detection algorithms such as CNNs, specialized people detection algorithms, and tracking algorithms suitable for UAV surveillance scenarios. It will also discuss the challenges associated with data collection and annotation specific to UAV imagery. Real-world applications and case studies will be presented to demonstrate the practicality and effectiveness of machine learning in UAV-based detection and tracking. Finally, the chapter will highlight future trends, challenges, and potential solutions, providing a roadmap for further advancements in this rapidly evolving field.

REFERENCES

Cai, Y., Du. D Zhang L, Wen L, Wang W, & Y. (2020). Guided attention network for object detection and counting on drones. In *Proceedings of the 28th ACM international conference on multimedia* (pp. 709–717). ACM.

Carrio, A., Sampedro, C., Rodriguez-Ramos, A., & Campoy, P. (2017). A review of deep learning methods and applications for unmanned aerial vehicles. *Journal of Sensors, 2017,* 1–13. doi:10.1155/2017/3296874

Cerro, J., Cruz Ulloa, C., Barrientos, A., & de León Rivas, J. (2021). Unmanned aerial vehicles in agriculture: A survey. *Agronomy (Basel), 11*(2), 203. doi:10.3390/agronomy11020203

Chandra, A. L., Desai, S. V., Guo, W., & Balasubramanian, V. N. (2020). *Computer vision with deep learning for plant phenotyping in agriculture: A survey.* Advanced Computing and Communications. doi:10.34048/ACC.2020.1.F1

Chang, X., Yang, C., Wu, J., Shi, X., & Shi, Z. (2018). A surveillance system for drone localization and tracking using acoustic arrays. In *Proceedings of the 2018 IEEE 10th sensor array and multichannel signal processing workshop (SAM)* (pp. 573–577). IEEE. 10.1109/SAM.2018.8448409

Chen, C. J., Huang, Y. Y., Li, Y. S., Chen, Y. C., Chang, C. Y., & Huang, Y. M. (2021). Identification of fruit tree pests with deep learning on embedded drone to achieve accurate pesticide spraying. *IEEE Access : Practical Innovations, Open Solutions, 9,* 21986–21997. doi:10.1109/ACCESS.2021.3056082

Chen, N., Chen, Y., You, Y., Ling, H., Liang, P., & Zimmermann, R. (2016). Dynamic urban surveillance video stream processing using fog computing. In *Proceedings of the 2016 IEEE second international conference on multimedia big data (BigMM)* (pp. 105–112). IEEE. 10.1109/BigMM.2016.53

Chen, Y., Lee, W. S., Gan, H., Peres, N., Fraisse, C., Zhang, Y., & He, Y. (2019). Strawberry yield prediction based on a deep neural network using high-resolution aerial orthoimages. *Remote Sensing (Basel), 11*(13), 1584. doi:10.3390/rs11131584

Ding G, Wu Q, Zhang L, Lin Y, Tsiftsis T A, & Yao Y D. (2018). An amateur drone surveillance system based on cognitive internet of things. *IEEE, 56*(1), 29–35.

Dramouskas I, Perikos I, & Hatzilygeroudis I. (2012). *A method for performing efficient real-time object tracing for drones.* Nimbus Vault.

Erdelj, M., Natalizio, E., Chowdhury, K. R., & Akyildiz, I. F. (2017). Help from the sky: Leveraging uavs for disaster management. *IEEE Pervasive Computing, 16*(1), 24–32. doi:10.1109/MPRV.2017.11

Faza, A., & Darma, S. (2020). Implementation of single shot detector for object finding in drone platform. *Journal of Physics: Conference Series, 1528*(1), 012005. doi:10.1088/1742-6596/1528/1/012005

Fradi, H., Bracco, L., Canino, F., & Dugelay, J. L. (2018). Autonomous person detection and tracking framework using unmanned aerial vehicles (UAVs). In *Proceedings of the 2018 26th European Signal Processing Conference (EUSIPCO)* (pp. 1047–1051). IEEE. 10.23919/EUSIPCO.2018.8553010

Gonzalez-TrejoJ.Mercado-RavellD. (2020). Dense crowds detection and surveillance with drones using density maps. ArXiv:2003.08766 [Cs]. https://arxiv.org/abs/2003.08766 doi:10.1109/ICUAS48674.2020.9213886

Han S, Shen W, & Liu Z. (2016). *Deep drone: object detection and tracking for smart drones on embedded system.* Stanford University.

Hii, M. S. Y., Courtney, P., & Royall, P. G. (2019). An evaluation of the delivery of medicines using drones. Multidisciplinary Digital Publishing Institute, 3(3), 52. 226. doi:10.3390/drones3030052

Hong, D., Gao, L., Yokoya, N., Yao, J., Chanussot, J., Du, Q., & Zhang, B. (2021). More diverse means better: Multimodal deep learning meets remote-sensing imagery classification. IEEE Trans. Geosci. Remote Sens., vol. 59, no. 5, pp. 4340–4354. *IEEE GRSM, 2021*, 19.

Hong, S. J., Han, Y., Kim, S. Y., Lee, A. Y., & Kim, G. (2019). Application of deep-learning methods to bird detection using unmanned aerial vehicle imagery. *Sensors (Basel)*, *19*(7), 1651. doi:10.339019071651 PMID:30959913

Hossain, S., & Lee, D. (2019). Deep learning-based real-time multiple-object detection and tracking from aerial imagery via a flying robot with GPU-based embedded devices. *Sensors (Basel)*, *19*(15), 3371. doi:10.339019153371 PMID:31370336

Hsieh, M. R., Lin, Y. L., & Hsu, W. H. (2017). Drone-based object counting by spatially regularized regional proposal network. In *Proceedings of the 2017 IEEE International Conference on Computer Vision (ICCV)* (pp. 4165–4173). IEEE. 10.1109/ICCV.2017.446

Hsu, H. J., & Chen, K. T. (2017). Drone face: An open dataset for drone research. In *Proceedings of the 8th ACM on multimedia systems conference* (pp. 187–192). ACM. 10.1145/3083187.3083214

Hwang, J., & Kim, H. (2019). Consequences of a green image of drone food delivery services: The moderating role of gender and age. *Business Strategy and the Environment*, *28*(5), 872–884. doi:10.1002/bse.2289

Hwang, J., Kim, J. J., & Lee, K. W. (2020). Investigating consumer innovativeness in the context of drone food delivery services: Its impact on attitude and behavioral intentions. Elsevier. *Article*, *120433*. doi:10.1016/j.techfore.2020.120433

Kalantar, A., Edan, Y., Gur, A., & Klapp, I. (2020). A deep learning system for single and overall weight estimation of melons using unmanned aerial vehicle images. *Computers and Electronics in Agriculture*, *178*, 105748. doi:10.1016/j.compag.2020.105748

Kalra, I., Singh, M., Nagpal, S., Singh, R., Vatsa, M., & Sujit, P. B. (2019). Drone SURF: Benchmark dataset for drone-based face recognition. In *Proceedings of the 2019 14th IEEE international conference on automatic face & gesture recognition (FG 2019)* (pp. 1–7). IEEE.

Kyrkou, C., & Theocharides, T. (2020). Emergency net: Efficient aerial image classification for drone-based emergency monitoring using atrous convolutional feature fusion. IEEE, 13, 1687–1699.

Lee, J., Wang, J., Crandall, D., Sabanovic, S., & Fox, G. (2017). Real-time, cloud-based object detection for unmanned aerial vehicles. In *Proceedings of the 2017 first IEEE international conference on robotic computing (IRC)* (pp. 36–43). IEEE. 10.1109/IRC.2017.77

Li, L., Huang, W., Gu, H., & Tian, Q. (2004). Statistical modeling of complex backgrounds for foreground object detection. *IEEE Transactions on Image Processing*, *13*(11), 1459–1472. doi:10.1109/TIP.2004.836169 PMID:15540455

Lygouras, E., Santavas, N., Taitzoglou, A., Tarchanidis, K., Mitropoulos, A., & Gasteratos, A. (2019). Unsupervised human detection with an embedded vision system on a fully autonomous UAV for search and rescue operations. *Sensors (Basel)*, *19*(16), 3542. doi:10.339019163542 PMID:31416131

Lyu, Y., Vosselman, G., Xia, G. S., Yilmaz, A., & Yang, M. Y. (2020). UA Vid: A semantic segmentation dataset for UAV imagery. *ISPRS Journal of Photogrammetry and Remote Sensing*, *165*, 108–119. doi:10.1016/j.isprsjprs.2020.05.009

Mishra B, Garg D, Narang P, & Mishra V. (2020). *Drone-surveillance for search and rescue in natural disaster*. Elsevier. . doi:10.1016/j.comcom.2020.03.012

Nuijten, R. J. G., Kooistra, L., & De Deyn, G. B. (2019). Using unmanned aerial systems (UAS) and object-based image analysis (OBIA) for measuring plant-soil feedback effects on crop productivity. *Drones (Basel)*, *3*(3), 54. doi:10.3390/drones3030054

Pi Y, Nath N D, & Behzadan A H. (2020). *Convolutional neural networks for object detection in aerial imagery for disaster response and recovery*. Elsevier.

Ramya, R., & Ramamoorthy, S. (2022). Survey on Edge Intelligence in IoT-Based Computing Platform. *Lecture Notes in Networks and Systems*, *356*, 549–561. doi:10.1007/978-981-16-7952-0_52

Ramya, R., & Ramamoorthy, S. (2022). Analysis of machine learning algorithms for efficient cloud and edge computing in the IoT. Challenges and Risks Involved in Deploying 6G and NextGen Networks, (pp. 72–90). Elsevier.

Ramya, R., & Ramamoorthy, S. (2022). Development of a framework for adaptive productivity management for edge computing based IoT applications. *AIP Conference Proceedings*, *2519*, 030068. doi:10.1063/5.0111710

Ramya, R., & Ramamoorthy, S. (2023). QoS in multimedia application for IoT devices through edge intelligence. *Multimedia Tools and Applications*. doi:10.100711042-023-15941-6

Ramya, R., & Ramamoorthy, S. (2023). Hybrid Fog-Edge-IoT Architecture for Real-time Data Monitoring. *International Journal of Intelligent Engineering and Systems*, *17*(1), 2024. doi:10.22266/ijies2024.0229.22

Ramya, R., & Ramamoorthy, S. (2023). Lightweight Unified Collaborated Relinquish Edge Intelligent Gateway Architecture with Joint Optimization. *IEEE Access : Practical Innovations, Open Solutions*, *11*, 90396–90409. doi:10.1109/ACCESS.2023.3307808

Rozenberg, G., Kent, R., & Blank, L. (2021). Consumer-grade UAV utilized for detecting and analyzing late-season weed spatial distribution patterns in commercial onion fields. *Precision Agriculture*, *22*(4), 1317–1332. doi:10.100711119-021-09786-y

Shao W, Kawakami R, Yoshihashi R, You S, Kawase H, & Naemura T. (2020). *Cattle detection and counting in UAV images based on convolutional neural networks*. Taylor & Francis. . doi:10.1080/01431161.2019.1624858

Wang S H, & Zhang Y D. (2020). Dense Net-201-based deep neural network with composite learning factor and precomputation for multiple sclerosis classification. *ACM Transactions on Multimedia Computing, Communications, and Applications (TOMM)*, *16*. ACM.

Wittstruck, L., Kühling, I., Trautz, D., Kohlbrecher, M., & Jarmer, T. (2020). UAV-based RGB imagery for Hokkaido pumpkin (Cucurbita max.) detection and yield estimation. *Sensors (Basel)*, *21*(1), 118. doi:10.339021010118 PMID:33375474

Yuan, W., & Choi, D. (2021). UAV-Based heating requirement determination for frost management in apple orchard. *Remote Sensing (Basel)*, *13*(2), 273. doi:10.3390/rs13020273

Zheng, J., Fu, H., Li, W., Wu, W., Yu, L., Yuan, S., Tao, W. Y. W., Pang, T. K., & Kanniah, K. D. (2021). Growing status observation for oil palm trees using unmanned aerial vehicle (UAV) images. *ISPRS Journal of Photogrammetry and Remote Sensing*, *173*, 95–121. doi:10.1016/j.isprsjprs.2021.01.008

Chapter 4
Applications ML in UAVs–Based Detecting and Tracking Objects and People

Rashid A. Saeed

iD https://orcid.org/0000-0002-9872-081X

Department of Computer Engineering, College of Computers and Information Technology, Taif University, Saudi Arabia

Nahla A. Nur Elmadina

iD https://orcid.org/0000-0002-0936-7322

Department of electrical engineering, Alzaiem Alazhari University, Sudan

ABSTRACT

This chapter provides an overview of the diverse applications of ML in UAVs for object and people detection and tracking. It begins by examining the current landscape of ML-driven UAV technologies and their potential. The related work section discusses the advancements in object and people detection and tracking. The subsequent sections delve into the technical aspects, focusing on the next generation of UAV convolutional neural network (CNN) backbones, including the contextual multi-scale region-based CNN (CMSRCNN), single shot multibox detector (SSD), and you only look once (YOLO), highlighting their significance in enhancing detection capabilities. Furthermore, it explores practical applications of ML in UAVs, encompassing object and people detection and tracking, path planning, navigation, and image and video analysis. Challenges and complexities in vision-based UAV navigation are addressed. Additionally, it showcases the potential for UAV networks to locate objects in real time.

DOI: 10.4018/979-8-3693-0578-2.ch004

1. INTRODUCTION

Unmanned Aerial Vehicles (UAVs), commonly known as drones, have witnessed extensive utilization across both military and civilian domains, ranging from search and rescue missions to exploration and surveillance (Telli et al., 2023). The integration of Machine Learning (ML) techniques into UAVs has unlocked a myriad of possibilities, including advanced object detection and tracking capabilities . The amalgamation of UAVs and ML has ushered in a new era of enhanced situational awareness and operational efficiency. Particularly noteworthy are the applications of ML in UAV-based object detection and tracking (Khalil et al., 2021) (Mohan et al., 2021)

(Zhu et al., 2017)introduced a Contextual Multi-Scale Region-based Convolutional Neural Network (CMS-RCNN) for unconstrained face detection, which was later extended for UAVs). Moreover, the capabilities of UAVs extend beyond individual object detection and tracking. (Oubbati et al., 2022) leveraged deep reinforcement learning for UAV-enabled mobile relaying systems, while Alqurashi et al. (2021) focused on Machine Learning Techniques in Internet of UAVs for Smart Cities Applications. These studies indicate the diversity of ML applications in UAVs, ranging from communication improvement to navigation assistance (Saeed M. M. et al., 2023).

However, while the synergy of UAVs and ML holds immense promise, the field is not devoid of challenges. The integration of ML algorithms in UAV systems necessitates addressing computational constraints and energy efficiency, ensuring real-time processing for swift decision-making, and maintaining data privacy and security (Bakri Hassan et al., 2022) . Thus, this introduction provides a glimpse into the exciting realm of ML applications in UAVs, while acknowledging the existing challenges that researchers and practitioners must navigate.

1.1 Motivation

The goal for this chapter is to explore the applications of machine learning in UAV-based object and people detection and tracking. The usage of unmanned aerial vehicles (UAVs) outfitted with thermal cameras has attracted interest in the field of object identification, recognition, and tracking. However, there are limitations in the existing frameworks, such as the inability to track things outside the field of view (FOV) of the UAV camera and the issue of discriminating between many objects in close proximity (Saeed M. M., et al., 2022).

To solve these shortcomings, this research provides a robust system that extends the automatic detection, recognition, and tracking architecture. The technology improves the tracking module's capacity to distinguish objects during revisitation by the UAV. It also extends the tracking method to track several objects in Earth-fixed coordinates, even when they are outside the FOV of the camera. Additionally, modifications are made to the UAV payload to enable onboard and real-time image processing (Saeed M. M. et al., 2023).

The combination of algorithms and UAV payload proposed in this paper forms a state-of-the-art system that excels in robustness. The system can track things for extended periods of time, even when they are outside the FOV of the camera(F. Huang et al., 2023). It also leverages thermal imaging properties for object detection, enabling improved difference between items in close proximity and recognizing objects re-entering the FOV. The report provides several experimental results from field tests that involve multi-object tracking scenarios with a fixed-wing UAV. The results illustrate the effectiveness and reliability of the suggested solution (Leira et al., 2021).

In summary, this chapter tries to overcome issues in UAV-based object detection and tracking by applying machine learning approaches. The suggested system achieves resilience by extending object tracking capabilities beyond FOV restrictions and exploiting thermal image properties for improved object detection. The testing findings demonstrate the usefulness of this strategy in numerous field tests scenarios (Guo et al., 2023; Wu et al., 2021).

1.2 Implications of Integrating UAVs With ML for Object and People Detection and Tracking

Unmanned aerial vehicles (UAVs) fitted with machine learning (ML) algorithms are effective for object and people detection in surveillance. Traditional methodologies are inadequate for real-time work, making UAVs a preferable choice. UAVs can efficiently use a single camera as the best sensor due to their lower size, weight, and power limits. Advances in computer vision, particularly deep learning, have led to the success of UAV systems in surveillance (Y.-T. Shen et al., 2023a).

Using UAVs and ML allows for automated surveillance without human interaction. Learning-based object detection algorithms combined with UAV systems enable real-time and dynamic object tracking. Deep learning-based perception approaches paired with 3D object posture tracking allow the system to monitor target objects throughout flights (Hoseini S. A., 2020). UAVs employing ML algorithms can overcome limited camera field of view (FoV) by navigating to track moving subjects. This ensures that a dynamic target remains within the FoV throughout surveillance operations. Including UAV path planning boosts the system's capacity to track and follow target object movements while following dynamic limitations (Zhang et al., 2023).

Flight experiments validate the benefits of utilizing UAVs with ML for item and people detection. The system's resilience, efficacy, and dependability in executing surveillance duties are demonstrated. The distribution of source code to the scientific community promotes continued development and reference for future investigations (Hoseini S. A., 2021). Overall, merging UAVs with ML algorithms provides several advantages for object and people detection in surveillance. It offers autonomous surveillance, real-time tracking of dynamic targets, increased perceptual performance through deep learning, and dependable outcomes proven by experimental testing. UAVs and ML have enormous promise in enhancing the efficiency and accuracy of detection and tracking in numerous real-world settings (F. Huang et al., 2023; Leira et al., 2021).

1.3. Challenges and Opportunities

Machine learning is being applied to UAV-based object and people detection and tracking, however there are issues that need to be addressed. One major improvement is the tracking module's ability to recognize items when revisiting them. The technology leverages thermal imaging properties for better item recognition (Wu et al., 2021). Real-time object detection is vital in emergency rescue and precision agriculture, but hardware and algorithm issues are typically disregarded. Challenges include object occupancy, low-resolution images, handling many objects, little labeled data, and erroneous localization (Leira et al., 2021).

Object identification techniques based on machine learning and deep learning struggle with multi-scale training, foreground-background class imbalance, detecting smaller objects, and restricted data availability. However, deep learning methods like Faster Convolutional neural networks, Cascade CNN,

You Only Look Once (YOLO), and Single Shot Multibox Detector (SSD) show promise for low-altitude UAV datasets. Further study is needed to increase the effectiveness of item detection and classification in UAV datasets (Cao et al., 2023; Mittal et al., 2020).

2. ML ALGORITHMS FOR OBJECT PEOPLE DETECTION AND TRACKING

2.1 Deep Learning

The applications of machine learning in UAV-based object and people detection and tracking have attracted substantial interest in recent years. Traditional image post-processing techniques used for object tracking on UAVs have proven to be insufficient for real-time surveillance applications (Hassan M. B. et al., 2022). These techniques are generally limited by size, weight, and power (SWaP) limits, which make it tough to add several cameras into the UAV system. However, with the developments in computer vision technologies, deep learning-based techniques have emerged as a promising alternative for autonomous surveillance employing UAVs (Ghorpade S. N., 2021).

A deep learning-based UAV system can leverage perception algorithms and filter-based 3D object pose tracking methods to monitor target objects during flights. This system can work in real-time without prior information about the environment, making it suited for dynamic surveillance missions (Eltahir A. A., et al., 2013). The fundamental contribution of this work is the integration of a real-time, learning-based object identification algorithm with the UAV embedded system to automatically locate targeted objects without human input. Additionally, a 3 Diminution (3D) posture tracking system is constructed employing object identification, stereo reconstruction techniques, and a Kalman filter to recognize, locate, and track target objects autonomously (Abdelgadir, 2019).

To enable effective surveillance missions, a UAV path planning algorithm is integrated in the system design. This technique enables the UAV to monitor and follow the movement of target objects while following dynamic limitations. The suggested system has been validated through trials including both moving objects and sensors. The results have proven good performance in terms of object detection and tracking (Eltahir A. A. et al., 2015).

In addition to the aforementioned contributions, there are other research efforts that have focused on deep learning-based algorithms for object detection and tracking in UAV settings. These research have studied many elements such as network designs, training methodologies, and performance evaluation criteria. By harnessing insights from these investigations, our research project intends to contribute to the expanding potential of UAV technology by developing an enhanced object detecting system (Amal E. A., et al., 2014).

Conventional object detection systems sometimes face limits in terms of coverage and accuracy. However, integrating drones, and machine learning algorithms can overcome these restrictions and illustrate the potential of advanced object detecting systems. The impact of distance between the UAV and the target person on the accuracy of object detection has been investigated, demonstrating a decrease in detection accuracy as the distance rises. This stresses the important relevance of distance in efficient object detection systems using UAVs (Diwan et al., 2023).

Overall, deep learning techniques have proven to be effective in UAV-based object and people detection and tracking. These algorithms have enabled autonomous surveillance missions by merging real-time, learning-based object detection with UAV embedded systems. With additional research and development, these systems can be tuned to boost coverage, accuracy, and efficiency in different applications such as surveillance, security, autonomous cars, robotics, environmental monitoring, precision agriculture, and traffic management. The future possibilities for Downlink -based UAV object identification and tracking algorithms are encouraging, especially when considering developments in network designs and training procedures (Cao et al., 2023; F. Huang et al., 2023).

2.2 Hybrid Approach

Hybrid techniques for machine learning algorithms in object and people detection and tracking utilizing unmanned aerial vehicles (UAVs) have garnered attention due to the requirement for precise and efficient systems. The key problem is the variance produced by the UAV's position, resulting to mismatches between pre-trained network domains and target domains. A unique methodology using a deeply supervised object detector (DSOD) trained exclusively on UAV pictures has been suggested, outperforming pre-trained-based detectors (Ahmed Z. E. et al., 2022).

Tracking observed items is vital for continuity in surveillance jobs, and Long-Short-Term Memory (LSTM) is employed for this purpose. The suggested hybrid technique, compared with pre-trained-based models, displays improved performance (Cao et al., 2023). The Archangel dataset, which includes UAV-specific metadata, provides excellent resources for precise model diagnostics and learning invariant characteristics. Existing datasets lack critical metadata, but Archangel solves these constraints by including actual and synthetic subsets with extensive metadata . Efficient computation is necessary for real-time processing; thus, over-segmentation and one-stage object detectors are applied (S. Zhao et al., 2023).

Real-time object detection based on UAV remote sensing is in high demand, and deep learning techniques have demonstrated promising results. However, issues in real-time processing, resource restrictions, and domain gaps need further research. The development of lightweight technology will contribute to the advancement of real-time object detection in UAV applications (Patterson et al., 2022; Y.-T. Shen et al., 2023a).

Table 0-1 show Researchers have made tremendous achievements in the field of unmanned aerial vehicle (UAV)-based object detection and tracking by developing unique algorithms and datasets that boost the accuracy and efficiency of these critical activities. A two-stage architecture that mixes classical target detection and deep learning techniques has been presented for real-time small object detection. A visible light mode dataset and a matching tracking method have been provided for UAV-based object recognition in visible light settings. An excellent tracking system that utilizes DeepSort and Histogram of Oriented Gradient (HOG) has been developed for reliable detection and tracking of moving objects. A benchmark dataset and a performance evaluation metric have been developed for multi-UAV multi-object tracking, giving significant tools for analyzing the effectiveness of alternative tracking methods (Mittal et al., 2020).

A comprehensive analysis of usable datasets and the potential of deep learning models for processing UAV-captured pictures has been published. An object recognition and tracking dataset that contains location and pose metadata has been introduced to assist more extensive model evaluation. The benefits of exploiting metadata during model evaluation have been established, stressing the need of considering contextual information for greater performance (Abdelgadir M., et al., 2016). A dataset specifically created for aerial-view person detection algorithms has been provided, and the generalization performance of state-of-the-art detection frameworks has been assessed, providing insights into the robustness of different approaches. These contributions have surely enhanced the field of UAV-based object detection and tracking, laying the framework for further improvements.

Table 1. Comparison of recent UAV-based datasets

Paper	Contribution	Method	Limitation
(Yu & Leung, 2023)	A real-time small object detection system with high speed and accuracy	A two-stage architecture that combines traditional target detection and deep learning	Conventional background subtraction and deep learning
(J. Zhao et al., 2022)	- Proposed a visible light mode dataset called DUT Anti-UAV - Developed a tracking algorithm combined with detect	- Detection algorithms trained on DUT Anti-UAV dataset - Tracking methods tested on tracking dataset.	NA
(Wang et al., 2023)	- Development of a tracking method named HOGSort. – Effective detection and tracking of move object	DeepSort and Histogram of Oriented Gradient (HOG) -Inter-frame difference algorithm	NA
(H. Shen et al., 2022)	Creation of a benchmark dataset for multi-UAV multi-object tracking - Proposal of a metric to evaluate performance	Creation of a dataset for multi-UAV multi-object tracking tasks - Proposal of a metric to evaluate performance	NA
(Shin et al., 2022)	A review of useful datasets for object detection from UAV images and videos	Deep learning models (e.g., federated learning)	Convolutional neural networks (CNN), recurrent neural networks (RNN), Long short-term memory (LSTM)
(Y.-T. Shen et al., 2023a)	The Archangel dataset with position and pose metadata and a demonstration of the benefits of leveraging metadata during model evaluation	Archangel dataset with real and synthetic subsets	Existing UAV-based benchmarks lack complete metadata.
(Symeonidis et al., 2022)	Introduction of AUTH-Persons dataset for aerial-view person detection algorithms. - Evaluation of generalization performance of state-of-the-art detection frameworks.	Lightweight Deep Neural Networks (DNNs)	Detection of individuals in dense crowds is challenging

3. UAV-BASED OBJECT AND PEOPLE DETECTION AND TRACKING SYSTEMS

3.1. System Components and Architecture

The system components and architecture for UAV-based item and people identification and tracking systems consist of several critical parts. Firstly, a learning-based UAV system is proposed, which leverages deep learning algorithms for autonomous surveillance. The system is meant to detect, track, and follow target objects without human interaction. The YOLOv4-Tiny algorithm is utilized for semantic object detection, which allows the UAV to identify and locate things in real-time (Saeed, 2022).

To increase the perception performance of the system, a 3D object poses estimation approach and Kalman filter are merged with the object identification algorithm. This combination improves the precision and reliability of the tracking procedure. The 3D posture tracking algorithm uses stereo reconstruction techniques to precisely predict the position of the target object in three-dimensional space (Saeed, 2023).

In addition to object identification and tracking, UAV path planning is included into the system to enable autonomous surveillance maneuvers. The path planning method takes into consideration dynamic restrictions to ensure that the UAV can properly track and follow the movement of the target item. This capability allows for continuous monitoring of the target within the limited field of view (FoV) of the camera. The perception module of the system is examined on a quadrotor UAV, while flight experiments are done to validate the performance of the overall system. The results reveal that the autonomous object tracking UAV system is resilient, effective, and reliable in completing surveillance duties (Abakar M. A. et al., 2010).

Overall, this system architecture blends deep learning-based object identification algorithms with 3D pose estimation, Kalman filtering, and UAV path planning to enable autonomous surveillance capabilities (F. Huang et al., 2023). It handles issues such as real-time surveillance requirements, limited processing resources, and dynamic target tracking within a narrow field of view. The integration of these components enables accurate and efficient detection and tracking of objects and people utilizing UAV technology (Leira et al., 2021; Micheal et al., 2020).

3.2. System Design Considerations

Developing reliable UAV-based object and people detection and tracking systems includes evaluating algorithm selection, sensor technology, data processing, and real-time performance (Wu et al., 2021). Deep learning techniques like CNNs are effective for object detection, while motion models like the Kalman filter improve tracking (Leira et al., 2021). Thermal cameras are often used for object detection but may require more complicated algorithms in less homogenous situations. Integrating navigation data helps accurately locate identified objects. Data association utilizing the Kuhn-Munkres method detects if a detected object is already tracked or new, based on physical distance and similarity in thermal pictures (Cao et al., 2023). Real-time performance can be increased by adopting efficient one-stage object detectors and developments in hardware technologies. Overall, incorporating these criteria leads to the development of dependable systems for surveillance, security, autonomous vehicles, and robotics applications (Y.-T. Shen et al., 2023a).

3.3. Performance Evaluation

This study covers a multiple object detection, recognition, and tracking system for unmanned aerial vehicles (UAVs). The technology employs machine vision to detect things in the camera's image stream and integrates navigation data to georeference each object. A tracking algorithm incorporating a Kalman filter is used to determine an object's position and velocity (Lo et al., 2021). A global-nearest-neighbor method is utilized for data association. Four field experiments were done at sea to validate the system's performance, displaying great accuracy in detecting and monitoring boat positions and velocities (Zhang et al., 2023).

The system obtained an accuracy of 5-15 meters in estimating boat placements from an altitude of 400 meters. However, the object detection algorithm may not perform well in non-uniform situations, thus future development should focus on enhancing its ability to filter out non-interesting detections.

Overall, our method enables UAVs to execute multi object tracking and situational awareness during maritime missions (Y.-T. Shen et al., 2023a).

Figure 1. Object tracking of a small drone surveillance system

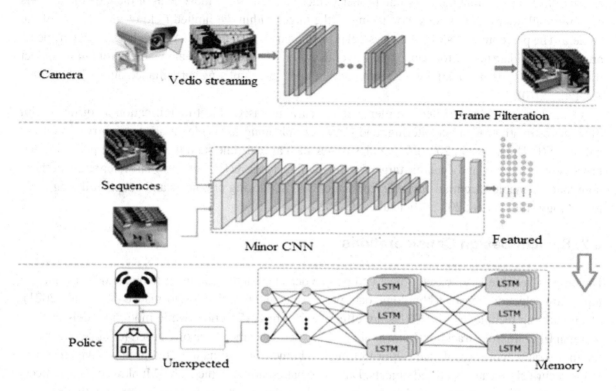

Figure 1. shows The suggested plan comprises four main stages: First, in the preprocessing phase, we train a simple CNN pilgrim's detector on a dataset of pilgrim images to choose specific video frames for more in-depth analysis. In the second stage, we create a lightweight CNN object detector to capture spatial features. Following that, we design an LSTM model to grasp spatio-temporal features for precise recognition of violent activities. Lastly, in the concluding step, the framework issues an alarm, notifying law enforcement agencies to take necessary actions in case of any violent activities. The entire process is illustrated in Figure 1 (Habib et al., 2021).

4. APPLICATIONS OF UAV-BASED OBJECT AND PEOPLE DETECTION AND TRACKING

4.1. Public Safety

Advancements in machine learning and computer vision algorithms have made it possible for UAVs outfitted with thermal cameras to detect, recognize, and track objects and people in real-time (Boudjit & Ramzan, 2022). By merging machine vision with navigation data, the system precisely georeferenced each item detection. A tracking technique based on a Kalman filter and constant velocity motion model calculates an object's position and velocity over time. Field experiments at sea have showed remarkable accuracy in detecting and tracking boats. Deep learning algorithms enable drones to independently recognize and track objects, boosting public safety in surveillance, search and rescue operations, transportation monitoring, etc (Lo et al., 2021).

Edge computing technologies like 5Generation networks feed UAV monitoring photos to cloud-based systems for analysis, boosting real-time tracking capabilities. Optimized network architectures and pre-training models unique to aerospace remote sensing datasets have increased object detection accuracy for UAV photos. Ongoing research intends to overcome issues in restricted aerial perspective, computing resources, and long-term tracking settings (Mittal et al., 2020; Y.-T. Shen et al., 2023a).

4.2. Surveillance and Monitoring

Surveillance and monitoring employing UAV-based item and people detection and tracking is significant in different sectors. Object detection has progressed over the years and is utilized in retail, autonomous driving, agriculture, security, transportation, healthcare, and more. Integrating machine learning techniques can boost the capabilities of commercial UAVs for object recognition. Deep learning approaches on powerful computer platforms have demonstrated promising outcomes in UAV data processing. The combination of object detection and tracking has increased tracking performance (Alawi M. A., et al., 2012).

An autonomous UAV tracking system utilizes deep learning methods, a Kalman filter for position estimation, and a maneuver state machine for autonomy. Future work includes combining vision-based and Global Navigation Satellite System (GNSS)based positioning systems and optimizing trajectory planning based on target motion prediction, obstacle constraints, and UAV limits. Machine learning in UAV-based surveillance offers enormous promise for increasing skills in numerous sectors (Cao et al., 2023; Diwan et al., 2023).

4.3. Disaster Relief

Disaster relief is a major use of UAV-based item and people detection and tracking. Drones equipped with deep learning algorithms may take real-time pictures and detect things of interest. Object detection with tracking gives stability and fine labels for objects in catastrophe circumstances (Mittal et al., 2020). Integrating several sensors on UAVs offers more robust tracking and detection. Challenges specific to UAV-based object recognition include fluctuations in altitude, viewing angles, camera movements, weather conditions, and item appearances (Zhang et al., 2023).

Researchers have produced datasets for UAV-based object detection that include metadata. Advancements in deep learning algorithms have enhanced the accuracy of object detection by employing convolutional neural networks and tracking-by-detection techniques. The combination of these approaches has proven improved performance in compared to standard trackers on UAV videos. Object detection serves a crucial part in computer vision tasks (Lo et al., 2021; Mohan et al., 2021; Y.-T. Shen et al., 2023a).

4.4. Search and Rescue

Machine learning in UAV-based object and people detection and tracking can considerably enhance search and rescue operations. Traditional image processing approaches have been utilized, involving searching for objects based on size and color. The collected photos are transformed to The captured photos undergo a transformation into the Hue, Saturation, and Value (HSV) color format to eliminate things that don't match the intended color. Other methods, such as adaptive background removal and color-based detection frameworks, have been developed for surveillance applications (F. Huang et al., 2023).

To increase accuracy, a three-layer architecture splits UAV images into stationary or moving categories using local features, applies moving feature clustering and segmentation, and follows objects using the Kalman filter. Deep learning-based techniques like CNNs and YOLO algorithms offer great accuracy and real-time detection speed. Object tracking is vital and requires assessing motion or forecasting trajectories. Tracking-by-detection algorithms and deep learning-based frameworks with Siamese-based tracking networks have demonstrated encouraging results. (Guo et al., 2023; Lo et al., 2021; Zhu et al., 2017).

4.5. Precision Agriculture

Precision agriculture utilizes UAV-based object and people recognition and monitoring to optimize crop management. Machine learning algorithms help farmers to track crops, collect data, and make informed decisions. Object detection helps counting animals, monitoring livestock, and evaluating agricultural product quality (Zhu et al., 2017). Damaged produce can also be identified during processing. UAVs offer cost-effectiveness and precision field monitoring compared to satellite images. Integrating sensors into drones helps protect crops from insects and weeds. Overall, UAV-based detection and monitoring are vital for optimizing crop management and enhancing agricultural productivity (Boudjit & Ramzan, 2022; Ramachandran & Sangaiah, 2021; Siemiątkowska, 2022).

4.6. Environmental Monitoring

UAV-based item and people detection and tracking have numerous uses in environmental monitoring. Retail can benefit from AI-based customer analysis to enhance store layouts and cut waiting times. Object detection in autonomous driving protects safety by recognizing people, traffic signs, and other cars. Agriculture uses object detection for purposes like animal monitoring and evaluating agricultural product quality (Siemiątkowska, 2022). Security programs detect people in restricted locations or automate inspection activities. Vehicle detection enhances traffic analysis and identifies autos stopping in unsafe spots. Healthcare benefits from medical feature recognition in disease diagnosis. Overall, these systems serve a key role in environmental monitoring across numerous industries (Cao et al., 2023; W. Huang et al., 2021). .

4.7. Asset Management

Asset management for UAV-based item and people recognition and monitoring is gaining popularity across numerous industries. UAVs offer advantages including minimal maintenance cost, compact size, and mobility, making them excellent for monitoring, surveillance, and target tracking. Research efforts are focused on merging machine learning, cloud computing, and 5Generation technologies to meet practical design challenges (Bithas et al., 2019). Deep learning-based object detection algorithms, including YOLO, Faster CNN and SSD, have shown promising results in real-time identification and classification of objects. However, there are still gaps and hurdles in enhancing performance specifically for UAV datasets. Fusion of UAV technology with deep learning algorithms has been effective in flight tests, exhibiting robustness against demanding situations. Further study is needed to better the accuracy and efficiency of item recognition and classification for UAV datasets (Lo et al., 2021; Micheal et al., 2020; Ranjith et al., 2023; Y.-T. Shen et al., 2023a).

Multiple target tracking is a complex process that requires a well-structured block diagram, effective data association schemes, and robust tracking algorithms. The new association scheme, as depicted in Figure 4-1 promises to enhance the accuracy and efficiency of tracking multiple targets in dynamic environments. This process requires robust algorithms that can efficiently handle data association, prediction, and filtering (Cao et al., 2023).

Figure 2. The data association tools employed for target identification

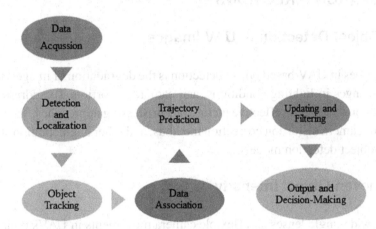

5. CASE STUDIES FOR REAL-WORLD

5.1 UAV-Based Object and People Detection and Tracking Specifically the Haram Area in Mecca, Kingdom of Saudi Arabia

In recent years, there has been a substantial increase in the applications of machine learning in unmanned aerial vehicle (UAV)-based object and people recognition and tracking. This technique has proven to be highly efficient and reliable in different real-world circumstances. In this section, we discuss some important case studies that show the successful implementation of UAV-based object and people identification and tracking (Mohsan et al., 2023).

The use of unmanned aerial vehicles (UAVs) for object and person recognition and tracking in the Haram area of Mecca, Kingdom of Saudi Arabia, has various possible applications. While there is no specific information about the employment of UAVs for this purpose in the Haram area in the search results, the general capabilities and applications of UAVs in public safety and security can be surmised. UAVs with object detection and tracking algorithms can be used to monitor big crowds and detect suspicious activity in the Haram area. Furthermore, as demonstrated in law enforcement applications, the use of UAVs for tracking individuals on foot (Al-Khaffaf et al., 2012).

Might potentially be customized for monitoring and maintaining the safety and security of individuals within the Haram region .It is vital to highlight that the usage of UAVs in the Haram region would need to comply with the drone regulations and laws in Saudi Arabia, as specified by the General Authority of Civil Aviation (GACA) . These restrictions are in place to ensure the safe and legal operating of drones in the country. In conclusion, while specific examples of UAV-based object and people detection and tracking in the Haram area in Mecca are not explicitly provided in the search results, the potential applications of UAVs in enhancing public safety and security in crowded areas, such as the Haram, can be inferred from the general capabilities and applications of UAV technology. Any specific usage of UAVs in the Haram region would need to adhere to the drone regulations and legislation in Saudi Arabia (UAV Coach 2023, n.d.; Habib et al., 2021).

6. FUTURE RESEARCH DIRECTIONS

6.1 Improving Object Detection in UAV Images

One of the primary issues in UAV-based object detection is the degradation of images due to factors such as fast movement, changes in lighting conditions, and camera distortion. To address this issue, future research should focus on developing effective picture pre-processing approaches. This can include noise reduction algorithms, camera distortion correction methods, and other augmentation strategies to assure the performance of object detection models.

6.2 Handling Uneven Object Intensity

The employment of wide-angle lenses and flexible camera movements in UAVs typically results to inconsistent object intensity in acquired photos. Some objects may be tightly packed and overlap several times, while others may be sparsely distributed, making detection problematic. Future study should investigate creative techniques to manage this challenge, such as building algorithms that can reliably distinguish things from their surrounds and successfully detect highly or sparsely distributed objects.

6.3 Addressing Small Object Size

UAV remote sensing photos can catch ground objects of varied sizes. Traditional deep learning-based algorithms suffer issues when dealing with small-sized objects, leading to false positives and missed detections. Future research should focus on building sophisticated algorithms that can reliably recognize and classify small-sized objects in UAV aerial photos. This could involve researching novel training algorithms or applying transfer learning techniques from larger datasets.

6.4 Real-Time Processing

Real-time processing is crucial for object detection and tracking activities in UAV surveillance applications. It is crucial to build fast algorithms that can rapidly and reliably find moving ground objects in drone recordings. Future research should study optimization techniques for real-time processing performance, including algorithmic optimizations, hardware acceleration, and parallel computing approaches.

6.5 Integration of Emerging Technologies

Incorporating new technologies into UAV-based object detection systems can considerably boost their capabilities. Areas for exploration include integrating machine learning techniques such as reinforcement learning or generative adversarial networks for increased object detection and tracking accuracy. Additionally, integrating cloud computing infrastructure for distributed processing and storage will enable more scalable and resource-efficient UAV-based surveillance systems. The incorporation of fifth-generation (5G) technology can also enable better connectivity and communication capabilities for real-time data transmission and collaboration among UAVs.

6.6 Autonomous Object Detection Algorithm

An important future direction is the development of self-tuning object identification systems for UAVs. Instead of manually specifying parameters such as threshold values and minimum item sizes, algorithms should be able to alter these parameters automatically or dynamically based on the unique application needs. This can involve combining artificial intelligence techniques, such as reinforcement learning, to enable algorithms to adapt and maximize their performance based on real-time feedback.

6.7 Enhancing Tracking Accuracy

Improving the tracking accuracy of UAV-based object identification systems is vital for reliable surveillance applications. Future study should focus on enhancing motion models inside tracking algorithms, including parameters such as UAV altitude, attitude, and the sort of object being tracked. By adjusting measurement noise and motion model noise depending on these characteristics, the tracking process can become more efficient and precisely predict the true position and velocity of objects (Ranjith et al., 2023).

6.8 Metadata Utilization

The application of metadata in UAV-based object identification models can greatly boost their performance and adaptability. Future study should explore strategies to exploit metadata during model evaluation, particularly in connection to diverse object poses and UAV positions. This can involve developing unique ways for data association in tracking algorithms that integrate feature vectors to adapt to modest changes in object attributes over time (Ramachandran & Sangaiah, 2021).

In conclusion, future research directions for UAV-based object detection and tracking involve addressing challenges related to image degradation, uneven object intensity, small object size, real-time processing performance, integration of emerging technologies, developing autonomous algorithms, improving tracking accuracy, and leveraging metadata for enhanced model evaluation. These developments will contribute towards more resilient and efficient surveillance systems using unmanned aerial vehicles (Guo et al., 2023; Habib et al., 2021; Mohan et al., 2021; Y.-T. Shen et al., 2023b).

REFERENCES

Abakar, M. A. (2010). *The challenges of wireless internet access in vehicular environments*. Proceeding of the 3rd International Conference on Information and Communication Technology for the Moslem World (ICT4M) 2010, Jakarta, Indonesia. 10.1109/ICT4M.2010.5971899

Abdelgadir, M. (2016). Vehicular Ad-hoc Networks (VANETs) dynamic performance estimation routing model for city scenarios. *2016 International Conference on Information Science and Communications Technologies (ICISCT)*, Tashkent, Uzbekistan. 10.1109/ICISCT.2016.7777397

Ahmed, Z. E. (2022). Optimization Procedure for Intelligent Internet of Things Applications. *2022 International Conference on Business Analytics for Technology and Security (ICBATS)*, Dubai, United Arab Emirates. 10.1109/ICBATS54253.2022.9759065

Al-Khaffaf, H., Haron, F., Sarmady, S., Talib, A., & Abu-Sulyman, I. (2012). Crowd Parameter Extraction from Video at the Main Gates of Masjid al-Haram. In Advances in Intelligent and Soft Computing. Springer. doi:10.1007/978-3-642-27552-4_96

Alawi, M. A. (2012). Cluster-based multi-hop vehicular communication with multi-metric optimization. *2012 International Conference on Computer and Communication Engineering (ICCCE)*, (pp. 22-27). Springer. 10.1109/ICCCE.2012.6271145

Amal, E. A. (2014). Vehicular Communication and Cellular Network Integration: Gateway Selection Perspective. *2014 International Conference on Computer and Communication Engineering*, Kuala Lumpur, Malaysia. 10.1109/ICCCE.2014.30

Bakri Hassan, M., Saeed, R., Khalifa, O., Sayed Ali Ahmed, E., Mokhtar, R., & Hashim, A. (2022). *Green Machine Learning for Green Cloud Energy Efficiency*. IEEE. doi:10.1109/MI-STA54861.2022.9837531

Bithas, P. S., Michailidis, E. T., Nomikos, N., Vouyioukas, D., & Kanatas, A. G. (2019). A Survey on Machine-Learning Techniques for UAV-Based Communications. *Sensors (Basel)*, *19*(23), 5170. doi:10.339019235170 PMID:31779133

Boudjit, K., & Ramzan, N. (2022). Human detection based on deep learning YOLO-v2 for real-time UAV applications. *Journal of Experimental & Theoretical Artificial Intelligence*, *34*(3), 527–544. doi:10.1080/0952813X.2021.1907793

Cao, Z., Kooistra, L., Wang, W., Guo, L., & Valente, J. (2023). Real-Time Object Detection Based on UAV Remote Sensing: A Systematic Literature Review. *Drones (Basel)*, *7*(10), 10. doi:10.3390/drones7100620

Diwan, T., Anirudh, G., & Tembhurne, J. V. (2023). Object detection using YOLO: Challenges, architectural successors, datasets and applications. *Multimedia Tools and Applications*, *82*(6), 9243–9275. doi:10.100711042-022-13644-y PMID:35968414

Drone Laws in Saudi Arabia. (2023). UAV Coach. https://uavcoach.com/drone-laws-in-saudi-arabia/

Eltahir, A. A. (2013). An enhanced hybrid wireless mesh protocol (E-HWMP) protocol for multihop vehicular communications. *2013 International Conference On Computing, Electrical And Electronic Engineering (ICCEEE)*, Khartoum, Sudan. 10.1109/ICCEEE.2013.6633899

Eltahir, A. A. (2015). Performance evaluation of an Enhanced Hybrid Wireless Mesh Protocol (E-HWMP) protocol for VANET. *2015 International Conference on Computing, Control, Networking, Electronics and Embedded Systems Engineering (ICCNEEE)*, Khartoum, Sudan. 10.1109/ICCNEEE.2015.7381437

Ghorpade, S. N., Zennaro, M., Chaudhari, B. S., Saeed, R. A., Alhumyani, H., & Abdel-Khalek, S. (2021). A Novel Enhanced Quantum PSO for Optimal Network Configuration in Heterogeneous Industrial IoT. *IEEE Access : Practical Innovations, Open Solutions*, 9, 134022–134036. doi:10.1109/ACCESS.2021.3115026

Guo, J., Liu, X., Bi, L., Liu, H., & Lou, H. (2023). UN-YOLOv5s: A UAV-Based Aerial Photography Detection Algorithm. *Sensors (Basel)*, 23(13), 5907. doi:10.339023135907 PMID:37447757

Habib, S., Hussain, A., Albattah, W., Islam, M., Khan, S., Khan, R. U., & Khan, K. (2021). Abnormal Activity Recognition from Surveillance Videos Using Convolutional Neural Network. *Sensors (Basel)*, 21(24), 8291. doi:10.339021248291 PMID:34960386

Hassan, M. B. (2022). Performance Evaluation of Uplink Shared Channel for Cooperative Relay based Narrow Band Internet of Things Network. *2022 International Conference on Business Analytics for Technology and Security (ICBATS)*, Dubai, United Arab Emirates. 10.1109/ICBATS54253.2022.9758935

Hassan, M. B. (2022). *Green Machine Learning for Green Cloud Energy Efficiency*. 2022 IEEE 2nd International Maghreb Meeting of the Conference on Sciences and Techniques of Automatic Control and Computer Engineering (MI-STA), Sabratha, Libya. 10.1109/MI-STA54861.2022.9837531

Hoseini, S. A., Bokani, A., Hassan, J., Salehi, S., & Kanhere, S. S. (2021). Energy and Service-Priority aware Trajectory Design for UAV-BSs using Double Q-Learning, 2021 IEEE 18th Annual Consumer Communications & Networking Conference. CCNC. doi:10.1109/CCNC49032.2021.9369472

Hoseini, S. A., Hassan, J., Bokani, A., & Kanhere, S. S. (2020). *Trajectory Optimization of Flying Energy Sources using Q-Learning to Recharge Hotspot UAVs*. IEEE INFOCOM 2020 - IEEE Conference on Computer Communications Workshops (INFOCOM WKSHPS), Toronto, ON, Canada. 10.1109/INFOCOMWKSHPS50562.2020.9162834

Huang, F., Chen, S., Wang, Q., Chen, Y., & Zhang, D. (2023). Using deep learning in an embedded system for real-time target detection based on images from an unmanned aerial vehicle: Vehicle detection as a case study. *International Journal of Digital Earth*, 16(1), 910–936. doi:10.1080/17538947.2023.2187465

Huang, W., Zhou, X., Dong, M., & Xu, H. (2021). Multiple objects tracking in the UAV system based on hierarchical deep high-resolution network. *Multimedia Tools and Applications*, 80(9), 13911–13929. doi:10.100711042-020-10427-1

Khalil, A. A., Byrne, A. J., Rahman, M. A., & Manshaei, M. H. (2021). Efficient UAV Trajectory-Planning using Economic Reinforcement Learning (arXiv:2103.02676). arXiv. https://arxiv.org/abs/2103.02676 doi:10.1109/SMARTCOMP52413.2021.00041

Leira, F. S., Helgesen, H. H., Johansen, T. A., & Fossen, T. I. (2021). Object detection, recognition, and tracking from UAVs using a thermal camera. *Journal of Field Robotics*, 38(2), 242–267. doi:10.1002/rob.21985

Lo, L.-Y., Yiu, C. H., Tang, Y., Yang, A.-S., Li, B., & Wen, C.-Y. (2021). Dynamic Object Tracking on Autonomous UAV System for Surveillance Applications. *Sensors (Basel)*, *21*(23), 7888. doi:10.339021237888 PMID:34883913

Micheal, A., Vani, K., Sanjeevi, S., & Lin, C.-H. (2020). Object Detection and Tracking with UAV Data Using Deep Learning. *Photonirvachak (Dehra Dun)*, *49*(3), 1–7. doi:10.100712524-020-01229-x

Mittal, P., Singh, R., & Sharma, A. (2020). Deep learning-based object detection in low-altitude UAV datasets: A survey. *Image and Vision Computing*, *104*, 104046. doi:10.1016/j.imavis.2020.104046

Mohan, M., Richardson, G., Gopan, G., Aghai, M. M., Bajaj, S., Galgamuwa, G. A. P., Vastaranta, M., Arachchige, P. S. P., Amorós, L., Corte, A. P. D., de-Miguel, S., Leite, R. V., Kganyago, M., Broadbent, E. N., Doaemo, W., Shorab, M. A. B., & Cardil, A. (2021). UAV-Supported Forest Regeneration: Current Trends, Challenges and Implications. *Remote Sensing (Basel)*, *13*(13), 13. Advance online publication. doi:10.3390/rs13132596

Mohsan, S. A. H., Othman, N. Q. H., Li, Y., Alsharif, M. H., & Khan, M. A. (2023). Unmanned aerial vehicles (UAVs): Practical aspects, applications, open challenges, security issues, and future trends. *Intelligent Service Robotics*, *16*(1), 109–137. doi:10.100711370-022-00452-4 PMID:36687780

Moradi, M., Bokani, A., & Hassan, J. (2020). *Energy-Efficient and QoS-aware UAV Communication using Reactive RF Band Allocation.* 2020 30th International Telecommunication Networks and Applications Conference (ITNAC), Melbourne, VIC, Australia. 10.1109/ITNAC50341.2020.9315157

Moradi, S., Bokani, A., & Hassan, J. (2022). *UAV-based Smart Agriculture: a Review of UAV Sensing and Applications.* 2022 32nd International Telecommunication Networks and Applications Conference (ITNAC), Wellington, New Zealand. 10.1109/ITNAC55475.2022.9998411

Oubbati, O. S., Lakas, A., & Guizani, M. (2022). Multi-Agent Deep Reinforcement Learning for Wireless-Powered UAV Networks. *IEEE Internet of Things Journal*, *9*(17), 16044–16059. doi:10.1109/JIOT.2022.3150616

Patterson, L., Pigorovsky, D., Dempsey, B., Lazarev, N., Shah, A., Steinhoff, C., Bruno, A., Hu, J., & Delimitrou, C. (2022). HiveMind: A hardware-software system stack for serverless edge swarms. *Proceedings of the 49th Annual International Symposium on Computer Architecture*, (pp. 800–816). ACM. 10.1145/3470496.3527407

Ramachandran, A., & Sangaiah, A. K. (2021). A review on object detection in unmanned aerial vehicle surveillance. *International Journal of Cognitive Computing in Engineering*, *2*, 215–228. doi:10.1016/j.ijcce.2021.11.005

Ranjith, C. P., Hardas, B. M., Mohideen, M. S. K., Raj, N. N., Robert, N. R., & Mohan, P. (2023). Robust Deep Learning Empowered Real Time Object Detection for Unmanned Aerial Vehicles based Surveillance Applications. *Journal of Mobile Multimedia*, (pp. 451–476). doi:10.13052/jmm1550-4646.1925

Saeed, M. M. (2022). *Green Machine Learning Approach for QoS Improvement in Cellular Communications.* 2022 IEEE 2nd International Maghreb Meeting of the Conference on Sciences and Techniques of Automatic Control and Computer Engineering (MI-STA), Sabratha, Libya. 10.1109/MI-STA54861.2022.9837585

Saeed, M. M. (2023). *Attacks Detection in 6G Wireless Networks using Machine Learning*. 2023 9th International Conference on Computer and Communication Engineering (ICCCE), Kuala Lumpur, Malaysia. 10.1109/ICCCE58854.2023.10246078

Saeed, M. M. (2023). *Machine Learning Techniques for Detecting DDOS Attacks*. 2023 3rd International Conference on Emerging Smart Technologies and Applications (eSmarTA), Taiz, Yemen. 10.1109/eSmarTA59349.2023.10293366

Salehi, S., Bokani, A., Hassan, J., & Kanhere, S. S. (2019). *AETD: An Application-Aware, Energy-Efficient Trajectory Design for Flying Base Stations*. 2019 IEEE 14th Malaysia International Conference on Communication (MICC), Selangor, Malaysia. 10.1109/MICC48337.2019.9037587

Salehi, S., Hassan, J., Bokani, A., Hoseini, S. A., & Kanhere, S. S. (2020). Poster Abstract: A QoS-aware, Energy-efficient Trajectory Optimization for UAV Base Stations using Q-Learning. 2020 19th ACM/IEEE International Conference on Information Processing in Sensor Networks (IPSN), Sydney, NSW, Australia. 10.1109/IPSN48710.2020.00-22

Shen, H., Yang, X., Lin, D., Chai, J., Huo, J., Xing, X., & He, S. (2022). A Benchmark for Vision-based Multi-UAV Multi-object Tracking. *2022 IEEE International Conference on Multisensor Fusion and Integration for Intelligent Systems (MFI)*, (pp. 1–7). IEEE. 10.1109/MFI55806.2022.9913874

Shen, Y.-T., Lee, Y., Kwon, H., Conover, D. M., Bhattacharyya, S. S., Vale, N., Gray, J. D., Leong, G. J., Evensen, K., & Skirlo, F. (2023a). Archangel: A Hybrid UAV-based Human Detection Benchmark with Position and Pose Metadata. *IEEE Access : Practical Innovations, Open Solutions*, *11*, 80958–80972. doi:10.1109/ACCESS.2023.3299235

Shen, Y.-T., Lee, Y., Kwon, H., Conover, D. M., Bhattacharyya, S. S., Vale, N., Gray, J. D., Leong, G. J., Evensen, K., & Skirlo, F. (2023b). Archangel: A Hybrid UAV-based Human Detection Benchmark with Position and Pose Metadata. *IEEE Access : Practical Innovations, Open Solutions*, *11*, 80958–80972. doi:10.1109/ACCESS.2023.3299235

Shin, J., & Piran, Md. J., Song, H.-K., & Moon, H. (2022). UAV-assisted and deep learning-driven object detection and tracking for autonomous driving. *Proceedings of the 5th International ACM Mobicom Workshop on Drone Assisted Wireless Communications for 5G and Beyond*, (pp. 7–12). ACM. 10.1145/3555661.3560856

Siemiątkowska, B. (2022). *Real-Time Object Detection and Classification by UAV Equipped With SAR. Sensors*. Academia. https://www.academia.edu/81075269/Real_Time_Object_Detection_and_Classification_by_UAV_Equipped_With_SAR

Suo, J., Wang, T., Zhang, X., Chen, H., Zhou, W., & Shi, W. (2023). HIT-UAV: A high-altitude infrared thermal dataset for Unmanned Aerial Vehicle-based object detection. *Scientific Data*, *10*(1), 1. doi:10.103841597-023-02066-6 PMID:37080987

Symeonidis, C., Mademlis, I., Pitas, I., & Nikolaidis, N. (2022). Auth-Persons: A Dataset for Detecting Humans in Crowds from Aerial Views. *2022 IEEE International Conference on Image Processing (ICIP)*, (pp. 596–600). 10.1109/ICIP46576.2022.9897612

Telli, K., Kraa, O., Himeur, Y., Ouamane, A., Boumehraz, M., Atalla, S., & Mansoor, W. (2023). A Comprehensive Review of Recent Research Trends on UAVs (arXiv:2307.13691). arXiv. https://arxiv.org/abs/2307.13691

Wang, Z., Li, D., Kuai, Y., & Sun, Y. (2023). A Model-Free Moving Object Detection and Tracking Framework Based on UAV Data. In W. Fu, M. Gu, & Y. Niu (Eds.), *Proceedings of 2022 International Conference on Autonomous Unmanned Systems (ICAUS 2022)* (pp. 3446–3456). Springer Nature. 10.1007/978-981-99-0479-2_318

Wu, X., Li, W., Hong, D., Tao, R., & Du, Q. (2021). Deep Learning for UAV-based Object Detection and Tracking. *Survey (London, England)*.

Yu, M., & Leung, H. (2023). Small-Object Detection for UAV-Based Images. *2023 IEEE International Systems Conference (SysCon)*, (pp.1–6). IEEE. 10.1109/SysCon53073.2023.10131084

Zhang, H., Shao, F., He, X., Zhang, Z., Cai, Y., & Bi, S. (2023). Research on Object Detection and Recognition Method for UAV Aerial Images Based on Improved YOLOv5. *Drones (Basel)*, 7(6), 6. doi:10.3390/drones7060402

Zhao, J., Zhang, J., Li, D., & Wang, D. (2022). Vision-Based Anti-UAV Detection and Tracking. *IEEE Transactions on Intelligent Transportation Systems*, 23(12), 25323–25334. doi:10.1109/TITS.2022.3177627

Zhao, S., Wang, W., Li, J., Huang, S., & Liu, S. (2023). Autonomous Navigation of the UAV through Deep Reinforcement Learning with Sensor Perception Enhancement. *Mathematical Problems in Engineering*, 2023, e3837615. doi:10.1155/2023/3837615

Zhu, C., Zheng, Y., Luu, K., & Savvides, M. (2017). CMS-RCNN: Contextual Multi-Scale Region-Based CNN for Unconstrained Face Detection. In B. Bhanu & A. Kumar (Eds.), *Deep Learning for Biometrics* (pp. 57–79). Springer International Publishing. doi:10.1007/978-3-319-61657-5_3

Chapter 5
Monitoring of Wildlife Using Unmanned Aerial Vehicle (UAV) With Machine Learning

Zeinab E. Ahmed

(iD) https://orcid.org/0000-0002-6144-8533

Department of Computer Engineering, University of Gezira, Sudan & Department of Electrical and Computer Engineering, International Islamic University Malaysia, Malaysia

Aisha H. A. Hashim

Department of Electrical and Computer Engineering, International Islamic University Malaysia, Malaysia

Rashid A. Saeed

(iD) https://orcid.org/0000-0002-9872-081X

Department of Computer Engineering, College of Computers and Information Technology, Taif University, Saudi Arabia

Mamoon M. Saeed

Department of Communications and Electronics Engineering, Faculty of Engineering, University of Modern Sciences (UMS), Yemen

ABSTRACT

Wildlife monitoring is critical for ecological study, conservation, and wildlife management, but traditional approaches have drawbacks. The combination of unmanned aerial vehicles (UAVs) with machine learning (ML) offers a viable approach to overcoming the limits of traditional wildlife monitoring methods and improving wildlife management and conservation tactics. The combination of UAVs and ML provides efficient and effective solutions for wildlife monitoring. UAVs with high-resolution cameras record airborne footage, while machine learning algorithms automate animal detection, tracking, and behavior analysis. The chapter discusses challenges, limitations, and future directions in using UAVs and ML for wildlife monitoring, addressing regulatory, technical, and ethical considerations, and emphasizing the need for ongoing research and technological advancements. Overall, the integration of UAVs and ML provides a promising solution to overcome the limitations of traditional wildlife monitoring methods and enhance wildlife management and conservation strategies.

DOI: 10.4018/979-8-3693-0578-2.ch005

1. INTRODUCTION

Wildlife monitoring is critical to scientific development and the decision-making process for wildlife protection (He et al., 2016). Collaboration efforts over a wide range of geographies and timelines provide vital insights into dynamic animal behavior, the impact of human activities, environmental changes, and critical aspects of wildlife, ecology, and the environment. As the effects of human-caused environmental change become more pronounced, large-scale collaborative wildlife surveillance is required to manage and safeguard animal resources successfully (Markovchick-Nicholls et al., 2008). To that aim, an integrated platform for collecting, analyzing, and managing large-scale multi-modal wildlife sensor data over the Internet infrastructure is critical. Technological advancements have found extensive application in wildlife monitoring and tracking various species (Xu et al., 2016). Various sensor-based devices are commonly used to relay animal data to a central station. However, monitoring animals in remote and expansive wildlife areas presents challenges due to hazardous conditions and unpredictable movement patterns. Additionally, conventional sensor networks face limitations in timely data transmission due to energy constraints, making it costly and impractical.

Various wildlife monitoring methods can be broadly categorized into Camera Traps, GPS Tracking, Remote Sensing, and Unmanned Aerial Vehicles (UAVs) (Nicheporchuk et al., 2020). UAVs have gained popularity in diverse applications due to their versatility, high speed, and durability. They offer different imaging techniques by integrating pictures from varying flight altitudes, enabling coverage of extensive areas, and producing detailed images (Šimek et al., 2017). UAVs act as independent mobile data collectors, gathering time-sensitive information. When utilized for animal monitoring, UAVs effectively overcome geographical challenges while ensuring no negative impact on the observed animals (Xu et al., 2016). In addition, UAVs use revolutionary monitoring techniques, such as group recognition and gender determination using visual or thermal imaging, to revolutionize ecological research.

Machine learning (ML) is highly effective in creating dependable correlations in data-driven systems through experiential learning. This knowledge derived from data can be tailored to tackle novel challenges and analyze unexplored data. The availability of abundant datasets from diverse spatiotemporal scales in wildlife monitoring is vital for the successful application of AI techniques through machine learning and interpretation (Sharma et al., 2022). ML empowers IT systems to autonomously identify patterns, establish rules, and develop solutions(Abang Abdurahman et al., 2022). Machine learning technology is occasionally used to detect and distinguish animals, as well as to recognize crucial behaviors such as running and walking, utilizing just seismic data generated by animals (Szenicer et al., 2022).

UAVs play a crucial role in efficient data collection and communication across various sectors. The integration of ML has advanced UAV operations, leading to improved automation and accuracy in tasks like communications, sensing, and data collection (Kurunathan et al., 2022). Integrating UAVs with ML enables additional functionalities like image processing, trajectory planning, and monitoring UAV-aided communication. ML enhances controlled mobility and trajectory decisions, making UAVs suitable for various AI-driven IoT paradigms. This integration adds an AI layer to existing UAV-enabled monitoring applications, enabling feature extraction and prediction capabilities. It creates new opportunities in real-time monitoring, data collection, and prediction across domains(Nahla, 2021) (Rashid, 2010). However, when applying ML to UAVs for wildlife conservation, there are significant challenges. These include obtaining high-quality data in remote settings, optimizing ML models for real-time processing and adaptability to diverse wildlife behaviors, and addressing privacy and ethical concerns. Other complex challenges involve energy-efficient UAV operation, reliable communication, multi-UAV coordination, algorithm complexity, cost-effectiveness, regulatory compliance, interoperability, and ensuring long-term sustainability through careful resource management and planning (Mona, 2020) (Nada, 2021).

1.1. Motivation and Contributions

This chapter explores the potential of integrating Unmanned Aerial Vehicles (UAVs) and machine learning techniques for wildlife monitoring. It aims to showcase the benefits, challenges, and applications of this approach in ecological research, conservation, and wildlife management. The motivation behind this exploration arises from the need for more efficient and effective methods of wildlife monitoring, as traditional approaches have limitations in coverage, accuracy, and cost-effectiveness (Ghorpade, 2021). The combination of UAV technology and machine learning offers an innovative solution to overcome these limitations and provides researchers and conservationists with valuable insights into wildlife populations, behavior, and habitat dynamics. This chapter makes significant contributions to the field of wildlife monitoring by highlighting key aspects:

- The chapter discusses the integration of UAVs and machine learning for wildlife monitoring, highlighting the advantages of combining these technologies for efficient and comprehensive data collection and analysis (Sayed, 2021) (Abbas, 2021).
- UAVs enable improved data collection by capturing high-resolution aerial imagery, behavioral data, and sensor readings, overcoming limitations of ground-based methods for comprehensive wildlife monitoring.
- Machine learning algorithms automate analysis tasks such as animal detection, tracking, and behavior analysis, extracting valuable insights from complex wildlife data collected by UAVs.
- UAVs and machine learning have significant conservation applications, aiding in habitat assessment, anti-poaching, population estimation, and environmental monitoring, enhancing wildlife management and conservation strategies (Zeinab, 2020) (Ahmed, 2020).
- The chapter discusses challenges, limitations, and future directions in using UAVs and machine learning for wildlife monitoring, addressing regulatory, technical, and ethical considerations, and emphasizing the need for ongoing research and technological advancements (Ali, 2022) (Elnour, 2023).

1.2. Chapter Organization

The chapter initiates by introducing the potential of integrating Unmanned Aerial Vehicles (UAVs) and machine learning techniques for wildlife monitoring. The initial part of the chapter explains the reasons behind and the contributions of this integration, emphasizing its significance in enhancing the efficiency and effectiveness of wildlife monitoring. The subsequent section delves into the technical aspects of Unmanned Aerial Vehicles, Machine Learning, and Wildlife Monitoring Methods. Furthermore, the chapter discusses real-world applications of UAVs and ML and presents examples of how these techniques can be applied to improve various systems, including wildlife tracking and population estimation, anti-poaching, and illegal wildlife trade prevention, as well as wildlife habitat mapping and conservation. In conclusion, the chapter provides a summary of the key points discussed and outlines future directions for research and development in UAVs and ML techniques for wildlife monitoring.

2. BACKGROUND AND OVERVIEW

This section begins with an introduction to Unmanned Aerial Vehicles (UAVs), machine learning and provides a comprehensive overview of wildlife monitoring methods. Furthermore, it delves into the specifics of integrating UAVs and ML techniques for wildlife monitoring (Omran, 2022) (Othman, 2022.

2.1. Unmanned Aerial Vehicles (UAVs)

UAV platforms merge the benefits of satellites and on-ground systems, offering innovative and efficient technologies (Bouguettaya et al., 2022). They excel in coverage, providing higher spatial and temporal resolution photos than satellites and at lower operational costs. Moreover, UAVs can handle aerial tasks beyond manned aviation's capabilities, leading to cost savings, environmental advantages, and reduced risks to human life (Outay et al., 2020). UAVs offer system designers the flexibility to equip different network units with diverse sensors, enabling a wider range of data capture. Additionally, flight formations with UAVs of varying sizes and configurations can handle complex tasks (Li & Savkin, 2021). Networked surveillance UAVs represent sensor-based, communication-enabled autonomous systems, demonstrating typical cyber-physical systems.

There are two primary types of UAVs: fixed-wing and rotary-wing, each with its specific strengths and weaknesses (Zeng et al., 2016) (Ahmed et al., 2022). The architecture of the multi-UAV communication framework is critical for intelligent control and autonomous coordination of multi-UAV systems(Jasim et al., 2022). Coordination entails resource sharing, as well as temporal and spatial coordination, with UAV synchronization ensuring temporal coordination. Spatial coordination ensures that UAVs operate safely and coherently with other UAVs and obstacles. Cooperation in the network includes sensing, control, and resource planning. Multi-UAV networks can be centralized or decentralized as indicated in Figure 1, with centralized systems necessitating many cognitive resources. Decentralized systems solve difficulties such as large-scale information distribution and real-time requirements. The control station connects with node members ad hoc in the decentralized architecture to manage duties for a group of autonomous UAVs) (Mohammad, 2022) (Lina, 2022).

Figure 1. Cooperation in the network includes sensing, control, and resource planning. Multi-UAV networks can be (a) centralized or (b) decentralized

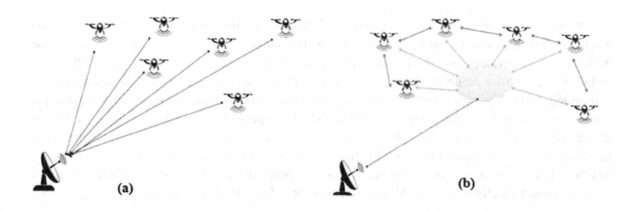

Significant efforts have recently been undertaken to create and use UAVs for specialized reasons. The classification of UAV systems is critical in highlighting their diverse capabilities. UAVs are classified depending on factors such as size, weight, range, endurance, maximum altitude, engine type, and configuration (Elmeseiry et al., 2021) (Velusamy et al., 2022), as shown in Figure 2. The goal is to aid in the selection of the best parameters for UAVs. UAVs offer various benefits, including portability, rapid deployment, proximity for surveying, enhanced safety through risk assessment, and cost-effectiveness due to the availability of off-the-shelf, camera-equipped UAVs (Giordan et al., 2020). These advantages make modern small and micro-UAVs suitable for fieldwork, as they can be easily transported, quickly maneuvered, operate at close distances, ensure safety, and are economically feasible.

2.2. Machine Learning

Machine learning (ML), a dynamic computational discipline emulating human intelligence by learning from its environment, is pivotal in the big data era. It has evolved into a crucial technique for harnessing data potential, enabling businesses to enhance innovation, efficiency, and sustainability across various sectors such as pattern recognition, computer vision, finance, entertainment, and medicine (Kreuzberger et al., 2023). To solve data challenges, machine learning employs a variety of algorithms. Data scientists like to point out that there is no one-size-fits-all type of algorithm that is best for solving an issue. The algorithm used is determined by the type of problem to be solved, the number of variables, the appropriate model to use, and so on. some of the most often-used algorithms in ML are illustrated in Figure 3 such as reinforcement learning (RL), supervised learning (SL), and unsupervised learning (UL) (Sejan et al., 2022). ML has the capacity to transform wireless communication technologies by improving channel estimation. Recent progress reveals that ML is effective in uncovering connections between input and output signals, resulting in more dependable channel estimation in various technological contexts.

Figure 2. Classification of UAVs

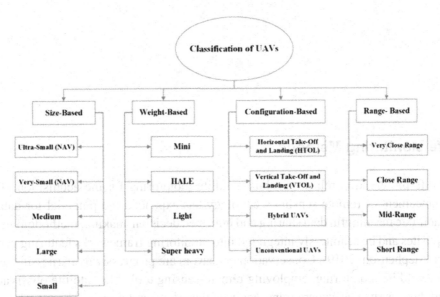

The machine learning application development cycle in the enterprise starts with problem specification (Patel, 2020). The cycle then proceeds to data consolidation through Extract-Transform-Load (ETL) or Extract-Load-Transform (ELT), involving data engineers and scientists, followed by labor-intensive feature engineering. Model development, training, and validation come next before deployment into the production environment. Monitoring, retraining, and iterative improvements are the final steps, involving the efforts of various professionals. Machine Learning addresses a range of prediction challenges, classified into the following categories (Kalathas et al., 2019): a) Classification: This involves sorting data into predefined categories to predict new data within a supervised context, b) Clustering: Unlike classification, clustering groups input data into categories that aren't predefined, typically in unsupervised learning scenarios, c) Regression: This deals with supervised problems where the output is continuous and not divided into categories, d) Density Estimation: It focuses on understanding the distribution of input data, and e) Dimension Reduction: This simplifies complex data with many variables by projecting it into a lower-dimensional space (Kalathas et al., 2019).

Figure 3. Some of the most often-used ML algorithms in UAVs

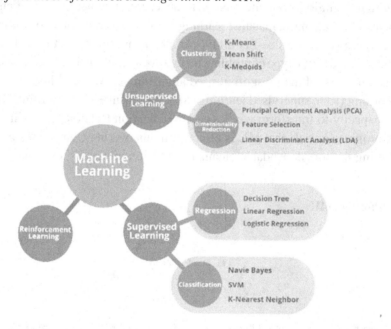

2.3. Wildlife Monitoring Methods

Effective wildlife preservation relies on robust wildlife monitoring for the acquisition of continuous data. The advancement of remote sensing technology has expanded the potential for data collection. However, to facilitate meaningful data sharing and informed decision-making, methodologies must align with local requisites and be seamlessly integrated into monitoring frameworks featuring pertinent goals and indicators (Stephenson, 2019). Conservation endeavors are progressively harnessing technological innovations for wildlife monitoring, employing remote-sensing tools like satellite observation, as well as Earth-based devices such as camera traps, acoustic recorders, and drones. These tools, coupled with emerging methodologies like environmental DNA and genetic monitoring, offer avenues for enriching data accuracy and quantity while concurrently streamlining on-site fieldwork activities. Remote sensing holds the potential to bridge data gaps, especially in regions abundant in biodiversity, thus enhancing both the temporal and spatial resolution of the collected information. we present some studies that reflect the diverse range of conventional and advanced methods used in wildlife monitoring, focusing on improving accuracy and data collection efficiency in large and complex natural habitats:

- Conventional Monitoring Methods: Various methods for wildlife monitoring exist, each differing in automation levels. These include manual wildlife surveys conducted by national park staff, invasive tracking using GPS collars without image data (Frair et al., 2004), camera traps capturing visual data in local memory cards (Burton et al., 2015), costly wireless cameras transmitting images via broadband (Zhang et al., 2014), and satellite-based remote sensing (Tibbetts, 2017). The choice of method depends on investigation goals, animal species, behavior, natural environment properties, and available technical resources. Traditional monitoring methods fall short in covering animals' movements throughout the day, risking conflicts, or accidents (Dhivya et al., 2022). To address this, the paper proposes using GPS tracking devices to monitor animals within predetermined zones. An alarm system is triggered if an animal crosses the defined area, alerting humans.
- Wireless Sensor Networks and UAVs: This article (Xu et al., 2016) introduced a novel approach merging wireless sensor networks (WSNs) and unmanned aerial vehicles (UAVs) for wildlife monitoring. The method aims to detect endangered species' locations in vast wildlife areas and monitor their movements without attachments. Sensors placed in the observation zone collect animal data, while a UAV retrieves information from these sensors. This project (Baig z & Shastry, 2023), a wireless tracking and health monitoring system for tigers is developed using Wireless Sensor Networks (WSN). The system uses WSN to communicate and monitor key physiological parameters like heart rate, temperature, sound signals, respiration rate, accelerometer data, and GPS info. Sensors within the network communicate remotely, sharing information among nodes. The authors (Hadji et al., 2022) highlight the need for ecosystem balance and cost-effective wildlife monitoring. It addresses challenges like data volume and redundancy. Solutions are proposed, involving image processing techniques, to tackle redundancy and counting issues encountered during monitoring tasks.
- Macro-Micro Monitoring Combination: Zhang et al. (Zhang et al., 2017) advocated the integration of macro and micro-monitoring techniques using Geographic Information Systems and remote sensing. This approach enhances spatial observation, positioning, and analysis capabilities in ecological monitoring scenarios.
- Improved Animal Monitoring: Zviedris et al. (Zviedris et al., 2010) developed LynxNet, a sensor system for lynx and wolf tracking, using TMote Mini sensor nodes, GPS, radio, and base stations at frequented locations. Their focus was on improved sensor node control and communication.

3. REAL-WORLD APPLICATIONS OF UAVS AND MACHINE LEARNING

The key issues affecting UAV performance are battery life, collision avoidance, and security (Elmeseiry et al., 2021). Proposed solutions for UAV issues are still incomplete, necessitating novel practical tactics.

The incorporation of machine learning into UAV systems opens new potential, particularly in resource allocation, obstacle avoidance, tracking, path planning, and battery scheduling. The progress of machine learning technologies and computational capability may enable the construction of more intelligent and compact UAV models capable of autonomous and collision-free operations. Precise data improves UAV activities such as intelligent control, trajectory planning, and visual processing (Mohsan et al., 2022). UAV cameras record a variety of images for further analysis. The application of machine learning in UAVs, including elements such as feature extraction and motion planning, has the potential to improve control, navigation, and manipulation (Elmeseiry et al., 2021). In Figure 4, we can illustrate the integration of Machine Learning (ML) and Unmanned Aerial Vehicles (UAVs) into three distinct steps:

a) Input Data or Database: This is the initial stage where data is collected and prepared for analysis. In the context of UAVs and ML, this step involves the acquisition of data from the UAV's sensors, cameras, or other onboard instruments. This data typically includes aerial imagery, videos, or sensor readings. It is essential to ensure that this data is cleaned, preprocessed, and organized for the subsequent ML analysis.

b) Learning Network: In this step, the ML algorithms come into play. The input data or database generated from the UAVs is fed into ML models, which can encompass a range of techniques, including deep learning neural networks. These models are trained to recognize patterns, features, or anomalies within the data. For instance, in the case of livestock monitoring, the ML model might be trained to identify and track specific animals or detect unusual behavior from aerial imagery. This step requires extensive training and optimization to ensure the ML model can make accurate predictions or classifications.

c) Output: The output stage is where the ML model's predictions or classifications are applied to real-world scenarios. Based on the analysis of the input data, the ML model generates actionable insights or decisions.

Figure 4. The integration of Machine Learning (ML) and Unmanned Aerial Vehicles (UAVs)

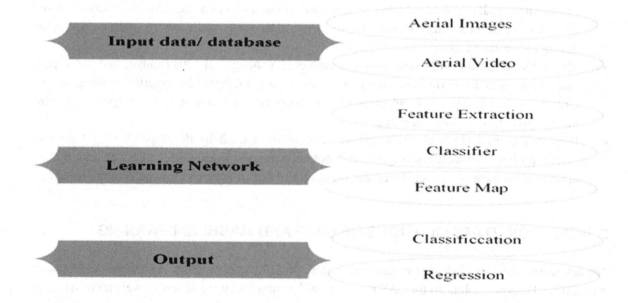

3.1. Wildlife Tracking and Population Estimation

Cardoso et al. used artificial intelligence models (CNN) to assess their usefulness in detecting cases of wildlife trade (Cardoso et al., 2023). The focus was on pangolins, a highly trafficked species that gained notoriety during the COVID-19 outbreak. Images from platforms such as iNaturalist, Flickr, and Google were used for training. Notably, the updated models detected possible occurrences of pangolin trade in the dataset with a detection rate of more than 90%. Aerial surveys are routinely used to monitor livestock density and land utilization. This article introduced HerdNet, an improved CNN architecture designed for identifying large mammals in aerial photos (Delplanque et al., 2023). HerdNet outperformed other models in terms of precision and speed, demonstrating its effectiveness in identifying and tallying animals up close. The study offers HerdNet to increase livestock monitoring through regular airborne operations.

Kulkarni et al. emphasized the significance of automated marine ecosystem monitoring for improved ecological understanding and policy formulation (Kuru et al., 2023). With extraordinary accuracy, the WILDetect platform, which combines supervised Machine Learning and Reinforcement Learning, detects, and enumerates maritime species, particularly birds, in aerial surveys. Authors highlights the effectiveness of automated data processing in streamlining marine wildlife censuses and ecological assessments, providing for more insight into species populations and ecological dynamics (Kuru et al., 2023). This article showcased the capability of generating effective training data for deep neural networks in situations where there is limited wildlife for automated image analysis (Chabot et al., 2022). Demonstrated using the instance of polar bears on sea ice, the strategy employs aerial images collected during live observer surveys. This method could be applicable to monitoring not only polar bears and Arctic wildlife, but also marine birds and predators in diverse environments. It presents a potential avenue for efficient remote aerial surveys, providing an alternative to conventional observer-dependent methods and benefiting from advancements in drone technology.

Under the One Health paradigm, this research investigates the concept of Integrated animal Monitoring, which integrates animal health monitoring and community observations to detect diseases and understand their patterns (Barroso et al., 2023). The study conducted a large-scale pilot test across Spain, using video traps and biomarker analysis to discriminate biodiversity and host populations in a variety of situations. The Eurasian wild boar emerged as a key indicator species, and the research found a link between biodiversity and disease susceptibility. The paper also discovered that human-caused factors such as urbanization and increased wildlife concentrations were associated with increased disease prevalence and inter-species transmission (Barroso et al., 2023). The goal of this research is to track wild birds to determine their habitats and population levels, with a special emphasis on migratory birds to predict potential disease transmission (Hong et al., 2019). The researchers develop deep-learning-powered object recognition systems using photos acquired by unmanned aerial vehicles (UAVs). The collection includes a variety of bird photos from various environments, such as lakesides and farmlands, as well as decoy images to diversify patterns. Multiple bird detection models were built and tested for accuracy and speed, with Faster R-CNN being the most accurate and YOLO being the fastest.

Öztürk et al. examined the utilization of synthetic images created by a game engine to train deep learning networks aimed at image classification, specifically targeting bird and rotary-wing unmanned aerial vehicle (RW-UAV) images, shown in Figure 5 (Öztürk & Erçelebi, 2021). The research introduces a corner detection and nearest three-point selection (CDNTS) layer and contrasts two experimental approaches. In the initial experiment, deep learning networks trained with synthetic data attain a test accuracy AUC of 72% on authentic data. Subsequently, in the second experiment, the incorporation of the CDNTS layer elevates the test accuracy AUC to 88.9%. In (Yousefi et al., 2022), authors illustrated the transformative impact of machine learning on swiftly identifying and classifying animals and their behaviors in wildlife imagery. Employing a swift review and bibliometric analysis, the study delved into the influence of machine learning in wildlife images, encompassing aspects such as species, image types, locations, algorithms, and results. To effectively harness machine learning's potential in advancing wildlife behavior understanding and conservation, the research suggests enhancing collaboration and knowledge-sharing strategies (Yousefi et al., 2022).

Figure 5. Image classification, specifically targeting bird and rotary-wing unmanned aerial vehicle (RW-UAV) images

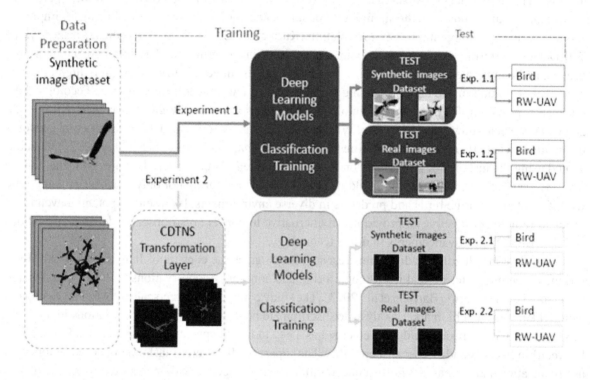

Monitoring marine animal populations for ecosystem protection is becoming increasingly important as the relevance of coral reef ecosystems and marine resources grows. Real-time environmental awareness is required for the evolution of Autonomous Underwater Vehicles (AUVs). This paper investigates marine animal detection utilizing deep neural network models, specifically YOLO-based approaches, to identify marine species in coral reef habitats rapidly and accurately (Zhong et al., 2022). Based on the assessment results, the results highlight successful recognition, and ideas for model enhancement are presented. Fang et al. focused on the use of small unmanned aerial vehicles (UAVs) in several sectors, including conservation management (Fang et al., 2021). The methodology involves incorporating atrous convolutional filters within a ResNet-50 backbone network to maintain feature map resolution while extracting more complex abstract features. Detection accuracy relies on the alignment between anchors and ground truth data, influenced by factors like image size and anchor selection. The newly introduced feature extraction technique proves effective in identifying small objects compared to alternative methods.

The goal of the article is to apply deep learning techniques to count wildlife and marine creatures in the context of human-induced difficulties (Singh et al., 2023). The study avoids the requirement for a separate detector by training with a UNet model with different backbones and Gaussian density maps. The approach is effective in counting dolphins and elephants in aerial photos, producing encouraging results with specific backbones that excel for each species. This novel approach permits accurate object counting using airborne remote sensing, so aiding wildlife conservation efforts and allowing humans to cohabit in harmony (Singh et al., 2023). The assessment of migratory waterbird populations holds vital importance in safeguarding coastal wetlands vulnerable to development. Despite the employment of video surveillance and unmanned technology, manual analysis remains a time-consuming process. This research introduced a two-stage automated waterbird monitoring approach that employs deep learning for segmentation, analysis, and enumeration of waterbirds (Wu et al., 2022). The method's efficacy was tested in a restored wetland, achieving an 85.59% accuracy rate and minimal standard error, thereby offering an effective means for precise data extraction from video surveillance to advance biodiversity monitoring within protected zones.

Abdulameer et al. addressed limitations in traditional classification systems, specifically in image classification, where accuracy and adaptability have been lacking (Abdulameer et al., 2022). It introduces an intelligent system utilizing Convolutional Neural Networks (CNNs) to identify bird types based on external appearance from bird shape images. The proposed CNN-based model significantly enhances accuracy by effectively extracting crucial features, especially for common bird classes, achieving high precision (approximately 0.99%), recall (about 0.95%), and F-measure (93%) scores. The system includes pre-processing and classification stages and demonstrates the superiority of the deep CNN algorithm over other machine learning classifiers such as Naive Bayes, Random Forest, Decision Tree, and K-NN (Abdulameer et al., 2022). The article highlights the influence of human activities on marine megafauna and suggests using advanced technologies like high-resolution cameras and machine learning for remote monitoring of marine animals (Berg et al., 2022). It introduces a customized patch distribution modeling method (PaDiM) to detect marine animals with weak supervision. The method's success is evidenced by enhanced F1 and recall scores on datasets containing high-resolution marine animal images. This strategy holds promise for improving marine animal identification during aerial surveys and simplifying annotation tasks through bounding box proposals within fully supervised detection setups.

The introduction of low-cost sensors such as cellphones, drones, and satellites has resulted in a wealth of animal-related data. However, successfully analyzing and obtaining useful insights from this data is difficult. Thalor et al. proposed that using deep learning methods within machine learning can help to alleviate this problem, resulting in better data interpretation, comprehension, and animal welfare (Thalor et al., 2023). The combination of machine learning with ecological processes may result in hybrid models in which machine learning delivers data-driven insights while ecological models set restrictions. This technique has the potential to provide more precise evaluations of animal populations, research of behaviors, and prevention of conflicts between humans and wildlife, all of which can tremendously help animal ecologists (Thalor et al., 2023). The rosette flight plan is a novel flight method for conducting animal population surveys utilizing Unmanned Aerial Systems (UAS) in this paper (Linchant et al., 2023). Although traditional manned planes can count huge ungulates, drones provide logistical advantages. The proposed flight plan uses triangular "petals" organized in rosettes to guide sampling, as opposed to methodical transects based on computer simulations. According to the findings, the accuracy of the rosette design improves with repeated iterations, making it especially ideal for species with greater dispersion patterns. Despite its demanding resource needs, this strategy is recommended for isolated parks that are having difficulty coordinating manned surveys, with potential future improvements linked to cost reduction and the introduction of solar-powered UAS (Linchant et al., 2023). Unmanned aerial systems (UAS) play an important role in ecology by obtaining data on wildlife abundance and distribution, but correcting detection mistakes is critical for accurate results (Brack et al., 2018). The paper focused on false-negative and false-positive mistakes that potentially influence UAS-derived counts. It investigates several error mitigation methods, including classic aerial survey solutions, auxiliary data inclusion, and new UAS-driven methodologies. The paper recommends strategic planning, hierarchical models, and data integration to optimize UAS-based wildlife abundance modelling while resolving various detection failures (Brack et al., 2018).

In (Xu et al., 2018), focused on using wireless sensor networks (WSNs) and unmanned aerial vehicles (UAVs) to track animals in broad wilderness areas without attaching sensors to the animals. The WSN configuration includes sensor node clusters and a UAV functioning as a mobile sink. The work introduces a model predictive control (MPC) technique for UAV path planning that uses learnt animal appearance patterns to anticipate real-time animal distributions. This method optimizes the UAV's trajectory to minimize message delay and maximize rewards. When compared to greedy and naive TSP techniques, simulation results show that this method is superior in terms of value of information (VoI) and event collection(Xu et al., 2018).

To improve animal surveys, authors used very high-resolution (VHR) photography, including data from unmanned aerial vehicles (UAVs) (Andrew & Shephard, 2017). The major purpose is too semi-automatically identify white-bellied sea eagle nests in aerial images of Australia's Houtman Abrolhos Islands. Despite problems posed by environmental unpredictability and insufficient training data, the work uses object-based image analysis and the Maxent machine learning classifier to detect nests accurately, with implications beyond animal surveys. The method also considers ways for making the best use of faulty or uncalibrated image data. A novel automated technique was developed that uses deep learning models to count sandhill cranes during their nighttime migration using thermal images (Luz-Ricca et al., 2023). In comparison to the object detection model, Faster R-CNN, the density estimation model, ASPDNet, displayed higher counting precision. Both models performed well with high-resolution imagery, demonstrating their ability to properly scan dense bird populations such as cranes and waterbirds in staging regions.

By this study, A convolutional neural network (CNN) was created to recognize terns and gulls in UAV photos of densely inhabited colonies (Kellenberger et al., 2021). CNN performed accurate detection of royal terns with quick annotation periods after being trained with minimum operator input utilizing the AIDE annotation platform. Despite issues with less common species, this strategy has the potential to improve monitoring precision and effectiveness in West African colonies, as well as provide new insights into breeding behaviors. Future efforts could focus on improving precision and evaluating the model's appropriateness across different ecosystems and settings. With an IoT detection system, this initiative aims to increase safety in forest corridors by addressing animal attacks on humans (Daniel Raj et al., 2023). It detects animals and alerts vehicles, which helps to reduce accidents. This system excels in reliably recognizing animals in images and videos, monitoring their habits, and facilitating wildlife population surveillance, making it an excellent fit for wildlife conservation operations. Traditional methods for detecting wildlife in aerial imagery are slow and prone to errors, while modern computer vision techniques are not widely adopted (Martini & Miller, 2021). This research employed e Cognition software for object-based image analysis (OBIA) to detect laughing gull nests in Jamaica Bay. The approach achieved an impressive 98% producer's accuracy, providing a more efficient and accurate method for monitoring wildlife populations and offering potential applications for other species and types of aerial imagery.

In summary, this collection of studies highlights the significant potential of machine learning and advanced technologies in transforming wildlife monitoring and conservation. These studies demonstrate the effectiveness of artificial intelligence models and innovative CNN architectures like HerdNet in addressing ecological challenges. They stress the importance of collaboration and knowledge sharing to fully utilize machine learning's potential for wildlife conservation. Whether it's tracking wild birds, monitoring marine ecosystems, or automating waterbird surveillance, these advancements enable more precise data analysis, ultimately benefiting the protection of diverse wildlife. Additionally, the integration of low-cost sensors and unmanned systems, like drones, enhances data collection, providing insights into animal populations, behaviors, and ecological dynamics. These innovations not only improve our understanding of wildlife but also promote coexistence between humans and animals (Moradi, 2020).

3.2. Anti-Poaching and Illegal Wildlife Trade Prevention

By this study (Hunter et al., 2023) highlights the use of digital data, such as social media, in understanding human-nature interactions, particularly animal exploitation. Automated systems are essential for organizing large datasets gathered from online searches. The author introduces a hierarchical text categorization pipeline that combines three binary tasks to sort through relevant data. Text classifiers, including transformer-based models, recognized texts related to bat hunting with an accuracy of about 90%. Population growth and greater biodiversity exacerbate the conflict between humans and wildlife, which has negative repercussions for both sides (Leonid et al., 2023). It is critical to detect and prevent wild animals from encroaching on human areas. Machine learning, namely the YOLO method, is used in this research to recognize endangered animals from a dataset of 10,000 photographs. The YOLO-centered technique outperforms prior models in detecting endangered wildlife, achieving an amazing 94% accuracy rate utilizing computer vision algorithms. Dujon et al emphasized the growing importance of machine learning in processing large amounts of wildlife photography data collected by unmanned aerial vehicles (UAVs) (Dujon et al., 2021). The study offers a machine learning algorithm built on a low-cost computer and evaluates its capacity to detect and monitor marine species. The programmer's performance differs depending on species with similar body sizes, regular behaviors, or uniform habitats, demonstrating that no single algorithm can capture the intricacies of different species in a single site. The article provides a semi-automated technique for processing UAV data for wildlife monitoring that combines machine learning with manual detection (Dujon et al., 2021).

3.3. Wildlife Habitat Mapping and Conservation

The objective of this research (Kulkarni & Di Minin, 2023) is to create machine vision models using Deep Neural Networks for the automatic identification of images depicting exotic pets being sold. This effort addresses the issue of unsustainable wildlife trade on the internet. By training 24 neural-net models with diverse data and approaches, the research improved the models' ability to generalize, leading to highly effective models. This research aimed to analyze changes in the intricate patterns of permafrost landscapes, specifically focusing on alterations in the coverage of bare peat in an Arctic region of north-western Russia between 2007 and 2015 (Räsänen et al., 2019). To achieve this, QuickBird and World-View-3 satellite images were combined with various one-class classifiers. These classifiers demonstrated diverse performance levels, with F-scores for bare peat area ranging from 0.77 to 0.96 in cross-validated training and 0.22 to 0.57 in independent test evaluations. Notably, a significant decrease of 21%-26% in the coverage of bare peat was identified over the 8-year period (Moradi, 2022).

This paper used high-resolution satellite data to successfully analyze Antarctic areas using geographic object-based analysis to identify penguin guano stains, which indicate nesting locations (Witharana & Lynch, 2016). The study assessed the quality of segmentation, classification accuracy, and the relevance of knowledge-based laws across various study sites. The findings highlight the success of detecting guano stains using object-based approaches, where updated rules gave comparable or better results. Sisodia et al. examined how AI and Industry 4.0 technologies are used in animal conservation, examining several techniques to amplify conservation results (Sisodia et al., 2023). It emphasizes AI's ability to take timely conservation actions while also recognizing the need for a more thorough study of its restrictions. The research aims to promote the integration of AI, Industry 4.0, and wildlife conservation by exploiting sensor and satellite data to improve protection and highlighting the ongoing exploration of AI's various contributions to advancing conservation projects. Authors provided examples of successful technology adoption, underlining the significance of collaborations between ecologists and machine learning professionals (Tuia et al., 2022). While acknowledging advances, the essay underlines the need to address challenges such as adding ecological insights into models and ensuring openness in deep learning approaches. It pushes for interdisciplinary collaboration to develop scalable solutions for biodiversity protection, bringing together computer scientists and ecologists to overcome technical and societal constraints.

4. CHALLENGES AND FUTURE DIRECTIONS

The studies discussed in the previous section emphasize the increasing significance of machine learning in handling vast collections of wildlife photography data gathered through unmanned aerial vehicles (UAVs) to monitor wildlife. They recognize the necessity for flexible methods due to variations in species and behaviors across diverse locations. However, the integration of machine learning (ML) and unmanned aerial vehicles (UAVs) for wildlife monitoring comes with its set of challenges:

- Data Management and Processing: UAVs can capture vast amounts of high-resolution imagery and video, resulting in massive datasets that require efficient storage and processing capabilities. Managing and analyzing this wealth of data can strain computational resources (Mukhtar, 2022) (Alatabani, 2021).
- Species and Habitat Diversity: Wildlife encompasses a wide range of species with varying behaviors, sizes, and habitats. Developing ML algorithms that can accurately detect, classify, and monitor this diversity demands extensive training data and adaptable models.
- Environmental Factors: Weather conditions, lighting, and terrain can affect the quality of data collected by UAVs. Adverse weather, such as rain or fog, can hinder image clarity, impacting the accuracy of ML algorithms (Ali, 2021) (Alqurashi, 2021).

- Real-Time Processing: In some wildlife monitoring applications, quick decision-making is vital, such as in conservation efforts to prevent poaching or address immediate threats. ML algorithms running on UAVs must process data rapidly to provide timely insights.
- Ethical Considerations: The use of UAVs and ML in wildlife monitoring must adhere to ethical guidelines, particularly concerning privacy and animal welfare. UAVs can inadvertently disturb animals and their habitats, raising concerns about the potential negative impact of these technologies on wildlife (Bakri, 2021) (Elmustafa, 2021).
- Cost Constraints can limit the adoption of ML and UAVs for wildlife monitoring, especially in conservation organizations with limited resources. The initial investment in UAVs and the development of ML models can be substantial, making it essential to demonstrate the cost-effectiveness of these technologies over time (Hassan, 2021) (Bakri, 2021).

The future of employing Machine Learning and Unmanned Aerial Vehicles for Wildlife Monitoring holds promising directions that can revolutionize conservation efforts and deepen our understanding of wildlife behavior. Here are some key areas of development:

- Improved Accuracy and Species Recognition: ML models will become increasingly accurate in recognizing and classifying diverse wildlife species. Deep learning techniques, like convolutional neural networks (CNNs), will continue to evolve, enabling UAVs to identify species with greater precision. This will be essential for monitoring rare and endangered species effectively.
- Integration of Sensor Technologies: UAVs will be equipped with a variety of sensors, including thermal imaging, LiDAR, and acoustic sensors. These technologies will complement visual data, allowing for comprehensive monitoring of wildlife, even in challenging conditions like dense forests or low-light environments (Bokani, 2018) (Hoseini, 2021).
- Privacy and Ethical Considerations: Future directions will also emphasize ethical considerations. UAVs will be designed with features to minimize disturbance to wildlife, and data collection will adhere to strict ethical guidelines to ensure the well-being of animals.
- Policy and Regulation: Governments and international bodies will play a significant role in shaping the future of UAV-based wildlife monitoring. Clear regulations and policies will need to balance the benefits of these technologies with potential environmental and privacy concerns (Elmustafa, 2023) (Askhedkar, 2023).
- Cost Reduction: As technology matures, the cost of UAVs and associated equipment is likely to decrease. This will make UAV-based wildlife monitoring more accessible to a broader range of conservation organizations, including those with limited resources.

5. CONCLUSION

The integration of Unmanned Aerial Vehicles (UAVs) and machine learning provides a promising solution to overcome the limitations of traditional wildlife monitoring methods and enhance wildlife management and conservation strategies. The chapter highlights the benefits, challenges, and future directions in wildlife monitoring using UAVs and machine learning. It emphasizes the need for ongoing research and technological advancements to address regulatory, technical, and ethical considerations. The combination of UAVs and machine learning offers efficient and effective alternatives for wildlife monitoring.

UAVs equipped with high-resolution cameras capture aerial imagery, while machine learning algorithms automate animal detection, tracking, and behavior identification. The combination enables habitat assessment, analyzing land cover changes and fragmentation. Thermal or infrared cameras on UAVs aid in anti-poaching efforts. Machine learning facilitates species identification and population estimation using visual or acoustic data. Environmental monitoring, including water quality and pollution levels, is possible with UAVs equipped with sensors. The integration of UAVs and machine learning provides efficient data collection, automated analysis, and actionable insights for wildlife research and conservation. Ethical considerations and collaboration with experts are crucial. The chapter aims to present the current state-of-the-art, highlighting benefits, challenges, and future directions in wildlife monitoring using UAVs and machine learning. The integration of UAVs and machine learning offers an innovative solution to overcome limitations in coverage, accuracy, and cost-effectiveness. It provides researchers and conservationists with valuable insights into wildlife populations, behavior, and habitat dynamics. The chapter discusses challenges, limitations, and future directions in using UAVs and machine learning for wildlife monitoring, addressing regulatory, technical, and ethical considerations, and emphasizing the need for ongoing research and technological advancements. Overall, the integration of UAVs and machine learning provides a promising solution to overcome the limitations of traditional wildlife monitoring methods and enhance wildlife management and conservation strategies.

REFERENCES

Abang Abdurahman, A. Z., Wan Yaacob, W. F., Md Nasir, S. A., Jaya, S., & Mokhtar, S. (2022). Using Machine Learning to Predict Visitors to Totally Protected Areas in Sarawak, Malaysia. *Sustainability (Basel), 14*(5), 2735. doi:10.3390u14052735

Abbas, A., & Rania, A. (2021). Quality of Services Based on Intelligent IoT WLAN MAC Protocol Dynamic Real-Time Applications in Smart Cities. Computational Intelligence and Neuroscience. Hindawi. doi:10.1155/2021/2287531

Abdulameer, M. H., Ahmed, H. W., & Ahmed, I. S. (2022). Bird Image Dataset Classification using Deep Convolutional Neural Network Algorithm. *2022 International Conference on Data Science and Intelligent Computing, ICDSIC 2022*, (pp. 81–86). IEEE. 10.1109/ICDSIC56987.2022.10075724

Ahmed, E., Rashid, A., Sheetal, N., & Amitava, M. (2020). Energy Optimization in LPWANs by using Heuristic Techniques. LPWAN Technologies for IoT and M2M Applications. Elsevier.

Ahmed, F., Mohanta, J. C., Keshari, A., & Yadav, P. S. (2022). Recent Advances in Unmanned Aerial Vehicles: A Review. *Arabian Journal for Science and Engineering, 47*(7), 7963–7984. doi:10.100713369-022-06738-0 PMID:35492958

Alaa, M. (2022). Performance Evaluation of Downlink Coordinated Multipoint Joint Transmission under Heavy IoT Traffic Load. Wireless Communications and Mobile Computing. IEEE. doi:10.1155/2022/6837780

Alatabani, L. E., & Ali, E. S. (2021). Deep Learning Approaches for IoV Applications and Services. In N. Magaia, G. Mastorakis, C. Mavromoustakis, E. Pallis, & E. K. Markakis (Eds.), *Intelligent Technologies for Internet of Vehicles. Internet of Things (Technology, Communications, and Computing)*. Springer. doi:10.1007/978-3-030-76493-7_8

Ali, E. S., & Hassan, M. B. (2021). Machine Learning Technologies on Internet of Vehicles. In N. Magaia, G. Mastorakis, C. Mavromoustakis, E. Pallis, & E. K. Markakis (Eds.), *Intelligent Technologies for Internet of Vehicles. Internet of Things (Technology, Communications, and Computing)*. Springer. doi:10.1007/978-3-030-76493-7_7

Ali, R. A., Ali, E. S., & Mokhtar, R. A. (2022). Blockchain for IoT-Based Cyber-Physical Systems (CPS): Applications and Challenges. In D. De, S. Bhattacharyya, & J. J. P. C. Rodrigues (Eds.), *Blockchain-based Internet of Things. Lecture Notes on Data Engineering and Communications Technologies* (Vol. 112). Springer. doi:10.1007/978-981-16-9260-4_4

Alqurashi, A., Alsolami, F., Abdel-Khalek, S., Sayed Ali, E., & Saeed, R. A. (2021). a; Abdel-Khalek, S.; (2021) 'Machine Learning Techniques in Internet of UAVs for Smart Cities Applications'. *Journal of Intelligent & Fuzzy Systems*, *42*(4), 1–24. doi:10.3233/JIFS-211009

Andrew, M. E., & Shephard, J. M. (2017). Semi-automated detection of eagle nests: An application of very high-resolution image data and advanced image analyses to wildlife surveys. *Remote Sensing in Ecology and Conservation*, *3*(2), 66–80. doi:10.1002/rse2.38

Askhedkar, A. R., Chaudhari, B. S., Abdelhaq, M., Alsaqour, R., Saeed, R., & Zennaro, M. (2023). LoRa Communication Using TVWS Frequencies: Range and Data Rate. *Future Internet*, *2023*(15), 270. doi:10.3390/fi15080270

Baig, T., & Shastry, C. (2023). Design of WSN Model with NS2 for Animal Tracking and Monitoring. *Procedia Computer Science, 218*, 2563–2574. doi:10.1016/j.procs.2023.01.230

Bakri, H., & Ali, E. (2021). Intelligent Internet of things in wireless networks. Intelligent Wireless Communications. IET Digital Library, doi:10.1049/PBTE094E_ch6

Barroso, P., Relimpio, D., Zearra, J. A., Cerón, J. J., Palencia, P., Cardoso, B., Ferreras, E., Escobar, M., Cáceres, G., López-Olvera, J. R., & Gortázar, C. (2023). Using integrated wildlife monitoring to prevent future pandemics through one health approach. *One Health, 16*. https://doi.org/ doi:10.1016/j.onehlt.2022.100479

Bakri, H., & Elmustafa, S. (2021). Machine Learning for Industrial IoT Systems. In J. Zhao & V. Vinoth Kumar (Eds.), *Handbook of Research on Innovations and Applications of AI, IoT, and Cognitive Technologies* (pp. 336–358). IGI Global. doi:10.4018/978-1-7998-6870-5.ch023

Berg, P., Maia, D. S., Pham, M. T., & Lefèvre, S. (2022). Weakly Supervised Detection of Marine Animals in High Resolution Aerial Images. *Remote Sensing (Basel)*, *14*(2), 339. doi:10.3390/rs14020339

Bokani, A., Hassan, J., & Kanhere, S. S. (2018). *Enabling Efficient and High Quality Zooming for Online Video Streaming using Edge Computing*. 2018 28th International Telecommunication Networks and Applications Conference (ITNAC), Sydney, NSW, Australia. 10.1109/ATNAC.2018.8615166

Bouguettaya, A., Zarzour, H., Taberkit, A. M., & Kechida, A. (2022). A review on early wildfire detection from unmanned aerial vehicles using deep learning-based computer vision algorithms. In *Signal Processing* (Vol. 190). Elsevier B.V. doi:10.1016/j.sigpro.2021.108309

Brack, I. V., Kindel, A., & Oliveira, L. F. B. (2018). Detection errors in wildlife abundance estimates from Unmanned Aerial Systems (UAS) surveys: Synthesis, solutions, and challenges. In Methods in Ecology and Evolution, 9(8), 1864–1873. doi:10.1111/2041-210X.13026

Burton, A. C., Neilson, E., Moreira, D., Ladle, A., Steenweg, R., Fisher, J. T., Bayne, E., & Boutin, S. (2015). REVIEW: Wildlife camera trapping: a review and recommendations for linking surveys to ecological processes. *Journal of Applied Ecology*, 52(3), 675–685. doi:10.1111/1365-2664.12432 PMID:26211047

Cardoso, A. S., Bryukhova, S., Renna, F., Reino, L., Xu, C., Xiao, Z., Correia, R., Di Minin, E., Ribeiro, J., & Vaz, A. S. (2023). Detecting wildlife trafficking in images from online platforms: A test case using deep learning with pangolin images. *Biological Conservation*, 279, 109905. doi:10.1016/j.biocon.2023.109905

Chabot, D., Stapleton, S., & Francis, C. M. (2022). Using Web images to train a deep neural network to detect sparsely distributed wildlife in large volumes of remotely sensed imagery: A case study of polar bears on sea ice. *Ecological Informatics*, 68, 101547. doi:10.1016/j.ecoinf.2021.101547

Daniel Raj, J. J., Sangeetha, C. N., Ghorai, S., & Das, S., Manish, & Ahmed, S. (2023). Wild Animals Intrusion Detection for Safe Commuting in Forest Corridors using AI Techniques. *Proceedings of 2023 3rd International Conference on Innovative Practices in Technology and Management, ICIPTM 2023*. IEEE. 10.1109/ICIPTM57143.2023.10117831

Delplanque, A., Foucher, S., Théau, J., Bussière, E., Vermeulen, C., & Lejeune, P. (2023). From crowd to herd counting: How to precisely detect and count African mammals using aerial imagery and deep learning? *ISPRS Journal of Photogrammetry and Remote Sensing*, 197, 167–180. doi:10.1016/j.isprsjprs.2023.01.025

Dhivya, K., Kumar, P. N., Hariharan, S., & Premalatha, G. (2022). A GPS based Tracking System for Wildlife Safety. *2022 3rd International Conference on Electronics and Sustainable Communication Systems (ICESC)*, (pp. 428–433). IEEE. 10.1109/ICESC54411.2022.9885423

Dujon, A. M., Ierodiaconou, D., Geeson, J. J., Arnould, J. P. Y., Allan, B. M., Katselidis, K. A., & Schofield, G. (2021). Machine learning to detect marine animals in UAV imagery: Effect of morphology, spacing, behaviour and habitat. *Remote Sensing in Ecology and Conservation*, 7(3), 341–354. doi:10.1002/rse2.205

Elmeseiry, N., Alshaer, N., & Ismail, T. (2021). A detailed survey and future directions of unmanned aerial vehicles (Uavs) with potential applications. *Aerospace (Basel, Switzerland)*, 8(12), 363. doi:10.3390/aerospace8120363

Elmustafa S. (2023). A systematic review on energy efficiency in the internet of underwater things (IoUT): Recent approaches and research gaps. *Journal of Network and Computer Applications, 213*. doi:10.1016/j.jnca.2023.103594

Elmustafa, S., & Mohammad, K. (2021). Machine Learning Technologies for Secure Vehicular Communication in Internet of Vehicles: Recent Advances and Applications. *Security and Communication Networks, 2021*, 1–23. doi:10.1155/2021/8868355

Elnour, R. A. M. (2023). Social Internet of Things (SIoT) Localization for Smart Cities Traffic Applications. In G. H. A. Salih & R. A. Saeed (Eds.), *Sustainability Challenges and Delivering Practical Engineering Solutions. Advances in Science, Technology & Innovation.* Springer. doi:10.1007/978-3-031-26580-8_24

Fang, Y., Du, S., Boubchir, L., & Djouani, K. (2021). Detecting African hoofed animals in aerial imagery using convolutional neural network. [IJRA]. *IAES International Journal of Robotics and Automation, 10*(2), 133. doi:10.11591/ijra.v10i2.pp133-143

Frair, J. L., Nielsen, S. E., Merrill, E. H., Lele, S. R., Boyce, M. S., Munro, R. H. M., Stenhouse, G. B., & Beyer, H. L. (2004). Removing GPS collar bias in habitat selection studies. *Journal of Applied Ecology, 41*(2), 201–212. doi:10.1111/j.0021-8901.2004.00902.x PMID:15146623

Ghorpade S. N. & Zennaro M. (2021). A Novel Enhanced Quantum PSO for Optimal Network Configuration in Heterogeneous Industrial IoT. *IEEE Access.* IEEE. . doi:10.1109/ACCESS.2021.3115026

Ghorpade S. N., Zennaro M., B. S. & Chaudhari, B. (2021). Enhanced Differential Crossover and Quantum Particle Swarm Optimization for IoT Applications. *IEEE Access.* IEEE. . doi:10.1109/ACCESS.2021.3093113

Giordan, D., Adams, M. S., Aicardi, I., Alicandro, M., Allasia, P., Baldo, M., De Berardinis, P., Dominici, D., Godone, D., Hobbs, P., Lechner, V., Niedzielski, T., Piras, M., Rotilio, M., Salvini, R., Segor, V., Sotier, B., & Troilo, F. (2020). The use of unmanned aerial vehicles (UAVs) for engineering geology applications. *Bulletin of Engineering Geology and the Environment, 79*(7), 3437–3481. doi:10.100710064-020-01766-2

Hadji, O., Kadri, O., Maimour, M., Rondeau, E., & Benyahia, A. (2022). Region of Interest and Redundancy Problem in Migratory Birds Wild Life Surveillance. *2022 International Conference on Advanced Aspects of Software Engineering (ICAASE),* (pp. 1–8). IEEE. 10.1109/ICAASE56196.2022.9931576

Hassan, M., Ali, E., & Nurelmadina, N. (2021). Artificial intelligence in IoT and its applications. Intelligent Wireless Communications. IET Digital Library. , doi:10.1049/PBTE094E_ch2

Hassan, M.B., Alsharif, S., & Alhumyani, H. (2021). An Enhanced Cooperative Communication Scheme for Physical Uplink Shared Channel in NB-IoT. Wireless Pers Commun., 120, 2367–2386. https://doi.org/ doi:10.100711277-021-08067-1

He, Z., Kays, R., Zhang, Z., Ning, G., Huang, C., Han, T. X., Millspaugh, J., Forrester, T., & McShea, W. (2016). Visual Informatics Tools for Supporting Large-Scale Collaborative Wildlife Monitoring with Citizen Scientists. *IEEE Circuits and Systems Magazine, 16*(1), 73–86. doi:10.1109/MCAS.2015.2510200

Hong, S. J., Han, Y., Kim, S. Y., Lee, A. Y., & Kim, G. (2019). Application of deep-learning methods to bird detection using unmanned aerial vehicle imagery. *Sensors (Basel), 19*(7), 1651. doi:10.339019071651 PMID:30959913

Hoseini, S. A., Bokani, A., Hassan, J., Salehi, S., & Kanhere, S. S. (2021). Energy and Service-Priority aware Trajectory Design for UAV-BSs using Double Q-Learning. 2021 IEEE 18th Annual Consumer Communications & Networking Conference. IEEE. doi:10.1109/CCNC49032.2021.9369472

Hunter, S. B., Mathews, F., & Weeds, J. (2023). Using hierarchical text classification to investigate the utility of machine learning in automating online analyses of wildlife exploitation. *Ecological Informatics*, *75*, 102076. doi:10.1016/j.ecoinf.2023.102076

Jasim, M. A., Shakhatreh, H., Siasi, N., Sawalmeh, A. H., Aldalbahi, A., & Al-Fuqaha, A. (2022). A Survey on Spectrum Management for Unmanned Aerial Vehicles (UAVs). *IEEE Access : Practical Innovations, Open Solutions*, *10*, 11443–11499. doi:10.1109/ACCESS.2021.3138048

Kalathas, I., Papoutsidakis, M., Piromalis, D., & Katsinoulas, L. (2019). Machine Learning: Prospects, Opportunities and Benefits to the Greek Railways. *International Journal of Computer Applications*, *178*(24), 26–32. doi:10.5120/ijca2019919038

Kellenberger, B., Veen, T., Folmer, E., & Tuia, D. (2021). 21 000 birds in 4.5 h: Efficient large-scale seabird detection with machine learning. *Remote Sensing in Ecology and Conservation*, *7*(3), 445–460. doi:10.1002/rse2.200

Khalifa, O. O., Roubleh, A., Esgiar, A., Abdelhaq, M., Alsaqour, R., Abdalla, A., Ali, E. S., & Saeed, R. (2022). An IoT-Platform-Based Deep Learning System for Human Behavior Recognition in Smart City Monitoring Using the Berkeley MHAD Datasets. *Systems*, *2022*(10), 177. doi:10.3390ystems10050177

Kreuzberger, D., Kuhl, N., & Hirschl, S. (2023). Machine Learning Operations (MLOps): Overview, Definition, and Architecture. *IEEE Access : Practical Innovations, Open Solutions*, *11*, 31866–31879. doi:10.1109/ACCESS.2023.3262138

Kulkarni, R., & Di Minin, E. (2023). Towards automatic detection of wildlife trade using machine vision models. *Biological Conservation*, *279*, 109924. doi:10.1016/j.biocon.2023.109924

Kuru, K., Clough, S., Ansell, D., McCarthy, J., & McGovern, S. (2023). WILDetect: An intelligent platform to perform airborne wildlife census automatically in the marine ecosystem using an ensemble of learning techniques and computer vision. *Expert Systems with Applications*, *231*, 120574. doi:10.1016/j.eswa.2023.120574

KurunathanH.HuangH.LiK.NiW.HossainE. (2022). Machine Learning-Aided Operations and Communications of Unmanned Aerial Vehicles: A Contemporary Survey. https://arxiv.org/abs/2211.04324

Leonid, T. T., & Kanna, H. (2023). *C. C., A S, H., & Lokesh, C* (Vol. J). Human Wildlife Conflict Mitigation Using YOLO Algorithm., doi:10.1109/ICONSTEM56934.2023.10142629

Li, X., & Savkin, A. V. (2021). Networked unmanned aerial vehicles for surveillance and monitoring: A survey. *Future Internet*, *13*(7), 174. doi:10.3390/fi13070174

Lina E. & Elmustafa, A. (2022). Deep and Reinforcement Learning Technologies on Internet of Vehicle (IoV) Applications: Current Issues and Future Trends. *Journal of Advanced Transportation*. doi:10.1155/2022/1947886

Linchant, J., Lejeune, P., Quevauvillers, S., Vermeulen, C., Brostaux, Y., Lhoest, S., & Michez, A. (2023). Evaluation of an Innovative Rosette Flight Plan Design for Wildlife Aerial Surveys with UAS. *Drones (Basel)*, *7*(3), 208. doi:10.3390/drones7030208

Luz-Ricca, E., Landolt, K., Pickens, B. A., & Koneff, M. (2023). Automating sandhill crane counts from nocturnal thermal aerial imagery using deep learning. *Remote Sensing in Ecology and Conservation*, *9*(2), 182–194. doi:10.1002/rse2.301

Markovchick-Nicholls, L., Regan, H. M., Deutschman, D. H., Widyanata, A., Martin, B., Noreke, L., & Ann Hunt, T. (2008). Relationships between Human Disturbance and Wildlife Land Use in Urban Habitat Fragments. *Conservation Biology*, *22*(1), 99–109. doi:10.1111/j.1523-1739.2007.00846.x PMID:18254856

Martini, B. F., & Miller, D. A. (2021). Using object-based image analysis to detect laughing gull nests. *GIScience & Remote Sensing*, *58*(8), 1497–1517. doi:10.1080/15481603.2021.1999376

Mohammad, K., & Taher, M. (2022). A review on security threats, vulnerabilities, and counter measures of 5G enabled Internet-of-Medical-Things. *IET Communications*, *16*(5), 421–432. doi:10.1049/cmu2.12301

Mohsan, S. A. H., Khan, M. A., Noor, F., Ullah, I., & Alsharif, M. H. (2022). Towards the Unmanned Aerial Vehicles (UAVs): A Comprehensive Review. In Drones, 6(6). MDPI. doi:10.3390/drones6060147

Mona, B., & Elmustafa, S. (2020). NB-IoT: Concepts, Applications, and Deployment Challenges. In B. Chaudhari & M. Zennaro (eds.) LPWAN Technologies for IoT and M2M Applications. Elsevier.

Moradi, M., Bokani, A., & Hassan, J. (2020). *Energy-Efficient and QoS-aware UAV Communication using Reactive RF Band Allocation*. 2020 30th International Telecommunication Networks and Applications Conference (ITNAC), Melbourne, VIC, Australia. 10.1109/ITNAC50341.2020.9315157

Moradi, S., Bokani, A., & Hassan, J. (2022). *UAV-based Smart Agriculture: a Review of UAV Sensing and Applications*. 2022 32nd International Telecommunication Networks and Applications Conference (ITNAC), Wellington, New Zealand. 10.1109/ITNAC55475.2022.9998411

Nada, M., Mohammad, K., & Zeinab, K. (2021). Internet of vehicle's resource management in 5G networks using AI technologies: Current status and trends. *IET Communications*, *2021*, 1–21. doi:10.1049/cmu2.12315

Nahla, N., Mohammad, K., & Imran, M. (2021). A Systematic Review on Cognitive Radio in Low Power Wide Area Network for Industrial IoT Applications. *Sustainability (Basel)*, *2021*(1), 338. Advance online publication. doi:10.3390u13010338

Nicheporchuk, V., Gryazin, I., & Favorskaya, M. N. (2020). *Framework for Intelligent Wildlife Monitoring*., doi:10.1007/978-981-15-5925-9_14

Omran, O., & Ahmed, M. Z. (2022). A Stochastic Approach for Blockchain Internet of Things Integration. *2022 International Conference on Advanced Computer Science and Information Systems (ICACSIS)*, (pp. 219-224). IEEE. 10.1109/ICACSIS56558.2022.9923464

Othman, O., & Ahmed, M. Z. (2022). Blockchain Security for 5G Network using Internet of Things Devices. *2022 7th International Workshop on Big Data and Information Security (IWBIS)*. IEEE. 10.1109/IWBIS56557.2022.9924937

Outay, F., Mengash, H. A., & Adnan, M. (2020). Applications of unmanned aerial vehicle (UAV) in road safety, traffic and highway infrastructure management: Recent advances and challenges. *Transportation Research Part A, Policy and Practice, 141*, 116–129. doi:10.1016/j.tra.2020.09.018 PMID:33024357

Öztürk, A. E., & Erçelebi, E. (2021). Real uav-bird image classification using cnn with a synthetic dataset. *Applied Sciences (Basel, Switzerland), 11*(9), 3863. doi:10.3390/app11093863

Patel, J. (2020). Unification of Machine Learning Features. *2020 IEEE 44th Annual Computers, Software, and Applications Conference (COMPSAC),* (pp. 1201–1205). IEEE. 10.1109/COMPSAC48688.2020.00-93

Rania, S., Sara, A., & Rania, A. (2020). *IoE Design Principles and Architecture; Book: Internet of Energy for Smart Cities: Machine Learning Models and Techniques.* CRC Press Publisher. doi:10.4018/978-1-7998-5101-1

Räsänen, A., Elsakov, V., & Virtanen, T. (2019). Usability of one-class classification in mapping and detecting changes in bare peat surfaces in the tundra. *International Journal of Remote Sensing, 40*(11), 4083–4103. doi:10.1080/01431161.2018.1558376

Rashid A. & Ahmed A. M. (2010). WiMAX, LTE and WiFi Interworking. *Journal of Computer Systems, Networks, and Communications, Hindawi Publishing Corporation.*

Sayed, A., & Zahraa, T. (2021). Algorithms Optimization for Intelligent IoV Applications. In J. Zhao & V. Vinoth Kumar (Eds.), *Handbook of Research on Innovations and Applications of AI, IoT, and Cognitive Technologies* (pp. 1–25). IGI Global. doi:10.4018/978-1-7998-6870-5.ch001

Sejan, M. A. S., Rahman, M. H., Shin, B. S., Oh, J. H., You, Y. H., & Song, H. K. (2022). Machine Learning for Intelligent-Reflecting-Surface-Based Wireless Communication towards 6G: A Review. In Sensors, 22(14). MDPI. doi:10.339022145405

Sharma, S., Sato, K., & Gautam, B. P. (2022). Bioacoustics Monitoring of Wildlife using Artificial Intelligence: A Methodological Literature Review. *Proceedings - 2022 International Conference on Networking and Network Applications.* IEEE. 10.1109/NaNA56854.2022.00063

Šimek, P., Pavlík, J., Jarolímek, J., Oèenášek, V., & Stoèes, M. (2017, September). Use of unmanned aerial vehicles for wildlife monitoring. In *Proceedings of the 8th International Conference on Information and Communication Technologies in Agriculture, Food and Environment (HAICTA 2017)* (pp. 21-24). Semantic Scholar.

SinghT.GangloffH.PhamM.-T. (2023). Object counting from aerial remote sensing images: application to wildlife and marine mammals. https://arxiv.org/abs/2306.10439 doi:10.1109/IGARSS52108.2023.10282150

Sisodia, S., Dhyani, S., Kathuria, S., Pandey, S., Chhabra, G., & Pandey, R. (2023). AI Technologies, Innovations and Possibilities in Wildlife Conservation. *International Conference on Innovative Data Communication Technologies and Application.* IEEE. 10.1109/ICIDCA56705.2023.10099721

Stephenson, P. J. (2019). Integrating Remote Sensing into Wildlife Monitoring for Conservation. *Environmental Conservation, 46*(3), 181–183. doi:10.1017/S0376892919000092

Szenicer, A., Reinwald, M., Moseley, B., Nissen-Meyer, T., Mutinda Muteti, Z., Oduor, S., McDermott-Roberts, A., Baydin, A. G., & Mortimer, B. (2022). Seismic savanna: Machine learning for classifying wildlife and behaviours using ground-based vibration field recordings. *Remote Sensing in Ecology and Conservation, 8*(2), 236–250. doi:10.1002/rse2.242

Thalor, M. A., Nagabhyrava, R., Rajkumar, K., Chakraborty, A., Singh, R., & Singh Aswal, U. (2023). Deep learning insights and methods for classifying wildlife. *2023 3rd International Conference on Advance Computing and Innovative Technologies in Engineering (ICACITE)*, (pp. 403–407). IEEE. 10.1109/ICACITE57410.2023.10183057

Tibbetts, J. H. (2017). Remote Sensors Bring Wildlife Tracking to New Level. *Bioscience, 67*(5), 411–417. doi:10.1093/biosci/bix033

Tuia, D., Kellenberger, B., Beery, S., Costelloe, B. R., Zuffi, S., Risse, B., Mathis, A., Mathis, M. W., van Langevelde, F., Burghardt, T., Kays, R., Klinck, H., Wikelski, M., Couzin, I. D., van Horn, G., Crofoot, M. C., Stewart, C. V., & Berger-Wolf, T. (2022). Perspectives in machine learning for wildlife conservation. In Nature Communications, 13(1). Nature Research. doi:10.103841467-022-27980-y

Velusamy, P., Rajendran, S., Mahendran, R. K., Naseer, S., Shafiq, M., & Choi, J. G. (2022). Unmanned aerial vehicles (Uav) in precision agriculture: Applications and challenges. In Energies, 15. doi:10.3390/en15010217

Witharana, C., & Lynch, H. J. (2016). An object-based image analysis approach for detecting penguin guano in very high spatial resolution satellite images. *Remote Sensing (Basel), 8*(5), 375. doi:10.3390/rs8050375

Wu, E., Wang, H., Lu, H., Zhu, W., Jia, Y., Wen, L., Choi, C.-Y., Guo, H., Li, B., Sun, L., Lei, G., Lei, J., & Jian, H. (2022). Unlocking the Potential of Deep Learning for Migratory Waterbirds Monitoring Using Surveillance Video. *Remote Sensing (Basel), 14*(3), 514. doi:10.3390/rs14030514

Xu, J., Solmaz, G., Rahmatizadeh, R., Boloni, L., & Turgut, D. (2018). Providing Distribution Estimation for Animal Tracking with Unmanned Aerial Vehicles. *2018 IEEE Global Communications Conference (GLOBECOM)*, (pp. 1–6). IEEE. 10.1109/GLOCOM.2018.8647784

XuJ.SolmazG.RahmatizadehR.TurgutD.BoloniL. (2016). Internet of Things Applications: Animal Monitoring with Unmanned Aerial Vehicle. arXiv. https://arxiv.org/abs/1610.05287

Yousefi, D. B. M., Rafie, A. S. M., Al-Haddad, S. A. R., & Azrad, S. (2022). A Systematic Literature Review on the Use of Deep Learning in Precision Livestock Detection and Localization Using Unmanned Aerial Vehicles. Institute of Electrical and Electronics Engineers Inc. doi:10.1109/ACCESS.2022.3194507

Zeinab, E., Hasan, K., & Rashid, A. (2020). Optimizing Energy Consumption for Cloud Internet of Things. *Frontiers in Physics (Lausanne), 8*, 2020. doi:10.3389/fphy.2020.00358

Zeng, Y., Zhang, R., & Lim, T. J. (2016). *Wireless Communications with Unmanned Aerial Vehicles: Opportunities and Challenges*. IEEE. doi:10.1109/MCOM.2016.7470933

Zhang, J., Luo, X., Chen, C., Liu, Z., & Cao, S. (2014). A Wildlife Monitoring System Based on Wireless Image Sensor Networks. In *Sensors & Transducers, 180*. http://www.sensorsportal.com

Zhang, J., Zhang, J., Du, X., Kang, H., & Qiao, M. (2017). An overview of ecological monitoring based on geographic information system (GIS) and remote sensing (RS) technology in China. *IOP Conference Series. Earth and Environmental Science, 94,* 012056. doi:10.1088/1755-1315/94/1/012056

Zhong, J., Li, M., Qin, J., Cui, Y., Yang, K., & Zhang, H. (2022). Real-time marine animal detection using yolo-based deep learning networks in the coral reef ecosystem. *International Archives of the Photogrammetry, Remote Sensing and Spatial Information Sciences - ISPRS Archives, 46*(3/W1-2022), 301–306. ISPRS. doi:10.5194/isprs-archives-XLVI-3-W1-2022-301-2022

Zviedris, R., Elsts, A., Strazdins, G., Mednis, A., & Selavo, L. (2010). LynxNet: Wild Animal Monitoring Using Sensor Networks, (pp. 170–173). Springer. doi:10.1007/978-3-642-17520-6_18

Chapter 6
Integration of Unmanned Aerial Vehicle Systems With Machine Learning Algorithms for Wildlife Monitoring and Conservation

R. Raffik
 https://orcid.org/0000-0001-8806-193X
Kumaraguru College of Technology, India

M. Mahima Swetha
Kumaraguru College of Technology, India

Rithish Ramamoorthy Sathya
Kumaraguru College of Technology, India

V. Vaishali
Kumaraguru College of Technology, India

B. Madhana Adithya
Kumaraguru College of Technology, India

S. Balavedhaa
Kumaraguru College of Technology, India

ABSTRACT

Two cutting-edge technologies, unmanned aerial vehicle (UAV) systems and deep learning algorithms, have the potential to completely change how wildlife is monitored and conserved. Data collection across wide areas, in challenging locations, and in real time are all possible with UAVs. Data collection via UAVs is possible in locations that are difficult or impossible to reach using conventional human approaches. Along with spotting strange behavior by wild creatures, the UAV can also spot it in human activity. Deep learning algorithms can be used to recognize certain animals, follow their motions, and categorize their behavior. The ecology of wildlife populations may be better understood using this knowledge, which can also be utilized to create more successful conservation plans. A novel technique that has promise for wildlife monitoring and conservation is the fusion of UAV systems and deep learning algorithms. The anticipation is even more creative and successful methods to use UAVs and deep learning to protect animals as technology progresses.

DOI: 10.4018/979-8-3693-0578-2.ch006

1. INTRODUCTION

The majority of the dangers to wildlife and its population are caused by habitat loss, degradation, poaching, overexploitation, and fragmentation. Additionally, abrupt climatic changes and pollution have an impact on habitat degradation. Several government and non-government organizations are attempting to stop wildlife. To avoid drought, new deserts, fires, and floods, it is essential to conserve wildlife. Additionally, by conserving the environment, future generations of people and animals will grow to love and appreciate it as well as comprehend the value of wildlife. The preservation of animals and flora promotes global ecological balance. By regulating the levels of oxygen and carbon dioxide in the environment, plants, for instance, contribute significantly to the maintenance of a healthy ecosystem. The improvement of food security is one of the most fundamental functions of wildlife protection for humans. The availability of different food products would rise if natural ecosystems were protected from deterioration and forests from deforestation. It is predicted that a sizable portion of animals and plants are yet to be discovered despite the expansion of animal studies over the past few decades (McComb, 2007). The majority of human drugs are derived from microbial, animal, and plant sources, which emphasizes the significance of protecting wildlife and its ecosystems. Future generations will not get the chance to witness some of the wild animals that are still around now if conservation efforts are not made. The number of wild animals is declining at an alarming rate as a result of human activity.

It is essential to preserve wildlife if we want to avoid drought, new deserts, fires, and flooding. Additionally, this conservation assures that future generations of people and wildlife will grow up in harmony with nature and appreciate it as well as comprehend the value of wildlife. The majority of the dangers to wildlife and its population are caused by habitat loss, degradation, poaching, excessive use, and fragmentation. Additionally, abrupt climatic changes and pollution have an impact on habitat degradation. A number of government and non-government organizations are attempting to stop wild-life. The preservation of animals and flora promotes global ecological balance. By regulating the levels of oxygen and carbon dioxide in the environment, plants, for instance, contribute significantly to the maintenance of a healthy ecosystem. The improvement of food security is one of the most fundamental functions of wildlife protection for humans. UAVs are useful in agriculture, (Senthilkumar, S. et al., 2021), for pesticide and weedicide spraying, harvesting and farmland monitoring purposes (Rakesh, D. et al., 2021). The availability of different food products would rise if natural ecosystems were protected from deterioration and forests from deforestation. It is predicted that a sizable portion of animals and plants are yet to be discovered despite the expansion of animal studies over the past few decades. The majority of human drugs are derived from microbial, animal, and plant sources, which emphasizes the significance of protecting wildlife and its ecosystems. Future generations won't be able to view a few of the wild animals that live today if conservation efforts are not made (Krausman and Johnsingh, 1990). Because of human activity, the number of wild animals is declining at an alarming rate. A cutting-edge technical solution is being pursued in response to the rising demand for original strategies to ensure wildlife preservation. Additionally, unmanned aircraft systems (UAVs) are promoted as a viable option or substitute for wildlife monitoring.

1.1 Advantages of UAVs in Wildlife Conservation

Comparing drones to more conventional approaches, there are several benefits to using them to monitor wildlife. Non-invasive data gathering, increased effectiveness and coverage, cost-effectiveness, and improved safety are a few of these. Drones make it possible to collect precise data and identify issues before they become serious, improving wildlife management (Brinkman, M. P, 2020). This technology also increases support for conservation efforts and public knowledge of them. Examples of specific drone applications include following koalas in Australia to assess their health and population reduction, monitoring elephant numbers in Kenya with infrared cameras, and securing sea turtle nests in the US by locating nesting places on beaches. Drones have a lot of potential to improve the effectiveness, precision, and efficiency of wildlife conservation efforts.

1.2 Types of UAVs in Wildlife Surveillance

A broad range of Unmanned Aerial Vehicles (UAVs), or drones, occupy the front stage in the field of wildlife surveillance. Fixed-wing UAVs, which look like little airplanes, excel at covering enormous areas, making them perfect for large-scale aerial surveys and tracking wildlife over long distances. Quadcopters and other multirotor UAVs provide stability and agility, making them ideal for close-range monitoring and obtaining high-resolution pictures (Hutcherson, Z. S, 2023). Hybrid UAVs combine fixed-wing endurance with multirotor flexibility, allowing for vertical takeoff and landing while switching to efficient fixed-wing flight. Solar-powered UAVs with solar panels have longer flight durations, making them ideal for long-term wildlife monitoring in isolated locations.

Tethered UAVs, which are connected to a ground station through a cable, provide continuous power and data transmission, making them ideal for stationary, long-term monitoring. Blimps and airships, with their quiet and slow-paced flights, provide for unobtrusive observation of species and environments. Vertical Takeoff and Landing (VTOL) UAVs combine the advantages of fixed-wing and multirotor drones, providing versatility for a wide range of surveillance jobs. Compact and lightweight miniature UAVs are ideal for close-range wildlife research and high-resolution image capturing. Furthermore, customized UAVs designed for specific research purposes frequently include specialized sensors such as infrared cameras or LiDAR for accurate wildlife monitoring activities. The choice of a UAV type is based on mission-specific parameters such as topography, flight duration, cargo capacity, and environmental circumstances, which must correspond with the specific goals of wildlife researchers and conservationists.

2. LITERATURE SURVEY

The situation of animal surveillance and conservation in recent years has created a picture of worldwide biodiversity degradation. The IUCN Red List of Threatened Species had identified a large number of species that were on the verge of extinction (Betts, J et al., 2020). Species extinction rates were exceeding the natural background rate due to human-caused factors such as habitat destruction, pollution, and climate change. The illicit wildlife trade remained a serious danger to several species, including elephants, rhinoceroses, and pangolins, with trafficking continuing for high-demand items such as ivory and rhino horn. As animals struggled to adapt to rapidly changing settings, climate change had a huge impact on wildlife, affecting habitats and behaviors.

Conservation efforts around the world have received significant financing, with an emphasis on habitat restoration, anti-poaching measures, and research (Krausman and Cain, 2022). Camera traps and satellite photography, for example, were important in monitoring and researching wildlife populations. Protected places, such as national parks and reserves, have remained vital in preserving critical habitats. Among these difficulties, there were also conservation success stories, demonstrating that focused efforts can help certain species recover from the brink of extinction. Consult credible sources and research publications from organizations such as WWF and IUCN for the most up-to-date and detailed statistical information.

In response to technology developments and the growing demand for real-time data, wildlife surveillance technologies have expanded substantially. One of the most notable changes is the incorporation of remote sensing technology, such as drones and satellite imagery, which provide an up-close perspective of wildlife habitats and allow for efficient monitoring across large areas. In addition, the usage of camera traps and audio monitoring systems has grown in popularity. These technologies provide non-intrusive methods for observing wildlife behavior, recording vocalizations, and capturing photographs and films.

Machine learning and artificial intelligence are progressively being used to analyze the massive volumes of data generated by these devices, allowing them to automatically identify species, track individuals, and spot patterns. Volunteers and communities are now able to actively participate in wildlife surveillance activities thanks to citizen science programs and collaborative platforms (Green, S et al., 2020). This strategy of distributed data collecting broadens and deepens monitoring while encouraging public involvement and awareness. These methodological changes have not only improved data collection accuracy and efficiency, but also promoted greater collaboration among researchers, environmentalists, and communities, eventually contributing to improved and environmentally friendly wildlife management practices in the modern world.

New advancements in wildlife surveillance technologies have greatly enhanced our understanding of wildlife populations and behaviours, which is essential for effective conservation efforts. A significant innovation is environmental DNA (eDNA) sampling, a non-invasive technique that detects DNA shed by organisms into their environment. Collected from water, soil, or other environmental samples, eDNA allows us to identify the species present in an area, providing a particularly efficient way to monitor wildlife populations, even rare or elusive species. This technology offers valuable insights without direct interaction, minimizing disturbance to ecosystems.

Another impactful development is the use of acoustic monitoring, which employs microphones to record animal sounds. This method is invaluable for identifying species, tracking individuals, and monitoring animal behaviour. Acoustic monitoring is particularly advantageous for studying nocturnal animals and species concealed in dense vegetation, providing a non-intrusive approach to understanding their ecological roles and behaviours. The data collected through this technology contributes significantly to wildlife research and aids conservationists in making informed decisions. Radiotelemetry, which tracks animal movements with radio collars, is still a highly effective method in wildlife surveillance. Through the analysis of movement trends, home range expansion, and habitat utilisation, radiotelemetry offers vital insights into the ecology of animal species. Through the discovery of new information on the geographical and temporal dynamics of wildlife, this technology has played a crucial role in helping to solve the mysteries surrounding animal behaviour and developing successful conservation policies.

Artificial intelligence (AI) has revolutionized wildlife surveillance, providing a plethora of applications to enhance monitoring and conservation efforts. AI is used to automatically identify animals in camera trap images, track individual movements, and detect poaching activity. AI algorithms' ability to swiftly analyse vast datasets contributes to efficient and accurate species identification, aiding researchers, and conservationists in their endeavours. Additionally, AI plays a crucial role in developing innovative conservation tools, such as software that can predict areas at high risk of poaching. By harnessing machine learning capabilities, AI enhances the predictive and analytical capacities of wildlife surveillance technologies, ultimately contributing to more effective conservation strategies. These advancements in wildlife surveillance technologies represent a comprehensive approach to understanding and protecting biodiversity. From non-invasive eDNA sampling to the acoustic monitoring of elusive species, and the spatial insights provided by radiotelemetry, these technologies collectively contribute to a thorough understanding of wildlife populations, behaviours, and ecological interactions.

2.1 Evolution of Wildlife Conservation Methodologies

Numerous governmental and non-governmental organizations have taken up the cause of protecting and conserving wildlife through the preservation of natural habitats, preservation of the viable number of species in protected areas, creation of Biosphere Reserves, safeguarding through legislation, imposition of export restrictions on rare plant and animal species and their products, improvement of the current conditions of protected areas, mass education, and declaration of some animals, trees, and flora as endangered.

The habitats of wildlife are unstable. Abiotic succession, retrogression, or unexpected natural or human-caused disruptions like fire, logging or lagging, flooding, construction activities, pollution, etc. are all causes of habitat changes. All wildlife species' access to nutrition, shelter, and other ecological resources is affected by these changes. Therefore, a generous portion of managing animal habitat involves managing succession, retrogression, and disturbance. By developing national parks, sanctuaries, reserve forests, and other conservation measures, it is possible to protect the habitat of species. Most of the typical habitat types in the nation are covered by these chains of protected areas, which offer security to both wild plants and animals. The Wildlife (Protection) Act of 1972, which established these safeguarded networks (National Parks, Sanctuaries, etc.), gives these places the much-needed legal support.

Many nations have passed legislation outlawing the slaughter of wildlife. The laws that have been established in India to protect wildlife are. Environmental protection and conservation are also connected to the 73rd Amendment to the Constitution (Panchayats) Act of 1992. Forests and animals are placed on the concurrent list according to the 42nd Amendment to the Indian Constitution (1976), which was passed. The state along with the Central Government have periodically made several numbers of Acts for the preservation of wild animals, and especially the endangered species.

To ensure the protection and conservation of wildlife, a multifaceted approach is necessary, encompassing various aspects of legal, ecological, and educational measures. Legal protection is paramount, and the enactment of legislation, such as the Indian Wildlife Protection Act established in 1972, serves as the cornerstone of conservation efforts. To provide safe havens for wildlife, the establishment of wildlife sanctuaries, national parks, and biosphere reserves is crucial, allowing fauna to thrive in protected environments. Furthermore, efforts to rehabilitate deforested areas and restore the original habitats of wildlife are essential, with initiatives like Vanmahotsav observed annually. Encouraging better living conditions for animals involves promoting their residence in dense grass, bushes, or trees, which are natural and conducive habitats. Education plays a pivotal role in wildlife conservation, with public awareness and understanding being key components of protection efforts. Educating the public about wildlife conservation fosters a sense of responsibility towards the environment and its inhabitants. Additionally, instruction on wildlife management is vital for wildlife forest officers and wildlife ecologists, equipping them with the knowledge and skills necessary for effective conservation strategies. In this holistic approach, legal, ecological, and educational measures converge to safeguard and preserve the rich biodiversity of our natural world.

All the tactics created by the Centre for the Conservation of Biological Diversity (CBD) aim to protect endangered species. All endangered species should be protected, and both natural and artificial habitats should be preserved by creating zoological and botanical gardens or parks. In addition, a variety of useful food crops, plants, animals, and microbes need to be maintained for national and international breeding programs, and wild plants and animals should be preserved as a gene bank for the latter. A protected area should be created to maintain the habitat of migratory or widely dispersed animal species, and it should be a primary priority to conserve the unique environment. Animal habits should also be carefully watched and protected. The ecosystem for exploited species will be determined, and trade and commerce involving wild animals and plants will be outlawed internationally.

Various methods are employed in wildlife surveys, each tailored to specific research objectives and the characteristics of the species being studied. These methods encompass both general and specialized techniques. General approaches include direct population counting, habitat sampling, full enumeration attempts, and plot-less sampling. Quadrate sampling involves dividing the sampling area into small squares, making it suitable for studying aquatic creatures, slow-moving animals, and plants. To estimate population size mathematically, animals are sampled, marked, and released, allowing them to mix with the broader population. Distance sampling techniques are widely used to assess the number of individuals and the availability of biological populations. Line transect methods involve an observer traveling along parallel lines or tracks, while site transects select random points to determine community size based on the organisms counted at each site.

One notable technology-driven method is camera trapping, which utilizes automated cameras triggered by moving animals to record medium to large-sized wildlife and bird species in their natural habitats. These photographs serve as verifiable evidence of the animal's presence. Active camera traps are among the variations, capturing only mobile animals, while inactive traps monitor video footage. Additional techniques employed in wildlife surveys encompass a diverse range, such as hand capture, noosing, trapping, marking, total counts, nesting or resting structure examination, aerial surveys, individual recognition, and tracking. These methods collectively contribute to our understanding of wildlife populations and behaviours.

2.2 Thermal Imaging Methodologies

The cost of thermal imaging technology has considerably decreased since the middle of the 2000s, enabling a variety of applications. The importance of wildlife conservation has been addressed via more accessible thermal imaging. For a fraction of the cost of other techniques, it can in this case permit widespread, major surveys and ongoing, passive monitoring. Thermal imaging is one powerful remote sensing technique that is used in many different sectors (Christiansen et al., 2014). Animal ecology field study can utilize thermal imaging, a completely passive, minimally disruptive tool, day, or night, in a variety of climates.

Various camera systems, including stationary hides, land-based roving robots, submersibles, helicopters, and drones, can gather image data in real-time. Thermal imaging transforms heat from infrared radiation into visual images that depict how different temperatures are distributed throughout a scene (Cilulko et al., 2013). It is significant to highlight that the technology records an object's emissivity against the background rather than comparing temperatures amongst objects in the picture. This enables them to capture images of warm-blooded creatures against a cold environment. Figure 1 depicts a system equipped with thermal imaging camera to identify animals based on its body temperature.

Thermographic cameras for thermal imaging pick up radiation between about 9 and 14 micrometers in the long-infrared spectrum. Thermal images are also known as thermograms, and these cameras produce them. Heat is released by everything that is above the freezing point (T> 0 K), and the amount released varies with surface quality and the object's temperature. Infrared (IR) cameras are used in modern thermal imaging cameras, which can detect heat emitted from objects. Images of the objects can be produced by radiation heat transfer at the speed of light, (Rojas et al., 2022).

The infrared camera's thermal images can be seen through a viewfinder, just like with a regular camcorder, or they can be seen on a TV screen while the camera records. Here, thermal energy—rather than visible light—is detected by the infrared camera, which also displays its geographic distribution. This makes it possible to see in conditions with low contrast, smoke, and total darkness. When eye observation is insufficient to identify a heat-emitting object from its backdrop, these cameras can also be utilized throughout the day to see heat-generated images. These cameras can also be used during the day to view images generated by heat when visual observation is insufficient to distinguish a heat-emitting object from its background. The imager detects all infrared-emitting objects in a specific scene. A procedure needs to be created and followed to determine whether the objects that were taken are relevant for any survey.

Thermal signatures are the objects of interest within the scene, and a thermal image is typically the location in space where the thermal energy coming from a scene is located. The spectral distribution (the infrared radiation wavelength band), geographical distribution (shape and size), and distribution intensity (temperature) of each signature enables us to differentiate it from the scene's background and other signatures. Additionally, these distributions have a temporal component that can be used to help analyze the gathered picture.

A multitude of factors, some of which will be covered in later sections, can influence these distributions. It is useful to look and investigate a typical thermal image To obtain a sense of some of these elements. It is crucial to understand that the object's surface and temperature have a significant impact on the captured distribution of energy. Thermal images are created by emitted intensity variation among objects and their backgrounds (Ward et al., 2016). In other words, the surface modifies the emissivity and the consequent distribution of energy radiating from the object, producing an "apparent" temperature difference rather than just a simple temperature difference that creates the image. The ambient radiation that is reflected and scattered also adds to the distribution of energy that produces the images. Figure 2 explains the color codes of a thermal imaging system. The brighter colors red, orange, and yellow indicate warmer temperatures due to heat and infrared radiation being emitted. Whilst purple, dark blues and black indicate cooler temperatures due to less heat and infrared radiation being emitted.

Figure 1. Thermal image of a deer

Figure 2. Thermal image with color codes

The requirement for detection to find animals, observe their behavior without upsetting them, and enabling counting to enable population estimations. If the animals are grouped together in huge numbers and spread individually over a wide region or are grouped together in small numbers and dispersed in groups, the counting procedure should be able to provide correct population densities (Christiansen et al., 2014). It is highlighted how adaptable IR imaging is as a non-intrusive method for conducting airborne and ground-based surveys, behavioral studies, figuring out the age of and sex traits of animal populations, and finding dens, lairs, and nests used by animals at any time over a diurnal cycle.

The earliest attempts to scan animals using thermal imaging were made in the late 1960s. Since then, there have been an increasing number of efforts to use infrared thermal sensors (thermal imagers) to perform airborne surveys and find and count large animals including deer, antelope, bears, and panthers. It is remarkable that thermal imagery is not utilized more frequently for animal surveys given that it eliminates one of the main causes of erroneous surveys, the issue of visible bias. It's possible that misconceptions about thermal imagers' capabilities and the absence of a set procedure for using them have slowed down their use. Early efforts to use thermal imaging for surveys had several problems, including insufficient sensor capabilities for the circumstances in which that they were used, a lack of knowledge about what thermal imaging was actually identifying, and perhaps more importantly, a reluctance on the part of researchers to adopt new technology, even if it could improve the accuracy and precision of earlier work.

The fact that the imagery is recorded creates a living document that can be examined over and over after the data is gathered and judgements on the relevance of the recorded images may be carefully analyzed is a very important side effect. Since the measurement is also influenced by solar heating, the insulating qualities of the animal's fur or feathery clothes, and the distance that exists between the animal and the device used for detection, the temperature measured is not the animal's real body temperature. Then, thermal signatures are used to extract features. Hot objects are identified based on a dynamic threshold, and feature extraction is then carried out (Lee, 2021). The unique feature extraction technique described in this research involves extracting the thermal signatures of each observed object and parameterizing those thermal signatures using the DCT algorithm.

IRT is a device with potential uses for wild animals kept under human supervision. When combined with other procedures, its non-invasiveness and capability for remote evaluation make it an appealing option for determining the health condition of wild species without the use of physical or chemical restraints has discovered viral diseases, inflammatory processes resulting from damage, and physiological states including gestation in a variety of feline, herbivore, avian, canine, and non-human primate species. Additionally, initiatives have been made to employ IRT to better comprehend the mental health of animals. However, IRT has individual, contextual, and technical constraints that must be taken into consideration when evaluating the thermal reactions of animals, as we are aware from experience with people and domesticated animals.

2.3 Real World Examples of Successful Wildlife Surveillance Projects Using UAVs and Machine Learning

Elephant populations in African savannas have been successfully monitored by unmanned aerial vehicles (UAVs) and machine learning algorithms. For example, in one study, researchers used unmanned aerial vehicles (UAVs) to gather aerial imagery of elephants in the Masai Mara National Reserve in Kenya. They then used machine learning algorithms to identify and count individual elephants in the photographs.

When compared to conventional ground-based techniques, this strategy for tracking elephant numbers proved to be more precise and effective.

To curb poaching, UAVs have been used in South Africa to track rhinoceroses. Because these unmanned aerial vehicles (UAVs) are fitted with thermal imaging cameras, they can identify rhinoceroses even in the dark or among thick foliage. Real-time maps of rhinoceros' whereabouts are produced using the data gathered by these UAVs, and anti-poaching teams use these maps to send out rangers to stop poaching.

UAVs with cameras have been effectively used by conservationists in Sumatra, Indonesia, to monitor wildlife, especially in hard-to-reach locations. These drones take high-resolution pictures, which are then analyzed using machine learning algorithms to look for evidence of poaching, illicit logging, and environmental degradation. The Sumatran orangutan is one of the endangered animals that technological innovation has helped to safeguard.

In Malawi's Liwonde National Park, African Parks, a nonprofit conservation organization, has used unmanned aerial vehicles (UAVs) to deal with poaching. Drones with thermal imaging cameras are used to keep an eye out for poachers in the area, particularly at night. By using machine learning algorithms to differentiate between humans and animals in thermal images, anti-poaching patrols can operate more effectively.

UAVs and machine learning have been utilized in the Himalayas to assist with snow leopard conservation. High-resolution camera-equipped drones monitor the wild landscape, and machine learning techniques are used to locate and monitor snow leopards. Researchers can collect vital information about snow leopard counts and their habitats with the assistance of this technology.

UAVs and machine learning have been used by Australian researchers to track koala populations. Drones carrying thermal cameras scan eucalyptus forests and the images are processed by machine learning algorithms, which use the heat signatures of the animals to identify koalas. This method aids in the estimation of population densities and habitat utilization.

2.4 Legal Considerations and Regulatory Framework

Unmanned Aerial Vehicle (UAV) activities are subject to aviation rules established by the International Civil Aviation Organization (ICAO) and enforced by national aviation authorities. These regulations provide guidelines for ensuring safe flight operations, encompassing restrictions on altitude, airspace categorizations, and licensing prerequisites. In India, the oversight of UAV operations falls under the purview of the Directorate General of Civil Aviation (DGCA). The DGCA has delineated specific Civil Aviation Regulations (CARs) for UAVs, outlining criteria for obtaining a UAV operator permit, ensuring airworthiness, and adhering to safety protocols. Beyond the general aviation guidelines, there are specialized regulations governing UAV operations in areas inhabited by wildlife. These regulations aim to mitigate disturbances to wildlife and mitigate potential human-wildlife conflicts. For instance, in India, the Wildlife (Protection) Act of 1972 explicitly prohibits the use of aircraft for hunting or harassing wildlife. Additionally, the Forest Conservation Act of 1980 regulates aircraft usage in forested regions, mandating prior authorization from the forest department. These measures collectively contribute to the responsible and regulated operation of UAVs in wildlife surveillance.

Apart from adhering to regulatory requirements, UAV operators must consider various legal considerations when engaging in wildlife surveillance. These factors encompass the following. Drones equipped with cameras or similar sensors have the capacity to gather highly detailed personal information, giving rise to concerns regarding potential breaches of privacy. Operators are obligated to ensure that the collection and handling of data adhere to relevant privacy laws, such as the Information Technology Act, 2000, in India. UAV activities should not inflict harm or disturbance upon wildlife. Operators need to be mindful of the legal safeguards provided to different species and take measures to prevent disruptions to their habitats or breeding areas. Images and footage of wildlife may be subject to copyright or other intellectual property rights. Operators must secure necessary permissions or licenses before utilizing such material.

To guarantee responsible and lawful drone operations for wildlife surveillance, operators need to acquaint themselves with relevant regulations and laws. This involves obtaining required permits and licenses, establishing operational guidelines to minimize wildlife disruption and privacy infringement, outfitting UAVs with suitable sensors and software for data collection while prioritizing privacy concerns, training pilots and staff in safe and responsible drone use, and collaborating with wildlife authorities and stakeholders to align operations with conservation objectives. Adhering to these guidelines allows operators to contribute to ethical and legally sound wildlife surveillance, ensuring effective and responsible practices.

In addition to obtaining permits, adhering to airspace regulations, and complying with wildlife protection laws, operators of Unmanned Aerial Vehicles (UAVs) should also consider the following factors when conducting operations in wildlife areas. UAVs have the capability to produce considerable noise, potentially causing disturbance to wildlife. To mitigate noise pollution, operators should employ strategies such as utilizing quieter UAV models or operating at elevated altitudes. The risk of collisions with wildlife, particularly birds, exists. Operators should be cognizant of the local wildlife species and implement precautions, such as flying at reduced speeds or utilizing obstacle avoidance systems, to minimize the potential for collisions. UAVs are capable of capturing images and videos of both people and animals. In line with privacy laws, operators should exercise discretion and refrain from gathering data that could be utilized for the identification or tracking of individuals.

2.5 Challenges Faced in Using UAVs and Machine Learning in Wildlife Surveillance

UAVs offer numerous advantages for wildlife surveillance, including their ability to cover large areas, collect high-resolution data, and access remote areas. However, their use is also associated with several challenges, such as limited battery life, susceptibility to adverse weather conditions, potential for wildlife disturbance, privacy concerns, and regulatory restrictions. Machine learning algorithms, while powerful tools for image and video analysis, also have limitations that affect their application in wildlife surveillance. These limitations include the need for high-quality training data, difficulties in accurately identifying individual species, challenges in interpreting complex behaviors, limited adaptability to new scenarios, and high computational demands.

Researchers and practitioners are continuously working to address these challenges and limitations. Some promising approaches include developing more efficient batteries, improving UAV navigation and obstacle avoidance, minimizing noise pollution, implementing privacy-preserving measures, enhancing machine learning algorithms, and developing hybrid approaches that combine UAV data with other sources of information. By addressing these challenges and limitations, UAVs and machine learning can continue to play an increasingly important role in wildlife surveillance, providing valuable insights for conservation efforts and biodiversity management.

3. COGNIZANCE OF MEGAFAUNA'S BIOMES/ECOSPHERE

Large-bodied creatures with average weights exceeding 100 kilograms (220 pounds) are known as megafauna. In a range of settings, such as woods, grasslands, and deserts, they may be found all over the world. Elephants, bison, deer, rhinoceroses, hippos, giraffes, zebras, lions, tigers, bears, whales, and dolphins are a few examples of megafauna. Megafaunas are crucial to the wellbeing and efficiency of ecosystems, yet many of their species are in risk of extinction because of habitat loss, hunting, and other human activities (Galetti et al., 2018). Megafauna populations and their habitats must be protected to preserve ecosystem health as well as the cultural and spiritual significance that megafauna carries for many people worldwide.

3.1 Panthera Tigris: The Tiger

Due to their remarkable level of adaptability, tigers may be found in several settings across their territory. Tropical Rainforests are located in places like areas of Southeast Asia and the Indian subcontinent, where animals must cross thick undergrowth and frequently hunt covertly. Tigers in mangrove swamps have evolved to hunting in mangrove forests, becoming good swimmers, and even collecting fish in places like the Sundarbans in Bangladesh and India (Sandom et al., 2014). Degradation of habitat for tigers to thrive, their habitat must have sizable unaltered portions. Nevertheless, logging, agriculture, and other development activities are destroying and fragmenting their habitat. Because of this, tigers have a harder time finding food and partners, and their likelihood of encountering people has also increased. Tigers are compelled to live closer to people as human populations increase and encroach on tiger habitat. Conflicts may result from this, such as when tigers kill cattle or assault people. To conserve essential tiger habitats, protected reserves, national parks, and wildlife corridors must be established and maintained. Although conservation measures have been made, tigers still face many difficulties. The demand for tiger parts in traditional Asian medicine and luxury markets means that the illegal wildlife trafficking still poses a serious danger (Szokalski et al., 2012). The appropriateness of habitats and the availability of prey might also shift because of climate change, which adds even another degree of uncertainty. A member of the genus Panthera and the largest extant cat species can be seen in Figure 3. Its orange fur with a white underside and dark vertical stripes are what make it most identifiable.

Figure 3. Panthera tigris

Due to their severely endangered status, tigers require careful monitoring and conservation measures. Protecting them could potentially be made simpler with the assistance of unmanned aerial vehicles (UAVs) equipped with cameras and machine learning (ML) models like Convolutional Neural Networks (CNN), Mask R-CNN, and YOLO (You Only Look Once). Tiger habitats include meadows and deep forests, and UAVs can take high-resolution images and videos of these areas. These habitats may be recognized and categorized using machine learning (ML) techniques, which offer important insights into the preferred tiger habitats. Comprehending these environments is essential for making informed decisions regarding conservation initiatives, including reforestation or safeguarding ecosystems.

Mask R-CNN and other machine learning models can recognize individual tigers based on their unique stripe patterns. This makes it easier to do in-depth research on tigers, their habits, and their migration routes. By identifying different behaviors, including hunting, resting, or mating, researchers can advance our knowledge of tiger ecology and the ways in which these animals interact with their environments. UAVs equipped with machine learning models are essential to anti-poaching efforts. With its real-time object identification capabilities, YOLO can quickly locate any dangers near tiger habitats. Furthermore, population estimation is made easier by the integration of UAVs with ML through the analysis of images and videos. Tiger population estimates can be estimated using CNN and YOLO models, which aid in conservation and management efforts.

3.2 Panthera Pardus: The Leopard

Leopards are exceptionally adaptable animals, able to survive in a variety of environments due to their opportunistic diet, physical characteristics, and behavioural flexibility. With their huge variety of prey and remarkable climbing and swimming skills, they can move about in a variety of habitats. Observable instances of their flexibility include their propensity for climbing trees in rainforests, their ability to blend in with their surroundings in savannahs, their nocturnal habits in deserts, and their capacity to adapt to urban environments (Jacobson et al., 2016). Leopards are solitary and territorial animals in addition to their dietary habits (Stein et al., 2017). Variables including the amount of available prey, the amount of foliage, and competition from other leopards all affect how big their area is. Conflict between leopards and humans develops when they fight over territory and resources, which can lead to assaults on people and cattle. Where their ecosystems intersect is where this conflict frequently arises. Competition for prey between leopards and people, who may both pursue similar animals like deer, antelope, and goats, is one reason why conflicts arise. This may result in leopard assaults on people, which may cause harm or even death. Human-leopard conflict is a major problem that endangers both people and leopards and damages the image of these majestic animals (Hayward et al., 2006). The disagreement may occasionally lead to demands for the eradication of leopards. Finally, it is crucial to inform people about leopards, their behavior, and how to prevent confrontation. One of the genera Panthera's five extant species is displayed in Figure 4. Its fur ranges in colour from light yellow to dark golden, with dark spots arranged in rosettes.

Figure 4. Panthera pardus

Unmanned Aerial Vehicles (UAVs) possess the ability to obtain high-definition pictures of leopard habitats, encompassing diverse ecosystems like savannahs and deep forests. By identifying and categorizing these areas, machine learning algorithms might shed insight into leopards' preferred habitats. The implementation of focused conservation initiatives, such as protecting important ecosystems and reducing habitat loss, depends on this knowledge. ML models for object detection and recognition can differentiate leopards from other animals or objects in the photos with appropriate training, which improves population monitoring and makes it easier to follow the movements of leopards. Using machine learning models such as Mask R-CNN, individual leopards may be identified by their distinct coat patterns. In addition, technology may be used to recognize and examine particular behaviors like mating, hunting, and resting, which offers important insights about the ecology of leopards and their interactions with their environment. The real-time object detection capabilities of YOLO facilitate the identification of possible threats within or close to leopard habitats. Furthermore, population estimate is streamlined by the combination of ML and UAVs. By analyzing images and videos, CNN and YOLO models can estimate leopard population sizes, which inform conservation strategies and wildlife management decisions.

3.3 Other Common Species

Every genus lives in certain habitats or ecosystems that offer them the resources they need to survive. This includes elements like temperature, humidity, flora, and natural features like burrows and nests. Each species has a unique ecological niche that it fills in relation to its function and location within its ecosystem. This pertains to its eating practices, relationships with other species, and resource use. Animals have a variety of physiological, physio-behavioral, and physical adaptations that enable them to flourish in their unique environments. Figure 5 depicts two species wherein one is of the genus Elephas that is distributed throughout the Indian subcontinent and the other is of the genus Bison which is a large bovine in the tribe Bovini. Physiological endurance to harsh environments, sophisticated digestive systems, and camouflaging coloring are a few examples. Birth, mortality, immigration, and emigration rates, among other variables, all have an impact on animal populations. A deer, a hoofed ruminant mammal belonging to the Cervidae family, is portrayed in Figure 6.

Figure 5. Elephas (Asian elephants) and bison

Unmanned aerial vehicles (UAVs) combined with advanced machine learning (ML) models like as Convolutional Neural Networks (CNN), Mask R-CNN, and YOLO (You Only Look Once) have great potential for monitoring and conservation of common animal species such as deer, bison, and elephants. UAVs with high-resolution cameras may take photographs of these creatures' environments, which can vary from vast fields to dense forests. To preserve these ecosystems and identify important environmental traits like vegetation types and land cover, machine learning (ML) methods are crucial to the interpretation of these images.

Figure 6. Cervidae (deer)

Apart from analyzing habitats, ML allows for the individual recognition of animals. Machine learning models like Mask R-CNN make it easier to identify and monitor the distinctive characteristics of individual animals. For instance, it makes it possible to identify individual elephants by their unique ear forms or bison by their particular horn patterns. This information advances our comprehension of the behaviors and movements of these organisms. Additionally, YOLO's real-time object identification skills improve anti-poaching initiatives by protecting these species from any dangers in their natural environments. Population estimation is made easier using UAVs and machine learning models, where CNN and YOLO are used to estimate the sizes of various animal species' populations. Making decisions on animal management and conservation methods is made much easier with the use of this data. By providing a comprehensive approach to wildlife monitoring and protection, these technological developments assure the preservation of these animals and their habitats for future generations.

4. DESIGN CONSIDERATIONS FOR WILDLIFE SURVEILLANCE UAV

Multirotor drones are available in various configurations such as quadcopters, hexacopters, and octacopters, where the wheelbase increases with more rotors, offering enhanced stability. PID Controllers are used for enhancing the stability control of UAVs (Ezhil, V. S., et al., 2022), and multiple UAV systems are also deployed to reduce the process lead time (Yan, L. et al., 2022). However, for navigating densely forested areas, it's advisable to opt for a quadcopter design with a shorter wheelbase to protect the propellers from potential impacts among tall trees and thick vegetation. Different structural investigations are carried out to create long-range UAVs (Raja, V. et al., 2022). A survey of market-available surveillance drones having a weight range less than 5 Kg was taken. Their maximum take-off weight with respective flight time and Battery weight was studied.

Table 1. Comparison of market available surveillance drones

Drone Name	Maximum Take-Off Weight (MTOW) (Kg)	Flight Time (mins)	Battery weight (Kg)	Battery to All Up Weight ratio
Aurelia X4	3.7	25	1.3	2.8: 1
Yuneec H520E	1.8	30	0.65	2.7: 1
Phantom 4	1.3	21	0.5	2.6: 1
Air 3S	0.7	45	0.26	2.7: 1
Inspire 3	3.9	28	0.94	4.1: 1
Mavic 3 pro cine	0.96	43	0.33	2.9: 1
Blade Chroma w/ 4K camera	1.3	30	0.54	2.3: 1
Average	1.95	31.7	0.65	2.9: 1

From the analyzed data, an average of 2.9: 1 shall be taken as the All up weight to battery weight ratio. We can assume that All up Weight to be less than or equal to 2 Kg, and therefore,

Dead weight of drone (without battery) = 1.29 Kg

Battery weight = 0.71 Kg

Maximum Take-Off Weight (MTOW) = 2 Kg

4.1 Thrust to Weight Ratio

The thrust required for drones differs according to their missions. Generally, drones for all applications other than FPV racing drones use a thrust-to-weight ratio of 2:1 (Putra et al., 2020). The thrust required for this drone can be calculated as follows:

Total thrust required = 2 x MTOW of drone (1)

MTOW=2 Kg

Thrust required = 4 Kg

Thrust required from each motor = 4/4 = 1 Kg

From the market-available motors, the MN4010 370 KV motor, capable of providing up to 1100g of thrust is chosen. The key factor in achieving optimum flight endurance is to use the largest possible propeller combination for that motor (Kauhanen et al., 2020). From the motor's datasheet, power consumption for 14*4.8 "propeller and 15*5" propeller was taken and a graph explaining the Thrust vs Power consumption relation was formed. The linear equations from graph charts can be used to calculate the power consumption during hovering conditions which is an important parameter to determine the flight endurance. The T-Motor Navigator MN4010, 370kV Outrunner Brushless Multi-Rotor Motor is a product designed for professional users and is shown in Figure 7. The specifications and parameters of the motor are mentioned in Figure 8.

Figure 7. Motor MN4010 370KV

Figure 8. Specifications of MN4010-370 KV

Test Report			
Test Item	MN4010 KV370	Report NO.	MN 00019
Specifications			
Internal Resistance	98mΩ	Configuration	18N24P
Shaft Diameter	4mm	Motor Dimensions	Φ44.7×30.5mm
Stator Diameter	40mm	Stator Height	10mm
AWG	18#	Cable Length	600mm
Weight Including Cables	137g	Weight Excluding Cables	112g
No.of Cells(Lipo)	4-8S	Idle Current@10v	0.8A
Max Continuous Power 180S	450W	Max Continuous Current 180S	20A

Load Testing Data									
Ambient Temperature				/		Voltage		DC Power Supplier	
Item No	Voltage (V)	Prop	Throttle	Current (A)	Power (W)	Thrust (G)	RPM	Efficiency (G/W)	Operating Temperature (°C)
		T-MOTOR 14*4.8CF	50%	2.1	31.08	360	3100	11.58	
			65%	3.1	45.88	510	3600	11.12	
			75%	4.1	60.68	640	3960	10.55	44
			85%	5.4	79.92	810	4400	10.14	
			100%	6.5	96.20	920	4700	9.56	
	14.8	T-MOTOR 15*5CF	50%	2.3	34.04	430	2800	12.63	
			65%	3.8	56.24	640	3400	11.38	
			75%	5.1	75.48	820	3800	10.86	44
			85%	6.9	102.12	1020	4250	9.99	
			100%	8.2	121.36	1160	4450	9.56	

*Figure 9. Thrust vs. power consumption for MN4010 370 KV – 14*4.8" Propeller*

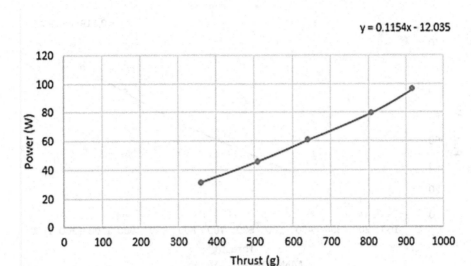

MN4010 370 KV - 14*4.8

Figure 9 explains the relationship between Thrust and power consumption and brings a linear equation for 14-inch propeller combination that can be used to predict the power consumption during hovering conditions.

Thrust required to hover = 2 Kg

Thrust required per motor to hover = 0.5 Kg

Substituting 0.5 Kg for x in equation $y = 0.1154x – 12.035$ (2)

$y = 45.664$ W

Therefore, for four motors = 222.66 W

Figure 10. Thrust vs. power consumption for MN4010 370 KV – 15*5" Propeller

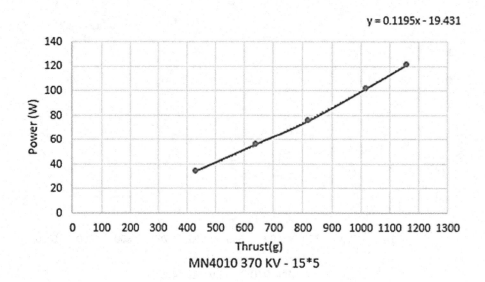

Figure 10 explains the relationship between Thrust and power consumption and brings a linear equation for 15-inch propeller combination that can be used to predict the power consumption during hovering conditions.

Similarly, Substituting 0.5 Kg for x in equation y = 0.1195x – 19.431 (3)

y = 40.319 W

Therefore, for four motors = 201.276 W

Comparing the power consumption for hovering conditions, the 15-inch propeller consumes less power, hence will offer a longer flight time.

4.2 Flight Time

Power consumption in a drone can be vastly split into two portions. One is for the motor unit and the other is for all other electronic components. In this motor consumes almost 90% of the power. The drone consumes more power while hovering than while pitching/rolling/yawing. To calculate the battery capacity and flight time, total power consumption by the drone in hovering conditions is needed (Putra et al., 2020). Four MN4010 370 KV motors with 15-inch propeller consume 201.276 W during hovering conditions. Along with this, miscellaneous power consumption from camera, onboard computer, and other avionics shall be estimated as 50W. So, a total power consumption of 251.276 W is expected from this drone model. Average flight time for surveillance drones is about 30 minutes (Teo and Choon Pei Jeremy, 2018). Also, from the market available drone survey from table 1, we have arrived at the value 31.2 minutes as average flight time. So, let us take 30 minutes as minimum required flight time and calculate the required battery capacity.

$$T = (Battery\ capacity\ in\ Ah * Voltage * 60 * 80\%) / (Total\ required\ power) \qquad (4)$$

30 = Battery capacity in Ah*14.8* 60*0.80 / (251.276)
Battery capacity = 10.63 Ah

In the above equation, the reference to 80% signifies the portion of energy that can be utilized. It's important to avoid fully depleting the battery and to maintain a reserve of energy to prolong the battery's lifespan. In this context, 20% of the battery's capacity is set aside as a reserve, leaving 80% available for use. This means that the battery is not discharged completely, with 80% of its capacity being the usable portion.

5. COMPONENTS OF WILDLIFE SURVEILLANCE DRONE

5.1 Motor and Propeller

BLDC (Brushless Direct Current) motors are extensively used in the drone industry, and they are characterized by their Kv rating, which indicates the motor's RPM per supplied voltage. For instance, a 1000Kv motor, when powered by a 2S battery (7.4 V), can reach speeds of up to 7400 RPM under no-load conditions. Based on equation (1), a motor capable of generating approximately 1 Kg of thrust is needed. The MN4010 is a 370Kv BLDC motor compatible with 4S-8S batteries, and it requires a 15" propeller to produce 1100g of thrust, consuming a maximum current of around 20 A and 450 W of power.

5.2 Electronic Speed Controller (ESC)

The Electronic Speed Controller (ESC) plays a crucial role in controlling the motor speed and converting the direct current (DC) from the drone's battery into alternating current (AC) signals required by the motor. The ESC consists of several key components, including MOSFETs (Metal-Oxide-Semiconductor Field-Effect Transistors). MOSFETs act as electronic switches within the ESC. When the ESC receives a command signal from the flight controller, it activates the appropriate MOSFETs to control the flow of current to the motor. To control motor speed, the ESC utilizes a technique called Pulse Width Modulation (PWM). It rapidly switches the MOSFETs on and off at varying durations, creating a series of pulses with different widths. By adjusting the width of these pulses, the ESC controls the average voltage and current delivered to the motor, thus controlling its speed. In addition to motor control, the ESC also converts the DC power from the battery to AC signals needed by the motor. The MOSFETs within the ESC rapidly switch the DC voltage, effectively creating an AC waveform. This alternating current is then fed to the motor windings, producing the rotating magnetic field necessary for motor operation. By intelligently controlling the MOSFETs, the ESC regulates motor speed and converts the DC power into AC signals, ensuring precise motor control and efficient performance in drones. The burst current of the motor from the source is identified as 20A. The current rating of ESC must be higher than the burst current of motor. So, a 30A, 4S ESC is chosen.

5.3 Battery (Ah)

Drones use various types of batteries for power, including lithium polymer (LiPo), lithium-ion (Li-ion), nickel-cadmium (NiCd), and nickel-metal hydride (NiMH). LiPo batteries are widely used due to their high energy density, lightweight design, and high discharge rates. Li-ion batteries offer a good balance of energy density and weight but have lower discharge rates. NiCd batteries have lower energy density and memory effect, while NiMH batteries provide moderate energy density and are less prone to memory effect. The choice of battery depends on factors such as flight time requirements, payload capacity, and specific drone configurations, each with their own advantages and considerations.

For our case we chose LiPo batteries. A 4S LiPo battery must be used to support the propulsion unit. The current capacity of the battery depends on the flight time requirements. Taking 30 minutes as the minimum required flight time, the required battery capacity is calculated as 10.6 AH. The closest value available in the market is a 10000 mAH 4S battery and the same is chosen for this application.

5.4 Telemetry

Data telemetry is essential for delivery drones, specifically quadcopters, as it enables real-time communication and information exchange between the drone and the ground control station. This technology provides operators with crucial flight data, including altitude, GPS coordinates, battery status, and payload conditions, ensuring safe and efficient operations. Telemetry systems allow for remote monitoring, waypoint management, and troubleshooting, enhancing control, precision, and reliability. For this application a 915 MHz telemetry is used.

5.5 Power Module

A power module is an essential component used with the Pixhawk Flight Control Board (FCB) to provide reliable and regulated power to the system. The power module acts as an intermediary between the main power source (typically a battery) and the Pixhawk FCB, ensuring stable voltage and current supply. It allows the FCB to receive consistent power, preventing voltage fluctuations and potential damage to sensitive electronic components. The power module also provides voltage and current monitoring capabilities, enabling real-time feedback on the battery's status and power consumption. This information is crucial for flight planning, battery management, and ensuring safe and reliable operation of the Pixhawk-based drone system.

5.6 Power Distribution Board

The power distribution board is responsible for distributing power from the main battery to various components of the drone, such as motors, ESCs, flight controller, and accessories. With a high amperage rating of 100 Amps, it ensures efficient and reliable power distribution during flight operations.

5.7 Receiver

The receiver is a crucial component that receives control signals from the transmitter and relays them to the flight controller. The S-Bus protocol allows for efficient communication between the receiver and the flight controller, providing a reliable and low-latency link for controlling the drone.

5.8 Transmitter

The transmitter is the handheld device used by the pilot to control the drone. Operating at the 2.4 GHz frequency, it wirelessly sends control signals to the receiver, allowing the pilot to maneuver the drone and activate various flight modes.

5.9 GPS Module

The GPS module provides accurate positioning and navigation data to the flight controller. It receives signals from multiple satellites and uses triangulation to determine the drone's precise location, altitude, and velocity. This information is crucial for autonomous flight modes, waypoint navigation, and precise positioning during payload delivery operations.

5.10 Computer Integration With UAV Flight Controllers

The options for combining onboard computers with UAV flight controllers are examined in this study. It talks about modern computing platforms like the Jetson Nano and emphasises how they might improve the efficiency and data processing power of UAVs. Figure 11 shows the onboard computer for this application which is Nvidia Jetson Nano. It provides a quad-core ARM Cortex A57 64-bit @ 1.43 GHz processor that smoothly connects with the flight controller. The Jetson Nano's GPU performance surpasses alternatives like the Raspberry Pi 4 and Beagle Bone boards by a wide margin. It is a viable option because of this.

These powerful computers provide increased computing power that enables data processing jobs and allows for accurate analysis of animal monitoring data. The UAV may perform real-time data processing and implement algorithms directly on board the UAV itself and provide the appropriate output for the operator by connecting the Jetson Nano to the flight controller. High-performance GPUs and neural network acceleration capabilities on the Jetson Nano make it possible to use deep learning algorithms for object detection, categorization, and tracking. With its amazing computer capacity, it is possible to analyse animal monitoring data instantly while requiring fewer post-processing steps.

Figure 11. NVIDIA Jetson Nano

6. DATA ACQUISITION IN WILDLIFE SURVEILLANCE

The collection of various data kinds from natural habitats to monitor and comprehend wildlife populations, behaviors, and ecological dynamics is referred to as data acquisition in wildlife surveillance. The process is essential for decoding animal behavior, protecting endangered species, and making knowledgeable choices concerning habitat maintenance. Camera traps, which capture images and videos of animals in motion, radio telemetry, which tracks animals through attached transmitters, GPS technology for precise movement tracking, and satellite tracking for animals with large ranges or migratory patterns are all common data collection strategies (Gonzalez et al., 2016). Acoustic monitoring records animal sounds, whilst drones and aerial surveys provide images of wildlife habitats from the air. Remote sensing and DNA sampling can provide details on ecosystem changes and genetic diversity. Environmental sensors monitor habitat conditions, and efficient data processing yields valuable information. Ethical issues highlight the significance of minimizing animal disruption and ensuring their well-being during the surveillance procedure.

This paper focuses on the methods and procedures for gathering information during animal monitoring missions with the help of Unmanned Aerial Vehicles (UAVs). The path planning, mission requirements, average endurance of the mission, real-time performance, forward speed, and interaction with the real world are studied. Quick response of sensors on board and cameras capturing images and videos are emphasized as the need for reliable and quality data sets are highlighted (Xu et al., 2026). The UAV is equipped with a real-time machine learning model, and a specialized approach is used to anticipate animal behavior, estimate movement patterns, and count animals. For training the machine learning model, two sets of data images are collected using various data collecting methodologies. The first data set includes images that show footprints of distinct species, while the second includes aerial images of wildlife animals.

Animal detection and movement prediction are significant concerns in animal monitoring applications. The application's goal is to determine the positions of various species in large-scale wildlife regions and to track animal movement without the use of any attached devices or sensors in the surrounding environment. A path planning strategy is proposed for the UAV to efficiently collect wildlife data. The drone explores the entire observation area and discovers various animal species in their respective regions (Alanezi et al., 2022). Now, the UAV prefers to return to previously discovered locations and identifies changes in the animal's position. The process of UAV path planning includes numerous interconnected processes. The first step in data collecting and preparation is to gather historical animal migration data as well as relevant spatial information. The data is then analyzed using AI algorithms that recognize patterns and behaviors of the target wildlife species. Path planning algorithms are built concurrently while AI analysis results are considered. Real-time integration of AI analysis and drone data stream is essential for generating waypoints for the drone's fly path which enhances monitoring of animal migration areas while maintaining safety and efficiency (Tuia et al., 2022). To enable smooth and obstacle-free drone movement, collision avoidance techniques, autonomous navigation algorithms, and real-time adaptation capabilities are implemented.

Using a machine learning (ML) model in conjunction with an unmanned aerial vehicle (UAV) to anticipate animal behavior, estimate migration trajectories, and count animals is a complicated process that requires careful preparation and execution. The first phase is data collection, which involves capturing real-time images with the UAV's onboard cameras. Preprocessing is used to improve relevant characteristics and decrease unwanted noise in the image data. To ensure that the data is appropriate for further analysis, techniques such as scaling, normalization, and noise reduction can be used (Dujon and Schofield, 2019). For animal detection and tracking, deep learning-based object detection models are used. However, tracking the animals over multiple frames is equally important. Historical tracking data is used alongside prediction models to anticipate an animal's movement pattern. This can be achieved using trajectory prediction models. To improve accuracy, environmental elements such as terrain, wind speed, and other conditions should be integrated into the prediction process. Animal counting uses the outcomes of object detection to determine the number of animals in each frame. The framework for model training is an annotated dataset of photos with labelled animal placements and movement patterns.

It is critical to ensure real-time inference. The trained model must be optimized to run efficiently on the hardware of the UAV. This optimization may include the use of hardware accelerators such as GPUs or specialized AI chips. The communication and integration part involves establishing a continuous link between the UAV and the base station. This framework allows for the transmission of picture data as well as predictions. A continual feedback loop informs improvements throughout the process (Chen et al., 2018). Gaining insights from the deployed system on a regular basis assist in identifying areas that want improvement. To retain its effectiveness, the model should be retrained with new data on a regular basis as conditions change. This paper briefs about three machine learning algorithms that can be used for the above-mentioned applications.

6.1 Data Analysis Using YOLO Algorithm

YOLO (You Only Look Once) is a real-time object detection algorithm that divides the input image into grid cells and predicts bounding boxes and class probabilities for each. It is well-known for its real-time performance and object detection accuracy. As training data, a huge dataset of annotated wildlife photographs translated to the YOLO format can be used. This is used to train the model based on YOLO architecture (Jiang et al., 2022). The model is evaluated using validation data to assess its performance. It includes performance metrics such as accuracy, precision, and recall score. Once trained, the YOLO model can be utilized for real-time animal detection and counting. Input the live camera feed or continually updated photos to the model, and it will forecast on each frame by recognizing animals and returning bounding box coordinates and class probabilities.

Due to the algorithm's unique architecture, it can recognize and categorize many objects in a single pass, making it ideal for on-the-fly applications. After detecting the object, a tracking algorithm is used to associate and predict the movement trajectories of the observed animals. This allows for a more in-depth analysis of animal behavior patterns and interactions. In addition, by exploiting YOLO's detections, a robust mechanism for animal counting is built, providing insights into population dynamics (Diwan et al., 2023), (Du, 2018). It is critical to integrate YOLO's detection results, path forecasts, and animal counts into the UAV's path planning system. This connectivity allows the UAV to alter its movement dynamically based on real-time data, effectively following animal movements and behaviors. The system ensures the most recent predictions, trajectories, and counts by continuously processing incoming frames. The visual display of detected animals, predicted trajectories, and counts in real time allows for a more straightforward comprehension of wildlife dynamics (Roy et al., 2023). Based on real-world observations, this integrated approach provides a feedback mechanism for improving the model's performance and configurations.

The algorithm includes a few necessary formulas and calculations. The Centre coordinates (x, y) and box dimensions (width w, height h) are projected relative to grid cells in bounding box predictions. The grid divides the view, with each cell in charge of detecting objects within it (Jintasuttisak et al., 2022). Anchor boxes with different aspect ratios help with handling different item sizes. The algorithm generates an object confidence score, which represents the probability of object presence and correct localization. Class probabilities are used in multi-class classification to forecast object classes (Li and Savkin, 2011). Non-Maximum Suppression (NMS) minimizes superfluous bounding boxes by evaluating confidence scores and Intersection over Union (IOU) metrics. YOLO's loss function refines accurate bounding box location, confidence estimate, and class assignment by optimizing predictions through localization loss, confidence loss, and classification loss. Along with matrix operations and neural network layers, these essential formulas create the complicated fabric of YOLO's real-time object detection process.

6.2 Data Analysis Using CNN Algorithm

Convolutional Neural Networks (CNNs) are widely used for image-based tasks and are particularly effective for object detection. Employing CNN for data analysis within the UAV system entails a multifaceted approach to address the specified objectives. CNNs can be trained to identify and localize animals within images, allowing for animal counting. An appropriate CNN architecture is chosen for animal detection and counting. VGGNet, ResNet, InceptionNet, and EfficientNet are examples of popular CNN designs (Cossa et al., 2023), (Adarsh et al., 2023). Multiple layers in these designs execute convolution, pooling, and fully linked operations to learn complicated characteristics from input images. The CNN model is trained using an optimization technique such as stochastic gradient descent (SGD) or Adam on the annotated dataset. During training, the model learns to detect and classify animals based on the training data presented, updating their weights and biases accordingly. The model is evaluated using unseen data and then applied to new pictures or video frames. The model will predict the presence of animals as well as their associated classes or labels (Neupane et al., 2022). Post-processing techniques are performed to the predicted outcomes to refine the detections and precisely count the animals.

CNN's abilities extend to real-time object detection, which is critical for wildlife tracking. As the model is trained on annotated data, it gains the capacity to recognize animals in photos. This identification, in conjunction with tracking algorithms, leads to trajectory predictions, allowing for greater understanding of animal behaviors and interactions. Meanwhile, CNN's object detection results transfer effortlessly into animal counting, providing an accurate estimate of the number of individual animals present. It is critical to incorporate these results into the course planning of the UAV. The UAV can modify its flight route on the fly by synchronizing object detection insights, trajectory predictions, and animal counts, efficiently adapting its movement to monitor animals and acquire vital data (Dhabekar). The system continuously processes incoming frames in real-time to enable accurate forecasts and trajectory evaluations. The system visualizes identified animals, predicted trajectories, and counts to aid comprehension, providing an intuitive summary of wildlife activity. In addition, the system generates detailed reports that include behavior patterns, trajectory dynamics, and population variations. In the meantime, the system's performance is being monitored, allowing for refining and hyperparameter tweaks to maintain accuracy and real-world usefulness.

The CNN determines bounding box coordinates (x, y, width, and height) and probability classes using anchor boxes for object detection. Localization loss (L1 loss between predicted and true box coordinates), confidence loss (binary cross-entropy for item existence), and classification loss (categorical cross-entropy for class probabilities) are all components of the loss function. Backpropagation calculates gradients during training, and optimization techniques like SGD (Stochastic Gradient Descent) modify the weights and biases to reduce loss (Ghosh et al., 2014), (He et al., 2017). The Kalman filter equations are used for state estimation when predicting paths, and prediction and update processes including transition matrices and covariance matrices are involved. Tracking algorithms anticipate the positions of the objects, and real positions are updated depending on measurements that have been taken. Both matrix multiplications and updating algorithms are used in the calculations.

The CNN object detection findings for animal counting immediately produce the count. The system counts the distinct occurrences of animals that are observed in the given areas (Li et al., 2021). The complex interaction of these calculations allows CNN to efficiently analyze the real-time visual data acquired by the UAV, offering perceptions into the population dynamics and behaviors of wildlife.

CNN determines the boundaries of the box (x, y, width, and height) and probability classes using anchor boxes for object detection. Localization loss (L1 loss between predicted and true box coordinates), confidence loss (binary cross-entropy for item existence), and classification loss (categorical cross-entropy for class probabilities) are all components of the loss function. Backpropagation calculates gradients during training, and optimization techniques like SGD (Stochastic Gradient Descent) modify the weights and biases to reduce loss (Albawi et al., 2017). The Kalman filter equations, which involve prediction and update steps using transition matrices and covariance matrices, are used for path prediction. Tracking algorithms anticipate the positions of the objects, and real positions are updated depending on measurements that have been taken. Both matrix multiplications and updating algorithms are used in the calculations.

The CNN object detection findings for animal counting immediately produce the count. The system counts the distinct occurrences of animals that are observed in the given areas. The complex interaction of these calculations allows CNN to efficiently analyze the real-time visual data acquired by the UAV, offering perceptions into the population dynamics and behaviors of wildlife.

6.3 Data Analysis Using Mask-R CNN Algorithm

Mask R-CNN is an effective algorithm for wildlife animal detection, as it combines object detection with instance-level segmentation. The training data should contain annotated wildlife images with bounding boxes and segmentation masks that are used to identify the animal species and its location in that specific image. A pre-trained Mask R-CNN can be used after updating the model parameters such as weights and biases. The training method typically entails optimizing the model's object detection and instance segmentation components. To evaluate the model's effectiveness in reliably recognizing and segmenting wildlife species, performance metrices are used for object identification and pixel-level accuracy, for instance segmentation. The model can be deployed for application with drone images (Xu et al., 2020). It will predict bounding boxes, class labels, and pixel-level masks that indicate the borders of the wildlife.

The system explores object detection and pixel-level instance segmentation by utilizing the Mask R-CNN architecture, an expansion of Faster R-CNN. This complex network setup consists of layers for mask prediction, region proposal network (RPN), and backbone architecture, all of which are designed to recognize objects, forecast their classes, and segment instances at the pixel level.

Mask R-CNN's abilities also extend to instance segmentation, making it possible to identify distinct animals with boundaries. The potential for real-time path prediction and behavior analysis is demonstrated by this instance-level data. Implementing tracking algorithms also makes it possible to connect detected events across frames, producing trajectory predictions that shed light on the interactions and behaviors of animals. The instance segmentation findings are quite helpful for counting animals because they allow for precise tallies of various animals inside frames. This vast amount of data combines smoothly with the UAV's path planning algorithm, enabling it to quickly change its trajectory to follow animals and collect data (Wall et al., 2014). Through the continuous processing of incoming frames, real-time analysis is maintained, guaranteeing that predictions, segmentations, and trajectory analyses are responsive and up to date. The visualization of identified animals, projected trajectories, segmentations, and counts enriches the visual narrative and provides a thorough depiction of wildlife activity. Insightful reports encapsulating behavior patterns, trajectory dynamics, and population variances are presented alongside these visualizations (Linchant et al., 2015). The system's performance is being closely monitored in the meantime, allowing for improvements and changes that will support accuracy and practical efficacy. In summary, the UAV system can effectively decipher animal behavior and population trends in real-time by incorporating Mask R-CNN for object identification, instance segmentation, and subsequent analysis.

In wildlife monitoring, the Mask R-CNN system employs complex formulas and calculations for object detection and instance segmentation. One important feature is Region Proposal Network (RPN) calculations, which create anchor box placements and scales and Intersection over Union (IOU) scores to establish probable object regions (Adams et al., 2020). Several matrix operations are used in the Forward Pass to convolve feature maps and forecast bounding box coordinates, class probabilities, and instance masks. The loss function contains multiple components, including localization loss, confidence loss (binary cross-entropy), and segmentation loss (pixel-wise softmax cross-entropy), where errors between predicted and ground-truth values are generated.

Backpropagation computes gradients during training, and optimization techniques like Stochastic Gradient Descent (SGD) fine-tune the model's weights and biases to minimize overall loss. The Instance Segmentation masks are created using pixel-wise labelling, which involves many matrix operations and sophisticated calculations. These computations act in tandem to enable the precise object detection and segmentation capabilities of Mask R-CNN in the context of wildlife surveillance.

7. RESULTS AND DISCUSSION

Using training and validation datasets of tiger and leopard photos, a CNN and a YOLOv8 model were developed in this chapter. The models are then tested and understood using the epoch versus training, validation, and accuracy curves. Finally, a single picture of a tiger and a leopard was used to evaluate the models. To evaluate how well the models perform throughout training, examine the accuracy and loss curves for each epoch versus training and validation. The models' ability to accurately categorize pictures in the training and validation datasets is depicted by the accuracy curve. The loss curve demonstrates how well the models can reduce the discrepancy between the expected and actual results.

7.1 YOLOv8 Algorithm

This section describes the implementation of the YOLOv8 algorithm for a binary image classification model. The model was trained on a dataset of 290 tiger images and 280 leopard images. Data augmentation was used to regularize the model and prevent overfitting due to the small dataset. A set 70 leopard images and 50 tiger images were taken for validation. The model was trained for 100 epochs but halted at 56 epochs dude to the lack of improvement in accuracy. Figure 12 represents the accuracy graph of the model where the final epoch showed an accuracy of 66.67% and the best result was obtained at the sixth epoch, with an accuracy of 75%. The model was then tested on the new images of tiger and leopard, and it was able to predict both images accurately. The model's speed, preprocess, and inference times were 1.0 mS, 5.0ms and 0.0mS, respectively.

The model's accuracy is quite poor, especially because its training data was somewhat limited. It is crucial to remember that binary image categorization can be difficult, particularly when the two classes are visually similar. Since data augmentation made the model more applicable to a wider variety of images, it probably helped to increase the model's accuracy. The model is appropriate for real-time applications due to its excellent speed and inference time. It's crucial to remember that only one picture was used to generate these findings. The findings shown, taken as a whole, are encouraging and show the YOLOv8 algorithm's potential for binary picture categorization.

Figure 12. Accuracy graph of YOLOv8 model

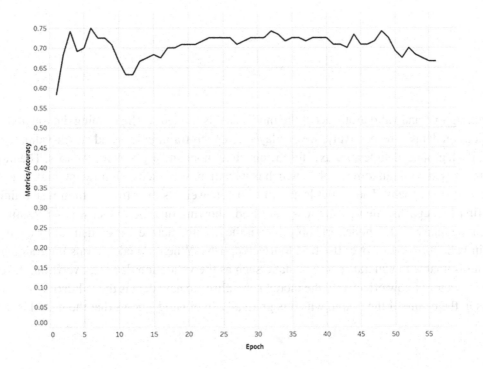

The model's accuracy as it is trained on the training dataset is displayed in the epoch-accuracy graph. The graph's epoch number is shown on the x-axis, while the model's accuracy is shown on the y-axis. The model's accuracy peaked during the sixth epoch, as seen by the apex of the graph at that time. The first epoch's dip on the graph shows when the model's accuracy was at its lowest. The final epoch of the graph shows the model's accuracy after 56 epochs of training. Through epochs one to twelve, accuracy fluctuated dramatically, most likely as a result of the model overfitting the training dataset. When a model learns the training dataset too well and is unable to generalise to new data, this is known as overfitting. Several methods, including data augmentation, regularisation, and early halting, can be employed to alleviate overfitting. The model was able to learn the training dataset without overfitting, as evidenced by the fact that it remained stable during the final epoch. This is encouraging since it shows that the model may generalise to different types of data.

Figure 13. Loss graph of YOLOv8 model

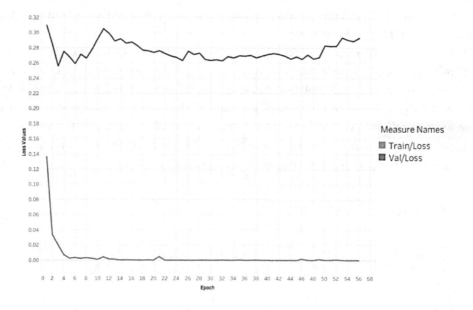

The training loss and validation loss of the model as it is trained on the training dataset and assessed on the validation dataset, respectively, are displayed as epoch-training loss and epoch-validation loss in Figure 13. Both graphs include an x-axis for the epoch number and a y-axis for the loss. The model was probably initialised with random weights, which is why there was such a significant amount of training loss in the first five epochs. The model learns to adjust its weights over time to minimise training loss. After the first five epochs, the training loss stabilised, showing that the model was successfully learning the training dataset. The model probably overfit the training dataset, as evidenced by the enormous variation in validation losses over the first fourteen epochs. When a model learns the training dataset too well and is unable to generalise to new data, such as the validation dataset, overfitting takes place. A reliable indicator of how effectively the model generalises to new data is the validation loss. The validation loss in the centre of the graph, which is gradually stabilising, shows that the model is beginning to learn the training dataset without overfitting. Nevertheless, the increase in validation losses in the last epochs raises the possibility that the model is once again beginning to overfit the training dataset.

The model was able to learn the training dataset and attain a decent accuracy on the validation dataset, according to the graphs of epoch-training loss and epoch-validation loss. It is crucial to remember that the performance of the model may differ based on the test dataset utilised.

7.2 CNN Algorithm

This section describes the implementation of Convolutional Neural Network for a Binary image classification model, with a training dataset of 290 tiger images and 280 leopard images. Data augmentation was used to regularize the model and prevent overfitting due to the small dataset. A set 70 leopard images and 50 tiger images were taken for validation. The model was trained for 80 epochs with the best results at forty sixth epoch with an accuracy of 70.91% and as of final epoch with 59.09%. Considering that the model's training data was relatively constrained, its accuracy is rather low. It is important to keep in mind that binary image classification can be challenging, especially when the two classes have a similar visual appearance. The model's applicability to new types of photos thanks to data augmentation likely contributed to its improved accuracy. The model's superior speed and inference time make it suitable for real-time applications.

Figure 14. Accuracy graph of CNN model

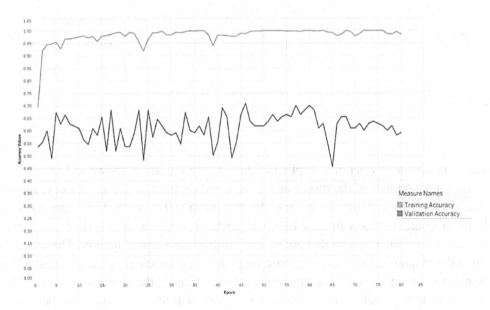

The accuracy of the model on the training dataset rises over time, as shown by the epoch-training accuracy graph. The accuracy of the model on the validation dataset evolves as it is trained, as seen by the epoch-validation accuracy graph in Figure 14. The training dataset could be being overfit by the model. As a result, the model cannot generalise to new data, such as the validation dataset since it is learning the training dataset too well. Machine learning approaches like data augmentation, regularisation, and early stopping could be implemented to solve this widespread issue. The validation dataset may not be reflective of the real-world data that the model will be applied to if it is too small. As a result, the validation accuracy graph may experience variations as the model continuously learns new information from the validation dataset. The validation accuracy graph may also see variations because of this. It would be beneficial to draw the epoch-loss graph for both the training and validation datasets to better analyse the problem. By doing so, we would be able to determine whether the model's loss on the validation dataset is rising, which would indicate overfitting. To ensure that the validation dataset is indicative of the real-world data that the model will be applied to, it would also be beneficial to examine its size and make any necessary alterations.

Figure 15. Loss graph of CNN model

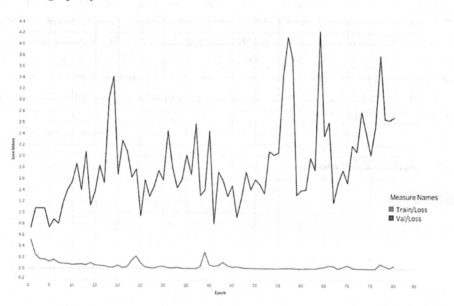

The model's training loss when it is applied to the training dataset is shown in the epoch-training loss graph. The validation loss of the model as it is assessed on the validation dataset is shown in the epoch-validation loss graph as Figure 15. It is possible that the model is successfully learning the training dataset if the training loss stabilises after the first five epochs. The validation loss fluctuating throughout the course of all epochs indicates that the model is overfitting the training dataset. The model is probably overfitting the training dataset if the epoch-training loss and epoch-validation loss graphs provide any indication. This is because while the training loss has stabilised, the validation loss is still varying across all epochs. Data augmentation, regularisation, or early halting techniques must be used to solve this problem. putting in place a different model architecture or fewer epochs. It is essential to remember that there is no one overfitting treatment that works for everyone. The ideal strategy will change based on the particular dataset and model architecture.

Several methods, including data augmentation, regularisation, and early stopping, can be utilised to alleviate the overfitting problem. By performing changes on the current training data, new training data is generated through data augmentation. To prevent overfitting, regularisation entails introducing limitations to the model's training procedure (Chen et al., 2019). To avoid overfitting, the training dataset, the training process must be stopped early. The findings indicate that tigers and leopards may be detected and classified in photos using CNNs and YOLOv8 models. This research may have uses in the protection of wildlife, where it may be used to track tigers, leopards, and other megafauna data and pinpoint vulnerable regions.

8. FUTURE ENDEAVOURS

During the training of machine learning models, epochs, training and validation accuracy, and loss curves are crucial for evaluating their performance. These indicators reveal trends in the model's development over time. As the model learns from the data, training accuracy often rises while training loss tends to fall. Several strategies may be used to improve the models' accuracy. One such method is data augmentation, which entails the generation of fresh training instances by the application of arbitrary changes like cropping, flipping, and rotation of pictures. This procedure aids in making the model more reliable and data adaptive. Another method to enhance the performance of the model is to modify the hyperparameters. For instance, how many epochs the model uses to iterate through the full training dataset depends on that amount. Finding the ideal balance is crucial since using too few or too many epochs might lead to underfitting or overfitting, respectively (Tuia, 2022). The step size the model takes when updating its parameters is controlled by the learning rate, another hyperparameter.

To get the best results, certain hyperparameters must be tuned. It is crucial to employ a sizable and varied training dataset in addition to these strategies. A varied dataset aids the model's ability to discover patterns and improve generalisation to new samples. Furthermore, to make sure that inaccurate inputs do not impair the model's accuracy, the data must be cleaned by eliminating mistakes or outliers. Making the right model architecture choice is also crucial. Different jobs could call for various architectures, and picking the right one might have a significant influence on performance (Duhart et al., 2019). Validation and test sets should be used to assess the model's performance since they give an indication of how effectively the model generalises to new data. The performance and accuracy of machine learning models may be greatly enhanced by putting these strategies into practise.

On enhancing wildlife surveillance efficiencies, some of the critical avenues for improvement in the future would be focussing on optimizing battery life for extending the flight endurance, and expanding the data telemetry, communication range for remote operations within the wilds. Performance charts for data storage growth, distance to latency rate, and flight time to coverage area will provide invaluable insights into the system's effectiveness (Edelblutte et al., 2023). Additionally, model will be optimized further by including human-in-the-loop decision making for complex scenarios, machine learning feedback loops for model refinement combined together will improve the effectiveness and reliability of wildlife surveillance with the NVIDIA Jetson Nano and Pixhawk integration in the multirotor model.

9. CONCLUSION

The use of deep learning algorithms for tracking wildlife has changed as artificial intelligence, especially in computer vision, has advanced. Animal classification, behaviour analysis, and reidentification have been greatly improved by the combination of large datasets, sensors, and Internet of Things technology.

The use of unmanned aerial vehicles (UAVs) in wildlife monitoring is a noteworthy development. Unmanned Aerial Vehicles (UAVs) provide economical, non-invasive, real-time data collection in expansive and difficult terrain. Compared to conventional ways, this technology works better since it can cover greater distances, is less expensive, and causes the least amount of disturbance to animals. UAVs with a range of sensors, including depth cameras and radar, can gather a variety of data for tracking animal populations, detecting threats, and evaluating conservation initiatives. Despite certain disadvantages, such as technological difficulties and legal concerns, the advantages of using UAVs for wildlife monitoring exceed these barriers. Unmanned Aerial Vehicles (UAVs) are an invaluable resource for researchers and conservationists due to their capacity to access isolated areas, collect vast amounts of data, and prevent harm to natural environments. In short, the combination of deep learning and unmanned aerial vehicle technologies signifies a revolutionary change in the field of wildlife study and preservation. Improved and thorough monitoring can help researchers understand wildlife populations on a deeper level. This method improves the capacity to recognise risks, evaluate conservation tactics, and support the general preservation of biodiversity. Unmanned Aerial Vehicles (UAVs) represent a viable path forward for the conservation of wildlife, providing a sophisticated and efficient way to protect a variety of habitats.

REFERENCES

Adams, K., Broad, A., Ruiz-García, D., & Davis, A. R. (2020). Continuous wildlife monitoring using blimps as an aerial platform: A case study observing marine megafauna. *Australian Zoologist*, *40*(3), 407–415. doi:10.7882/AZ.2020.004

Adarsh, M. S., Aaron, B., Shubhang, B., Sumathi, V., Sakthivel, G., & Jegadeeshwaran, R. (2023, July). AI enabled drones for detecting injured animals in wildlife. In AIP Conference Proceedings. AIP Publishing. doi:10.1063/5.0149348

Alanezi, M. A., Shahriar, M. S., Hasan, M. B., Ahmed, S., Yusuf, A., & Bouchekara, H. R. (2022). Livestock management with unmanned aerial vehicles: A review. *IEEE Access : Practical Innovations, Open Solutions*, *10*, 45001–45028. doi:10.1109/ACCESS.2022.3168295

Albawi, S., Mohammed, T. A., & Al-Zawi, S. (2017, August). Understanding of a convolutional neural network. In 2017 international conference on engineering and technology (ICET) (pp. 1-6). IEEE. doi:10.1109/ICEngTechnol.2017.8308186

Betts, J., Young, R. P., Hilton-Taylor, C., Hoffmann, M., Rodríguez, J. P., Stuart, S. N., & Milner-Gulland, E. J. (2020). A framework for evaluating the impact of the IUCN Red List of threatened species. *Conservation Biology*, *34*(3), 632–643. doi:10.1111/cobi.13454 PMID:31876054

Brinkman, M. P. (2020). Applying UAV systems in wildlife management. In *Proceedings of the Vertebrate Pest Conference* (Vol. 29, No. 29). OA.

Chen, R., Little, R., Mihaylova, L., Delahay, R., & Cox, R. (2019). Wildlife surveillance using deep learning methods. *Ecology and Evolution*, *9*(17), 9453–9466. doi:10.1002/ece3.5410 PMID:31534668

Chen, Y. P., Li, Y., & Wang, G. (2018). An Enhanced Region Proposal Network for object detection using deep learning method. *PLoS One*, *13*(9), e0203897. doi:10.1371/journal.pone.0203897 PMID:30235238

Christiansen, P., Steen, K. A., Jørgensen, R. N., & Karstoft, H. (2014). Automated detection and recognition of wildlife using thermal cameras. *Sensors (Basel)*, *14*(8), 13778–13793. doi:10.3390140813778 PMID:25196105

Christiansen, P., Steen, K. A., Jørgensen, R. N., & Karstoft, H. (2014). Automated detection and recognition of wildlife using thermal cameras. *Sensors (Basel)*, *14*(8), 13778–13793. doi:10.3390140813778 PMID:25196105

Cilulko, J., Janiszewski, P., Bogdaszewski, M., & Szczygielska, E. (2013). Infrared thermal imaging in studies of wild animals. *European Journal of Wildlife Research*, *59*(1), 17–23. doi:10.100710344-012-0688-1

Cossa, D., Cossa, M., Timba, I., Nhaca, J., Macia, A., & Infantes, E. (2023). Drones and machine-learning for monitoring dugong feeding grounds and gillnet fishing. *Marine Ecology Progress Series*, *716*, 123–136. doi:10.3354/meps14361

Dhabekar, A. K. (2022). Integrated Technologies for Effective Wildlife Monitoring in India: A Proposed System. Research Gate.

Diwan, T., Anirudh, G., & Tembhurne, J. V. (2023). Object detection using YOLO: Challenges, architectural successors, datasets and applications. *Multimedia Tools and Applications*, *82*(6), 9243-9275.

Du, J. (2018, April). Understanding of object detection based on CNN family and YOLO. []. IOP Publishing.]. *Journal of Physics: Conference Series*, *1004*, 012029. doi:10.1088/1742-6596/1004/1/012029

Duhart, C., Dublon, G., Mayton, B., Davenport, G., & Paradiso, J. A. (2019, June). Deep learning for wildlife conservation and restoration efforts. In *36th International conference on machine learning, Long Beach* (Vol. 5). PMLR.

Dujon, A. M., & Schofield, G. (2019). Importance of machine learning for enhancing ecological studies using information-rich imagery. *Endangered Species Research*, *39*, 91–104. doi:10.3354/esr00958

Edelblutte, É., Krithivasan, R., & Hayek, M. N. (2023). Animal agency in wildlife conservation and management. *Conservation Biology*, *37*(1), e13853. doi:10.1111/cobi.13853 PMID:35262968

Ezhil, V. S., Sriram, B. R., Vijay, R. C., Yeshwant, S., Sabareesh, R. K., Dakkshesh, G., & Raffik, R. (2022). Investigation on PID controller usage on Unmanned Aerial Vehicle for stability control. *Materials Today: Proceedings*, *66*, 1313–1318. doi:10.1016/j.matpr.2022.05.134

Galetti, M., Moleón, M., Jordano, P., Pires, M. M., Guimaraes, P. R. Jr, Pape, T., Nichols, E., Hansen, D., Olesen, J. M., Munk, M., de Mattos, J. S., Schweiger, A. H., Owen-Smith, N., Johnson, C. N., Marquis, R. J., & Svenning, J. C. (2018). Ecological and evolutionary legacy of megafauna extinctions. *Biological Reviews of the Cambridge Philosophical Society*, *93*(2), 845–862. doi:10.1111/brv.12374 PMID:28990321

Ghosh, R., Mishra, A., Orchard, G., & Thakor, N. V. (2014, October). Real-time object recognition and orientation estimation using an event-based camera and CNN. In 2014 IEEE Biomedical Circuits and Systems Conference (BioCAS) Proceedings (pp. 544-547). IEEE. doi:10.1109/BioCAS.2014.6981783

Gonzalez, L. F., Montes, G. A., Puig, E., Johnson, S., Mengersen, K., & Gaston, K. J. (2016). Unmanned aerial vehicles (UAVs) and artificial intelligence revolutionizing wildlife monitoring and conservation. *Sensors (Basel)*, *16*(1), 97. doi:10.339016010097 PMID:26784196

Goodrich, J., Lynam, A., Miquelle, D., Wibisono, H., Kawanishi, K., Pattanavibool, A., & Karanth, U. (2015). *Panthera tigris*. The IUCN Red List of Threatened Species 2015: e. T15955A50659951.

Green, S. E., Rees, J. P., Stephens, P. A., Hill, R. A., & Giordano, A. J. (2020). Innovations in camera trapping technology and approaches: The integration of citizen science and artificial intelligence. *Animals (Basel)*, *10*(1), 132. doi:10.3390/ani10010132 PMID:31947586

Hayward, M. W., Henschel, P., O'Brien, J., Hofmeyr, M., Balme, G., & Kerley, G. I. (2006). Prey preferences of the leopard (Panthera pardus). *Journal of Zoology (London, England)*, *270*(2), 298–313. doi:10.1111/j.1469-7998.2006.00139.x

He, K., Gkioxari, G., Dollár, P., & Girshick, R. (2017). Mask r-cnn. In *Proceedings of the IEEE international conference on computer vision* (pp. 2961-2969). IEEE.

Hutcherson, Z. S. (2023). *A Literary Review on the Current State of Drone Technology in Regard to Conservation*.

Jacobson, A. P., Gerngross, P., Lemeris, J. R. Jr, Schoonover, R. F., Anco, C., Breitenmoser-Würsten, C., Durant, S. M., Farhadinia, M. S., Henschel, P., Kamler, J. F., Laguardia, A., Rostro-García, S., Stein, A. B., & Dollar, L. (2016). Leopard (Panthera pardus) status, distribution, and the research efforts across its range. *PeerJ*, *4*, e1974. doi:10.7717/peerj.1974 PMID:27168983

Jiang, P., Ergu, D., Liu, F., Cai, Y., & Ma, B. (2022). A Review of Yolo algorithm developments. *Procedia Computer Science*, *199*, 1066–1073. doi:10.1016/j.procs.2022.01.135

Jintasuttisak, T., Leonce, A., Sher Shah, M., Khafaga, T., Simkins, G., & Edirisinghe, E. (2022, March). Deep learning based animal detection and tracking in drone video footage. *In Proceedings of the 8th International Conference on Computing and Artificial Intelligence* (pp. 425-431). ACM. 10.1145/3532213.3532280

Kauhanen, H., Rönnholm, P., Vaaja, M., & Hyyppä, H. (2020). Designing and building a cost-efficient survey drone. *The International Archives of the Photogrammetry, Remote Sensing and Spatial Information Sciences*, *43*, 165–172. doi:10.5194/isprs-archives-XLIII-B1-2020-165-2020

Krausman, P. R., & Cain, J. W. (Eds.). (2022). *Wildlife management and conservation: contemporary principles and practices*. JHU Press. doi:10.56021/9781421443973

Krausman, P. R., & Johnsingh, A. J. T. (1990). Conservation and wildlife education in India. *Wildlife Society Bulletin (1973-2006)*, *18*(3), 342-347

Lee, S., Song, Y., & Kil, S. H. (2021). Feasibility analyses of real-time detection of wildlife using UAV-derived thermal and RGB images. *Remote Sensing (Basel)*, *13*(11), 2169. doi:10.3390/rs13112169

Li, X., & Savkin, A. V. (2021). Networked unmanned aerial vehicles for surveillance and monitoring: A survey. *Future Internet*, *13*(7), 174. doi:10.3390/fi13070174

Li, Z., Liu, F., Yang, W., Peng, S., & Zhou, J. (2021). A survey of convolutional neural networks: Analysis, applications, and prospects. *IEEE Transactions on Neural Networks and Learning Systems*. PMID:34111009

Linchant, J., Lisein, J., Semeki, J., Lejeune, P., & Vermeulen, C. (2015). Are unmanned aircraft systems (UAS s) the future of wildlife monitoring? A review of accomplishments and challenges. *Mammal Review*, *45*(4), 239–252. doi:10.1111/mam.12046

Markowitz, H., Aday, C., & Gavazzi, A. (1995). Effectiveness of acoustic "prey": Environmental enrichment for a captive African leopard (Panthera pardus). *Zoo Biology*, *14*(4), 371–379. doi:10.1002/zoo.1430140408

McComb, B. C. (2007). *Wildlife habitat management: concepts and applications in forestry*. CRC Press. doi:10.1201/9781420007633

McGuire, K., Coppola, M., De Wagter, C., & de Croon, G. 2017, September. Towards autonomous navigation of multiple pocket-drones in real-world environments. In *2017 IEEE/RSJ International Conference on Intelligent Robots and Systems (IROS)* (pp. 244-249). IEEE. 10.1109/IROS.2017.8202164

Mota-Rojas, D., Pereira, A. M., Martínez-Burnes, J., Domínguez-Oliva, A., Mora-Medina, P., Casas-Alvarado, A., Rios-Sandoval, J., de Mira Geraldo, A., & Wang, D. (2022). Thermal Imaging to Assess the Health Status in Wildlife Animals under Human Care: Limitations and Perspectives. *Animals (Basel)*, *12*(24), 3558. doi:10.3390/ani12243558 PMID:36552478

Myanmar, W., & Lao, P. D. R. (2022). *Tiger IUCN Status Category: Endangered*. WCS.

Neupane, S. B., Sato, K., & Gautam, B. P. (2022). A literature review of computer vision techniques in wildlife monitoring. *IJSRP*, *16*, 282–295.

Petso, T., Jamisola, R. S. Jr, Mpoeleng, D., Bennitt, E., & Mmereki, W. (2021). Automatic animal identification from drone camera based on point pattern analysis of herd behaviour. *Ecological Informatics*, *66*, 101485. doi:10.1016/j.ecoinf.2021.101485

Putra, H. M., Fikri, M. R., Riananda, D. P., Nugraha, G., Baidhowi, M. L., & Syah, R. A. 2020, April. Propulsion selection method using motor thrust table for optimum flight in multirotor aircraft. In AIP Conference Proceedings (Vol. 2226, No. 1, p. 060008). AIP Publishing LLC. doi:10.1063/5.0004809

Raja, V., Gnanasekaran, R. K., Rajendran, P., Mohd Ali, A., Rasheed, R., AL-bonsrulah, H. A. Z., & Al-Bahrani, M. (2022). Asymmetrical damage aspects based investigations on the disc brake of long-range UAVs through verified computational coupled approaches. *Symmetry*, *14*(10), 2035. doi:10.3390ym14102035

Rakesh, D., Kumar, N. A., Sivaguru, M., Keerthivaasan, K. V. R., Janaki, B. R., & Raffik, R. (2021, October). Role of UAVs in innovating agriculture with future applications: A review. In *2021 International Conference on Advancements in Electrical, Electronics, Communication, Computing and Automation (ICAECA)* (pp. 1-6). IEEE. 10.1109/ICAECA52838.2021.9675612

Roy, A. M., Bhaduri, J., Kumar, T., & Raj, K. (2023). WilDect-YOLO: An efficient and robust computer vision-based accurate object localization model for automated endangered wildlife detection. *Ecological Informatics, 75*, 101919. doi:10.1016/j.ecoinf.2022.101919

Sandom, C., Faurby, S., Sandel, B., & Svenning, J. C. (2014). Global late Quaternary megafauna extinctions linked to humans, not climate change. *Proceedings of the Royal Society B: Biological Sciences, 281*(1787), 20133254. 10.1098/rspb.2013.3254

Senthilkumar, S., Anushree, G., Kumar, J. D., Vijayanandh, R., Raffik, R., Kesavan, K., & Prasanth, S. I. (2021, October). Design, dynamics, development and deployment of hexacopter for agricultural applications. In *2021 International Conference on Advancements in Electrical, Electronics, Communication, Computing and Automation (ICAECA)* (pp. 1-6). IEEE. 10.1109/ICAECA52838.2021.9675753

Shen, C. H., Albert, F. Y. C., Ang, C. K., Teck, D. J., & Chan, K. P. (2017, December). Theoretical development and study of takeoff constraint thrust equation for a drone. In *2017 IEEE 15th Student Conference on Research and Development (SCOReD)* (pp. 18-22). IEEE. 10.1109/SCORED.2017.8305428

Stein, A. B., Athreya, V., Gerngross, P., Balme, G., Henschel, P., Karanth, U., & Ghoddousi, A. (2017). *Panthera pardus (amended version of 2019 assessment)*. WCS.

Szokalski, M. S., Litchfield, C. A., & Foster, W. K. (2012). Enrichment for captive tigers (Panthera tigris): Current knowledge and future directions. *Applied Animal Behaviour Science, 139*(1-2), 1–9. doi:10.1016/j.applanim.2012.02.021

Teo, C. P. J. (2018). *Persistent perimeter surveillance using multiple swapping multi-rotor uas.* [Ph. D. dissertation, the Naval Postgraduate School Monterey United States].

Tuia, D., Kellenberger, B., Beery, S., Costelloe, B. R., Zuffi, S., Risse, B., Mathis, A., Mathis, M. W., van Langevelde, F., Burghardt, T., Kays, R., Klinck, H., Wikelski, M., Couzin, I. D., van Horn, G., Crofoot, M. C., Stewart, C. V., & Berger-Wolf, T. (2022). Perspectives in machine learning for wildlife conservation. *Nature Communications, 13*(1), 792. doi:10.103841467-022-27980-y PMID:35140206

Tuia, D., Kellenberger, B., Beery, S., Costelloe, B. R., Zuffi, S., Risse, B., Mathis, A., Mathis, M. W., van Langevelde, F., Burghardt, T., Kays, R., Klinck, H., Wikelski, M., Couzin, I. D., van Horn, G., Crofoot, M. C., Stewart, C. V., & Berger-Wolf, T. (2022). Perspectives in machine learning for wildlife conservation. *Nature Communications, 13*(1), 792. doi:10.103841467-022-27980-y PMID:35140206

Wall, J., Wittemyer, G., Klinkenberg, B., & Douglas-Hamilton, I. (2014). Novel opportunities for wildlife conservation and research with real-time monitoring. *Ecological Applications, 24*(4), 593–601. doi:10.1890/13-1971.1 PMID:24988762

Ward, S., Hensler, J., Alsalam, B., & Gonzalez, L. F. (2016, March). Autonomous UAVs wildlife detection using thermal imaging, predictive navigation and computer vision. In 2016 IEEE aerospace conference. IEEE.

Warrier, R., Noon, B. R., & Bailey, L. (2020). Agricultural lands offer seasonal habitats to tigers in a human-dominated and fragmented landscape in India. *Ecosphere, 11*(7), e03080. doi:10.1002/ecs2.3080

Xu, B., Wang, W., Falzon, G., Kwan, P., Guo, L., Sun, Z., & Li, C. (2020). Livestock classification and counting in quadcopter aerial images using Mask R-CNN. *International Journal of Remote Sensing*, *41*(21), 8121–8142. doi:10.1080/01431161.2020.1734245

Xu, J., Solmaz, G., Rahmatizadeh, R., Turgut, D., & Boloni, L. (2016). Internet of things applications: Animal monitoring with unmanned aerial vehicle. arXiv preprint arXiv:1610.05287.

Yan, L., Ahmad, M. W., Jawarneh, M., Shabaz, M., Raffik, R., & Kishore, K. H. (2022). Single-Input Single-Output System with Multiple Time Delay PID Control Methods for UAV Cluster Multiagent Systems. *Security and Communication Networks*, *2022*, 2022. doi:10.1155/2022/3935143

Chapter 7
Machine Learning and Deep Learning–Based Prediction and Monitoring of Forest Fires Using Unmanned Aerial Vehicle

Rishi Chhabra

 https://orcid.org/0009-0009-3159-7237

Madhav Institute of Technology and Science, Gwalior, India

Aditya Bhagat

G.H. Raisoni College of Engineering, Nagpur, India

Gaurav Mishra

Visvesvaraya National Institute of Technology, Nagpur, India

Ashish Tiwari

Visvesvaraya National Institute of Technology, Nagpur, India

M. M. Dhabu

Visvesvaraya National Institute of Technology, Nagpur, India

ABSTRACT

Wildfires, also referred to as forest fires, pose serious risks to heavily vegetated forested areas, demanding the development of sophisticated techniques for accurate forecasting and early detection. Unmanned aerial vehicles (UAV) and machine learning integration has been identified as a possible strategy to improve forest fire prediction systems. This thorough study seeks to provide an overview of the research that has been done in the field of machine learning-based UAV-based forest fire prediction. It discusses the benefits of using UAVs for data collection, the use of machine learning techniques, current difficulties, and potential future developments in this area. The main goal of this research is to clearly explain the state-of-the-art UAV-based forest fire prediction in order to facilitate future research projects and practical applications. Drones with sensors and imaging equipment make it possible to collect vital information on vegetation, weather, and fire behavior in real-time, which aids in more efficient wildfire management.

DOI: 10.4018/979-8-3693-0578-2.ch007

1. INTRODUCTION

Forest fires, commonly referred to as wildfires or blazes, are unattended flames that can cause great destruction in forested areas with a lot of vegetation. Due to conditions like high temperatures, aridity, and the presence of combustible elements like dead leaves and branches, these flames quickly spread across dry vegetation. High gusts and dry weather can make the spread speed worse. Forest fires can range greatly in size from little, isolated flames to enormous infernos that consume vast swaths of land. The forest fire is a particular variety of wildfire that only appears in wooded areas. In forests, there is a high concentration of trees and other flammable plants, which can result in extremely disastrous fires. Fires may spread quickly, even though the forest canopy, thanks to the fuel provided by dry leaves, branches, and other forest debris. Depending on regional and contextual variances, the phrases "wildfire" and "forest fire" are occasionally used synonymously. The word "bushfire" may occasionally be used to describe fires that predominantly harm shrubland or a forest (Arbez, 2002).

Forest fires have a significant influence on society, the economy, and the environment. These fires cause ecosystem disruption, forest degradation, and animal habitat destruction, reducing biodiversity and having long-term ecological repercussions. Large volumes of carbon dioxide are released into the atmosphere during the burning of plants, which contributes to air pollution and climate change. Forest fires destroy infrastructure, agricultural fields, and wood resources, which incur considerable costs to individuals, communities, and governments. Additionally, forest fires directly endanger human life by uprooting villages, displacing people, inflicting harm, and even resulting in fatalities. Both people and animals may suffer negative health impacts from the smoke and potentially dangerous substances these flames release. Affected people and communities may suffer long-term psychological and emotional effects (Arbez 2002; Stephens, 2005).

There are several factors, including both natural and human processes, that contribute to forest fires. Lightning strikes during thunderstorms, volcanic eruptions, and spontaneous combustion under particular dry circumstances are examples of natural sources of ignition. Unattended campfires, abandoned cigarettes, slash-and-burn farming techniques, poor garbage disposal, and deliberate arson are only a few examples of human-related causes of forest fires. Fires can also start as a result of mechanical failures, equipment sparks, and improper pyrotechnic use. Implementing preventative measures and efficient fire control methods depends on understanding these reasons. Reducing fire occurrences caused by people requires increasing awareness, sharing information through public service announcements, and encouraging adherence to fire safety standards. Rapid reaction and efficient fire control are made possible by early detection technology like monitoring networks and surveillance equipment. To further reduce the incidence and severity of forest fires, strict rules, good maintenance of firefighting equipment, and encouraging responsible conduct in fire-prone regions are all necessary (Arbez, 2002; Stephens, 2005).

Forest fires are complex, dynamic occurrences that are impacted by a wide range of factors, including their own behavior. To successfully manage, avoid, and lessen the effects of forest fires, it is necessary to understand these dynamics and causes. The behavior of a fire includes elements like its pace of spread, the length of its flame, the intensity of its fireline, and smoke and heat emission indications. Depending on the type of vegetation, the weather, the topography, and other environmental factors, these components change. For instance, estimating the path and possible effects of a fire depends critically on the pace at which it spreads, which is affected by wind speed, slope steepness, and fuel conditions. Flame length, which is influenced by wind, fuel load, and moisture content, sheds light on the fire's intensity. Information on possible harm and dangers is provided by fireline intensity, which gauges the amount of heat energy released per unit of fire front width. Having a good grasp of these aspects improves modeling systems for forecasting fire behavior, early detection, and the creation of successful fire management plans (Stephens, 2005; Chandler, 1983).

The range of fire severity reflects the degree of harm and effect a fire has on an area. Understanding the factors influencing fire intensity is essential to understanding the origins and effects of forest fires. Decision-making and tactics for controlling, avoiding, and mitigating the incidence and impacts of big forest fires are informed by knowledge about the intensity of the fire. Fire intensity is influenced by elements including fuel properties, weather patterns, geography, and proximity to populated areas. Considering burn size, area, and impacts on soil, plant, and wildlife habitats is common when describing a fire's intensity. The severity of a fire incident can change, with varying amounts of devastation and ecological repercussions. Fire intensity is largely influenced by fuel type and quantity, with dry, plentiful fuels like dead vegetation and downed trees causing more severe flames. Strong winds, low humidity, and extreme temperatures can all lead to more serious flames. Steep slopes can allow faster fire spread and more severe burns, therefore the geography of an area also matters. The hazards of forest fires are increased by nearby human infrastructure and constructions. It is possible to lessen the intensity of fires and the hazards they pose by developing tactics like controlled burning, fuel management, and constructing defensible areas around populations. The impact of major forest fires can be reduced by educating the public and increasing knowledge of fire safety and preparedness (Chandler, 1983; Halpern, 2022).

Forest fires pose significant threats to human regions, animals, and ecosystems. Manual tactics continue to be crucial for managing and controlling fires despite technological and firefighting equipment developments. Building firebreaks entails selectively removing vegetation to provide barriers that slow the spread of the fire. The direct attack strategy entails actively putting out the fire using shovels, hoses, and axes. Burns that are purposely started and use more fuel help lower the possibility of larger, uncontrollable flames. Activities like monitoring and surveillance help with resource allocation and decision-making by providing essential information on the behavior of fires. Backburning, in which flames are started against the wind, reduces the amount of fuel available and slows the spread of the fire. These manual methods, along with state-of-the-art technology, provide a thorough plan to save ecosystems, animals, and communities from the devastation caused by forest fires (Davis, 1959; Dimopoulou, 2004). The classification of techniques of forest fire detection and monitoring is shown in Figure 1.

Figure 1. Classification of detection and prevention of forest fire

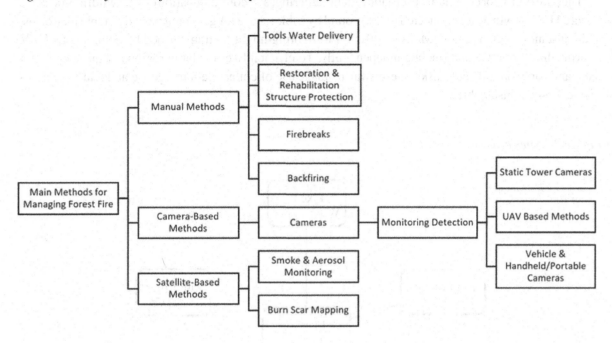

Due to their sophisticated sensors, cameras, and navigational systems, drones, also known as unmanned aerial vehicles (UAVs), have revolutionized the detection and management of forest fires. By providing early identification, real-time monitoring, and precise mapping of fire perimeters, these UAVs play a crucial role in contemporary wildfire control, leading to more successful firefighting efforts (Cazaurang, 2020; Espinoza-Fraire, 2023).

UAVs are excellent at accessing difficult-to-reach isolated and rocky places that ground-based crews find difficult to access. They traverse challenging terrain, dense cover, and hazardous areas while gathering crucial aerial data to comprehend fire dynamics (Cazaurang, 2020). UAVs support the analysis of fire behavior, the location of hotspots, and the identification of risk zones by delivering high-resolution photos, infrared imaging, and other sensor data from various heights (Cazaurang, 2020).

Early fire detection is made possible by UAVs' capacity to quickly scan vast areas for warning indicators, enabling quick action by emergency personnel (Cazaurang, 2020). UAVs also provide real-time observation, taking exact pictures and videos that help with resource allocation, firefighting strategies, and evacuation planning (Cazaurang, 2020). Making wise judgments when conducting firefighting operations requires the use of this information.

The capacity of UAVs to provide high-resolution maps that show the extent and size of a fire improves fire management tactics. Fixed-wing UAVs with cutting-edge sensors and cameras offer thorough surveillance and early fire detection, helping with resource allocation and planning for containment (Cazaurang, 2020). Due to their mobility and stability, multirotor UAVs, often known as drones, excel in localized surveillance and close-range inspections (Espinoza-Fraire, 2023). Hybrid UAVs also incorporate multirotor and fixed-wing elements, enabling extended observation and varied flying capabilities, which aid in effective fire control (Mohsan, 2022).

They are useful for continual observation, data gathering, and communication during wildfires because tethered UAVs, which are connected to the ground by cables, have longer flight periods, stable platforms, and constant power supplies (Mohsan, 2022). Firefighting might be transformed by autonomous UAV swarms that cooperate and operate independently. To efficiently cover large regions, acquire essential data, and carry out difficult tasks, these swarms make use of collective intelligence and real-time communication (Mohsan, 2022).

Figure 2. Types of UAVs

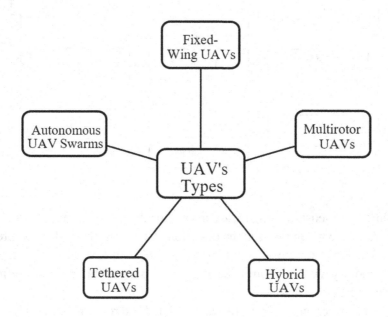

Forest fire control benefits significantly from a range of UAV types, including fixed-wing, multirotor, tethered, and autonomous UAV swarms. They aid in early identification, ongoing monitoring, precise mapping, and targeted reaction, all of which improve the efficiency of firefighting operations and lessen the effects of wildfires (Cazaurang, 2020; Espinoza-Fraire, 2023; Mohsan, 2022). **UAV based approaches are divided into two parts such as UAV based tasks and algorithms. Figure 3 and 4 denote the classification of the UAV based tasks and algorithms respectively.**

Figure 3. Classification of UAV based tasks

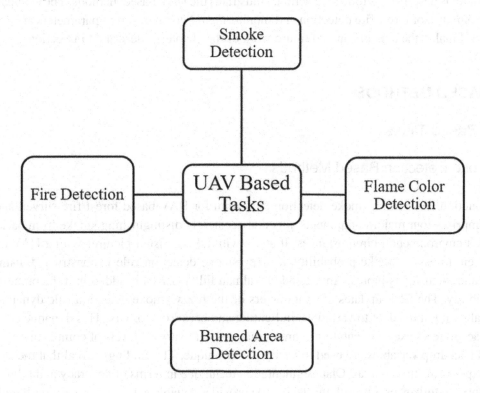

Figure 4. Classification of UAV based methods

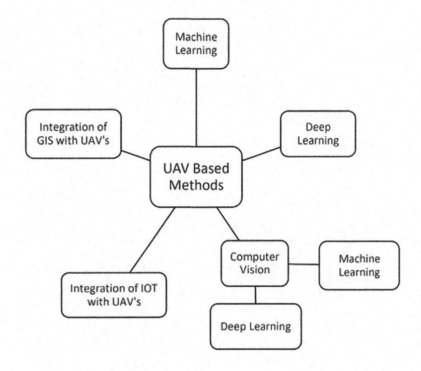

This chapter is described as follows. Section 2 illustrates the UAV based methods. The Comparison of different techniques of forest fire detection and monitoring based on different parameters are described in Section 3. Finally, the conclusion and future work of the chapter is described in Section 4.

2.UAV BASED METHODS

2.1 UAV Based Tasks

2.1.1 Smoke Detection Based Methods

This introduction describes a smoke detection algorithm for UAV-based forest fire surveillance. The process comprises four major components aimed at accurately distinguishing smoke from background under varied environmental circumstances. It starts with taking visual pictures with a UAV-mounted camera. Then, to assess smoke probability, a fuzzy smoke detection rule is constructed, using RGB difference and intensity as inputs. An Extended Kalman Filter (EKF) is added into the process to improve flexibility. The EKF updates the parameters of the fuzzy smoke detection rule dynamically in real-time, allowing it to adapt to variations in lighting and backdrop colours. This dynamic adjustment allows for accurate smoke segmentation. Three situations with varying levels of complexity in terms of smoke and backdrop variables are used to verify the technique. The findings reveal that the suggested strategy outperforms the standard Otsu segmentation technique in terms of accuracy and robustness to environmental disturbances. Overall, this technique provides a viable solution for learning-based smoke detection in UAV-based forest fire monitoring, allowing for precise and flexible detection (Yuan, 2019). Figure 5 shows the forest fire detection based on smoke.

Figure 5. Forest fire detection based on smoke five
(Jiao, 2020)

2.1.2 Flame Detection Based Methods

By integrating the colour and dynamic properties of flames, fire detection systems have attempted to increase recognition accuracy. However, little study has been conducted especially on fire detection in forest contexts. Unmanned aerial vehicles (UAVs) have gained significant popularity in recent years as efficient and cost-effective platforms for a variety of jobs. Because of their versatility and agility, they have the potential to be used in fire detection. This introduction emphasizes the necessity for more extensive research concentrating on fire detection in forest ecosystems, as well as the growing usage of unmanned aerial vehicles (UAVs) as a viable tool for such applications. Unmanned aerial vehicles (UAVs) outfitted with vision-based systems have a lot of potential for monitoring, identifying, and fighting forest fires. Their advantages, such as quick manoeuvrability, increased operational range, and greater worker safety, make them ideal for these duties. UAV-based forest fire suppression technology has made significant progress in recent years. This introduction emphasizes the rising interest in using unmanned aerial vehicles (UAVs) for forest fire monitoring, detection, and suppression. The overview focuses on

Figure 6. Forest fire detection based on the flame
(Nguyen, 2021)

UAV development and system design in this context, as well as a brief discussion of important technologies such as fire detection, diagnosis, and prognosis methodologies, image vibration removal techniques, and cooperative UAV control. Furthermore, the introduction highlights the existing obstacles and possible solutions related with using unmanned aerial vehicles (UAVs) to battle forest fires (Yuan, 2015).

To avoid possible calamities, forest fire detection is a key responsibility that necessitates precise and effective approaches. This section introduces a two-stage forest fire detection system that focuses on colour feature extraction and motion analysis. The approach seeks to properly detect fire zones in photos or videos by utilizing the particular colour features and motion patterns associated with fire. Colour feature extraction begins with translating the input picture into an appropriate colour space and then using a colour thresholding approach to divide the image into fire and non-fire areas based on particular colour attributes. The second step employs motion analysis to identify fire within the segmented zones. A backdrop subtraction approach is used to isolate moving items from the static background by assuming that fire causes motion owing to flickering flames. These moving items are then analysed for fire based on their motion characteristics. The suggested technique is tested utilizing a UAV-based forest fire detection system on real aerial films of forest fires and indoor experimental experiments, displaying great accuracy and low false alarm rates. Overall, this method provides a strong approach to forest fire detection, leveraging colour and motion information to increase detection effectiveness in a variety of settings (Yuan, 2017).

Flame detection in films and precise fire propagation estimation are critical for successful fire prevention and catastrophe management. To achieve these goals, this introduction introduces a complete technique that combines flame detection algorithms with a 3D visualization tool. To select potential flame locations, the proposed technique includes many processing phases, including background removal and colour analysis. Further processing is used to differentiate between genuine flames and fire-coloured objects by identifying spatiotemporal properties specific to fires. Based on these retrieved characteristics, a classifier is used to reach the ultimate conclusion on flame detection. In terms of accuracy, comparative assessments show that the proposed technique is superior. The introduction also emphasizes the 3D visualization tool, which gives a visual picture of fire spread. The program assists in early fire detection and efficient catastrophe mitigation by modelling various situations. Overall, this integrated technique provides a viable solution for reliable flame identification in films as well as useful insights for calculating fire spread in real-world settings (Dimitropoulos, 2012). **The flame based forest fire detection is shown in figure 6.**

2.2 UAV Based Algorithms

2.2.1 Computer Vision Based Methods

The goal of the academic area and technology known as computer vision is to give computers a deep understanding of visual data. It entails the creation of algorithms and methods that enable computers to decipher, examine, and extract valuable data from pictures or movies. The computer can recognize and classify things, locate and detect specific features, comprehend spatial relationships, and make judgements based on visual inputs using these algorithms that can be taught on massive datasets of photos.

For detecting wildfires, there are two basic categories of computer vision algorithms. The first kind is conventional machine learning, which entails choosing and creating characteristics from pictures, including colours and patterns, by hand. This method takes time, and selecting the appropriate characteristics calls for expertise. It also has trouble solving challenging issues, such as finding fires in forested areas with a lot of background noise.

The second kind of method uses deep learning algorithms to automatically extract valuable and powerful information from photos. Thanks to updated hardware and software technologies, deep learning has made considerable strides recently. Convolutional neural networks (CNNs), in particular, have revolutionised deep learning architectures and made it feasible to complete previously unsolvable complicated problems.

The performance of computer vision techniques is, nevertheless, susceptible to a number of difficulties. These difficulties include shifting points of view, shifting illumination, shifting how flames and smoke appear, scale problems, occlusion, crowded settings, and shifting item classes (Bouguettaya, 2022). **Figure 7 shows the forest fire detection using computer vision techniques.**

Figure 7. Forest fire detection using computer vision techniques
(Nguyen, 2021)

2.2.2 Computer Vision Based Machine Learning Methods

Artificial intelligence (AI) has an area called machine learning that focuses on creating algorithms and models that let computers learn and make predictions or judgements without having to be explicitly programmed.

The suggested visual real-time fire detection approach is intended to improve real-time fire monitoring utilising drones. It is made up of a number of parts that all work together to effectively detect fires. The method makes use of a cheap camera to take high-definition pictures of the surroundings. These pictures provide essential visual information for spotting fires. The photos are then analysed by a small companion computer, which employs the Single Shot MultiBox Detector (SSD), a sophisticated object detection technique. The SSD algorithm has a reputation for being effective and precise at locating objects within photos, including possible fire situations. The system includes a flight controller, which controls the drone's movement and trajectory, to guarantee optimal coverage and navigation. As a result, the UAV can effectively scan broad regions, like woods, for signs of fire. The system also incorporates localization and telemetry modules that enable the transmission of detection findings to a ground station or central monitoring station while tracking the UAV's position in real-time. The process starts with the development of a large dataset with a variety of fire photos and detailed annotations identifying the locations of the flames in each image. Using this dataset and well-known deep learning frameworks like TensorFlow or PyTorch, the SSD algorithm is trained. The dataset is expanded during the training phase to boost its size and variety. The photos are altered using methods including rotation, scaling, and flipping to improve the algorithm's capacity to identify fires in a variety of settings. To increase detection accuracy, model initialization and optimisation phases modify the algorithm's weights. The UAV platform incorporates the object detection algorithm after it has been trained. Real-time photos are captured by the camera and processed using the SSD method by the small companion computer. The system examines the photographs and finds situations where a fire may have occurred. The localization and telemetry modules follow the UAV's position and relay the detection findings to a monitoring centre, while the flight controller maintains the UAV's effective coverage and manoeuvrability. Performance measurements including accuracy, recall, and the F1 score are used to assess the usefulness of the suggested solution. These metrics evaluate the system's precision and effectiveness in identifying fires in real-world situations. The outcomes show that the suggested strategy is better than conventional fire detection techniques. In conclusion, the suggested visual real-time fire detection method offers an integrated strategy that improves fire monitoring by utilising drones. The system's parts, which include the inexpensive camera, portable companion computer, flight controller, and localization and telemetry modules, cooperate to detect fires effectively and precisely. The technique assures the system's efficacy from dataset development through algorithm training and execution. This approach is a huge development in fire safety since it has the power to completely change how fire monitoring activities are carried out (Nguyen, 2021).

Early detection of fires is critical for averting catastrophic occurrences and protecting lives and property. Traditional fire and smoke detection sensors, which are usually used inside, sometimes rely on the accumulation of smoke before triggering an alert, whereas outside conditions such as woods and wild regions make their deployment difficult. Vision based fire detection systems, on the other hand, have the benefit of detecting fires using cameras immediately, making them suited for early response. These systems are inexpensive, simple to set up, and may be installed to unmanned aerial vehicles (UAVs) for large-scale fire detection. Various vision-based fire detection approaches have been presented in the literature, with colour models, motion analysis, and spatial and temporal aspects all playing a key role due to the unique properties of fire. These algorithms often use background removal to identify moving pixels before employing colour models to find fire zones. These regions are subjected to further research in order to capture the erratic and flickering patterns associated with fire. Most present techniques, however, are confined to fixed surveillance cameras. Such limits are solved in this study by utilizing deep learning techniques, notably deep convolutional neural networks (CNNs), to create feature representations and train discriminative classifiers for fire area identification. This study makes an important addition by introducing a benchmark dataset for fire detection, which addresses the lack of a standardized dataset in the area. This comprehensive dataset includes both previously studied fire sequences and newly obtained data, including patch-level annotations for benchmarking and supporting future study in the field of fire detection. A review of existing vision-based fire detection methods is followed by a presentation of the newly introduced benchmark dataset, the proposed CNN-based fire detection method, experimental results on the benchmark dataset, and a concluding section summarizing the key findings and highlighting future research directions (Zhang, 2016).

The suggested technique is centered on the design and implementation of a complete and efficient forest fire detection system based on a UAV-based platform and the YOLOv3 algorithm. The goal is to use the UAV's capabilities and sophisticated deep learning algorithms to enable real-time fire detection, assisting in the prevention and management of forest fires. The platform consists of a six-rotor unmanned aerial vehicle outfitted with cutting edge technology, such as high-definition digital picture transmission, and a ground station outfitted with a video capture card and a powerful GPU. This connection provides smooth picture acquisition from the forest environment as well as effective image transmission to the ground station for real-time processing. The use of unmanned aerial vehicles (UAVs) in fire detection has various advantages, including a larger search area coverage, flexible deployment, and the capacity to visit remote or inaccessible sites. Because of these characteristics, it is a good platform for early fire detection in large-scale outdoor areas such as forests. The suggested technique is built around the YOLOv3 algorithm, a popular and robust object detection system noted for its speed and accuracy. The algorithm is made up of two layers: a feature extraction layer and a processing output layer. The feature extraction layer collects relevant information from input photos, whereas the processing output layer predicts the bounding boxes and class probabilities of identified items such as fires. The algorithm's strength is its ability to recognize and categories items of diverse sizes and scales, making it suitable for spotting both large-scale flames and tiny fire-related factors like smoke. A large collection of forest fire photos is used for testing and validation to assess the algorithm's performance. This dataset includes a variety of situations, such as varying fire sizes, backdrops, lighting settings, and environmental elements. The dataset is meticulously chosen to guarantee a representative and diverse sample of forest fire photos, allowing for an in-depth evaluation of the algorithm's capabilities. Accuracy, precision, recall, and F1 score are among the assessment measures employed, offering a full knowledge of the algorithm's effectiveness in fire detection. The experimental findings show that the proposed technique is effective and efficient. The YOLOv3 algorithm, which is integrated into the UAV-FFD platform, is extremely accurate and has real-time fire detection capabilities. Because of the algorithm's speed and precision, fires may be identified and located quickly, allowing for prompt reaction and mitigation efforts. The technique achieves quick processing speeds by exploiting the computational capabilities of the ground station's GPU, allowing for real-time analysis of the recorded photos. This skill is crucial in fire control since early identification allows for quick response, avoiding fire spread and minimizing possible damage to forests and adjacent regions. Furthermore, the suggested technique emphasizes the need of ongoing improvement and benchmarking in the detection of forest fires. A specialized fire detection benchmark is being created in order to create a standardized assessment framework for evaluating various fire detection technologies. This benchmark comprises a wide variety of fire sequences from prior research as well as freshly gathered data, guaranteeing that fire detection systems are thoroughly evaluated. The availability of such standards allows for more study and improvements in the sector, enabling the development of more accurate and resilient fire detection systems. Finally, the suggested UAVbased forest fire detection approach, which incorporates the YOLOv3 algorithm, provides a reliable and efficient solution for real-time fire detection in forest environments. The system delivers accurate and fast information to help in the prevention, control, and mitigation of forest fires by using the capabilities of UAVs and modern deep learning algorithms. The incorporation of a large dataset, benchmarking initiatives, and performance review all help to develop fire detection technologies. The suggested technique has the potential to significantly improve the capacities of forest fire detection systems, resulting in more effective fire control methods and the protection of natural resources (Jiao, 2020).

PreVM (Preferred Vector Machine), a revolutionary pixel-precision approach, is proposed in this work for fire detection and recognition in forest monitoring systems. By giving equal consideration to fire and non-fire samples and introducing a new L0 norm requirement for the fire class, the technique addresses the problem of fire miss-detection. This restriction ensures a high rate of fire detection and precision management.

In order to improve training efficiency and lower error warning rates, a kernel-based L1 norm PreVM (L1-PreVM) is described. Extensive testing on real forest fire photos and videos shows that L1-PreVM performs well in real-time detection settings while PreVM obtains greater fire detection rates and lower error warning rates when compared to state-of-the-art approaches. The various techniques for detecting forest fires that are now in use can be divided into three categories: colour- or rule-based detection, motion-based techniques, and model-based fire detection employing computer vision and machine learning algorithms. These approaches, however, frequently have drawbacks, such as giving both fire and non-fire samples the same amount of attention, which leads to high miss-detection rates. By focusing on high fire detection rates while limiting the error warning rate, the suggested PreVM (Preferred Vector Machine) method seeks to address these difficulties. The PreVM technique promises possible improvements in fire detection accuracy and robustness by combining L0-norm and L1-norm constraints and utilising shallow learning for interpretability. Theoretical justifications, mathematical support for norm kernelization, and useful problem-solving strategies are all contributions of the method. Comparative analyses show that PreVM is more effective than current state-of-the-art techniques (Yang, 2023). The flow chart of the machine learning based forest fire detection is shown in Figure 8.

Figure 8. Flow chart of machine learning based detection and monitoring of forest fire

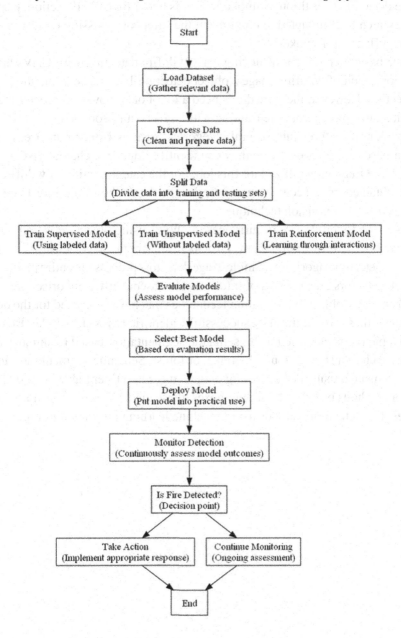

2.2.3 Deep Learning-Based Computer Vision Methods

Despite these challenges, deep learning-based computer vision approaches have shown significant results in a number of areas, including the detection of vehicles, face recognition, self-driving vehicles, and the diagnosis of plant diseases.

UAVs are being utilized more often in forestry applications, such as forest scouting, search and rescue missions, measuring forest resource availability, and battling forest fires. UAVs are preferred over other technologies due to their low cost, flexibility, and ability to fly at various heights. UAVs can now analyse intricate visual data onboard thanks to improvements in hardware and software.

Deep learning-based computer vision algorithms have attracted a lot of attention recently because they can be used for early wildfire detection using UAVs. Flame and smoke are the two primary visual elements employed in wildfire detection. While some studies concentrate on detecting fires by flame, others emphasize detecting fires through smoke, which is better for early detection, particularly in deep woods. Recent research has attempted to circumvent the limits of focussing on just one item by simultaneously detecting flame and smoke.

There are three basic methods for achieving early wildfire detection with UAVs and deep learning algorithms: categorization of wildfire images, object detection-based detection, and semantic segmentation-based detection. However, these methods need a lot of data, powerful processing, careful choice of the ideal architecture, and appropriate training with useful data (Bouguettaya, 2022).

The categorization of pictures into several categories, such as fire or non-fire, is the basis of image classification-based approaches. Since they can identify important characteristics in pictures, deep CNN architectures are frequently utilized for this job. For the categorization of wildfire images, several researchers have obtained great accuracy using CNNs. Figure 9 shows the forest fire detection using deep learning-based computer vision techniques.

In order to locate and identify fire occurrences in photos using object detection-based approaches, bounding boxes are often drawn around them. Two-stage and single-stage detectors are the two primary categories of object detection algorithms. Single-stage detectors process the entire picture in a single pass, whereas two-stage detectors create zones of interest and subsequently categorise them. Faster R-CNN, YOLO, and SSD are a few object identification techniques that have been used for the detection of wildfires. In UAV images, these algorithms have successfully identified fires and smoke (Bouguettaya, 2022).

Each pixel in a picture is classified using semantic segmentation-based techniques according to the item it represents, such as a flame, cloud of smoke, or forest. Semantic segmentation in wildfire detection has been implemented using deep learning architectures like DeepLabV3+ and U-Net. Compared to object detection methods based on bounding boxes, these algorithms deliver more accurate findings. The steps of forest fire detection methods using machine learning are shown in Figure 11.

Figure 9. Forest fire detection using deep learning-based computer vision techniques
(Zhang, 2016)

Figure 10. Flowchart of computer vision-based methods for forest fire detection

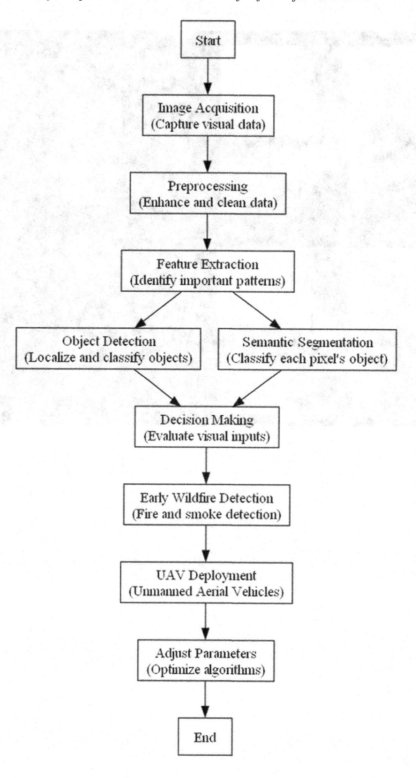

2.2.4 Integration of Internet of Things With UAV Based Methods

The Internet of Things is referred to as IoT. It describes a network of actual physical objects, including machinery, automobiles, appliances, and other machinery, that are equipped with sensors, software, and networking capabilities to gather and exchange data online. IoT devices typically include connectivity modules (such as Wi-Fi, Bluetooth, or cellular) that enable communication with other devices and the internet, sensors or actuators that gather data from their environment or carry out actions, and micro-controllers or processors that process the data and manage the device's operations.

EdgeFireSmoke++ is a proposed technique that seeks to stream video in real-time to monitor small patches of forest reserves. The EdgeFireSmoke approach is expanded upon, and deep learning and artificial neural networks are used. It aims to go beyond the capabilities of satellite-based monitoring systems by doing this to improve forest monitoring and surveillance.

The EdgeFireSmoke++ algorithm that has been proposed shows good results in identifying forest fires. Based on the assessed dataset, it detected forest fires with an accuracy of 95.41% and 95.49%. Additionally, it performed admirably in real-time tests using Internet Protocol cameras, averaging 33 frames per second. Comparatively, it performed better than procedures that had been tested in the literature before.

The EdgeFireSmoke++ method can assist in early detection and quick response to forest fires by offering real-time monitoring capabilities. The effects of flames on the environment and populated areas can both be lessened with this prompt intervention. By concentrating on tiny portions of forest reserves, it complements already-existing monitoring systems and tackles the shortcomings of satellite-based monitoring.

Overall, the suggested algorithm shows potential in enhancing the monitoring and surveillance of forest fires, providing practical answers to the problems encountered in this area (Almeida, 2021).

The EdgeFireSmoke++ algorithm's approaches are discussed here: -

2.2.5 Colour Conversion

The method changes input photos from RGB to HSV (Hue, Saturation, Value) format, which is more effective for processing in conditions of forest fires.

2.2.6 Histogram and its Normalization

Using the histogram and its normalization, the digital image is converted into a condensed statistical representation. It aids in analysing how the image's pixel intensities are distributed.

2.2.7 Histogram Comparison

This method determines how closely the input image resembles the patterns of interest. For each comparison pattern, it outputs a vector of coefficients, enabling pattern identification and categorization.

2.2.8 Artificial Neural Network (ANN)

To address misclassifications that could happen during the histogram comparison stage, the technique uses an ANN. The ANN aids in raising the detecting process's level of precision.

The EdgeFireSmoke++ algorithm's real-time forest fire detection and visualisation capabilities are enhanced by the combination of these approaches (Almeida, 2021). The steps of IoT based Forest fire detection and prevention is described in Figure 12.

Figure 11. Flow chart of fire forest detection using integration of internet of things with UAV based methods

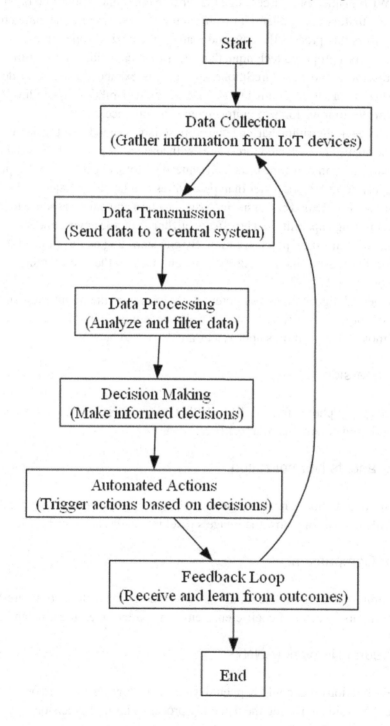

2.2.9 Integration of Geographic Information System (GIS) With UAV Based Methods

The Geographic Information System is referred to as GIS. It is a technique that integrates spatial (coordinates and shapes) and attribute (descriptive) data with geographic (knowledge about locations on the Earth's surface) data to build, analyse, and visualise maps and spatial connections. GIS enables users to digitally store, manage, process, and show geographic information. It offers a framework for gathering, compiling, and presenting data in a spatial context, allowing users to recognise patterns, connections, and trends that would not be immediately obvious in tabular data.

The automatic early warning system is intended to guard against fire dangers at archaeological and cultural sites. It monitors temperature, humidity, and meteorological conditions using cutting-edge surveillance technologies including cameras and wireless sensors. Intelligent algorithms are used to analyse the obtained data and look for probable fire patterns or abnormalities. Automatic warning signals are produced for local authorities when a risky condition is found.

Based on elements such as fuel, wind speed, and topography, the system can also predict how far the fire will travel. Its objective is to deliver crucial information and early alerts to protect these priceless locations from fire threats. There are numerous techniques and technologies that can be used for early detection and fire monitoring in the context of fire surveillance for cultural assets and archaeological sites. These consist of:

2.2.10 Human Surveillance

Human observers are stationed at observation points like lookout towers or through video surveillance systems in this conventional mode of monitoring. But relying only on human observation may not be effective.

2.2.11 Systems Based on Satellites

Satellite photography can be used to spot fires before they spread. Data for monitoring vast areas is provided by systems like the Moderate Resolution Imaging Spectroradiometer (MODIS) and the Advanced Very High-Resolution Radiometer (AVHRR). The accuracy and dependability of satellite-based systems can be impacted by weather conditions and low resolution, and satellite coverage may not be constant.

2.2.12 Airborne Systems

These systems monitor and identify fires using sensors and cameras placed on helicopters or aeroplanes. They provide adaptability, prompt responses, and data of high resolution. Because they are inexpensive and can fly in bad weather, unmanned aerial vehicles (UAVs) are being employed more and more for fire detection.

2.2.13 Terrestrial systems

These systems use thermal, infrared (IR), or video cameras to detect fire. Smoke and fire can be seen by visible-range cameras, while heat signatures can be detected by IR cameras. The range of thermal sensors is constrained; therefore, IR cameras can be pricey.

2.2.14 Wireless Sensor Networks (WSNs)

WSNs are made up of tiny sensor nodes that work together to monitor a space and transmit data wirelessly to a hub. WSNs are capable of detecting ambient temperature, humidity, and other characteristics crucial to the detection of fires. They offer adequate protection and can change their data gathering times based on the likelihood of a fire. WSNs can communicate via wireless technologies like IEEE 802.15.4/Zigbee.

These techniques can be combined into a multi-sensor early warning system to remotely monitor the risk of fire at archaeological and cultural heritage sites. Data from numerous sensors, including temperature, humidity, optical cameras, and infrared cameras, are combined by the system. A monitoring centre receives the data collection and processes it using sophisticated computer vision algorithms and data fusion techniques. In the event of a critical situation, automatic warning signals can be issued for local authorities.

The estimation of fire propagation utilising plant models, wind speed, slope, and ground surface aspect can also be added to fire detection systems. To aid in decision-making for the suppression of forest fires, geographic information systems (GIS) can be used to visualise expected fire propagation in three dimensions.

It's vital to remember that the precise application and efficiency of these techniques may change depending on elements like site characteristics, resources available, and local laws (Grammalidis, 2011). The steps for monitoring and detecting the forest fire using geographic information system (GIS) is shown in Figure 13.

Figure 12. Flow chart of forest fire detection and monitoring using integration of GIS with UAV based methods

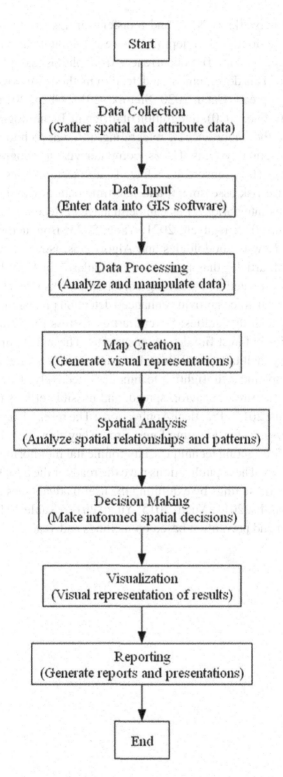

2.2.15 The Special Comments That These Publications Make

Deep convolutional neural networks (CNNs) and transfer learning are two examples of cutting-edge detection approaches that are discussed in depth in the research publications. The studies show better accuracy and resilience in recognizing fire occurrences from photos taken by UAVs by utilizing these cutting-edge methodologies. This development in detection methods improves attempts to identify and respond to fires before they spread (Catal, 2020; Sharma, 2017; Chen, 2018; Jiao, 2019; Ghali, 2022; Nguyen, 2021; Zhang, 2016; Jiao, 2020). Integration of different Technologies: A number of the papers in the collection emphasize the importance of integrating different technologies to develop thorough and efficient forest fire detection systems. UAVs, computer vision, geographic information systems (GIS), and Internet of Things (IoT) sensors are a few of these technologies. Researchers want to offer complete monitoring, precise risk assessment, and real-time data processing capabilities by merging these techniques. Due to this integration, fires can be managed effectively and decisions can be made quickly (Chen, 2018; Ghali, 2022; Nguyen, 2021; Yang, 2023; Bouguettaya, 2022; Almeida, 2021; Yuan, 2015; Yuan, 2017). New methodologies and Algorithms: New algorithms and methodologies are presented in the research articles that are created particularly for UAV-based forest fire detection. For instance, it has been investigated to use cutting-edge frameworks like YOLOv3, deep learning, and transfer learning. These novel methods provide enhanced detection precision, flexibility, and scalability, precisely addressing the special difficulties. Several articles stress the value of real-time monitoring and visualization capabilities in forest fire detection systems. These technologies aid in prompt action and situational awareness by facilitating real-time data capture, processing, and visualization. In order to allocate resources and implement firefighting techniques effectively, decision-makers can get up-to-date information regarding the fire's behavior, spread, and possible effects (Ghali, 2022; Islam, 2019; Almeida, 2021; Grammalidis, 2011). Practical Applications: The research articles provided information on the use of UAV-based systems for detecting forest fires. They show how these systems may be used for early warning systems, firefighting techniques, environmental monitoring, and cultural asset protection, among other applications. These publications pave the road for the adoption and use of UAV-based detection systems in real-world settings by exhibiting the useful advantages and success stories (Ghali, 2022; Yang, 2023; Grammalidis, 2011; Yuan, 2015; Yuan, 2017). Table 1 shows some recent publications of forest fire detection and prevention based on methods and year.

Table 1. Classification of forest fire detection and prevention based on techniques and year

Approach Description	Detection Method	Year
GIS-based 3D visualization for fire assistance (Arbez, 2002)	3D GIS Assisting fire & Decision Making	2011
3D visualization using flame colour for fire detection (Dimitropoulos, 2012)	3D Visualization with flames and Fire-colour	2012
Detection based on flame colour (Dimitropoulos, 2012)	Flame Colour Detection	2015, 2017
CNN-SVM approach using CIFAR 10 network (Sharma, 2017)	CNN with SVM & CIFAR 10 network	2016
Smoke detection using RGB and Extended Kalman Filter (Yuan, 2019)	Smoke Detection with RGB & Extended Kalman Filter (EKF)	2018
CNN-SVM with RBF and Region of Interest (Sharma, 2017)	CNN with SVM's Radial Basic Function (RBF) & ROI	2018
YOLOv3 implementation on UAV-FFD platform (Jiao, 2019)	YOLOv3 Algo into the UAV-FFD platform	2020
Lightweight IoT-human interface algorithm for real-time detection (Almeida, 2021)	EdgeFireSmoke++	2023
CNN with Transfer Learning (VGG16, ResNet50) (Catal, 2020)	Using Deep Convolutional Neural Network with Transfer Learning Approach	2023
Detection using preferred vector machine (Yang, 2023)	Preferred Vector Machine for Forest Fire Detection	2023
Detection from UAVs using Computer Vision (Bouguettaya, 2022)	Early Wildfire Detection from UAVs using Deep Learning-based CV Algorithms	2021
CNN with Vision Transformer architecture (Ghali, 2022)	CNN with Vision Transformer (ViT) Architecture	2022

3. COMPARISON OF DIFFERENT TECHNIQUES OF FOREST FIRE DETECTION AND MONITORING BASED ON METHODS, USE CASE, AND LIMITATIONS

Unmanned aerial vehicles (UAVs), which use a range of techniques to improve their capabilities, are essential in the detection of forest fires. These techniques include the use of thermal cameras and optical sensors to detect flame and smoke. UAVs are able to locate hot spots and spot the presence of flames by analysing thermal photos. Images and smoke plumes are captured using visual cameras and specialised sensors, which are then analysed using image processing techniques to find patterns or changes suggestive of a fire. Flames and smoke are obvious markers of an ongoing fire; hence this strategy works well for doing so. The location and severity of a fire can be revealed in real time. However, it might not be able to detect fires in thickly wooded regions where the flames might be partially hidden or the smoke might not be as noticeable. It works best when there are active fires that are spewing forth smoke and visible flames. The inability to identify fires early on or in situations when flames are not apparent, such as smouldering or subterranean fires, is one drawback of depending entirely on flame and smoke detection. Additionally, the efficiency of this strategy may be impacted by the presence of dense vegetation or adverse weather, such as thick fog or smoke, which can make flames and smoke less visible.

Another crucial element of UAV-based fire detection is the integration of geographic information systems (GIS). Georeferenced data, such as information on the location and spread of fires as well as terrain and vegetation kinds, is gathered by UAVs with GPS and other sensors. This information is then included into a GIS system, which offers a thorough overview of the fire situation and facilitates efficient resource allocation and decision-making. When it comes to managing and analysing geospatial data on forest fires, GIS is incredibly effective. It enables precise mapping of the location and spread of fires as well as other crucial elements like terrain and plant kinds. Effective resource allocation and decision-making are made possible by GIS integration. This approach is particularly beneficial for long-term fire control plans, post-fire analysis, and strategic planning.

Convolutional neural networks (CNNs), in particular, are frequently used in UAV systems for forest fire detection. Deep learning algorithms can analyse photos and accurately detect fire-related patterns by using vast information collected by UAVs. CNNs are capable of picking up on intricate details and recognising flames, smoke, or other fire signs, greatly enhancing the precision and effectiveness of fire detection. Deep learning methods, like CNNs, are very effective in analysing big datasets and accurately identifying patterns connected to fires. Even under difficult circumstances, they can pick up complicated details and recognise flames, smoke, or other fire signs. Deep learning is excellent at analysing images, and by giving UAVs the ability to automatically identify fires, it can increase their effectiveness. To attain high accuracy, deep learning models often need a lot of labelled training data. It might be difficult and time-consuming to collect this information for the purpose of detecting forest fires. Deep learning models can also be computationally demanding, necessitating strong hardware resources for both training and inference, which may restrict their real-time application in resource-constrained UAV systems.

Additionally, using previous data and current sensor readings, machine learning algorithms are used to forecast the likelihood of a fire. Machine learning algorithms can determine the potential of fire breakouts by examining meteorological variables including temperature, humidity, wind speed, and plant moisture content. UAVs with sensors gather real-time data that machine learning algorithms use to anticipate fires more accurately and implement preventative fire management techniques. In order to forecast the likelihood of a fire, machine learning algorithms can effectively analyse both historical and current sensor data. They can offer insightful information regarding the possibility of fire breakouts by taking into account a variety of environmental parameters. When it comes to proactive fire control, machine learning is very helpful since it makes early warning systems possible and supports decision-making. The quality and representativeness of the training data have a significant impact on how well machine learning algorithms perform. The availability of various and comprehensive datasets that cover the spectrum of climatic variables and fire occurrences can be constrained in the case of forest fire forecast. The accuracy and generalizability of the machine learning models may be impacted by this.

Integration of the Internet of Things (IoT) improves UAV capabilities for forest fire detection. IoT gadgets like environmental sensors that measure temperature, humidity, and carbon monoxide levels can be added to UAVs. Realtime data transmission and collecting make it easier to analyse and respond to fire situations quickly, allocating resources effectively and hastening decision-making. The effective collection of real-time environmental data by IoT devices embedded into UAVs can improve situational awareness during fire detection missions. Rapid transmission and analysis of the data enables quick reaction and resource allocation. Real-time decision-making is supported by IoT integration, which enables efficient monitoring of changing fire conditions. A strong and dependable network connection is necessary for IoT devices installed into UAVs for real-time data collecting. However, network coverage might be patchy or non-existent in distant or heavily wooded locations. The timely and efficient nature of fire detection and response may be hampered as a result of this impeding the transfer of real-time data.

A variety of approaches are utilised in UAV-based fire detection under the heading of computer methods. These techniques use data analysis, pattern recognition, and image processing to find patterns connected to fires, extract characteristics, and arrive at judgements. UAVs can successfully analyse collected pictures and sensor data by using computer algorithms, assisting in the prompt and precise identification of forest fires. For the purpose of detecting fires, computer technologies such as pattern recognition and image processing can analyse pictures and sensor data effectively. These techniques have the ability to extract pertinent characteristics and find fire-related patterns. By automating the analytical process and delivering timely information for decision-making, they improve the overall efficiency of UAV systems. Image quality, illumination, and other environmental elements can have an impact on how computer algorithms, in particular image processing and pattern recognition, perform. The accuracy and dependability of the computer-based analysis may be impacted by poor image quality or difficult weather circumstances, such as heavy smoke or poor visibility. Comparison of different methods based on methods, use case and limitations- are shown in Table 2.

Table 2. Comparison of different methods based on methods, use case and limitations

Method	Limitations	Efficiency compared to other methods	Use Cases
Flame and Smoke Detection	Flame and smoke detection has the drawback of being most effective in detecting current flames. Early-stage fire detection, as well as fires with partially or completely hidden flames, may not be as accurate. Additionally, this method's efficiency might be diminished by unfavourable meteorological circumstances like thick smoke or heavy fog, which can obscure flames and reduce their visibility.	Moderate	In real-time fire detection and active fire monitoring, flame and smoke detection are especially helpful. It offers immediate information on the location and severity of the fire, facilitating quick response actions.
GIS Integration	The availability and accuracy of geographic data are crucial for GIS integration, despite the fact that it provides strong data management and decision-making skills. It might be difficult to find current, high-quality data, especially in rural or places with poor data coverage. In some situations, the processing and administration of massive volumes of geographic data may be constrained by the need for computational resources and expertise.	High	GIS integration is useful for long-term fire management plans, strategic planning, post-fire analysis, and fire mapping and visualisation. It offers a thorough analysis of the fire situation, assisting with resource allocation and well-informed decisionmaking.
Deep Learning	Convolutional neural networks (CNNs), one type of deep learning technology, have strong analytical skills. To obtain high accuracy, a substantial amount of labelled training data is necessary, which is one of the major restrictions. It might be difficult and time-consuming to collect this information for the purpose of detecting forest fires. Deep learning algorithms can also be computationally demanding, requiring strong hardware resources for both training and inference. This may restrict the realtime use of these models in resource-constrained UAV systems.	High	Deep learning is very helpful in automating fire detection, analysing photos taken by UAVs, and accurately recognising patterns connected to fires. It increases the effectiveness of UAV systems and offers insightful information on monitoring and detecting fires.
Machine Learning	The performance of machine learning algorithms depends on the availability of extensive and representative training data. Acquiring broad and high-quality datasets that record a variety of climatic circumstances and fire occurrences might be difficult when it comes to detecting forest fires. The calibre and representativeness of the training data can have an impact on the accuracy and generalizability of machine learning models. In order to maintain optimal performance over time, model retraining may also be required on a regular basis.	Moderate	Utilising both past and current sensor data, machine learning can forecast the likelihood of a fire occurring and give early warning systems. By facilitating prompt reaction actions and resource allocation, it supports proactive fire management tactics.
IoT Integration	Even while IoT integration improves real-time monitoring capabilities, it is dependent on reliable network access, which can be difficult in rural or heavily wooded locations where fires frequently break out. The timely transmission of real-time data from IoT devices on UAVs may be hampered by a lack of network coverage or inconsistent connections, which might have an impact on the efficiency of fire detection and response activities.	Moderate	Real-time environmental monitoring made possible by IoT integration in UAV systems provides speedy analysis of changing fire conditions. It facilitates quick data transfer and improves situational awareness, supporting wise decision-making and effective resource management.

Table 3. Comparison of different UAV based algorithms based on accuracy

Algorithm	Publication Year	Accuracy (F1 Score)	Reference Titles
Deep CNN	2022	98%	"A Review on Early Wildfire Detection from Unmanned Aerial Vehicles using Deep Learning-based Computer Vision Algorithms" (Bouguettaya, 2022)
YOLOv3	2022	91%	"A Review on Early Wildfire Detection from Unmanned Aerial Vehicles using Deep Learning-based Computer Vision Algorithms" (Bouguettaya, 2022)
YOLOv3	2019	81%	"A Deep Learning Based Forest Fire Detection Approach Using UAV and YOLOv3" (Jiao, 2019)
YOLOv3	2020	81%	"A YOLOv3-based Learning Strategy for Real-time UAV-based Forest Fire Detection" (Jiao, 2020)

With respect to their publication years and related accuracy in terms of F1 scores, the table presents a comparative analysis of several wildfire detection systems. With varied degrees of precision, these algorithms—Deep CNN and YOLOv3—have demonstrated their efficacy in precisely detecting wildfires when applied to the crucial task of early wildfire detection using unmanned aerial vehicles. This comparison provides important context for understanding how techniques and technology are developing to improve forest fire prevention and management.

3.2 Comparison of UAV Hybrid Techniques Based on Computational Power

The accessibility of adequate computing power is essential for the effective application of UAV-based forest fire detection. In order to identify and monitor forest fires and enable early identification and efficient management, UAVs with superior computing capabilities are essential. These UAV systems analyse fire patterns, evaluate dangers, and give situational awareness in real time by combining data from a variety of sources, including photography, sensor readings, and geographic information. Several variables affect the amount of computing power needed for UAV-based forest fire detection. First and foremost, an important factor is the complexity of the algorithms employed for fire detection and analysis. To analyse enormous datasets and extract valuable insights, advanced algorithms like deep learning and machine learning approaches sometimes need a lot of computer power. Based on past data and current sensor readings, these algorithms allow for the detection of trends connected to fires and the forecast of fire occurrences. Second, the amount of processing power required depends on the volume and complexity of the data being processed. High-resolution imaging, sensor data from multiple sources, and geographic data are all collected by UAVs; this data must all be processed and analysed in real-time or very close to it. For early fire detection and decision-making, it is essential to be able to manage and analyse this data rapidly and efficiently. The required processing power is also influenced by the desired level of accuracy and effectiveness. Higher accuracy and precision in fire detection frequently require the use of more complicated algorithms and in-depth analysis, which in turn requires more processing power. It is essential to carefully evaluate the computing power needs for various use cases and modify the system in accordance with the results in order to ensure the effective deployment of UAV-based forest fire detection. This entails taking into account the UAV platform's computational capabilities, including memory size, parallel computing capabilities, and onboard computer processing power. Optimizing the performance of fire detection systems and cutting processing time need the effective use of computer resources. the necessity of taking into account processing capacity in the system design by stressing the computational elements of UAV-based forest fire detection. UAVs can greatly help to the prompt discovery and control of forest fires by using sufficient processing capacity, minimizing possible damages, and enabling efficient response tactics to safeguard people and the environment. Computational power of different methods are shown in Figure 14. Table 3 shows the comparison of different methods on various parameters.

Table 4. Comparison of different UAV based fire forest detection techniques based on computational power

Algorithm	Computational Power Required	Computational Techniques	UAV Type Used	Computational Power Calculation	Research Paper References
Deep Learning (CNN)	High	GPU acceleration	DJI Phantom 4 Pro	Number of layers × Number of neurons per layer × FLOPs	(Catal, 2020; Sharma, 2017; Chen, 2018; Jiao, 2019; Ghali, 2022; Nguyen, 2021; Zhang, 2016; Jiao, 2020)
Machine Learning	Moderate to High	Parallel processing, distributed computing	DJI Matrice 600 Pro	Number of training samples × Number of features × FLOPs	(Chen, 2018; Ghali, 2022; Nguyen, 2021; Yang, 2023; Bouguettaya, 2022; Almeida, 2021; Yuan, 2015; Yuan, 2017)
Image Processing	Moderate	Image filtering, feature extraction	DJI Inspire 2	DJI Inspire 2 Number of pixels × Number of image filters × FLOPs	(Ghali, 2022; Islam, 2019; Almeida, 2021; Grammalidis, 2011)
Data Analysis	Moderate	Statistical analysis, data mining	DJI Mavic 2 Pro	Number of data points × Number of features × FLOPs	(Ghali, 2022; Yang, 2023; Grammalidis, 2011; Yuan, 2015; Yuan, 2017)
Pattern Recognition	Moderate	Feature detection, classification	Parrot Bebop 2	Number of input patterns × Number of pattern features × FLOPs	(Ghali, 2022; Nguyen, 2021; Yang, 2023; Grammalidis, 2011; Yuan, 2015; Yuan, 2017)
AI Algorithms	High	Neural network training, model optimization	Yuneec Typhoon H Pro	Number of training samples × Number of model	(Chen, 2018; Jiao, 2019; Jiao, 2020; Bouguettaya, 2022; Yuan, 2019)

Figure 13. Computational power required for different algorithms

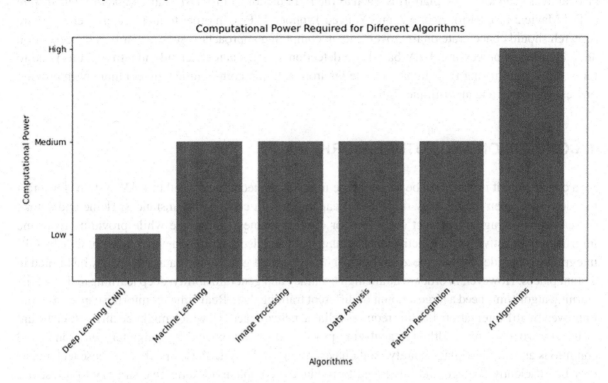

Depending on the particular methods used, different algorithms for UAV-based forest fire detection need different amounts of computer resources. Convolutional Neural Networks (CNN) and other deep learning algorithms often require a lot of processing power because of their intricate network structures and extensive training procedures. Machine learning algorithms demand a moderate to high level of computational capacity, particularly when distributed computing or parallel processing methods are applied for effective training. Moderate computational capacity is required for operations like image filtering, feature extraction, statistical analysis, and data mining when using image processing and data analysis techniques. Pattern recognition algorithms, which deal with activities like feature identification and categorization, also come under the category of moderate computational power. AI algorithms use a wide range of methodologies and may demand different amounts of computing resources. Calculations based on variables such as the number of layers, neurons, training samples, pixels, data points, and FLOPs may be used to determine the computing capacity for each method. There are many different types of UAVs that may be utilized for implementation, with DJI Phantom 4 Pro, DJI Matrice 600 Pro, DJI Inspire 2, DJI Mavic 2 Pro, Parrot Bebop 2, and Yuneec Typhoon H Pro being a few examples. The estimation of computing power offers information about the need for resources and aids in improving algorithm performance.

Conclusion: Depending on the specific approaches employed, the computational power needed for UAV-based forest fire detection systems can vary, with deep learning algorithms often requiring significant computational resources. Moderate computational capacity is needed for machine learning, image processing, and pattern recognition algorithms. For algorithm performance and resource allocation, estimation and optimization of computing resources are essential. For specialized fire detection capabilities, it's critical to use suitable UAV platforms, such as the DJI Phantom 4 Pro, DJI Matrice 600 Pro, DJI Inspire 2, DJI Mavic 2 Pro, Parrot Bebop 2, and Yuneec Typhoon H Pro. In order to increase efficiency, future research should concentrate on improvements in computing approaches, such as hardware acceleration and cloud-based processing. UAV-based fire detection systems can efficiently identify and respond to forest fires, minimizing their impact on the environment and communities, by continually improving processing power and algorithmic skills.

4. CONCLUSION AND FUTURE WORK

As a conclusion, it is critical to be aware of the limits of the techniques used in UAV systems for forest fire detection, even though they offer useful capabilities. In certain circumstances, flame and smoke detection may struggle to detect early fires or covered flames and smoke while providing real-time information on active fires. Effective data management and decision-making are made possible by GIS integration, but it depends on the availability and precision of geographic data, which may be limited in distant places. However, in order to attain high accuracy and generalizability, deep learning and machine learning algorithms need a large amount of different training data. Real-time monitoring capabilities are improved by IoT integration, but this requires reliable network access, which might be difficult in distant or heavily wooded areas. Although analyzing procedures are automated by computers, environmental conditions and varying image quality might have an impact. Despite these drawbacks, these techniques may be efficiently coupled and integrated to produce a complete and effective strategy to forest fire detection, enabling prompt and precise reaction measures that are suited to each unique circumstance. The efficiency of UAV-based forest fire detection and control activities may be greatly improved with additional improvements and a comprehensive integration of various techniques, helping to preserve priceless ecosystems and safeguard people and property.

Unmanned aerial vehicles (UAVs) have come a long way in terms of detecting forest fires, but there is still room for development. More accurate fire information may be obtained by improving sensor technology, for as by employing sophisticated multispectral and thermal sensors. By creating autonomous UAV systems using AI algorithms, complex forest settings can support autonomous flying and adaptive reactions. For thorough fire detection, collaborative UAV networks and data fusion approaches can enhance coverage, data collecting, and analysis. Real-time data transmission may be improved by enhancing interoperability and communication between UAVs and ground-based command centers. For system performance evaluation and algorithm improvement, field testing and validation are crucial.

REFERENCES

Alejo, D., & Cobano, J. A. (2014). Optimal Reciprocal Collision Avoidance with mobile and static obstacles for multi-UAV systems. In *2014 International Conference on Unmanned Aircraft Systems (ICUAS)*. IEEE. 10.1109/ICUAS.2014.6842383

Almeida, J. S., Jagatheesaperumal, S. K., Nogueira, F. G., & Albuquerque, V. H. C. (2021). *EdgeFireSmoke++: A novel lightweight algorithm for real-time forest fire detection and visualization using internet of things-human machine interface*. Department of Electrical Engineering, Federal University of Ceará.

Arbez, M., Birot, Y., & Carnus, J. M. (Eds.). (2002). Risk Management and Sustainable Forestry. In *EFI Proceedings No. 45*. European Forest Institute.

Bouguettaya, A., Zarzour, H., Taberkit, A. M., & Kechida, A. (2022). *A review on early wildfire detection from unmanned aerial vehicles using deep learning-based computer vision algorithms. Research Centre in Industrial Technologies (CRTI)*. Department of Mathematics and Computer Science, Souk Ahras University.

Catal Reis, H. (2020). *Detection of forest fire using deep convolutional neural networks with a transfer learning approach*. Department of Geomatics Engineering, Gumushane University.

Cazaurang, F., Cohen, K., & Kumar, M. (2020). *Multi-Rotor Platform-based UAV Systems*.

Chandler, C., Cheney, P., Thomas, P., Trabaud, L., & Williams, D. (1983). *Fire in forestry*. Forest fire management and organization.

Chen, X., Zhao, M., & Yin, L. (2020). *Dynamic Path Planning of the UAV Avoiding Static and Moving Obstacles*.

Chen, Y., Zhang, Y., Xin, J., Yi, Y., Liu, D., & Liu, H. (2018). A UAV-based Forest Fire Detection Algorithm Using Convolutional Neural Network. In *Proceedings of the 37th Chinese Control Conference*. IEEE. 10.23919/ChiCC.2018.8484035

Chung, Y.-S., & Le, H. V. (1984). Detection of forest-fire smoke plumes by satellite imagery. *Atmospheric Environment, 18*(10), 2143–2151. doi:10.1016/0004-6981(84)90201-4

Davis, K. P. (1959). *Forest fire, control, and use*. SRP.

Dimitropoulos, K., Tsalakanidou, F., & Grammalidis, N. (2012). Flame detection for video-based early fire warning systems and 3D visualization of fire propagation. In *13th IASTED International Conference on Computer Graphics and Imaging (CGIM 2012)*. ACTA Press. 10.2316/P.2012.779-011

Dimopoulou, M., & Giannikos, I. (2004). Towards an integrated framework for forest fire control. *European Journal of Operational Research, 152*(2), 476–486. doi:10.1016/S0377-2217(03)00038-9

Espinoza-Fraire, A. T., Dzul López, A. E. (2023). *Design of Control Laws and State Observers for Fixed-Wing UAVs*.

Ghali, R., Akhloufi, M. A., & Mseddi, W. S. (2022). Deep Learning and Transformer Approaches for UAV-Based Wildfire Detection and Segmentation. *Sensors (Basel), 22*(5), 1977. doi:10.339022051977 PMID:35271126

Grammalidis, N. C., Dimitropoulos, K., Tsalakanidou, F., Kose, K., Gunay, O., Gouverneur, B., Torri, D., Kuruoglu, E., & Tozzi, S. (2011). A multi-sensor network for the protection of cultural heritage. In *2011 19th IEEE European Signal Processing Conference*. IEEE.

Halpern, C. B., & Antos, J. A. (2022). Burn severity and pre-fire seral state interact to shape vegetation responses to fire in a young, western Cascade Range Forest. *Forest Ecology and Management, 507*, 120028. doi:10.1016/j.foreco.2022.120028

Ham, Y., Han, K. K., Lin, J. J., & Golparvar-Fard, M. (2016). Visual monitoring of civil infrastructure systems via camera-equipped Unmanned Aerial Vehicles (UAVs): A review of related works. *Visualization in Engineering, 4*(1).

FAO. (1999). *International Handbook on Forest Fire Protection Technical guide for the countries of the Mediterranean basin.* Ministère de L'aménagement du Territoire et de L'environnement (France). F.A.O. (Food and Agriculture Organization of the United Nations).

Islam, S., Huang, Q., Afghah, F., Fule, P., & Razi, A. (2019). Fire Frontline Monitoring by Enabling UAV-Based Virtual Reality with Adaptive Imaging Rate. In *2019 53rd Asilomar Conference on Signals, Systems, and Computers.*

Jaiswal, R. K., Mukherjee, S., Raju, K. D., & Saxena, R. (2002). Forest fire risk zone mapping from satellite imagery and GIS. *International Journal of Applied Earth Observation and Geoinformation, 4*(1), 1–10. doi:10.1016/S0303-2434(02)00006-5

Jiao, Z., Zhang, Y., Mu, L., Xin, J., Jiao, S., Liu, H., & Liu, D. (2020). A YOLOv3-based Learning Strategy for Real-time UAV-based Forest Fire Detection. In *2020 Chinese Control And Decision Conference (CCDC 2020).* IEEE. 10.1109/CCDC49329.2020.9163816

Jiao, Z., Zhang, Y., Mu, L., Xin, J., Yi, Y., & Liu, D. (2019). A Deep Learning Based Forest Fire Detection Approach Using UAV and YOLOv3. In *2019 1st International Conference on Industrial Artificial Intelligence (IAI).* IEEE. 10.1109/ICIAI.2019.8850815

Kraus, D., & Schmerbeck, J. (2021). Forest Fire Management Manual, India, Himalayas. In Indo-German Biodiversity Programme Conservation and Sustainable Use of Biodiversity in India. Himachal Pradesh Forest Ecosystem Services Project (HP-FES).

Mohsan, S. A. H., Khan, M. A., Noor, F., Ullah, I., & Alsharif, M. H. (2022). Towards the Unmanned Aerial Vehicles (UAVs): A Comprehensive Review. *Drones (Basel), 6*(6), 147. doi:10.3390/drones6060147

Nguyen, A. Q., Nguyen, H. T., Tran, V. C., Pham, H. X., & Pestana, J. (2021). A Visual Real-time Fire Detection using Single Shot MultiBox Detector for UAV-based Fire Surveillance. In *2020 IEEE Eighth International Conference on Communications and Electronics (ICCE).* IEEE. 10.1109/ICCE48956.2021.9352080

Rauste, Y., Herland, E., Frelander, H., Soini, K., Kuoremaki, T., & Ruokari, A. (2010). Satellite-based forest fire detection for fire control in boreal forests. *International Journal of Remote Sensing, 18*(12), 2641–2656. doi:10.1080/014311697217512

Sharma, J., Granmo, O.-C., Goodwin, M., & Fidje, J. T. (2017). Deep convolutional neural networks for fire detection in images. In *International Conference on Engineering Applications of Neural Networks.* Springer. 10.1007/978-3-319-65172-9_16

Stephens, S. L. (2005). Forest fire causes and extent on United States Forest Service lands. *International Journal of Wildland Fire, 14*(3), 213–222. doi:10.1071/WF04006

Tadesse, E., & Seboko, B. (2013). *Forest/Wildland Fire Prevention and Control For Sustainable Forest Management. Manual.* Hawassa University, Wondo Genet College of Forestry and Natural Resources.

Xiao-rui, T., Mcrae, D. J., Li-fu, S., Ming-yu, W., & Hong, L. (2005). Satellite remote-sensing technologies used in forest fire management. *Journal of Forestry Research*, *16*(1), 73–78. doi:10.1007/BF02856861

Yang, X., Hua, Z., Zhang, L., Zhang, L., Fan, X., Zhang, L., Ye, Q., & Fu, L. (2023). *Preferred vector machine for forest fire detection*. Institute of Forest Resource Information Techniques, Chinese Academy of Forestry. doi:10.1016/j.patcog.2023.109722

Yuan, C., Liu, Z. X., & Zhang, Y. M. (2017). Aerial images-based forest fire detection for firefighting using optical remote sensing techniques and unmanned aerial vehicles. *Journal of Intelligent & Robotic Systems*, *88*(2-4), 635–654. doi:10.100710846-016-0464-7

Yuan, C., Liu, Z. X., & Zhang, Y. M. (2019). Learning-based smoke detection for unmanned aerial vehicles applied to forest fire surveillance. *Journal of Intelligent & Robotic Systems*, *93*(1-2), 337–349. doi:10.100710846-018-0803-y

Yuan, C., Zhang, Y. M., & Liu, Z. X. (2015). A survey on technologies for automatic forest fire monitoring, detection, and fighting using unmanned aerial vehicles and remote sensing techniques. *Canadian Journal of Forest Research*, *45*(7), 783–792. doi:10.1139/cjfr-2014-0347

Zhang, Q. J., Xu, J. L., Xu, L., & Guo, H. F. (2016). Deep convolutional neural networks for forest fire detection. In *2016 International Forum on Management, Education and Information Technology Application*. Atlantis Press. 10.2991/ifmeita-16.2016.105

194

Chapter 8
Comprehensive Framework for Control and Coordination of UAV Swarms in Wildfire Management

Sanoufar Abdul Azeez

Kerala University of Digital Sciences, Innovation, and Technology, India

Sumedha Arora

Kerala University of Digital Sciences, Innovation, and Technology, India

ABSTRACT

Wildfires pose a significant threat to ecosystems and human lives, underscoring the necessity of early detection and rapid response to mitigate the devastating effects of these fires. In recent times, advancements in unmanned aerial vehicle (UAV) technology have provided new avenues for enhancing wildfire monitoring and response. This chapter explores the potential of an innovative framework for UAV swarms that can be controlled and coordinated autonomously for managing wildfires. The comprehensive framework also integrates other technologies such as computer vision, sensor networks, swarm intelligence, and reinforcement learning algorithms to enable collaborative and autonomous UAV swarm operation. The framework addresses navigation challenges in dense forest environments, facilitates swarm coordination, and enables data-driven decision-making for wildfires and diverse real-world applications. This chapter also provides insights into the method of implementation in a simulated 100X100 2D grid environment, showcasing its potential and effectiveness in realistic scenarios.

DOI: 10.4018/979-8-3693-0578-2.ch008

Copyright © 2024, IGI Global. Copying or distributing in print or electronic forms without written permission of IGI Global is prohibited.

1. INTRODUCTION

In recent days wildfires have become increasingly prevalent and destructive, posing significant challenges to the environment, wildlife, human lives, and infrastructure. Early detection and efficient monitoring are critical to mitigating the devastating effects of these fires. The timely response to wildfires can help prevent the spread of the fire and minimize its impact on the ecosystem and human communities. The development of unmanned aerial vehicles (UAVs) in recent years has opened up new possibilities for monitoring and responding to wildfires. UAV systems have emerged as a promising technology for enhancing forest fire monitoring and response and they have attracted researchers' interest in several aspects, including forest monitoring, fire detection, and fighting applications.

This chapter, analyzes the potential of an innovative architectural framework for wildfire monitoring that harnesses the power of controlled coordination autonomous drone swarms. The multi-drone systems play a crucial role in enhancing the efficiency and effectiveness of missions combining various cutting-edge technologies further detailed in this chapter. It aims to revolutionize the way wildfires are detected, monitored, and mitigated.

1.1 Problem Statement

The increasing frequency and intensity of wildfires necessitate an urgent need for advanced monitoring and disaster[14] response systems. Traditional methods of wildfire monitoring face several challenges including limited coverage, delayed response time, and the inability to efficiently monitor large forested areas, real-time situational monitoring, damage assessment, and resource allocation. Additionally, the unpredictable nature of wildfires, with rapidly changing patterns and behaviors, makes it challenging for human responders to keep pace and make informed decisions in real time.

To address these challenges, the proposed architectural framework leverages the capabilities of autonomous drone swarms to provide real-time monitoring and rapid response to wildfire events. Employing computer vision, sensor fusion, and SI, RL, and machine learning, algorithms, the aim is to enhance wildfire monitoring accuracy, speed, and efficiency, minimizing the ecological and socioeconomic impact. These systems are also capable enough to adopt various roles in addressing specific challenges and requirements.

The objectives of this chapter are to outline the shortcomings of traditional forest fire monitoring methods emphasizing more innovative solutions for reliable detection of wildfire in a complex, noisy, potentially false positive environment. Energy optimization for internet drones is also a major concern and the

Further in this chapter it details how intelligent drone swarms can significantly enhance world fire management. By leveraging AI technologies such as computer vision, machine learning, Swarm Intelligence[12], Reinforcement Learning, and Sensor Fusion[19] to enhance the accuracy, speed, and efficiency of situational monitoring and real-time damage assessment during forest fires. This approach aims to detect fires early and facilitate rapid response thereby minimizing ecological and socioeconomic impacts.

1.2 Novelty of the Proposed Framework

This chapter tackles a fundamental challenge in the realm of drone-assisted forest fire monitoring—the autonomous navigation and coordination of drone swarms. The gravity of this challenge is underlined by the chapter's central focus on eliminating human control and emphasizing the need for self-navigation and inter-drone communication. Achieving such autonomy necessitates the development of efficient algorithms that can control and coordinate drones in various environmental settings, including forests. This level of efficiency is crucial for drone swarms to promptly detect and respond to forest fire events.

To achieve a substantial level of autonomy in drone swarms, the chapter puts forth the adoption of collective intelligence behavior. This behavior, characterized by decentralization, self-organization, and adaptability to dynamic situations, becomes imperative for effective hotspot detection and rapid response in forest fire events.

Acknowledging the complexity of the Control and Coordination of a swarm of aerial drone, that this is a multifaceted problem requiring interdisciplinary integration and the development of advanced algorithms. These algorithms, as highlighted, are geared towards optimizing drone behavior to ensure not only effective hotspot detection[15] but also swift responses in the face of evolving forest fire scenarios.

The proposed framework emerges as an innovative integration of Reinforcement Learning (RL) and Swarm Intelligence (SI) algorithms. By combining RL's strategic decision-making prowess with SI's decentralized self-organization, the framework aims to enhance swarm autonomy and agility.

Ultimately, this chapter unfolds a step-by-step methodology for controlling and coordinating UAV swarms. While the potential of drones for wildfire monitoring[16] is clear, the chapter emphasizes the need for further research and development to improve the methodology's effectiveness. This effort has the potential to enhance the usefulness of swarms in a variety of real-world applications. Moreover, this chapter explores the navigation of aerial swarms in complex wild environments, leveraging the autonomy of individual drones. Beyond its immediate application, this holistic study is positioned as a significant contribution to the advancement of wildfire management[17] practices. The research seeks to transcend existing limitations and enrich the practicality of swarm technology, thus offering a nuanced perspective on the potential applications of this technology in various scenarios.

Figure 1. UAV swarms in action during a wildfire: A creative visualization

2. REVIEW OF RELATED WORKS

Internet of Robotic Things Based Autonomous Fire Fighting Mobile Robot by Anantha Raj and Srivani(2018) uses a path planning algorithm to navigate a mobile robot to a fire. The robot can also perform firefighting actions, such as spraying water or foam, and can stream video of the fire back to a control center. However, the robot is limited to early-stage firefighting actions and cannot extinguish large fires.

AI for UAV-Assisted IoT Applications: A Comprehensive Review by N. Cheng et al.(2023) uses a swarm of autonomous drones to monitor and mitigate forest fires. The solution uses AI for fire detection, tracking fire spread, and assessing damage.. However, the paper does not provide a scalability analysis for the proposed system.

A Coalition Formation Approach to Coordinated Task Allocation in Heterogeneous UAV Networks by Fatemeh Afghah et al. (2018) uses coalition formation approaches to allocate tasks to a swarm of drones. The drones can perform a variety of tasks, such as firefighting, search and rescue, and surveillance. However, the paper does not consider the time-consuming nature of coalition formation algorithms or their computational complexity.

Wildfire Monitoring in Remote Areas using Autonomous Unmanned Aerial Vehicles by Afghah, F. et al. (2019) Proposes a drone-based wildfire monitoring system for remote and hard-to-reach areas using autonomous UAVs. It does not evaluate the system's performance in real-world wildfire scenarios.

Distributed Control for Groups of Unmanned Aerial Vehicles Performing Surveillance Missions and Providing Relay Communication Network Services by de Moraes, R. S. et al.(2018) Presents an autonomous and distributed movement coordination algorithm for UAV swarms in communication relay networks and surveillance missions. Primarily addresses surveillance missions and communication, not wildfire management.

Fire Detection Using Unmanned Aerial Vehicle by Nabeel, M et al. (2023) proposes a drone-based wildfire monitoring system for remote and hard-to-reach areas. Tested, system achieving 99.79% accuracy in detecting fires using a pre-trained CNN model (MobileNetv2). It Uses a distributed leader-follower coalition formation model for efficient coverage.

Energy-efficient deployment of IoT applications in remote rural areas using UAV networks by Galan-Jiménez et al. (2022) address IoT application deployment in remote areas, lacking a thorough examination of real-world challenges like scalability and reliability. The simulation's insights might not fully represent the complexities of practical implementation in diverse terrains, and the paper doesn't extensively discuss hurdles associated with deploying UAVs in challenging conditions, limiting its applicability to dynamic rural environments. Economic aspects and long-term cost-effectiveness of maintaining UAVs in remote areas remain unexplored in the paper.

Optimal energy management of UAV-based cellular networks powered by solar panels and batteries: Formulation and solutions Amorosi et al. (2019) offer a detailed optimization model for energy management in UAV-based networks but overlook real-world challenges like adverse weather or technical malfunctions. The trade-off analysis could benefit from considering additional variables such as terrain complexity, impacting the practicality of the proposed solution. The paper lacks exploration of security and privacy concerns associated with deploying UAVs in rural areas, raising doubts about the model's feasibility in addressing these critical issues. The evaluation's focus on representative case studies may limit the findings' generalizability across diverse geographical and environmental contexts.

Table 1. Summarized review of related works

Author	Summary	Limitations
Raj, P. A. et al.(2018)	Proposes integrating an autonomous firefighting mobile robot into traditional fire safety IoT systems for early intervention.	The article does not discuss the challenges of implementing such a system in real-world environments, such as cost, scalability, and reliability. Focuses on specific aspects of firefighting, lacking a comprehensive approach. Does not explicitly address autonomy and scalability for large wildfires.
N. Cheng et al.(2023)	Provides a comprehensive analysis of AI's impact on key IoT technologies, tasks, and applications in UAV-assisted networks.	The article is primarily theoretical and does not include any case studies or empirical results.- Lacks a holistic approach to wildfire management. and not a comprehensive wildfire solution
Fatemeh Afghah et al.(2018)	Introduces a leader-follower coalition formation model where the first UAV locating a target becomes the leader, forming a group of follower UAVs to complete tasks.	The article does not consider the impact of communication constraints and environmental factors on the performance of the proposed coalition formation algorithm.Only Focused on monitoring rather than a comprehensive wildfire management system
Afghah, F. et al. (2019)	Proposes a drone-based wildfire monitoring system for remote and hard-to-reach areas using autonomous UAVs.	The article does not evaluate the system's performance in real-world wildfire scenarios.
de Moraes, R. S. et al.(2023)	Presents an autonomous and distributed movement coordination algorithm for UAV swarms in communication relay networks and surveillance missions.	Primarily addresses surveillance missions and communication, not wildfire management.
Nabeel, M et al.(2023)	Presents a tested system achieving 99.79% accuracy in detecting fires using a pre-trained CNN model (MobileNetv2).	The article does not evaluate the system's performance in challenging environmental conditions, such as smoke and fog. Limited discussion on scalability and autonomy for large wildfires.
J Galán-Jiménez et al.(2022)	Proposes an UAV-based network architecture and an energy-efficient algorithm to deploy IoT applications Decomposes IoT applications into microservices, deploying them across a subset of UAVs to overcome limitations imposed by individual UAVs' battery and computation constraints. This prevents running the entire IoT application on a single UAV, which could result in suboptimal outcomes.	- Lack of consideration for scalability and reliability in diverse environments. - Simulation-based evaluation might not fully reflect practical complexities. - Insufficient discussion on potential hurdles and trade-offs in deploying UAVs in challenging conditions. - Limited exploration of economic aspects and cost-effectiveness in maintaining UAVs in remote areas.
Amorosi et al.(2019)	Focuses on maximizing energy stored in UAVs and ground sites by optimizing UAV mission scheduling over space and time. Decomposition-Based Approach: Proposes a decomposition-based strategy to address the complexity of the problem. Genetic Algorithm: Introduces a novel genetic algorithm to optimize energy storage and coverage.	- Assumption of an ideal scenario without explicit consideration of real-world challenges like wild fire monitoring. - Inadequate inclusion of additional variables, like terrain complexity, in the trade-off analysis. - Lack of discussion on security and privacy concerns related to UAV deployment in rural areas. - Potential limitations in the generalizability of findings due to the focus on specific case studies.

Upon comprehensively reviewing related works in UAV swarm technology for wildfire management, several key limitations and challenges emerge concerning the proposed Aerial UAV Swarm Architecture. First and foremost, the existing literature predominantly emphasizes only on specifc aspects of firefighting rather than a comprehensive approach, such as forest fire detection and monitoring, with limited focus on extinguishing large fires. Scalability becomes a critical concern, necessitating effective operation with a substantial number of UAVs in intricate and dynamic environments. The computational complexity of coalition formation algorithms raises challenges, urging the development of efficient real-time implementations. Moreover, the cost and complexity of ground-based systems must be carefully considered for the deployment of an affordable and user-friendly UAV swarm system. Collision-free path planning remains a formidable task, particularly in dynamic wildfire zones, calling for the development of real-time algorithms capable of handling numerous UAVs in complex environments. Additional challenges include establishing reliable communication and coordination mechanisms in harsh wildfire environments, ensuring security and privacy to guard against unauthorized access, and addressing public concerns to gain acceptance for UAV swarm use in wildfire management. Despite these challenges, the Aerial UAV Swarm Architecture holds transformative potential, and by addressing these limitations, a robust and effective system can be developed to revolutionize wildfire management, ultimately saving lives and property.

3. METHODOLOGY

The proposed methodology leverages the strengths of UAV swarm that controls and coordinates its action with the help of Swarm Intelligence and Reinforcement Learning algorithms. Moreover, the UAVs use Computer vision algorithms to detect and localize forest fires using onboard multiple cameras for navigation and thermal cameras of hot spot identification in real-time, various onboard sensors are used in the system like CO_2 sensors (non-dispersive infrared (NDIR) sensors) that can measure as lower up to 5% CO_2 levels, Barometric pressure sensors, humidity, and mini ultrasonic wind sensors, to collect real-time sensor fusion data to enhance situational awareness about the environment, that will help to firefighters and other first-line responders to integrate remedial actions, using the same data along with the collection GIS information about the spot, the machine learning algorithms can generate 3D models of the affected area for further analysis and can predict fire behavior and its spread. Based on the insights the firefighting team can strategize task allocation, resource utilization, diagnosis, monitoring, fighting, and risk mitigation. Control and Coordination of Swarms are done through the combination of model-free RL that enables drones to navigate complex environments and make intelligent decisions, and swarm intelligence algorithms facilitate optimized communication and collaboration between the UAVs of its actions.

Figure 2. UAV swarms collectively gathering real-time data

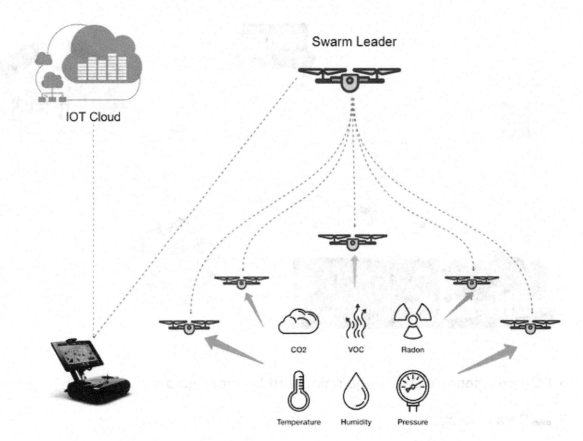

The proposed forest fire detection and response framework (Figure 2, Figure 3) commences with a leader patrolling UAV, equipped with thermal cameras and computer vision capabilities, conducting routine forest patrols while continuously capturing environmental images or videos. Real-time computer vision algorithms analyze this data to detect signs of a forest fire, like smoke or flames, subsequently notifying the ground station control with precise fire details. Upon receiving this alert, the ground station assesses the situation and instructs selected follower drones to autonomously navigate to the fire's location using advanced obstacle avoidance techniques. Swarm intelligence algorithms ensure coordinated drone movement, establishing specific formations for optimized monitoring. These formations facilitate real-time data collection, including fire size, intensity, and environmental conditions, transmitted via reliable communication networks. Machine learning algorithms process this data alongside historical records and weather conditions to predict the fire's future behavior and spread. The ground station then generates recommendations for mitigation strategies, such as resource allocation or deploying firefighting drones, if necessary, to effectively combat the fire.

Figure 3. Comprehensive process flow of proposed forest fire monitoring UAVs and risk mitigation

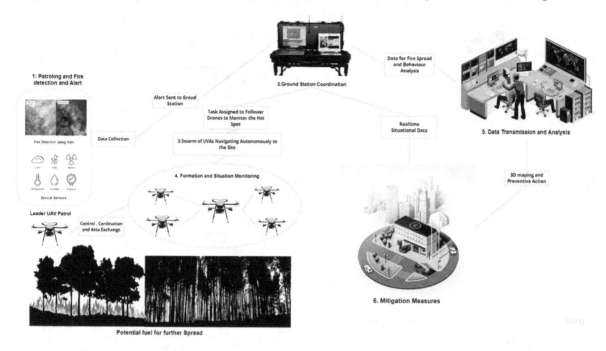

3.1 Comprehensive Data Acquisition and Sensor Fusion

3.1.1 Data Collection

The first step is to collect various data from the forest environment using the UAV swarm. This data can be collected using a variety of sensors, such as thermal cameras, air quality sensors, and weather sensors. Drones can provide real-time information to firefighters and other first responders with information like

- **Fire Location:** Accurate mapping of the fire's location.
- **Fire Size:** Measuring the dimensions of the fire.
- **Fire Direction:** Determining the path and direction of fire spread.
- **Terrain Characteristics:** Assessing the topography and landscape ruggedness.
- **Weather Conditions:** Monitoring critical meteorological factors influencing fire behavior.

3.1.2 Sensor Selection

Choosing the right sensors is pivotal for accurate data collection in forest fire monitoring. The array of sensors includes:

- **Thermal Cameras:** To detect heat signatures, often indicative of fires.
- **Air Quality Sensors:** For measuring air pollutants, particularly in smoke-heavy environments.
- **Weather Sensors:** To monitor meteorological conditions like wind speed, humidity, and temperature.

- **GPS Sensors:** For tracking the drones' positions and fire locations.
- **Infrared Sensors:** To complement thermal cameras in detecting heat.
- **Gas Sensors:** For identifying specific gases associated with fires.

Data collected from different sensors can provide a comprehensive understanding of the fire situation, including its location, size, and intensity. Using the data, you can also determine what factors are contributing to the fire, such as weather conditions, fuel availability, and human activity. The data collected can be used to track the spread of the fire, predict its future behavior, and assess the risks associated with the spread to the surrounding area.

3.1.3 Strategic Information Gathering

UAV swarms are equipped with advanced sensors, including LiDAR (Light Detection and Ranging) and high-resolution cameras. This allows us to capture intricate topographical information, enabling us to:

- Assess terrain ruggedness.
- Identify potential obstacles.
- Determine proximity to critical infrastructure.
- Plan effective firefighting strategies.
- Identify safe access routes for first responders.

Fuel Types: A combination of optical cameras, multispectral sensors, and hyperspectral sensors on drones can capture detailed images of vegetation types. These sensors allow experts to identify and classify various fuel types based on their reflectance properties, aiding in assessing the fire's potential behavior and spread patterns.

Wind Levels: Drones can carry anemometers and wind sensors that measure wind speed and direction at different altitudes. By flying at different heights, drones can create a vertical profile of wind conditions, providing valuable insights into wind patterns that influence fire behavior.

Slope and Aspect: LiDAR sensors can accurately measure the slope and aspect of the terrain, creating detailed elevation models. This data, combined with imagery, helps experts understand how the landscape's features may affect fire progression, including uphill spread due to steep slopes.

Fuel Moisture: Near-infrared (NIR) and thermal sensors can assess the moisture content of vegetation. NIR sensors detect differences in reflectance related to moisture levels, while thermal sensors capture temperature variations that indicate moisture content. This information aids in evaluating the potential fire susceptibility of vegetation.

Temperature: Thermal cameras mounted on drones can measure ground temperatures and identify areas with higher heat signatures. By monitoring temperature variations, experts can infer the potential ignition risk and assess areas of active fire.

Relative Humidity: Weather sensors on drones can measure temperature and humidity levels at different altitudes. This data helps experts understand the atmospheric conditions affecting fuel moisture and the fire's potential to spread.

By fusing data from these different sensors, it is possible to create a more accurate and complete understanding of the fire situation. The use of swarm intelligence algorithms for sensor fusion can help to improve the efficiency and effectiveness of the process. Swarm intelligence algorithms can enable drones to collaborate and share information in real time. This can help to ensure that the data from all of the sensors is fused together quickly and accurately. It can be used to fuse data from multiple sensors, such as thermal cameras, air quality sensors, and weather sensors, to obtain a more accurate and comprehensive understanding of the fire situation. This can help to improve the efficiency and effectiveness of wildfire monitoring and suppression

3.2 Computer Vision for Fire Detection and Localization

The localization of wildfire detection and monitoring processes can be done using YOLOv7[18]. YOLOv7 is a real-time object detection algorithm that can be used to detect and localize fires in images and videos, which can identify the presence of smoke, flames, or other fire-related patterns in the images captured by drones. It is a Convolutional Neural Network (CNN) [20] that is trained on a large dataset of images that contain fires.

Computer Vision for Fire Detection: Computer vision[20] algorithms play a vital role in detecting and localizing fires. By analyzing the visual data captured by the drones, computer vision algorithms can identify the presence of smoke, flames, or other fire-related patterns. This early detection is crucial for prompt response and containment efforts.

Fire detection and localization: Is used to determine the precise location of the detected fire and localize the fire using the fused data[19]. This entails the utilization of computer vision algorithms adept at recognizing smoke, flames, or fire-induced patterns

- The fire detection and localization algorithms are used to detect fires early before they have a chance to spread.
- The algorithm is also used to localize fires, which will help firefighters to target their resources more effectively.
- The algorithm is used to keep track of the spread of fire and to predict their future behavior.

Below (Table 2) shown are the datasets that are all publicly available. They contain a variety of images of forest smoke, both with and without smoke, which will help the YOLOv7 model to learn to distinguish between the two.

Table 2. Forest fire smoke datasets and specification for YOLOv7 model training

Dataset	Smoke Images	Non-Smoke Images	Source
Wildfire Smoke Dataset	737	737	Roboflow
Forest Fire Smoke Dataset	1,000	1,000	Google
Smoke Detection Dataset	1,200	1,200	Kaggle
Forest Fire Detection Dataset	2,000	2,000	Flickr
Smoke and Haze Dataset	3,000	3,000	Bing

3.2.1 Fire Detection Process With YOLOv7

1. The drone captures an image or video of the forest area.
2. The image or video is pre-processed to remove noise and improve the contrast.
3. The image or video is passed to the YOLOv7 CNN.
4. The YOLOv7 CNN outputs a set of bounding boxes, each of which corresponds to a potential fire.
5. The bounding boxes are then passed to a post-processing algorithm to refine their positions and remove false positives.
6. The final output of the system is a list of detected fires, along with their locations and sizes.

The YOLOv7 algorithm has been shown to be very effective at detecting and localizing fires in a variety of conditions. It is also relatively fast, making it suitable for use in real-time applications.

Benefits of YOLOv7 for Wildfire Detection:

- **Real-Time Capability:** YOLOv7 operates in real-time, enabling immediate fire detection.
- **High Accuracy:** Achieving over 90% detection rate, YOLOv7 ensures reliability.
- **Robust Performance:** It maintains accuracy amidst noise and lighting variations.
- **Versatility:** Effective in various settings like forests, grasslands, and urban areas.

3.2.2 Enhanced Fire Detection With Thermal Imaging and Visual Spectrum Cameras

Using Thermal imaging cameras and visual spectrum cameras, (Figure 4) the fire detection and localization can be done more effective in a number of ways.

- **Thermal imaging cameras:** Thermal imaging cameras detect heat, which can be used to identify fires, even in smoke or darkness. Thermal imaging cameras can also be used to detect hotspots deep inside the peat, which are sometimes undetected by satellite sensors due to thick smoke or the small fires that limit satellite sensing capabilities.
- **Visual spectrum cameras:** Visual spectrum cameras detect visible light, which can be used to identify fires, smoke, and other fire-related features. Visual spectrum cameras can also be used to identify the size and shape of a fire, which can be helpful for firefighters to target their resources effectively.

Figure 4. Thermal imaging drones can read heat signatures and detect forest fires in the early stages (https://www.borneonaturefoundation.org/news/thermal-drone-ne w-technology-to-detect-fires/)

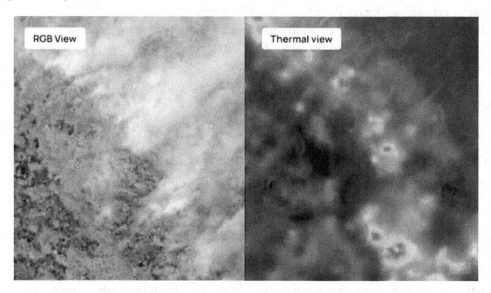

3.3 Machine Learning for Fire Prediction and Spread Analysis

Machine learning algorithms can analyze historical fire data, weather patterns, and other relevant variables to predict the behavior and spread of forest fires. By sharing their individual predictions and insights, the swarm can collectively generate more accurate predictions of fire behavior and spread. This collaborative approach enables better decision-making regarding resource allocation, evacuation routes, and firefighting strategies.

3.3.1 Predictive Analysis of Fire Behavior and Spread

The third step is to predict the behavior and spread of the fire using sensor fusion and machine learning algorithms. Analyzing the spread and behavior of wildfires involves considering various factors that collectively influence how a fire progresses and the extent of its impact This information can be used to make decisions about resource allocation, evacuation routes, and firefighting strategies.

- The fire prediction and spread analysis algorithms can be used to predict the behavior and spread of fires.
- This information can be used to make decisions about resource allocation, evacuation routes, and firefighting strategies.
- The algorithms can be used to improve the accuracy of the fire detection and localization algorithms.

3.3.2 Sensor Fusion for Comprehensive Monitoring

The heart of the methodology lies in the fusion of data from these diverse sensors. By integrating data intelligently in real-time using swarm intelligence algorithms, This process achieves several critical goals:

- **Enhanced Accuracy and Reliability:** The fusion process significantly improves data accuracy and reliability by cross-verifying information from various sources.
- **Identification of Patterns and Trends:** By amalgamating data allows discernment of different patterns and trends that individual sensors might not capture.
- **Improved Fire Detection and Localization:** The combined data boosts the precision of the fire detection and localization algorithms.
- **Informed Decision-Making:** This comprehensive dataset assists in strategic decision-making, such as firefighter deployment and resource allocation.

3.3.3 Data Processing and Analysis

The data collected by drones are transmitted in real-time to a ground station, where advanced algorithms process and do a predictive analysis based on the gathered information. Incorporating data from drones provides accurate, up-to-date, and comprehensive information about the fire's environment, aiding in early detection, assessment, and response. Machine learning techniques are employed to create predictive models that simulate fire behavior based on the collected data, allowing firefighters and emergency responders to make informed decisions about resource allocation, evacuation planning, and containment strategies.

3.4 Enhancing Coordination and Communication among Drones Using Swarm Intelligence

3.4.1 Swarm Intelligence Empowering Collaborative Drones

SI refers to the collective behavior exhibited by a group of autonomous agents, such as drones, that coordinate their actions to achieve a common goal. In the context of forest fire monitoring, swarm intelligence algorithms can enable drones to collaborate and share information in real time. Drones can communicate their observations, coordinate their movements, and distribute tasks efficiently. By leveraging swarm intelligence, drones can cover larger areas, enhance the accuracy of fire detection, and dynamically adapt their strategies based on the evolving fire situation.

3.4.2 Coordinated Communication

The fourth step is to coordinate and communicate between the drones in the swarm. This can be done using swarm intelligence algorithms, which can enable drones to collaborate and share information in real time.

- The coordination and communication between the drones in the swarm can help to improve the efficiency and effectiveness of the fire monitoring system.
- The drones can share information about the fire situation in real time, which can help them to work together to detect, localize, and track fires.
- The drones can also communicate with a ground control station, which can provide them with additional information and instructions.

3.5 Leveraging Leader-Follower Architecture and Efficient Task Management

3.5.1 Leader-Follower Architecture

A leader-follower architecture is a swarm intelligence concept where one or more drones take on the role of leaders, guiding the behavior of the other follower drones. In the context of autonomous drone swarms for forest fire monitoring, a leader-follower architecture can be employed to ensure coordinated and efficient swarm behavior. The leader drones can be responsible for high-level decision-making, such as task assignment, while the follower drones execute the assigned tasks. This hierarchical approach enables better coordination and organization within the swarm, enhancing the overall effectiveness of forest fire monitoring operations.

3.5.2 Optimized Task Assignment

The fifth step involves the precise assignment of tasks to the drones within the swarm. This strategic allocation can be achieved through the adoption of the leader-follower architecture, where selected drones assume leadership roles, guiding the behavior of the follower drones. This approach ensures that each drone is assigned tasks that align with their inherent capabilities, optimizing the fire monitoring system's efficiency and effectiveness.

- The task assignment process streamlines the deployment of drones, capitalizing on their strengths.
- This meticulous assignment enhances both the efficiency and effectiveness of the fire monitoring system.
- Variables such as fire location, size, and drone capabilities inform the task allocation process.

3.5.3 Synergy of Swarm Intelligence and AI Techniques

By incorporating swarm intelligence algorithms into the AI techniques discussed earlier, autonomous drone swarms can exhibit collective intelligence, adaptability, and robustness in forest fire monitoring. These algorithms foster collaborative decision-making, decentralized data analysis, and harmonized behavior among drones, mitigating the catastrophic impact of forest fires.

3.6 Autonomous Drone Navigation Enhanced by Reinforcement Learning

3.6.1 Model-Free Reinforcement Learning for Dynamic Navigation

The sixth step is to use a reinforcement learning algorithm that involves leveraging autonomous drones to navigate and adapt their flight paths within complex and unpredictable surroundings. By capitalizing on real-time sensor data and reinforcement signals - rewards for task completion or penalties for deviations - drones can refine their flight trajectories. This ability enables them to autonomously explore forest areas, identify fire-prone regions, and collect data without human intervention. This self-sufficiency significantly boosts the efficiency and scope of drones in wildfire monitoring endeavors. Model-free reinforcement learning algorithms act as the driving force behind training drones to navigate complex environments. This is accomplished by using rewards to reinforce positive behaviors and imposing penalties for deviations. Consequently, drones become adept at optimizing their trajectories based on real-time sensor data.

- Model-free reinforcement learning algorithms are pivotal for training drone performance.
- These algorithms significantly enhance the efficiency of drones in autonomously accomplishing tasks.
- A trial-and-error approach facilitates drones in mastering task execution with improved effectiveness.

3.6.2 ARS and ABC Optimization Strategies

Augmented Random Search (ARS): ARS is an optimization algorithm that involves randomly perturbing the parameters of a policy and evaluating the performance of these perturbed policies.

Artificial Bee Colony (ABC): ABC is a swarm intelligence optimization algorithm inspired by the foraging behavior of honey bees.

The combination of Augmented Random Search (ARS) and Artificial Bee Colony (ABC) can leverage these features to optimize the behavior of drone swarms in complex environments, addressing challenges such as trajectory optimization, path planning, and coordination. This approach can provide a comprehensive solution materializing the intricate task of control and coordination of autonomous drone swarms in real-world scenarios.

- ARS and ABC synergize to enhance control and coordination in complex environments.
- The randomness of ARS and the precision of ABC together refine the algorithm's effectiveness.
- This fusion optimizes drone behavior and decision-making, enhancing the swarm's agility in responding to fire incidents.

Control Coordination Strategy: The combination of ARS and ABC (Figure 5) is to leverage the exploration capability of ARS, which helps in avoiding local optima, and the exploitation capability of ABC, which helps find a better solution within the local search space. This combined strategy aims to achieve better optimization results by taking advantage of the strengths of both algorithms. Integrating the strengths of both RL and SI algorithms for enhanced control and coordination of multiple drones. The inherent randomness in the search strategy achieved by the combination of the RL with the ABC algorithm plays a crucial role in improving its effectiveness. By optimizing the behavior and decision-making processes of the drones, this framework aims to enhance the autonomy and efficiency of the swarm's agile movement to the hotspots in detecting and responding to forest fire events. Ultimately, fortifying their role in safeguarding forests from the ravages of fire.

Figure 5. ARS+ ABC hybrid algorithm for autonomous navigation of drones

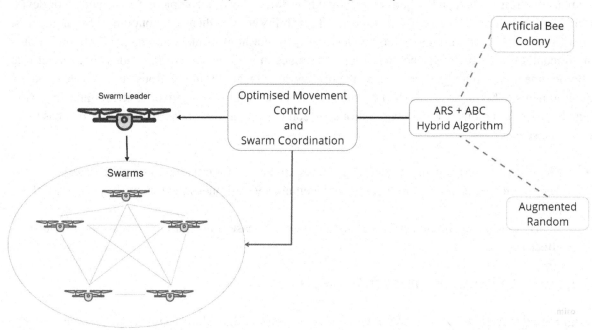

Autonomous Learning through Experience: Through repeated interactions with their environment, drones acquire a wealth of experiential knowledge. The combination of rewards and penalties within the reinforcement learning framework guides drones toward making informed decisions. This iterative process of learning by doing significantly elevates their performance.

4. EXPERIMENTAL SETUP FOR FOREST FIRE MONITORING AND RISK MITIGATION

In this section, we outline the meticulous design and execution of our experimental setup geared towards forest fire monitoring and risk mitigation. The success of our proposed framework relies on robust testing and validation under diverse conditions, mimicking real-world scenarios.

4.1 Hardware and Software Specifications for YOLOv7 Forest Fire Detection

The specified hardware configuration for YOLOv7 forest fire detection training on a desktop computer encompasses a robust combination of components, including dual GeForce 1080 GPUs for parallel processing, an Intel Core i5 11600K 11th Gen Processor for high-performance deep learning tasks, DDR4

32 GB RAM for efficient data processing, and a storage setup consisting of a 512 GB SSD and two 2 TB HDDs. The Intel motherboard ensures compatibility and support for high-performance elements, and the operating system of choice is Ubuntu Desktop, Version 18.04 LTS, known for its compatibility with deep learning tools. This comprehensive hardware arrangement is meticulously designed to optimize computational efficiency and facilitate effective model training for YOLOv7-based forest fire detection.

Figure 6. Performance YOLOv7 compared to prior models of YOLOv3, YOLOv5

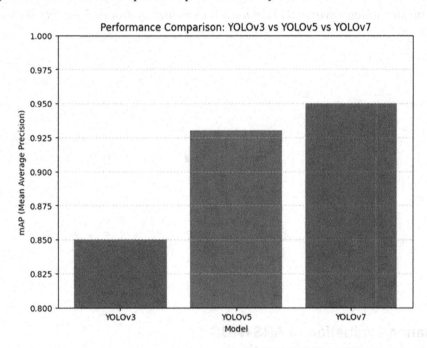

When the performance of YOLOv7 is compared against its previous models YOLOv3 and YOLOv5, YOLOv7 (Figure 6) shows significant accuracy of 95%. Mean Average Precision (mAP) is a common metric used to evaluate the accuracy and effectiveness of object detection models like YOLO (You Only Look Once) in identifying objects of interest within images or video frames.

4.2 Test Environment for Proposed Leader-Follower Architecture for the UAV Swarm

In the experimental framework, we have employed a grid simulation environment measuring 100x100 units. This grid is enriched with obstacles to represent trees and hills, simulating a dynamic landscape mimicking a forest terrain. To introduce variability and dynamic behavior into the environment, we randomize the number of drones and obstacles, as well as the origin and goal positions for each run of the experiment.

Effectively navigating this challenging environment and simulating swarm behavior involves embracing a leader-follower architecture. In this construct, a single drone assumes the role of a leader, guiding other drones (followers) towards designated goal positions. The leader drone may possess specialized capabilities, such as advanced perception or strategic planning skills, enabling it to efficiently steer the swarm. The followers, on the other hand, mimic the leader's actions, thereby forming a coherent movement pattern within the swarm as shown in (Figure 7).

The leader-follower framework fosters cooperative behavior among the drones, wherein they synchronize their actions to collectively attain the set of objectives while evading collisions. Integrated is a decentralized decision-making mechanism with predefined rules governing the behavior of followers.

Figure 7. 2D grid simulation environment demonstrates swarm of drones following the leader drone

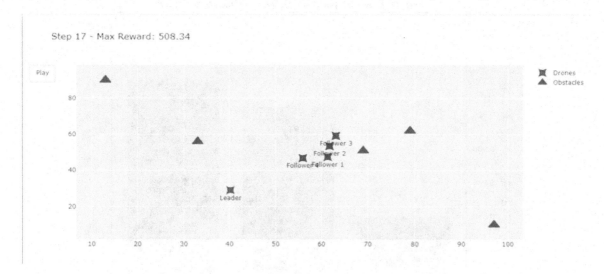

4.3 Performance Evaluation of ARS+ABC Algorithm for Autonomous Navigation

In this section, we delve into the comprehensive evaluation of the ARS+ABC algorithm for autonomous navigation, a pivotal aspect of our proposed framework. The integration of Augmented Random Search (ARS) and Artificial Bee Colony (ABC) algorithms is examined under for Path efficiency to assess its effectiveness in guiding unmanned aerial vehicles (UAVs) within dynamic and challenging environments.

Improved Path Efficiency:

The path efficiency of the proposed algorithm is evaluated in a dynamic context. Figure 8 illustrates the optimal path efficiency achieved by employing the approach with five drones over 100 episodes in a 100x100 grid environment. Fluctuations in path efficiency indicate an inherent exploration-exploitation trade-off, where exploration phases lead to suboptimal paths, but efficiency improves progressively as drones learn from experiences.

In the context of reinforcement learning, the relationship between reward and episode for path efficiency is visualized using a plot with:

X- axis (Episode): The number of episodes or iterations during the learning process.
Y- axis (Reward): The reward obtained by the learning agent in each episode, indicative of path efficiency.

Figure 8. Optimal path efficiency obtained for five drones for 100 episodes for a grid size of 100

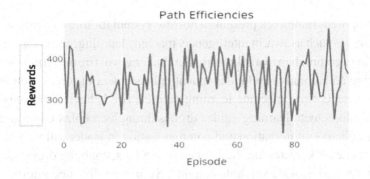

5. DISCUSSIONS

The proposed framework exhibits notable strengths, positioning itself at the forefront of UAV swarm technology for forest fire monitoring. Key among its contributions is the adept integration of Swarm Intelligence (SI) and Reinforcement Learning (RL) algorithms, fostering dynamic navigation, adaptability to complex environments, and autonomous decision-making within the UAV swarm. A significant innovation lies in the realm of sensor data collection, where the methodology emphasizes comprehensive Sensor Fusion. This involves the harmonious integration of diverse data from thermal cameras, air quality sensors, and weather sensors, facilitated by swarm intelligence algorithms. The fusion of these data sets enhances decision-making accuracy. The approach to fire detection and localization is commendable, employing the robust YOLOv7 computer vision system with real-time capabilities and high accuracy. Furthermore, the integration of thermal imaging and visual spectrum cameras contributes to effective fire detection, particularly in challenging conditions like smoke or darkness. Machine learning algorithms play a pivotal role in predicting and analyzing fire spread, enabling proactive decision-making for resource allocation, evacuation planning, and firefighting strategies. The implementation of a Swarm Intelligence and Leader-Follower Architecture ensures real-time collaboration among drones, optimizing fire monitoring efficiency. Reinforcement Learning strategies, specifically the Augmented Random Search (ARS) and Artificial Bee Colony (ABC) optimization, present an innovative approach to addressing challenges in trajectory optimization and coordination, thereby enhancing overall efficiency in real-world scenarios. The experimental setup's hardware specifications, including GPUs, CPU, RAM, and storage, underscore a robust infrastructure for YOLOv7 model implementation and training, ensuring efficient processing. The evaluation of the ARS+ABC algorithm reflects its capacity to achieve improved path efficiency, with due acknowledgment of the exploration-exploitation trade-off and emphasis on the learning process for progressive improvement. While acknowledging these strengths, the framework is not without challenges. The exploration-exploitation trade-off presents fluctuations in path efficiency, suggesting future work could delve into minimizing suboptimal paths during exploration. Additionally, to enhance realism, incorporating additional real-world complexities in dynamic environment simulations is proposed for future consideration.

6. CONCLUSION

In conclusion, the proposed framework presents a holistic system for forest fire monitoring. It integrates cutting-edge technologies such as swarm intelligence, machine learning, computer vision, and reinforcement learning, offering a comprehensive solution to the challenges of fire detection, prediction, and swarm coordination, fostering collaborative and independent enhancement of forest fire monitoring systems.

Computer vision detects fires, machine learning predicts fire behavior and sensor fusion enhances decision-making. Reinforcement learning guides drones through complex environments, while swarm intelligence ensures effective coordination and communication in leader follower architecture.

This innovative framework overcomes traditional limitations, enabling drones to cover larger areas, detect fires in real time, and provide valuable insights. Swarm intelligence improves coordination and adaptability. The integration of multiple technologies and the collaborative approach of the UAV swarm make this framework a promising avenue for advancing forest fire monitoring systems.

Overall, this framework provides a real-time solution for forest fire monitoring and mitigation. Through the synergy of sensor networks and advanced algorithms, autonomous drone swarms adeptly detect, respond to, and contain fires, thereby minimizing damage and significantly enhancing the system's efficiency in managing forest fires.

REFERENCES

Afghah, F., Razi, A., Chakareski, J., & Ashdown, J. (2019, April). Wildfire monitoring in remote areas using autonomous unmanned aerial vehicles. In *IEEE INFOCOM 2019-IEEE Conference on Computer Communications Workshops (INFOCOM WKSHPS)* (pp. 835-840). IEEE. 10.1109/INFCOMW.2019.8845309

Afghah, F., Zaeri-Amirani, M., Razi, A., Chakareski, J., & Bentley, E. (2018, June). A coalition formation approach to coordinated task allocation in heterogeneous UAV networks. In *2018 Annual American Control Conference (ACC)* (pp. 5968-5975). IEEE. 10.23919/ACC.2018.8431278

Akhloufi, M. A., Couturier, A., & Castro, N. A. (2021). Unmanned aerial vehicles for wildland fires: Sensing, perception, cooperation and assistance. *Drones (Basel), 5*(1), 15. doi:10.3390/drones5010015

Al-Smadi, Y., Alauthman, M., Al-Qerem, A., Aldweesh, A., Quaddoura, R., Aburub, F., Mansour, K., & Alhmiedat, T. (2023). Early Wildfire Smoke Detection Using Different YOLO Models. *Machines, 11*(2), 246. doi:10.3390/machines11020246

Amorosi, L., Chiaraviglio, L., & Galan-Jimenez, J. (2019). Optimal energy management of UAV-based cellular networks powered by solar panels and batteries: Formulation and solutions. *IEEE Access : Practical Innovations, Open Solutions, 7*, 53698–53717. doi:10.1109/ACCESS.2019.2913448

Bezas, K., Tsoumanis, G., Angelis, C. T., & Oikonomou, K. (2022). Coverage path planning and point-of-interest detection using autonomous drone swarms. *Sensors (Basel), 22*(19), 7551. doi:10.339022197551 PMID:36236651

Cheng, N., Wu, S., Wang, X., Yin, Z., Li, C., Chen, W., & Chen, F. (2023). AI for UAV-Assisted IoT Applications: A Comprehensive Review. *IEEE Internet of Things Journal, 10*(16), 14438–14461. doi:10.1109/JIOT.2023.3268316 de Moraes, R. S., & de Freitas, E. P. (2018). Distributed control for groups of unmanned aerial vehicles performing surveillance missions and providing relay communication network services. *Journal of Intelligent & Robotic Systems*, *92*(3-4), 645–656. doi:10.100710846-017-0726-z

de Venancio, P. V. A., Lisboa, A. C., & Barbosa, A. V. (2022). An automatic fire detection system based on deep convolutional neural networks for low-power, resource-constrained devices. *Neural Computing & Applications*, *34*(18), 15349–15368. doi:10.100700521-022-07467-z

Galán-Jiménez, J., Vegas, A. G., & Berrocal, J. (2022, October). Energy-efficient deployment of IoT applications in remote rural areas using UAV networks. In *2022 14th IFIP Wireless and Mobile Networking Conference (WMNC)* (pp. 70-74). IEEE. 10.23919/WMNC56391.2022.9954292

Grari, M., Idrissi, I., Boukabous, M., Moussaoui, O., Azizi, M., & Moussaoui, M. (2022). Early wildfire detection using machine learning model deployed in the fog/edge layers of IoT. *Indonesian Journal of Electrical Engineering and Computer Science*, *27*(2), 1062–1073. doi:10.11591/ijeecs.v27.i2.pp1062-1073

Grari, M., Idrissi, I., Boukabous, M., Moussaoui, O., Azizi, M., & Moussaoui, M. (2022). Early wildfire detection using machine learning model deployed in the fog/edge layers of IoT. *Indonesian Journal of Electrical Engineering and Computer Science*, *27*(2), 1062–1073. doi:10.11591/ijeecs.v27.i2.pp1062-1073

Janik, P., Zawistowski, M., Fellner, R., & Zawistowski, G. (2021). Unmanned aircraft systems risk assessment based on sora for first responders and disaster management. *Applied Sciences (Basel, Switzerland)*, *11*(12), 5364. doi:10.3390/app11125364

Kanand, T., Kemper, G., König, R., & Kemper, H. (2020). Wildfire detection and disaster monitoring system using UAS and sensor fusion technologies. *The International Archives of the Photogrammetry, Remote Sensing and Spatial Information Sciences*, *43*, 1671–1675. doi:10.5194/isprs-archives-XLIII-B3-2020-1671-2020

Karaboga, D., Gorkemli, B., Ozturk, C., & Karaboga, N. (2014). A comprehensive survey: Artificial bee colony (ABC) algorithm and applications. *Artificial Intelligence Review*, *42*(1), 21–57. doi:10.100710462-012-9328-0

Liang, J. H., & Lee, C. H. (2015). Efficient collision-free path-planning of multiple mobile robots system using efficient artificial bee colony algorithm. *Advances in Engineering Software*, *79*, 47–56. doi:10.1016/j.advengsoft.2014.09.006

Moon, H., Martinez-Carranza, J., Cieslewski, T., Faessler, M., Falanga, D., Simovic, A., Scaramuzza, D., Li, S., Ozo, M., De Wagter, C., de Croon, G., Hwang, S., Jung, S., Shim, H., Kim, H., Park, M., Au, T.-C., & Kim, S. J. (2019). Challenges and implemented technologies used in autonomous drone racing. *Intelligent Service Robotics*, *12*(2), 137–148. doi:10.100711370-018-00271-6

Nabeel, M. M., & Al-Shammari, S. W. (2023). Fire Detection Using Unmanned Aerial Vehicle. *Al-Iraqia Journal for Scientific Engineering Research*, *2*(1), 47–56.

Raj, P. A., & Srivani, M. (2018, December). Internet of robotic things based autonomous fire fighting mobile robot. In 2018 IEEE international conference on computational intelligence and computing research (ICCIC) (pp. 1-4). IEEE.

Saffre, F., Hildmann, H., Karvonen, H., & Lind, T. (2022). Monitoring and Cordoning Wildfires with an Autonomous Swarm of Unmanned Aerial Vehicles. *Drones (Basel)*, *6*(10), 301. doi:10.3390/drones6100301

Tang, J., Duan, H., & Lao, S. (2023). Swarm intelligence algorithms for multiple unmanned aerial vehicles collaboration: A comprehensive review. *Artificial Intelligence Review*, *56*(5), 4295–4327. doi:10.100710462-022-10281-7

Tiwari, A. K., & Nadimpalli, S. V. (2019). Augmented random search for quadcopter control: An alternative to reinforcement learning. *arXiv preprint arXiv:1911.12553*.

Chapter 9
Machine Learning in UAV–Assisted Smart Farming

Simeon Okechukwu Ajakwe
https://orcid.org/0000-0002-6973-530X
Hanyang University, Seoul, South Korea

Ihunanya Udodiri Ajakwe
https://orcid.org/0009-0004-9922-2320
Federal University of Technology, Owerri, Nigeria

Nkechi Faustina Esomonu
Federal University of Technology, Owerri, Nigeria

Jae-Min Lee
Kumoh National Institute of Technology, Gumi, South Korea

Opeyemi Deji-Oloruntoba
https://orcid.org/0009-0004-4332-0837
Inje University, Gimhae, South Korea

Dong Seong Kim
Kumoh National Institute of Technology, Gumi, South Korea

ABSTRACT

Over the years, economic loss in the agricultural sector has been attributed to the late detection of varying plant diseases due to incongruent detection technologies. With the advent of disruptive technologies and their deployment, such as incorporating artificial intelligence (AI) models into unmanned autonomous vehicles for real-time monitoring, the curtailment of losses and inadvertent waste of agricultural produce can be significantly addressed. This study examines the role of deploying AI models in improving the early and accurate detection of crop lesions for prompt, intuitive, and decisive action to forestall recurrence and guarantee a return on investment to farmers. Furthermore, the chapter established scientific basis for the acceleration of crop yields through allied mechano-biosynthesis in a quest to cushion the effect of the contemporary global food crisis. Connected intelligence in smart farming can be achieved through convergence technology for cost effective agro-allied production by improving the limitations of UAVs and AI-models.

DOI: 10.4018/979-8-3693-0578-2.ch009

1.0 INTRODUCTION

Agriculture is among the most prevailing sectors contributing to the world's economy, as the consumption of farm produce is integral to man's existence and survival. However, agricultural yield is susceptible to biotic stresses caused by pathogens (that is, viruses, bacteria, and fungi) in plants leading to significant losses in terms of decreased productivity (Kulkarni, 2018), when not attended to during the early stages. With the increasing number of farmers around the world and the adoption of emerging technologies, it is still very challenging to provide adequate food to the constantly growing population of humans. Crop disease inhibits food availability (Gao et al., 2020), promotes food scarcity, and incurs agricultural and economic losses to farmers. According to Ahmad et al. (2021), annual crop losses worldwide caused by plant disease are approximately $60billion. Regrettably, a substantial proportion of exported fruits are rejected annually due to symptoms of fruit diseases (Kulkarni, 2018). Therefore, early disease detection using cognitive capabilities innovative technologies guarantees quality crop output (Zhang et al., 2020). The introduction of technology as an enabler to accelerate the overall farming process and guarantee increased productivity is termed smart farming or smart agriculture. It involves the deployment of cognitive methods and machines for responsive, timely, tractable, and trustworthy evaluation of agricultural activities such as crop monitoring, disease detection, livestock management, etc. With smart farming, expended efforts by farmers can be eased while increasing the quantity, quality, and efficiency of the agricultural production process. However, these cognitive methods and machines need to work synergistically to optimize their utility in any agricultural setting and ensure good returns on investment.

Smart farming/agriculture for early plant disease detection entails the convergence of varied disruptive technologies such as the embedded cognition capacity of artificial intelligence (AI) algorithms, edge computing, and networks, coupled with the autonomous navigation capability of unmanned aerial vehicles (UAVs) otherwise called drones, for real-time monitoring of the developmental stages and healthiness of plants for intuitive inferencing and evidence-based conclusions and decisions. Currently, advancement in agriculture is engineered via converging technologies such as UAVs, Internet of Things (IoT), Deep Learning (DL) algorithms, wireless sensor networks, and cloud computing (Ajakwe et al., 2023d; Ramli et al., 2020). These technological advancements are to necessitate precision agriculture (PA). PA is an act that gathers, maps, and analyses data based on agricultural land variability and helps to draw relevant and useful inferences for proactive farm management decisions based on the results of such analysis, coupled with a proper application of pesticides and fertilizers in a controlled manner. Crop disease monitoring and control is a crucial aspect of smart agriculture facilitated by PA with regards to timely intervention. Manual monitoring of crop disease is capital and labor-intensive, time-consuming, and highly erroneous, thereby reducing production targets. The introduction of modifiable UAVs to enable agricultural processes is one of the phenomenal benefits of PA.

UAVs are flying robots remotely controlled by a ground control station or can autonomously fly with the aid of software-controlled flight plans in their embedded systems in conjunction with inbuilt sensors (Ajakwe et al., 2023b). UAVs have made renowned contributions to agriculture, such as crop monitoring, autonomous detection of pest infestation, disease, weed detection, field mapping, and plant population census (Moradi et al., 2022). Deploying UAVs on farms guarantees the collection of large amounts of images (data) via the aid of mounted cameras and embedded sensors, as well as enabling comprehensive farm monitoring (Kouadio et al., 2023). When the cognitions of these UAVs are controlled by the pattern discovery and learning characterizations of AI algorithms (via feature engineering and extractions enabled by feedback from edge networks), the benefits are enormous in actualizing the sustainable availability of farm produce (Ihekoronye et al., 2021). With AI algorithms embedded on the mounted cameras of UAVs deployed for surveillance over a farm settlement, different tasks such as classification, clustering and predictions of captured farm data can carried out synergistically in real-time over a network (Megat et al., 2021; Kharim et al., 2022; Yu et al., 2020; Ajakwe et al., 2022e) for timely intervention and avert losses.

However, despite the proliferation of the use of UAVs for different purposes, the acquisition of modifiable UAVs by farmers is capital-intensive. Also, most high accuracy object detection-based AI algorithms (DL) for precision-based detection of tiniest plant lesions have high computational complexities. This makes these DL algorithms virtually infeasible to be deployed onboard UAVs instead UAVs use low-computational DL algorithms for real-time crop monitoring for speedy curtailment of the spread of crop disease and avert economic and human resource waste which inherently limits their overall performance. A pertinent question therefore arises; to what extent has the convergence and deployment of DL object detection algorithms and UAV applications helped to achieve effective crop monitoring and facilitated quick intervention in averting the spread of crop disease that ultimately results in increased crop production? What are the economic values of deploying UAVs for real-time monitoring of crops? How can energy-efficient and resource-friendly AI paradigms be deployed in UAVs to achieve cost-effective smart farming for accelerative smart farming?

1.1 Motivation and Contribution

The chapter provides empirical-based answers to these questions by examining the significant impact of AI algorithms and UAV application in plant recognition and yield predictions for sustainable food security. It is motivated by the need to provide cutting-edge solutions and insights for the seamless integration of AI algorithms and UAVs in achieving increased crop monitoring, disease control, and overall security food for sustainable development. The chapter focuses on the adoption of disruptive and convergence technologies (especially AI algorithms and UAVs) for the curtailment of agricultural product wastage and uninterrupted availability of farm produce, through automatic detection, recognition, and classification of plant diseases. Specifically, the chapter examined different precautionary measures against wastage through conscious collocative monitoring. Then, it assayed bio-mechanic approaches to monitoring crop disease and their shortcomings. Furthermore, it highlighted the fundamental technological advancements in the deployment of computer vision technology and AI algorithms for smart agriculture. Moreso, the chapter x-rayed the convergence of AI algorithms and autonomous vehicles in achieving smart farming, especially crop monitoring and security. Thereafter, it discussed the likely botherations inhibiting expansive deployment of UAVs and AI algorithms for inclusive agro-allied production. Finally, expert-based deductions and road map for sustainable convergence and deployment of UAVs and AI algorithms in actualizing effective and efficient crop monitoring and yield production was provided.

2.0 CLOSE CROP MONITORING (CCM): A CASE FOR CONSCIOUS COLOCATIVE PRECAUTIONARY MEASURE AGAINST WASTAGE

Crop diseases may have a variety of impacts on plants, with substantial economic and environmental repercussions, viz; reduced crop quality, reduced agricultural output, increased production cost, loss of genetic diversity, implications on global food security, environmental consequences, and altered ecosystem which all ultimately affect the economic benefits of such crops (Ristaino et al., 2021). Various interventions have been employed for the improvement of crop disease, Crop rotation, resistant cultivars (Dar et al., 2020), sanitation measures, and integrated pest control are all effective disease management strategies. These are very critical for reducing the effects of plant diseases while also protecting the overall plant health and output (Egan et al.,2020; Lundin et al., 2021).

Crop disease management frequently necessitates the use of fungicides, insecticides, or other control techniques (Nayak & Solanki, 2021). These policies raise farmers' production expenses. includes the costs of obtaining and using pesticides and the personnel costs associated with disease monitoring and control (Ristaino et al., 2021; Yu et al., 2020). Furthermore, excessive and indiscriminate usage has been related to biodiversity and ecosystem degradation, as well as increased threats to food safety and consumer and agricultural workers' health (Kalyabina et al., 2021). The stakeholders of the Strategic Approach to International Chemicals Management, which includes the Food and Agricultural Organization (FAO), United Nations Environmental Program (UNEP), and the World Health Organization (WHO), as well as many other organizations, have voiced concern about the dangers that highly hazardous pesticides (HHPs) can bring to people and the environment (Pathak et al., 2022). To mitigate the hazards caused by pesticides, particularly HHPs, global action from all stakeholders is required (Leong et al., 2020). Close crop monitoring (CCM), as highlighted by precision agriculture thus becomes imperative not just for healthy consumption, but also for improved economic benefits. Close crop monitoring (CCM) is the technique of examining and measuring the status and development of crops on a regular basis during their growth cycle. It entails gathering data and information regarding numerous criteria such as plant health, growth rate, the absence or presence of pests and diseases, nutrient levels, and environmental conditions followed by proper decision-making (Maimaitijiang et al., 2020). Reliable data from CCM facilitates early risk identification and timely intervention. Thereby resulting in an improvement in crop yield and quality (Figure 1). Overall, CCM forms a major part of an improved farm management package. The regularity of CCM helps in the early detection of major plant issues such as disease outbreaks and pest infestations. Since this is normally followed by prompt interventions, CCM therefore helps to improve yield and quality and in the optimization of materials. A combination of CCM and Soil monitoring helps in Nitrogen management. Thereby helping in the optimization of crop Nitrogen in vegetable crop production (Padilla et al.,2020). More interestingly, CCM provides a series of benefits for smart agriculture as shown in Figure 1. CCM is highly essential for controlling pests, weeds, and diseases in crops, offering relevant information about the present state of the crop, and giving an insight into futuristic occurrences and helping to birth pathways for interventions.

Figure 1. Advantages of close crop monitoring (CCM)
(Source: author)

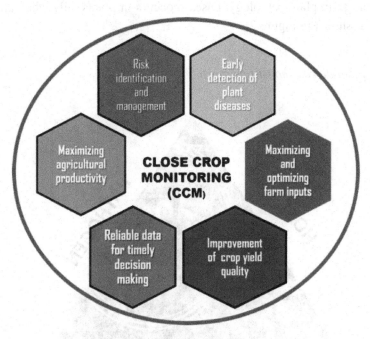

Image-based methods are now being used to increase disease identification and severity assessment precision (Dong et al., 2021). More so, databases for agrochemicals, biological control, and biopesticides make it easier to locate active substances for plant disease treatment (Cunningham et al., 2019). AI and Machine Learning (ML) systems can process vast amounts of agricultural data to detect trends, estimate crop yields, and enables farmers to do more with less, thereby optimizing farming techniques with a futuristic potential of driving agricultural revolution (Liu, 2020, Ihekoronye et al., 2021; Ajakwe et al., 2023a). These technologies may also evaluate nutritional data to create individualized diet plans and offer dietary adjustments depending on an individual's particular needs. This is specifically important to boost smart nutrition (Javaid et al., 2022). Advanced farming technologies such as LED lighting, hydroponics, and automatic temperature control systems are also used by Controlled environmental agriculture (CEA). These methods provide exact control over growing conditions, allowing for year-round production, optimal nutrient delivery, and improved yields (Ragaveena et al., 2021). A broader analysis of crop disease and indigenous mechano-cognitive efforts at tackling and curtailing them provides basis for innovative developments of disruptive technologies and their impact on food security.

3.0 COLOCATIVE COGNITIONS IN CROP MONITORING AND COPIOUS YIELD

Crop lesions refer to abnormal or damaged areas that appear on the foliage or stems of crops, typically caused by various biotic and abiotic factors (Whitfield et al., 2018). These lesions can be symptomatic of diseases, pests, or environmental stressors, and their identification is crucial for effective crop management and disease control. The occurrence of plant disease in any plant system depends on three compulsory components namely, Host: a susceptible host plant; Pathogen: a virulent pathogen; and Environment: a favorable environment (Wokorach et al., 2018). These constituents form the plant disease triangle, which is a fundamental concept in plant pathology. Disease occurs in plants only when all three sides of the triangle are present as shown in Figure 2.

Figure 2. Tripartite plant disease constituents
(Source: author)

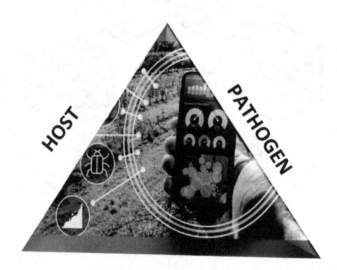

Table 1 highlights common types of crop lesions

Table 1. Crop lesions, types, and descriptions

No.	Crop Lesions	Image	Brief Description
1	**Necrotic Lesions**		Dark and dead areas on the plant tissue, often resulting from fungal, bacterial, or viral infections. It may have defined edges and vary in size and shape depending on the specific pathogen causing the damage.
2	**Chlorotic Lesions**		Yellowing of plant tissues due to a lack of chlorophyll, caused by nutrient deficiencies or viral infections. Chlorotic lesions appear as yellowish patches on the leaves.
3	**Ring or Target Lesions**		Have distinct concentric rings or target-like patterns, caused by certain fungal diseases like anthracnose or Corynespora leaf spot.
4	**Water-soaked Lesions**		Caused by bacteria, and appear as wet, slimy, and translucent areas on the plant tissue. They may eventually turn brown or black as the tissue dies.
5	**Cankers**		Occur on stems or branches, often caused by fungi or bacteria. They appear as sunken, necrotic areas and can lead to the death of the affected plant parts
6	**Rust Pustules**		Causes reddish-brown to orange pustules on the plant surface, which release spores. These pustules contain the fungal spores that spread the infection to other plants.
7	**Scabs**		Rough and raised areas on the plant surface, caused by various fungi. They are common on fruit trees and can affect the marketability of the produce.
8	**Mosaic Patterns**		Appear as irregular, mottled areas on the leaves, often due to viral infections. These patterns are characterized by light and dark green patches.
9	**Shot Hole Lesions**		Small, circular lesions that resemble bullet holes, commonly caused by certain fungi. They are prevalent on leaves and fruits of various crops.

According to Kouadio et al (2023), the causing pathogens of these plant diseases can be classified into six (6) groups namely, fungi, fungi-like oomycetes, bacteria, viruses, stramenopila, and nematode. Of these groups, fungi accounted for more than half of the pathogens followed by bacteria. UAV-based pathogen detection mounted with various types of sensors and cameras can collect high spatial and spectral resolution data for plant disease detection and monitoring. Each of these classes of plant diseases if not detected timely portends a hazard to global food security and increased vulnerability to famine and malnutrition, especially in agriculturally depleted countries (Ristaino et al., 2021; Mason-D'Croz et al., 2020). It could lead to a dangerous economic impact that extends beyond the immediate consequences on crop yield. It has the potential to have an impact on agricultural sectors, the local economy, and world trade. Disease outbreaks can restrict exports, increase import reliance, cause job losses, and create economic instability in impacted areas (Mason-D'Croz et al., 2020). Although various technologies have attempted to solve the problem of plant diseases, thereby reducing its negative effects on agriculture, various bottlenecks have been identified (Zou et al., 2020). Isothermal DNA amplification technologies for point of need plant disease diagnosis have a lot of drawbacks ranging from sensitivity, cost, simplicity, and the need for large quantities of target DNA for amplification (Zou et al., 2020). Although biogenic volatiles are a rich source of information that might be extremely useful in current precision agriculture, real-time monitoring of microbe-induced plant volatiles (MIPVs), for example, might enable for the quick and noninvasive diagnosis of plant illnesses. Bacterial volatiles have also shown considerable promise in the field as fertilizers or inducers of natural plant defenses.

However, they are limited in their application due to their high vapor pressure (Sharifi & Ryu, 2018). Also, the incorporation of microbiological agents such as yeasts in plant protection can assist to reduce or eliminate the usage of agrichemicals while also improving plant quality. However, these biological plant protection products must fulfill certain stringent requirements such as high level of pathogen inhibition. More so, for both in vitro and in plant-based research, the development and implementation take several years and are very expensive, and the process is difficult. The beneficial effect of agricultural-friendly Nano compounds has been proven by recent findings (Agri et al., 2022). They are often mixed with bioinoculants and may be used as an alternative to chemical fertilizers in sustainable agriculture, a major characteristic of interest in smart food development.

To pioneer and stabilize an easier process that is both fast and cost effective requires the use of disruptive technologies for collaborative agricultural monitoring and improved nutritional quality, not just in terms of their economic benefits in accelerative crop output but also in relation to achieving the food security and food safety, both of which are global concerns and major factors with respect to the sustainable development goals. It thus becomes imperative to arm farmers and researchers with relevant technological tools with a clear perspective of IoT applications and IoT-based software (Gómez-Chabla, et al., 2018). IoT devices and sensors may be put in agricultural fields to collect real-time data on environmental factors like temperature, humidity, soil moisture, and nutrient levels. This information may be shared with farmers, researchers, and agricultural specialists to improve crop management techniques and maintain optimal plant nutrition. Adopting a Smart Food (SF) approach can address several significant direct and indirect concerns of plant diseases, including environmental pollution, malnutrition and diet-related health problems, rural poverty, adaptation to and mitigation of climate change, and others (Bacco et al., 2022; Panetto et al., 2020). SF is the concept underlying such a movement, which aims to address all parts of the global food system by being beneficial for the consumer's health and wellness, enhancing environmental sustainability, and being a profitable venture for the farmer (Ristaino et al., 2021; Bacco et al., 2022; Whitfield et al., 2018). The timely, accurate, and exact visual detection of crop diseases is critical for proper analysis and elicitation of effected plants, right prescriptions of curtailment measures, and proactive response to forestall future recurrence which ultimately holds significant economic and agricultural importance for farmers, the food industry, and the overall economy. The role of computer vision (CV) technologies and object detection models empowered by AI in achieving this lofty goal cannot be over-emphasized.

4.0 COMPUTER VISION AND ARTITCIAL INTELLIGENCE FOR PERCEPTIVE PLANT RECOGNITION: INGENUITY AND ISSUES

According to Singh et al (2018), image-based digital technologies are now being used to identify plant diseases to avoid them (Singh et al., 2018). A significant quantity of visual data is collected in real time, and various artificial intelligence (AI) algorithms are applied to deliver optimum judgments. This has resulted in lower costs and is used by most farmers. These strategies aim to enhance the quality of plant disease rating data by decreasing human mistakes (Dong et al., 2021; Singh et al., 2018). Remote sensing and satellite imaging technologies, such as satellite imaging and aerial drones, give significant information regarding crop health, soil conditions, and vegetation indices. Farmers and researchers may now monitor agricultural landscapes, diagnose nutrient shortages, and take prompt interventions to increase crop quality and nutritional content by evaluating resulting data. The various techniques for plant disease image data curation and analysis are visual analysis, computer vision (CV), and VI-based analysis (Kouadio et al., 2023). CV techniques are the most widely used method for plant disease due to its ability to extract meaningful information from captured images in real-time especially when such techniques work with AI algorithms to distinguish between various plant types and diseases based on their peculiarities and patterns. Hence, AI algorithms are now being greatly explored in various agricultural processes beyond crop disease monitoring and detection. Figure 3 shows that with an AI-based application, it is possible for recognize, count, and geolocate plants, as well as assess plant height and canopy size, and create plant health maps, with various systems for assessing digital representations of objects using ML techniques (Ampatzidis et al., 2020).

Figure 3. Applications of AI in agriculture
(Source: author)

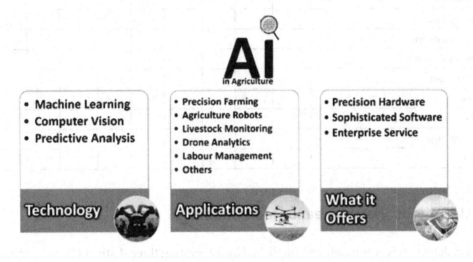

To distinguish between plant types and diseases, CV-based-AI algorithms use features such texture, color, shape, and spectral-based characteristics to make its deductions. Therefore, CV-based-AI algorithms for crop disease detection perform color-based analysis, texture-based analysis, shape-based analysis, and/or spectral-based analysis on plants to ascertain its state of healthiness at any given instance. However, combining multiple features (texture and color) has proven to achieve a comprehensive representation and precise plant disease symptoms recognition and subsequent elicitation (Zhang et al., 2019; Dang et al., 2020). This capability of ML techniques for complex feature extraction and pattern discovery has given rise to its popularity and continuous adoption as a first-choice candidate technique for plant disease detection and monitoring. To be precise, Kouadio et al (2023) posited that of all plant disease detection techniques adopted between 2013-2022, ML-based techniques was about 67% as summarized in Table 2.

Table 2. Overview of methods for plant disease symptoms recognition as reported in published articles between 2013-2022

Methods for Plant Disease Symptoms Identification	Year									
	2013	2014	2016	2017	2018	2019	2020	2021	2022	Total
Analysis of Variance (ANOVA)			1					1	3	5
Clustering analysis							2			2
Correlation analysis							2	1		3
Geo-statistics/GIS					1			1	1	3
Machine learning (ML)				2	3	5	15	6	12	43
ML/Deep learning (DL)				1	1	4	4	3	10	23
ML and Deep learning					1				1	2
ML and regression models								1		1
ML and statistical comparison							1			1
Pixel-wise comparison						3	1			4
Regression models	1	1			2		1	2	2	9
Threshold-based colour analysis			1		1					2
Vegetation health mapping								2		2
Visual analysis						1		1	1	3

4.1 CV-AI Methods Plant Disease Recognition

Visual object detection is commonly accomplished by integrating three distinct CV techniques: the conventional method of feature engineering (encompassing motion and appearance features), ML approach, and multiple DL (CNN) approaches (Ajakwe et al., 2022b). This integration aims to enhance detection speed and accuracy as highlighted in Figure 4.

Figure 4. Computer vision object detectors for crop detection
(Source: author)

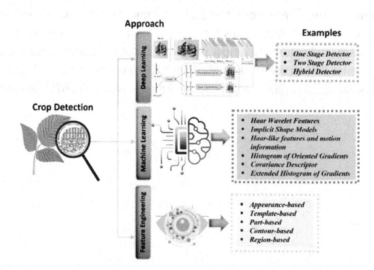

Different factors determine the choice of method for plant disease symptoms recognition. These factors include data complexity and scale, system complexity and computational resource, training data diversity, interoperability of model, etc. (Bouguettaya et al., 2022). In the context of object detection, the classical feature engineering method involves utilizing an object's visual characteristics such as its color, contour lines, geometric shapes, edges, and its motion attributes by analyzing sequential frames within the captured image. Vegetation Index (VI) is the second most popular classical feature engineering plant disease detection method based on UAV imagery (Kouadio et al., 2023). Examples of VI methods include normalized difference vegetation index (NDVI), green NDVI, triangular greenness index, simple ratio index. To achieve better analysis of disease severity and variability, map vegetation health status, and assess the homogeneity of data, these Vis are combined with ML approaches as baseline predictors (Megat et al., 2021; Kharim et al., 2022; Yu et al., 2020).

Similarly, the ML approach fuses traditional computer vision methods to achieve better object classification and detection results. Generally, AI algorithms can be in the form of supervised learning, semi-supervised learning, unsupervised learning, and reinforcement learning, depending on the model training process, data acquisition method, and other environmental dynamics (). Traditional ML-based supervised learning methods for plant disease symptoms recognition include random forest (RF), support vector machine (SVM), naïve bayes (NB), k-nearest neighbour (KNN), logistics regression, linear discriminant analysis, ensemble learning (EL), and artificial neural networks (ANN) (Ajakwe et al., 2020). A work conducted by Deng et al (2019) on classification of healthy, symptomatic HLB infected, and asymptomatic HLB-infected citrus leaf disease, the SVM algorithm achieved a 90.8% accuracy for binary classification and 96% accuracy for multiclass classification better than other ML classifiers. On the other hand, EL gives a robust analysis and classification of data samples by checking different ML classifiers' performance behaviour with increase in data variability and sample across different metrics through a concept known as majority voting (Ajakwe et al., 2023c). However, EL has high computational complexity. Another study conducted by Lan et al (2020) on citrus disease detection proves the robustness and superiority of EL and ANN over normal ML classifiers with AdaBoost achieving a 100% classification accuracy while NN achieved a 97.28% accuracy as against the 96% accuracy achieved by SVM in the works of Deng et al (2019). Notwithstanding, as the volume and variability of data complexity increases, conventional ML approaches perform poorly in extracting important features (tiny features) needed for specific on-the point deductions. This is where DL approaches steps in for better and exact visual pattern discovery, elicitation, and representation of plant disease symptoms.

DL approaches are an extension of NN in terms of width and depth which makes them achieve higher prediction superiority than classical ML classifiers. DL approaches to plant disease symptoms recognition and elicitation comes in the form of back-propagation neural networks (BPNN), multilayer perceptron (MLP), and convolutional neural networks (CNN). In recent times, there is an increase adoption of MLP in plant disease recognition (Kouadio et al., 2023) due to demand for ultra-precision-low-complexity systems. This notwithstanding, when precise visual representation of detected plant disease is key to final decision, CNN models are preferred to BPNN and MLP. CNN-based object detection models are grouped as One-stage Detectors, Two-stage detectors, or Hybrid detectors (Ajakwe et al., 2022b). This categorization is based on tradeoff between timeliness and accuracy when deciding the choice of CNN model to be deployed for crop disease monitoring, analysis and detection given the available system resource. According to Ajakwe et al (2023a), One-stage detectors, otherwise called Single Stage Detectors (SSD), perform sequential image detection and processing, which makes them very fast but with low detection accuracy. SSDs include Single Shot Multibox Detectors, RetinaNet, MobileNet, and You

Only Look Once (YOLO) family. Two-stage Detectors also known as Region-based Convolution Neural Networks (R-CNN) perform more accurate image detection and feature extraction than SSD but require more memory and power to run, use complex pipeline, and adopts a sliding window method that is expensive. Common examples include R-CNN and Faster R-CNN. Hybrid detectors fuse SSD and R-CNN to blend speed and accuracy in performance—for example, Visual Geometry Group (VGG)Net, ShuffleNetV2, COCO Model, ResNet-101, and Yolov5. In practice, CNN models deployed for plant disease detection are generally categorized as either classical CNN architectures or customizable CNN architectures. Popular classical CNN architectures for plant disease detection include ResNet (Rangarajan et al, 2022), U-Net (Van et al., 2022), DarkNet53 (Zhao et al., 2022), LeNet-5 (Kerkech et al., 2018), SqueezeNet (Rangarajan et al, 2022), GoogleNet (Dang et al., 2020), and DeepLabv3+ (Deng et al., 2022). Customizable CNN architectures are a combination or modification of classical CNN architectures. Examples of customizable CNN architectures include EfficientNet-EfficientDet network (Prasad et al., 2022), the vine disease detection network (VddNet) (Kerkech et al., 2020), the MobiResNet (a combination of ResNet50 and MobileNet (Ksibi et al., 2022), Inception-ResNet (combination of Inception and ResNet) (Zhang et al., 2019), and the CropdocNet, (a combination of three encoders i.e., spectral information, spectral–spatial feature, and class-capsule encoders, and a decoder) (Shi et al., 2022), CenterNet", (Liang et al., 2022), and efficient dual flow U-Net, employed (Zhang et al., 2022). The performance of CNN models in the detection and classification of plant disease depends largely on the quality of dataset, its sampling variability, representativeness, and proper annotation during dataset curation (Ajakwe et al., 2023a; 2023d). Unreliable datasets lead to wrong predictions by CNN models. On the other hand, invariable dataset samples lead to model overfitting problems because of misclassification. The dependence on public datasets for robust model training rather than in-house dataset curation and development is a major drawback for CNN model training and validation. The development of a reliable, and robust dataset that can serve multiple purposes is both resource and capital intensive. Little wonder there is scarcity of reliable and quality dataset for robust AI model training, testing and validation before full scale deployment in real-life scenario. This gap in simulation and real-world deployment of CNN models has overtime cast doubt on the reliability of these models in real-word scenario. Considerably, the effort made by Plant village (Hughes & Salathé, 2015) and VisioDECT (Ajakwe et al., 2022f) dataset in bridging this gap is quite commendable. Notwithstanding, more quality and diverse datasets are needed to supplement the existing efforts towards availability of reliable datasets.

4.2 Selection of Plant Disease Detection Method

In selecting the right method for plant disease monitoring and detection, the problem domain, nature of task to be performed, and expectation defines the method to deploy. The nature of the task could be regression (time series), classification, clustering (grouping), or detection. Nowadays, classical ML methods such as the Bayesian network, logistic regression, decision tree, etc. are used when the dataset features are not too complex and visual representation does not matter (Ben-Ayed & Hanana, 2021) in carrying out time series analysis of data to predict the likely projections of crop yields or outbreak of farm diseases which could hamper harvest and result in food supply shortages. For instance, Kumar et al (2015) proposed the CSM (Crop Selection Method) to tackle crop selection challenges and aid boost crop net yield rate across the season which is a time series method. Also, for increased efficiency and economic feasibility, Choudhary et al (2019) used PLSR and other regression algorithms as an artificial intelligence tool in conjunction with sensors for data gathering and Internet of things hardware deployment. However, when the objective function is visual detection of plant diseases, DL approaches becomes crucial and mandatory. For instance, in a study to detect maize leaves infected with fall armyworms (faw), Ishengoma et al (2021) utilized automated recognition algorithm models based on the convolution neural network (CNN), namely VGG16, VGG19, InceptionV3, and MobileNetV2 and achieved a corresponding increase in detection accuracy ranging from 96%, 93.08%, 96.75% and 98.25% to 99.92%, 99.67%, 100% and 100%, respectively. Nowadays, computer vision-based and AI-empowered object detection models can detect tiniest and distant objects of all shades and forms albeit with some shortfalls (Ihekoronye et al., 2022; Ajakwe et al., 2022). These results undoubtedly reveal the capacity and capability of CV-based-AI-empowered algorithms for efficient plant disease monitoring and detection.

However, it is worthy to note that all the discussed plant disease symptoms recognition methods will achieve better and faster result when each method works in synergy with UAVs as means for data capturing and acquisition. This is because the need to identify the precise location on the field or plantation where each infection has occurred is a crucial subject requiring urgent attention for immediate curtailment before widespread contamination.

5.0 CONVERGENCE OF DRONES MOBILITY AND CHARACTERIZATION FOR ACCELERATIVE CROP SURVEILLANCE

5.1 Crop Lesion Detection via UAVs Imagery

Unmanned Aerial Vehicles (UAVs), commonly known as drones, are autonomous or remotely piloted aircraft that have gained significant popularity in various industries, including agriculture.

The cost-effectiveness, easier deployment, adaptive applicability, and mobility friendliness of UAVs informs their sporadic usage across all domains including the agricultural sector (Ajakwe et al., 2023b). Recently, UAVs have become valuable tools for precision farming and crop monitoring, revolutionizing traditional agricultural practices. In developed nations, agricultural applications now constitute 20% of the overall UAV market, demonstrating their growing significance as tools for farmers and researchers to aid decision-making and tackle agricultural difficulties (Hogan et al., 2017). These small, versatile aircraft are equipped with cameras, sensors, and GPS technology, enabling them to capture high-resolution imagery and collect real-time data from fields.

UAVs can be categorized according to their purpose, such as photography, aerial mapping, surveillance, and cinematography (Ajakwe et al., 2023d). However, a more effective classification can be based on their specific features. In a paper by Vroegindeweij et al., 2014, various types of UAVs used in agriculture were examined and divided into three main groups: fixed-wing, Vertical Take Off and Landing (VTOL), and bird/insect-like UAVs. The authors concluded that VTOL UAVs, due to their agility, exceptional maneuverability, and hovering capabilities, are particularly well-suited for agricultural applications. According to Sylvester (2018), fixed-wing UAVs were advocated as a preferable option due to their extended flight duration and high speed when compared to VTOL UAVs, which have shorter flight times and slower speeds. Conversely, Chapman et al. (2014) and Sugiura (2018) argued in favor of unmanned helicopters like the monocopter or single-rotor UAVs. These types of UAVs possess extended flight times, can operate at various altitudes, and exhibit excellent hovering capabilities. Nonetheless, they require more intricate piloting techniques. Recently, UAVs have been classified into distinct types based on their design, purpose, and capabilities. It is worthy to note that technology is constantly evolving, and new types of UAVs emerge daily based on user-demands. Figure 5 highlights the different types of UAVs for crop lesion monitoring and detection.

Figure 5. Common UAVs for crop lesion detection
(Source: author)

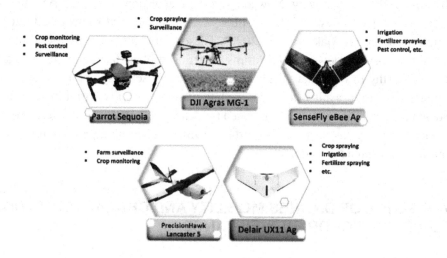

One of the standout features of the DJI Agras MG-1 is its advanced sensing technology. It utilizes radar and intelligent algorithms to maintain a consistent and safe flying height above the crops. The drone can adapt its flight path to the terrain, ensuring an even and accurate distribution of the sprayed substances. This precision spraying not only maximizes the effectiveness of the chemicals but also minimizes waste and environmental impact. Overall, the DJI Agras MG-1 is a cutting-edge agricultural drone that brings efficiency, accuracy, and sustainability to crop spraying operations. On the other hand, the Parrot Sequoia is a cutting-edge multispectral camera system designed primarily for agricultural applications. The camera's high-resolution imagery and multispectral capabilities make it a valuable tool for various tasks, such as crop monitoring, disease detection, irrigation management, and yield prediction. One of the major advantages of the Parrot Sequoia is its user-friendly and integrated platform, which includes software for data processing and analysis. By capturing data in the near-infrared range, the Sequoia can reveal information about plant health that is not visible to the human eye, helping farmers optimize their agricultural practices and maximize crop yields while minimizing resource usage.

The PrecisionHawk Lancaster 5 drone is equipped with advanced sensing technologies and carries a range of sensors, such as multispectral and RGB cameras, LiDAR, and other data collection devices. One of the key features of the Lancaster 5 is its compatibility with PrecisionHawk's data analytics and software platform, which facilitates easy data processing, analysis, and integration with various precision agriculture and mapping tools. This integration streamlines the data-to-decision process, empowering farmers, environmentalists, and other users to make informed choices based on the collected aerial data. Furthermore, the Delair UX11 Ag is an advanced fixed-wing drone designed specifically for agricultural applications. One of the standout features of the Delair UX11 Ag is its integrated multispectral camera system. This camera captures data in multiple spectral bands, including infrared, red edge, and visible light, enabling the drone to collect detailed and accurate information about crop health and vegetation status. The data collected by the UX11 Ag allows farmers to detect early signs of stress, disease, or nutrient deficiencies in their crops, thus enabling them to take proactive measures to mitigate potential yield losses. Finally, the SenseFly eBee Ag is an advanced agricultural drone designed to revolutionize modern farming practices. The eBee Ag is equipped with a high-resolution multispectral camera, capable of capturing detailed images of crops in different spectral bands. These images provide valuable insights into crop health, identifying stress factors, pest infestations, nutrient deficiencies, and other potential issues that might not be visible to the naked eye. One of the key features of the eBee Ag is its user-friendly interface and seamless data integration capabilities. The SenseFly eBee Ag serves as a powerful tool in modern precision agriculture, helping farmers enhance productivity while minimizing resource usage and environmental impact.

UAVs detect crop lesions via different cameras and sensor types (individual or combination) that are mounted on them to gather high spatial and spectral resolution data of plant diseases. These sensors include multispectral sensors (Zhang et al., 2022; Su et al., 2019), red-green-blue (RGB) cameras (Pan et al., 2021; Deng et al., 2022), hyperspectral sensors (Zhang et al., 2019; Guo et al., 2021), and RGB + multispectral sensors (Su et al., 2021) depending on the nature and symptom of the plant disease. To achieve a high degree of detection accuracy and precision, most UAVs use mounted cameras with combination of sensors (Shahi et al., 2023). According to Kouadio et al (2023) several experiments were conducted using various combinations of sensors. Multispectral + digital, multispectral + thermal, multispectral + RGB, hyperspectral + RGB, RGB + near infrared, thermal + multispectral + RGB, thermal infrared + RGB, multispectral + hyperspectral + Thermal, and hyperspectral + RGB + Light Detection and Ranging (LiDAR) were among the combinations of sensors as summarized in Figure 6.

Figure 6. UAV sensor types distribution and plant diseases
(Source: Kouadio et al., 2023)

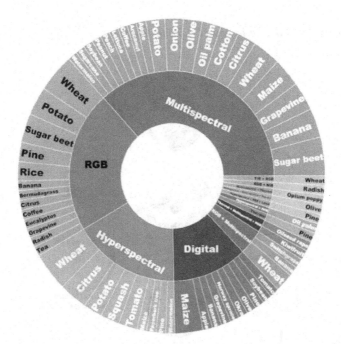

Most of the studies using more than one sensor used the data obtained from them directly to identify symptoms of the disease. In several cases, though, the processing of information from multiple sensors was enhanced by data from one sensor to help identify symptoms of the disease. One example is the research conducted by Yu et al (2022), which used LiDAR, RGB, and hyperspectral sensors. Hyperspectral data pre-processing involved the use of LiDAR sensor data, or digital elevation model data. The information obtained from the RGB and hyperspectral sensors was then used to identify the symptoms of the pine wilt disease (Yu et al., 2022). As mentioned previously, the crop disease symptoms analysis and detection are carried out by the mounted camera on the UAVs via different AI-assisted and CV-based object detection techniques; conventional, ML, and DL methods. Some studies have investigated extensively crop diseases recognition based on UAVs and DL methods (Bouguettaya et al., 2021; Bouguettaya et al., 2022; Kuswidiyanto et al., 2022; Messina & Modica, 2020; Shahi et al., 2023). These studies indicate that using UAV imagery, crop lesion estimation can be properly carried out in real-time especially in a networked smart farm to avert spread of such disease among other UAV use cases in a smart farm environment.

5.2 Common Use Cases and Scenarios of Drone in Smart Agriculture

One of the primary benefits of unmanned aerial vehicles (UAVs) in the field of agriculture, specifically in crop monitoring, lies in their capacity to offer precise and prompt data regarding the health and growth of crops. Through flying at low heights over fields, drones can obtain images and infrared data that facilitate the identification of disparities in crop health, detection of diseases, and recognition of nutrient deficiencies. Consequently, farmers can proactively address potential problems and enhance crop productivity by utilizing this valuable information. Figure 7 highlights the various use cases of drones in smart agriculture which inadvertently reflects on its economic values to real-time monitoring of crops and farming practice in general.

Figure 7. Common use cases of drone in smart agriculture
(Source: author)

In China, plant-protection UAV development has been accelerated since 2018 with increased areas of unified prevention and spraying operations, purchased plant-protection UAV for unified prevention services, and raised the drone subsidy standards. With the government's unwavering support, the plant-protection UAV industry grew quickly and accounted for 41.5% of the industrial UAV market in 2018 (Lan & Wang, 2018). Eurostat statistics show that the value of products imported and exported between Poland and China was USD 12.40 billion in the first half of 2019. This represents an increase of 10.7% (Wang et al., 2022). Thanks to the bilateral agreement between China and Poland on the plant-protection UAV initiative. Specifically, in 2019, the total cultivated area of fruit trees in Poland was 430,000 hm2, with a total output of 3.93327 million tons. In particular, Poland's total cultivated fruit tree area in 2019 was 430,000 hm2, and its entire production was 3.93327 million tons. The output dropped 22.5% from 2018 due to spring frost, soil-water constraints, and high temperatures, which increased the cost of most fruits. Poland had the highest apple production, accounting for almost 78.3% of all fruit produced. The cherry is the second-biggest fruit, and the others are the strawberry, raspberry, chokeberry, highbush blueberry, blackcurrant, plum, and pear. Poland's imports came to USD 3.34 billion, a 32.4% rise (Wang et al., 2022). With a 15.5% annual growth, the two nations' trade volume reached a record high of about USD 24.524 billion in 2018.

The use of UAVs in agriculture is cost-effective compared to traditional methods like manned aerial surveys or ground-based inspections. Drones are relatively affordable to operate, and they cover large areas efficiently in a short amount of time, reducing labor and fuel costs (Ajakwe et al., 2023d). The data collected by UAVs also helps farmers optimize resource usage, such as water and fertilizers, leading to significant savings in the long run. Furthermore, UAVs provide a level of accessibility and flexibility that was previously unattainable in agriculture. They can be deployed quickly and easily, enabling farmers to monitor crops more frequently, especially in remote or hard-to-reach areas. This agility allows for early detection of potential problems, mitigating risks and increasing the chances of successful harvests. The data gathered by UAVs is not only useful for crop monitoring but also plays a crucial role in decision-making and planning. By analyzing the data, farmers can create detailed field maps, assess crop health, and generate prescription maps for targeted treatments. This precision agriculture approach ensures that resources are applied precisely where needed, reducing waste and environmental impact.

Ultimately, UAVs have emerged as a transformative technology in agriculture, particularly for crop monitoring. Their ability to capture high-resolution imagery and collect real-time data allows farmers to make informed decisions, optimize resource usage, and proactively manage crop health. With their cost-effectiveness, accessibility, and speed of data analysis, drones have become indispensable tools for modern precision farming practices, helping farmers increase productivity, reduce costs, and promote sustainable agriculture. Several factors have contributed to the growing utilization of unmanned aerial vehicles (UAVs). Primarily, the reduced prices of UAVs equipped for agricultural functions have steadily declined, with the majority now available for less than $10,000 (Barbedo & Koenigkan, 2018). Although there are additional costs involved in operating UAVs, such as maintenance, insurance, and software (Mulero-Pázmány et al., 2014), the advantages they provide outweigh these expenses. Furthermore, regulations governing UAV usage are increasingly finding a balance between safety and usability (Barbedo & Koenigkan, 2018), particularly in rural regions with lower population density, which helps alleviate concerns regarding safety and privacy. Additionally, rural properties are often extensive, making it challenging to identify issues solely through ground scouting. By combining UAVs with ground sensors (Gabriel et al., 2015), they can efficiently cover large areas much faster than humans on foot, offering an effective solution for scouting purposes. Additionally, advancements in imaging sensors have enabled UAVs to capture high-resolution images, allowing for early problem detection before they escalate altitudes (Barbedo & Koenigkan 2018; Anderson & Gaston, 2013).

5.3 Critical Limitations of UAV Usage in Smart Agriculture and Crop Monitoring

Despite the enormous advantages that the usage of UAVs portends to agriculture due to their versatility, accessibility, and cost-effectiveness, like any technology, UAVs also have certain limitations (Ajakwe et al., 2023d). Careful consideration of these limitations highlights the pathways for inventive improvements.

1. **Limited Flight Time**: Most consumer-grade UAVs have a limited flight time, typically ranging from 15 to 30 minutes, depending on the model and battery capacity. This constraint restricts the amount of time a UAV can stay airborne for certain tasks, such as surveillance, mapping large areas, or conducting lengthy missions.

2. **Lower Payload Capacity:** UAVs have weight limitations, which can restrict their ability to carry heavy equipment or larger payloads. This limitation may hinder the use of UAVs in applications that require specialized or heavy equipment, such as certain scientific or industrial tasks (Ajakwe et al., 2023d).

3. **Laborious Weather Conditions:** Adverse weather conditions, such as strong winds, rain, snow, or extreme temperatures, can significantly impact UAV flight performance and pose safety risks (Ajakwe et al., 2023a). Flying in challenging weather conditions may lead to instability, reduced battery life, or even complete loss of the UAV.

4. **Legal and Regulatory Restrictions:** Governments and aviation authorities have established strict regulations and guidelines for UAV operations to ensure safety and protect airspace. Compliance with these regulations can limit the areas where UAVs can operate or require specific certifications for certain applications (Ajakwe et al., 2023d).

5. **Limited Range:** UAVs are typically limited in their operating range, especially consumer-grade models. This limitation can restrict their use in applications that require long-distance flights, such as large-scale surveying or remote inspections.

6. **Line of Sight and Communication Range Constraint:** Most UAVs rely on radio frequency communication, which can be limited by line-of-sight constraints or interference from other signals (Ajakwe et al., 2023e). This limitation can affect control and data transmission, particularly in remote or obstructed areas.

7. **Large Volume of Data Processing and Storage:** High-quality cameras and sensors mounted on UAVs can generate large amounts of data during flights. Processing and storing this data in real-time can be challenging, requiring powerful onboard computing or a reliable data link to ground stations.

8. **Laws on Privacy Concerns:** The proliferation of UAVs raises concerns about privacy, as they can be equipped with cameras and potentially used for intrusive surveillance or data gathering without consent (Ajakwe et al., 2023d).

9. **Loose to Hacking:** UAVs are susceptible to cybersecurity threats, and if compromised, they can pose serious safety and security risks. Hackers could take control of a drone, steal data, or use it for malicious purposes (Ahakonye et al., 2022; Ihekoronye et al., 2022a).

10. **Limited Autonomy:** While advancements in AI and autonomous technologies have enabled some level of automation, most UAVs still require human operators for complex tasks and decision-making

(Ajakwe et al., 2022c). Full autonomy for UAVs is still a developing field, and safety concerns limit its implementation in many scenarios.

Despite these limitations, ongoing research and technological advancements continue to address some of these challenges, making UAVs increasingly capable and valuable tools for various applications. However, it is essential to understand and consider these limitations while utilizing UAVs for different tasks to ensure safe and effective operations.

6.0 CONNECTED INTELLIGENCE FOR COST EFFECTIVE FARMING: THE ROAD MAP

Leveraging the mobility and other unique characteristics of UAVs with the sophistication of AI object detection models, cost effective farming and crop yield can be achieved through connected intelligence (CI) and connected innovation intelligence (CII). According to Ajakwe et al (2023c), CI and CII help to create value and improve the reliability of the system's decision-making capacity. Specifically, the CII paradigm aims to improve the competitive value, econometric indices (cost-effectiveness), ergonomics (user perception), and technical scalability of a design or ideation process (Ajakwe et al., 2022a). The development of lightweight AI object detection models that are mounted on electro-optical cameras of UAVs is fundamental in revolutionizing the landscape of agro-allied productions. Although there are about 570 million farms worldwide and 95% of them are less than 5 hectares, AI solutions are majorly implemented on farms with over 100 hectares of land due to the high cost of implementation, the agricultural drone market is predicted to expand from $1.2 billion (USD) in 2019 to $4.8 billion (USD) in 2024 and it is expected to grow at a compound annual growth rate (CAGR) of 23.1%. Drone data collected on farms is frequently utilized to better inform agronomic choices as part of a system known as precision agriculture (PA). According to some reports, adopting precision farming techniques can enhance yields by up to 5% (Amarasingam et al., 2022).

Precision farming is an act that gathers, maps and analyses data based on agricultural land variability and helps to draw relevant and useful inferences for proactive farm management decisions based on the results of such analysis, coupled with a proper application of pesticides and fertilizers in a controlled manner. The UAVs in PA consist of different integrating sensors (high-resolution RGB, multispectral, hyperspectral, LiDAR, and thermal), Internet connectivity, flight mission, data collection, image processing, and AI (Amarasingam et al., 2022) as shown in Figure 4. AI is now being greatly explored in various agricultural processes (Figure 6), an AI-based application for recognizing, counting, and geolocating plants, as well as assessing plant height and canopy size and creating plant health maps now exist, with various systems for assessing digital photographs of citrus trees using machine learning techniques (Ampatzidis et al., 2020).

Figure 8. *Major plant parameters captured with UAV with AI-empowered camera*
NO IMAGE PROVIDED
(Source: author)

For an effective monitoring of the plant diseases at the field size, which is critical for disease control, an unmanned aerial vehicle (UAV) outfitted with a hyperspectral sensor to capture hyperspectral pictures at the field size have been utilized and have helped to establish a standard for reliable disease surveillance with UAV hyperspectral photos in wheat production (Guo et al, 2021). Phenology detection is highly essential for crop management, yield estimation and estimation of harvest time. However, prior methods of estimation were limited in that the performance of these approaches is determined by the time-series data's duration and temporal resolution. UAV have helped to overcome this limitation as it has now been used to estimate plant phenology, through its identification of the principal growth stages in rice with a top accuracy of 83.9% and a mean absolute error (MAE) of 0.18 (Yang et al., 2020). Plant nitrogen concentration (PNC) is an important biomarker of crop Nitrogen (N) status that may be utilized for N nutrition diagnosis and control. While most other measurement methods were found to be only weakly related to PNC, UAV imagery processing did not only explain the 61% and 51% variations in groups and seasons, but it significantly improved the accuracy of PNC detection in rice, thus making its integration a desirable technique for crop growth monitoring (Zheng et al., 2018). Gao et al. also used hyperspectral datasets and the AlexNet CNN deep learning network to categorize strawberry fruits into early-ripe and ripe phases and obtained 98.6% classification accuracy (Gao et al., 2020).

The connected intelligence achieved through the convergence of onboard, edge-friendly, and AI-empowered electro-optical cameras mounted on UAVs can be summarized as timely and accurate data availability which plays a crucial role in decision-making processes. When it comes to detecting crop lesions, accurate data analysis and prediction via UAV-enabled-AI-empowered cognitive tool is essential for:

1. **Effective Disease Identification:** Accurate data provides a reliable basis for identifying crop lesions and distinguishing them from other types of damage or abnormalities. Correct identification is crucial for implementing appropriate disease management strategies and minimizing crop losses.
2. **Efficient and Precise Treatment:** Accurate data enables farmers and agronomists to select the most suitable treatment options for crop lesions. This precision ensures that the chosen interventions effectively target the specific disease, minimizing the use of unnecessary chemicals or resources.
3. **Early Detection:** Accurate data enables the early detection of crop lesions, even at their initial stages when the visual symptoms might be subtle. Early detection enhances the chances of successful disease management and prevents the spread of diseases to neighboring plants or fields.
4. **Evaluation and Monitoring of Disease Progression:** Accurate data allows for precise monitoring of the progression of crop lesions over time. This information helps in assessing the effectiveness of treatment methods and making timely adjustments if necessary.
5. **Exogenic Surveillance:** Accurate physical surveillance of smart farming geographical settings against external aggressors, climate change, and unsolicited intrusion into the physical farm space.

To facilitate accelerate crop disease monitoring and by extension guarantee sustainable food security through the deployment of UAV-AI empowered technologies for surveillance, studies focusing on the real-time implementation of transparent AI models for UAV are highly recommended. There is a need to go beyond supervised learning AI models (that require laborious data annotations) to semi-supervised and reinforcement models. The application of models in the actual world is unquestionably a crucial indicator of how well an idea is performing. Most UAVs have not yet adopted cutting-edge AI models for greater sophistication and performance. Research effort must be directed into developing customizable AI architectures that incorporates explainable AI algorithms (XAI), semi-supervised learning (SSL) algorithm, federated learning (FL) algorithms, edge AI algorithms (EAI), and reinforcement learning (RL) algorithms. The incorporation of these algorithms into UAVs for crop monitoring and disease detection will encourage efficient resource allocation, scalable and large-scale compliance, less human intervention in model training and learning, efficient representation learning, light-weight computing complexity, increase mobility and communication capacity, tractable and transparent paradigm for factual data analysis, and decomposable reverse engineering process, among other intangible benefits. Also, since the UAV-AI cognition for crop monitoring and disease curtailment works synergistically over a network, security of both the physical infrastructure and communication protocol is critical against intrusion and unauthorized access (Ajakwe et al., 2022d). Finally, constant collaborative training and retraining of engineers (AI engineers, mechatronics, agricultural engineers, etc.) is crucial for cross fertilization of ideas and latest updates of emerging trends in their designs in the quest to circumvent the dynamic changes in crop monitoring, plant disease detection and prevention, and other activities in a farming settlement. This is to guarantee overall food security and sustainable deployment of technology that ensures positive returns on investment.

7.0 CONCLUSION

The deployment of fast and efficient unmanned aerial vehicles (UAVs) that are empowered by AI models for crop lesion detection and monitoring can provide several direct benefits for farmers. Early detection of crop lesions through advanced multispectral or thermal camera will undoubtedly foster faster response in eliciting the causes and nipping the problem at the bud. This will directly result in precise monitoring, time and cost savings, enhanced disease management, data-driven decision-making, and environmental sustainability due to rapid global climate changes. By addressing the fundamental issues in UAV designs, operational regulations, battery management, etc. as well as the computational complexity issues of object detection models, there will be quantum leap in the application of drones to achieve increased crop monitoring, proactive disease control, accelerative food security for sustainable development. As connected innovation intelligence continues to thrive, a measurable increase in agricultural portfolio is guaranteed.

REFERENCES

Agri, U., Chaudhary, P., Sharma, A., & Kukreti, B. (2022). Physiological response of maize plants and its rhizospheric microbiome under the influence of potential bioinoculants and nanochitosan. *Plant and Soil, 474*(1-2), 451–468. doi:10.100711104-022-05351-2

Ahakonye, L. A. C., Nwakanma, C. I., Ajakwe, S. O., Lee, J. M., & Kim, D. S. (2022, February). Countering DNS vulnerability to attacks using ensemble learning. In *2022 International Conference on Artificial Intelligence in Information and Communication (ICAIIC)* (pp. 007-010). IEEE.

Ahmad, M., Abdullah, M., Moon, H., & Han, D. (2021). Plant disease detection in imbalanced datasets using efficient convolutional neural networks with stepwise transfer learning. *IEEE Access : Practical Innovations, Open Solutions, 9*, 140565–140580. doi:10.1109/ACCESS.2021.3119655

Ajakwe, S., Kim, D. S., & Lee, J. M. (2023b). Radicalization of Airspace Security: Prospects and Botheration of Drone Defense System Technology. *The Journal of Intelligence, Conflict, and Warfare*, 6(1), 23–48. doi:10.21810/jicw.v6i1.5274

Ajakwe, S. O., Ajakwe, I. U., Jun, T., Kim, D. S., & Lee, J. M. (2023c). CIS-WQMS: Connected intelligence smart water quality monitoring scheme. *Internet of Things : Engineering Cyber Physical Human Systems*, 23, 100800. doi:10.1016/j.iot.2023.100800

Ajakwe, S. O., Ihekoronye, V. U., Ajakwe, I. U., Jun, T., Kim, D. S., & Lee, J. M. (2022a, October). Connected Intelligence for Smart Water Quality Monitoring System in IIoT. In *2022 13th International Conference on Information and Communication Technology Convergence (ICTC)* (pp. 2386-2391). IEEE. 10.1109/ICTC55196.2022.9952785

Ajakwe, S. O., Ihekoronye, V. U., Ajakwe, I. U., Jun, T., Kim, D. S., & Lee, J. M. (2022e). Connected Intelligence for Smart Water Quality Monitoring System in IIoT. *In 2022 13th International Conference on Information and Communication Technology Convergence (ICTC)* (pp. 2386-2391). IEEE.

Ajakwe, S. O., Ihekoronye, V. U., Kim, D. S., & Lee, J. M. (2022, September). Tractable minacious drones aerial recognition and safe-channel neutralization scheme for mission critical operations. In *2022 IEEE 27th International Conference on Emerging Technologies and Factory Automation (ETFA)* (pp. 1-8). IEEE. 10.1109/ETFA52439.2022.9921494

Ajakwe, S. O., Ihekoronye, V. U., Kim, D. S., & Lee, J. M. (2022b). DRONET: Multi-tasking framework for real-time industrial facility aerial surveillance and safety. *Drones (Basel)*, 6(2), 46. doi:10.3390/drones6020046

Ajakwe, S. O., Ihekoronye, V. U., Kim, D. S., & Lee, J. M. (2022c). AI-trust in intelligent autonomous decision-centric systems: Introspection of security architectures. 1–2. *In 2022 Korean Institute of Communication and Information Science*. NIH.

Ajakwe, S. O., Ihekoronye, V. U., Kim, D. S., & Lee, J. M. (2022d). Pervasive intrusion detection scheme to mitigate sensor attacks on UAV Networks. *In 2022 Korean Institute of Communication and Information Sciences (KICS) summer conference*, 1267-1268.

Ajakwe, S. O., Ihekoronye, V. U., Kim, D. S., & Lee, J. M. (2022e, October). SimNet: UAV-integrated sensor nodes localization for communication intelligence in 6G networks. In *2022 27th Asia Pacific Conference on Communications (APCC)* (pp. 344-347). IEEE.

Ajakwe, S. O., Ihekoronye, V. U., Kim, D. S., & Lee, J. M. (2023a). ALIEN: Assisted Learning Invasive Encroachment Neutralization for Secured Drone Transportation System. *Sensors (Basel)*, 23(3), 1233. doi:10.339023031233 PMID:36772272

Ajakwe, S. O., Ihekoronye, V. U., Mohtasin, G., Akter, R., Aouto, A., Kim, D. S., & Lee, J. M. (2022f). *VisioDECT Dataset: An Aerial Dataset for Scenario-Based Multi-Drone Detection and Identification*. IEEE Dataport.

Ajakwe, S. O., Kim, D. S., & Lee, J. M. (2023d). Drone Transportation System: Systematic Review of Security Dynamics for Smart Mobility. *IEEE Internet of Things Journal*, 10(16), 14462–14482. doi:10.1109/JIOT.2023.3266843

Ajakwe, S. O., Nwakanma, C. I., Lee, J. M., & Kim, D. S. (2020, October). Machine learning algorithm for intelligent prediction for military logistics and planning. In *2020 International Conference on Information and Communication Technology Convergence (ICTC)* (pp. 417-419). IEEE. 10.1109/ICTC49870.2020.9289286

Amarasingam, N., Salgadoe, A. S. A., Powell, K., Gonzalez, L. F., & Natarajan, S. (2022). A review of UAV platforms, sensors, and applications for monitoring of sugarcane crops. *Remote Sensing Applications: Society and Environment, 26*, 100712. doi:10.1016/j.rsase.2022.100712

Ampatzidis, Y., Partel, V., & Costa, L. (2020). Agroview: Cloud-based application to process, analyze and visualize UAV-collected data for precision agriculture applications utilizing artificial intelligence. *Computers and Electronics in Agriculture, 174*, 105457. doi:10.1016/j.compag.2020.105457

Anderson, K., & Gaston, K. J. (2013). Lightweight Unmanned Aerial Vehicles Will Revolutionize Spatial Ecology. *Frontiers in Ecology and the Environment, 11*(3), 138–146. doi:10.1890/120150

Bacco, M., Brunori, G., Rolandi, S., & Scotti, I. (2022). Smart and sustainable food: What is ahead? In *Future Foods* (pp. 39–48). Academic Press. doi:10.1016/B978-0-323-91001-9.00015-3

Barbedo, J. G. A., & Koenigkan, L. V. (2018). Perspectives on The Use of Unmanned Aerial Systems to Monitor Cattle. *Outlook on Agriculture, 47*(3), 214–222. doi:10.1177/0030727018781876

Ben Ayed, R., & Hanana, M. (2021). Artificial intelligence to improve the food and agriculture sector. *Journal of Food Quality, 2021*, 1–7. doi:10.1155/2021/5584754

Bouguettaya, A., Zarzour, H., Kechida, A., & Taberkit, A. M. (2021, July). Recent advances on UAV and deep learning for early crop diseases identification: A short review. In *2021 International Conference on Information Technology (ICIT)* (pp. 334-339). IEEE. 10.1109/ICIT52682.2021.9491661

Bouguettaya, A., Zarzour, H., Kechida, A., & Taberkit, A. M. (2022). Deep learning techniques to classify agricultural crops through UAV imagery: A review. *Neural Computing & Applications, 34*(12), 9511–9536. doi:10.100700521-022-07104-9 PMID:35281624

Chapman, S., Merz, T., Chan, A., Jackway, P., Hrabar, S., Dreccer, M., Holland, E., Zheng, B., Ling, T., & Jimenez-Berni, J. (2014). Pheno-copter: A low-altitude, autonomous remote-sensing robotic helicopter for high-throughput fieldbased phenotyping. *Agronomy (Basel), 4*(2), 279–301. doi:10.3390/agronomy4020279

Choudhary, S., Gaurav, V., Singh, A., & Agarwal, S. (2019). Autonomous crop irrigation system using artificial intelligence. *International Journal of Engineering and Advanced Technology, 8*(5), 46–51. doi:10.35940/ijeat.E1010.0585S19

Cunningham, F., Achuthan, P., Akanni, W., Allen, J., Amode, M. R., Armean, I. M., Bennett, R., Bhai, J., Billis, K., Boddu, S., Cummins, C., Davidson, C., Dodiya, K. J., Gall, A., Girón, C. G., Gil, L., Grego, T., Haggerty, L., Haskell, E., & Flicek, P. (2019). Ensembl 2019. *Nucleic Acids Research, 47*(D1), D745–D751. doi:10.1093/nar/gky1113 PMID:30407521

Dang, L. M., Hassan, S. I., & Suhyeon, I. (2020). UAV based wilt detection system via convolutional neural networks. *Sustainable Computing: Informatics and Systems*, *28*, 100250. doi:10.1016/j.suscom.2018.05.010

Dar, M. H., Waza, S. A., Shukla, S., Zaidi, N. W., Nayak, S., Hossain, M., Kumar, A., Ismail, A. M., & Singh, U. S. (2020). Drought tolerant rice for ensuring food security in Eastern India. *Sustainability (Basel)*, *12*(6), 2214. doi:10.3390u12062214

Deng, J., Zhou, H., Lv, X., Yang, L., Shang, J., Sun, Q., Zheng, X., Zhou, C., Zhao, B., Wu, J., & Ma, Z. (2022). Applying convolutional neural networks for detecting wheat stripe rust transmission centers under complex field conditions using RGB-based high spatial resolution images from UAVs. *Computers and Electronics in Agriculture*, *200*, 107211. doi:10.1016/j.compag.2022.107211

Deng, X., Huang, Z., Zheng, Z., Lan, Y., & Dai, F. (2019). Field detection and classification of citrus Huanglongbing based on hyperspectral reflectance. *Computers and Electronics in Agriculture*, *167*, 105006. doi:10.1016/j.compag.2019.105006

Dong, A. Y., Wang, Z., Huang, J. J., Song, B. A., & Hao, G. F. (2021). Bioinformatic tools support decision-making in plant disease management. *Trends in Plant Science*, *26*(9), 953–967. doi:10.1016/j.tplants.2021.05.001 PMID:34039514

Egan, P. A., Dicks, L. V., Hokkanen, H. M., & Stenberg, J. A. (2020). Delivering integrated pest and pollinator management (IPPM). *Trends in Plant Science*, *25*(6), 577–589. doi:10.1016/j.tplants.2020.01.006 PMID:32407697

Gabriel, J. L., Zarco-Tejada, P. J., López-Herrera, P. J., Pérez-Martín, E., Alonso-Ayuso, M., & Quemada, M. (2017). Airborne and Ground Level Sensors for Monitoring Nitrogen Status in A Maize Crop. *Biosystems Engineering*, *160*, 124–133. doi:10.1016/j.biosystemseng.2017.06.003

Gao, D., Sun, Q., Hu, B., & Zhang, S. (2020). A framework for agricultural pest and disease monitoring based on internet-of-things and unmanned aerial vehicles. *Sensors (Basel)*, *20*(5), 1487. doi:10.339020051487 PMID:32182732

Gómez-Chabla, R., Real-Avilés, K., Morán, C., Grijalva, P., & Recalde, T. (2018, December). IoT applications in agriculture: A systematic literature review. In *2nd International conference on ICTs in agronomy and environment* (pp. 68-76). Cham: Springer International Publishing.

Guo, A., Huang, W., Dong, Y., Ye, H., Ma, H., Liu, B., Wu, W., Ren, Y., Ruan, C., & Geng, Y. (2021). Wheat yellow rust detection using UAV-based hyperspectral technology. *Remote Sensing (Basel)*, *13*(1), 123. doi:10.3390/rs13010123

Hogan, S. D., Kelly, M., Stark, B., & Chen, Y. (2017). Unmanned Aerial Systems for Agriculture and Natural Resources. *California Agriculture*, *71*(1), 5–14. doi:10.3733/ca.2017a0002

Hughes, D., & Salathé, M. (2015). *An open access repository of images on plant health to enable the development of mobile disease diagnostics*. arXiv preprint arXiv:1511.08060.

Ihekoronye, V. U., Ajakwe, S. O., Kim, D. S., & Lee, J. M. (2021). UAV Assisted Real-Time Detection and Recognition of Citrus Disease in Smart Farm using Deep Learning. *In 2021 Korean Institute of Communication and Information Science*, (pp. 453-454). Research Gate.

Ihekoronye, V. U., Ajakwe, S. O., Kim, D. S., & Lee, J. M. (2022, February). Aerial supervision of drones and other flying objects using convolutional neural networks. In *2022 International Conference on Artificial Intelligence in Information and Communication (ICAIIC)* (pp. 069-074). IEEE. 10.1109/ICAIIC54071.2022.9722702

Ihekoronye, V. U., Ajakwe, S. O., Kim, D. S., & Lee, J. M. (2022a, November). Hierarchical intrusion detection system for secured military drone network: A perspicacious approach. In MILCOM 2022-2022 IEEE Military Communications Conference (MILCOM) (pp. 336-341). IEEE. doi:10.1109/MILCOM55135.2022.10017532

Ishengoma, F. S., Rai, I. A., & Said, R. N. (2021). Identification of maize leaves infected by fall army-worms using UAV-based imagery and convolutional neural networks. *Computers and Electronics in Agriculture*, *184*, 106124. doi:10.1016/j.compag.2021.106124

Javaid, M., Haleem, A., Singh, R. P., & Suman, R. (2022). Enhancing smart farming through the applications of Agriculture 4.0 technologies. *International Journal of Intelligent Networks*, *3*, 150–164. doi:10.1016/j.ijin.2022.09.004

Kalyabina, V. P., Esimbekova, E. N., Kopylova, K. V., & Kratasyuk, V. A. (2021). Pesticides: Formulants, distribution pathways and effects on human health–a review. *Toxicology Reports*, *8*, 1179–1192. doi:10.1016/j.toxrep.2021.06.004 PMID:34150527

Kerkech, M., Hafiane, A., & Canals, R. (2018). Deep leaning approach with colorimetric spaces and vegetation indices for vine diseases detection in UAV images. *Computers and Electronics in Agriculture*, *155*, 237–243. doi:10.1016/j.compag.2018.10.006

Kerkech, M., Hafiane, A., & Canals, R. (2020). VddNet: Vine disease detection network based on multispectral images and depth map. *Remote Sensing (Basel)*, *12*(20), 3305. doi:10.3390/rs12203305

Kharim, M. N. A., Wayayok, A., Abdullah, A. F., Shariff, A. R. M., Husin, E. M., & Mahadi, M. R. (2022). Predictive zoning of pest and disease infestations in rice field based on UAV aerial imagery. *The Egyptian Journal of Remote Sensing and Space Sciences*, *25*(3), 831–840. doi:10.1016/j.ejrs.2022.08.001

Khattak, A., Asghar, M. U., Batool, U., Asghar, M. Z., Ullah, H., Al-Rakhami, M., & Gumaei, A. (2021). Automatic detection of citrus fruit and leaves diseases using deep neural network model. *IEEE Access : Practical Innovations, Open Solutions*, *9*, 112942–112954. doi:10.1109/ACCESS.2021.3096895

Kouadio, L., El Jarroudi, M., Belabess, Z., Laasli, S.-E., Roni, M. Z. K., Amine, I. D. I., Mokhtari, N., Mokrini, F., Junk, J., & Lahlali, R. (2023). A Review on UAV-Based Applications for Plant Disease Detection and Monitoring. *Remote Sensing (Basel)*, *2023*(15), 4273. doi:10.3390/rs15174273

Ksibi, A., Ayadi, M., Soufiene, B. O., Jamjoom, M. M., & Ullah, Z. (2022). MobiRes-net: A hybrid deep learning model for detecting and classifying olive leaf diseases. *Applied Sciences (Basel, Switzerland)*, *12*(20), 10278. doi:10.3390/app122010278

Kulkarni, O. (2018, August). Crop disease detection using deep learning. In 2018 Fourth international conference on computing communication control and automation (ICCUBEA) (pp. 1-4). IEEE. 10.1109/ICCUBEA.2018.8697390

Kumar, R., Singh, M. P., Kumar, P., & Singh, J. P. (2015, May). Crop Selection Method to maximize crop yield rate using machine learning technique. In 2015 international conference on smart technologies and management for computing, communication, controls, energy and materials (ICSTM) (pp. 138-145). IEEE. doi:10.1109/ICSTM.2015.7225403

Kuswidiyanto, L. W., Noh, H. H., & Han, X. (2022). Plant Disease Diagnosis Using Deep Learning Based on Aerial Hyperspectral Images: A Review. *Remote Sensing (Basel)*, *14*(23), 6031. doi:10.3390/rs14236031

Lan, Y., Huang, Z., Deng, X., Zhu, Z., Huang, H., Zheng, Z., Lian, B., Zeng, G., & Tong, Z. (2020). Comparison of machine learning methods for citrus greening detection on UAV multispectral images. *Computers and Electronics in Agriculture*, *171*, 105234. doi:10.1016/j.compag.2020.105234

Lan, Y., & Wang, G. (2018). Development situation and prospects of China's crop protection UAV industry. *Nongye Gongcheng Jishu*, *38*, 17–27.

Leong, W. H., Teh, S. Y., Hossain, M. M., Nadarajaw, T., Zabidi-Hussin, Z., Chin, S. Y., Lai, K.-S., & Lim, S. H. E. (2020). Application, monitoring and adverse effects in pesticide use: The importance of reinforcement of Good Agricultural Practices (GAPs). *Journal of Environmental Management*, *260*, 109987. doi:10.1016/j.jenvman.2019.109987 PMID:32090796

Liang, D., Liu, W., Zhao, L., Zong, S., & Luo, Y. (2022). An improved convolutional neural network for plant disease detection using unmanned aerial vehicle images. *Nature Environment and Pollution Technology*, *21*(2), 899–908. doi:10.46488/NEPT.2022.v21i02.053

Liu, S. Y. (2020). Artificial intelligence (AI) in agriculture. *IT Professional*, *22*(3), 14–15. doi:10.1109/MITP.2020.2986121

Lundin, O., Rundlöf, M., Jonsson, M., Bommarco, R., & Williams, N. M. (2021). Integrated pest and pollinator management–expanding the concept. *Frontiers in Ecology and the Environment*, *19*(5), 283–291. doi:10.1002/fee.2325

Mason-D'Croz, D., Bogard, J. R., Herrero, M., Robinson, S., Sulser, T. B., Wiebe, K., Willenbockel, D., & Godfray, H. C. J. (2020). Modelling the global economic consequences of a major African swine fever outbreak in China. *Nature Food*, *1*(4), 221–228. doi:10.103843016-020-0057-2 PMID:33634268

Megat Mohamed Nazir, M. N., Terhem, R., Norhisham, A. R., Mohd Razali, S., & Meder, R. (2021). Early monitoring of health status of plantation-grown eucalyptus pellita at large spatial scale via visible spectrum imaging of canopy foliage using unmanned aerial vehicles. *Forests*, *12*(10), 1393. doi:10.3390/f12101393

Messina, G., & Modica, G. (2020). Applications of UAV thermal imagery in precision agriculture: State of the art and future research outlook. *Remote Sensing (Basel)*, *12*(9), 1491. doi:10.3390/rs12091491

Moradi, S., Bokani, A., & Hassan, J. (2022, November). UAV-based Smart Agriculture: a Review of UAV Sensing and Applications. In *2022 32nd International Telecommunication Networks and Applications Conference (ITNAC)* (pp. 181-184). IEEE.

Mulero-Pázmány, M., Stolper, R., Essen, L., Negro, J. J., & Sassen, T. (2014). Remotely Piloted Aircraft Systems as A Rhinoceros Anti-Poaching tool In Africa. *PLoS One*, *9*(1), e83873. doi:10.1371/journal.pone.0083873 PMID:24416177

Nayak, P., & Solanki, H. (2021). Pesticides and Indian agriculture—A review. *Int J Res Granthaalayah*, *9*(5), 250–263. doi:10.29121/granthaalayah.v9.i5.2021.3930

Pan, Q., Gao, M., Wu, P., Yan, J., & Li, S. (2021). A deep-learning-based approach for wheat yellow rust disease recognition from unmanned aerial vehicle images. *Sensors (Basel)*, *21*(19), 6540. doi:10.339021196540 PMID:34640873

Panetto, H., Lezoche, M., Hormazabal, J. E. H., Diaz, M. D. M. E. A., & Kacprzyk, J. (2020). Special issue on Agri-Food 4.0 and digitalization in agriculture supply chains-New directions, challenges and applications. *Computers in Industry*, *116*, 103188. doi:10.1016/j.compind.2020.103188

Pathak, V. M., Verma, V. K., Rawat, B. S., Kaur, B., Babu, N., Sharma, A., Dewali, S., Yadav, M., Kumari, R., Singh, S., Mohapatra, A., Pandey, V., Rana, N., & Cunill, J. M. (2022). Current status of pesticide effects on environment, human health and it's eco-friendly management as bioremediation: A comprehensive review. *Frontiers in Microbiology*, *13*, 2833. doi:10.3389/fmicb.2022.962619 PMID:36060785

Prasad, A., Mehta, N., Horak, M., & Bae, W. D. (2022). A Two-Step Machine Learning Approach for Crop Disease Detection Using GAN and UAV Technology. *Remote Sensing (Basel)*, *14*(19), 4765. doi:10.3390/rs14194765

Ragaveena, S., Shirly Edward, A., & Surendran, U. (2021). Smart controlled environment agriculture methods: A holistic review. *Reviews in Environmental Science and Biotechnology*, *20*(4), 887–913. doi:10.100711157-021-09591-z

Ramli, M. R., Daely, P. T., Kim, D. S., & Lee, J. M. (2020). IoT-based adaptive network mechanism for reliable smart farm system. *Computers and Electronics in Agriculture*, *170*, 105287. doi:10.1016/j.compag.2020.105287

Rangarajan, A. K., Balu, E. J., Boligala, M. S., Jagannath, A., & Ranganathan, B. N. (2022). A low-cost UAV for detection of Cercospora leaf spot in okra using deep convolutional neural network. *Multimedia Tools and Applications*, *81*(15), 21565–21589. doi:10.100711042-022-12464-4

Rangarajan, A. K., Balu, E. J., Boligala, M. S., Jagannath, A., & Ranganathan, B. N. (2022). A low-cost UAV for detection of Cercospora leaf spot in okra using deep convolutional neural network. *Multimedia Tools and Applications*, *81*(15), 21565–21589. doi:10.100711042-022-12464-4

Ristaino, J. B., Anderson, P. K., Bebber, D. P., Brauman, K. A., Cunniffe, N. J., Fedoroff, N. V., Finegold, C., Garrett, K. A., Gilligan, C. A., Jones, C. M., Martin, M. D., MacDonald, G. K., Neenan, P., Records, A., Schmale, D. G., Tateosian, L., & Wei, Q. (2021). The persistent threat of emerging plant disease pandemics to global food security. *Proceedings of the National Academy of Sciences of the United States of America*, *118*(23), e2022239118. doi:10.1073/pnas.2022239118 PMID:34021073

Shahi, T. B., Xu, C. Y., Neupane, A., & Guo, W. (2023). Recent Advances in Crop Disease Detection Using UAV and Deep Learning Techniques. *Remote Sensing (Basel)*, *15*(9), 2450. doi:10.3390/rs15092450

Sharifi, R., & Ryu, C. M. (2018). Biogenic volatile compounds for plant disease diagnosis and health improvement. *The Plant Pathology Journal*, *34*(6), 459–469. doi:10.5423/PPJ.RW.06.2018.0118 PMID:30588219

Shi, Y., Han, L., Kleerekoper, A., Chang, S., & Hu, T. (2022). Novel cropdocnet model for automated potato late blight disease detection from unmanned aerial vehicle-based hyperspectral imagery. *Remote Sensing (Basel)*, *14*(02), 396. doi:10.3390/rs14020396

Singh, A. K., Ganapathysubramanian, B., Sarkar, S., & Singh, A. (2018). Deep learning for plant stress phenotyping: Trends and future perspectives. *Trends in Plant Science*, *23*(10), 883–898. doi:10.1016/j.tplants.2018.07.004 PMID:30104148

Su, J., Liu, C., Hu, X., Xu, X., Guo, L., & Chen, W. H. (2019). Spatio-temporal monitoring of wheat yellow rust using UAV multispectral imagery. *Computers and Electronics in Agriculture*, *167*, 105035. doi:10.1016/j.compag.2019.105035

Su, J., Yi, D., Su, B., Mi, Z., Liu, C., Hu, X., Xu, X., Guo, L., & Chen, W. H. (2020). Aerial visual perception in smart farming: Field study of wheat yellow rust monitoring. *IEEE Transactions on Industrial Informatics*, *17*(3), 2242–2249. doi:10.1109/TII.2020.2979237

Sugiura, R., Noguchi, N., & Ishii, K. (2005). Remote-sensing technology for vegetation monitoring using an unmanned helicopter. *Biosystems Engineering*, *90*(4), 369–379. doi:10.1016/j.biosystemseng.2004.12.011

Sylvester, G. (2018). *E-Agriculture in Action: Drones for Agriculture*. Food and Agriculture Organization of the United Nations and International Telecommunication Union.

Tokunaga, H., Anh, N. H., Dong, N. V., Ham, L. H., Hanh, N. T., Hung, N., Ishitani, M., Tuan, L. N., Utsumi, Y., Vu, N. A., & Seki, M. (2020). An efficient method of propagating cassava plants using aeroponic culture. *Journal of Crop Improvement*, *34*(1), 64–83. doi:10.1080/15427528.2019.1673271

Van De Vijver, R., Mertens, K., Heungens, K., Nuyttens, D., Wieme, J., Maes, W. H., Van Beek, J., Somers, B., & Saeys, W. (2022). Ultra-High-Resolution UAV-Based Detection of Alternaria solani Infections in Potato Fields. *Remote Sensing (Basel)*, *14*(24), 6232. doi:10.3390/rs14246232

Vroegindeweij, B. A., van Wijk, S. W., & van Henten, E. (2014). Autonomous unmanned aerial vehicles for agricultural applications. In: *Proceeding. International Conference of Agricultural Engineering (AgEng)*. Zurich, p. 8

Wang, L., Huang, X., Li, W., Yan, K., Han, Y., Zhang, Y., Pawlowski, L., & Lan, Y. (2022). Progress in Agricultural Unmanned Aerial Vehicles (UAVs) Applied in China and Prospects for Poland. *Agriculture*, *2022*(12), 397. doi:10.3390/agriculture12030397

Weinblum, N., Cna'Ani, A., Yaakov, B., Sadeh, A., Avraham, L., Opatovsky, I., & Tzin, V. (2021). Tomato cultivars resistant or susceptible to spider mites differ in their biosynthesis and metabolic profile of the monoterpenoid pathway. *Frontiers in Plant Science*, *12*, 630155. doi:10.3389/fpls.2021.630155 PMID:33719301

Whitfield, S., Challinor, A. J., & Rees, R. M. (2018). Frontiers in climate smart food systems: Outlining the research space. *Frontiers in Sustainable Food Systems*, 2, 2. doi:10.3389/fsufs.2018.00002

Wokorach, G., Edema, H., & Echodu, R. (2018). Sweet potato seed exchange systems and knowledge on sweetpotato viral diseases among local farmers in Acholi Sub Region-Northern Uganda. *African Journal of Agricultural Research*, 13(45). PMID:33282145

Yang, Q., Shi, L., Han, J., Yu, J., & Huang, K. (2020). A near real-time deep learning approach for detecting rice phenology based on UAV images. *Agricultural and Forest Meteorology*, 287, 107938. doi:10.1016/j.agrformet.2020.107938

Yu, K. D. S., & Aviso, K. B. (2020). Modelling the economic impact and ripple effects of disease outbreaks. *Process Integration and Optimization for Sustainability*, 4(2), 183–186. doi:10.100741660-020-00113-y

Yu, R., Huo, L., Huang, H., Yuan, Y., Gao, B., Liu, Y., Yu, L., Li, H., Yang, L., Ren, L., & Luo, Y. (2022). Early detection of pine wilt disease tree candidates using time-series of spectral signatures. *Frontiers in Plant Science*, 13, 1000093. doi:10.3389/fpls.2022.1000093 PMID:36311089

Zhang, T., Yang, Z., Xu, Z., & Li, J. (2022). Wheat yellow rust severity detection by efficient DF-UNet and UAV multispectral imagery. *IEEE Sensors Journal*, 22(9), 9057–9068. doi:10.1109/JSEN.2022.3156097

Zhang, X., Han, L., Dong, Y., Shi, Y., Huang, W., Han, L., González-Moreno, P., Ma, H., Ye, H., & Sobeih, T. (2019). A deep learning-based approach for automated yellow rust disease detection from high-resolution hyperspectral UAV images. *Remote Sensing (Basel)*, 11(13), 1554. doi:10.3390/rs11131554

Zhang, Y., Song, C., & Zhang, D. (2020). Deep learning-based object detection improvement for tomato disease. *IEEE Access : Practical Innovations, Open Solutions*, 8, 56607–56614. doi:10.1109/ACCESS.2020.2982456

Zhao, X. H., Zhang, J. C., Tang, A. L., Yu, Y. F., Yan, L. J., Chen, D. M., & Yuan, L. (2022). The stress detection and segmentation strategy in tea plant at canopy level. *Frontiers in Plant Science*, 13, 9054. doi:10.3389/fpls.2022.949054 PMID:35873976

Zheng, H., Cheng, T., Li, D., Yao, X., Tian, Y., Cao, W., & Zhu, Y. (2018). Combining unmanned aerial vehicle (UAV)-based multispectral imagery and ground-based hyperspectral data for plant nitrogen concentration estimation in rice. *Frontiers in Plant Science*, 9, 936. doi:10.3389/fpls.2018.00936 PMID:30034405

Zou, Y., Mason, M. G., & Botella, J. R. (2020). Evaluation and improvement of isothermal amplification methods for point-of-need plant disease diagnostics. *PLoS One*, 15(6), e0235216. doi:10.1371/journal.pone.0235216 PMID:32598374

Chapter 10
Applicability of UAV in Crop Health Monitoring Using Machine Learning Techniques

Tej Bahadur Shahi
https://orcid.org/0000-0002-0616-3180
Central Queensland University, Australia

Ram Bahadur Khadka
https://orcid.org/0000-0002-1810-7493
Nepal Agricultural Research Council, Nepal

Arjun Neupane
Central Queensland University, Australia

ABSTRACT

Food demands are increasing globally. Various issues such as urbanization, climate change, and desertification increasingly favour crop pests and diseases that limit crop productivity. Elaborating and discussing the pragmatic knowledge and information on recent advances in tools and techniques for crop monitoring developed in recent decades might help agronomists make more informed decisions. This chapter discusses the progress and development of new techniques equipped with recent sensors and platforms such as drones that have revolutionized the way of understanding plant physiology and stresses. It begins with the introduction to various tools available for crop stress estimation, mainly based on optical imaging such as multispectral, thermal, and hyperspectral imaging. An overview of unmanned aerial vehicle (UAV) -based image processing pipeline is presented and shed light on the possible avenues of UAV-based remote sensing for crop health monitoring using machine learning approaches.

DOI: 10.4018/979-8-3693-0578-2.ch010

1. INTRODUCTION

Global food requirements by 2050 are expected to double the amount consumed in 2005 (Schaeffer et al., 2013). However, annual global productivity gains have been decelerating over the past two decades, and crop production area has decreased due to industrialization, desertification and urbanization, further constraining future food availability (Schaeffer et al., 2013). Despite these identifiable challenges, global agriculture is facing a severe threat from the changing climate, which is increasingly favourable to crop pests including diseases, insects and weeds that damage crop plants (Lamichhane et al., 2015). Furthermore, the changing climate also increases the pressure of abiotic stresses such as high temperature, water deficit, soil salinity and acidity. About 34% of global crop production is lost annually due to biotic and abiotic stresses (Oerke, 2006). The 2007 Intergovernmental Panel on Climate Change (Solomon, 2007) predicted that air temperature and the intensity and frequency of extreme weather events worldwide would increase significantly in the near term. These changes impact soil temperature and moisture regimes and may result in a higher risk of increasing impacts of plant threats (Manici et al., 2014).

Plants that provide food, fibre, and shelter to millions of lives on the earth, are always threatened by various biotic and abiotic stressors (Dresselhaus & Hückelhoven, 2018). These stressors could be unfavourable environments (e.g., extreme temperature, water stress, etc.), soil factors such as nutrient deficiencies, and toxicity or biotic factors such as pests, pathogens, and weeds. Plants have the capacity to tolerate these stresses at a certain level. During these phases, the impact of these stresses may remain hidden externally but has a significant impact on the plant's physiology and ultimately reduces the yield and quality of the crop (Bita & Gerats, 2013). Most of the time, the infected plants demonstrate the visible symptoms due to these stressors to the point where further management is either not possible or has already exacerbated the plant physiology to significantly lowered productivity and quality (Nazarov et al., 2020). The early detection of plant stresses could be achieved using optical imaging and machine-learning techniques (Butte et al., 2021). This field is emerging rapidly and can potentially change crop productivity more unprecedentedly.

Conventional crop disease assessment and monitoring methods, such as manual scouting, are not only time-consuming and labour-intensive but also prone to human biases, making it difficult to obtain accurate data (Shahi et al., 2023a). Therefore, the researchers have been exploring alternative technologies such as sensors, cameras and GPS to support the agriculture field data acquisitions. Ground or satellite-based remote sensing (RS) offers a quick and unbiased method for detecting and assessing crop diseases (Shahi et al., 2022b). Here, ground-based sensors can produce high-resolution imagery, but moving these sensors from one location to another location to measure crop disease is time-consuming. On the other hand, satellite-based remote sensing provides a wider view of the agricultural field and covers large geographical areas, but it has its own limitations in terms of revisiting time and sensor capabilities. In this context, unmanned aerial vehicles (UAVs) have the ability to avoid these and provide more accurate crop disease assessments (Nebikar et al., 2016).

Recent advances in UAV-based image processing techniques combined with available optical sensors have revolutionized the understanding of plant physiology and stresses. For instance, non-invasive sensors such as hyperspectral imaging equipped with UAVs have been utilized for the early detection of crop diseases (Thomas et al., 2018). Therefore, assessing the progress made so far and the challenges faced in applying optical sensors to monitor plant health is essential. Furthermore, it is also beneficial to know the potential applicability of recently introduced technologies such as UAVs and artificial intelligence (AI) for crop health monitoring (Su et al., 2022).

This study aims to compile the insights and expertise generated over the past few decades about the various tools and techniques for early crop disease estimation and monitoring, with a primary focus on Unmanned Aerial Vehicles (UAVs) and machine learning techniques. Furthermore, it discusses the various tools utilized for crop monitoring using optical sensors and drones or UAVs. Finally, it underscores the challenges and opportunities of UAV-based remote sensing for crop health monitoring. We believe that this study will serve as a valuable resource for readers and stakeholders, encompassing farmers and precision agriculture researchers, by providing insights into the effective utilization of UAV technology and machine learning for improved crop health monitoring practices.

The rest of the chapter is organized as follows. Section 2 introduces the various tools for crop health monitoring, including thermal, multispectral, and hyperspectral imaging. Section 3 discusses the UAV-based imaging systems for plant health monitoring, Section 4 illustrates plant stressors' monitoring using UAVs and ML techniques, and Sections 5 and 6 provide the discussion, conclusion, and recommendations.

2. TOOLS FOR CROP HEALTH MONITORING

Crop health monitoring is essential as plants are subjected to various stresses such as pests, insects, extreme temperatures, drought, water and so on. There has been consistent development of tools for enhancing crop monitoring efficiently and accurately. Initially, traditional methods such as visual inspection and human scouting were used for crop monitoring which is a tedious and time-consuming process. Furthermore, it might be biased as it relies on human observations. As technology progressed and advanced sensors were developed, remote sensing techniques emerged that utilized field-oriented sensors and satellite imagery to non-destructively evaluate crop health status. While ground-based sensors can offer finely detailed spatial imagery, relocating these sensors to measure field variations is a time-consuming process (Shahi et al., 2023a). On the other hand, satellite-based remote sensing can provide a broader view of agricultural fields on a global or regional scale but is bound by its own scheduling and sensor capabilities. Additionally, it may not offer real-time farm data. UAV-based remote sensing has progressed notably in recent years, which mitigates many of the constraints linked to satellite or aircraft-based remote sensing. For instance, UAVs introduce a level of flexibility, permitting users to revisit fields whenever weather conditions permit, resulting in the capture of imagery with a high temporal resolution. This innovation has fundamentally transformed crop health monitoring by supplying farmers with intricate and precise insights into their crops (Nex et al., 2022).

Here, we discuss the various sensors and tools used to monitor crop stress, primarily focusing on optical sensors (see Table 1).

Table 1. Tools used for crop health monitoring

Tools	Sectors	References
Thermal sensors	Crop stress estimation	(Messina & Modica, 2020)
Multispectral sensors	Crop disease estimation	(Shahi et al., 2023a)
Hyperspectral sensors	Early crop disease detection	(Lacotte et al., 2022)
Wearable Sensors	Plant health monitoring	(Lee et al., 2021)
Vivo plant sensors	Plant health monitoring	(Roper et al., 2021)
Field Robot	Early plant health monitoring system	(Rizk & Habib, 2018)
Nano-sensors	Monitoring plant health	(Giraldo & Kruss, 2023)
Handheld spectrophotometry	Nitrogen status estimation in crop	(Li et al., 2008)
Handheld photosynthesis system	Crop disease diagnosis	(Watanabe et al., 2022)

2.1 Thermal Imaging

Thermal imaging includes the thermal camera, which carries sensors that recognize the infrared radiation emitted by the object (Messina & Modica, 2020). The infrared radiation is then converted into an electronic image representing the object's surface temperature under consideration. It provides a non-invasive and efficient way of gathering crop data related to plant stress. Most of the existing works on thermal imaging are employed to measure the water stress in the plant. Also, they can be utilized to recognize the stress caused by pests and diseases (Awais et al., 2022). The thermal sensors embedded with the drone can capture infrared images of crop fields, which can be used for crop stress, such as water and temperature (see Figure 1). For instance, Zhou et al. (2022) assess the water status in grapevine using ground-based thermal imaging. They captured the thermal image of the grapevine during the growing season and derived the crop water stress index (CWSI). A strong correlation ($R^2=0.67$) between CWSI and leaf water potential (ψ) was found. Besides, Matese et al. (2018) estimated the water stress on grape vines using thermal images acquired with UAV and proximal sensors. Their results showed that UAV-based remote sensing can be used to assess the spatial variability of crop water stress along with proximal sensors.

Figure 1. An illustration of thermal imaging for crop stress monitoring using ground-vehicle. Adapted from Zhou et al. (2022)

2.2 Multispectral Imaging

Multispectral imaging systems capture multiple wavebands, including red, green, blue, and near-infrared (NIR) wavelengths (Shahi et al., 2022b). These sensors are extensively utilized in precision agriculture due to the NIR band's significant reflection by green vegetation, enabling the distinction of vegetation attributes such as plant stress and chlorophyll content. In the context of crop disease detection, these multispectral images are processed to extract the specific features that distinguish the diseased vs. healthy corps (see Figure 2). The vegetation indices such as normalized difference vegetation index (NDVI), and normalized difference red edge (NDRE) are widely used for feature extractions (Shahi et al. 2022b). This integration of VI and other crop-related data, such as canopy cover and plant density, has shown some success in crop disease detection (Singh et al., 2020).

Figure 2. An illustration of multispectral imagery of crop field a) RGB images b) Vegetation index image (NDVI). Adapted from Shahi et al. (2022b)

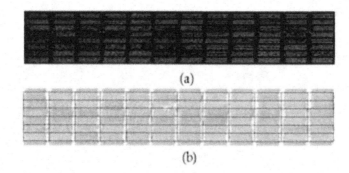

(a)

(b)

2.3 Hyperspectral Imaging

Hyperspectral sensors consist of hundreds or even thousands of narrower and contiguous spectral bands, providing detailed information about the reflectance properties of crops (Thomas et al., 2018). This enables more precise identification and differentiation of various crop traits, including healthy and diseased crops. Hyperspectral imaging can detect subtle spectral changes in plants caused by diseases even before visible symptoms appear. This early detection allows for timely intervention, disease management, and yield losses minimized (Lacotte et al., 2022). However, the large amount of hyperspectral data requires sophisticated processing techniques for analysis and significant computational resources compared to other imaging such as multispectral and thermal (Fuentes & Chang, 2022). For instance, the data captured in the hypercube includes the hundreds of bands that need to be further processed to extract useful information (Ortega et al., 2020). Here, dimensional reduction techniques such as principal component analysis (PCA) are used to extract the useful features (Rodarmel & Shan, 2002), so that they can be further utilized into model building processes such as crop stress estimation or disease detection (see Figure 3).

Figure 3. An illustration of hyperspectral image processing workflow. Adopted from Kashyap and Kumar (2021)

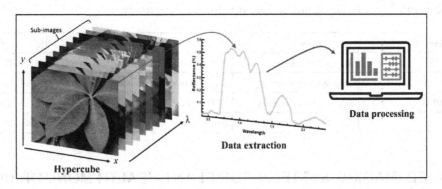

2.4 Handheld Spectrophotometry

A spectrophotometer is based on the principle of absorption, transmission, or light reflection by an object or sample. The spectrometer emits a beam of light across a range of wavelengths and measures the amount of light that is absorbed, transmitted, or reflected by the sample. The following are the most widely used spectrophotometers.

VIS-NIR spectroscopy, which can acquire the wavelength in visible and near-infrared regions, is essentially based on a lamp and a photodetector (Farber et al., 2019). It is easy to set up and inexpensive. The researchers are attracted to using it for crop stress estimation. For instance, Mishra et al. (2012) utilized the VIS-NIR for citrus greening disease detection. Nitrogen (N) status was estimated by Li et al. (2008) using spectral vegetation indices derived from handheld spectrometer data. The red ratio vegetation index (RVI) produced the highest coefficient of determination ($R^2=0.60$) while predicting the nitrogen status of winter wheat in North China.

2.5 Handheld Photosynthesis System

The portable photosynthesis system is an innovative technological advancement designed to measure and analyze parameters intricately linked to plant photosynthesis. This device is crucial for researchers, agronomists, and scientists, enabling deep exploration of photosynthetic efficiency and plant well-being (Chaerle & Van Der Straeten, 2000). Notably, it conducts non-destructive and instant assessments. The system integrates critical components and advanced sensors, harmoniously providing insights into plant physiological processes. It includes a controlled light source emitting precise wavelengths, triggering photosynthesis. Gas exchange chambers attached to leaves measure gas exchange rates, including carbon dioxide uptake and oxygen release (Maimaitiyiming et al., 2017).

By measuring the photosynthetic processes of plants, this handheld system can provide valuable insights into their overall health status. Diseases often impact a plant's ability to carry out efficient photosynthesis, leading to changes in physiological parameters. The system's ability to perform these measurements in real-time and non-destructively makes it a valuable tool for diagnosing crop diseases at an early stage, enabling timely interventions to mitigate the spread of infections (Watanabe et al., 2022). The summary of performance of various optical sensors used for crop monitoring are reported in Table 2.

Table 2. The performance of various optical sensors for crop health monitoring. Note that R^2 and Acc. represents the coefficient of determination and accuracy respectively

Reference	Sensor type	Application	Results
(Zhou et al., 2022)	Thermal imaging	Water status assessment	R^2=0.67
(Shahi et al., 2023a)	Multispectral imaging	Late leaf spot estimation in peanut	R^2=0.79
(Mishra et al., 2012)	Handheld spectrometry	Citrus greening	Acc=97%
(Li et al., 2008)	Handheld spectrometry	Nitrogen status estimation in wheat	R^2=0.60

3. UAV-BASED IMAGING SYSTEMS FOR PLANT HEALTH MONITORING

An UAV, also known as a drone, is a remotely controlled aerial vehicle that operates without a human pilot onboard. Initially, UAVs were designed for tasks considered monotonous, unclean, or hazardous (van Lieshout & Friedewald, 2018). However, now, they are used in a wide range of applications such as precision agriculture, surveying, environmental conservation, search and rescue, mining, etc.

Drones come in various sizes and designs, ranging from small quadcopters to large fixed-wing aircraft. They are equipped with a combination of sensors, cameras, GPS systems, communication devices, and sometimes even specialized equipment for specific tasks. Once the UAV platform and sensors (refer to section 2) are selected, the pre-flight preparations are completed by performing various tasks such as crop field, timing, locations, and other supporting equipment. With all set-in places, the UAV flight is conducted, which returns a large number of images (e.g. RGB, multispectral etc.). These individual image tiles need to be further processed which includes necessary image corrections such as radiometric and geometric corrections and image stitching. These activities are usually carried out using off-the-self UAV image processing software such as Pix4dMapper, Agsoft and so on (see Figure 4).

Figure 4. illustration of different types of a) drones, b) sensors, and c) software for UAV image processing

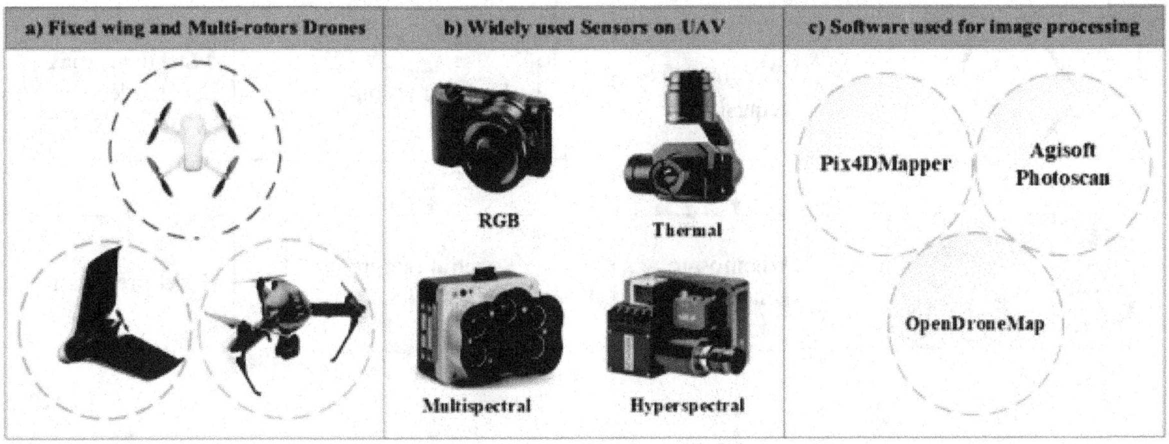

4. MONITORING OF PLANT STRESSORS USING UAV AND ML TECHNIQUES

Machine learning (ML) has revolutionized different areas, including precision agriculture and crop disease detection (Shahi et al., 2023b). ML is an advanced data analysis technique that attempts to reveal the hidden patterns in the given data. The learning methods for such patterns may be either supervised or unsupervised. In the supervised method, training samples are collected along with their corresponding actual outputs (Shahi et al., 2022a). The learning algorithm enhances its accuracy through these training samples by comparing its predictions with the provided inputs. Whereas the unsupervised learning algorithm attempts to find the hidden patterns in the given data without pre-defined labels (Alzubi et al., 2018).

The general pipeline includes the three stages (see Figure 5). Firstly, the raw UAV images were captured, and processed by following the standard UAV image processing software. It includes various pre-processing tasks such as orthomosaic generation, and soil vs. crop segmentation using the vegetation index. Second, the pre-processed images or reflectance maps were divided into a region of interest, and plot-level data extraction was carried out. The plot level data extraction might include the calculation of spectral features such as various vegetation indices such as normalized difference vegetation index (NDVI), normalized difference red edge (NDRE) etc. Thirdly, the machine learning models such as support vector machine and random forest for crop disease or stress estimation. These models are generally the regression models that follow the supervised learning strategy. Once the prediction model is built, it is validated with out-of-sample data and the disease maps are generated by visualizing the prediction on field maps.

Figure 5. The overall UAV image processing pipeline for machine learning-based crop disease prediction

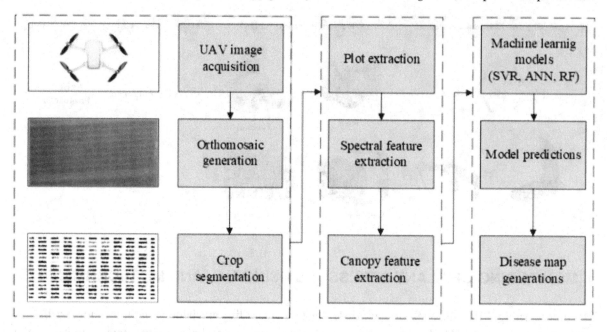

4.1 Monitoring Germination, Crop Stands and Plant Population in the Early Stage

A plant stand count is useful for calculating yield, gauging planter effectiveness, and assessing seed quality. Traditional techniques for manually measuring and counting plants take a lot of time and are prone to mistakes. In comparison, ground-based sensing methods are restricted to smaller areas. In order to analyze plant stand count, which directly affects yield, high spatial resolution images from UAV can be utilized in conjunction with computer vision algorithms. Despite the significance of high-throughput plant stand counting in row crop agriculture, there isn't any compiled data on the topic.

Both farmers and academics value and attempt to maximize plant population or plant stand count to get a good yield. A plant stand count is another tool for evaluating the planter's effectiveness and the seeds' quality, including emergence and germination rates. The survival rate during the seedling phase can be calculated by counting the plants during emergence and harvest (Ampatzidis et al., 2020). Numerous variables, including nutrient and water availability (including soil texture, moisture content, and temperature), seed depth, herbicide injury, weather, pest infestations, and sunlight, have an impact on plant population and uniformity (Al-Kaisi & Hanna, 2006). These elements eventually affect production output and quality. For instance, numerous other factors might cause corn output to decrease, including aborted kernels, barren stalks, and uneven population (Hashemi et al., 2005).

In addition to nurseries, counting plants is also done in the field (Leiva et al., 2016). Manual counting is a lot of work, takes a long time, and is vulnerable to subjectivity and human error (Bullock et al., 1998). In addition to visual inspection, traditional counting techniques for plants in the field include hoops and graduated sticks (Conley & Robinson, 2007). Shirzadifar et al. (2020) segmented the pixels containing maize plants in the mosaicked pictures using the excess green index (EXG) approach and the k-means clustering-segmentation technique. They reported a mean accuracy of 46% in the EXG method with 91% accuracy in the k-means clustering-segmentation method. Additionally, the consistency of maize plant planting was assessed using three indices: miss index, multiple indices, and coefficient of precision. These results indicated that the values set on the planting machine were more closely matched by the plant stand assessment utilizing mosaicked images. Vong et al. (2022) used UAV imagery and deep learning (DL)-based modelling to estimate maize stand count in field conditions. They used three parameters quantified with plant density, plant spacing standard deviation (PSstd), and mean days to imaging after emergence (DAEmean) for calculating plant count. Their reported estimation accuracy for plant density, PSstd, and DAEmean was 0.97, 0.73, and 0.95, respectively. Wilke et al. (2021) reported that the prediction accuracy of UAV in estimated plant density was an R^2 value of 0.83 and a mean absolute error of less than 21 plants m^{-2}.

4.2 Early Prediction of Biotic Stresses

Plants are often at risk of attack by various biotic and abiotic stresses. The biotic stresses include plant pathogens such as fungi, bacteria, viruses, nematodes, phanerogams, insects, and weeds. Insects and weeds are visible, and it is easy to predict the damage in the early stage to inform management, however, plant pathogens are microscopic and hard to see the damage at the beginning through bare eyes. When symptoms are available to detect the damage due to plant pathogens, the plants have already lost their potential to quality yield and pathogens have already colonized the plant tissues at the level where disease management is either not economically feasible or possible. Therefore, early predictions are quite critical for plant disease management. Infection of plant pathogens creates specific biochemical and physiological changes in plant cells and tissues which could be detected by nondestructive methods such as NIR, multispectral or hyperspectral imagery or, spectrophotometry. Several studies have been conducted in this perspective. For example, Nebikar et al. (2016) reported the high efficacy of a high-end multispectral multiSPEC 4C camera mounted in UAV in determining the early-stage infestation of thrips in onions and infection of potato blight using high geometric resolutions. Abdulridha et al. (2020) reported 99%, accuracy of multilayer perceptron neural network classification methods in a multispectral image taken from UAV-mounted cameras in detecting bacterial spots and target spots of tomatoes in field conditions. These two diseases are often difficult to distinguish visually due to the development of similar field symptoms. Diagnosing plant viruses and phytoplasma requires quite sophisticated techniques such as polymerase chain reaction (PCR) and enzyme-linked immunoassay (ELISA) for detection, which is time-consuming and expensive. Instead, the use of UAV-based could be a strong alternative for these. Several workers demonstrated the high efficiency of UAV-based imagery in detecting crop diseases caused by plant viruses and phytoplasmas. e.g. UAV-based multispectral imagery resulted in 81.75% efficiency in detecting citrus greening diseases (DadrasJavan et al., 2019).

4.3 Monitoring Insect and Weed Populations

Drone has great potential for being used in insect and weed monitoring. Drones can be used to gather data and insights about the presence and distribution of insects and weeds in agricultural fields. Drones equipped with various sensors, cameras, and imaging technologies offer a valuable tool for detecting, classifying, and categorizing weeds from the crops (see Figure 6). For example, Dos et al. (2017) implemented a convolutional neural network (CNN) to discern weeds within aerial images. Their study encompassed the acquisition of aerial photographs of soybean fields in Brazil, captured via drone. Then, they established a database comprising over fifteen thousand images, encompassing diverse categories such as soil, soybeans, broadleaf plants, and grassy weeds. Their proposal yielded a classification accuracy of 98% when identifying broadleaf and grassy weeds, showing the great potential of employing drones in weed detection.

Figure 6. The UAV image processing pipeline for deep learning-based weed detection. Weed images are adapted from Krestenitis et al. (2022)

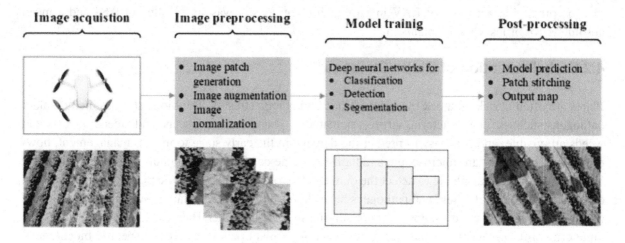

5. RESULTS AND DISCUSSION

We have explored the potential of a UAV in precision agriculture, especially for crop health monitoring using machine learning techniques. We discussed the various tools for crop health monitoring, including thermal imaging, multispectral imaging, hyperspectral imaging, handheld spectro-photometry, and photosynthesis systems. Most importantly, this chapter investigated monitoring of the plant stressors using UAV and machine learning techniques, which play a significant role in extracting meaningful information from a large amount of UAV images. In this section, we assimilate and summarize the various prospects of UAV and machine learning in precision agriculture. We first discuss the utilization of UAVs in smart agriculture. Furthermore, the recent advances in Big data and AI are elaborated, considering their application in crop monitoring. Similarly, the regulation and safety considerations of UAVs and their associated challenges are discussed. Finally, we report the future challenges and opportunities of UAVs for crop health monitoring.

5.1 Smart Agriculture and UAV

In recent decades, there has been notable progress in UAV-based remote sensing. Due to the improved capabilities of sensors and drones, it is worth noting that the use of UAVs for crop monitoring and disease mapping is increasing. For this, fixed-wing UAVs such as quadcopters and octocopters are the most utilized. The appeal of multi-rotor UAVs lies in their enhanced flexibility, manoeuvrability, and cost-effectiveness, which motivate their use in crop health monitoring and related precision agriculture tasks.

5.2 Big Data and AI for Crop Monitoring

UAVs can collect high-resolution imagery including multispectral, hyperspectral, and thermal measurements, which consists of a rich source of information about crop health. This Big data can be supplemented with other agricultural data such as weather data, historical crop data and irrigation data thereby providing a holistic view of crop health management and helping farmers to make well-informed decisions.

Artificial intelligence (AI) and ML techniques for UAV-based remote sensing are mainly used for analyzing the crop disease features and patterns in the UAV images. This can be achieved by training the AI algorithms on massive collected by UAVs. Evident signs of crop diseases encompass alterations in plant colour and morphology, prominently manifested in leaves. Such symptoms include leaf spots, leaf yellowing, and analogous changes. Hence, extracting the canopy feature is essential to estimate crop disease and assess crop health accurately. Here, the UAV with advanced sensors such as hyperspectral and thermal can capture the narrow details of crop canopy, enabling early detection of disease symptoms. This might not be possible with the naked eye or visible cameras such as RGB images. The early detection of crop disease allows timely intervention for the disease and prevents possible epidemics.

The combination of UAV, big data and AI can magnify the real-time crop monitoring which will allow the farmers to practice adaptive farm management where farmers can adjust inputs such as irrigation, fertilization, and pest control based on the targeted area of agricultural fields.

5.3 UAV Regulation and Safety

Despite the evident benefits of UAVs, the surge in drone flights has raised public apprehensions regarding safety and privacy issues. As they represent the new objects in the airspaces and can capture images, video and sounds from public spaces, they pose risks and challenges to users' privacy and safety (Stöcker et al., 2017). Therefore, it is necessary to formulate regulations for drone operations that could ensure safety and privacy while operating the drones. Many countries have already put regulations in place that make them part of aviation regulation and safety. Furthermore, Organizations such as the International Civil Aviation Organization (ICAO) are working to establish global standards for UAV operations, while regional bodies like the European Union Aviation Safety Agency (EASA) are developing harmonized regulations for their members (Ayamga et al., 2021).

5.4 Challenge and Opportunity of UAV for Crop Monitoring

UAV technology has produced some successful results in crop monitoring tasks such as plant stand count, early predictions of biotic stressors and weed monitoring. Furthermore, the advancement of various sensors and UAV technology creates numerous opportunities for precision agriculture researchers and farmers in general and crop health monitoring in particular. For instance, the high-resolution imagery acquired with UAVs can enable real-time monitoring of crop growth. Similarly, the massive amount of data produced through the UAV mission can enable the training of AI algorithms thereby automating the crop stand count, early prediction of crop disease and weed monitoring. However, it also brings challenges such as expert skills in data analysis and interpretations, and regulatory and technical limitations.

6. CONCLUSION

In this chapter, we presented the various applicability of UAVs in crop health monitoring using ML techniques, a powerful transformative opportunity to apply emerging technology in the agriculture industry. This work highlighted harnessing cutting-edge technologies and tools to address the growers/farmers faced by modern agriculture. Adopting these emerging innovations, from early disease detection to precision agricultural techniques, offers a promising pathway to enhance agricultural productivity, sustainability, and resilience. By empowering growers/farmers with the tools they need to make driven decisions to optimize crop yield and reduce the cost, precision, and environmental sustainability.

Future research should include deeper insight into the applicability of UAVs in crop health monitoring and integrating various machine learning techniques. Investigating how UAVs are equipped with robust machine learning algorithms and artificial intelligence can provide real-time crop monitoring, pest infestations, and nutrient deficiencies will be instrumental.

7. FUTURE DIRECTIONS

7.1 Digital Agriculture and Agricultural Robots

Modern technology such as UAV, ML and data analytics enable digital agriculture and help make better decisions for farmers and stakeholders towards smart farm management. In future, the combinations of ground-based vehicles such as agricultural robots and aerial vehicles such as UAVs will offer the opportunity that help increase crop productivity, resource efficiency and sustainability. The automation of farm activities that these technologies will bring into the field can benefit the farmers by reducing labour costs, and risk associated with hazards such as spraying pesticides and herbicides. More importantly, these technologies will enable the precise application of irrigation, pesticides, herbicides, and fertilizers.

7.2 Advancement in UAV and AI

Automation in precision agriculture in the present era of the Internet of Things (IoT), Big data and AI has made significant progress, which truly revolutionized farming practice. The combination of GPS-enabled devices and connectivity with other sensors can now measure the precise information on soil moisture, temperature and nutrients that help farmers to make more informed decisions. The availability of drones or UAVs integrated with such sensors makes it possible to collect crop information at a larger scale compared to manual or ground-based measurement which ultimately helps make more accurate decisions for farm management activities. Furthermore, the UAV swarms are composed of several UAVs functioning as a collective unit, interconnected through a shared network to exchange agricultural data. Their synchronized and collaborative methodology allows them to address particular tasks, such as efficiently applying pesticides over a large area.

REFERENCES

Abdulridha, J., Ampatzidis, Y., Kakarla, S. C., & Roberts, P. (2020). Detection of target spot and bacterial spot diseases in tomato using UAV-based and benchtop-based hyperspectral imaging techniques. *Precision Agriculture*, *21*(5), 955–978. doi:10.100711119-019-09703-4

Al-Kaisi, M., & Hanna, H. M. (2006, June 19). Field soil variability and its impact on crop stand uniformity. *Integrated Crop Management news*. https://works.bepress.com/mark_hanna/144/

Alzubi, J., Nayyar, A., & Kumar, A. (2018). Machine Learning from Theory to Algorithms: An Overview. *Journal of Physics: Conference Series*, *1142*, 012012. doi:10.1088/1742-6596/1142/1/012012

Ampatzidis, Y., Partel, V., & Costa, L. (2020). Agroview: Cloud-based application to process, analyze and visualize UAV-collected data for precision agriculture applications utilizing artificial intelligence. *Computers and Electronics in Agriculture*, *174*, 105457. doi:10.1016/j.compag.2020.105457

Awais, M., Li, W., Cheema, M. J. M., Zaman, Q. U., Shaheen, A., Aslam, B., & Liu, C. (2022). UAV-based remote sensing in plant stress imagine using high-resolution thermal sensor for digital agriculture practices: A meta-review. *International Journal of Environmental Science and Technology*, *20*(1), 1135–1152. doi:10.100713762-021-03801-5

Bita, C. E., & Gerats, T. (2013). Plant tolerance to high temperature in a changing environment: Scientific fundamentals and production of heat stress-tolerant crops. *Frontiers in Plant Science*, *4*, 273. doi:10.3389/fpls.2013.00273 PMID:23914193

Bullock, D. G., Bullock, D. S., Nafziger, E. D., Doerge, T. A., Paszkiewicz, S. R., Carter, P. R., & Peterson, T. A. (1998). Does variable rate seeding of corn pay? *Agronomy Journal*, *90*(6), 830–836. doi:10.2134/agronj1998.00021962009000060019x

Butte, S., Vakanski, A., Duellman, K., Wang, H., & Mirkouei, A. (2021). Potato crop stress identification in aerial images using deep learning-based object detection. *Agronomy Journal*, *113*(5), 3991–4002. doi:10.1002/agj2.20841

Chaerle, L., & Van Der Straeten, D. (2000). Imaging techniques and the early detection of plant stress. *Trends in Plant Science*, *5*(11), 495–501. doi:10.1016/S1360-1385(00)01781-7 PMID:11077259

Conley, S., & Robinson, A. (2007). Thin soybean stands: Should I replant, fill in, or leave them alone? *Coop. Ext. Serv. SPS-104-W*. https://www.extension.purdue.edu/extmedia/sps/sps-104-w.pdf

DadrasJavan, F., Samadzadegan, F., Seyed Pourazar, S. H., & Fazeli, H. (2019). UAV-based multispectral imagery for fast Citrus Greening detection. *Journal of Plant Diseases and Protection*, *126*(4), 307–318. doi:10.100741348-019-00234-8

dos Santos Ferreira, A., Freitas, D. M., da Silva, G. G., Pistori, H., & Folhes, M. T. (2017). Weed detection in soybean crops using ConvNets. *Computers and Electronics in Agriculture*, *143*, 314–324. doi:10.1016/j.compag.2017.10.027

Dresselhaus, T., & Hückelhoven, R. (2018). Biotic and abiotic stress responses in crop plants. *Agronomy (Basel)*, *8*(11), 267. doi:10.3390/agronomy8110267

Farber, C., Mahnke, M., Sanchez, L., & Kurouski, D. (2019). Advanced spectroscopic techniques for plant disease diagnostics. A review. *Trends in Analytical Chemistry*, *118*, 43–49. doi:10.1016/j.trac.2019.05.022

Fuentes, S., & Chang, J. (2022). Methodologies Used in Remote Sensing Data Analysis and Remote Sensors for Precision Agriculture. *Sensors (Basel)*, *22*(20), 7898. doi:10.339022207898 PMID:36298248

Giraldo, J. P., & Kruss, S. (2023). Nanosensors for monitoring plant health. *Nature Nanotechnology*, *18*(2), 107–108. doi:10.103841565-022-01307-w PMID:36609485

Hashemi, A. M., Herbert, S. J., & Putnam, D. H. (2005). Yield response of corn to crowding stress. *Agronomy Journal*, *97*(3), 839–846. doi:10.2134/agronj2003.0241

Kashyap, B., & Kumar, R. J. I. (2021). Sensing methodologies in agriculture for monitoring biotic stress in plants due to pathogens and pests. *Inventions, 6*(2), 29. https://doi.org/10.3390/inventions6020029

Krestenitis, M., Raptis, E. K., Kapoutsis, A. C., Ioannidis, K., Kosmatopoulos, E. B., Vrochidis, S., & Kompatsiaris, I. (2022). CoFly-WeedDB: A UAV image dataset for weed detection and species identification. *Data in Brief*, *45*, 108575. doi:10.1016/j.dib.2022.108575 PMID:36131952

Lacotte, V., Peignier, S., Raynal, M., Demeaux, I., Delmotte, F., & da Silva, P. (2022). Spatial–spectral analysis of hyperspectral images reveals early detection of downy mildew on grapevine leaves. *International Journal of Molecular Sciences*, *23*(17), 10012. doi:10.3390/ijms231710012 PMID:36077411

Lamichhane, J. R., Barzman, M., Booij, K., Boonekamp, P., Desneux, N., Huber, L., & Ricci, P. (2015). Robust cropping systems to tackle pests under climate change. A review. *Agronomy for Sustainable Development*, *35*(2), 443–459. doi:10.100713593-014-0275-9

Lee, G., Wei, Q., & Zhu, Y. (2021). Emerging wearable sensors for plant health monitoring. *Advanced Functional Materials*, *31*(52), 2106475. doi:10.1002/adfm.202106475

Leiva, J. N., Robbins, J., Saraswat, D., She, Y., & Ehsani, R. (2016). Effect of plant canopy shape and flowers on plant count accuracy using remote sensing imagery. *Agricultural Engineering International: CIGR Journal*, *18*(2), 73–82.

Li, F., Gnyp, M. L., Jia, L., Miao, Y., Yu, Z., Koppe, W., & Zhang, F. (2008). Estimating N status of winter wheat using a handheld spectrometer in the North China Plain. *Field Crops Research*, *106*(1), 77–85. doi:10.1016/j.fcr.2007.11.001

Maimaitiyiming, M., Ghulam, A., Bozzolo, A., Wilkins, J. L., & Kwasniewski, M. T. (2017). Early Detection of Plant Physiological Responses to Different Levels of Water Stress Using Reflectance Spectroscopy. *Remote Sensing (Basel)*, *9*(7), 745. doi:10.3390/rs9070745

Manici, L., Bregaglio, S., Fumagalli, D., & Donatelli, M. (2014). Modelling soil-borne fungal pathogens of arable crops under climate change. *International Journal of Biometeorology*, *58*(10), 2071–2083. doi:10.100700484-014-0808-6 PMID:24615638

Matese, A., Baraldi, R., Berton, A., Cesaraccio, C., Di Gennaro, S. F., Duce, P., Facini, O., Mameli, M., Piga, A., & Zaldei, A. (2018). Estimation of water stress in grapevines using proximal and remote sensing methods. *Remote Sensing (Basel)*, *10*(1), 114. doi:10.3390/rs10010114

Messina, G., & Modica, G. (2020). Applications of UAV Thermal Imagery in Precision Agriculture: State of the Art and Future Research Outlook. *Remote Sensing (Basel)*, *12*(9), 1491. doi:10.3390/rs12091491

Mishra, A. R., Karimi, D., Ehsani, R., & Lee, W. S. (2012). Identification of Citrus Greening (HLB) Using a VIS-NIR Spectroscopy Technique. *Transactions of the ASABE*, *55*(2), 711–720. doi:10.13031/2013.41369

Nazarov, P. A., Baleev, D. N., Ivanova, M. I., Sokolova, L. M., & Karakozova, M. V. (2020). Infectious plant diseases: Etiology, current status, problems and prospects in plant protection. *Acta Naturae (English Ed.)*, *12*(3), 46–59. doi:10.32607/actanaturae.11026 PMID:33173596

Nebiker, S., Lack, N., Abächerli, M., & Läderach, S. (2016). Light-weight multispectral UAV sensors and their capabilities for predicting grain yield and detecting plant diseases. *The International Archives of the Photogrammetry, Remote Sensing and Spatial Information Sciences*, *41*(B1), 963–970. doi:10.5194/isprs-archives-XLI-B1-963-2016

Nex, F., Armenakis, C., Cramer, M., Cucci, D. A., Gerke, M., Honkavaara, E., & Skaloud, J. (2022). UAV in the advent of the twenties: Where we stand and what is next. *ISPRS Journal of Photogrammetry and Remote Sensing*, *184*, 215–242. doi:10.1016/j.isprsjprs.2021.12.006

Oerke, E. C. (2006). Crop losses to pests. *Journal of Agricultural Science*, *144*(1), 31–43. doi:10.1017/S0021859605005708

Ortega, S., Halicek, M., Fabelo, H., Callico, G. M., & Fei, B. (2020). Hyperspectral and multispectral imaging in digital and computational pathology: A systematic review. *Biomedical Optics Express*, *11*(6), 3195–3233. doi:10.1364/BOE.386338 PMID:32637250

Rizk, H., & Habib, M. K. (2018). Robotized early plant health monitoring system. *IECON 2018-44th Annual Conference of the IEEE Industrial Electronics Society*. IEEE.10.1109/IECON.2018.8592833

Roper, J. M., Garcia, J. F., & Tsutsui, H. (2021). Emerging technologies for monitoring plant health in vivo. *ACS Omega*, *6*(8), 5101–5107. doi:10.1021/acsomega.0c05850 PMID:33681550

Schaeffer, M., Hare, B., Rocha, M., & Rogelj, J. (2013). *Adequacy and feasibility of the 1.5 C long-term global limit*. Climate Action Network Europe.

Shahi, T. B., Sitaula, C., Neupane, A., & Guo, W. (2022a). Fruit classification using attention-based MobileNetV2 for industrial applications. *PLoS One*, *17*(2), e0264586. doi:10.1371/journal.pone.0264586 PMID:35213643

Shahi, T. B., Xu, C.-Y., Neupane, A., Fresser, D., O'Connor, D., Wright, G., & Guo, W. (2023a). A cooperative scheme for late leaf spot estimation in peanut using UAV multispectral images. *PLoS One*, *18*(3), e0282486. doi:10.1371/journal.pone.0282486 PMID:36972266

Shahi, T. B., Xu, C.-Y., Neupane, A., & Guo, W. (2022b). Machine learning methods for precision agriculture with UAV imagery: A review. *Electronic Research Archive*, *30*(12), 4277–4317. doi:10.3934/era.2022218

Shahi, T. B., Xu, C.-Y., Neupane, A., & Guo, W. (2023b). Recent Advances in Crop Disease Detection Using UAV and Deep Learning Techniques. *Remote Sensing (Basel)*, *15*(9), 2450. doi:10.3390/rs15092450

Shirzadifar, A., Maharlooei, M., Bajwa, S. G., Oduor, P. G., & Nowatzki, J. F. (2020). Mapping crop stand count and planting uniformity using high resolution imagery in a maize crop. *Biosystems Engineering*, *200*, 377–390. doi:10.1016/j.biosystemseng.2020.10.013

Singh, V., Sharma, N., & Singh, S. (2020). A review of imaging techniques for plant disease detection. *Artificial Intelligence in Agriculture*, *4*, 229–242. doi:10.1016/j.aiia.2020.10.002

Solomon, S. (2007). *Climate change 2007-the physical science basis: Working group I contribution to the fourth assessment report of the IPCC* (Vol. 4). Cambridge University Press.

Su, J., Zhu, X., Li, S., & Chen, W.-H. (2022). AI meets UAVs: A survey on AI empowered UAV perception systems for precision agriculture. *Neurocomputing*, *518*, 242–270. doi:10.1016/j.neucom.2022.11.020

Thomas, S., Kuska, M. T., Bohnenkamp, D., Brugger, A., Alisaac, E., Wahabzada, M., & Mahlein, A.-K. (2018). Benefits of hyperspectral imaging for plant disease detection and plant protection: A technical perspective. *Journal of Plant Diseases and Protection*, *125*(1), 5–20. doi:10.100741348-017-0124-6

van Lieshout, M., & Friedewald, M. (2018). Drones–dull, dirty or dangerous?: The social construction of privacy and security technologies. In *Socially Responsible Innovation in Security* (pp. 25–43). Routledge. doi:10.4324/9781351246903-3

Vong, C. N., Conway, L. S., Feng, A., Zhou, J., Kitchen, N. R., & Sudduth, K. A. (2022). Corn emergence uniformity estimation and mapping using UAV imagery and deep learning. *Computers and Electronics in Agriculture*, *198*, 107008. doi:10.1016/j.compag.2022.107008

Watanabe, K., Agarie, H., Aparatana, K., Mitsuoka, M., Taira, E., Ueno, M., & Kawamitsu, Y. (2022). Fundamental Study on Water Stress Detection in Sugarcane Using Thermal Image Combined with Photosynthesis Measurement Under a Greenhouse Condition. *Sugar Tech*, *24*(5), 1382–1390. doi:10.100712355-021-01087-y

Wilke, N., Siegmann, B., Postma, J. A., Muller, O., Krieger, V., Pude, R., & Rascher, U. (2021). Assessment of plant density for barley and wheat using UAV multispectral imagery for high-throughput field phenotyping. *Computers and Electronics in Agriculture*, *189*, 106380. doi:10.1016/j.compag.2021.106380

Zhou, Z., Diverres, G., Kang, C., Thapa, S., Karkee, M., Zhang, Q., & Keller, M. J. A. (2022). Ground-based thermal imaging for assessing crop water status in grapevines over a growing season. *Agronomy*, *12*(2), 322. https://doi.org/10.3390/agronomy12020322

Chapter 11
UAV–Based Warehouse Management Using Multi–Agent RL:
Applications, Challenges, and Solutions

Arefeh Esmaili

Tarbiat Modares University, Tehran, Iran

Mehdy Roayaei

https://orcid.org/0000-0001-9843-5886

Tarbiat Modares University, Tehran, Iran

ABSTRACT

This chapter aims to investigate the applications of reinforcement learning (RL) and Multi-Agent RL (MARL) in UAV networks in warehouse management. Different applications of UAVs in warehousing and different applications of RL in UAV networks are reviewed. Currently, most research in this area relies on single-agent RL approaches. Transitioning from single-agent RL to MARL offers the opportunity can potentially achieve higher levels of optimization, scalability, and adaptability in warehouse management using UAV networks. However, the application of multi-agent approaches in UAV-based warehouse management is still in its early stages, and may introduce new challenges. Thus, this chapter specifically focuses on the challenges and solutions associated with adopting MARL in the context of UAV-based warehouse management tasks. This includes addressing challenges such as non-stationary, partial observability, credit assignment, scalability, and task allocation. The authors highlight challenges and present some of the widely-used approaches to address these challenges.

DOI: 10.4018/979-8-3693-0578-2.ch011

1 INTRODUCTION

The digital transformation towards Industry 4.0 is now an essential step for companies as it enhances their flexibility, agility, and responsiveness. This transformation affects logistics significantly, bringing about profound changes in logistics processes and operations with the support of revolutionary Industry 4.0 technologies (Richnák, 2022).

Warehousing or warehouse management stands as a crucial element within the supply chain and logistics, playing a fundamental role in managing inventory. The effectiveness of warehouse operations significantly influences the effectiveness of realized goods flows. Thus, digitization and automation of warehouse operations increase the demand for research in this area. This is confirmed by the growing number of recent publications related to this topic (Tubis & Rohman, 2023).

UAVs have emerged as a key solution for achieving nearly automated or intelligent warehouse operations. They facilitate timely and enhanced efficiency in operations such as receiving, picking, storage, and shipping processes (Malang et al., 2023). A UAV, is an unmanned aerial vehicle that lacks a human operator on board. It can operate autonomously or be controlled remotely. UAVs are typically either remotely piloted by a ground-based operator or operate autonomously following pre-defined flight plans or advanced dynamic automation systems. (A. Gupta et al., 2021).

Utilizing machine learning, particularly MARL, in warehouse management offers a compelling approach to address the evolving demands and complexities of modern supply chains. Traditional warehouse management systems often struggle to adapt to dynamic and unpredictable environments, optimize tasks and resource allocation, and rely on manual processes prone to errors. However, by employing machine learning techniques, warehouses can enhance their operational efficiency, scalability, and adaptability. MARL, in particular, introduces the capability for multiple autonomous agents, such as UAVs, to collaborate and learn from each other in real-time. This collaborative learning enables them to collectively optimize tasks, allocate resources, and respond dynamically to changing conditions. Moreover, machine learning empowers warehouses to make data-driven decisions, reducing human intervention, minimizing errors, and improving overall productivity. By harnessing the potential of machine learning, especially MARL, warehouses can revolutionize their management operations, achieving higher levels of efficiency, accuracy, and responsiveness in an increasingly competitive and fast-paced business landscape.

1.1 Warehouse Management

Warehouse management is a critical component of modern supply chain operations, playing a pivotal role in ensuring the efficient flow of goods from production to distribution and ultimately into the hands of customers. It encompasses a wide array of tasks and processes designed to optimize the storage, retrieval, and movement of inventory within a warehouse facility.

Traditional warehouse management systems (WMS) have long been the backbone of supply chain operations, but they come with inherent challenges that can limit their effectiveness in today's rapidly changing business environment. Among the limitations are increased operational costs, high labor expenses, human errors, order delays, and potential risks to operators' safety, to name a few.

Traditional WMS functioned primarily through manual processes. Warehouse workers received paper-based instructions for tasks such as order picking, packing, and inventory tracking. These manual processes were not only time-consuming but also error-prone, leading to inefficiencies in the warehouse. Scalability was a concern as business operations grew, and hiring more staff didn't always result in proportional increases in efficiency. Inaccurate data entry was another common issue, affecting inventory accuracy and order fulfillment.

Visibility into warehouse operations was limited in traditional WMS. Managers often had to rely on periodic reports or physical checks to understand inventory levels and order statuses. This lack of real-time information made it challenging to respond quickly to changing demands or address issues within the warehouse. Consequently, decision-making regarding resource allocation and order prioritization suffered.

Automation was limited in traditional WMS. While basic conveyor systems and barcode scanners were in use, comprehensive automation was uncommon. Workers spent significant time on routine, repetitive tasks that could have been automated, leading to inefficiency and higher labor costs.

Furthermore, traditional WMS often operated in isolation from other enterprise systems, creating data silos that hindered the flow of information across the organization. This lack of integration made it challenging to achieve seamless data exchange between departments, impeding decision-making and overall efficiency.

With the growth of e-commerce and global trade, the demands on warehouse management have escalated, compelling businesses to seek innovative solutions that enhance productivity, reduce costs, and improve customer satisfaction. The goal is to minimize errors, reduce handling time, maximize space utilization, and ensure accurate, on-time deliveries to meet customer expectations.

In recent years, the integration of advanced technologies, such as automation, robotics, Internet of Things (IoT), and artificial intelligence, has brought about a transformation in the field of warehouse management. These technologies have revolutionized the way warehouses operate, making them smarter, more responsive, and capable of adapting to the ever-changing demands of the global market.

Intelligent warehouse management leverages advanced technologies and data-driven strategies to optimize operations and improve overall efficiency. Some key technologies and approaches in intelligent warehouse management include IoT (Khan et al., 2022), data visualization (Cogo et al., 2020), cloud computing (Sivakumar et al., 2020), blockchain (Prasad Tripathy et al., 2020), and UAV (Roca-Riu & Monica Menendez, 2019). A comparative analysis between traditional and modern warehouse management systems is presented in Table 1.

Table 1. Comparative analysis between traditional and modern WMS

Aspect	Traditional WMS	Modern WMS
Automation	Minimal automation; reliance on manual processes	Extensive automation, including the use of robots, IoT devices, and AI-driven systems.
Inventory Visibility	Limited real-time visibility; often relies on periodic reports or manual checks.	Real-time inventory tracking and visibility enabled by IoT sensors and AI analytics.
Data Accuracy	Prone to human errors in data entry and documentation.	Improved data accuracy with reduced human involvement due to automation and AI.
Scalability	Limited scalability; adding more staff may not proportionally increase efficiency.	Highly scalable with the ability to adapt to changing business needs through technology.
Integration	Often operates in isolation from other enterprise systems, creating data silos.	Integrated with other systems and channels, enabling seamless data exchange and decision-making.
Sustainability	Minimal focus on sustainability; energy and resource consumption often not optimized.	Emphasis on sustainability with eco-friendly practices, energy efficiency, and waste reduction.
Order Fulfillment Speed	Slower order fulfillment due to manual processes and limited visibility.	Faster order fulfillment with optimized processes and real-time tracking.
Environmental Impact	Often has a higher environmental impact due to inefficiencies and waste.	Reduced environmental impact through sustainable practices and green technologies.
Cost Efficiency	Potentially higher operational costs due to inefficiencies and errors.	Improved cost efficiency through automation, reduced labor, and resource optimization.
Adaptability	Less adaptable to market changes and evolving business requirements.	Highly adaptable, capable of quickly responding to changing demands and challenges.

Despite the advantages of modern warehouse management, these systems also come with challenges that should be handled before it can be widely used in practice. For instance, these challenges encompass the scalability and adaptability of the process, the limited observability of autonomous agents, and the dynamicity and complexity of warehouse environments.

RL is a promising area of machine learning that can address and improve some unique challenges in the warehousing industry, including automatically scale and optimize to handle business needs, reducing the reliance on manual interaction and improving efficiency and profitability.

1.2 UAVs

UAVs, also known as drones, have emerged as a transformative technology with a wide range of applications across various domains. UAVs are aircraft that operate without a human pilot onboard, controlled either autonomously by onboard computers or remotely by human operators. Their versatility, agility, and capacity to access hard-to-reach or hazardous areas have made them invaluable tools in industries such as agriculture, environmental monitoring, surveillance, disaster management, and logistics.

UAVs come in various sizes and configurations, from small quadcopters used for aerial photography to large fixed-wing drones employed in long-range surveying missions. They are equipped with an array of sensors, cameras, and communication systems, enabling them to gather real-time data and relay it to ground stations for analysis. This capability has opened up new possibilities for data collection, remote sensing, and decision-making.

UAVs are often equipped with various types of cameras, including RGB cameras, infrared cameras, and multispectral cameras. These cameras capture visual and thermal imagery. Cameras provide real-time visual data of warehouse operations. They can monitor inventory levels, track the movement of goods, and identify potential issues such as congestion or damage. Infrared cameras can detect temperature variations, helping identify hotspots or equipment malfunctions.

Also, UAVs may be equipped with LiDAR (Light Detection and Ranging) that are sensors which use laser beams to measure distances and create detailed 3D maps of the environment. LiDAR enables UAVs to create high-resolution warehouse maps. This data is crucial for path planning, collision avoidance, and assessing the layout of goods within the warehouse. LiDAR can also identify obstacles and calculate precise distances, enhancing navigation and safety.

Another equipment available in some UAVs is GPS. GPS receivers determine the UAV's exact location by communicating with satellites. GPS is essential for accurate geo-spatial positioning during warehouse tasks. It ensures the UAV follows predefined routes, marks specific locations for inventory tracking, and assists in creating georeferenced maps of the warehouse. GPS data enhances overall navigation and geospatial awareness.

Also, UAVs should be with communication systems that facilitate data transfer between the UAV and ground stations or remote operators. Communication systems ensure real-time data transmission, allowing operators to monitor the UAV's progress, receive live video feeds, and make informed decisions promptly. These systems also enable remote control and communication with other devices within the warehouse.

Another equipment available in UAVs is sensors for payload handling. Some UAVs designed for warehouse management tasks may include specialized sensors for payload handling. These sensors can detect and adjust cargo position, weight, and attachment status. payload handling sensors ensure precise cargo handling and release. They help prevent accidents during the loading and unloading of goods, enhancing both safety and operational efficiency.

The first appearances of UAV were in the military, but modern trends and globalization scattered UAV applications in the spectrum of commercial applications (Škrinjar et al., 2019). UAVs have received attention in the last decade because of their low cost, small size, and programmable features.

While the military remains the largest market for UAVs at present, the commercial sector is experiencing the most rapid growth potential. Within the commercial sector, the infrastructure industry appears to have the highest growth prospects, followed by agriculture and transportation (A. Gupta et al., 2021). There are expectations that this market will expand by $29 billion by 2027, demonstrating an annual growth rate of nearly 20% (MarketsandMarkets, 2019).

Commercial UAVs find applications in various sectors, including agriculture, construction, transportation, traffic management, inspections, public safety, and many other civil-government purposes. (Škrinjar et al., 2019). They Also have interesting applications in smart cities from monitoring traffic flow to measuring and detecting floods and natural disasters by using wireless sensors (Mohammed et al., 2014). Other applications of UAVs include forest fire monitoring (Skorput et al., 2016), wildfire mapping, buildings and bridges inspections, powerlines surveys, pipelines monitoring, and many others (A. Gupta et al., 2021).

The increasing utilization of UAVs is largely driven by the expanding e-commerce sector and the rising demands for quicker delivery services. As automation becomes more prevalent in the transportation industry, UAVs are expected to have a significant role in the development of a fully automated transportation system (A. Gupta et al., 2021).

Recent technological progress in UAVs, including visual-based navigation and advanced sensors, has opened possibilities for their indoor applications. The fourth industrial revolution is also making a significant impact on warehouses, leading to their increased digitalization and connectivity, often referred to as "warehouse 4.0." Emerging scanning technologies like barcodes, QR codes, RFID, and AI are enabling automation powered by UAVs within warehouses. Furthermore, the presence of onboard computing capabilities and efficient algorithms is facilitating the development of UAV applications. (Wawrla et al., 2019).

In addition to the progress in UAV technology, a significant factor behind warehouse automation shift is the expansion of warehouse sizes, driven by the expansion of global e-commerce. UAVs can play a role in automating inventory audits and intralogistics tasks. Large warehouses are aiming to increase efficiency by investing more in automation and robotics. This is not without precedence since the cost of warehousing operations account for 30% of the total costs in logistics. Furthermore, difficulty to attract skilled labors, increasing demand for customer services and the rise of e-commerce have intensified the need to further increase efficiency in warehouse operations (Wawrla et al., 2019). The presence of an uneven terrain within a warehouse and the storage of items at higher locations, beyond the reach of a grounded robot, necessitates using a flying system.

The warehouse management using autonomous UAVs is beneficial in terms of cost, time, safety of human workers, reducing inventory costs, significantly shortening the process, and reducing use of human resources. Civilian UAVs are commonly regarded as recoverable drones. Due to their unmanned nature, UAVs typically provide a safer operational environment compared to manned aerial vehicles, if they are regulated appropriately. UAVs can serve as a viable choice for carrying out riskier missions and tasks, eliminating the potential danger to operators' lives. (A. Gupta et al., 2021).

Moreover, UAVs have economic benefits by minimizing labor costs and reducing operational downtime associated with inventory tracking. They achieve this by providing near-continuous inventory inspection, optimizing operational decision-making processes (Karamitsos et al., 2021), (L. Gupta et al., 2016).

In general, a group or fleet of UAVs that work together to achieve a holistic goal is known as a UAV network. As can be seen in Figure 1, a heterogenous network of UAVs with different capabilities and sensors can integrated with control station and Unmanned Ground Vehicle (UGV) to handle different activities in warehouse management.

Figure 1. Representation of a UAV network in warehouse management

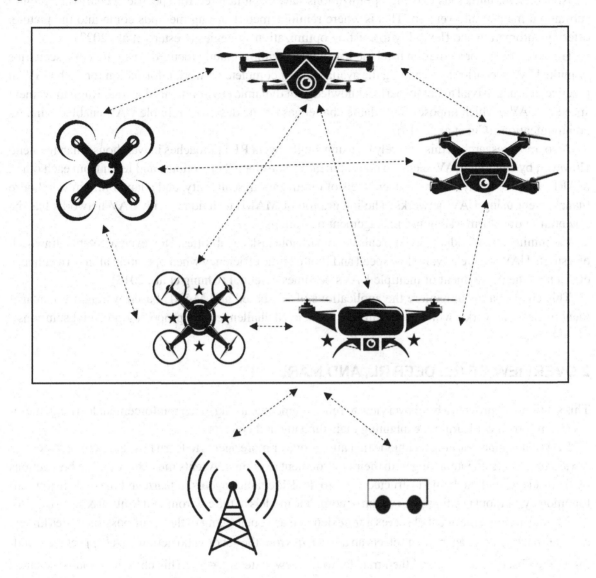

1.3 MARL in UAV-Based Warehouse Management

While, the UAVs are assigned a very specific task in a warehouse management (for example searching for RFID tags), the UAVs cannot be programmed to follow a specific policy (path) because different warehouses have different layouts. Warehouses may also change their layouts periodically based on business needs. Thus, machine learning and artificial intelligence is required to allow the UAVs to make clever decision and adapt to unfamiliar environment and dynamic obstacles. Artificial intelligence can also help the UAVs optimized their path decisions to minimize the amount of time used to complete the task based on previous trajectory pattern (Ong et al., 2007).

Nonetheless, numerous existing optimizations have been tailored for specific scenarios or require substantial manual intervention. This is where reinforcement learning methods come into the picture, offering automation and flexibility to existing optimization strategies (Cestero et al., 2022).

However, the prior studies on machine learning algorithms mainly focused on single UAV scenarios or multi-UAV scenarios by assuming the availability of complete network information for each UAV. In practice, it is non-trivial to obtain perfect knowledge of dynamic environments due to the high movement speed of UAVs, which imposes formidable challenges on the design of reliable UAV-enabled wireless communications (Cui et al., 2019).

Also, most research in this area rely on using single-agent RL approaches in warehouse management. However, by enabling UAV agents to communicate, coordinate their actions, and learn from each other, MARL can potentially achieve higher levels of optimization, scalability, and adaptability in warehouse management using UAV networks. The integration of MARL techniques with UAV networks has the potential to transform warehouse management operations.

Examining an individual UAV reveals its remarkable task capabilities. However, a notable drawback of a single UAV is its relatively slow speed and limited time efficiency when operating alone. To enhance efficiency, the deployment of multiple UAVs becomes essential (Chung et al., 2018).

This chapter aims to explore the applications of RL-based and MARL-based warehouse management in UAV networks, while addressing the associated challenges and proposing potential solutions.

2 OVERVIEW OF RL, DEEP RL, AND MARL

This section will provide a brief overview to reinforcement learning, deep reinforcement learning, multi-agent reinforcement learning, explaining their fundamental concepts.

RL is a machine-learning technique that allows one or more agents to learn how to maximize the total reward they get from interacting with their environment over time. Agents must discover the best actions by themselves, without being instructed what to do. RL enables agents to learn and make decisions autonomously, without needing supervision or complete models of the environment (Sutton & Barto, 2018).

At time period t, the agent observes a *state* denoted as s_t, belonging to the set of possible states known as state space $\mathcal{S}$. The agent then selects an *action*, a_t, from the set of valid actions, $\mathcal{A}\left(s_t\right)$, corresponding to the observed state s_t, and then transfer to the new state $s_{t+1} \in \mathcal{S}$. This chosen action is executed on the *environment*, resulting in a *reward*, denoted by $r(s_t, a_t, s_{t+1}) \in \mathbb{R}$ (Figure 2). This process continues for a duration of T time-steps, culminating in the end of an episode.

The concept of Markov Decision Process (MDP) is employed to model and analyze this problem, if the agent possesses complete knowledge of the current state. In an MDP, the goal of the agent is to find a policy, denoted as $\pi : \mathcal{S} \to \mathcal{A}$, which maps states from the state space $\mathcal{S}$ to corresponding actions from the action space $\mathcal{A}$. The goal of this policy is to maximize the overall cumulative rewards over the long term, considering a discount factor γ for future rewards as stated in Eq. (1):

$$argmax_i : r(\pi_i) = \sum_{t=0}^{T} \gamma^t r\left(s_t, a_t, s_{t+1}\right) \qquad (1)$$

Figure 2. Agent interaction with environment in reinforcement learning

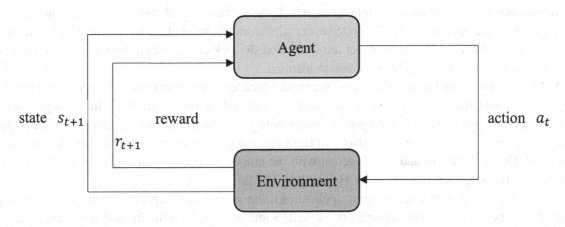

Deep Reinforcement Learning (DRL) is a general paradigm which combines RL and deep learning. DRL uses neural network modeling in traditional RL algorithms (as depicted in Figure 3). It uses deep neural networks to approximate the optimal policy in complex and high-dimensional environments. DRL is typically employed when traditional RL methods face challenges or limitations due to the large state space or action space (H. Wang et al., 2020).

Figure 3. Neural network in deep reinforcement learning

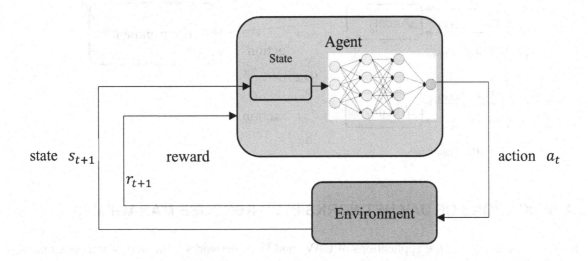

Initial applications of DRL mostly focused on using one single agent to solve the problem and has achieved success in a variety of applications including games (Roohi et al., 2020), robot control (Han et al., 2023), traffic signal control (Bouktif et al., 2023), autonomous vehicles (Pérez-Gil et al., 2022), healthcare (Esteva et al., 2019), and finance (Jin, 2023).

Although single agent RL have had many successful applications, many real-world applications require the participation of more than one single agent, which should be modeled systematically as multi-agent RL problems (Zhang et al., 2021). Robotic soccer (Catacora Ocana et al., 2019), multi-UAV coverage (Tolstaya et al., 2021), multi-robot object transportation (Rezeck et al., 2021), and traffic management (Antonio & Maria-Dolores, 2022) are a few to mention.

MARL algorithms tackle the challenge of sequential decision-making in systems comprising multiple agents like robots, machines, or cars, all interacting in a shared environment. The primary objective of MARL algorithms is to enable each agent to learn a policy that contributes to the collective goal of the system (Figure 4). These agents can adapt and learn optimal policies dynamically during their interactions with the environment and other agents, with the aim of maximizing the cumulative discounted reward over the long term (Oroojlooy & Hajinezhad, 2022).

In addition to inherently multi-agent applications, the use of multi-agent reinforcement learning methods has benefits for other applications as well. Some of these benefits include better exploration of environments and sample efficiency, robustness and resilience, time-saving, and parallel learning.

Figure 4. Multi-agent reinforcement learning

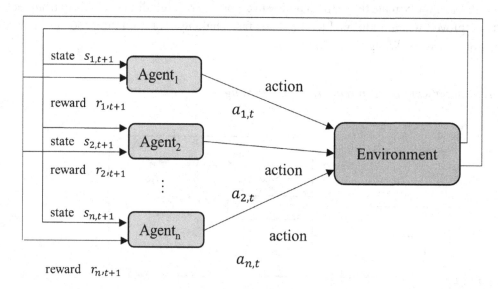

3 APPLICATIONS OF UAV NETWORKS IN WAREHOUSE MANAGEMENT

This section will explore the applications of UAVs and UAV networks in modern warehouse management. It will highlight how UAVs can help to automate different tasks in warehouse management such as inventory management, logistics, and inspection and surveillance. The advantages of using UAV networks, such as increased efficiency, flexibility, and adaptability, will also be emphasized, along with their potential impact on optimizing warehouse management processes.

The operation of warehouse management, as shown in Figure 5, can be classified into three major groups, *inventory management* (Beul et al., 2018), (C. Li et al., 2021) (including inventory audit, stock management, cycle counting item search, buffer stock maintenance, stocktaking), *intra-logistics of items*

(UAV-based deliveries), and *inspection and surveillance* (including monitoring and inspection and regular surveillance) (Malang et al., 2023).

Figure 5. Warehouse management tasks

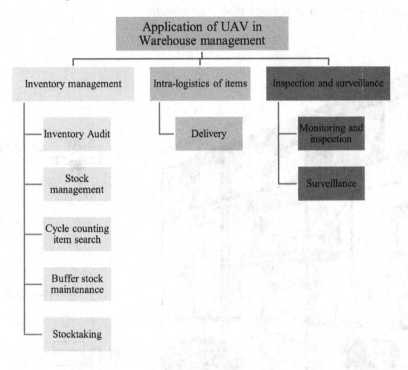

3.1 Inventory Management

Inventory management refers to the strategic process of overseeing and controlling an organization's inventory of items. An inventory audit involves comparing real, tangible inventory quantities with financial records to validate the accuracy of inventory bookkeeping. Stock management entails a methodical strategy for acquiring, storing, and selling inventory items.

Cycle counting is an inventory management technique that enables companies to verify the alignment between actual inventory counts and their recorded inventory data. This approach involves conducting periodic counts of physical items across various sections of the warehouse, avoiding the need to tally the entire inventory. Subsequently, adjustments for specific products are documented based on the findings. Buffer stock management involves determining and upholding an appropriate quantity of extra inventory to minimize holding expenses while guaranteeing the timely fulfillment of customer orders.

Finally, Stocktaking involves the manual verification and recording of the existing inventory held by businesses. Carrying out stocktaking may necessitate temporarily halting all business operations to enable the physical counting of each item. This procedure additionally encompasses examining the categories of stock and validating the status of stock movement and their respective locations.

Harik et al. (Harik et al., 2016) proposed an autonomous warehouse inventory where UAVs can be integrated alongside UGVs to achieve a fully automated inventory management system, as depicted in Figure 6.

Figure 6. Autonomous warehouse inventory global architecture
(Harik et al., 2016)

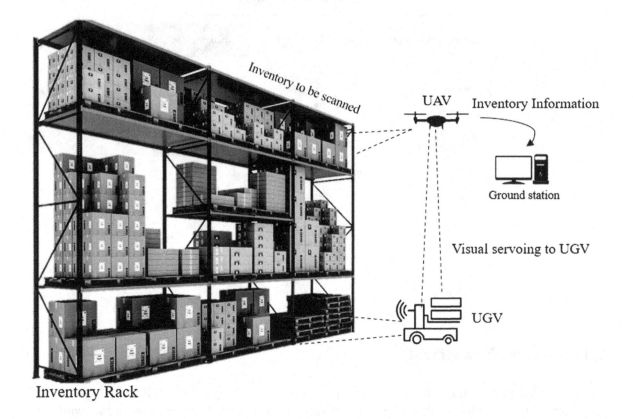

In their proposed architecture, UGV serves as the transport platform and acts as a ground reference for guiding the indoor flight of the UAV. The UAV functions as a mobile scanning device. It UGV navigates through rows of storage racks while carrying the UAV. When positioned at the base of a designated rack for scanning, the UGV halts its movement, allowing the UAV to take off and ascend vertically to scan the items within that rack. Once the UAV reaches the top of the rack, the UGV advances to the subsequent rack. Given that the UAV uses the UGV as its ground reference, it trails behind it, thereby positioning itself at the top of the subsequent rack to commence a top-to-bottom scanning process. This sequence is reiterated until all racks in the row have been comprehensively scanned. Subsequently, the UAV lands on the UGV, where it recharges its battery while the UGV progresses to the next row of racks.

Fernández-Caramés et al. detailed the creation and examination of UAVs integrated with RFID for the purpose of scanning warehouse inventory (Fernández-Caramés et al., 2019). The acquired inventory information from the UAV was suggested to be transmitted via blockchain technology. Bae et al. explored inventory management within an outdoor warehouse using UAVs and RFIDs, successfully establishing a prototype system to showcase the viability of this approach (Bae et al., 2016).

A practical instance of the application of UAVs in real-world warehouse inventory management can be observed in the case of Doks Innovation, a German company. They employ UAVs for the purpose of streamlining warehouse management and sustaining inventory control through automation. These UAVs have the capacity to locate items both within warehouse premises and outdoor spaces, actively tracking barcodes and RFID tags. This integration enables seamless inclusion within warehouse administrative systems, resulting in time and cost savings, as well as error reduction (*Doks. Innovation*, n.d.).

Moura et al. addressed the development of a vision-based Graph-SLAM approach for UAV indoor localization without predefined warehouse markers positions. Their framework is developed to support different commercial UAV platforms, allowing the estimation in real-time of the UAV position and attitude (Moura et al., 2021).

Karamitsos et al. proposed a system established in an industrial facility layout enabling the 24/7 operation of a UAV for inventory listing. Operational activities include the automation of processes (navigation, routing, identification of inventory levels) and the communication with the IT infrastructure. Their proposed integrated scenario provides a web-based multifunctional interface for monitoring inventory levels (Karamitsos et al., 2021).

Kalinov et al. proposed a hybrid UAV-based robotic system for real-time barcode detection and scanning using Convolutional Neural Networks (CNN). Their approach improves the UAV's localization using scanned barcodes as landmarks in a real warehouse with lowlight conditions, which results in UAV trajectory optimization for autonomous warehouse stocktaking (Kalinov et al., 2020).

Liu et al. proposed a hybrid differential evolution algorithm for UAV stocktaking task-planning for industrial warehouses (H. Liu et al., 2022). They proposed a trajectory planning model for UAVs equipped with RFID readers based on inventory tasks.

Chen et al. proposed a warehouse management system with UAV based on digital twin and 5G in order to realize intelligent, controllable, and convenient warehouse management (Chen et al., 2020). They used cloud as data processing center and 5G communication as the core exchange means. The flight data and item information of the entity warehouse with UAV are uploaded to cloud through 5G communication, and then are sent to the digital twin platform to get real-time warehouse data and visual feedback.

3.2 Logistic

Utilizing UAVs for efficient package delivery holds significant promise. This application has the potential to transform global delivery practices, offering expedited and cost-effective options. Particularly in situations such as disaster relief efforts or the transportation of pharmaceutical resources to remote destinations, UAV deployment can substantially reduce the expenses and time associated with unconventional delivery networks. Nevertheless, despite its potential, this technology is currently in its initial testing phases and is limited to a specific geographic area.

UAV delivery presents several advantages compared to traditional delivery methods. UAV delivery is much faster, as it remains largely unaffected by road systems and traffic congestion. When authorized, UAVs follow an optimal aerial route between the point of departure and the destination. Furthermore, UAV delivery proves to be cost-efficient in terms of delivery duration and environmentally friendly. In comparison to conventional road-based delivery approaches, such as truck-based package delivery, UAV delivery generates significantly fewer carbon emissions, thus contributing to a reduced environmental footprint (Yoo et al., 2018).

Intra-logistics for an item can be described as the logistical operations carried out within a warehouse utilizing UAVs. These operations encompass tasks like storage, movement of items or information, transportation, and delivery of items, tools, and spare parts within the confines of the warehouses. Additionally, this term encompasses activities such as selecting and preparing end products for customers, exemplified by services like UAV-assisted delivery.

As real-world example, Figure 7, within the United States, Amazon Prime Air, DHL, Google, Mercedes-Benz, and UPS, represents an innovative delivery service with the objective of delivering packages to customers utilizing UAVs. Simultaneously, they endeavor to adhere to diverse regulations governing the utilization of UAVs within the urban logistics sphere (Roca-Riu & Monica Menendez, 2019).

Figure 7. Logistics in Modern WMS

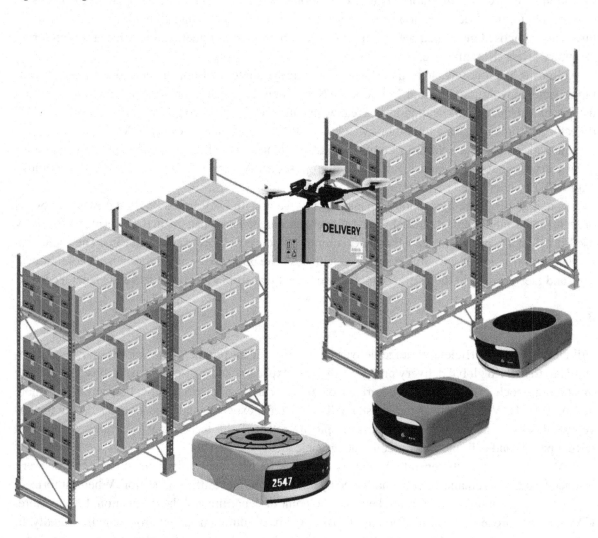

An essential concern in logistics using UAVs is trajectory tracking. Addressing this challenge, Rafo et al. introduced a non-linear control approach designed to manage the transportation of suspended loads. The proposed control strategy achieved system stabilization during trajectory tracking, even when faced with external disturbances, uncertainties in parameters, unmodeled dynamics, and imprecise measurements containing noise (Raffo & Almeida, 2018).

Another challenge in logistics of warehouse management is navigating UAVs while avoiding obstacles in route to guarantee effective delivery. Pizetta et al. examined the significance of integrating obstacle avoidance methods into the navigation of UAVs within forested surroundings. Considering UAV-cargo system navigating towards a desired position where the load should be delivered, they modeled UAV-cargo system using Euler-Lagrange equations models, guaranteed its stability using a non-linear controller that rejects load oscillations (Pizetta et al., 2018).

Kwon et al. presented an integrated system for autonomous UAV-based delivery in warehouses (Kwon et al., 2020). They proposed a low-cost sensing system with an Extended Kalman Filter (EKF)-based multi-sensor fusion framework to achieve practical autonomous navigation of UAVs in warehouse environments.

3.3 Inspection and Surveillance

Warehouse monitoring and inspection entail a proactive safety protocol designed to detect potential risks that could jeopardize the safety, reliability, and quality of stored items within a warehouse. The objective of this process is to guarantee the well-being of employees, secure inventory, and enhance workflows and procedures. Alternatively, regular surveillance serves as an alternate inspection approach to identify and counteract key warehouse threats, notably theft and other undesirable activities.

The warehouse management frequently presents complexities, as it involves maneuvering around numerous identical tall racks stocked with items during the process of material procurement. This activity is often time-consuming and carries the risk of worker injuries due to the elevated nature of the racks and the weight of the procured items. Consequently, these factors contribute to elevated operational expenses coupled with limited output. The automation of inventory management systems utilizing UAVs holds the potential to yield substantial time savings, significantly reduce costs, and mitigate the occurrence of worker injuries.

UAVs have been known for their surveillance capabilities due to their cost-effectiveness, manageable size, and programmable functionalities. Similarly, UAVs hold significant potential in enhancing surveillance endeavors within the warehouse management. They can be harnessed for the monitoring of ongoing logistics operations and other warehousing tasks. Moreover, their accessibility to difficult to reach areas makes them valuable for security and surveillance purposes in warehousing. Aerial surveillance facilitated by UAVs can efficiently oversee vast regions, requiring less effort compared to human-powered methods.

As a real-world example, Figure 8, Abu Dhabi Ports has introduced the utilization of UAVs to enhance protection and safeguard vessels transporting valuable or sensitive materials (A. Gupta et al., 2021). Also, to enhance the security of items within the railway network, PKP Cargo, a freight company based in Poland, conducted trials of surveillance UAVs. The company observed a significant decrease of 44% in theft incidents on the network as a result (Marsh, 2015).

Figure 8. Inspection and surveillance in modern WMS

Yang et al. introduced a novel panoramic UAV surveillance system. The proposed system is based on the unique structure-free fisheye camera array and has the capability of real-time UAV detection, 3D localization, tracking, and recycling capacity over a very wide field of view. They demonstrated effectiveness of their method in challenging situations, such as poor weather conditions, using a variety of UAVs (Yang et al., 2019).

Kwak et al. focus on generating UAV flight paths and control strategies for monitoring various targets in different environments. It involves measuring the UAV's position in its surroundings, specifying monitoring targets, and recording flight data. Flight paths are created based on this recorded data, enabling UAVs to navigate around obstacles and reach their destinations. These flight paths are applicable for indoor and outdoor UAV operations. Additionally, tailored flight paths are generated for different surveillance objectives, both indoors and outdoors. Pilots can easily manage UAVs using these predefined paths, capturing surveillance images using various methods based on object properties (Kwak et al., 2021).

Sharma et al. suggested a low-power wide-area network communication protocol to tackle the constrained energy challenges of UAVs. Handling the energy consumption issue improves the UAV coverage and ensure energy-efficient surveillance with low power (Sharma et al., 2018).

To achieve continuous surveillance using UAVs, Jung et al. utilized solar-powered hybrid UAVs, and developed a photovoltaic energy control system for UAVs. They predicted the duration of UAV flights using a method to estimate battery charge levels. The findings indicated that hybrid UAVs could achieve extended flight durations in normal weathers compared to traditional multi-rotor UAVs (Jung et al., 2019).

Although applications of a single UAV received many attentions in warehouse management in recent years using a single standalone agent ((Moura et al., 2021), (Kwon et al., 2020), (Ong et al., 2007), (Škrinjar et al., 2019), (H. Liu et al., 2022)) or the hybrid autonomous system of two robots including a UAV and an UGV ((Harik et al., 2016), (Kalinov et al., 2020)), the application of multi-UAVs in warehouse management is still in its early stages.

4 APPLICATIONS OF RL IN UAV NETWORKS

In this section, we will review specific applications and potential advantages of RL-based warehouse management using UAV networks. It will discuss how RL and MARL can optimize warehouse management tasks such as inventory management, order fulfillment, path planning, and surveillance.

In the previous section, different tasks in warehouse management which can be done utilizing UAVs were reviewed. One of the key challenges of using UAV in warehousing is optimizing their performance in dynamic and complex environments. RL offers a promising approach to enhance the UAV network capabilities by enabling autonomous learning and decision-making processes. In this section, we delve into the ways and rationale behind incorporating RL techniques into UAV networks to improve their inherent tasks.

Combining RL with UAV networks equips these autonomous flying platforms with the ability to learn, adapt, and optimize their actions based on experience and real-time feedback. Beyond traditional rule-based algorithms, RL empowers UAVs to autonomously navigate through obstacles, allocate resources fairly, and collaborate seamlessly in multi-agent environments. This combination of artificial intelligence and aerial capabilities holds the potential to redefine the boundaries of what UAVs can achieve across their inherent tasks. Advantage of using RL in UAV networks can be summarized as follows:

- **Adaptive Learning**: RL enables UAVs to learn and adapt their behaviors based on real-time interactions with the environment. This adaptability allows them to respond to changing conditions, such as weather, terrain, or mission objectives, improving their overall effectiveness.
- **Autonomous Decision-Making**: By using RL, UAVs can make decisions autonomously without requiring explicit programming for every possible scenario. This autonomy reduces the need for constant human intervention, freeing up human operators for higher-level tasks.
- **Collaborative Behavior**: In multi-UAV scenarios, RL enables UAVs to learn collaborative behaviors, enhancing coordination and teamwork. They can share information, coordinate actions, and optimize their collective performance to achieve complex tasks.
- **Learning from Experience**: UAVs can learn from their past experiences, both successes and failures. RL algorithms can help them remember and build upon previous knowledge, improving their decision-making over time.
- **Complex Task Solving**: RL enables UAVs to tackle complicated tasks that may involve multiple variables and interactions. This capability is particularly valuable in scenarios like search and rescue missions or environmental monitoring.

Extending RL to MARL in UAV networks (Figure 9) is essential for efficiently and effectively handling multiple UAVs operating simultaneously. MARL enables these unmanned vehicles to collaborate, communicate, and coordinate their actions to achieve common objectives while adapting to dynamic environments. Each UAV becomes an agent that learns not only from its own experiences but also from the actions and outcomes of other UAVs. This allows the UAVs to collectively learn better strategies and policies for tasks such as surveillance, inventory management, or intra-logistics. Here are some key reasons highlighting the necessity of this extension:

- **Collaborative Tasks**: Many UAV applications, such as surveillance, search and rescue, or environmental monitoring, require multiple UAVs to collaborate and work together. MARL enables UAVs to learn and adapt joint strategies, optimizing their actions to achieve shared objectives. This collaboration enhances mission efficiency and effectiveness.
- **Communication and Coordination**: MARL enables UAVs to communicate and coordinate their actions, which is crucial to prevent collisions, share information, and synchronize tasks. Through joint learning, UAVs can develop communication protocols and coordination strategies that enhance safety and efficiency.
- **Exploration of Solution Space**: MARL facilitates the exploration of a broader solution space by leveraging the experiences of multiple UAVs. This can lead to the discovery of more optimal and innovative solutions that a single UAV might not achieve.
- **Learning from Others**: In MARL, UAVs can learn from the successes and failures of their peers. This accelerates the learning process and enables faster convergence towards effective strategies, benefiting from the collective knowledge of the UAV network.
- **Faster Task Completion**: MARL allows for faster task completion as UAVs can parallelize their efforts and strategies to achieve tasks more efficiently, reducing the time required to accomplish objectives.

Figure 9. Main components of MARL-based warehousing using UAV networks

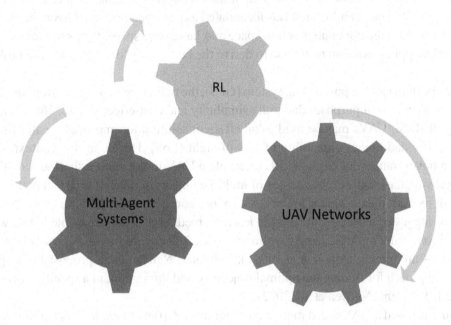

Previous research on using RL and MARL in UAV networks can be categorized into three main applications: trajectory design, resource management and scheduling, and delivery and transportation (as depicted in Figure 10). In the following, we will review main researches in these categories.

Figure 10. Various applications of RL and MARL in UAV networks

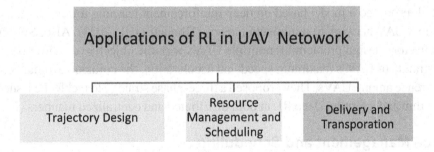

4.1 Trajectory Design

Trajectory design in a UAV network is the task of planning paths for a group of UAVs. It's about finding the best routes for each UAV to fly, making sure they don't bump into each other and use fuel wisely. This helps the UAVs work together smoothly for tasks such as auditing, monitoring, and surveillance.

Zhao et al. proposed a method called MADDPG to tackle the joint trajectory design and power allocation optimization problem in multi-UAV networks. They introduced a MARL strategy to maximize the long-term network utility and meet the quality of service demands of user equipment. Additionally, since each UAV's utility relies on the network environment and the actions of other UAVs, the problem of trajectory design and power allocation was formulated as a stochastic game. Given the computational challenges arising from the continuous action space and large state space, they suggested a multi-agent deep deterministic policy gradient technique to derive the best policy for addressing the problem (Zhao et al., 2020).

In the absence of the global positioning system (GPS), the radio received signal strength index (RSSI) can be used for localization purposes due to its simplicity and cost-effectiveness. However, due to the low accuracy of RSSI, UAVs may be used as an efficient solution for improved localization accuracy due to their agility and higher probability of line-of-sight (LoS). Hence, in this context, Ebrahimi et al. proposed a novel framework based on RL to enable a UAV to autonomously find its trajectory that results in improving the localization accuracy of multiple objects in shortest time and path length, fewer signal-strength measurements, and/or lower UAV energy consumption (Ebrahimi et al., 2021).

Moon et al. suggested a deep reinforcement learning method to control multiple UAVs with the primary goal of monitoring multiple targets within complex 3-D environments, even when obstacles and visual occlusions are present (Moon et al., 2021). Similarly, Nguyen et al. proposed a deep reinforcement learning approach for finding the optimal trajectory and throughput in a specific coverage area in a UAV-based IoT system (Nguyen et al., 2022).

Wang et al. proposed a UAV-aided mobile edge computing framework, in which a trajectory control algorithm based on multi-agent deep reinforcement learning is introduced. The algorithm independently manages the flight path of each UAV, employing the well-known Multi-Agent Deep Deterministic Policy Gradient (MADDPG) technique (L. Wang et al., 2021).

UAVs faces difficulty in determining their trajectories due to the dynamic environments, where other UAVs dynamically establish their trajectories and compete for the limited spectrum resources concurrently. In response, Hu et al. utilized reinforcement learning as a solution for the decentralized UAV trajectory design challenge. They presented an improved multi-UAV Q-learning algorithm to address the decentralized problem of UAV trajectory design (Hu et al., 2019).

Dhuheir et al. proposed a model based on deep reinforcement learning for distributed collaborative path planning in a UAV network to minimized latency (Dhuheir et al., 2023). Also, Similarly, Xu et al. investigated trajectory design problem for multiple UAVs with the objective of minimizing the mission time with constraints of UAV's maximum speed and acceleration, the collision avoidance, and communication interference among UAVs. They proposed a three-phase strategy to tackle the issue, utilizing the K-means algorithm and adopting Deep RL in both distributed and centralized manners (Xu et al., 2022).

4.2 Resource Management and Scheduling

Resource management and scheduling in a UAV network involves the strategic allocation and optimization of various resources and capabilities to ensure the efficient and effective operation of multiple UAVs. This encompasses critical tasks, including the fair distribution of energy resources to UAVs, dynamic assignment of UAVs to specific tasks or regions for optimal coverage and data collection, as well as the coordination of communication bandwidth to facilitate real-time information exchange among UAVs and ground stations.

Cui et al. (Cui et al., 2019) used independent learners Q-learning based approaches in MARL to propose an autonomous resource allocation of multiple UAVs. In their proposed method, each UAV is considered as an agent and learns its best strategy according to its local observations. Also, UAVs share their knowledge through Q-table.

Peng et al. (Peng & Shen, 2021) studied multi-dimensional resource management in the Mobile Edge Computing (MEC) and UAV-assisted vehicular networks. To cooperatively support the heterogeneous and delay-sensitive vehicular applications, they used an MADDPG-based scheme to distributively manage the spectrum, computing, and caching resources available to the MEC-mounted UAVs.

Sixing et al. (Yin & Yu, 2022) addressed the decentralized resource allocation and trajectory design problem in a downlink cellular network where multiple UAVs serve as aerial base stations for ground users through frequency-division multiple access (FDMA). They modeled the problem as a decentralized partially observable Markov decision process (Dec-POMDP) and proposed multi-agent reinforcement learning as a solution.

Sacco et al. (Sacco et al., 2021) proposed a distributed architecture based on a MARL technique to dynamically offload tasks from UAVs to the edge cloud. Nodes of the system co-operate to jointly minimize the overall latency perceived by the user and the energy usage on UAVs by continuously learning from the environment the best action, which entails the decision of offloading and, in this case, the best transmission technology, i.e., Wi-Fi or cellular.

Oubbati et al. (Oubbati et al., 2022) addressed the problem of energy limitation of UAV networks, when UAVs are used as base stations to complement the wireless network. To do this, they took advantage of adjustable flying energy sources (FESs) to power UAVs onboard batteries and avoid disrupting their trajectories. They leveraged a multi-agent deep reinforcement learning method to optimize the task of energy transfer between FESs and UAVs.

Spectrum management is one of the key challenges in UAV networks, since spectrum shortage can impede the operation of these networks. In response, Shamsoshoara et al. (Shamsoshoara et al., 2019) proposed a distributed multi-agent reinforcement learning algorithm for spectrum sharing among UAVs. Their approach offers a practical solution for scenarios where the UAV network might require access to additional spectrum when facing congested frequency bands or when it has to modify its operating frequency due to security concerns.

4.3 Delivery and Transportation

UAV networks are reshaping delivery and transportation by utilizing UAVs to rapidly transport items. These unmanned vehicles navigate with precision, from urban deliveries to remote supply transport, offering efficiency, reduced costs, and minimal environmental impact. Integrating with existing systems and adhering to regulations are key for maximizing their potential in revolutionizing modern logistics.

To overcome the delivery range and payload capacity limitations of UAVs, the combination of trucks and UAVs is gaining more attention. By using trucks as a flight platform for UAVs and supporting their take-off and landing, the delivery range and capacity can be greatly extended. Bi et al. (Bi et al., 2023) focused on mixed truck-drone delivery and utilized reinforcement learning to address the problem. Similarly, Wu et al. (Wu et al., 2023) investigated using UAV networks to deliver medical supplies home-quarantined people during the pandemic. They took advantage of reinforcement learning to achieve safe and effective truck-UAV coordinated delivery.

Hachiya et al. (Hachiya et al., 2022) focused on using UAVs for transportation of emergency relief items due to their convenience regardless of the disaster conditions. They suggested an approach for planning transportation that introduces three essential performance measures, the speed of supply, the priority of supply, and the fairness of supply quantities. They formulated the transportation problem as a multi-objective, multi-trip, multi-item, and multi-UAV problems, and then utilized Q-learning to optimize this problem.

Faust et al. (Faust et al., 2017) presented a reinforcement learning approach for aerial cargo delivery tasks in environment with static obstacles. Also, Panetsos et al. addressed the problem of ensuring the safe transportation of the load, the swinging motion. They used a policy-based reinforcement learning algorithm to mitigate the load oscillations (Panetsos et al., 2022).

5 CHALLENGES OF USING MARL IN UAV-BASED WAREHOUSE MANAGEMENT

Multi-UAV systems have the potential to perform tasks more effectively and economically than single-UAV systems when working together. However, numerous challenges need to be addressed to ensure the stability and reliability of UAVs for context-specific networks. (L. Gupta et al., 2016).

Also, implementing MARL in distributed and cooperative tasks such as UAV networks-based warehouse management introduces unique challenges. This section will discuss main challenges such as non-stationarity of environments (Marinescu et al., 2017), partial observability (Gronauer & Diepold, 2022), reward design (Oroojlooy & Hajinezhad, 2022), scalability issues (Cassano et al., 2021), and task allocation and load balancing (D. Liu et al., 2023). Understanding and addressing these challenges is essential for effective MARL-based warehouse management using UAV networks. In the following section, we will introduce these challenges and the primary factors that can lead to their occurrence in UAV-based warehouse management.

5.1 Non-Stationary

The non-stationary challenge refers to the problem of dealing with environments where the dynamics, goals, or policies of agents are subject to change over time. In traditional single-agent reinforcement learning, the environment is usually assumed to be stationary, meaning that the underlying dynamics do not change during the learning process (Marinescu et al., 2017). However, in MARL, each agent's learning process can affect the environment, which in turn can lead to changes in the environment's dynamics. There are several factors that can introduce non-stationarity in MARL-based warehouse management using UAV networks:

- **Changing Agent Policies**: In a multi-agent system, as agents (UAVs) learn and improve their policies, they may adopt different strategies over time. These shifts in strategies can lead to changes in the overall behavior of the system, making it difficult for agents to adapt to the dynamic environment.
- **Environmental Changes**: The warehouse environment itself may change over time due to shifting, insertion, or removal of items. These environmental shifts can affect the dynamics of the interactions between agents and lead to non-stationary conditions.
- **Communication and Cooperation**: In MARL-based warehouse management, the effectiveness of communication and coordination between UAVs can vary over time due to their distance or the presence of obstacles between them, leading to non-stationary behavior and challenges in learning effective joint policies.

MARL can address this challenge by allowing the robots to learn and adapt to these changes. Each robot can adapt its inventory placement strategies, picking procedures, and routing decisions based on real-time observations and changes in the warehouse environment. For example, during the holiday season, when there's a significant shift in the types of products being stored and orders being processed, MARL-equipped robots can autonomously reconfigure their operations to accommodate the non-stationary conditions. This adaptability ensures that the warehouse can efficiently handle fluctuations in inventory and demand, optimizing storage and retrieval processes to match the evolving needs of the environment.

5.2 Partial Observability

The partial observability challenge refers to the difficulty agents face when they have limited or incomplete information about the state of the environment and the actions of other agents (Gronauer & Diepold, 2022). In this scenario, each agent can only observe a partial view of the overall system, and they do not have access to the complete state information. There are several factors that can introduce partial observability in MARL-based warehouse management:

- **Limited Sensing Range**: UAVs may have a restricted sensing range, meaning they can only observe a portion of the warehouse at any given time. This limited view can lead to incomplete knowledge about the locations of goods, obstacles, and other agents in the warehouse.
- **Noisy or Inaccurate Sensing**: Even within the sensing range, the UAVs' sensors may suffer from noise, inaccuracies, or occlusions. This can result in unreliable or imprecise observations, making it difficult for the agents to accurately perceive the state of the environment.
- **Communication Delays**: In a multi-agent setting, different UAVs may communicate their observations to each other, and there can be delays or limitations in this communication process. As a result, agents may not have access to real-time information from all other agents, leading to partial observability of the overall system state.
- **Environment Obstacles**: Warehouse layouts, shelves, and obstacles can obstruct the line of sight, causing partial visibility of agents and objects.

Traditional warehouse systems often deal with partial observability, as robots have limited visibility of the entire warehouse. MARL can overcome this issue by enabling robots to communicate and collaborate effectively. For instance, if one robot identifies a low-stock item or encounters an obstacle in its path, it can share this information with other robots. This collaborative approach allows the team of robots to collectively optimize their actions, ensuring that the entire warehouse operates efficiently despite partial observability.

5.3 Credit Assignment

The credit assignment challenge in MARL refers to the difficulty of properly attributing credit to individual agents in a multi-agent system when their actions jointly contribute to achieving collective goals. It involves aligning the credit assignment with the agents' actual contributions to the overall performance of the system (Gronauer & Diepold, 2022).

For example, consider Figure 11, where in a sample traffic gridlock, it's not easy to pinpoint which individuals or factors were primarily responsible for causing the problem. Similarly, once the gridlock is resolved, it becomes a challenge to accurately attribute credit to specific contributing factors or agents when using a global reward system. This illustrates the concept of credit assignment, where determining who or what deserves credit or blame in a complex system can be quite intricate.

Figure 11. Credit assignment example in traffic
(Eric Liang & Richard Liaw, 2018)

In a warehouse management system, multiple UAVs (and probably UGVs) work together to perform various tasks, such as item retrieval, inventory management, and order fulfillment. These tasks are often interdependent, and the overall system's performance depends on the coordinated efforts of all UAVs. However, determining the specific contributions of each agent to the system's success can be challenging due to the following reasons:

- **Collective Decision-Making**: In a multi-agent setting, UAVs make decisions based on their local observations and the information shared by other UAVs. The joint actions of all UAVs collectively impact the overall system's performance, making it challenging to isolate the impact of an individual UAV's actions.

- **Sparse Rewards**: The rewards in a MARL system may be sparse or delayed, meaning that the consequences of an action may not be immediately apparent. As a result, associating specific actions with long-term rewards becomes difficult.
- **Interaction Dependencies**: The actions of one UAV can influence the state of the environment and, consequently, the opportunities and challenges for other UAVs. Credit assignment must account for these interaction dependencies.

Credit assignment in traditional systems can be challenging when assessing the individual contributions of robots in a team. MARL can address this by using a reward-based system. Each robot learns to associate its actions with rewards, which can be assigned based on their impact on overall warehouse performance. This way, each robot can receive credit commensurate with its contributions, facilitating fair performance evaluation.

5.4 Scalability

The scalability challenge refers to the difficulty of effectively handling and coordinating a large number of UAVs as the size of the warehouse or the complexity of the tasks increases (Aleksandar Krnjaic et al., 2023). As the number of UAVs in the system grows, the interactions and dependencies between them increase exponentially, leading to a combinatorial explosion of possible joint actions and observations. This makes the coordination and communication among UAVs more complex and resource-intensive, which poses significant scalability challenges. The scalability challenge can occur in warehouse management for several reasons:

- **Combinatorial Complexity**: As the number of UAVs increases or warehouse environment becomes larger or more complex, the size of the action and observation spaces grows exponentially, making it computationally infeasible to explore all possible policies.
- **Communication Overhead**: In a multi-UAV system, communication is necessary for coordination. With a large number of UAVs, the communication overhead can become substantial, leading to delays and inefficiencies.
- **Coordination Bottlenecks**: Centralized coordination approaches might become a bottleneck when dealing with a large number of UAVs, leading to reduced responsiveness and slower decision-making.
- **Learning**: Training MARL algorithms in a large-scale setting can be time-consuming and require a vast amount of data, leading to slow learning and high computational requirements.

As a warehouse's operations expand or contract, traditional systems may struggle to adapt to the changing scale. MARL provides scalability by allowing the seamless integration of new robots or the reconfiguration of existing ones. These agents can quickly adapt to the new workload and collaborate with the existing robots to maintain efficient operations. As the warehouse grows or shrinks, MARL ensures that the system can easily accommodate these changes.

5.5 Task Allocation and Load Balancing

The task allocation and load balancing challenge refer to the difficulty of optimally assigning tasks to individual UAVs while ensuring a balanced distribution of workload among them (D. Liu et al., 2023). In a warehouse management system, multiple tasks need to be performed simultaneously, such as item retrieval, inventory management, or order fulfillment. These tasks can vary in complexity, priority, and spatial distribution within the warehouse. The challenge lies in efficiently allocating these tasks to UAVs based on current state of UAV network to ensure that the system operates effectively and with minimal delays. The challenge can occur due to the following reasons:

- **Heterogeneous UAV Capabilities**: UAVs may have different capabilities, such as flight range, payload capacity, or task execution speed. Task allocation should consider these variations to assign tasks that match UAV capabilities.
- **Spatial Distribution of Tasks**: Tasks in the warehouse may be scattered across different locations. Allocating tasks to UAVs in a way that minimizes their travel distances and optimizes the overall travel time is a challenging optimization problem.
- **Task Dependencies**: Some tasks might be dependent on others, requiring specific sequences or coordination among UAVs to ensure successful execution. Managing task dependencies is essential for efficient task allocation.
- **Dynamic Task Priorities**: Task priorities may change over time based on customer demand, inventory levels, or other factors. Adapting task allocation to changing priorities is crucial for responsive warehouse management.

Task allocation and load balancing are critical in warehouse management. MARL can optimize these aspects by enabling robots to autonomously allocate tasks and collaborate to ensure efficient order fulfillment. When a surge in orders occurs, MARL-equipped robots can collectively decide how to distribute tasks among themselves, optimizing the load balance and minimizing idle time. This dynamic allocation ensures that orders are processed efficiently, even during peak periods.

6 SOLUTIONS AND APPROACHES

In this section, we have tried to address all mentioned challenges associated with MARL-based UAV networks in warehouse management. For each challenge, most popular approaches to overcome will be discussed. The section will provide insights into how these solutions can enhance the coordination, scalability, and decision-making capabilities of UAV agents in warehouse management scenarios.

6.1 Non-Stationary

One of the key challenges in MARL is the non-stationarity of the learning environment when multiple agents are learning concurrently. When multiple agents are learning and updating their policies concurrently, the transition dynamics and rewards, and environments, are not stationary from a single agent's point of view since the next state of the environment is a function of the joint action of all agents and not only that agent's own action.

This dynamic issue disrupts the Markov assumption typically relied upon in single-agent RL algorithms, resulting in continuous adjustments by multiple agents as they react to each other's policy changes. In the following, two main scenarios are described to handle the non-stationary issue.

6.1.1 Centralized Training With Decentralized Execution

One approach, as can be seen in Figure 12, which is commonly used in the literature to circumvent the challenge of non-stationarity is to assume that agents are trained in an environment where information about all agents is exploited during training but not execution. This learning paradigm is called *Centralized Training with Decentralized Execution* (CTDE) (Gronauer & Diepold, 2022). In this approach, the agents have the option to utilize extra global state data for centralized guidance during training while basing their decisions solely on decentralized local policies. This extra information is discarded in the execution phase. Thus, agents can achieve a local policy using global information in training phase which can hopefully achieve good results in execution phase using only local information.

Sharing mutual information during training can streamline the process and enhance the learning speed when compared to agents trained independently. Furthermore, agents can overcome non-stationarity by having access to additional information about the actions chosen by all agents during training, allowing them to attribute the outcomes of actions to the respective agents. The CTDE paradigm has been used both in homogenous networks (Ahilan & Dayan, 2019), (Kyunghwan Son, Daewoo Kim, Wan Ju Kang, David Earl Hostallero, 2019), and heterogenous networks (Lowe et al., 2017), (Bono et al., 2019).

Figure 12. Centralized training decentralized execution approach

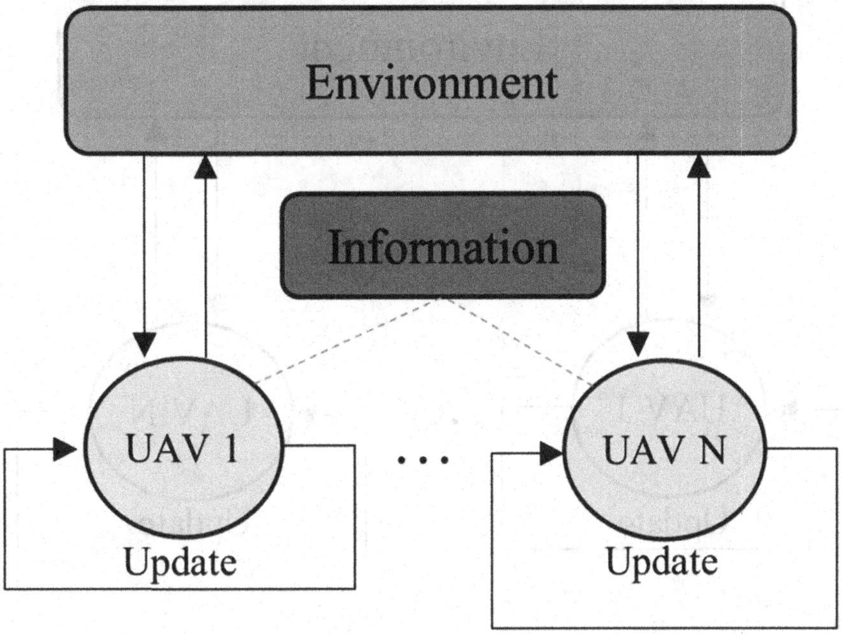

6.1.2 Distributed Training With Decentralized Execution

Although CTDE can circumvent the conceptual challenges of non-stationarity of the environment, it is not an ideal solution in all scenarios. CTDE is only applicable when there is access to the observations and actions of all agents. It is not always possible to construct such a centralized training, especially in online real-world settings. For example, self-driving cars cannot share their policies and observations with other cars on the road in real-time.

In latter scenario, *Distributed Training, and Decentralized Execution* (DTDE) approach is used, where each agent has an associated policy which maps its local observations to a distribution over individual action (Figure 13). No information is shared between agents such that each agent learns independently (Gronauer & Diepold, 2022).

The primary limitation of the DTDE paradigm is that, from the perspective of a single agent, the environment seems non-stationary. This is because agents lack access to the information of other agents and do not perceive joint actions.

Li et al. (W. Li et al., 2020) proposed a fully decentralized approach in which in order to mitigate the impact of information loss resulting from decentralized settings, an approach known as the modeling-other-agents (MOA) technique was employed. This technique relies on the theory-of-mind (TOM) concept, and utilizes online supervised learning to estimate the information of other agents while making decisions based on local observation.

Figure 13. Decentralized training decentralized execution approach

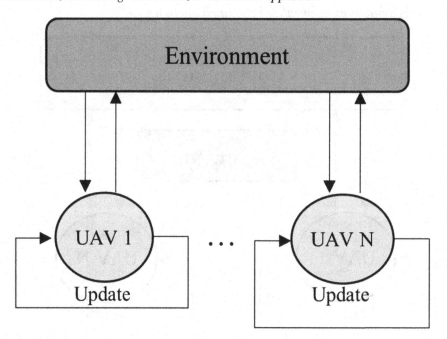

6.2 Partial Observability

Another key challenge in MARL is partial observability. It arises when UAVs lack complete information about the warehouse environment. In such scenarios, each agent's observation is typically limited to its local sensory input or a partial view of the environment, making it challenging to make informed decisions. To handle partial observability in warehouse environments different approaches can be used including learn to communicate and memory mechanism.

6.2.1 Learn to Communicate

The Learn to Communicate approach in focuses on enabling agents in a multi-agent system to learn how to effectively communicate with each other. This approach is especially relevant in scenarios where agents need to cooperate or coordinate their actions to achieve common goals. It allows agents to autonomously develop communication skills that facilitate teamwork and coordination, leading to improved performance in complex, multi-agent scenarios.

Intelligent agents need to make choices not just about what information to communicate but also about the timing and the recipients of their communication. In such settings, agents are required to learn communication protocols to exchange necessary information for task-solving (Jakob Foerster et al., 2016).

For instance, literature on communication types can be categorized according to the direction of message flow. The first category, Figure 14(a), is when the broadcasting is used, where sent messages are received by all agents (Jakob Foerster et al., 2016). The second category, Figure 14(b), is when the targeted messages are learned to determine recipients (Abhishek Das et al., 2019). The third category, Figure 14(c), is when communications happen in networked settings where we examine communication within networked settings, where agents communicate only with their local neighborhood instead of the whole population (Chu et al., 2020).

Figure 14. Different communication types: (a): Broadcasting, (b) targeted communication, and (c) networked communication
(Gronauer & Diepold, 2022).

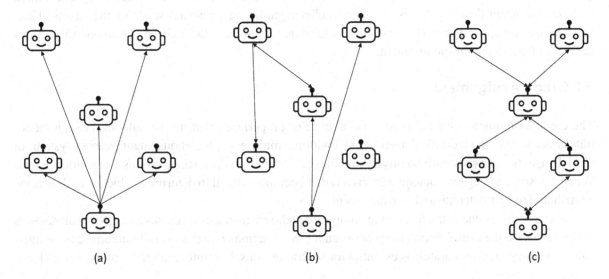

6.2.2 Memory Mechanism

To tackle the challenge of partial observability, a commonly adopted approach involves the use of deep recurrent neural networks (RNNs). RNN is a type of artificial neural network designed for processing sequences of data. Unlike traditional feedforward neural networks, RNNs have connections that loop back on themselves, allowing them to maintain a form of memory (depicted in Figure 15). These RNNs offer agents a memory mechanism, allowing them to store relevant information and past experiences as a compensatory factor for the partiality of information (X. Li et al., 2015). However, making decisions with long-term dependencies becomes complex, as experiences observed further in the past may fade from memory.

Figure 15. RNN as a memory mechanism in RL
(X. Li et al., 2015)

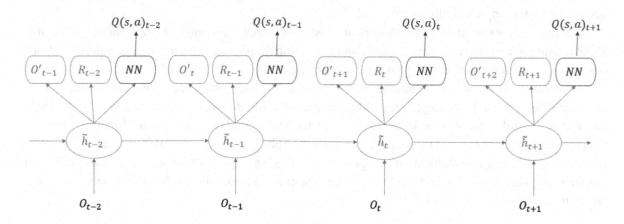

As an example, Foerster et al. (Jakob Foerster et al., 2019) employed a Bayesian approach to address the challenge of partial observability within MARL. They leveraged all openly accessible environment features and agent data to establish a shared belief regarding the internal states of the agents. Their method uses an approximate Bayesian update to obtain a public belief that conditions on the actions taken by all agents in the environment.

6.3 Credit Assignment

The credit assignment issue refers to the challenge of properly attributing the outcomes of a joint action or decision to the individual agent (UAV) within a multi-agent warehouse management system. In MARL, agents often work collaboratively to achieve a common goal, and their actions are interdependent. When a positive or negative outcome is observed, it becomes crucial to determine which agent's actions contributed to that outcome and to what extent.

This issue arises due to the fact that in complex warehouse management tasks and environments with multiple UAVs, the causal relationship between a UAV's actions and the overall outcome can be intricate. Assigning credit accurately is essential for several reasons. In reinforcement learning, agents learn by receiving rewards based on their actions. Accurate credit assignment ensures that agents receive the appropriate rewards for their contributions to the team's success or failure. Agents use credit assignment to update their policies and strategies. If credit is assigned incorrectly, agents may learn ineffective or suboptimal behaviors, hindering the overall performance of the team.

Solving the credit assignment problem in MARL is a complex task because it involves disentangling the interactions among agents and their effects on the environment. Two well-known approaches for credit assignment in MARL are value function decomposition and inverse reinforcement learning.

6.3.1 Value Function Decomposition

Decomposition approaches concentrate on leveraging inter-agent dependencies to break down the reward allocation among agents, considering their genuine contributions to the overall reward (Figure 16). The learning challenge becomes more manageable as the task is divided into smaller sub-problems, simplifying the overall problem through decomposition.

Figure 16. Value decomposition paradigm
(S. Liu et al., 2023)

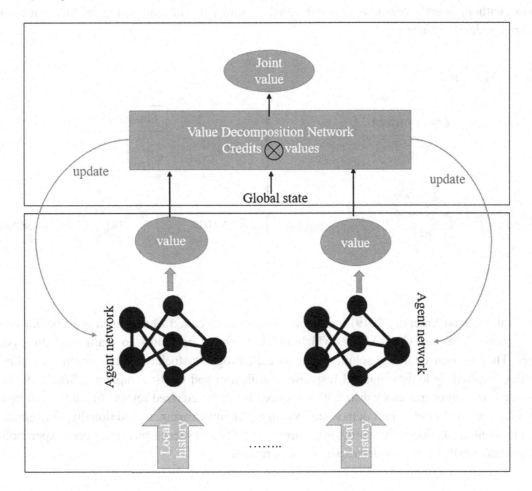

Sunehag et al. (Sunehag et al., 2018) introduced the concept of the value decomposition network, which decomposes the joint action-value function into a linear combination of individual action-value functions. The approach is designed to learn the optimal allocation of individual rewards based on each agent's performance, effectively clarifying the joint reward signal regarding an agent's influence. Rashid et al. (Rashid et al., 2020) presented another approach using deep neural network to enhance value function decomposition. Their approach learns a centralized action-value function, which is further decomposed into individual agent action-value functions through non-linear combinations.

6.3.2 Inverse Reinforcement Learning

Problems with credit assignment can stem from poorly designed reinforcement learning problems. Misinterpretations by agents can lead to failures because unintentional strategies may be explored, particularly if the reward function fails to encompass all essential aspects of the underlying task. Hence, the reward function is a critical component in problem design; and designing an appropriate reward function can be a complicated task for complex problems.

In response, another approach to tackle the credit assignment problem is by employing inverse reinforcement learning (IRL). This method enables an agent to learn a reward function that explains expert behavior, without direct access to the reward signal (Figure 17). The learned reward function can then be utilized to devise strategies.

Figure 17. RL vs. IRL

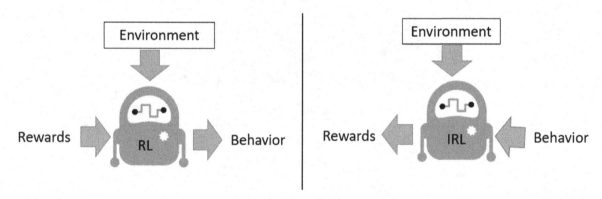

Yu et al. (Lantao Yu et al., 2019) introduced a framework called Multi-Agent Adversarial Inverse Reinforcement Learning (MA-AIRL), which imitates expert behaviors to learn high-dimensional policies. They introduced a new solution concept called logistic stochastic best response equilibrium (LSBRE), inspired by logistic quantal response equilibrium and Gibbs sampling. LSBRE allows for the characterization of trajectory distribution induced by parameterized reward functions and handles the bounded rationality of expert demonstrations in a principled manner. Additionally, they employed maximum pseudo-likelihood estimation to ensure tractability and successfully recovered expert policies for individual agents from provided expert demonstrations.

6.4 Scalability

The scalability issue in MARL, particularly in the context of warehouse management, refers to the challenge of effectively applying MARL techniques to large-scale and complex environments with numerous agents (UAVs), states, and actions. This challenge becomes increasingly pronounced as the size and complexity of the warehouse operations grow. Among others, two important approaches for handling scalability issues in MARL are knowledge reuse and curriculum learning.

6.4.1 Knowledge Reuse

Training individual learning models becomes less efficient as the number of UAVs increases, mainly due to the growing computational complexity resulting from the various possible combinations. To address this issue and make reinforcement learning more scalable for complex problems, strategies involving the reuse of knowledge are implemented. Knowledge reuse (Figure 18) entails leveraging previously acquired knowledge and applying it to new tasks, which can be employed in various ways including parameter sharing and transfer learning (Felipe Leno Da Silva et al., 2018).

Figure 18. Knowledge reuse in MARL
(F. L. Da Silva & Costa, 2020)

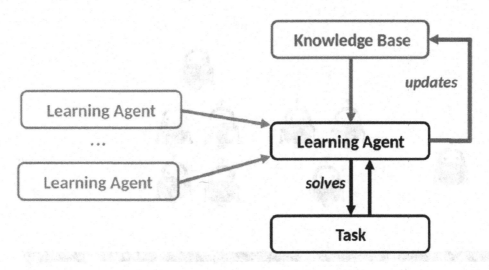

Agents can employ a parameter sharing method when they possess similar structures, such as sharing specific parts or the entire learning model, such as the weights in a neural network, with other agents. Sharing policy parameters facilitates an efficient training process that can be expanded to accommodate any number of agents, thereby enhancing the learning process (J. K. Gupta et al., 2017).

Also, knowledge reuse can take the form of transfer learning, where the experience gained while learning one task can enhance performance in a related yet distinct task. Da Silva et al. (F. Da Silva & Costa, 2017) employed a knowledge database, allowing an agent to extract previous solutions from related tasks and incorporate this information into its current training for the task at hand.

6.4.2 Curriculum Learning

Curriculum learning can be employed to address the challenge of scaling to a large number of UAVs in large and complex warehouse environments. As tasks become challenging, more complex, and time-consuming to train for with an increasing number of UAVs, starting from scratch can be challenging.

Curriculum learning, as depicted in Figure 19, initiates training with a small group of agents and then gradually expands the agent count as the training progresses. This gradual enlargement within the curriculum has been shown to yield better-performing policies compared to training without a curriculum, as demonstrated by Long et al. (Long et al., 2020). Moreover, curriculum learning approaches have the potential to enhance the generalization capabilities of agents and faster policy convergence.

Figure 19. Concept of curriculum learning in MARL

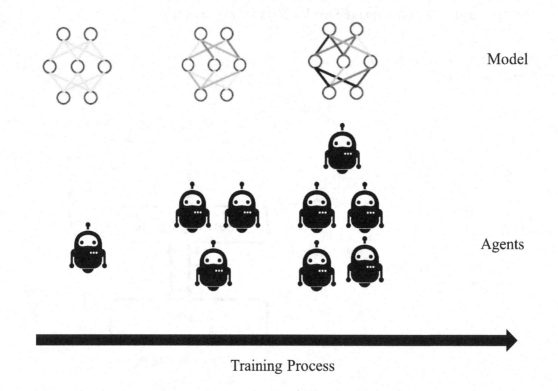

Training Process

6.5 Task Allocation and Load Balancing

Task allocation and load Balancing is a significant issue in MARL, especially in the context of warehouse management. In a warehouse environment, there are various and different tasks to be performed by multiple UAVs in order to optimize the overall operational efficiency. The primary challenge lies in distributing these tasks among the UAVs efficiently while ensuring a balanced workload and minimizing delays.

Solving the task allocation and load balancing issue in MARL involves designing algorithms and strategies that enable agents to collaborate in a decentralized manner to make optimal task allocation decisions. These algorithms should consider real-time factors like agent availability, task urgency, and the overall system performance. Current approaches to handle this issue can be categorized into two groups including centralized and distributed methods.

6.5.1 Centralized Methods

In a centralized configuration, the coordination, signal transmission, and overall control among the UAVs within the system are all managed by a single central control planner. This places significant computational demands on the ground-based control center, allowing the UAVs themselves to be constructed in a smaller and more cost-effective manner.

Moradi et al. (Moradi, 2016) used a centralized reinforcement learning method to present an adaptable, scalable, and model-independent method for job scheduling to attain a desired level of load distribution and overall system efficiency. The method uses task information and completion times to assess resource efficiency.

6.5.2 Distributed Methods

Distributed task allocation refers to the process of assigning tasks or responsibilities to multiple UAVs or entities within a network or system in a decentralized manner. This method is particularly valuable in scenarios where a central authority or controller may not be feasible or efficient due to factors such as scalability, redundancy, or dynamic changes in the environment. Distributed task allocation systems often employ algorithms and protocols that facilitate communication and coordination among agents to ensure that tasks are allocated optimally, considering factors like resource availability, task complexity, and agent expertise.

Cui et al. (Cui et al., 2020) proposed a dynamic multi-UAV resource allocation framework utilizing collaborative multi-agent reinforcement learning. They introduced the Independent Learner (ILs) based MARL algorithm to address the challenge of reducing information exchange overhead in multi-UAV networks. This development is characterized by an agent-independent approach, where each UAV agent autonomously makes decisions. Each UAV employs a standard Q-learning algorithm to determine its optimal strategy by independently learning its optimal Q-value. The illustration in Figure 20 depicts the illustration of multi-UAV communication networks established by them. The UAVs fly over the designated area based on predefined user trajectories, establishing communication links with users. The dynamic resource allocation considers parameters such as the number of users, power levels, and subchannel selections in multi-UAV networks.

Figure 20. Illustration of multi-UAV communication networks
(Cui et al., 2020)

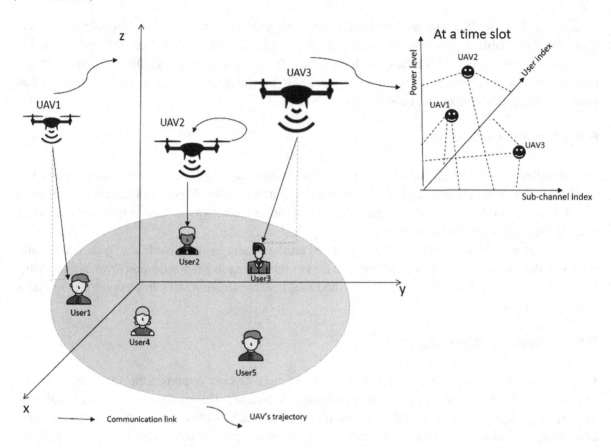

7. CONCLUSION AND FUTURE TRENDS

In this chapter, we reviewed the potentiality of using UAV network in warehouse management using multi-agent reinforcement learning as its algorithmic framework. We reviewed the basic concepts in reinforcement learning and multi-agent reinforcement learning.

We reviewed different applications of UAVs in warehouse management including inventory management, logistic, and inspection and surveillance. We also reviewed different applications of reinforcement learning in UAV networks including trajectory design, resource management, delivery and transportation, and task scheduling and load balancing.

Currently, most of the research in this field depends on single-agent reinforcement learning approaches. These single-agent RL techniques concentrate on enhancing the performance of individual UAV agents operating within a warehouse environment. However, in real-world warehouse situations, the coordination and collaboration of multiple agents are vital for achieving efficient and effective operations. Shifting from single-agent RL to multi-agent reinforcement learning presents the chance to tackle these challenges and leverage the combined intelligence of UAV agents in warehouse management tasks.

However, applying multi-agent reinforcement learning to manage UAV networks introduce new challenges and issues, which should be handled. We highlighted main challenges including non-stationary, partial observability, credit assignment, scalability, and task allocation and load balancing, and presented some of the popular approaches to handle these challenges.

Certainly, there are some future trends in modern warehouse management. Robotics and automation are revolutionizing warehouse operations. Autonomous Mobile Robots (AMRs) are increasingly used for material handling and order picking. These robots can work alongside human operators, improving efficiency and reducing labor costs. Robotic Process Automation (RPA) is also being deployed to automate various warehouse tasks, such as data entry and inventory management.

AI and Machine Learning are playing a crucial role in warehouse management. Predictive analytics powered by AI can forecast inventory demands, optimize order picking routes, and identify potential issues before they disrupt operations. Advanced AI-driven forecasting models are helping warehouses anticipate customer demands and optimize inventory levels more effectively.

IoT sensors are providing real-time data on warehouse conditions, including temperature, humidity, and equipment performance, ensuring product quality and safety. IoT-enabled asset tracking solutions are improving inventory visibility, reducing the risk of stockouts and overstocking.

Augmented Reality (AR) and Virtual Reality (VR) are enhancing warehouse operations. AR glasses are guiding workers to the precise location of items, improving order fulfillment accuracy and speed. VR is being used for employee training, allowing them to familiarize themselves with warehouse layouts and operations in a safe, simulated environment.

Blockchain technology is enhancing supply chain transparency. It enables better tracking of product origins, authenticity, and quality, enhancing trust and accountability in the supply chain. Also, cloud-based WMS Systems offer scalability and flexibility. These solutions allow warehouses to adapt to changing business needs without significant IT investments.

REFERENCES

Ahilan, S., & Dayan, P. (2019). *Feudal Multi-Agent Hierarchies for Cooperative Reinforcement Learning*. ArXiv.

Antonio, G.-P., & Maria-Dolores, C. (2022). Multi-Agent Deep Reinforcement Learning to Manage Connected Autonomous Vehicles at Tomorrow's Intersections. *IEEE Transactions on Vehicular Technology*, *71*(7), 7033–7043. doi:10.1109/TVT.2022.3169907

Bae, S. M., Han, K. H., Cha, C. N., & Lee, H. Y. (2016). Development of Inventory Checking System Based on UAV and RFID in Open Storage Yard. *2016 International Conference on Information Science and Security (ICISS)*, (pp. 1–2). IEEE. 10.1109/ICISSEC.2016.7885849

Beul, M., Droeschel, D., Nieuwenhuisen, M., Quenzel, J., Houben, S., & Behnke, S. (2018). Fast autonomous flight in warehouses for inventory applications. *IEEE Robotics and Automation Letters*, *3*(4), 3121–3128. doi:10.1109/LRA.2018.2849833

Bi, Z., Guo, X., Wang, J., Qin, S., & Liu, G. (2023). Deep Reinforcement Learning for Truck-Drone Delivery Problem. *Drones (Basel)*, *7*(7), 445. doi:10.3390/drones7070445

Bono, G., Dibangoye, J. S., Matignon, L., Pereyron, F., & Simonin, O. (2019). Cooperative Multi-agent Policy Gradient. Springer. doi:10.1007/978-3-030-10925-7_28

Bouktif, S., Cheniki, A., Ouni, A., & El-Sayed, H. (2023). Deep reinforcement learning for traffic signal control with consistent state and reward design approach. *Knowledge-Based Systems*, *267*, 110440. doi:10.1016/j.knosys.2023.110440

Cassano, L., Yuan, K., & Sayed, A. H. (2021). Multiagent Fully Decentralized Value Function Learning with Linear Convergence Rates. *IEEE Transactions on Automatic Control*, *66*(4), 1497–1512. doi:10.1109/TAC.2020.2995814

Cestero, J., Quartulli, M., Metelli, A. M., & Restelli, M. (2022). Storehouse: a Reinforcement Learning Environment for Optimizing Warehouse Management. *2022 International Joint Conference on Neural Networks (IJCNN)*, (pp. 1–9). IEEE. 10.1109/IJCNN55064.2022.9891985

Chen, S., Meng, W., Xu, W., Liu, Z., Liu, J., & Wu, F. (2020). A Warehouse Management System with UAV Based on Digital Twin and 5G Technologies. *2020 7th International Conference on Information, Cybernetics, and Computational Social Systems*, (pp. 864–869). IEEE. 10.1109/ICCSS52145.2020.9336832

Chu, T., Wang, J., Codeca, L., & Li, Z. (2020). Multi-agent deep reinforcement learning for large-scale traffic signal control. *IEEE Transactions on Intelligent Transportation Systems*, *21*(3), 1086–1095. doi:10.1109/TITS.2019.2901791

Chung, S.-J., Paranjape, A. A., Dames, P., Shen, S., & Kumar, V. (2018). A Survey on Aerial Swarm Robotics. *IEEE Transactions on Robotics*, *34*(4), 837–855. doi:10.1109/TRO.2018.2857475

Cogo, E., Zunic, E., Besirevic, A., Delalic, S., & Hodzic, K. (2020). Position based visualization of real world warehouse data in a smart warehouse management system. *2020 19th International Symposium INFOTEH-JAHORINA (INFOTEH)*, (pp. 1–6). IEEE. 10.1109/INFOTEH48170.2020.9066323

Cui, J., Liu, Y., & Nallanathan, A. (2019). The application of multi-agent reinforcement learning in UAV networks. *2019 IEEE International Conference on Communications Workshops, ICC Workshops 2019 - Proceedings*. IEEE. 10.1109/ICCW.2019.8756984

Cui, J., Liu, Y., & Nallanathan, A. (2020). Multi-Agent Reinforcement Learning-Based Resource Allocation for UAV Networks. *IEEE Transactions on Wireless Communications*, *19*(2), 729–743. doi:10.1109/TWC.2019.2935201

Da Silva, F., & Costa, A. (2017). Accelerating Multiagent Reinforcement Learning through Transfer Learning. *Proceedings of the AAAI Conference on Artificial Intelligence*, *31*(1). Advance online publication. doi:10.1609/aaai.v31i1.10518

Da Silva, F. L., & Costa, A. H. R. (2020). Methods and Algorithms for Knowledge Reuse in Multiagent Reinforcement Learning. *Anais Do Concurso de Teses e Dissertações Da SBC (CTD-SBC 2020)*, 1–6. doi:10.5753/ctd.2020.11360

Da Silva, F. L., Taylor, M. E., & Anna, H. R. C. (2018). Autonomously reusing knowledge in multiagent reinforcement learning. *Proceedings of the Twenty-Seventh International Joint Conference on Artificial Intelligence (IJCAI-18)*. IEEE. 10.24963/ijcai.2018/774

Das, A., Gervet, T., Romoff, J., Batra, D., Parikh, D., Rabbat, M., & Pineau, J. (2019). TarMAC: Targeted Multi-Agent Communication. *Proceedings of the 36th International Conference on Machine Learning.* IEEE.

Dhuheir, M. A., Baccour, E., Erbad, A., Al-Obaidi, S. S., & Hamdi, M. (2023). Deep Reinforcement Learning for Trajectory Path Planning and Distributed Inference in Resource-Constrained UAV Swarms. *IEEE Internet of Things Journal, 10*(9), 8185–8201. doi:10.1109/JIOT.2022.3231341

Doks. Innovation. (n.d.). Doks Innovation. https://doks-innovation.com/

Ebrahimi, D., Sharafeddine, S., Ho, P.-H., & Assi, C. (2021). Autonomous UAV Trajectory for Localizing Ground Objects: A Reinforcement Learning Approach. *IEEE Transactions on Mobile Computing, 20*(4), 1312–1324. doi:10.1109/TMC.2020.2966989

Esteva, A., Robicquet, A., Ramsundar, B., Kuleshov, V., DePristo, M., Chou, K., Cui, C., Corrado, G., Thrun, S., & Dean, J. (2019). A guide to deep learning in healthcare. *Nature Medicine, 25*(1), 24–29. doi:10.103841591-018-0316-z PMID:30617335

Faust, A., Palunko, I., Cruz, P., Fierro, R., & Tapia, L. (2017). Automated aerial suspended cargo delivery through reinforcement learning. *Artificial Intelligence, 247*, 381–398. doi:10.1016/j.artint.2014.11.009

Fernández-Caramés, T. M., Blanco-Novoa, O., Froiz-Míguez, I., & Fraga-Lamas, P. (2019). Towards an Autonomous Industry 4.0 Warehouse: A UAV and Blockchain-Based System for Inventory and Traceability Applications in Big Data-Driven Supply Chain Management. *Sensors (Basel), 19*(10), 2394. doi:10.339019102394 PMID:31130644

Foerster, J. (2016). Advances in Neural Information Processing Systems: Vol. 29. *Ioannis Alexandros Assael, Nando de Freitas, & Shimon Whiteson.* Learning to Communicate with Deep Multi-Agent Reinforcement Learning.

Foerster, J., Song, F., Hughes, E., Burch, N., Dunning, I., Whiteson, S., Botvinick, M., & Bowling, M. (2019). Bayesian Action Decoder for Deep Multi-Agent Reinforcement Learning. *Proceedings of the 36th International Conference on Machine Learning.* IEEE.

Gronauer, S., & Diepold, K. (2022). Multi-agent deep reinforcement learning: A survey. *Artificial Intelligence Review, 55*(2), 895–943. doi:10.100710462-021-09996-w

Gupta, A., Afrin, T., Scully, E., & Yodo, N. (2021). Advances of UAVs toward Future Transportation: The State-of-the-Art, Challenges, and Opportunities. *Future Transportation, 1*(2), 326–350. doi:10.3390/futuretransp1020019

Gupta, J. K., Egorov, M., & Kochenderfer, M. (2017). Cooperative Multi-agent Control Using Deep Reinforcement Learning. Lecture Notes in Computer Science (Including Subseries Lecture Notes in Artificial Intelligence and Lecture Notes in Bioinformatics), 10642 LNAI, (pp. 66–83). Springer. doi:10.1007/978-3-319-71682-4_5

Gupta, L., Jain, R., & Vaszkun, G. (2016). Survey of Important Issues in UAV Communication Networks. *IEEE Communications Surveys and Tutorials, 18*(2), 1123–1152. doi:10.1109/COMST.2015.2495297

Hachiya, D., Mas, E., & Koshimura, S. (2022). A Reinforcement Learning Model of Multiple UAVs for Transporting Emergency Relief Supplies. *Applied Sciences (Basel, Switzerland)*, *12*(20), 10427. doi:10.3390/app122010427

Han, D., Mulyana, B., Stankovic, V., & Cheng, S. (2023). A Survey on Deep Reinforcement Learning Algorithms for Robotic Manipulation. *Sensors (Basel)*, *23*(7), 3762. doi:10.339023073762 PMID:37050822

Harik, E. H. C., Guerin, F., Guinand, F., Brethe, J.-F., & Pelvillain, H. (2016). Towards An Autonomous Warehouse Inventory Scheme. *2016 IEEE Symposium Series on Computational Intelligence (SSCI)*, (pp. 1–8). IEEE. 10.1109/SSCI.2016.7850056

Hu, J., Zhang, H., & Song, L. (2019). Reinforcement Learning for Decentralized Trajectory Design in Cellular UAV Networks With Sense-and-Send Protocol. *IEEE Internet of Things Journal*, *6*(4), 6177–6189. doi:10.1109/JIOT.2018.2876513

Jin, B. (2023). A Mean-VaR Based Deep Reinforcement Learning Framework for Practical Algorithmic Trading. *IEEE Access : Practical Innovations, Open Solutions*, *11*, 28920–28933. doi:10.1109/ACCESS.2023.3259108

Jung, S., Jo, Y., & Kim, Y.-J. (2019). Flight Time Estimation for Continuous Surveillance Missions Using a Multirotor UAV. *Energies*, *12*(5), 867. doi:10.3390/en12050867

Kalinov, I., Petrovsky, A., Ilin, V., Pristanskiy, E., Kurenkov, M., Ramzhaev, V., Idrisov, I., & Tsetserukou, D. (2020). WareVision: CNN Barcode Detection-Based UAV Trajectory Optimization for Autonomous Warehouse Stocktaking. *IEEE Robotics and Automation Letters*, *5*(4), 6647–6653. doi:10.1109/LRA.2020.3010733

Karamitsos, G., Bechtsis, D., Tsolakis, N., & Vlachos, D. (2021). Unmanned aerial vehicles for inventory listing. *International Journal of Business and Systems Research*, *15*(6), 748–756. doi:10.1504/IJBSR.2021.118776

Khan, M. G., Huda, N. U., & Zaman, U. K. U. (2022). Smart Warehouse Management System: Architecture, Real-Time Implementation and Prototype Design. *Machines*, *10*(2), 150. doi:10.3390/machines10020150

Krnjaic, A., Steleac, R. D., Thomas, J. D., Papoudakis, G., Schäfer, L., Andrew, W. K. T., Lao, K.-H., Cubuktepe, M., Haley, M., Börsting, P., & Albrecht, S. V. (2023). *Scalable Multi-Agent Reinforcement Learning for Warehouse Logistics with Robotic and Human Co-Workers*. ArXiv.

Kwak, J., Park, J. H., & Sung, Y. (2021). Emerging ICT UAV applications and services: Design of surveillance UAVs. *International Journal of Communication Systems*, *34*(2), e4023. doi:10.1002/dac.4023

Kwon, W., Park, J. H., Lee, M., Her, J., Kim, S. H., & Seo, J. W. (2020). Robust Autonomous Navigation of Unmanned Aerial Vehicles (UAVs) for Warehouses' Inventory Application. *IEEE Robotics and Automation Letters*, *5*(1), 243–249. doi:10.1109/LRA.2019.2955003

Li, C., Tanghe, E., Suanet, P., Plets, D., Hoebeke, J., De Poorter, E., & Joseph, W. (2021). ReLoc 2.0: UHF-RFID Relative Localization for Drone-Based Inventory Management. *IEEE Transactions on Instrumentation and Measurement*, *70*, 1–13. doi:10.1109/TIM.2021.3069377

Li, W., Jin, B., Wang, X., Yan, J., & Zha, H. (2020). *F2A2: Flexible Fully-decentralized Approximate Actor-critic for Cooperative Multi-agent Reinforcement Learning*.

LiX.LiL.GaoJ.HeX.ChenJ.DengL.HeJ. (2015). *Recurrent Reinforcement Learning: A Hybrid Approach*. arXiv. https://arxiv.org/abs/1509.03044

Liang, E., & Liaw, R. (2018). *Scaling Multi-Agent Reinforcement Learning*. Berkeley Artificial Intelligence Research. https://bair.berkeley.edu/blog/2018/12/12/rllib/

Liu, D., Dou, L., Zhang, R., Zhang, X., & Zong, Q. (2023). Multi-Agent Reinforcement Learning-Based Coordinated Dynamic Task Allocation for Heterogenous UAVs. *IEEE Transactions on Vehicular Technology*, *72*(4), 4372–4383. doi:10.1109/TVT.2022.3228198

Liu, H., Chen, Q., Pan, N., Sun, Y., An, Y., & Pan, D. (2022). UAV Stocktaking Task-Planning for Industrial Warehouses Based on the Improved Hybrid Differential Evolution Algorithm. *IEEE Transactions on Industrial Informatics*, *18*(1), 582–591. doi:10.1109/TII.2021.3054172

Liu, S., Zhou, Y., Song, J., Zheng, T., Chen, K., Zhu, T., Feng, Z., & Song, M. (2023). Contrastive Identity-Aware Learning for Multi-Agent Value Decomposition. *Proceedings of the AAAI Conference on Artificial Intelligence*, (pp. 11595–11603). AAAI. 10.1609/aaai.v37i10.26370

Long, Q., Zhou, Z., Gupta, A., Fang, F., Wu, Y., & Wang, X. (2020). *Evolutionary Population Curriculum for Scaling Multi-Agent Reinforcement Learning*.

Lowe, R., Wu, Y. I., Tamar, A., Harb, J., Pieter Abbeel, O., & Mordatch, I. (2017). Multi-Agent Actor-Critic for Mixed Cooperative-Competitive Environments. *Advances in Neural Information Processing Systems*, 30.

Malang, C., Charoenkwan, P., & Wudhikarn, R. (2023). Implementation and Critical Factors of Unmanned Aerial Vehicle (UAV) in Warehouse Management: A Systematic Literature Review. *Drones (Basel)*, *7*(2), 80. doi:10.3390/drones7020080

Marinescu, A., Dusparic, I., & Clarke, S. (2017). Prediction-Based Multi-Agent Reinforcement Learning in Inherently Non-Stationary Environments. *ACM Transactions on Autonomous and Adaptive Systems*, *12*(2), 1–23. doi:10.1145/3070861

Markets and Markets. (2019). *Unmanned Aerial Vehicles (UAV) market*. Markets and Markets. https://www.marketsandmarkets.com/Market-Reports/unmanned-aerial-vehicles-uav-market

Marsh, I. (2015). *Drones-a View into the Future for the Logistics Sector*.

Mohammed, F., Idries, A., Mohamed, N., Al-Jaroodi, J., & Jawhar, I. (2014). UAVs for smart cities: Opportunities and challenges. *2014 International Conference on Unmanned Aircraft Systems, ICUAS 2014 - Conference Proceedings*, (pp. 267–273). IEEE. 10.1109/ICUAS.2014.6842265

Moon, J., Papaioannou, S., Laoudias, C., Kolios, P., & Kim, S. (2021). Deep Reinforcement Learning Multi-UAV Trajectory Control for Target Tracking. *IEEE Internet of Things Journal*, *8*(20), 15441–15455. doi:10.1109/JIOT.2021.3073973

Moradi, M. (2016). A centralized reinforcement learning method for multi-agent job scheduling in Grid. *2016 6th International Conference on Computer and Knowledge Engineering (ICCKE)*, (pp. 171–176). 10.1109/ICCKE.2016.7802135

Moura, A., Antunes, J., Dias, A., Martins, A., & Almeida, J. (2021). Graph-SLAM Approach for Indoor UAV Localization in Warehouse Logistics Applications. *2021 IEEE International Conference on Autonomous Robot Systems and Competitions, ICARSC 2021*, (pp. 4–11). IEEE. 10.1109/ICARSC52212.2021.9429791

Nguyen, K. K., Duong, T. Q., Do-Duy, T., Claussen, H., & Hanzo, L. (2022). 3D UAV Trajectory and Data Collection Optimisation Via Deep Reinforcement Learning. *IEEE Transactions on Communications*, *70*(4), 2358–2371. doi:10.1109/TCOMM.2022.3148364

Ocana, C., Martin, J., Riccio, F., Capobianco, R., & Nardi, D. (2019). Cooperative Multi-Agent Deep Reinforcement Learning in Soccer Domains. *In Proceedings of the 18th International Conference on Autonomous Agents and MultiAgent Systems*. IEEE.

Ong, J. H., Sanchez, A., & Williams, J. (2007). Multi-UAV system for inventory automation. *2007 1st Annual RFID Eurasia*. IEEE. doi:10.1109/RFIDEURASIA.2007.4368142

Oroojlooy, A., & Hajinezhad, D. (2022). A review of cooperative multi-agent deep reinforcement learning. *Applied Intelligence*. doi:10.100710489-022-04105-y

Oubbati, O. S., Lakas, A., & Guizani, M. (2022). Multiagent Deep Reinforcement Learning for Wireless-Powered UAV Networks. *IEEE Internet of Things Journal*, *9*(17), 16044–16059. doi:10.1109/JIOT.2022.3150616

Panetsos, F., Karras, G. C., & Kyriakopoulos, K. J. (2022). A Deep Reinforcement Learning Motion Control Strategy of a Multi-rotor UAV for Payload Transportation with Minimum Swing. *2022 30th Mediterranean Conference on Control and Automation (MED)*, 368–374. 10.1109/MED54222.2022.9837220

Peng, H., & Shen, X. (2021). Multi-Agent Reinforcement Learning Based Resource Management in MEC- And UAV-Assisted Vehicular Networks. *IEEE Journal on Selected Areas in Communications*, *39*(1), 131–141. doi:10.1109/JSAC.2020.3036962

Pérez-Gil, Ó., Barea, R., López-Guillén, E., Bergasa, L. M., Gómez-Huélamo, C., Gutiérrez, R., & Díaz-Díaz, A. (2022). Deep reinforcement learning based control for Autonomous Vehicles in CARLA. *Multimedia Tools and Applications*, *81*(3), 3553–3576. doi:10.100711042-021-11437-3

Pizetta, I. H. B., Brandao, A. S., & Sarcinelli-Filho, M. (2018). Control and Obstacle Avoidance for an UAV Carrying a Load in Forestal Environments. *2018 International Conference on Unmanned Aircraft Systems (ICUAS)*, (pp. 62–67). IEEE. 10.1109/ICUAS.2018.8453399

Prasad Tripathy, R., Ranjan Mishra, M., & Dash, S. R. (2020). Next Generation Warehouse through disruptive IoT Blockchain. *2020 International Conference on Computer Science, Engineering and Applications (ICCSEA)*, (pp. 1–6). IEEE. 10.1109/ICCSEA49143.2020.9132906

Raffo, G. V., & de Almeida, M. M. (2018). A Load Transportation Nonlinear Control Strategy Using a Tilt-Rotor UAV. *Journal of Advanced Transportation*, *2018*, 1–20. doi:10.1155/2018/1467040

Rashid, T., Samvelyan, M., De Witt, C. S., Farquhar, G., Foerster, J., & Whiteson, S. (2020). Monotonic value function factorisation for deep multi-agent reinforcement learning. *Journal of Machine Learning Research*, 21.

Rezeck, P., Assuncao, R. M., & Chaimowicz, L. (2021). Cooperative Object Transportation using Gibbs Random Fields. *2021 IEEE/RSJ International Conference on Intelligent Robots and Systems (IROS)*, (pp. 9131–9138). IEEE. 10.1109/IROS51168.2021.9635928

Richnák, P. (2022). Current Trend of Industry 4.0 in Logistics and Transformation of Logistics Processes Using Digital Technologies: An Empirical Study in the Slovak Republic. *Logistics*, 6(4), 79. doi:10.3390/logistics6040079

Roca-Riu, M., & Monica Menendez. (2019). Logistic deliveries with drones: State of the art of practice and research. *19th Swiss Transport Research Conference (STRC 2019)*. IEEE.10.1145/3410404.3414235

Sacco, A., Esposito, F., Marchetto, G., & Montuschi, P. (2021). Sustainable Task Offloading in UAV Networks via Multi-Agent Reinforcement Learning. *IEEE Transactions on Vehicular Technology*, 70(5), 5003–5015. doi:10.1109/TVT.2021.3074304

Shamsoshoara, A., Khaledi, M., Afghah, F., Razi, A., & Ashdown, J. (2019). Distributed Cooperative Spectrum Sharing in UAV Networks Using Multi-Agent Reinforcement Learning. *2019 16th IEEE Annual Consumer Communications and Networking Conference, CCNC 2019*. IEEE. 10.1109/CCNC.2019.8651796

Sharma, V., You, I., Pau, G., Collotta, M., Lim, J., & Kim, J. (2018). LoRaWAN-Based Energy-Efficient Surveillance by Drones for Intelligent Transportation Systems. *Energies*, 11(3), 573. doi:10.3390/en11030573

Sivakumar, V., Ruthramathi, R., & Leelapriyadharsini, S. (2020). Challenges of Cloud Computing in Warehousing Operations with Respect to Chennai Port Trust. *Proceedings of the 2020 the 3rd International Conference on Computers in Management and Business*, (pp. 162–165). IEEE. 10.1145/3383845.3383895

Skorput, P., Mandzuka, S., & Vojvodic, H. (2016). The use of Unmanned Aerial Vehicles for forest fire monitoring. *Proceedings Elmar - International Symposium Electronics in Marine, 2016-Novem*, 93–96. 10.1109/ELMAR.2016.7731762

Škrinjar, J. P., Škorput, P., & Furdić, M. (2019). Application of Unmanned Aerial Vehicles in Logistic Processes. In Lecture Notes in Networks and Systems (Vol. 42, pp. 359–366). doi:10.1007/978-3-319-90893-9_43

Son, K., Kim, D., Wan, J. K., Hostallero, D. E., & Yi, Y. (2019). Qtran: Learning to factorize with transformation for cooperative multi-agent reinforcement learning. *31st International Conference On Machine Learning*. IEEE.

Sunehag, P., Lever, G., Gruslys, A., Czarnecki, W. M., Zambaldi, V., Jaderberg, M., Lanctot, M., Sonnerat, N., Leibo, J. Z., Tuyls, K., & Graepel, T. (2018). Value-decomposition networks for cooperative multi-agent learning based on team reward. *Proceedings of the International Joint Conference on Autonomous Agents and Multiagent Systems, AAMAS, 3*, (pp. 2085–2087). AAMAS.

Sutton, R. S., & Barto, A. G. (2018). *Reinforcement Leaning*.

Tolstaya, E., Paulos, J., Kumar, V., & Ribeiro, A. (2021). Multi-Robot Coverage and Exploration using Spatial Graph Neural Networks. *2021 IEEE/RSJ International Conference on Intelligent Robots and Systems (IROS)*, (pp. 8944–8950). IEEE. 10.1109/IROS51168.2021.9636675

Tubis, A. A., & Rohman, J. (2023). Intelligent Warehouse in Industry 4.0—Systematic Literature Review. *Sensors (Basel)*, *23*(8), 4105. doi:10.339023084105 PMID:37112446

Wang, H., Liu, N., Zhang, Y., Feng, D., Huang, F., Li, D., & Zhang, Y. (2020). Deep reinforcement learning: A survey. *Frontiers of Information Technology & Electronic Engineering*, *21*(12), 1726–1744. doi:10.1631/FITEE.1900533

Wang, L., Wang, K., Pan, C., Xu, W., Aslam, N., & Hanzo, L. (2021). Multi-Agent Deep Reinforcement Learning-Based Trajectory Planning for Multi-UAV Assisted Mobile Edge Computing. *IEEE Transactions on Cognitive Communications and Networking*, *7*(1), 73–84. doi:10.1109/TCCN.2020.3027695

Wawrla, L., & Maghazei, O. (2019). Applications of drones in warehouse operations. *ETH Zurich*.

Wu, G., Fan, M., Shi, J., & Feng, Y. (2023). Reinforcement Learning Based Truck-and-Drone Coordinated Delivery. *IEEE Transactions on Artificial Intelligence*, *4*(4), 754–763. doi:10.1109/TAI.2021.3087666 PMID:37954545

Xu, S., Zhang, X., Li, C., Wang, D., & Yang, L. (2022). Deep Reinforcement Learning Approach for Joint Trajectory Design in Multi-UAV IoT Networks. *IEEE Transactions on Vehicular Technology*, *71*(3), 3389–3394. doi:10.1109/TVT.2022.3144277

Yang, T., Li, Z., Zhang, F., Xie, B., Li, J., & Liu, L. (2019). Panoramic UAV Surveillance and Recycling System Based on Structure-Free Camera Array. *IEEE Access : Practical Innovations, Open Solutions*, *7*, 25763–25778. doi:10.1109/ACCESS.2019.2900167

Yin, S., & Yu, F. R. (2022). Resource Allocation and Trajectory Design in UAV-Aided Cellular Networks Based on Multiagent Reinforcement Learning. *IEEE Internet of Things Journal*, *9*(4), 2933–2943. doi:10.1109/JIOT.2021.3094651

Yoo, W., Yu, E., & Jung, J. (2018). Drone delivery: Factors affecting the public's attitude and intention to adopt. *Telematics and Informatics*, *35*(6), 1687–1700. doi:10.1016/j.tele.2018.04.014

Yu, L., Song, J., & Ermon, S. (2019). Multi-Agent Adversarial Inverse Reinforcement Learning. *Proceedings of the 36th International Conference on Machine Learning*. IEEE.

Zhang, K., Yang, Z., & Başar, T. (2021). *Multi-Agent Reinforcement Learning: A Selective Overview of Theories and Algorithms.*, doi:10.1007/978-3-030-60990-0_12

Zhao, N., Liu, Z., & Cheng, Y. (2020). Multi-Agent Deep Reinforcement Learning for Trajectory Design and Power Allocation in Multi-UAV Networks. *IEEE Access : Practical Innovations, Open Solutions*, *8*, 139670–139679. doi:10.1109/ACCESS.2020.3012756

Chapter 12
Enhancing Medical Services Through Machine Learning and UAV Technology:
Applications and Benefits

Rashid A. Saeed

 https://orcid.org/0000-0002-9872-081X

Department of Computer Engineering, College of Computers and Information Technology, Taif University, Saudi Arabia

Mamoon M. Saeed

Department of Communications and Electronics Engineering, Faculty of Engineering, University of Modern Sciences, Yemen

Zeinab E. Ahmed

 https://orcid.org/0000-0002-6144-8533

Department of Computer Engineering, University of Gezira, Sudan & Department of Electrical and Computer Engineering, International Islamic University Malaysia, Malaysia

Aisha H. A. Hashim

Department of Electrical and Computer Engineering, International Islamic University Malaysia, Malaysia

ABSTRACT

This chapter focuses on the enhancement of medical services through the integration of unmanned aerial vehicle (UAV) technology and machine learning algorithms. It explores the broad spectrum of applications and benefits that arise from combining these two technologies. By employing UAVs for automated delivery, medical supplies can be efficiently transported to remote or inaccessible regions, thereby improving access to vital items. Remote patient monitoring, facilitated through UAVs and machine learning, enables real-time data collection and analysis, enabling the early identification of health issues. UAVs equipped with medical equipment and machine learning capabilities enhance emergency medical response by providing immediate assistance during critical situations. Disease surveillance and outbreak management can benefit from the use of UAVs and machine-learning algorithms to identify disease hotspots and predict the spread of illnesses.

DOI: 10.4018/979-8-3693-0578-2.ch012

1. INTRODUCTION

Unmanned aerial vehicles (UAVs) and machine learning can completely change the way medical services are delivered. UAVs are remotely controlled or self-flying aircraft. Machine learning is the ability of computer systems to learn from experience and make improvements without being explicitly programmed (Pathak, Damle, Pal, & Yadav, 2019). These two technologies working together can have a huge impact on the medical industry. Figure 1 illustrates how machine learning algorithms can be used to evaluate vast volumes of medical data and find patterns that can be utilized to enhance illness detection, treatment, and prevention.

Figure 1. Working steps for implementing medical service through UAV

UAVs, on the other hand, can be used to carry patients and deliver medical supplies in locations that are challenging to access with conventional transportation. The use of UAVs and machine learning in emergency response is among the medical industry's most promising uses. Time is of the essence in emergencies, and a quick response could be the difference between life and death. UAVs can be used to quickly deliver medical supplies to remote locations or disaster situations, such as blood and medication. To estimate the severity of the problem and prioritize response times, machine learning algorithms can also be utilized to analyze data from emergency response calls (Motlagh et al., 2023).

Application in disease surveillance and outbreak response is yet another promising area. To find possible disease outbreaks, machine learning algorithms can be used to examine data from a variety of sources, including social media and news reports. Then, to gather samples and transport medical supplies to the impacted areas, UAVs can be used.

Machine learning and UAVs can also be used to enhance patient care in addition to these applications. For instance, patient data can be analyzed using machine learning algorithms to determine the best courses of action for specific patients. Patients can obtain care without having to go far thanks to the usage of UAVs for transporting medical supplies and equipment (Estrada & Ndoma, 2019).

1.1 Overview of UAVs and Machine Learning

Drones, commonly referred to as unmanned aerial vehicles (UAVs), are aircraft that are flown remotely or automatically without a human pilot present. Due to their adaptability and capacity for a variety of activities, including aerial surveillance, mapping, package delivery, and search and rescue missions, UAVs have grown in popularity in recent years (Motlagh et al., 2023).

A branch of artificial intelligence called machine learning (ML) involves teaching computer systems to recognize patterns and make predictions based on data. Numerous applications, such as image identification, natural language processing, and predictive analytics, use machine learning (ML) methods.

There are several methods to combine UAVs and machine learning to allow new capabilities and enhance already existing ones. Machine learning techniques, for instance, can be used to analyze data from UAV sensors, like cameras and lidar, to automatically detect and classify items of interest, like structures, moving vehicles, and people (Yao, Qin, & Chen, 2019). UAVs may be able to carry out activities more effectively and precisely as a result, including monitoring traffic, inspecting infrastructure, and carrying out search and rescue missions.

By allowing UAVs to make decisions based on real-time data from their sensors, machine learning can also be utilized to increase their autonomy. A UAV with machine learning algorithms, for instance, may automatically modify its fly route to avoid obstacles or navigate through difficult settings.

1.2 Motivation and Contributions

Machine learning and unmanned aerial vehicle technologies have the potential to improve medical services in a variety of ways. The following are some of the main drivers and contributions of this technology in the medical field:

1. Quick delivery of medical equipment and supplies: UAVs are capable of delivering drugs, vaccines, blood samples, and other supplies to inaccessible or remote locations. To ensure that goods are delivered on schedule, UAV routing and scheduling can be improved using machine learning methods.
2. Aerial surveillance and imaging: UAVs with cameras and other sensors can be used to inspect disaster areas and evaluate damage, as well as to monitor and track disease outbreaks. The data gathered by UAVs can be analyzed using machine learning techniques to spot trends and pinpoint problem areas.
3. Remote patient monitoring: UAVs can be utilized to monitor patients remotely, especially those who live in rural or remote places. For instance, UAVs with medical sensors can be used to continuously check vital signs and relay information to medical specialists. This data can be analyzed using machine learning techniques to look for patterns and possible health problems.
4. Emergency response and search and rescue: UAVs can deliver emergency medical services in far-off or inaccessible locations, such as in the wake of a disaster. Data gathered by UAVs can be analyzed using machine learning algorithms to pinpoint regions that urgently require medical care.

The benefits of using machine learning and UAV technology in the medical field include:

1.   Better access to medical services: UAVs can be used to deliver medical supplies and equipment to remote or inaccessible locations, enhancing locals' access to medical care.
2.   Shorter response times: UAVs can be immediately deployed in emergency circumstances, shortening response times and perhaps saving lives.
3.   Better data analysis: Machine learning algorithms can evaluate data acquired by UAVs more rapidly and correctly than traditional techniques, allowing healthcare practitioners to make better judgments.
4.   Better patient outcomes: Remote monitoring and early identification of health problems can result in earlier intervention and better patient outcomes

1.3 Chapter Organization

The chapter contributes by providing an overview of the book's focus on enhancing medical services by integrating machine learning and unmanned aircraft (UAV) technology. It highlights the potential applications and benefits these technologies can bring to healthcare. Figure 2 shows the class organization.

Figure 2. Chapter organization

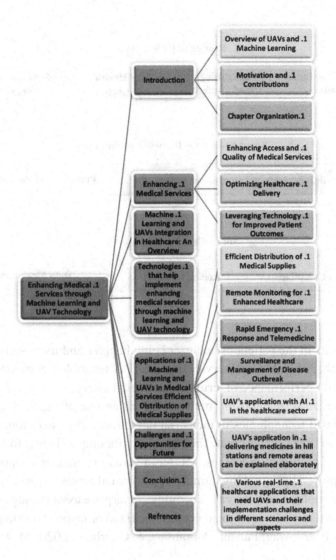

2. ENHANCING MEDICAL SERVICES

Enhancing medical services is a critical aspect of healthcare delivery that can benefit from the use of machine learning and UAV technology. The implementation process for medical services through UAV in the healthcare system is shown in Figure 3. First, the procedure begins with the collection of patient data and records of the patient's prior medical information. The recorded patient data is further analyzed using intelligent technologies, such as cloud computing, artificial intelligence, machine learning, and the Internet of Things. The compilation of the data after analysis and the creation of enhanced patient records marks the conclusion of this execution process.

Figure 3. Working steps for implementing medical service through UAV

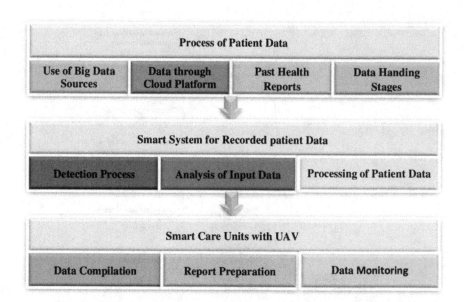

This ultimately results in the patient or end user being happier and more satisfied (Dimitrov, 2016; Javaid, Khan, & research, 2021). Medical service through UAV technologies aims to enhance operational performance, particularly performance in terms of health and safety.

Therefore, there is a close relationship between the rising use of medical services through UAV technologies and AI-based technologies in industrial operations. The operations of these technologies are characterized by data flows, which create the framework for employing AI to assist and even directly oversee the execution of industrial processes. ML has a variety of industrial applications. Deep learning algorithms are employed by a growing number of automated process control systems in the process industries. To maximize uptime and decrease downtime, enterprise asset management systems also rely on ML techniques to predict when equipment needs to be fixed or inspected (Manogaran, Thota, Lopez & Sundarasekar 2017; Pourdowlat, Panahi, Pooransari, & Ghorbani, 2020; M. M. Saeed, R. A. Saeed, M. A. Azim, et al., 2022).

Examples of how these technologies can be used to improve medical care include the following (Z. H. Chen et al., 2021; Jamshidi et al., 2020):

1. Diagnosis and treatment: To increase the precision of diagnosis and treatment decisions, machine learning algorithms can be used to assess patient data, including medical imaging and electronic health records. By lowering the possibility of misdiagnosis and optimizing treatment strategies, this can enhance patient outcomes.
2. Medical research: Machine learning algorithms can be used to examine enormous volumes of data from medical research to spot patterns and trends that human researchers would miss. Facilitating the creation of novel cures and treatments can quicken the speed of medical research.
3. Patient monitoring: UAVs with sensors and cameras can be used to remotely monitor patients with long-term problems while also keeping an eye on them in real-time. Providing early detection and intervention for potential health risks can enhance patient outcomes.

4. Medical education and training: Based on each healthcare professional's unique learning style and knowledge gaps, machine learning algorithms can be utilized to develop customized training programs. This could raise the standard of medical instruction and training, which would benefit patients.

5. Precision medicine: Algorithms based on machine learning can examine genetic and other data to produce individualized treatment regimens based on a person's particular traits. This can increase the effectiveness of medical therapies and lower the chance of negative side effects (Kononenko, 2001).

2.1 Enhancing Access and Quality of Medical Services

The change in healthcare has an impact on how physicians manage, monitor, and diagnose their patients' health. While delivering the agility needed to enhance operations, compliance, and patient experience, it seeks to keep costs as low as possible. The healthcare industry is currently dealing with the digital problem and trying to restructure its processes to save costs, increase access, and provide better care. To make the shift to the digital era, hospitals adopt cutting-edge technologies and operational improvements that prioritize quality, efficiency, and convenience. Healthcare providers have started converting their processes from analog to digital using technology. EHRs are frequently employed to monitor patient health, check for potentially harmful drug interactions, and help medical decision-making. Clinical staff and patients may communicate about their health while on the go thanks to mobile health technologies. By utilizing a network and information technology to provide distant healthcare and improve access to medical services in rural areas, telemedicine transcends geographical borders (Taiwo & Ezugwu, 2020).

A crucial component of healthcare delivery that can profit from the application of machine learning and UAV technology is the improvement of access and quality of medical services (Haleem, Javaid, Singh & Suman, 2022). Here are some instances of how these technologies can be used to increase the availability and caliber of medical care (Mbunge, Muchemwa, & Batani, 2021):

1. Telemedicine: Algorithms for machine learning can be used to examine patient data, such as vital signs and medical history, and offer recommendations for remote diagnosis and therapy. For telemedicine consultations, UAVs can be utilized to transport medical professionals and supplies to far-off areas. Patients in rural or difficult-to-reach places may benefit from better access to healthcare services as a result.

2. Patient engagement: To deliver individualized treatment and raise patient involvement, machine learning algorithms can be utilized to analyze patient behavior and preferences. Empowering patients to actively participate in their care, can enhance patient outcomes.

3. Precision medicine: Algorithms for machine learning can evaluate genetic and other data to produce individualized treatment regimens based on a person's particular traits. This can increase the effectiveness of medical procedures and lower the possibility of negative side effects.

4. Autonomous UAVs: To enable autonomous operation, UAVs can be fitted with AI-powered navigation and obstacle detection systems, increasing efficiency and lowering the demand for human intervention. This can decrease the possibility of errors while also improving the speed and accuracy of medical supply delivery.

5. Individualized care: To deliver individualized treatment plans and predictive analytics, machine learning algorithms can examine data on patient health conditions and usage behaviors. Adapting therapy to each patient's unique needs can enhance patient outcomes.

2.2 Optimizing Healthcare Delivery

Self-driving and self-flying vehicles are rapidly approaching the age of drones. It's exciting to think about how drones might be used in the medical field. Infectious disease outbreaks might be stopped if medicines, supplies, and vaccines are delivered quickly to the infection site. In areas where critical infrastructure damage would prevent typical ground or air supply, speedy delivery of communication equipment, transportable technology, and portable shelter are only a few examples (Ray, Dash & De, 2019; Sodhro, Luo, Sangaiah, & Baik, 2019; Young & Aquilina, 2021). In the future, tiny indoor drones might deliver medication from a pharmacy to a patient's bedside, replacing some human processes. Faster and less error-prone pharmaceutical administration would result from this. Since supplies can be ordered to be sent to the patient's bedside rather than having to spend time gathering the necessary items, nurses and pharmacists can work more efficiently. Drones may deliver medications and supplies to patients who receive care at home as opposed to in a hospital setting (M. Chen, Li, Hao, Qian, & Humar, 2018; X. Li, Huang, Li, Yu, & Shu, 2019; Oueida, Kotb, Aloqaily, Jararweh, & Baker, 2018; Uddin, 2019). In the future, hospital-based therapy will be replaced by outpatient care and possibly home-based care. Delivering this type of at-home care for many ailments could become simpler and safer thanks to drone technology. When a doctor visits a patient at home, blood can be drawn and sent right away by drone to the lab for analysis. Drones may deliver the medications, treatments, and therapies the practitioner has prescribed to the patient's home (Anbaroğlu, 2021; Nyaaba & Ayamga, 2021; Pustokhina et al., 2020). The baby boomer generation's freedom may increase as a result of this technology, which may allow more residents of nursing homes to receive care at home for longer periods. Drones enable the supply of blood, immunizations, contraceptives, snakebite serum, and other medical supplies to far-flung areas, as well as the ability to reach victims in need of immediate medical attention in a matter of minutes. They can move medications between medical buildings, transport blood, and provide elderly patients with devices to help them age in place (Ndiaye, Salhi, Madani, & Logistics, 2020; Pathak et al., 2019; Poljak & Šterbenc, 2020). Several ways that machine learning and UAV technology can improve healthcare delivery include:

1. Quick and effective delivery of medical supplies: UAVs can be used to carry medical supplies and equipment to inaccessible or remote locations. To ensure prompt delivery of goods, machine learning algorithms can be used to schedule and route UAVs more effectively.
2. Individualized treatment plans: To create individualized treatment plans, machine learning algorithms can be employed to assess patient data, including genetic data and medical records. By adapting the treatment to the demands of each patient, this can enhance patient outcomes.
3. More accurate diagnosis and disease detection: Medical images and other data can be analyzed using machine learning algorithms to increase the accuracy of diagnosis and disease detection. Early intervention and therapy may result from this, improving patient outcomes.
4. Real-time monitoring: Especially in isolated or rural locations, UAVs fitted with medical sensors can be used to keep an eye on patients in real-time. This may entail keeping track of vital signs and sending data for analysis and interpretation to medical specialists.

5. Disease monitoring and outbreak detection: UAVs can be used to monitor and track disease outbreaks, enabling early identification and action. These drones are outfitted with cameras and other sensors. This data can be analyzed using machine learning techniques to look for patterns and possible health problems.
6. Training and education: Machine learning algorithms can be utilized to create healthcare professional training and education resources. Ensuring that healthcare personnel are knowledgeable about the most recent research and methods, can enhance the quality of care.

2.3 Leveraging Technology for Improved Patient Outcomes

Participating in one's healthcare has a positive impact on the standard of care and enhances patient safety, health outcomes, and satisfaction. New technologies are making it possible for patients to participate more actively in their care (Aiken et al., 2012). The rapid development of these technologies is also affecting workflows, care delivery models, and nursing professional practice across the continuum. Nurse executives are in a unique position to lead care transformation that uses technology to engage patients at the point of care, reinvent nursing practice, and enhance empirical outcomes in the face of a sustained and ongoing technology explosion. Various ways utilizing technology can help to enhance patient outcomes (Cassano, 2014; Mukati et al., 2023):

1. Remote patient monitoring: Patients can manage chronic diseases and receive medical care in the convenience of their own homes with the use of telemedicine and other remote patient monitoring technology. Allowing for earlier intervention and lowering the need for hospital visits, can improve patient outcomes.
2. Imaging and diagnosis in medicine: Machine learning algorithms can examine data, including medical pictures, to increase the precision of disease detection and diagnosis. Early intervention and therapy may result from this, improving patient outcomes.
3. Patient education: With the aid of technology, patients can better understand their conditions and available treatments by watching films and using interactive apps. Encouraging people to actively participate in their treatment, can enhance patient outcomes.
4. Monitoring and preventing health issues: Machine learning algorithms can be used to assess health information, including patient records and environmental data, to spot potential health hazards and create prevention plans. This can assist patients in changing their lifestyles to enhance their general health and delay the emergence of chronic illnesses.

3. MACHINE LEARNING AND UAV INTEGRATION IN HEALTHCARE

The use of UAVs and machine learning in healthcare has the potential to completely change how medical treatments are provided. UAVs can be used to transfer medical supplies and equipment to inaccessible or remote locations, and machine learning algorithms can be used to schedule and route UAVs more efficiently to guarantee prompt delivery of the necessary supplies (Ghazal et al., 2021). UAVs with medical sensors can also be used to remotely monitor patients, particularly those who live in rural or isolated places, and send real-time data to medical specialists. This data can be analyzed using machine learning techniques to look for patterns and possible health problems as shown in Figure 4.

Figure 4. Machine learning and UAV integration in healthcare

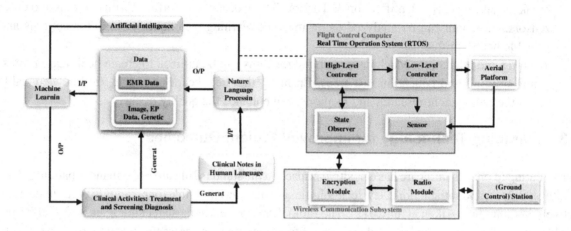

Patterns linked to illnesses and other health issues have been found using machine learning algorithms. Typically, historical datasets of patient data, such as medical records, are used to train machine-learning models. Recent developments in machine learning technology have aided healthcare systems in underdeveloped nations in coming up with innovative, long-lasting treatments for chronic illnesses including cancer detection and treatment (Huang et al., 2020; Magna, Allende-Cid, Taramasco, Becerra, & Figueroa, 2020; M. M. Saeed, Ali, & Saeed, 2023; Wiens et al., 2019). Classifying intricate patterns in data is a task that machine learning systems excel at. Machine learning techniques are thus employed extensively in the medical industry, particularly in those applications that rely on cutting-edge proteomics and genomics studies. In many disease detection and diagnosis issues, machine learning methods are fundamentally utilized. Classification and regression trees (CART), fuzzy logic, k-nearest neighbors (KNN), support vector machines (SVM), and naïve Bayes (NB) classification are a few examples of machine learning models based on various methods that are employed in healthcare applications (Norgeot, Glicksberg, & Butte, 2019; Ricciardi et al., 2022; M. M. Saeed, Saeed, et al., 2023). Table 1 provides an overview of reviews and research articles pertinent to innovative applications in healthcare powered by machine learning.

Table 1. An overview of healthcare applications based on machine learning

Title	Accuracy	Relative Demerit
Using a naïve Bayes algorithm to detect heart disorders (Vembandasamy, Sasipriya & Deepa, 2015)	86.41%	Built on data mining methods for categorizing data patterns and recognizing heart diseases, the system is considered to be the best algorithm for many healthcare issues. The naive Bayes algorithm does well with categorical data but poorly with numerical data in the training set.
SVM and CNN are used to classify disorders related to diabetes (Qomariah, Tjandrasa, & Fatichah, 2019)	95.83%, 95.24%	Reduced the amount of time needed to do the classification process using CNN with fine-tuning by employing transfer learning from CNN as the input features. Due to the short dataset, only 2 out of 8 CNN architectures provide 90+ accuracy.
Thyroid disease diagnosis using SVM (Shankar, Lakshmanaprabu, Gupta, Maseleno, & De Albuquerque, 2020)	97.49%	Use a kernel-based classifier and the best feature selection to categorize thyroid data. requires lengthy computation.
Thyroid disease diagnosis using SVM (Asri, Mousannif, Al Moatassime, & Noel, 2016)	SVM = 99.10%	Analyze each algorithm's efficiency and efficacy in accurately identifying data.
Breast cancer detection with the use of SVM and DT (Sivakami & Saraswathi, 2015)	91%	A trustworthy breast cancer diagnosis prediction model using data mining techniques.
Six algorithms are used to identify Type-2 diabetes (Tigga & Garg, 2020)	RF = 94.10%	predicts the risk associated with type 2 diabetes.
Breast cancer data classification using J48 (Ortega et al., 2020)	95.00%	The J48 decision tree algorithm was used by the researchers to develop a technique for automatically determining whether a tumor is malignant or benign. Classification is done by examining the cell features that the X-cyt algorithm returned.
Breast cancer classification using a decision tree (Venkatesan & Velmurugan, 2015)	J48 = 99%	Using the performance of decision tree classification algorithms, the optimal model for breast cancer data was examined.
Using SVM, random forest, and K-NN for COVID-19 identification (Eljamassi & Maghari, 2020)	98.14, 96.29, 88.89%	combining chest X-ray pictures and machine learning algorithms to identify COVID-19 patients to stop the spread of this pandemic as soon as feasible.
Utilizing DT, SVM, and NN for swallowing detection (Santoso et al., 2019)	93.2, 86.2, 93.7%	Machine learning methods were used to recognize binary eating with great accuracy from audio recordings.
Kidney disease diagnosis using SVM (Amirgaliyev, Shamiluulu, & Serek, 2018)	93%	Renal disease diagnosis using low-cost, secure, and noninvasive physical examinations, clinical history, and machine learning algorithms.
Kidney disease diagnosis using CNN-SVM (Bhaskar & Manikandan, 2019)	98.04%	Deep learning capabilities can be combined with the suggested sensing module to recognize the CKD dataset more effectively than current methods.
Six methods for the diagnosis of kidney disease (Qin et al., 2019)	RF = 99.75%, LR + RF = 99.83%	Suitable in terms of diagnostic imputation samples. Due to the short number of data samples that are currently available for model construction, the generalization performance may be constrained. Since the dataset only contains two categories of data samples, such as CKD and NOTCKd, the model is unable to determine the severity of CKD.
Five algorithms are used to diagnose Alzheimer's disease (Subha, Nayana, & Selvadass, 2022)	NN = 98.36%	use computer learning methods to identify Alzheimer's in its early stages. It will lessen the likelihood that patients with Alzheimer's disease will develop new difficulties.

UAVs can be used to take medical images, such as X-rays and ultrasounds, and then communicate those images to healthcare specialists for analysis and interpretation. UAVs are outfitted with high-resolution cameras and other sensors. These photos can be analyzed using machine learning algorithms to spot potential health problems and help with diagnosis (Muhammad, Alqahtani, & Alelaiwi, 2021).

Additionally, UAVs can be employed to deliver emergency medical care in inhospitable or isolated locations, like in the wake of a disaster. UAVs containing medical equipment and supplies, including defibrillators, can be promptly deployed to provide these items to patients in need. Data gathered by UAVs can be analyzed using machine learning algorithms to pinpoint regions that urgently require medical care.

Especially in distant or inaccessible places, the integration of machine learning and UAVs in healthcare has the potential to transform the way medical services are provided and enhance patient outcomes. UAVs can be used to transport medical equipment and supplies to distant or inaccessible locations. To ensure prompt delivery of goods, machine learning algorithms can be used to schedule and route UAVs more effectively.

Healthcare workers can increase the effectiveness and precision of the delivery of medical services by incorporating machine learning algorithms with UAV technology. Healthcare practitioners can recognize patterns and potential health risks in real-time by using machine learning algorithms to examine the vast amounts of data that UAVs collect. Early intervention and therapy are possible as a result, which can improve patient outcomes and save lives (Abir, Islam, Anwar, Mahmood, & Oo, 2020).

Figure 5 shows a potential reference layer architecture for using the aforementioned technologies to create machine learning-based healthcare applications.

Figure 5. Conceptual Layered architecture of ML for healthcare applications

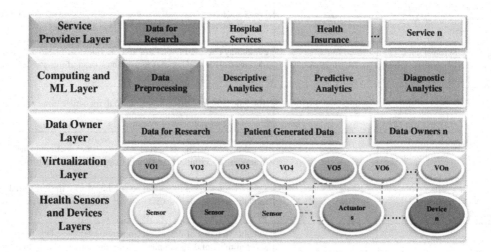

4. TECHNOLOGIES THAT HELP IMPLEMENT ENHANCING MEDICAL SERVICES THROUGH MACHINE LEARNING AND UAV TECHNOLOGY

Several supplementary technologies can help improve medical care by integrating machine learning and UAV technology (Comtet & Johannessen, 2022; Imran et al., 2021). A few of these technologies are as follows:

1. 5G connectivity: 5G networks enable ultra-fast, low-latency communication capabilities, which are essential for real-time data transmission between UAVs, healthcare organizations, and medical equipment. High-quality video streaming, remote monitoring, and data interchange are made possible by 5G, which improves telemedicine applications and supports UAV operations in real-time medical settings (R. Gupta, Kumari, & Tanwar, 2021; Mourtzis, Angelopoulos, & Panopoulos, 2021).

2. Edge Computing: Edge computing involves reducing latency and enhancing real-time analysis by processing data closer to the source. UAVs can execute on-board data processing and AI algorithms by utilizing edge computing capabilities, which enables quicker decision-making and reduces reliance on distant cloud infrastructure. When real-time analysis of medical data is necessary for prompt interventions and therapy, this is very advantageous (Cao, Liu, Meng, & Sun, 2020; M. M. Saeed, Saeed, Mokhtar, et al., 2023).

3. Internet of Things (IoT): An interconnected system of gadgets that can gather and share data is referred to as the IoT. IoT devices, including wearable sensors, remote monitoring equipment, and medical equipment, can give real-time patient data in the context of improving medical services through machine learning and UAV technology. Machine learning algorithms can make use of this data to provide insights, guide treatment choices, and enhance UAV operations (Nikhat & Yusuf, 2020).

4. Big Data Analytics: To uncover significant patterns and insights, big data analytics entails processing and analyzing enormous amounts of data. UAVs may assess a variety of data sources, such as patient records, environmental data, and geographic information, using machine learning algorithms to produce relevant insights for healthcare providers. Big data analytics can help with precision medicine, disease surveillance, and UAV operational optimization in healthcare settings (Najafabadi et al., 2015; M. M. Saeed, Ali & Saeed, 2023).

5. Cloud Computing: Cloud computing offers scalable and instant access to computing resources, simplifying data processing, storage, and analysis. Cloud infrastructure can be used by UAVs to offload complex computing operations, store a lot of data, and access machine learning models for in-depth analysis. Along with allowing remote consultations and knowledge exchange, cloud computing also facilitates data sharing and collaboration among healthcare providers (Hashem et al., 2015).

6. Augmented reality (AR) and virtual reality (VR): By delivering immersive and engaging experiences, AR and VR technologies can improve telemedicine applications. AR and VR can be used by medical practitioners to virtually consult with patients, visualize patient data from a distance, and direct UAV operations. These innovations facilitate better decision-making, communication, and training, which boosts the efficacy and efficiency of medical services provided by UAVs (Almousa et al., 2021).

It's crucial to remember that these technologies must be implemented successfully and that strong infrastructure, adherence to privacy and security standards, and legislative frameworks that control their use in healthcare are all necessary. Additionally, to use these technologies efficiently and guarantee the delivery of safe and effective medical services using machine learning and UAV technology, interdisciplinary collaboration between healthcare providers, technological specialists, and regulatory agencies is essential.

5. APPLICATIONS OF MACHINE LEARNING AND UAVS IN MEDICAL SERVICES EFFICIENT DISTRIBUTION OF MEDICAL SUPPLIES

The more popular term "drone" was first used to describe ancient military unmanned target aircraft because of how it sounded to a male bee, loud and rhythmic. Despite being widely accepted by the general public, the word has faced fierce resistance from regulators and aviation experts. Unmanned aerial vehicles (UAVs) are multipurpose, autonomous, remotely controlled aircraft that can carry payloads and are propelled by aerodynamic forces. The term unmanned aerial vehicle (UAV) was originally used in the 1980s (Eisenbeiss, 2004). The contrast between UAVs and other airborne systems, such as ballistic vehicles, gliders, balloons, and cruise missiles, was outlined by this term. Unmanned aerial systems (UAS), which are more commonly used in professional contexts, are any one or more unmanned aerial vehicles that are equipped with a data terminal, a sensing array, and an electronic data link. The words remotely piloted vehicle (RPV) and remotely piloted aircraft system (RPAS) are also used to refer to the drone. RPV has primarily been used in military contexts, whereas RPAS is a more official and widely used term. This essay will refer to drones throughout for ease of use (Ahmad, Ordoñez, Cartujo, & Martos, 2020; Casagrande, Sik, & Szabó, 2018).

An airframe, a propulsion system, and a navigation system are the basic components of drones. They contain several different aircraft design variations as well as auxiliary equipment that supports varied uses. Although this technology is not new, it has only just started to meet normal business applications by offering a more affordable, quicker, and superior alternative to full-size aircraft. Drone designs have improved in capability, cost, and accessibility thanks to the development of micro miniaturization and mass production of the underlying technologies, such as processors, micro-electrical mechanical systems (MEMS) sensors, and batteries created for smart devices. Medical supplies can be distributed effectively using machine learning and UAVs, especially in isolated or difficult-to-reach locations (Nedelea et al., 2022). Table 2 provides examples of machine learning and UAV applications in the efficient distribution of medical supplies.

Table 2. Examples of machine learning and UAV applications in the efficient distribution of medical supplies

Application	Description
Inventory management	Real-time inventory data analysis by machine learning algorithms can improve supply chain operations and avoid stockouts.
Predictive analytics	To forecast future demand for medical goods, machine learning algorithms can examine data on usage trends, patient demographics, and disease prevalence.
Routing optimization	Delivery route optimization using machine learning algorithms can shorten delivery times and increase delivery effectiveness.
Emergency medical supply delivery	UAVs can deliver emergency medical supplies and equipment to hard-to-reach places, enhancing supply chain operations in the process.
Last-mile delivery	UAVs can be used to deliver last-mile medical supplies, especially in cities where road congestion might cause delivery times to be delayed.
Inventory monitoring	Real-time inventory monitoring by UAVs with sensors and cameras can provide crucial information for inventory management and supply chain improvement.

Here are some examples of particular uses:

1. Improving supply chain logistics: To ensure prompt delivery of medical supplies, machine learning algorithms can be utilized to improve the routing and scheduling of UAVs. To do this, data on weather patterns, road conditions, and other variables that can affect delivery times can be analyzed.
2. Delivering medical supplies to disaster areas: In areas where conventional routes of transportation may be affected, UAVs can convey medical supplies and equipment. Data gathered by UAVs can be analyzed using machine learning algorithms to pinpoint regions that urgently require medical care.
3. Delivering vaccines and blood samples: UAVs can deliver vaccines and blood samples swiftly and effectively to far-off or inaccessible locations. To make sure that these supplies are delivered promptly and safely, UAV routing and scheduling can be optimized using machine learning methods.
4. Providing quick access to emergency medical supplies: Time is of the essence in an emergency. UAVs can be quickly deployed to provide medical equipment and supplies to patients in need, including defibrillators and emergency medications. Data gathered by UAVs can be analyzed using machine learning algorithms to pinpoint regions that urgently require medical care.
5. Inventory management: To make sure that medical supplies are always available when needed, machine learning algorithms can be used to assess data on inventory levels, consumption trends, and expiration dates. This can assist healthcare facilities in reducing waste and stockouts.

5.1 Efficient Distribution of Medical Supplies

Efficient distribution of medical supplies is essential for ensuring that healthcare providers have access to the equipment, medications, and other supplies they need to provide high-quality care to patients. Inefficient distribution systems can lead to shortages, delays, and other problems that can compromise patient care.

Efficient distribution of medical supplies requires careful planning and coordination between healthcare providers, suppliers, and logistics professionals. This may involve the use of advanced technologies such as inventory management systems, predictive analytics, and real-time tracking tools to optimize supply chain operations and ensure that supplies are delivered to the right place at the right time (Schneller, Abdulsalam, Conway, & Eckler, 2023).

One key factor in the efficient distribution of medical supplies is effective inventory management. This involves tracking inventory levels, forecasting demand, and ensuring that supplies are ordered promptly to avoid shortages or overstocking. It also involves ensuring that supplies are stored and transported in the appropriate conditions to maintain their quality and effectiveness. Another important factor is effective logistics management. This involves coordinating the movement of supplies from manufacturers or distributors to healthcare providers, using the most efficient and cost-effective transportation methods. This may involve the use of centralized distribution centers, regional warehouses, or other logistics hubs to streamline the supply chain and reduce transportation costs.

Efficient distribution of medical supplies is particularly important in emergencies, such as natural disasters or disease outbreaks. In these situations, healthcare providers may require large quantities of supplies on short notice, and efficient distribution systems are essential for ensuring that these supplies are delivered quickly and effectively.

This dispersion is based on demographic trends, where healthcare network managers try to make it simpler for individuals to remain in their homes by bringing healthcare services closer to the patients (Garagiola, Creazza, & Porazzi, 2020). Since there is a physical separation between the patient and the doctor via telemedicine, for instance, modern information technologies stress this concept. The latest telemedicine technology allows for long-distance diagnosis by enabling remote monitoring of fundamental vital signs. A new dispersion of healthcare professionals is being created by the adoption of this technology in workplaces. The SC should have more flexibility to distribute the pharmaceuticals and medical supplies that the patient needs after a particular consultation for this distribution of healthcare services to be successful.

A crucial component of healthcare delivery that can profit from the application of machine learning and UAV technology is the efficient distribution of medical supplies. Examples of how these technologies can be used to enhance the delivery of medical supplies are given below (Schneller et al., 2023; Tan et al., 2022):

1. Routing optimization: To cut travel time and increase delivery efficiency, delivery routes can be optimized using machine learning algorithms. This helps expedite and more precisely distribute medical supplies, especially in distant or difficult-to-reach places.
2. Delivery of emergency medical supplies: UAVs can be used to transport emergency medical equipment and supplies to hard-to-reach places, speeding up patient care and response times. In the wake of calamities or natural disasters, this can be especially helpful.
3. Last-mile delivery: UAVs can be used to transport last-mile medical supplies, especially in cities where traffic jams can cause delivery delays. This can decrease the chance of stockouts and enhance the speed and accuracy of the delivery of medical supplies.

5.2 Remote Monitoring for Enhanced Healthcare

A technology-enabled approach to healthcare called remote monitoring enables healthcare professionals to remotely monitor patients outside of conventional clinical settings. With remote monitoring, patients can watch their vital signs and health condition via wearable tech, mobile apps, or other linked devices, and instantly share that information with their healthcare professionals. In particular, for patients with chronic diseases or those residing in rural places, this strategy offers the potential to enhance patient outcomes, lower healthcare expenses, and increase access to care. Patients who suffer from long-term illnesses including diabetes, heart disease, or chronic obstructive pulmonary disease (COPD) may find remote monitoring to be very helpful (Sobnath et al., 2017). Through remote monitoring, medical professionals may keep tabs on their patient's vital signs, medication compliance, and other crucial health indicators and take prompt action if there are any indications that their condition is deteriorating. Patient's quality of life may be improved, and fewer hospitalizations and ER visits may be necessary as a result. By lowering the need for in-person visits and hospital stays, remote monitoring can not only improve patient outcomes but also lower healthcare expenses. Patients who need frequent monitoring or who reside in rural places with limited access to healthcare may find this to be very helpful. However, there are certain difficulties with remote monitoring as well. Patients can be reluctant to use the technology, for instance, or they might not have access to the required equipment or internet connectivity. The management and interpretation of the massive amounts of data produced by remote monitoring devices may provide difficulties for healthcare providers.

From diverse clinical data, the artificial neural network base's multiple layered layers of neurons can learn intricate correlations between characteristics and labels (H. Li, Zhao, Zhang, & Zio, 2020). Convolutional neural networks, deep neural networks, deep belief networks, and recurrent neural networks are the four subcategories of deep learning used to implement pattern recognition and predictive modeling on large, high-dimensional data sets. Multitasking, automatic building of intricate features, digitalization of EHR and image-based data, integrating heterogeneous data sets compiled from diverse sources, and integrating with wearables for remote monitoring are some of its capabilities. It is fundamentally a fundamentally different paradigm in ML. A technology-enabled method called remote monitoring enables medical personnel to follow and track patients' health conditions from a distance (Haleem, Javaid, Singh, & Suman, 2023). Patients with chronic diseases or people who reside in rural places without regular access to healthcare services may find this to be very helpful. The following ways can remote monitoring and machine learning be combined to improve healthcare (Panesar, 2019; Xu, Sanders, Li, & Chow, 2021):

1. Early health issue detection: Machine learning algorithms can examine data gathered by remote monitoring devices to find patterns and trends that can point to the beginning of a health problem. This allows medical experts to act quickly and stop the illness from getting worse.
2. Personalized care: To develop individualized treatment plans for specific patients, machine learning algorithms can be utilized to analyze data obtained from remote monitoring devices. This can include advice on altering one's lifestyle, using particular medications, and engaging in other actions that can enhance one's health.
3. Predictive analytics: Data gathered by remote monitoring devices can be analyzed using machine learning algorithms to forecast future health outcomes. This may make it possible for medical practitioners to take early action and stop the emergence of significant health problems.
4. Virtual consultations: Patients who are unable to travel to a medical center can receive virtual consultations from healthcare specialists thanks to remote monitoring. To provide individualized advice and treatment programs, machine learning algorithms can be utilized to analyze the data gathered during these consultations.

5. Greater effectiveness: Reducing the need for in-person consultations can save time and money for both patients and medical staff. The effectiveness of remote monitoring can be increased by using machine learning algorithms to automate data analysis and send real-time alerts to medical experts.

5.3 Rapid Emergency Response and Telemedicine

Telemedicine and quick emergency response are two effective technologies that can enhance emergency medical care and potentially save lives. Even if patients are placed far from a hospital or healthcare facility, medical experts can still give remote medical care to them in an emergency through the use of telemedicine. Systems for rapid emergency response are created to quickly recognize and address medical situations. Typically, these systems feature a central monitoring station that responds to distress signals sent by patients or carers and sends out emergency responders to provide medical assistance. Rapid emergency response and telemedicine enable medical professionals to assess a patient's health quickly, administer immediate care, and collaborate with nearby emergency responders to make sure the patient gets the right care (Al-Wathinani et al., 2023).

Patients in isolated or underserved locations can receive medical care using telemedicine. Healthcare providers can remotely diagnose and treat patients, give medical advice, and coordinate care with local healthcare professionals by using videoconferencing and other remote communication technology. Patients who live in rural or distant places with limited access to healthcare may find this to be of special value. Rapid emergency response and telemedicine are connected with several difficulties, nevertheless. For instance, technical difficulties could make it difficult for healthcare professionals to communicate with patients or coordinate care with regional emergency responders. In some circumstances, telemedicine use may also be constrained by legal and regulatory restrictions. Machine learning can have a big impact on healthcare in two areas (Haleem, Javaid, Singh, & Suman, 2021):

1. Quick response to emergencies: In an emergency, every second matters. To find people who are most likely to have a medical emergency, machine learning algorithms can be used to examine data from a variety of sources, including medical records, vital signs, and patient history. This allows medical experts to act quickly and stop the illness from getting worse. Machine learning can also be used to plan and route emergency response teams more effectively, enabling them to get to the patient as soon as feasible.
2. Telemedicine: Telemedicine is the practice of delivering medical care remotely. In telemedicine, machine learning algorithms can be used to assess patient data and offer individualized advice and treatment regimens. To give patients real-time feedback and support, this may involve evaluating data from wearable technology, remote monitoring tools, and other sources. The effectiveness of telemedicine services can be increased by automating processes like triage, diagnosis, and treatment planning.

5.4 Surveillance and Management of Disease Outbreak

To restrict the spread of infectious illnesses and stop epidemics, public health initiatives must prioritize the surveillance and management of disease outbreaks. While management tactics are used to contain and control outbreaks once they start, surveillance systems are used to track the development of illnesses and spot epidemics. There are many different types of surveillance systems, including more conventional ones like laboratory testing and case reporting as well as more cutting-edge ones like syndromic surveillance and digital disease surveillance. Syndromic surveillance entails keeping an eye on social media, electronic health records, and other data sources to spot sickness patterns that might point to an outbreak. To spot trends of illness propagation, digital disease monitoring entails examining data from social media, internet searches, and other digital sources. When an outbreak is discovered, management techniques are employed to stop the disease's spread. A few of these tactics might be contact tracing, isolation, quarantine, public health campaigns to encourage handwashing, social seclusion, and other steps to stop the spread of disease (Şerban et al., 2019).

To effectively manage and monitor disease outbreaks, public health officials, healthcare professionals, and other stakeholders must work closely together. Analyzing and comprehending massive amounts of data in real-time also necessitates the employment of cutting-edge technologies and data analytics tools. However, monitoring and controlling disease outbreaks also present some difficulties. For instance, public health officials might not be able to execute efficient surveillance and management techniques due to resource limitations. The collection and use of personal health information in surveillance systems may also raise ethical and legal questions.

Disease outbreaks can have a catastrophic effect on both the economy and public health (Banda Chitsamatanga & Malinga, 2021). The following are some methods that machine learning can be applied to the management and surveillance of disease outbreaks (Du & Guo, 2022; Riswantini & Nugraheni, 2022):

1. Early detection: To predict potential illness outbreaks early, machine learning algorithms can scan data from a variety of sources, including social media, news stories, and medical records. This can make it possible for medical personnel to respond quickly to stop the outbreak and stop it from spreading.
2. Predictive analytics: Data on population demographics, travel habits, and other elements that could affect the spread of disease can be analyzed using machine learning. This makes it possible for medical experts to forecast how quickly a disease outbreak will spread and to deploy resources accordingly.
3. Contact tracing: To find people who may have been exposed to the disease, machine learning can be used to evaluate data on the whereabouts and contacts of sick people. This can make it possible for medical experts to carry out focused testing and quarantine measures, which will stop the sickness from spreading.
4. Treatment optimization: Data on the efficacy of various treatment choices for a specific condition can be analyzed using machine learning. This can help medical providers tailor treatment plans to each patient, which will lead to better patient outcomes.
5. Resource distribution: To guarantee that resources are distributed where they are most required during an illness, machine learning can be used to assess data on the availability and distribution of resources like hospital beds, medical supplies, and employees.

5.5 UAV's Application With AI in the Healthcare Sector

Drones, also referred to as unmanned aerial vehicles (UAVs), have shown promise in several industries, including the medical field. UAVs can change healthcare delivery by offering effective and cutting-edge solutions when integrated with artificial intelligence (AI) (Ampatzidis, Partel, Costa, & Agriculture, 2020; Euchi, 2021; Tahir et al., 2023). Here, we look at the use of AI-equipped UAVs in the healthcare industry.

Delivery of Medical Supplies: UAVs with AI technology can be used to deliver medical supplies, including drugs, vaccines, and blood samples, to hard-to-reach places. In emergency scenarios or during natural catastrophes, AI algorithms can improve the route planning and navigation of UAVs, assuring fast and accurate delivery (Abdelhaleem, 2022), (Alatabani, 2021), (Ali, 2021).

1. Telemedicine support: UAVs connected to AI-driven telemedicine platforms can deliver remote medical support. They can enable video consultations between medical staff and patients in distant places, enabling in-the-moment evaluations and direction. AI algorithms can assist in the analysis of medical data supplied by UAVs, assisting in the decision-making process for diagnosis and treatment, (Alqurashi, 2021), (Asif, 2022).
2. Emergency Response: In emergency response circumstances, UAVs with AI and thermal imaging capabilities can be used. They can scan disaster-affected areas swiftly, find survivors, and communicate crucial information to rescue crews. Rescue operations may be prioritized using AI algorithms, and they can also offer important information for disaster management, (Aswathy, 2022), (Bokani, 2018), (Elmustafa, 2021), (Faroug, 2021), (Hassan, 2021).
3. Monitoring and Surveillance: UAVs with AI algorithms may monitor expansive areas, such as hospital lobbies or public places, for patient monitoring and security purposes. They can spot irregularities, pinpoint potential dangers, and instantly notify medical staff. The mobility of patients within healthcare institutions can also be tracked using AI-powered picture recognition, assuring their security (Hoseini, 2021), (Khalifa, 2022), (Lina, 2022).
4. Precision Medicine and Personalized Care: By gathering and analyzing patient data from distant areas, UAVs linked with AI technology can support precision medicine. They can collect DNA samples, keep track of vital signs, and take pictures that can be processed by AI algorithms to produce individualized treatment plans and improve medical procedures, (Mamoon, 2022), (Mamoon, 2023).
5. Disease Surveillance and Outbreak Management: UAVs with AI algorithms are useful for managing disease outbreaks and surveillance. To locate possible disease hotspots or track the transmission of infectious illnesses, they might gather environmental data, keep track of population movements, and evaluate patterns. The use of this information by healthcare administrators can help them allocate resources and plan efficient containment initiatives, (Mansour, 2022).

While UAVs with AI present the healthcare industry with incredible prospects, several issues need to be resolved. Regulation compliance, privacy issues, establishing a dependable communication infrastructure, and seamlessly integrating UAV operations with current healthcare systems are a few of these (Mohanty, Ravindra, Narayana, Pattnaik, & Sirajudeen, 2023).

5.6 UAV's Application in Delivering Medicines in Hill Stations and Remote Areas Can Be Explained Elaborately

Drones, commonly referred to as unmanned aerial vehicles (UAVs), have gained popularity as a possible alternative to traditional transportation methods for delivering medications to distant locations and hill stations. Speed, accessibility, and affordability are just a few benefits of using UAVs in the delivery of medications (F. Saeed et al., 2021; Valavanis, 2008). Let's examine the complex use of UAVs in delivering medications to these areas.

1. Overcoming Geographical Challenges: Hill stations and distant locales may include rocky terrain, scant road infrastructure, and difficult-to-reach locations. These difficult terrains are easily negotiated by UAVs, which can avoid obstructions and quickly reach distant locations. UAVs are the perfect option for delivering medicines to remote areas because they can fly over mountains, jungles, and other tough terrain, (Mohammed, 2022), (Mohammed, 2023).

2. Route Optimization and Navigation: UAVs equipped with AI algorithms can choose the best delivery routes based on distance, weather, and terrain analyses, among other variables. These formulas can figure out the most effective route, avoiding hazards and assuring the timely and safe delivery of medications. Real-time navigation technologies further improve the UAVs' capacity to change course in response to environmental changes during delivery.

3. Cold Chain Management: To retain their efficacy, certain medications, particularly vaccines and treatments that are sensitive to temperature, need to be handled with extreme care. To maintain the integrity of the drugs during transport, UAVs can be fitted with refrigeration equipment or temperature-controlled containers. To ensure that the medications are given in the best possible settings, AI algorithms can monitor and control temperature conditions, (Mona, 2021).

4. Tracking and Monitoring: Tracking and Monitoring systems that offer real-time updates on the condition and location of the medications throughout travel can be installed on UAVs. This increases accountability and lowers the danger of theft or loss by giving healthcare professionals total visibility into and control over the distribution process, (Moradi, 2020), (Moradi, 2022).

5. Cost-Effectiveness: UAVs provide a cost-effective solution for delivering medications in hill stations and isolated locations as compared to conventional transportation methods, such as road or air transport. They can dramatically lower the costs of logistics connected with conventional transportation techniques and they do it without the need for extensive infrastructure development.

To make sure that UAVs for drug delivery are successfully implemented, several issues must be taken into account. These include establishing a suitable communication infrastructure and complying with laws governing airspace, safety procedures, privacy issues, and UAV operations (Fahlstrom, Gleason, & Sadraey, 2022).

5.7 Various Real-Time Healthcare Applications That Need Uavs and Their Implementation Challenges in Different Scenarios and Aspects

Unmanned aerial vehicles (UAVs) are used in real-time healthcare applications, which have the potential to significantly enhance patient care and healthcare delivery. However, using UAVs in many contexts and facets of healthcare has its own unique set of difficulties. Let's look at a few real-time healthcare applications that make use of UAVs and the difficulties that each one has in implementation (Kumar et al., 2021).

1. Emergency Medical Response:

Using UAVs to carry vital medical supplies like defibrillators, blood units, or emergency drugs to the scene of an emergency is a real-time healthcare application in emergency medical response. Regulatory compliance, adhering to airspace limits, and acquiring required licenses and clearances for UAV operations are challenges in this scenario (Mills et al., 2019).

- Safety and Reliability: Ensuring the UAVs' safety and dependability in emergency response scenarios, including navigating congested locations, bad weather, and sustaining communication links, (Nada, 2022).
- Precision Delivery: Overcoming obstacles to accurate and precise delivery to the specific emergency location, particularly in urban settings with complex structures and constrained landing zones, (Othman, 2022).
    2. Remote Area Healthcare Delivery:

To reach rural places with little access to medical facilities, UAVs can be used to transport medications, vaccinations, and diagnostic samples (Olatomiwa, Blanchard, Mekhilef & Akinyele, 2018). Among the difficulties in this scenario are:

- Geographical Restrictions: Addressing issues with difficult terrain, unpredictable weather, and sparse infrastructure in remote places, (Rania, 2020).
- Payload Capacity: Enhancing the UAV's payload capacity and design to transport the required medical supplies while ensuring their safe storage and transportation.
- Navigation and localization: Using reliable navigation technologies to guarantee accurate UAV positioning and delivery in regions with spotty or nonexistent GPS service, (Rashid, 2014).
    3. Telemedicine Support:

By enabling real-time video conferencing and remote diagnostics, UAVs can help telemedicine consultations (Wootton & telecare, 2008). The following issues must be addressed in this scenario:

- Connectivity and Bandwidth: Ensuring dependable and high-bandwidth communication lines between the UAV and medical personnel, especially in distant or underdeveloped regions with inadequate network infrastructure, (Rofida, 2017), (Salehi, 2019).
- Data Security and Privacy: Enacting strong encryption and security measures to safeguard patient data transmitted during telemedicine sessions and ensuring adherence to privacy laws.
- Integration with Healthcare Systems: To facilitate effective information interchange and continuity of treatment, UAV-based telemedicine solutions must be seamlessly integrated with current healthcare systems, electronic medical records, and communication platforms, (Salehi, 2019), (Sayed, 2021).
    4. Disaster Response and Public Health:

By offering capabilities for aerial surveillance, disease surveillance, and environmental monitoring, UAVs can help in situations involving disaster response and public health (Lurie, Manolio, Patterson, Collins, & Frieden, 2013). Among the difficulties in this scenario are:

- Real-Time Data Analysis: Making use of AI algorithms and image recognition tools to process and analyze massive amounts of data gathered by UAVs in real-time so that decisions can be made quickly.
- Interoperability and Collaboration: Creating standards and procedures for interoperability to facilitate seamless data exchange and collaboration between several UAVs, healthcare organizations, and disaster response teams.

- Ethical Considerations: Addressing ethical issues relating to data gathering, privacy, and potential stigma connected with illness tracking and aerial surveillance in the context of public health.

6. CHALLENGES AND OPPORTUNITIES FOR THE FUTURE

A good amount of skepticism is there along with new dangers and challenges that come with machine learning-based applications in the healthcare industry, even though they have a fresh and progressive potential. Here, we discuss the main concerns to be aware of, such as the probability of prediction errors and their consequences, privacy and security problems in the systems, and even the lack of data availability for producing verifiable results (M. Saeed et al., 2022; R. A. Saeed, Saeed, Mokhtar, Alhumyani, & Abdel-Khalek, 2021). There are many obstacles, including ethical concerns and the loss of the human aspect of healthcare, as well as the interpretability and practical applicability of the concepts to bedside settings.

One of the biggest risks of machine learning-based algorithms is the reliance on probabilistic distribution and the likelihood of inaccurate diagnosis and prognosis. Additionally, it promotes a healthy dose of skepticism about the dependability and precision of predictions generated using ML-based techniques. Even while the likelihood of inaccuracy and reliance on probability is strongly ingrained in many aspects of health care, the repercussions of ML-based operations that result in human mortality are grave. Before implementing these machine learning-based technologies, one solution is to require strong institutional and legal authorization from numerous entities (Froomkin, Kerr, & Pineau, 2019; Gupta, Kumar, & Medicine, 2023). Another strategy that can be used to prevent false-positive or false-negative diagnoses (such as the diagnosis of depression or breast cancer) involves human oversight and intervention from a skilled healthcare professional in highly sensitive applications. The involvement of current healthcare professionals in developing and putting these techniques into practice may boost adaptation rates and lessen worries about the workforce decreasing or providing fewer career options for people (Cook et al., 2020).

Another issue with applying ML and deep learning algorithms to the healthcare sector is the availability of high-quality training and testing data with adequate sample sizes to ensure high reliability and reproducibility of the predictions. One cannot overestimate the importance of high-quality data because ML and deep learning-based approaches 'learn' on data. The enormous amounts of feature-rich data required for various learning networks and algorithms, which are generally hard to get by, may also be a representation of the population sample's limited distribution. Additionally, the data that have been gathered across some healthcare segments are heterogeneous, lacking, and have far more features than samples (M. M. Saeed, Saeed, Gaid, et al., 2023). These challenges must be taken seriously while developing and evaluating the results of ML-based approaches.

These challenges might be overcome thanks to the recent drive for open scientific initiatives and the sharing of research data. One should consider the privacy risk and ethical repercussions while applying ML-based technologies in healthcare. Several machine learning (ML) based procedures are developed and implemented using cloud-based technologies, but it should be noted that these methods call for sizable, easily scalable data storage as well as reasonably high computing capacity. Given the sensitive nature of healthcare data and privacy concerns, increased data security and accountability have to be one of the first elements taken into account well before model design (Dang, Tatipamula, & Nguyen, 2021; M. M. Saeed, R. A. Saeed, R. A. Mokhtar, et al., 2022).

Concerning ethical issues, researchers using ML-based methods in healthcare can easily learn from the field of genetic engineering, which has been the subject of intense ethical discussion. There is ongoing debate concerning the use of genetic engineering to produce long-lasting genetic improvements and cures. Finding and correcting deleterious genetic abnormalities, like the HTT mutation that causes Huntington's disease, may lead to life-altering medical interventions. On the other hand, developing genome-altering therapies when they are still prohibitively expensive may widen the socioeconomic gap for populations who cannot afford such treatment (Habehh & Gohel, 2021; M. M. A. Saeed, Ahmed, Saeed, & Azim). Guidelines for the creation of AI machinery have recently begun to appear. A Model Artificial Intelligence Governance Framework was put forth by Singapore in 2019 to direct businesses in the private sector in the creation and ethical application of AI (Palladino, 2023; M. M. Saeed, M. K. Hasan, et al., 2022). Even though they are stringent, these rules and guidelines have been established to guarantee the development and conduct of ethical research.

A fundamental challenge in the use of ML in healthcare is the interpretation and clinical value of the data. The complexity of ML-based methods, especially deep learning-based approaches, makes it very challenging to distinguish and isolate the contribution of the original characteristics to the prediction. Even while this may not be a serious concern in other ML applications (such as web searches), a lack of transparency has considerably hampered the ability of ML-based approaches in healthcare to be adapted (Muehlematter, Daniore, & Vokinger, 2021). Figure 6 shows the challenges of machine learning and UAV technology in healthcare.

Figure 6. Challenges for machine learning and UAV technology in healthcare

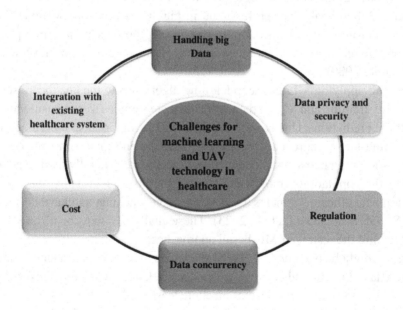

In the healthcare sector, it is common knowledge that the solution approach is equally as important as the actual solution. It is necessary to make a systematic shift to identify and quantify the underlying data attributes that are employed for prediction. Increased acceptance rates may also result from the development, use, and testing of ML-based methods with input from medical professionals. Additionally, these techniques offer a unique opportunity to increase involvement, even though there is reason to be cautious about the likelihood that a patient's and PCP's relationship may suffer as a result of the increased usage of ML-based approaches. Studies show that about 25% of Americans do not have a primary care doctor, and the doctor-patient relationship is already a dying concept (Botrugno, 2021).

In this situation, ML can provide unique chances to increase involvement when patients discuss the results of potential diagnoses and increase the efficiency of outreach programs. Patients who follow a healthy lifestyle may also gain from early prognosis brought on by ML-based therapy, according to discussions they have with their PCPs. Last but not least, a survey of physicians found that 56% saw patients for no longer than 16 minutes and 56% for no longer than 9 minutes (Hobbs & Erhardt, 2002). Reducing stress and giving doctors more one-on-one time with their patients are two benefits of using AI approaches for diagnosis and symptom monitoring, which will also boost patient satisfaction and outcomes.

Through machine learning and UAV technology, there are numerous opportunities and difficulties for the future of medical services (Ullah, Al-Turjman, Mostarda, & Gagliardi, 2020). Here are a few illustrations of Tables 3,4 and 5 that show the difficulties and possibilities for the application of machine learning and UAV technology in the healthcare sector in the future:

Table 3. Challenges for machine learning and UAV technology in healthcare

Challenge	Description
Data privacy and security	Healthcare data must be safeguarded from unauthorized access and disclosure since it is sensitive.
Integration with existing healthcare systems	To achieve smooth integration and effective data sharing, machine learning and UAV technology must be integrated into the current healthcare systems.
Regulation	Regulations and standards like those set forth by the HIPAA and FDA must be adhered to by machine learning and UAV technology.
Cost	The adoption of UAV and machine learning technology may be hampered by the expense of setup and maintenance.

Table 4. Opportunities for machine learning and UAV technology in healthcare

Opportunity	Description
Personalized care	To deliver individualized care plans and predictive analytics, machine learning algorithms can examine data on patient health conditions and usage trends.
Medical supply delivery	UAVs can deliver emergency medical supplies and equipment to hard-to-reach places, enhancing supply chain operations in the process.
Disease surveillance	To gather information on disease outbreaks and reveal patterns of disease transmission, UAVs can be fitted with sensors and cameras.
Drug discovery	Machine learning algorithms can examine large datasets of chemical compounds to identify potential therapeutic candidates.

Table 5. Future directions for machine learning and UAV technology in healthcare

Direction	Description
Integration with electronic health records	Electronic health records can be combined with UAV and machine learning technologies to give real-time data analysis and decision support.
Patient engagement	To deliver individualized care and boost patient engagement, machine learning algorithms can be employed to analyze patient behavior and preferences.
Precision medicine	To create individualized treatment plans based on a person's particular features, machine learning algorithms can be used to examine genetic data and other types of data.
Autonomous UAVs	AI-driven navigation and obstacle detection technologies can be added to UAVs to enable autonomous operation, increase efficiency, and lessen the need for human involvement.

7. CONCLUSION

Let's sum up by saying that the combination of machine learning and UAV technology has the potential to improve medical services in some ways. This technology has the potential to boost healthcare delivery's effectiveness and precision, especially in remote or underserved areas, by streamlining the distribution of medical supplies and enabling remote access to healthcare services. Personalized treatment plans, predictive analytics, and inventory management can all be provided by machine learning algorithms that assess data on patient health status, usage habits, and inventory levels. UAVs can be used to deliver medical equipment and supplies to inaccessible or remote locations, enhancing supply chain operations and providing emergency medical supplies.

Furthermore, the application of machine learning and unmanned aerial vehicles (UAVs) to healthcare services can enhance disease surveillance and management by facilitating precise contact tracing, early identification, and forecasting of disease outbreaks. The advantages of machine learning and UAV technology in medical services are obvious, despite the difficulties in implementing this technology, which include data privacy and security, legislation, integration with current healthcare systems, and cost. With the ability to enhance patient outcomes and lower costs, this technology has the power to completely change the way healthcare is provided. As a result, the continuous development and application of UAV and machine learning technology in medical services give a promising prospect for advancement and innovation in the healthcare sector.

8. REFERENCES

Abdelhaleem, R.S., Omri, M., Abdel-Khalek, S. et al. (2022), Optimal path planning for drones based on swarm intelligence algorithm. *Neural Comput & Applic*. doi:10.1007/s00521-022-06998-9

Abir, S. A. A., Islam, S. N., Anwar, A., Mahmood, A. N., & Oo, A. M. T. (2020). Building resilience against COVID-19 pandemic using artificial intelligence, machine learning, and IoT: A survey of recent progress. *IoT*, *1*(2), 506–528. doi:10.3390/iot1020028

Ahmad, A., Ordoñez, J., Cartujo, P., & Martos, V. (2020). Remotely piloted aircraft (RPA) in agriculture: A pursuit of sustainability. *Agronomy (Basel)*, *11*(1), 7. doi:10.3390/agronomy11010007

Aiken, L. H., Sermeus, W., Van den Heede, K., Sloane, D. M., Busse, R., McKee, M., Bruyneel, L., Rafferty, A. M., Griffiths, P., Moreno-Casbas, M. T., Tishelman, C., Scott, A., Brzostek, T., Kinnunen, J., Schwendimann, R., Heinen, M., Zikos, D., Sjetne, I. S., Smith, H. L., & Kutney-Lee, A. (2012). Patient safety, satisfaction, and quality of hospital care: Cross sectional surveys of nurses and patients in 12 countries in Europe and the United States. *BMJ (Clinical Research Ed.)*, *344*(mar20 2), 344. doi:10.1136/bmj.e1717 PMID:22434089

Al-Wathinani, A. M., Alhallaf, M. A., Borowska-Stefańska, M., Wiśniewski, S., Sultan, M. A. S., Samman, O. Y., & Goniewicz, K. (2023, May). Elevating Healthcare: Rapid Literature Review on Drone Applications for Streamlining Disaster Management and Prehospital Care in Saudi Arabia. []). MDPI]. *Health Care*, *11*(11), 1575. PMID:37297715

Alatabani, L. E., Ali, E. S., & Saeed, R. A. (2021). Deep Learning Approaches for IoV Applications and Services. In N. Magaia, G. Mastorakis, C. Mavromoustakis, E. Pallis, & E. K. Markakis (Eds.), *Intelligent Technologies for Internet of Vehicles. Internet of Things (Technology, Communications, and Computing)*. Springer. doi:10.1007/978-3-030-76493-7_8

Ali, E. H. A., Zahraa, T. M., Hassan, M. B., & Saeed, R. (2021). Algorithms Optimization for Intelligent IoV Applications. In J. Zhao & V. Vinoth Kumar (Eds.), *Handbook of Research on Innovations and Applications of AI, IoT, and Cognitive Technologies* (pp. 1–25). IGI Global. doi:10.4018/978-1-7998-6870-5.ch001

Almousa, O., Zhang, R., Dimma, M., Yao, J., Allen, A., Chen, L., Heidari, P., & Qayumi, K. (2021). Virtual reality technology and remote digital application for tele-simulation and global medical education: An innovative hybrid system for clinical training. *Simulation & Gaming*, *52*(5), 614–634. doi:10.1177/10468781211008258

Alqurashi, F. A., & Alsolami, F.a; Abdel-Khalek, S.; S. Ali, E.; et al. (. (2021). 'Machine Learning Techniques in the Internet of UAVs for Smart Cities Applications. *Journal of Intelligent & Fuzzy Systems*, *24*(4), 1–24. doi:10.3233/JIFS-211009

Amirgaliyev, Y., Shamiluulu, S., & Serek, A. (2018, October). Analysis of chronic kidney disease dataset by applying machine learning methods. In *2018 IEEE 12th International Conference on Application of Information and Communication Technologies (AICT)* (pp. 1-4). IEEE] 10.1109/ICAICT.2018.8747140

Ampatzidis, Y., Partel, V., & Costa, L. (2020). Agroview: Cloud-based application to process, analyze and visualize UAV-collected data for precision agriculture applications utilizing artificial intelligence. *Computers and Electronics in Agriculture*, *174*, 105457. doi:10.1016/j.compag.2020.105457

Anbaroğlu, B. (2021). Drones in healthcare: An extended discussion on humanitarian logistics. In *Research Anthology on Reliability and Safety in Aviation Systems, Spacecraft, and Air Transport* (pp. 973-994). IGI Global]

Asif, K., Jian, P. L., Mohammad, K. H., Naushad, V., Zulkefli, M., & Shayla, I., & (2022). PackerRobo: Model-based robot vision self-supervised learning in CART. *Alexandria Engineering Journal*, *61*(12), 12549–12566. doi:10.1016/j.aej.2022.05.043

Asri, H., Mousannif, H., Al Moatassime, H., & Noel, T. (2016). Using machine learning algorithms for breast cancer risk prediction and diagnosis. *Procedia Computer Science*, *83*, 1064–1069. doi:10.1016/j.procs.2016.04.224

Aswathy, R. H., Suresh, P., Sikkandar, M. Y., & Abdel-Khalek, S. (2022). Optimized Tuned Deep Learning Model for Chronic Kidney Disease Classification. *CMC-Computers. Materials & Continua*, *70*(2), 2097–2111. doi:10.32604/cmc.2022.019790

Banda Chitsamatanga, B., & Malinga, W. (2021). 'A tale of two paradoxes in response to COVID-19': Public health system and socio-economic implications of the pandemic in South Africa and Zimbabwe. *Cogent Social Sciences*, *7*(1), 1869368. doi:10.1080/23311886.2020.1869368

Bhaskar, N., & Manikandan, S. (2019). A deep-learning-based system for automated sensing of chronic kidney disease. *IEEE Sensors Letters*, *3*(10), 1–4. doi:10.1109/LSENS.2019.2942145

Bokani, A., Hassan, J., & Kanhere, S. S. (2018). *Enabling Efficient and High Quality Zooming for Online Video Streaming using Edge Computing*. 2018 28th International Telecommunication Networks and Applications Conference (ITNAC), Sydney, NSW. 10.1109/ATNAC.2018.8615166

Botrugno, C. (2021). Information technologies in healthcare: Enhancing or dehumanising doctor–patient interaction? *Health*, *25*(4), 475–493. doi:10.1177/1363459319891213 PMID:31849239

Cao, K., Liu, Y., Meng, G., & Sun, Q. (2020). An overview on edge computing research. *IEEE Access : Practical Innovations, Open Solutions*, *8*, 85714–85728. doi:10.1109/ACCESS.2020.2991734

Casagrande, G., Sik, A., & Szabó, G. (Eds.). (2018). *Small Flying Drones*. Springer. doi:10.1007/978-3-319-66577-1

Cassano, C. (2014). The right balance-technology and patient care. *On-Line Journal of Nursing Informatics*, *18*(3).

Chen, M., Li, W., Hao, Y., Qian, Y., & Humar, I. (2018). Edge cognitive computing based smart healthcare system. *Future Generation Computer Systems*, *86*, 403–411. doi:10.1016/j.future.2018.03.054

Chen, Z. H., Lin, L., Wu, C. F., Li, C. F., Xu, R. H., & Sun, Y. (2021). Artificial intelligence for assisting cancer diagnosis and treatment in the era of precision medicine. *Cancer Communications*, *41*(11), 1100–1115. doi:10.1002/cac2.12215 PMID:34613667

Comtet, H. E., & Johannessen, K. A. (2022). A socio-analytical approach to the integration of drones into health care systems. *Information (Basel)*, *13*(2), 62. doi:10.3390/info13020062

Cook, T. M., El-Boghdadly, K., McGuire, B., McNarry, A. F., Patel, A., & Higgs, A. (2020). Consensus guidelines for managing the airway in patients with COVID-19: Guidelines from the Difficult Airway Society, the Association of Anaesthetists the Intensive Care Society, the Faculty of Intensive Care Medicine and the Royal College of Anaesthetists. *Anaesthesia*, *75*(6), 785–799. doi:10.1111/anae.15054 PMID:32221970

Dang, H. V., Tatipamula, M., & Nguyen, H. X. (2021). Cloud-based digital twinning for structural health monitoring using deep learning. *IEEE Transactions on Industrial Informatics*, *18*(6), 3820–3830. doi:10.1109/TII.2021.3115119

Dimitrov, D. V. (2016). Medical internet of things and big data in healthcare. *Healthcare Informatics Research*, *22*(3), 156–163. doi:10.4258/hir.2016.22.3.156 PMID:27525156

Du, Y., & Guo, Y. (2022). Machine learning techniques and research framework in foodborne disease surveillance system. *Food Control*, *131*, 108448. doi:10.1016/j.foodcont.2021.108448

Eisenbeiss, H. (2004). A mini unmanned aerial vehicle (UAV): system overview and image acquisition. *International Archives of Photogrammetry. Remote Sensing and Spatial Information Sciences, 36*(5/ W1), 1-7.

Eljamassi, D. F., & Maghari, A. Y. (2020, December). COVID-19 detection from chest X-ray scans using machine learning. In *2020 International Conference on Promising Electronic Technologies (ICPET)* (pp. 1-4). IEEE. 10.1109/ICPET51420.2020.00009

Elmustafa, S. A., Mohammad, K. H., & Rosilah, H. (2021). Machine Learning Technologies for Secure Vehicular Communication in Internet of Vehicles: Recent Advances and Applications [SCN]. *Security and Communication Networks*, *2021*, 1–23. doi:10.1155/2021/8868355

Estrada, M. A. R., & Ndoma, A. (2019). The uses of unmanned aerial vehicles–UAV's-(or drones) in social logistic: Natural disasters response and humanitarian relief aid. *Procedia Computer Science*, *149*, 375–383. doi:10.1016/j.procs.2019.01.151

Euchi, J. (2021). Do drones have a realistic place in a pandemic fight for delivering medical supplies in healthcare systems problems? *Chinese Journal of Aeronautics*, *34*(2), 182–190. doi:10.1016/j.cja.2020.06.006

Fahlstrom, P. G., Gleason, T. J., & Sadraey, M. H. (2022). *Introduction to UAV systems*. John Wiley & Sons.

Faroug, M. O., Ali, E. S., & Saeed, R. A. (2021). Cyber-Physical System for Smart Grid. In A. K. Luhach & A. Elçi (Eds.), *Artificial Intelligence Paradigms for Smart Cyber-Physical Systems* (pp. 301–323). IGI Global. doi:10.4018/978-1-7998-5101-1.ch014

Froomkin, A. M., Kerr, I., & Pineau, J. (2019). When AIs outperform doctors: Confronting the challenges of a tort-induced over-reliance on machine learning. *Arizona Law Review*, *61*, 33.

Garagiola, E., Creazza, A., & Porazzi, E. (2020). Analyzing the performance of health technologies distribution models in primary care services. *Measuring Business Excellence*, *25*(4), 452–474. doi:10.1108/MBE-11-2019-0109

Ghazal, T. M., Hasan, M. K., Alshurideh, M. T., Alzoubi, H. M., Ahmad, M., Akbar, S. S., Al Kurdi, B., & Akour, I. A. (2021). IoT for smart cities: Machine learning approaches in smart healthcare—A review. *Future Internet*, *13*(8), 218. doi:10.3390/fi13080218

Gupta, N. S., & Kumar, P. (2023). Perspective of artificial intelligence in healthcare data management: A journey towards precision medicine. *Computers in Biology and Medicine*, *162*, 107051. doi:10.1016/j.compbiomed.2023.107051 PMID:37271113

Gupta, R., Kumari, A., & Tanwar, S. (2021). Fusion of blockchain and artificial intelligence for secure drone networking underlying 5G communications. *Transactions on Emerging Telecommunications Technologies*, *32*(1), e4176. doi:10.1002/ett.4176

Habehh, H., & Gohel, S. (2021). Machine learning in healthcare. *Current Genomics*, *22*(4), 291–300. doi:10.2174/1389202922666210705124359 PMID:35273459

Haleem, A., Javaid, M., Singh, R. P., & Suman, R. (2021). Telemedicine for healthcare: Capabilities, features, barriers, and applications. *Sensors International*, *2*, 100117. doi:10.1016/j.sintl.2021.100117 PMID:34806053

Haleem, A., Javaid, M., Singh, R. P., & Suman, R. (2022). Medical 4.0 technologies for healthcare: Features, capabilities, and applications. *Internet of Things and Cyber-Physical Systems*, *2*, 12–30. doi:10.1016/j.iotcps.2022.04.001

Haleem, A., Javaid, M., Singh, R. P., & Suman, R. (2023). Exploring the revolution in healthcare systems through the applications of digital twin technology. *Biomedical Technology*, *4*, 28–38. doi:10.1016/j.bmt.2023.02.001

Hashem, I. A. T., Yaqoob, I., Anuar, N. B., Mokhtar, S., Gani, A., & Khan, S. U. (2015). The rise of "big data" on cloud computing: Review and open research issues. *Information Systems*, *47*, 98–115. doi:10.1016/j.is.2014.07.006

Hassan, M. B., Ali, E. S., & Nurelmadina, N. (2021). Artificial intelligence in IoT and its applications (Telecommunications, 2021). Intelligent Wireless Communications'. IET Digital Library. , doi:10.1049/PBTE094E_ch2

Hobbs, F. R., & Erhardt, L. (2002). Acceptance of guideline recommendations and perceived implementation of coronary heart disease prevention among primary care physicians in five European countries: the Reassessing European Attitudes about Cardiovascular Treatment (REACT) survey. *Family practice*, *19*(6), 596-604.

Hoseini, S. A., Bokani, A., Hassan, J., Salehi, S., & Kanhere, S. S. (2021). Energy and Service-Priority aware Trajectory Design for UAV-BSs using Double Q-Learning. *2021 IEEE 18th Annual Consumer Communications & Networking Conference. CCNC*. doi:10.1109/CCNC49032.2021.9369472

Huang, L., Wang, L., Hu, X., Chen, S., Tao, Y., Su, H., Yang, J., Xu, W., Vedarethinam, V., Wu, S., Liu, B., Wan, X., Lou, J., Wang, Q., & Qian, K. (2020). Machine learning of serum metabolic patterns encodes early-stage lung adenocarcinoma. *Nature Communications*, *11*(1), 3556. doi:10.103841467-020-17347-6 PMID:32678093

Imran, M., Zaman, U., Imran, Imtiaz, J., Fayaz, M., & Gwak, J. (2021). Comprehensive survey of iot, machine learning, and blockchain for health care applications: A topical assessment for pandemic preparedness, challenges, and solutions. *Electronics (Basel)*, *10*(20), 2501. doi:10.3390/electronics10202501

Jamshidi, M., Lalbakhsh, A., Talla, J., Peroutka, Z., Hadjilooei, F., Lalbakhsh, P., Jamshidi, M., Spada, L. L., Mirmozafari, M., Dehghani, M., Sabet, A., Roshani, S., Roshani, S., Bayat-Makou, N., Mohamadzade, B., Malek, Z., Jamshidi, A., Kiani, S., Hashemi-Dezaki, H., & Mohyuddin, W. (2020). Artificial intelligence and COVID-19: Deep learning approaches for diagnosis and treatment. *IEEE Access : Practical Innovations, Open Solutions*, 8, 109581–109595. doi:10.1109/ACCESS.2020.3001973 PMID:34192103

Javaid, M., & Khan, I. H. (2021). Internet of Things (IoT) enabled healthcare helps to take the challenges of COVID-19 Pandemic. *Journal of Oral Biology and Craniofacial Research*, 11(2), 209–214. doi:10.1016/j.jobcr.2021.01.015 PMID:33665069

Khalifa, O. O., Roubleh, A., Esgiar, A., Abdelhaq, M., Alsaqour, R., Abdalla, A., Ali, E. S., & Saeed, R. (2022). An IoT-Platform-Based Deep Learning System for Human Behavior Recognition in Smart City Monitoring Using the Berkeley MHAD Datasets. *Systems*, 2022(10), 177. doi:10.3390ystems10050177

Kononenko, I. (2001). Machine learning for medical diagnosis: History, state of the art and perspective. *Artificial Intelligence in Medicine*, 23(1), 89–109. doi:10.1016/S0933-3657(01)00077-X PMID:11470218

Kumar, A., Sharma, K., Singh, H., Srikanth, P., Krishnamurthi, R., & Nayyar, A. (2021). Drone-based social distancing, sanitization, inspection, monitoring, and control room for COVID-19. *artificial intelligence and machine learning for covid-19*, 153-173.

Li, H., Zhao, W., Zhang, Y., & Zio, E. (2020). Remaining useful life prediction using multi-scale deep convolutional neural network. *Applied Soft Computing*, 89, 106113. doi:10.1016/j.asoc.2020.106113

Li, X., Huang, X., Li, C., Yu, R., & Shu, L. (2019). EdgeCare: Leveraging edge computing for collaborative data management in mobile healthcare systems. *IEEE Access : Practical Innovations, Open Solutions*, 7, 22011–22025. doi:10.1109/ACCESS.2019.2898265

Lina, E. A., Elmustafa, S. A., & Rania, A. (2022). Deep and Reinforcement Learning Technologies on Internet of Vehicle (IoV) Applications: Current Issues and Future Trends. *Journal of Advanced Transportation*, 2022, 1947886. doi:10.1155/2022/1947886

Lurie, N., Manolio, T., Patterson, A. P., Collins, F., & Frieden, T. (2013). Research as a part of public health emergency response. *The New England Journal of Medicine*, 368(13), 1251–1255. doi:10.1056/NEJMsb1209510 PMID:23534565

Magna, A. A. R., Allende-Cid, H., Taramasco, C., Becerra, C., & Figueroa, R. L. (2020). Application of machine learning and word embeddings in the classification of cancer diagnosis using patient anamnesis. *IEEE Access : Practical Innovations, Open Solutions*, 8, 106198–106213. doi:10.1109/ACCESS.2020.3000075

Mamoon, S. M., Ahmed, E. S. A., Saeed, R. A., & Azim, M. A. (2022). Green machine learning protocols for cellular communication. In *Green Machine Learning Protocols for Future Communication Networks* (pp. 15–62). CRC Press.

Mamoon, S. M., & Kamrul, H. (2022). Preserving Privacy of User Identity Based on Pseudonym Variable in 5G. *Computers, Materials & Continua*, 70(3).

Mamoon, S. M., Saeed, R. A., Gaid, A. S., Mokhtar, R. A., Khalifa, O. O., & Ahmed, Z. E. (2023, August). Attacks Detection in 6G Wireless Networks using Machine Learning. In *2023 9th International Conference on Computer and Communication Engineering (ICCCE)* (pp. 6-11). IEEE.

Manogaran, G., Thota, C., Lopez, D., & Sundarasekar, R. (2017). Big data security intelligence for healthcare industry 4.0. *Cybersecurity for Industry 4.0: Analysis for Design and Manufacturing*, 103-126.

Mansour, R. F., Alfar, N. M., Abdel-Khalek, S., Abdelhaq, M., Saeed, R. A., & Alsaqour, R. (2022). Optimal deep learning based fusion model for biomedical image classification. *Expert Systems: International Journal of Knowledge Engineering and Neural Networks*, 39(3), e12764. doi:10.1111/exsy.12764

Mbunge, E., Muchemwa, B., & Batani, J. (2021). Sensors and healthcare 5.0: Transformative shift in virtual care through emerging digital health technologies. *Global Health Journal (Amsterdam, Netherlands)*, 5(4), 169–177. doi:10.1016/j.glohj.2021.11.008

Mills, E. H. A., Aasbjerg, K., Hansen, S. M., Ringgren, K. B., Dahl, M., Rasmussen, B. S., Torp-Pedersen, C., Søgaard, P., & Kragholm, K. (2019). Prehospital time and mortality in patients requiring a highest priority emergency medical response: A Danish registry-based cohort study. *BMJ Open*, 9(11), e023049. doi:10.1136/bmjopen-2018-023049 PMID:31753864

Mohammed, S. M. (2023). Task Reverse Offloading with Deep Reinforcement Learning in Multi-Access Edge Computing. In *2023 9th International Conference on Computer and Communication Engineering (ICCCE)* (pp. 322-327). IEEE.

Mohammed S. M., Ali, E. S., & Saeed, R. A. (2023). Data-Driven Techniques and Security Issues in Wireless Networks. *Data-Driven Intelligence in Wireless Networks: Concepts, Solutions, and Applications*, 107.

Mohammed, S. M., Saeed, R. A., Azim, M. A., Ali, E. S., Mokhtar, R. A., & Khalifa, O. (2022, May). Green Machine Learning Approach for QoS Improvement in Cellular Communications. In *2022 IEEE 2nd International Maghreb Meeting of the Conference on Sciences and Techniques of Automatic Control and Computer Engineering (MI-STA)* (pp. 523-528). IEEE.

Mohanty, S. N., Ravindra, J. V. R., Narayana, G. S., Pattnaik, C. R., & Sirajudeen, Y. M. (Eds.). (2023). *Drone Technology: Future Trends and Practical Applications*. John Wiley & Sons. doi:10.1002/9781394168002

Mona, H. B., Elmustafa, S. A., & Saeed, R. A. (2021). Machine Learning for Industrial IoT Systems. In J. Zhao & V. Vinoth Kumar (Eds.), *Handbook of Research on Innovations and Applications of AI, IoT, and Cognitive Technologies* (pp. 336–358). IGI Global. doi:10.4018/978-1-7998-6870-5.ch023

Moradi, M., Bokani, A., & Hassan, J. (2020). *Energy-Efficient and QoS-aware UAV Communication using Reactive RF Band Allocation*. 2020 30th International Telecommunication Networks and Applications Conference (ITNAC), Melbourne, VIC, Australia. 10.1109/ITNAC50341.2020.9315157

Moradi, S., Bokani, A., & Hassan, J. (2022). *UAV-based Smart Agriculture: a Review of UAV Sensing and Applications*. 2022 32nd International Telecommunication Networks and Applications Conference (ITNAC), Wellington, New Zealand. 10.1109/ITNAC55475.2022.9998411

Motlagh, N. H., Kortoçi, P., Su, X., Lovén, L., Hoel, H. K., Haugsvær, S. B., Srivastava, V., Gulbrandsen, C. F., Nurmi, P., & Tarkoma, S. (2023). Unmanned Aerial Vehicles for Air Pollution Monitoring: A survey. *IEEE Internet of Things Journal*, 1. doi:10.1109/JIOT.2023.3290508

Mourtzis, D., Angelopoulos, J., & Panopoulos, N. (2021). Smart manufacturing and tactile internet based on 5G in industry 4.0: Challenges, applications and new trends. *Electronics (Basel)*, *10*(24), 3175. doi:10.3390/electronics10243175

Muehlematter, U. J., Daniore, P., & Vokinger, K. N. (2021). Approval of artificial intelligence and machine learning-based medical devices in the USA and Europe (2015–20): A comparative analysis. *The Lancet. Digital Health*, *3*(3), e195–e203. doi:10.1016/S2589-7500(20)30292-2 PMID:33478929

Muhammad, G., Alqahtani, S., & Alelaiwi, A. (2021). Pandemic management for diseases similar to COVID-19 using deep learning and 5G communications. *IEEE Network*, *35*(3), 21–26. doi:10.1109/MNET.011.2000739

Mukati, N., Namdev, N., Dilip, R., Hemalatha, N., Dhiman, V., & Sahu, B. (2023). Healthcare assistance to COVID-19 patient using internet of things (IoT) enabled technologies. *Materials Today: Proceedings*, *80*, 3777–3781. doi:10.1016/j.matpr.2021.07.379 PMID:34336599

Nada, M., & Kamrul, H. (2022). Internet of vehicle's resource management in 5G networks using AI technologies: Current status and trends. *IET Communications*, *16*(5), 400–420. doi:10.1049/cmu2.12315

Najafabadi, M. M., Villanustre, F., Khoshgoftaar, T. M., Seliya, N., Wald, R., & Muharemagic, E. (2015). Deep learning applications and challenges in big data analytics. *Journal of Big Data*, *2*(1), 1–21. doi:10.118640537-014-0007-7

Ndiaye, M., Salhi, S., & Madani, B. (2020). When green technology meets optimization modeling: the case of routing drones in logistics, agriculture, and healthcare. *Modeling and Optimization in Green Logistics*, 127-145.

Nedelea, P. L., Popa, T. O., Manolescu, E., Bouros, C., Grigorasi, G., Andritoi, D., Pascale, C., Andrei, A., & Cimpoesu, D. C. (2022). Telemedicine System Applicability Using Drones in Pandemic Emergency Medical Situations. *Electronics (Basel)*, *11*(14), 2160. doi:10.3390/electronics11142160

Nikhat, A., & Yusuf, P. (2020). The internet of nano things (IoNT) existing state and future Prospects. *GSC Advanced Research and Reviews*, *5*(2), 131–150. doi:10.30574/gscarr.2020.5.2.0110

Norgeot, B., Glicksberg, B. S., & Butte, A. J. (2019). A call for deep-learning healthcare. *Nature Medicine*, *25*(1), 14–15. doi:10.103841591-018-0320-3 PMID:30617337

Nyaaba, A. A., & Ayamga, M. (2021). Intricacies of medical drones in healthcare delivery: Implications for Africa. *Technology in Society*, *66*, 101624. doi:10.1016/j.techsoc.2021.101624

Olatomiwa, L., Blanchard, R., Mekhilef, S., & Akinyele, D. (2018). Hybrid renewable energy supply for rural healthcare facilities: An approach to quality healthcare delivery. *Sustainable Energy Technologies and Assessments*, *30*, 121–138. doi:10.1016/j.seta.2018.09.007

Ortega, J. H. J. C., Resureccion, M. R., Natividad, L. R. Q., Bantug, E. T., Lagman, A. C., & Lopez, S. R. (2020). An analysis of classification of breast cancer dataset using J48 algorithm. *Int. J. Adv. Trends Comput. Sci. Eng, 9*.

Othman, O. (2022). Vehicle Detection for Vision-Based Intelligent Transportation Systems Using Convolutional Neural Network Algorithm. *Journal of Advanced Transportation, 2022*, 9189600. doi:10.1155/2022/9189600

Oueida, S., Kotb, Y., Aloqaily, M., Jararweh, Y., & Baker, T. (2018). An edge computing based smart healthcare framework for resource management. *Sensors (Basel), 18*(12), 4307. doi:10.339018124307 PMID:30563267

Palladino, N. (2023). A 'biased' emerging governance regime for artificial intelligence? How AI ethics get skewed moving from principles to practices. *Telecommunications Policy, 47*(5), 102479. doi:10.1016/j.telpol.2022.102479

Panesar, A. (2019). *Machine learning and AI for healthcare*. Apress. doi:10.1007/978-1-4842-3799-1

Pathak, P., Damle, M., Pal, P. R., & Yadav, V. (2019). Humanitarian impact of drones in healthcare and disaster management. *Int. J. Recent Technol. Eng, 7*(5), 201–205.

Poljak, M., & Šterbenc, A. J. C. M. (2020). Use of drones in clinical microbiology and infectious diseases: Current status, challenges and barriers. *Clinical Microbiology and Infection, 26*(4), 425–430. doi:10.1016/j.cmi.2019.09.014 PMID:31574337

Pourdowlat, G., Panahi, P., Pooransari, P., & Ghorbani, F. (2020). Prophylactic recommendation for healthcare workers in COVID-19 pandemic. *Frontiers in Emergency Medicine, 4*(2s), e39–e39.

Pustokhina, I. V., Pustokhin, D. A., Gupta, D., Khanna, A., Shankar, K., & Nguyen, G. N. (2020). An effective training scheme for deep neural network in edge computing enabled Internet of medical things (IoMT) systems. *IEEE Access : Practical Innovations, Open Solutions, 8*, 107112–107123. doi:10.1109/ACCESS.2020.3000322

Qin, J., Chen, L., Liu, Y., Liu, C., Feng, C., & Chen, B. (2019). A machine learning methodology for diagnosing chronic kidney disease. *IEEE Access : Practical Innovations, Open Solutions, 8*, 20991–21002. doi:10.1109/ACCESS.2019.2963053

Qomariah, D. U. N., Tjandrasa, H., & Fatichah, C. (2019, July). Classification of diabetic retinopathy and normal retinal images using CNN and SVM. In *2019 12th International Conference on Information & Communication Technology and System (ICTS)* (pp. 152-157). IEEE. 10.1109/ICTS.2019.8850940

Rania, S. A., Sara, A. M., Rania, A. M., Elmustafa, S. A., & Saeed, R. A. (2020). *IoE Design Principles and Architecture; Book: Internet of Energy for Smart Cities: Machine Learning Models and Techniques*. CRC Press Publisher. doi:10.4018/978-1-7998-5101-1

Rashid, A. S., Mohammed, A., & Rania, A. M. (2014). "Machine-to-Machine Communication", IGI Global, Encyclopedia of Information Science and Technology, Third Edition, , pp. 152-157). IEEE. 6195-6206. doi:10.4018/978-1-4666-5888-2

Ray, P. P., Dash, D., & De, D. (2019). Edge computing for Internet of Things: A survey, e-healthcare case study and future direction. *Journal of Network and Computer Applications*, *140*, 1–22. doi:10.1016/j.jnca.2019.05.005

Ricciardi, C., Ponsiglione, A. M., Scala, A., Borrelli, A., Misasi, M., Romano, G., Russo, G., Triassi, M., & Improta, G. (2022). Machine learning and regression analysis to model the length of hospital stay in patients with femur fracture. *Bioengineering (Basel, Switzerland)*, *9*(4), 172. doi:10.3390/bioengineering9040172 PMID:35447732

Riswantini, D., & Nugraheni, E. (2022). Machine learning in handling disease outbreaks: A comprehensive review. *Bulletin of Electrical Engineering and Informatics*, *11*(4), 2169–2186. doi:10.11591/eei.v11i4.3612

Rofida, O. D., Rashid, A. S., Mohammad, K. H., & Musse, M. (2017). Persistent Overload Control for Backlogged Machine to Machine Communications in Long Term Evolution Advanced Networks [JTEC]. *Journal of Telecommunication, Electronic and Computer Engineering*, *9*(3).

Saeed, F., Mehmood, A., Majeed, M. F., Maple, C., Saeed, K., Khattak, M. K., Wang, H., & Epiphaniou, G. (2021). Smart delivery and retrieval of swab collection kit for COVID-19 test using autonomous Unmanned Aerial Vehicles. *Physical Communication*, *48*, 101373. doi:10.1016/j.phycom.2021.101373

Saeed, M. M., Hasan, M. K., Obaid, A. J., Saeed, R. A., Mokhtar, R. A., Ali, E. S., Akhtaruzzaman, M., Amanlou, S., & Hossain, A. Z. (2022). A comprehensive review on the users' identity privacy for 5G networks. *IET Communications*, *16*(5), 384–399. doi:10.1049/cmu2.12327

Saeed, M. M., Saeed, R. A., Abdelhaq, M., Alsaqour, R., Hasan, M. K., & Mokhtar, R. A. (2023). Anomaly Detection in 6G Networks Using Machine Learning Methods. *Electronics (Basel)*, *12*(15), 3300. doi:10.3390/electronics12153300

Saeed, M. M., Saeed, R. A., Mokhtar, R. A., Alhumyani, H., & Ali, E. S. (2022). A novel variable pseudonym scheme for preserving privacy user location in 5G networks. *Security and Communication Networks*, *2022*, 2022. doi:10.1155/2022/7487600

Saeed, R. A., Saeed, M. M., Mokhtar, R. A., Alhumyani, H., & Abdel-Khalek, S. (2021). Pseudonym Mutable Based Privacy for 5G User Identity. *Computer Systems Science and Engineering*, *39*(1). Advance online publication. doi:10.32604/csse.2021.015593

Salehi, S., Bokani, A., Hassan, J., & Kanhere, S. S. (2019). *AETD: An Application-Aware, Energy-Efficient Trajectory Design for Flying Base Stations.* 2019 IEEE 14th Malaysia International Conference on Communication (MICC), Selangor, Malaysia, pp. 19-24, 10.1109/MICC48337.2019.9037587

Salehi, S., Hassan, J., & Bokani, A. (2022) "An Optimal Multi-UAV Deployment Model for UAV-assisted Smart Farming," 2022 IEEE Region 10 Symposium (TENSYMP), Mumbai, India, pp. 1-6, 10.1109/TENSYMP54529.2022.9864512

Santoso, L. F., Baqai, F., Gwozdz, M., Lange, J., Rosenberger, M. G., Sulzer, J., & Paydarfar, D. (2019, July). Applying machine learning algorithms for automatic detection of swallowing from sound. In *2019 41st Annual International Conference of the IEEE Engineering in Medicine and Biology Society (EMBC)* (pp. 2584-2588). IEEE] 10.1109/EMBC.2019.8857937

Sayed, E. A., Hassan, M. B., & Sae ed, R. A. (2021). Machine Learning Technologies on Internet of Vehicles. In N. Magaia, G. Mastorakis, C. Mavromoustakis, E. Pallis, & E. K. Markakis (Eds.), *Intelligent Technologies for Internet of Vehicles. Internet of Things (Technology, Communications, and Computing)*. Springer., doi:10.1007/978-3-030-76493-7_7

Schneller, E., Abdulsalam, Y., Conway, K., & Eckler, J. (2023). *Strategic management of the health care supply chain*. John Wiley & Sons.

Şerban, O., Thapen, N., Maginnis, B., Hankin, C., & Foot, V. (2019). Real-time processing of social media with SENTINEL: A syndromic surveillance system incorporating deep learning for health classification. *Information Processing & Management*, 56(3), 1166–1184. doi:10.1016/j.ipm.2018.04.011

Shankar, K., Lakshmanaprabu, S. K., Gupta, D., Maseleno, A., & De Albuquerque, V. H. C. (2020). Optimal feature-based multi-kernel SVM approach for thyroid disease classification. *The Journal of Supercomputing*, 76(2), 1128–1143. doi:10.100711227-018-2469-4

Sivakami, K., & Saraswathi, N. (2015). Mining big data: Breast cancer prediction using DT-SVM hybrid model. [IJSEAS]. *International Journal of Scientific Engineering and Applied Science*, 1(5), 418–429.

Sobnath, D. D., Philip, N., Kayyali, R., Nabhani-Gebara, S., Pierscionek, B., Vaes, A. W., Spruit, M. A., & Kaimakamis, E. (2017). Features of a mobile support app for patients with chronic obstructive pulmonary disease: Literature review and current applications. *JMIR mHealth and uHealth*, 5(2), e4951. doi:10.2196/mhealth.4951 PMID:28219878

Sodhro, A. H., Luo, Z., Sangaiah, A. K., & Baik, S. W. (2019). Mobile edge computing based QoS optimization in medical healthcare applications. *International Journal of Information Management*, 45, 308–318. doi:10.1016/j.ijinfomgt.2018.08.004

Subha, R., Nayana, B. R., & Selvadass, M. (2022, December). Hybrid Machine Learning Model Using Particle Swarm Optimization for Effectual Diagnosis of Alzheimer's Disease from Handwriting. In *2022 4th International Conference on Circuits, Control, Communication and Computing (I4C)* (pp. 491-495). IEEE.

Tahir, M. N., Lan, Y., Zhang, Y., Wenjiang, H., Wang, Y., & Naqvi, S. M. Z. A. (2023). Application of unmanned aerial vehicles in precision agriculture. In *Precision Agriculture* (pp. 55–70). Academic Press. doi:10.1016/B978-0-443-18953-1.00001-5

Taiwo, O., & Ezugwu, A. E. (2020). Smart healthcare support for remote patient monitoring during covid-19 quarantine. *Informatics in Medicine Unlocked*, 20, 100428. doi:10.1016/j.imu.2020.100428 PMID:32953970

Tan, M., Xu, Y., Gao, Z., Yuan, T., Liu, Q., Yang, R., Zhang, B., & Peng, L. (2022). Recent advances in intelligent wearable medical devices integrating biosensing and drug delivery. *Advanced Materials*, 34(27), 2108491. doi:10.1002/adma.202108491 PMID:35008128

Tigga, N. P., & Garg, S. (2020). Prediction of type 2 diabetes using machine learning classification methods. *Procedia Computer Science*, 167, 706–716. doi:10.1016/j.procs.2020.03.336

Uddin, M. Z. (2019). A wearable sensor-based activity prediction system to facilitate edge computing in smart healthcare system. *Journal of Parallel and Distributed Computing, 123*, 46–53. doi:10.1016/j.jpdc.2018.08.010

Ullah, Z., Al-Turjman, F., Mostarda, L., & Gagliardi, R. (2020). Applications of artificial intelligence and machine learning in smart cities. *Computer Communications, 154*, 313–323. doi:10.1016/j.comcom.2020.02.069

Valavanis, K. P. (Ed.). (2008). *Advances in unmanned aerial vehicles: state of the art and the road to autonomy.*

Vembandasamy, K., Sasipriya, R., & Deepa, E. (2015). Heart diseases detection using Naive Bayes algorithm. *International Journal of Innovative Science. Engineering & Technology, 2*(9), 441–444.

Venkatesan, E. V., & Velmurugan, T. (2015). Performance analysis of decision tree algorithms for breast cancer classification. *Indian Journal of Science and Technology, 8*(29), 1–8. doi:10.17485/ijst/2015/v8i1/84646

Wiens, J., Saria, S., Sendak, M., Ghassemi, M., Liu, V. X., Doshi-Velez, F., Jung, K., Heller, K., Kale, D., Saeed, M., Ossorio, P. N., Thadaney-Israni, S., & Goldenberg, A. (2019). Do no harm: A roadmap for responsible machine learning for health care. *Nature Medicine, 25*(9), 1337–1340. doi:10.103841591-019-0548-6 PMID:31427808

Wootton, R. (2008). Telemedicine support for the developing world. *Journal of Telemedicine and Telecare, 14*(3), 109–114. doi:10.1258/jtt.2008.003001 PMID:18430271

Xu, L., Sanders, L., Li, K., & Chow, J. C. (2021). Chatbot for health care and oncology applications using artificial intelligence and machine learning: Systematic review. *JMIR Cancer, 7*(4), e27850. doi:10.2196/27850 PMID:34847056

Yao, H., Qin, R., & Chen, X. (2019). Unmanned aerial vehicle for remote sensing applications—A review. *Remote Sensing (Basel), 11*(12), 1443. doi:10.3390/rs11121443

Compilation of References

Abakar, M. A. (2010). *The challenges of wireless internet access in vehicular environments.* Proceeding of the 3rd International Conference on Information and Communication Technology for the Moslem World (ICT4M) 2010, Jakarta, Indonesia. 10.1109/ICT4M.2010.5971899

Abang Abdurahman, A. Z., Wan Yaacob, W. F., Md Nasir, S. A., Jaya, S., & Mokhtar, S. (2022). Using Machine Learning to Predict Visitors to Totally Protected Areas in Sarawak, Malaysia. *Sustainability (Basel)*, *14*(5), 2735. doi:10.3390u14052735

Abbas, A., & Rania, A. (2021). Quality of Services Based on Intelligent IoT WLAN MAC Protocol Dynamic Real-Time Applications in Smart Cities. Computational Intelligence and Neuroscience. Hindawi. doi:10.1155/2021/2287531

Abdelgadir, M. (2016). Vehicular Ad-hoc Networks (VANETs) dynamic performance estimation routing model for city scenarios. *2016 International Conference on Information Science and Communications Technologies (ICISCT)*, Tashkent, Uzbekistan. 10.1109/ICISCT.2016.7777397

Abdelhaleem, R.S., Omri, M., Abdel-Khalek, S. et al. (2022), Optimal path planning for drones based on swarm intelligence algorithm. *Neural Comput & Applic.* doi:10.1007/s00521-022-06998-9

Abdel-Razeq, S., Shakhatreh, H., Alenezi, A., Sawalmeh, A., Anan, M., & Almutiry, M. (2021). PSO-based UAV deployment and dynamic power allocation for UAV-enabled uplink NOMA network. *Wireless Communications and Mobile Computing*, *2021*, 1–17. doi:10.1155/2021/2722887

Abdulameer, M. H., Ahmed, H. W., & Ahmed, I. S. (2022). Bird Image Dataset Classification using Deep Convolutional Neural Network Algorithm. *2022 International Conference on Data Science and Intelligent Computing, ICDSIC 2022*, (pp. 81–86). IEEE. 10.1109/ICDSIC56987.2022.10075724

Abdulridha, J., Ampatzidis, Y., Kakarla, S. C., & Roberts, P. (2020). Detection of target spot and bacterial spot diseases in tomato using UAV-based and benchtop-based hyperspectral imaging techniques. *Precision Agriculture*, *21*(5), 955–978. doi:10.100711119-019-09703-4

Abir, S. A. A., Islam, S. N., Anwar, A., Mahmood, A. N., & Oo, A. M. T. (2020). Building resilience against COVID-19 pandemic using artificial intelligence, machine learning, and IoT: A survey of recent progress. *IoT*, *1*(2), 506–528. doi:10.3390/iot1020028

Adams, K., Broad, A., Ruiz-García, D., & Davis, A. R. (2020). Continuous wildlife monitoring using blimps as an aerial platform: A case study observing marine megafauna. *Australian Zoologist*, *40*(3), 407–415. doi:10.7882/AZ.2020.004

Adarsh, M. S., Aaron, B., Shubhang, B., Sumathi, V., Sakthivel, G., & Jegadeeshwaran, R. (2023, July). AI enabled drones for detecting injured animals in wildlife. In AIP Conference Proceedings. AIP Publishing. doi:10.1063/5.0149348

Afghah, F., Razi, A., Chakareski, J., & Ashdown, J. (2019, April). Wildfire monitoring in remote areas using autonomous unmanned aerial vehicles. In *IEEE INFOCOM 2019-IEEE Conference on Computer Communications Workshops (INFOCOM WKSHPS)* (pp. 835-840). IEEE. 10.1109/INFOCOMW.2019.8845309

Afghah, F., Zaeri-Amirani, M., Razi, A., Chakareski, J., & Bentley, E. (2018, June). A coalition formation approach to coordinated task allocation in heterogeneous UAV networks. In *2018 Annual American Control Conference (ACC)* (pp. 5968-5975). IEEE. 10.23919/ACC.2018.8431278

Agri, U., Chaudhary, P., Sharma, A., & Kukreti, B. (2022). Physiological response of maize plants and its rhizospheric microbiome under the influence of potential bioinoculants and nanochitosan. *Plant and Soil*, *474*(1-2), 451–468. doi:10.100711104-022-05351-2

Ahakonye, L. A. C., Nwakanma, C. I., Ajakwe, S. O., Lee, J. M., & Kim, D. S. (2022, February). Countering DNS vulnerability to attacks using ensemble learning. In *2022 International Conference on Artificial Intelligence in Information and Communication (ICAIIC)* (pp. 007-010). IEEE.

Ahilan, S., & Dayan, P. (2019). *Feudal Multi-Agent Hierarchies for Cooperative Reinforcement Learning*. ArXiv.

Ahmad, A., Ordoñez, J., Cartujo, P., & Martos, V. (2020). Remotely piloted aircraft (RPA) in agriculture: A pursuit of sustainability. *Agronomy (Basel)*, *11*(1), 7. doi:10.3390/agronomy11010007

Ahmad, M., Abdullah, M., Moon, H., & Han, D. (2021). Plant disease detection in imbalanced datasets using efficient convolutional neural networks with stepwise transfer learning. *IEEE Access : Practical Innovations, Open Solutions*, *9*, 140565–140580. doi:10.1109/ACCESS.2021.3119655

Ahmed, E., Rashid, A., Sheetal, N., & Amitava, M. (2020). Energy Optimization in LPWANs by using Heuristic Techniques. LPWAN Technologies for IoT and M2M Applications. Elsevier.

Ahmed, F., Mohanta, J. C., Keshari, A., & Yadav, P. S. (2022). Recent Advances in Unmanned Aerial Vehicles: A Review. *Arabian Journal for Science and Engineering*, *47*(7), 7963–7984. doi:10.100713369-022-06738-0 PMID:35492958

Ahmed, N., Pawase, C. J., & Chang, K. (2021). Distributed 3-D path planning for multi-UAVs with full area surveillance based on particle swarm optimization. *Applied Sciences (Basel, Switzerland)*, *11*(8), 3417. doi:10.3390/app11083417

Ahmed, Z. E. (2022). Optimization Procedure for Intelligent Internet of Things Applications. *2022 International Conference on Business Analytics for Technology and Security (ICBATS)*, Dubai, United Arab Emirates. 10.1109/ICBATS54253.2022.9759065

Aiken, L. H., Sermeus, W., Van den Heede, K., Sloane, D. M., Busse, R., McKee, M., Bruyneel, L., Rafferty, A. M., Griffiths, P., Moreno-Casbas, M. T., Tishelman, C., Scott, A., Brzostek, T., Kinnunen, J., Schwendimann, R., Heinen, M., Zikos, D., Sjetne, I. S., Smith, H. L., & Kutney-Lee, A. (2012). Patient safety, satisfaction, and quality of hospital care: Cross sectional surveys of nurses and patients in 12 countries in Europe and the United States. *BMJ (Clinical Research Ed.)*, *344*(mar20 2), 344. doi:10.1136/bmj.e1717 PMID:22434089

Ajakwe, S. O., Ihekoronye, V. U., Ajakwe, I. U., Jun, T., Kim, D. S., & Lee, J. M. (2022a, October). Connected Intelligence for Smart Water Quality Monitoring System in IIoT. In *2022 13th International Conference on Information and Communication Technology Convergence (ICTC)* (pp. 2386-2391). IEEE. 10.1109/ICTC55196.2022.9952785

Ajakwe, S. O., Ihekoronye, V. U., Ajakwe, I. U., Jun, T., Kim, D. S., & Lee, J. M. (2022e). Connected Intelligence for Smart Water Quality Monitoring System in IIoT. *In 2022 13th International Conference on Information and Communication Technology Convergence (ICTC)* (pp. 2386-2391). IEEE.

Ajakwe, S. O., Ihekoronye, V. U., Kim, D. S., & Lee, J. M. (2022, September). Tractable minacious drones aerial recognition and safe-channel neutralization scheme for mission critical operations. In *2022 IEEE 27th International Conference on Emerging Technologies and Factory Automation (ETFA)* (pp. 1-8). IEEE. 10.1109/ETFA52439.2022.9921494

Ajakwe, S. O., Ihekoronye, V. U., Kim, D. S., & Lee, J. M. (2022d). Pervasive intrusion detection scheme to mitigate sensor attacks on UAV Networks. *In 2022 Korean Institute of Communication and Information Sciences (KICS) summer conference,* 1267-1268.

Ajakwe, S. O., Ihekoronye, V. U., Kim, D. S., & Lee, J. M. (2022e, October). SimNet: UAV-integrated sensor nodes localization for communication intelligence in 6G networks. In *2022 27th Asia Pacific Conference on Communications (APCC)* (pp. 344-347). IEEE.

Ajakwe, S. O., Ajakwe, I. U., Jun, T., Kim, D. S., & Lee, J. M. (2023c). CIS-WQMS: Connected intelligence smart water quality monitoring scheme. *Internet of Things : Engineering Cyber Physical Human Systems*, *23*, 100800. doi:10.1016/j.iot.2023.100800

Ajakwe, S. O., Ihekoronye, V. U., Kim, D. S., & Lee, J. M. (2022b). DRONET: Multi-tasking framework for real-time industrial facility aerial surveillance and safety. *Drones (Basel)*, *6*(2), 46. doi:10.3390/drones6020046

Ajakwe, S. O., Ihekoronye, V. U., Kim, D. S., & Lee, J. M. (2022c). AI-trust in intelligent autonomous decision-centric systems: Introspection of security architectures. 1–2. *In 2022 Korean Institute of Communication and Information Science*. NIH.

Ajakwe, S. O., Ihekoronye, V. U., Kim, D. S., & Lee, J. M. (2023a). ALIEN: Assisted Learning Invasive Encroachment Neutralization for Secured Drone Transportation System. *Sensors (Basel)*, *23*(3), 1233. doi:10.339023031233 PMID:36772272

Ajakwe, S. O., Ihekoronye, V. U., Mohtasin, G., Akter, R., Aouto, A., Kim, D. S., & Lee, J. M. (2022f). *VisioDECT Dataset: An Aerial Dataset for Scenario-Based Multi-Drone Detection and Identification*. IEEE Dataport.

Ajakwe, S. O., Kim, D. S., & Lee, J. M. (2023d). Drone Transportation System: Systematic Review of Security Dynamics for Smart Mobility. *IEEE Internet of Things Journal*, *10*(16), 14462–14482. doi:10.1109/JIOT.2023.3266843

Ajakwe, S. O., Nwakanma, C. I., Lee, J. M., & Kim, D. S. (2020, October). Machine learning algorithm for intelligent prediction for military logistics and planning. In *2020 International Conference on Information and Communication Technology Convergence (ICTC)* (pp. 417-419). IEEE. 10.1109/ICTC49870.2020.9289286

Ajakwe, S., Kim, D. S., & Lee, J. M. (2023b). Radicalization of Airspace Security: Prospects and Botheration of Drone Defense System Technology. *The Journal of Intelligence, Conflict, and Warfare*, *6*(1), 23–48. doi:10.21810/jicw.v6i1.5274

Akhloufi, M. A., Couturier, A., & Castro, N. A. (2021). Unmanned aerial vehicles for wildland fires: Sensing, perception, cooperation and assistance. *Drones (Basel)*, *5*(1), 15. doi:10.3390/drones5010015

Alaa, M. (2022). Performance Evaluation of Downlink Coordinated Multipoint Joint Transmission under Heavy IoT Traffic Load. Wireless Communications and Mobile Computing. IEEE. doi:10.1155/2022/6837780

Alanezi, M. A., Shahriar, M. S., Hasan, M. B., Ahmed, S., Yusuf, A., & Bouchekara, H. R. (2022). Livestock management with unmanned aerial vehicles: A review. *IEEE Access : Practical Innovations, Open Solutions*, *10*, 45001–45028. doi:10.1109/ACCESS.2022.3168295

Alatabani, L. E., & Ali, E. S. (2021). Deep Learning Approaches for IoV Applications and Services. In N. Magaia, G. Mastorakis, C. Mavromoustakis, E. Pallis, & E. K. Markakis (Eds.), *Intelligent Technologies for Internet of Vehicles. Internet of Things (Technology, Communications, and Computing)*. Springer. doi:10.1007/978-3-030-76493-7_8

Alawi, M. A. (2012). Cluster-based multi-hop vehicular communication with multi-metric optimization. *2012 International Conference on Computer and Communication Engineering (ICCCE)*, (pp. 22-27). Springer. 10.1109/ICCCE.2012.6271145

Albawi, S., Mohammed, T. A., & Al-Zawi, S. (2017, August). Understanding of a convolutional neural network. In 2017 international conference on engineering and technology (ICET) (pp. 1-6). IEEE. doi:10.1109/ICEngTechnol.2017.8308186

Alejo, D., & Cobano, J. A. (2014). Optimal Reciprocal Collision Avoidance with mobile and static obstacles for multi-UAV systems. In *2014 International Conference on Unmanned Aircraft Systems (ICUAS)*. IEEE. 10.1109/ICUAS.2014.6842383

Al-Hourani, A., Kandeepan, S., & Lardner, S. (2014). Optimal LAP Altitude for Maximum Coverage. *IEEE Wireless Communications Letters*, *3*(6), 569–572. doi:10.1109/LWC.2014.2342736

Ali, E. S., & Hassan, M. B. (2021). Machine Learning Technologies on Internet of Vehicles. In N. Magaia, G. Mastorakis, C. Mavromoustakis, E. Pallis, & E. K. Markakis (Eds.), *Intelligent Technologies for Internet of Vehicles. Internet of Things (Technology, Communications, and Computing)*. Springer. doi:10.1007/978-3-030-76493-7_7

Ali, R. A., Ali, E. S., & Mokhtar, R. A. (2022). Blockchain for IoT-Based Cyber-Physical Systems (CPS): Applications and Challenges. In D. De, S. Bhattacharyya, & J. J. P. C. Rodrigues (Eds.), *Blockchain-based Internet of Things. Lecture Notes on Data Engineering and Communications Technologies* (Vol. 112). Springer. doi:10.1007/978-981-16-9260-4_4

Aljalaud, F., Kurdi, H., & Youcef-Toumi, K. (2023). Bio-Inspired Multi-UAV Path Planning Heuristics: A Review. *Mathematics*, *11*(10), 2356. doi:10.3390/math11102356

Al-Kaisi, M., & Hanna, H. M. (2006, June 19). Field soil variability and its impact on crop stand uniformity. *Integrated Crop Management news*. https://works.bepress.com/mark_hanna/144/

Al-Khaffaf, H., Haron, F., Sarmady, S., Talib, A., & Abu-Sulyman, I. (2012). Crowd Parameter Extraction from Video at the Main Gates of Masjid al-Haram. In Advances in Intelligent and Soft Computing. Springer. doi:10.1007/978-3-642-27552-4_96

Almeida, J. S., Jagatheesaperumal, S. K., Nogueira, F. G., & Albuquerque, V. H. C. (2021). *EdgeFireSmoke++: A novel lightweight algorithm for real-time forest fire detection and visualization using internet of things-human machine interface*. Department of Electrical Engineering, Federal University of Ceará.

Almousa, O., Zhang, R., Dimma, M., Yao, J., Allen, A., Chen, L., Heidari, P., & Qayumi, K. (2021). Virtual reality technology and remote digital application for tele-simulation and global medical education: An innovative hybrid system for clinical training. *Simulation & Gaming*, *52*(5), 614–634. doi:10.1177/10468781211008258

Alqurashi, A., Alsolami, F., Abdel-Khalek, S., Sayed Ali, E., & Saeed, R. A. (2021). a; Abdel-Khalek, S.; (2021) 'Machine Learning Techniques in Internet of UAVs for Smart Cities Applications'. *Journal of Intelligent & Fuzzy Systems*, *42*(4), 1–24. doi:10.3233/JIFS-211009

Al-Smadi, Y., Alauthman, M., Al-Qerem, A., Aldweesh, A., Quaddoura, R., Aburub, F., Mansour, K., & Alhmiedat, T. (2023). Early Wildfire Smoke Detection Using Different YOLO Models. *Machines*, *11*(2), 246. doi:10.3390/machines11020246

Al-Wathinani, A. M., Alhallaf, M. A., Borowska-Stefańska, M., Wiśniewski, S., Sultan, M. A. S., Samman, O. Y., & Goniewicz, K. (2023, May). Elevating Healthcare: Rapid Literature Review on Drone Applications for Streamlining Disaster Management and Prehospital Care in Saudi Arabia. []. MDPI]. *Health Care*, *11*(11), 1575. PMID:37297715

Alzubi, J., Nayyar, A., & Kumar, A. (2018). Machine Learning from Theory to Algorithms: An Overview. *Journal of Physics: Conference Series*, *1142*, 012012. doi:10.1088/1742-6596/1142/1/012012

Amal, E. A. (2014). Vehicular Communication and Cellular Network Integration: Gateway Selection Perspective. *2014 International Conference on Computer and Communication Engineering*, Kuala Lumpur, Malaysia. 10.1109/ICCCE.2014.30

Amarasingam, N., Salgadoe, A. S. A., Powell, K., Gonzalez, L. F., & Natarajan, S. (2022). A review of UAV platforms, sensors, and applications for monitoring of sugarcane crops. *Remote Sensing Applications: Society and Environment, 26*, 100712. doi:10.1016/j.rsase.2022.100712

Amirgaliyev, Y., Shamiluulu, S., & Serek, A. (2018, October). Analysis of chronic kidney disease dataset by applying machine learning methods. In *2018 IEEE 12th International Conference on Application of Information and Communication Technologies (AICT)* (pp. 1-4). IEEE. 10.1109/ICAICT.2018.8747140

Amorosi, L., Chiaraviglio, L., & Galan-Jimenez, J. (2019). Optimal Energy Management of UAV-Based Cellular Networks Powered by Solar Panels and Batteries: Formulation and Solutions. *IEEE Access : Practical Innovations, Open Solutions, 7*, 53698–53717. doi:10.1109/ACCESS.2019.2913448

Ampatzidis, Y., Partel, V., & Costa, L. (2020). Agroview: Cloud-based application to process, analyze and visualize UAV-collected data for precision agriculture applications utilizing artificial intelligence. *Computers and Electronics in Agriculture, 174*, 105457. doi:10.1016/j.compag.2020.105457

Anbaroğlu, B. (2021). Drones in healthcare: An extended discussion on humanitarian logistics. In Research Anthology on Reliability and Safety in Aviation Systems, Spacecraft, and Air Transport (pp. 973-994). IGI Global.

Anderson, K., & Gaston, K. J. (2013). Lightweight Unmanned Aerial Vehicles Will Revolutionize Spatial Ecology. *Frontiers in Ecology and the Environment, 11*(3), 138–146. doi:10.1890/120150

Andrew, M. E., & Shephard, J. M. (2017). Semi-automated detection of eagle nests: An application of very high-resolution image data and advanced image analyses to wildlife surveys. *Remote Sensing in Ecology and Conservation, 3*(2), 66–80. doi:10.1002/rse2.38

Antonio, G.-P., & Maria-Dolores, C. (2022). Multi-Agent Deep Reinforcement Learning to Manage Connected Autonomous Vehicles at Tomorrow's Intersections. *IEEE Transactions on Vehicular Technology, 71*(7), 7033–7043. doi:10.1109/TVT.2022.3169907

Arbez, M., Birot, Y., & Carnus, J. M. (Eds.). (2002). Risk Management and Sustainable Forestry. In *EFI Proceedings No. 45*. European Forest Institute.

Arshad, M. A., Khan, S. H., Qamar, S., Khan, M. W., Murtza, I., Gwak, J., & Khan, A. (2022). Drone Navigation Using Region and Edge Exploitation-Based Deep CNN. *IEEE Access : Practical Innovations, Open Solutions, 10*, 95441–95450. doi:10.1109/ACCESS.2022.3204876

Asif, K., Jian, P. L., Mohammad, K. H., Naushad, V., Zulkefli, M., & Shayla, I., & (2022). PackerRobo: Model-based robot vision self-supervised learning in CART. *Alexandria Engineering Journal, 61*(12), 12549–12566. doi:10.1016/j.aej.2022.05.043

Askhedkar, A. R., Chaudhari, B. S., Abdelhaq, M., Alsaqour, R., Saeed, R., & Zennaro, M. (2023). LoRa Communication Using TVWS Frequencies: Range and Data Rate. *Future Internet, 2023*(15), 270. doi:10.3390/fi15080270

Aslan, M. F., Durdu, A., Sabanci, K., Ropelewska, E., & Gültekin, S. S. (2022). A comprehensive survey of the recent studies with UAV for precision agriculture in open fields and greenhouses. *Applied Sciences (Basel, Switzerland), 12*(3), 1047. doi:10.3390/app12031047

Asri, H., Mousannif, H., Al Moatassime, H., & Noel, T. (2016). Using machine learning algorithms for breast cancer risk prediction and diagnosis. *Procedia Computer Science, 83*, 1064–1069. doi:10.1016/j.procs.2016.04.224

Aswathy, R. H., Suresh, P., Sikkandar, M. Y., & Abdel-Khalek, S. (2022). Optimized Tuned Deep Learning Model for Chronic Kidney Disease Classification. *CMC-Computers. Materials & Continua, 70*(2), 2097–2111. doi:10.32604/cmc.2022.019790

Awais, M., Li, W., Cheema, M. J. M., Zaman, Q. U., Shaheen, A., Aslam, B., & Liu, C. (2022). UAV-based remote sensing in plant stress imagine using high-resolution thermal sensor for digital agriculture practices: A meta-review. *International Journal of Environmental Science and Technology, 20*(1), 1135–1152. doi:10.100713762-021-03801-5

Bacco, M., Brunori, G., Rolandi, S., & Scotti, I. (2022). Smart and sustainable food: What is ahead? In *Future Foods* (pp. 39–48). Academic Press. doi:10.1016/B978-0-323-91001-9.00015-3

Bae, S. M., Han, K. H., Cha, C. N., & Lee, H. Y. (2016). Development of Inventory Checking System Based on UAV and RFID in Open Storage Yard. *2016 International Conference on Information Science and Security (ICISS)*, (pp. 1–2). IEEE. 10.1109/ICISSEC.2016.7885849

Baig, T., & Shastry, C. (2023). Design of WSN Model with NS2 for Animal Tracking and Monitoring. *Procedia Computer Science, 218*, 2563–2574. doi:10.1016/j.procs.2023.01.230

Bakri Hassan, M., Saeed, R., Khalifa, O., Sayed Ali Ahmed, E., Mokhtar, R., & Hashim, A. (2022). *Green Machine Learning for Green Cloud Energy Efficiency*. IEEE. doi:10.1109/MI-STA54861.2022.9837531

Bakri, H., & Ali, E. (2021). Intelligent Internet of things in wireless networks. Intelligent Wireless Communications. IET Digital Library, doi:10.1049/PBTE094E_ch6

Bakri, H., & Elmustafa, S. (2021). Machine Learning for Industrial IoT Systems. In J. Zhao & V. Vinoth Kumar (Eds.), *Handbook of Research on Innovations and Applications of AI, IoT, and Cognitive Technologies* (pp. 336–358). IGI Global. doi:10.4018/978-1-7998-6870-5.ch023

Banda Chitsamatanga, B., & Malinga, W. (2021). 'A tale of two paradoxes in response to COVID-19': Public health system and socio-economic implications of the pandemic in South Africa and Zimbabwe. *Cogent Social Sciences, 7*(1), 1869368. doi:10.1080/23311886.2020.1869368

Barbedo, J. G. A., & Koenigkan, L. V. (2018). Perspectives on The Use of Unmanned Aerial Systems to Monitor Cattle. *Outlook on Agriculture, 47*(3), 214–222. doi:10.1177/0030727018781876

Barroso, P., Relimpio, D., Zearra, J. A., Cerón, J. J., Palencia, P., Cardoso, B., Ferreras, E., Escobar, M., Cáceres, G., López-Olvera, J. R., & Gortázar, C. (2023). Using integrated wildlife monitoring to prevent future pandemics through one health approach. *One Health, 16*. https://doi.org/ doi:10.1016/j.onehlt.2022.100479

Ben Ayed, R., & Hanana, M. (2021). Artificial intelligence to improve the food and agriculture sector. *Journal of Food Quality, 2021*, 1–7. doi:10.1155/2021/5584754

Berg, P., Maia, D. S., Pham, M. T., & Lefèvre, S. (2022). Weakly Supervised Detection of Marine Animals in High Resolution Aerial Images. *Remote Sensing (Basel), 14*(2), 339. doi:10.3390/rs14020339

Betts, J., Young, R. P., Hilton-Taylor, C., Hoffmann, M., Rodríguez, J. P., Stuart, S. N., & Milner-Gulland, E. J. (2020). A framework for evaluating the impact of the IUCN Red List of threatened species. *Conservation Biology, 34*(3), 632–643. doi:10.1111/cobi.13454 PMID:31876054

Beul, M., Droeschel, D., Nieuwenhuisen, M., Quenzel, J., Houben, S., & Behnke, S. (2018). Fast autonomous flight in warehouses for inventory applications. *IEEE Robotics and Automation Letters, 3*(4), 3121–3128. doi:10.1109/LRA.2018.2849833

Bezas, K., Tsoumanis, G., Angelis, C. T., & Oikonomou, K. (2022). Coverage path planning and point-of-interest detection using autonomous drone swarms. *Sensors (Basel)*, 22(19), 7551. doi:10.339022197551 PMID:36236651

Bhaskar, N., & Manikandan, S. (2019). A deep-learning-based system for automated sensing of chronic kidney disease. *IEEE Sensors Letters*, 3(10), 1–4. doi:10.1109/LSENS.2019.2942145

Bita, C. E., & Gerats, T. (2013). Plant tolerance to high temperature in a changing environment: Scientific fundamentals and production of heat stress-tolerant crops. *Frontiers in Plant Science*, 4, 273. doi:10.3389/fpls.2013.00273 PMID:23914193

Bithas, P. S., Michailidis, E. T., Nomikos, N., Vouyioukas, D., & Kanatas, A. G. (2019). A Survey on Machine-Learning Techniques for UAV-Based Communications. *Sensors (Basel)*, 19(23), 5170. doi:10.339019235170 PMID:31779133

Bi, Z., Guo, X., Wang, J., Qin, S., & Liu, G. (2023). Deep Reinforcement Learning for Truck-Drone Delivery Problem. *Drones (Basel)*, 7(7), 445. doi:10.3390/drones7070445

Bokani, A., Hassan, J., & Kanhere, S. S. (2018). *Enabling Efficient and High Quality Zooming for Online Video Streaming using Edge Computing*. 2018 28th International Telecommunication Networks and Applications Conference (ITNAC), Sydney, NSW, Australia. 10.1109/ATNAC.2018.8615166

Bono, G., Dibangoye, J. S., Matignon, L., Pereyron, F., & Simonin, O. (2019). Cooperative Multi-agent Policy Gradient. Springer. doi:10.1007/978-3-030-10925-7_28

Bor-Yaliniz, R. I., El-Keyi, A., & Yanikomeroglu, H. (2016, May 1). *Efficient 3-D placement of an aerial base station in next generation cellular networks*. IEEE Xplore. https://doi.org/ doi:10.1109/ICC.2016.7510820

Botrugno, C. (2021). Information technologies in healthcare: Enhancing or dehumanising doctor–patient interaction? *Health*, 25(4), 475–493. doi:10.1177/1363459319891213 PMID:31849239

Boudjit, K., & Ramzan, N. (2022). Human detection based on deep learning YOLO-v2 for real-time UAV applications. *Journal of Experimental & Theoretical Artificial Intelligence*, 34(3), 527–544. doi:10.1080/0952813X.2021.1907793

Bouguettaya, A., Zarzour, H., Kechida, A., & Taberkit, A. M. (2021, July). Recent advances on UAV and deep learning for early crop diseases identification: A short review. In *2021 International Conference on Information Technology (ICIT)* (pp. 334-339). IEEE. 10.1109/ICIT52682.2021.9491661

Bouguettaya, A., Zarzour, H., Kechida, A., & Taberkit, A. M. (2022). Deep learning techniques to classify agricultural crops through UAV imagery: A review. *Neural Computing & Applications*, 34(12), 9511–9536. doi:10.100700521-022-07104-9 PMID:35281624

Bouguettaya, A., Zarzour, H., Taberkit, A. M., & Kechida, A. (2022). A review on early wildfire detection from unmanned aerial vehicles using deep learning-based computer vision algorithms. In *Signal Processing* (Vol. 190). Elsevier B.V. doi:10.1016/j.sigpro.2021.108309

Bouguettaya, A., Zarzour, H., Taberkit, A. M., & Kechida, A. (2022). *A review on early wildfire detection from unmanned aerial vehicles using deep learning-based computer vision algorithms*. Research Centre in Industrial Technologies (CRTI). Department of Mathematics and Computer Science, Souk Ahras University.

Bouktif, S., Cheniki, A., Ouni, A., & El-Sayed, H. (2023). Deep reinforcement learning for traffic signal control with consistent state and reward design approach. *Knowledge-Based Systems*, 267, 110440. doi:10.1016/j.knosys.2023.110440

Boursianis, A. D., Papadopoulou, M. S., Diamantoulakis, P., Liopa-Tsakalidi, A., Barouchas, P., Salahas, G., Karagiannidis, G., Wan, S., & Goudos, S. K. (2020). Internet of Things (IoT) and Agricultural Unmanned Aerial Vehicles (UAVs) in smart farming: A comprehensive review. *Internet of Things : Engineering Cyber Physical Human Systems*, 100187. doi:10.1016/j.iot.2020.100187

Brack, I. V., Kindel, A., & Oliveira, L. F. B. (2018). Detection errors in wildlife abundance estimates from Unmanned Aerial Systems (UAS) surveys: Synthesis, solutions, and challenges. In Methods in Ecology and Evolution, 9(8), 1864–1873. doi:10.1111/2041-210X.13026

Brinkman, M. P. (2020). Applying UAV systems in wildlife management. In *Proceedings of the Vertebrate Pest Conference* (Vol. 29, No. 29). OA.

Brockman, G., Cheung, V., Pettersson, L., Schneider, J., Schulman, J., Tang, J., & Zaremba, W. (2016). *OpenAI Gym.* ArXiv.org. https://arxiv.org/abs/1606.01540

Bullock, D. G., Bullock, D. S., Nafziger, E. D., Doerge, T. A., Paszkiewicz, S. R., Carter, P. R., & Peterson, T. A. (1998). Does variable rate seeding of corn pay? *Agronomy Journal*, *90*(6), 830–836. doi:10.2134/agronj1998.00021962009000060019x

Burton, A. C., Neilson, E., Moreira, D., Ladle, A., Steenweg, R., Fisher, J. T., Bayne, E., & Boutin, S. (2015). REVIEW: Wildlife camera trapping: a review and recommendations for linking surveys to ecological processes. *Journal of Applied Ecology*, *52*(3), 675–685. doi:10.1111/1365-2664.12432 PMID:26211047

Butte, S., Vakanski, A., Duellman, K., Wang, H., & Mirkouei, A. (2021). Potato crop stress identification in aerial images using deep learning-based object detection. *Agronomy Journal*, *113*(5), 3991–4002. doi:10.1002/agj2.20841

Cai, Y., Du. D Zhang L, Wen L, Wang W, & Y. (2020). Guided attention network for object detection and counting on drones. In *Proceedings of the 28th ACM international conference on multimedia* (pp. 709–717). ACM.

Cao, K., Liu, Y., Meng, G., & Sun, Q. (2020). An overview on edge computing research. *IEEE Access : Practical Innovations, Open Solutions*, *8*, 85714–85728. doi:10.1109/ACCESS.2020.2991734

Cao, Z., Kooistra, L., Wang, W., Guo, L., & Valente, J. (2023). Real-Time Object Detection Based on UAV Remote Sensing: A Systematic Literature Review. *Drones (Basel)*, *7*(10), 10. doi:10.3390/drones7100620

Cao, Z., Li, D., Zhang, B., & Gou, K. (2023). Multi-UAV collaborative trajectory planning for emergency response mapping based on PSO. *International Conference on Geographic Information and Remote Sensing Technology (GIRST 2022)*. Spie. 10.1117/12.2667401

Cardoso, A. S., Bryukhova, S., Renna, F., Reino, L., Xu, C., Xiao, Z., Correia, R., Di Minin, E., Ribeiro, J., & Vaz, A. S. (2023). Detecting wildlife trafficking in images from online platforms: A test case using deep learning with pangolin images. *Biological Conservation*, *279*, 109905. doi:10.1016/j.biocon.2023.109905

Carrio, A., Sampedro, C., Rodriguez-Ramos, A., & Campoy, P. (2017). A review of deep learning methods and applications for unmanned aerial vehicles. *Journal of Sensors*, *2017*, 1–13. doi:10.1155/2017/3296874

Casagrande, G., Sik, A., & Szabó, G. (Eds.). (2018). *Small Flying Drones.* Springer. doi:10.1007/978-3-319-66577-1

Cassano, C. (2014). The right balance-technology and patient care. *On-Line Journal of Nursing Informatics*, *18*(3).

Cassano, L., Yuan, K., & Sayed, A. H. (2021). Multiagent Fully Decentralized Value Function Learning with Linear Convergence Rates. *IEEE Transactions on Automatic Control*, *66*(4), 1497–1512. doi:10.1109/TAC.2020.2995814

Catal Reis, H. (2020). *Detection of forest fire using deep convolutional neural networks with a transfer learning approach.* Department of Geomatics Engineering, Gumushane University.

Cazaurang, F., Cohen, K., & Kumar, M. (2020). *Multi-Rotor Platform-based UAV Systems.*

Cerro, J., Cruz Ulloa, C., Barrientos, A., & de León Rivas, J. (2021). Unmanned aerial vehicles in agriculture: A survey. *Agronomy (Basel)*, *11*(2), 203. doi:10.3390/agronomy11020203

Cestero, J., Quartulli, M., Metelli, A. M., & Restelli, M. (2022). Storehouse: a Reinforcement Learning Environment for Optimizing Warehouse Management. *2022 International Joint Conference on Neural Networks (IJCNN)*, (pp. 1–9). IEEE. 10.1109/IJCNN55064.2022.9891985

Chabot, D., Stapleton, S., & Francis, C. M. (2022). Using Web images to train a deep neural network to detect sparsely distributed wildlife in large volumes of remotely sensed imagery: A case study of polar bears on sea ice. *Ecological Informatics*, *68*, 101547. doi:10.1016/j.ecoinf.2021.101547

Chaerle, L., & Van Der Straeten, D. (2000). Imaging techniques and the early detection of plant stress. *Trends in Plant Science*, *5*(11), 495–501. doi:10.1016/S1360-1385(00)01781-7 PMID:11077259

Chandler, C., Cheney, P., Thomas, P., Trabaud, L., & Williams, D. (1983). *Fire in forestry*. Forest fire management and organization.

Chandra, A. L., Desai, S. V., Guo, W., & Balasubramanian, V. N. (2020). *Computer vision with deep learning for plant phenotyping in agriculture: A survey*. Advanced Computing and Communications. doi:10.34048/ACC.2020.1.F1

Chang, X., Yang, C., Wu, J., Shi, X., & Shi, Z. (2018). A surveillance system for drone localization and tracking using acoustic arrays. In *Proceedings of the 2018 IEEE 10th sensor array and multichannel signal processing workshop (SAM)* (pp. 573–577). IEEE. 10.1109/SAM.2018.8448409

Chapman, S., Merz, T., Chan, A., Jackway, P., Hrabar, S., Dreccer, M., Holland, E., Zheng, B., Ling, T., & Jimenez-Berni, J. (2014). Pheno-copter: A low-altitude, autonomous remote-sensing robotic helicopter for high-throughput fieldbased phenotyping. *Agronomy (Basel)*, *4*(2), 279–301. doi:10.3390/agronomy4020279

Chen, S., Meng, W., Xu, W., Liu, Z., Liu, J., & Wu, F. (2020). A Warehouse Management System with UAV Based on Digital Twin and 5G Technologies. *2020 7th International Conference on Information, Cybernetics, and Computational Social Systems*, (pp. 864–869). IEEE. 10.1109/ICCSS52145.2020.9336832

Chen, X., Zhao, M., & Yin, L. (2020). *Dynamic Path Planning of the UAV Avoiding Static and Moving Obstacles*.

Chen, C. J., Huang, Y. Y., Li, Y. S., Chen, Y. C., Chang, C. Y., & Huang, Y. M. (2021). Identification of fruit tree pests with deep learning on embedded drone to achieve accurate pesticide spraying. *IEEE Access : Practical Innovations, Open Solutions*, *9*, 21986–21997. doi:10.1109/ACCESS.2021.3056082

Cheng, N., Wu, S., Wang, X., Yin, Z., Li, C., Chen, W., & Chen, F. (2023). AI for UAV-Assisted IoT Applications: A Comprehensive Review. *IEEE Internet of Things Journal*, *10*(16), 14438–14461. doi:10.1109/JIOT.2023.3268316

Chen, J., Du, C., Zhang, Y., Han, P., & Wei, W. (2022). A Clustering-Based Coverage Path Planning Method for Autonomous Heterogeneous UAVs. *IEEE Transactions on Intelligent Transportation Systems*, *23*(12), 25546–25556. doi:10.1109/TITS.2021.3066240

Chen, J., Ling, F., Zhang, Y., You, T., Liu, Y., & Du, X. (2022). Coverage path planning of heterogeneous unmanned aerial vehicles based on ant colony system. *Swarm and Evolutionary Computation*, *69*, 101005. doi:10.1016/j.swevo.2021.101005

Chen, J., Ma, R., & Oyekan, J. (2023). A deep multi-agent reinforcement learning framework for autonomous aerial navigation to grasping points on loads. *Robotics and Autonomous Systems*, *167*, 104489. doi:10.1016/j.robot.2023.104489

Chen, M., Li, W., Hao, Y., Qian, Y., & Humar, I. (2018). Edge cognitive computing based smart healthcare system. *Future Generation Computer Systems*, *86*, 403–411. doi:10.1016/j.future.2018.03.054

Chen, N., Chen, Y., You, Y., Ling, H., Liang, P., & Zimmermann, R. (2016). Dynamic urban surveillance video stream processing using fog computing. In *Proceedings of the 2016 IEEE second international conference on multimedia big data (BigMM)* (pp. 105–112). IEEE. 10.1109/BigMM.2016.53

Chen, R., Little, R., Mihaylova, L., Delahay, R., & Cox, R. (2019). Wildlife surveillance using deep learning methods. *Ecology and Evolution*, *9*(17), 9453–9466. doi:10.1002/ece3.5410 PMID:31534668

Chen, Y. P., Li, Y., & Wang, G. (2018). An Enhanced Region Proposal Network for object detection using deep learning method. *PLoS One*, *13*(9), e0203897. doi:10.1371/journal.pone.0203897 PMID:30235238

Chen, Y., Dong, Q., Shang, X., Wu, Z., & Wang, J. (2022). Multi-UAV autonomous path planning in reconnaissance missions considering incomplete information: A reinforcement learning method. *Drones (Basel)*, *7*(1), 10. doi:10.3390/drones7010010

Chen, Y., Lee, W. S., Gan, H., Peres, N., Fraisse, C., Zhang, Y., & He, Y. (2019). Strawberry yield prediction based on a deep neural network using high-resolution aerial orthoimages. *Remote Sensing (Basel)*, *11*(13), 1584. doi:10.3390/rs11131584

Chen, Y., Zhang, Y., Xin, J., Yi, Y., Liu, D., & Liu, H. (2018). A UAV-based Forest Fire Detection Algorithm Using Convolutional Neural Network. In *Proceedings of the 37th Chinese Control Conference*. IEEE. 10.23919/ChiCC.2018.8484035

Chen, Z. H., Lin, L., Wu, C. F., Li, C. F., Xu, R. H., & Sun, Y. (2021). Artificial intelligence for assisting cancer diagnosis and treatment in the era of precision medicine. *Cancer Communications*, *41*(11), 1100–1115. doi:10.1002/cac2.12215 PMID:34613667

Chi, K., Li, F., Zhang, F., Wu, M., & Xu, C. (2022). AoI Optimal Trajectory Planning for Cooperative UAVs: A Multi-Agent Deep Reinforcement Learning Approach. *2022 IEEE 5th International Conference on Electronic Information and Communication Technology (ICEICT)*. IEEE. PMID:35033326

Choudhary, S., Gaurav, V., Singh, A., & Agarwal, S. (2019). Autonomous crop irrigation system using artificial intelligence. *International Journal of Engineering and Advanced Technology*, *8*(5), 46–51. doi:10.35940/ijeat.E1010.0585S19

Christiansen, P., Steen, K. A., Jørgensen, R. N., & Karstoft, H. (2014). Automated detection and recognition of wildlife using thermal cameras. *Sensors (Basel)*, *14*(8), 13778–13793. doi:10.3390140813778 PMID:25196105

Chung, S.-J., Paranjape, A. A., Dames, P., Shen, S., & Kumar, V. (2018). A Survey on Aerial Swarm Robotics. *IEEE Transactions on Robotics*, *34*(4), 837–855. doi:10.1109/TRO.2018.2857475

Chung, Y.-S., & Le, H. V. (1984). Detection of forest-fire smoke plumes by satellite imagery. *Atmospheric Environment*, *18*(10), 2143–2151. doi:10.1016/0004-6981(84)90201-4

Chu, T., Wang, J., Codeca, L., & Li, Z. (2020). Multi-agent deep reinforcement learning for large-scale traffic signal control. *IEEE Transactions on Intelligent Transportation Systems*, *21*(3), 1086–1095. doi:10.1109/TITS.2019.2901791

Cilulko, J., Janiszewski, P., Bogdaszewski, M., & Szczygielska, E. (2013). Infrared thermal imaging in studies of wild animals. *European Journal of Wildlife Research*, *59*(1), 17–23. doi:10.100710344-012-0688-1

Cogo, E., Zunic, E., Besirevic, A., Delalic, S., & Hodzic, K. (2020). Position based visualization of real world warehouse data in a smart warehouse management system. *2020 19th International Symposium INFOTEH-JAHORINA (INFOTEH)*, (pp. 1–6). IEEE. 10.1109/INFOTEH48170.2020.9066323

Comtet, H. E., & Johannessen, K. A. (2022). A socio-analytical approach to the integration of drones into health care systems. *Information (Basel)*, *13*(2), 62. doi:10.3390/info13020062

Conley, S., & Robinson, A. (2007). Thin soybean stands: Should I replant, fill in, or leave them alone? *Coop. Ext. Serv. SPS-104-W*. https://www.extension.purdue.edu/extmedia/sps/sps-104-w.pdf

Cook, T. M., El-Boghdadly, K., McGuire, B., McNarry, A. F., Patel, A., & Higgs, A. (2020). Consensus guidelines for managing the airway in patients with COVID-19: Guidelines from the Difficult Airway Society, the Association of Anaesthetists the Intensive Care Society, the Faculty of Intensive Care Medicine and the Royal College of Anaesthetists. *Anaesthesia, 75*(6), 785–799. doi:10.1111/anae.15054 PMID:32221970

Cossa, D., Cossa, M., Timba, I., Nhaca, J., Macia, A., & Infantes, E. (2023). Drones and machine-learning for monitoring dugong feeding grounds and gillnet fishing. *Marine Ecology Progress Series, 716*, 123–136. doi:10.3354/meps14361

Cruz, G., & Touchard, G. (2018). *Enabling Rural Coverage - Regulatory and policy recommendations to foster mobile broadband coverage in developing countries.* GSMA. https://www.gsma.com/mobilefordevelopment/wp-content/uploads/2018/02/Enabling_Rural_Coverage_English_February_2018.pdf

Cui, J., Liu, Y., & Nallanathan, A. (2019). The application of multi-agent reinforcement learning in UAV networks. *2019 IEEE International Conference on Communications Workshops, ICC Workshops 2019 - Proceedings.* IEEE. 10.1109/ICCW.2019.8756984

Cui, J., Liu, Y., & Nallanathan, A. (2020). Multi-Agent Reinforcement Learning-Based Resource Allocation for UAV Networks. *IEEE Transactions on Wireless Communications, 19*(2), 729–743. doi:10.1109/TWC.2019.2935201

Cunningham, F., Achuthan, P., Akanni, W., Allen, J., Amode, M. R., Armean, I. M., Bennett, R., Bhai, J., Billis, K., Boddu, S., Cummins, C., Davidson, C., Dodiya, K. J., Gall, A., Girón, C. G., Gil, L., Grego, T., Haggerty, L., Haskell, E., & Flicek, P. (2019). Ensembl 2019. *Nucleic Acids Research, 47*(D1), D745–D751. doi:10.1093/nar/gky1113 PMID:30407521

Da Silva, F. L., & Costa, A. H. R. (2020). Methods and Algorithms for Knowledge Reuse in Multiagent Reinforcement Learning. *Anais Do Concurso de Teses e Dissertações Da SBC (CTD-SBC 2020)*, 1–6. doi:10.5753/ctd.2020.11360

Da Silva, F. L., Taylor, M. E., & Anna, H. R. C. (2018). Autonomously reusing knowledge in multiagent reinforcement learning. *Proceedings of the Twenty-Seventh International Joint Conference on Artificial Intelligence (IJCAI-18).* IEEE. 10.24963/ijcai.2018/774

Da Silva, F., & Costa, A. (2017). Accelerating Multiagent Reinforcement Learning through Transfer Learning. *Proceedings of the AAAI Conference on Artificial Intelligence, 31*(1). Advance online publication. doi:10.1609/aaai.v31i1.10518

DadrasJavan, F., Samadzadegan, F., Seyed Pourazar, S. H., & Fazeli, H. (2019). UAV-based multispectral imagery for fast Citrus Greening detection. *Journal of Plant Diseases and Protection, 126*(4), 307–318. doi:10.100741348-019-00234-8

Dang, H. V., Tatipamula, M., & Nguyen, H. X. (2021). Cloud-based digital twinning for structural health monitoring using deep learning. *IEEE Transactions on Industrial Informatics, 18*(6), 3820–3830. doi:10.1109/TII.2021.3115119

Dang, L. M., Hassan, S. I., & Suhyeon, I. (2020). UAV based wilt detection system via convolutional neural networks. *Sustainable Computing: Informatics and Systems, 28*, 100250. doi:10.1016/j.suscom.2018.05.010

Daniel Raj, J. J., Sangeetha, C. N., Ghorai, S., & Das, S., Manish, & Ahmed, S. (2023). Wild Animals Intrusion Detection for Safe Commuting in Forest Corridors using AI Techniques. *Proceedings of 2023 3rd International Conference on Innovative Practices in Technology and Management, ICIPTM 2023.* IEEE. 10.1109/ICIPTM57143.2023.10117831

Dar, M. H., Waza, S. A., Shukla, S., Zaidi, N. W., Nayak, S., Hossain, M., Kumar, A., Ismail, A. M., & Singh, U. S. (2020). Drought tolerant rice for ensuring food security in Eastern India. *Sustainability (Basel), 12*(6), 2214. doi:10.3390u12062214

Das, A., Gervet, T., Romoff, J., Batra, D., Parikh, D., Rabbat, M., & Pineau, J. (2019). TarMAC: Targeted Multi-Agent Communication. *Proceedings of the 36th International Conference on Machine Learning.* IEEE.

Davis, K. P. (1959). *Forest fire, control, and use.* SRP.

De Castro, G. G., Pinto, M. F., Biundini, I. Z., Melo, A. G., Marcato, A. L., & Haddad, D. B. (2023). Dynamic Path Planning Based on Neural Networks for Aerial Inspection. *Journal of Control. Automation and Electrical Systems, 34*(1), 85–105.

de Moraes, R. S., & de Freitas, E. P. (2018). Distributed control for groups of unmanned aerial vehicles performing surveillance missions and providing relay communication network services. *Journal of Intelligent & Robotic Systems, 92*(3-4), 645–656. doi:10.100710846-017-0726-z

de Venancio, P. V. A., Lisboa, A. C., & Barbosa, A. V. (2022). An automatic fire detection system based on deep convolutional neural networks for low-power, resource-constrained devices. *Neural Computing & Applications, 34*(18), 15349–15368. doi:10.100700521-022-07467-z

Delplanque, A., Foucher, S., Théau, J., Bussière, E., Vermeulen, C., & Lejeune, P. (2023). From crowd to herd counting: How to precisely detect and count African mammals using aerial imagery and deep learning? *ISPRS Journal of Photogrammetry and Remote Sensing, 197*, 167–180. doi:10.1016/j.isprsjprs.2023.01.025

Deng, J., Zhou, H., Lv, X., Yang, L., Shang, J., Sun, Q., Zheng, X., Zhou, C., Zhao, B., Wu, J., & Ma, Z. (2022). Applying convolutional neural networks for detecting wheat stripe rust transmission centers under complex field conditions using RGB-based high spatial resolution images from UAVs. *Computers and Electronics in Agriculture, 200*, 107211. doi:10.1016/j.compag.2022.107211

Deng, X., Huang, Z., Zheng, Z., Lan, Y., & Dai, F. (2019). Field detection and classification of citrus Huanglongbing based on hyperspectral reflectance. *Computers and Electronics in Agriculture, 167*, 105006. doi:10.1016/j.compag.2019.105006

Dhabekar, A. K. (2022). Integrated Technologies for Effective Wildlife Monitoring in India: A Proposed System. Research Gate.

Dhivya, K., Kumar, P. N., Hariharan, S., & Premalatha, G. (2022). A GPS based Tracking System for Wildlife Safety. *2022 3rd International Conference on Electronics and Sustainable Communication Systems (ICESC),* (pp. 428–433). IEEE. 10.1109/ICESC54411.2022.9885423

Dhuheir, M. A., Baccour, E., Erbad, A., Al-Obaidi, S. S., & Hamdi, M. (2023). Deep Reinforcement Learning for Trajectory Path Planning and Distributed Inference in Resource-Constrained UAV Swarms. *IEEE Internet of Things Journal, 10*(9), 8185–8201. doi:10.1109/JIOT.2022.3231341

Dhulkefl, E., Durdu, A., & Terzioğlu, H. (2020). Dijkstra algorithm using UAV path planning. *Konya Journal of Engineering Sciences, 8*, 92–105. doi:10.36306/konjes.822225

Dimitropoulos, K., Tsalakanidou, F., & Grammalidis, N. (2012). Flame detection for video-based early fire warning systems and 3D visualization of fire propagation. In *13th IASTED International Conference on Computer Graphics and Imaging (CGIM 2012).* ACTA Press. 10.2316/P.2012.779-011

Dimitrov, D. V. (2016). Medical internet of things and big data in healthcare. *Healthcare Informatics Research, 22*(3), 156–163. doi:10.4258/hir.2016.22.3.156 PMID:27525156

Dimopoulou, M., & Giannikos, I. (2004). Towards an integrated framework for forest fire control. *European Journal of Operational Research, 152*(2), 476–486. doi:10.1016/S0377-2217(03)00038-9

Ding G, Wu Q, Zhang L, Lin Y, Tsiftsis T A, & Yao Y D. (2018). An amateur drone surveillance system based on cognitive internet of things. *IEEE, 56*(1), 29–35.

Diwan, T., Anirudh, G., & Tembhurne, J. V. (2023). Object detection using YOLO: Challenges, architectural successors, datasets and applications. *Multimedia Tools and Applications, 82*(6), 9243-9275.

Diwan, T., Anirudh, G., & Tembhurne, J. V. (2023). Object detection using YOLO: Challenges, architectural successors, datasets and applications. *Multimedia Tools and Applications*, *82*(6), 9243–9275. doi:10.100711042-022-13644-y PMID:35968414

Doks. Innovation. (n.d.). Doks Innovation. https://doks-innovation.com/

Dong, A. Y., Wang, Z., Huang, J. J., Song, B. A., & Hao, G. F. (2021). Bioinformatic tools support decision-making in plant disease management. *Trends in Plant Science*, *26*(9), 953–967. doi:10.1016/j.tplants.2021.05.001 PMID:34039514

dos Santos Ferreira, A., Freitas, D. M., da Silva, G. G., Pistori, H., & Folhes, M. T. (2017). Weed detection in soybean crops using ConvNets. *Computers and Electronics in Agriculture*, *143*, 314–324. doi:10.1016/j.compag.2017.10.027

Dramouskas I, Perikos I, & Hatzilygeroudis I. (2012). *A method for performing efficient real-time object tracing for drones*. Nimbus Vault.

Dresselhaus, T., & Hückelhoven, R. (2018). Biotic and abiotic stress responses in crop plants. *Agronomy (Basel)*, *8*(11), 267. doi:10.3390/agronomy8110267

Drone Laws in Saudi Arabia. (2023). UAV Coach. https://uavcoach.com/drone-laws-in-saudi-arabia/

Duhart, C., Dublon, G., Mayton, B., Davenport, G., & Paradiso, J. A. (2019, June). Deep learning for wildlife conservation and restoration efforts. In *36th International conference on machine learning, Long Beach* (Vol. 5). PMLR.

Du, J. (2018, April). Understanding of object detection based on CNN family and YOLO. []. IOP Publishing.]. *Journal of Physics: Conference Series*, *1004*, 012029. doi:10.1088/1742-6596/1004/1/012029

Dujon, A. M., Ierodiaconou, D., Geeson, J. J., Arnould, J. P. Y., Allan, B. M., Katselidis, K. A., & Schofield, G. (2021). Machine learning to detect marine animals in UAV imagery: Effect of morphology, spacing, behaviour and habitat. *Remote Sensing in Ecology and Conservation*, *7*(3), 341–354. doi:10.1002/rse2.205

Dujon, A. M., & Schofield, G. (2019). Importance of machine learning for enhancing ecological studies using information-rich imagery. *Endangered Species Research*, *39*, 91–104. doi:10.3354/esr00958

Du, Y., & Guo, Y. (2022). Machine learning techniques and research framework in foodborne disease surveillance system. *Food Control*, *131*, 108448. doi:10.1016/j.foodcont.2021.108448

Ebrahimi, D., Sharafeddine, S., Ho, P.-H., & Assi, C. (2021). Autonomous UAV Trajectory for Localizing Ground Objects: A Reinforcement Learning Approach. *IEEE Transactions on Mobile Computing*, *20*(4), 1312–1324. doi:10.1109/TMC.2020.2966989

Edelblutte, É., Krithivasan, R., & Hayek, M. N. (2023). Animal agency in wildlife conservation and management. *Conservation Biology*, *37*(1), e13853. doi:10.1111/cobi.13853 PMID:35262968

Egan, P. A., Dicks, L. V., Hokkanen, H. M., & Stenberg, J. A. (2020). Delivering integrated pest and pollinator management (IPPM). *Trends in Plant Science*, *25*(6), 577–589. doi:10.1016/j.tplants.2020.01.006 PMID:32407697

Eisenbeiss, H. (2004). A mini unmanned aerial vehicle (UAV): system overview and image acquisition. *International Archives of Photogrammetry. Remote Sensing and Spatial Information Sciences*, *36*(5/W1), 1-7.

Eljamassi, D. F., & Maghari, A. Y. (2020, December). COVID-19 detection from chest X-ray scans using machine learning. In *2020 International Conference on Promising Electronic Technologies (ICPET)* (pp. 1-4). IEEE. 10.1109/ICPET51420.2020.00009

Elmeseiry, N., Alshaer, N., & Ismail, T. (2021). A detailed survey and future directions of unmanned aerial vehicles (Uavs) with potential applications. *Aerospace (Basel, Switzerland)*, *8*(12), 363. doi:10.3390/aerospace8120363

Elmustafa S. (2023). A systematic review on energy efficiency in the internet of underwater things (IoUT): Recent approaches and research gaps. *Journal of Network and Computer Applications, 213*. doi:10.1016/j.jnca.2023.103594

Elmustafa, S., & Mohammad, K. (2021). Machine Learning Technologies for Secure Vehicular Communication in Internet of Vehicles: Recent Advances and Applications. *Security and Communication Networks, 2021*, 1–23. doi:10.1155/2021/8868355

Elnabty, I. A., Fahmy, Y., & Kafafy, M. (2022). A survey on UAV placement optimization for UAV-assisted communication in 5G and beyond networks. *Physical Communication, 51*, 101564. doi:10.1016/j.phycom.2021.101564

Elnour, R. A. M. (2023). Social Internet of Things (SIoT) Localization for Smart Cities Traffic Applications. In G. H. A. Salih & R. A. Saeed (Eds.), *Sustainability Challenges and Delivering Practical Engineering Solutions. Advances in Science, Technology & Innovation*. Springer. doi:10.1007/978-3-031-26580-8_24

Eltahir, A. A. (2013). An enhanced hybrid wireless mesh protocol (E-HWMP) protocol for multihop vehicular communications. *2013 International Conference On Computing, Electrical And Electronic Engineering (ICCEEE)*, Khartoum, Sudan. 10.1109/ICCEEE.2013.6633899

Eltahir, A. A. (2015). Performance evaluation of an Enhanced Hybrid Wireless Mesh Protocol (E-HWMP) protocol for VANET. *2015 International Conference on Computing, Control, Networking, Electronics and Embedded Systems Engineering (ICCNEEE)*, Khartoum, Sudan. 10.1109/ICCNEEE.2015.7381437

Erdelj, M., Natalizio, E., Chowdhury, K. R., & Akyildiz, I. F. (2017). Help from the Sky: Leveraging UAVs for Disaster Management. *IEEE Pervasive Computing, 16*(1), 24–32. doi:10.1109/MPRV.2017.11

Ergunsah, S., Tümen, V., Kosunalp, S., & Demir, K. (2023). Energy-efficient animal tracking with multi-unmanned aerial vehicle path planning using reinforcement learning and wireless sensor networks. *Concurrency and Computation, 35*(4), e7527. doi:10.1002/cpe.7527

Espinoza-Fraire, A. T., Dzul López, A. E. (2023). *Design of Control Laws and State Observers for Fixed-Wing UAVs*.

Esteva, A., Robicquet, A., Ramsundar, B., Kuleshov, V., DePristo, M., Chou, K., Cui, C., Corrado, G., Thrun, S., & Dean, J. (2019). A guide to deep learning in healthcare. *Nature Medicine, 25*(1), 24–29. doi:10.103841591-018-0316-z PMID:30617335

Estrada, M. A. R., & Ndoma, A. (2019). The uses of unmanned aerial vehicles–UAV's-(or drones) in social logistic: Natural disasters response and humanitarian relief aid. *Procedia Computer Science, 149*, 375–383. doi:10.1016/j.procs.2019.01.151

Euchi, J. (2021). Do drones have a realistic place in a pandemic fight for delivering medical supplies in healthcare systems problems? *Chinese Journal of Aeronautics, 34*(2), 182–190. doi:10.1016/j.cja.2020.06.006

Ezhil, V. S., Sriram, B. R., Vijay, R. C., Yeshwant, S., Sabareesh, R. K., Dakkshesh, G., & Raffik, R. (2022). Investigation on PID controller usage on Unmanned Aerial Vehicle for stability control. *Materials Today: Proceedings, 66*, 1313–1318. doi:10.1016/j.matpr.2022.05.134

Fahlstrom, P. G., Gleason, T. J., & Sadraey, M. H. (2022). *Introduction to UAV systems*. John Wiley & Sons.

Fakhreddine, A., Raffelsberger, C., Sende, M., & Bettstetter, C. (2022, December 1). *Experiments on Drone-to-Drone Communication with Wi-Fi, LTE-A, and 5G*. IEEE Xplore. https://doi.org/doi:10.1109/GCWkshps56602.2022.10008743

Fang, Y., Du, S., Boubchir, L., & Djouani, K. (2021). Detecting African hoofed animals in aerial imagery using convolutional neural network. [IJRA]. *IAES International Journal of Robotics and Automation, 10*(2), 133. doi:10.11591/ijra.v10i2.pp133-143

FAO. (1999). *International Handbook on Forest Fire Protection Technical guide for the countries of the Mediterranean basin*. Ministère de L'aménagement du Territoire et de L'environnement (France). F.A.O. (Food and Agriculture Organization of the United Nations).

Farber, C., Mahnke, M., Sanchez, L., & Kurouski, D. (2019). Advanced spectroscopic techniques for plant disease diagnostics. A review. *Trends in Analytical Chemistry*, *118*, 43–49. doi:10.1016/j.trac.2019.05.022

Faroug, M. O., Ali, E. S., & Saeed, R. A. (2021). Cyber-Physical System for Smart Grid. In A. K. Luhach & A. Elçi (Eds.), *Artificial Intelligence Paradigms for Smart Cyber-Physical Systems* (pp. 301–323). IGI Global. doi:10.4018/978-1-7998-5101-1.ch014

Faust, A., Palunko, I., Cruz, P., Fierro, R., & Tapia, L. (2017). Automated aerial suspended cargo delivery through reinforcement learning. *Artificial Intelligence*, *247*, 381–398. doi:10.1016/j.artint.2014.11.009

Faza, A., & Darma, S. (2020). Implementation of single shot detector for object finding in drone platform. *Journal of Physics: Conference Series*, *1528*(1), 012005. doi:10.1088/1742-6596/1528/1/012005

Fernández-Caramés, T. M., Blanco-Novoa, O., Froiz-Míguez, I., & Fraga-Lamas, P. (2019). Towards an Autonomous Industry 4.0 Warehouse: A UAV and Blockchain-Based System for Inventory and Traceability Applications in Big Data-Driven Supply Chain Management. *Sensors (Basel)*, *19*(10), 2394. doi:10.339019102394 PMID:31130644

Foerster, J. (2016). Advances in Neural Information Processing Systems: Vol. 29. *Ioannis Alexandros Assael, Nando de Freitas, & Shimon Whiteson*. Learning to Communicate with Deep Multi-Agent Reinforcement Learning.

Foerster, J., Song, F., Hughes, E., Burch, N., Dunning, I., Whiteson, S., Botvinick, M., & Bowling, M. (2019). Bayesian Action Decoder for Deep Multi-Agent Reinforcement Learning. *Proceedings of the 36th International Conference on Machine Learning*. IEEE.

Fotouhi, A., Qiang, H., Ding, M., Hassan, M., Giordano, L. G., Garcia-Rodriguez, A., & Yuan, J. (2019). Survey on UAV Cellular Communications: Practical Aspects, Standardization Advancements, Regulation, and Security Challenges. *IEEE Communications Surveys and Tutorials*, *21*(4), 3417–3442. doi:10.1109/COMST.2019.2906228

Fradi, H., Bracco, L., Canino, F., & Dugelay, J. L. (2018). Autonomous person detection and tracking framework using unmanned aerial vehicles (UAVs). In *Proceedings of the 2018 26th European Signal Processing Conference (EUSIPCO)* (pp. 1047–1051). IEEE. 10.23919/EUSIPCO.2018.8553010

Frair, J. L., Nielsen, S. E., Merrill, E. H., Lele, S. R., Boyce, M. S., Munro, R. H. M., Stenhouse, G. B., & Beyer, H. L. (2004). Removing GPS collar bias in habitat selection studies. *Journal of Applied Ecology*, *41*(2), 201–212. doi:10.1111/j.0021-8901.2004.00902.x PMID:15146623

Froomkin, A. M., Kerr, I., & Pineau, J. (2019). When AIs outperform doctors: Confronting the challenges of a tort-induced over-reliance on machine learning. *Arizona Law Review*, *61*, 33.

Fuentes, S., & Chang, J. (2022). Methodologies Used in Remote Sensing Data Analysis and Remote Sensors for Precision Agriculture. *Sensors (Basel)*, *22*(20), 7898. doi:10.339022207898 PMID:36298248

Gabriel, J. L., Zarco-Tejada, P. J., López-Herrera, P. J., Pérez-Martín, E., Alonso-Ayuso, M., & Quemada, M. (2017). Airborne and Ground Level Sensors for Monitoring Nitrogen Status in A Maize Crop. *Biosystems Engineering*, *160*, 124–133. doi:10.1016/j.biosystemseng.2017.06.003

Galán-Jiménez, J., Vegas, A. G., & Berrocal, J. (2022, October 1). *Energy-efficient deployment of IoT applications in remote rural areas using UAV networks*. IEEE Xplore. doi:10.23919/WMNC56391.2022.9954292

Galán-Jiménez, J., Moguel, E., García-Alonso, J., & Berrocal, J. (2021). Energy-efficient and solar powered mission planning of UAV swarms to reduce the coverage gap in rural areas: The 3D case. *Ad Hoc Networks*, *118*, 102517. doi:10.1016/j.adhoc.2021.102517

Galetti, M., Moleón, M., Jordano, P., Pires, M. M., Guimaraes, P. R. Jr, Pape, T., Nichols, E., Hansen, D., Olesen, J. M., Munk, M., de Mattos, J. S., Schweiger, A. H., Owen-Smith, N., Johnson, C. N., Marquis, R. J., & Svenning, J. C. (2018). Ecological and evolutionary legacy of megafauna extinctions. *Biological Reviews of the Cambridge Philosophical Society*, *93*(2), 845–862. doi:10.1111/brv.12374 PMID:28990321

Gan, W., Qu, X., Song, D., Sun, H., Guo, T., & Bao, W. (2022, October 1). *Research on Key Technology of Unmanned Surface Vehicle Motion Simulation Based on Unity3D*. IEEE Xplore. doi:10.1109/OCEANS47191.2022.9977285

Gao, D., Sun, Q., Hu, B., & Zhang, S. (2020). A framework for agricultural pest and disease monitoring based on internet-of-things and unmanned aerial vehicles. *Sensors (Basel)*, *20*(5), 1487. doi:10.339020051487 PMID:32182732

Garagiola, E., Creazza, A., & Porazzi, E. (2020). Analyzing the performance of health technologies distribution models in primary care services. *Measuring Business Excellence*, *25*(4), 452–474. doi:10.1108/MBE-11-2019-0109

García Gil, S., Gómez de la Hiz, J. A., & Ramos Ramos, D. (2023, June 15). *sgarciatz/coverageOptimization*. GitHub. https://github.com/sgarciatz/coverageOptimization

Ghali, R., Akhloufi, M. A., & Mseddi, W. S. (2022). Deep Learning and Transformer Approaches for UAV-Based Wildfire Detection and Segmentation. *Sensors (Basel)*, *22*(5), 1977. doi:10.339022051977 PMID:35271126

Ghazal, T. M., Hasan, M. K., Alshurideh, M. T., Alzoubi, H. M., Ahmad, M., Akbar, S. S., Al Kurdi, B., & Akour, I. A. (2021). IoT for smart cities: Machine learning approaches in smart healthcare—A review. *Future Internet*, *13*(8), 218. doi:10.3390/fi13080218

Ghorpade S. N., Zennaro M., B. S. & Chaudhari, B. (2021). Enhanced Differential Crossover and Quantum Particle Swarm Optimization for IoT Applications. *IEEE Access*. IEEE. . doi:10.1109/ACCESS.2021.3093113

Ghorpade, S. N., Zennaro, M., Chaudhari, B. S., Saeed, R. A., Alhumyani, H., & Abdel-Khalek, S. (2021). A Novel Enhanced Quantum PSO for Optimal Network Configuration in Heterogeneous Industrial IoT. *IEEE Access : Practical Innovations, Open Solutions*, *9*, 134022–134036. doi:10.1109/ACCESS.2021.3115026

Ghosh, R., Mishra, A., Orchard, G., & Thakor, N. V. (2014, October). Real-time object recognition and orientation estimation using an event-based camera and CNN. In 2014 IEEE Biomedical Circuits and Systems Conference (BioCAS) Proceedings (pp. 544-547). IEEE. doi:10.1109/BioCAS.2014.6981783

Giordan, D., Adams, M. S., Aicardi, I., Alicandro, M., Allasia, P., Baldo, M., De Berardinis, P., Dominici, D., Godone, D., Hobbs, P., Lechner, V., Niedzielski, T., Piras, M., Rotilio, M., Salvini, R., Segor, V., Sotier, B., & Troilo, F. (2020). The use of unmanned aerial vehicles (UAVs) for engineering geology applications. *Bulletin of Engineering Geology and the Environment*, *79*(7), 3437–3481. doi:10.100710064-020-01766-2

Giraldo, J. P., & Kruss, S. (2023). Nanosensors for monitoring plant health. *Nature Nanotechnology*, *18*(2), 107–108. doi:10.103841565-022-01307-w PMID:36609485

Gómez-Chabla, R., Real-Avilés, K., Morán, C., Grijalva, P., & Recalde, T. (2018, December). IoT applications in agriculture: A systematic literature review. In *2nd International conference on ICTs in agronomy and environment* (pp. 68-76). Cham: Springer International Publishing.

Gonzalez, L. F., Montes, G. A., Puig, E., Johnson, S., Mengersen, K., & Gaston, K. J. (2016). Unmanned aerial vehicles (UAVs) and artificial intelligence revolutionizing wildlife monitoring and conservation. *Sensors (Basel)*, *16*(1), 97. doi:10.339016010097 PMID:26784196

Gonzalez-TrejoJ.Mercado-RavellD. (2020). Dense crowds detection and surveillance with drones using density maps. ArXiv:2003.08766 [Cs]. https://arxiv.org/abs/2003.08766 doi:10.1109/ICUAS48674.2020.9213886

Goodrich, J., Lynam, A., Miquelle, D., Wibisono, H., Kawanishi, K., Pattanavibool, A., & Karanth, U. (2015). *Panthera tigris*. The IUCN Red List of Threatened Species 2015: e. T15955A50659951.

Grammalidis, N. C., Dimitropoulos, K., Tsalakanidou, F., Kose, K., Gunay, O., Gouverneur, B., Torri, D., Kuruoglu, E., & Tozzi, S. (2011). A multi-sensor network for the protection of cultural heritage. In *2011 19th IEEE European Signal Processing Conference*. IEEE.

Grari, M., Idrissi, I., Boukabous, M., Moussaoui, O., Azizi, M., & Moussaoui, M. (2022). Early wildfire detection using machine learning model deployed in the fog/edge layers of IoT. *Indonesian Journal of Electrical Engineering and Computer Science*, *27*(2), 1062–1073. doi:10.11591/ijeecs.v27.i2.pp1062-1073

Greco, C., Pace, P., Basagni, S., & Fortino, G. (2021). Jamming detection at the edge of drone networks using multi-layer perceptrons and decision trees. *Applied Soft Computing*, *111*, 107806. doi:10.1016/j.asoc.2021.107806

Green, S. E., Rees, J. P., Stephens, P. A., Hill, R. A., & Giordano, A. J. (2020). Innovations in camera trapping technology and approaches: The integration of citizen science and artificial intelligence. *Animals (Basel)*, *10*(1), 132. doi:10.3390/ani10010132 PMID:31947586

Gronauer, S., & Diepold, K. (2022). Multi-agent deep reinforcement learning: A survey. *Artificial Intelligence Review*, *55*(2), 895–943. doi:10.100710462-021-09996-w

Guo, A., Huang, W., Dong, Y., Ye, H., Ma, H., Liu, B., Wu, W., Ren, Y., Ruan, C., & Geng, Y. (2021). Wheat yellow rust detection using UAV-based hyperspectral technology. *Remote Sensing (Basel)*, *13*(1), 123. doi:10.3390/rs13010123

Guo, J., Liu, X., Bi, L., Liu, H., & Lou, H. (2023). UN-YOLOv5s: A UAV-Based Aerial Photography Detection Algorithm. *Sensors (Basel)*, *23*(13), 5907. doi:10.339023135907 PMID:37447757

Guo, Z., Chen, H., & Li, S. (2023). Deep Reinforcement Learning-Based UAV Path Planning for Energy-Efficient Multitier Cooperative Computing in Wireless Sensor Networks. *Journal of Sensors*, *2023*, 2023. doi:10.1155/2023/2804943

Gupta, J. K., Egorov, M., & Kochenderfer, M. (2017). Cooperative Multi-agent Control Using Deep Reinforcement Learning. Lecture Notes in Computer Science (Including Subseries Lecture Notes in Artificial Intelligence and Lecture Notes in Bioinformatics), 10642 LNAI, (pp. 66–83). Springer. doi:10.1007/978-3-319-71682-4_5

Gupta, A., Afrin, T., Scully, E., & Yodo, N. (2021). Advances of UAVs toward Future Transportation: The State-of-the-Art, Challenges, and Opportunities. *Future Transportation*, *1*(2), 326–350. doi:10.3390/futuretransp1020019

Gupta, L., Jain, R., & Vaszkun, G. (2016). Survey of Important Issues in UAV Communication Networks. *IEEE Communications Surveys and Tutorials*, *18*(2), 1123–1152. doi:10.1109/COMST.2015.2495297

Gupta, N. S., & Kumar, P. (2023). Perspective of artificial intelligence in healthcare data management: A journey towards precision medicine. *Computers in Biology and Medicine*, *162*, 107051. doi:10.1016/j.compbiomed.2023.107051 PMID:37271113

Gupta, R., Kumari, A., & Tanwar, S. (2021). Fusion of blockchain and artificial intelligence for secure drone networking underlying 5G communications. *Transactions on Emerging Telecommunications Technologies*, *32*(1), e4176. doi:10.1002/ett.4176

Haas, J. K. (2014). *A History of the Unity Game Engine*. Www.semanticscholar.org. https://www.semanticscholar.org/paper/A-History-of-the-Unity-Game-Engine-Haas/5e6b2255d5b7565d11e71e980b1ca141aeb3391d

Habehh, H., & Gohel, S. (2021). Machine learning in healthcare. *Current Genomics, 22*(4), 291–300. doi:10.2174/138 9202922666210705124359 PMID:35273459

Habib, S., Hussain, A., Albattah, W., Islam, M., Khan, S., Khan, R. U., & Khan, K. (2021). Abnormal Activity Recognition from Surveillance Videos Using Convolutional Neural Network. *Sensors (Basel), 21*(24), 8291. doi:10.339021248291 PMID:34960386

Hachiya, D., Mas, E., & Koshimura, S. (2022). A Reinforcement Learning Model of Multiple UAVs for Transporting Emergency Relief Supplies. *Applied Sciences (Basel, Switzerland), 12*(20), 10427. doi:10.3390/app122010427

Hadji, O., Kadri, O., Maimour, M., Rondeau, E., & Benyahia, A. (2022). Region of Interest and Redundancy Problem in Migratory Birds Wild Life Surveillance. *2022 International Conference on Advanced Aspects of Software Engineering (ICAASE),* (pp. 1–8). IEEE. 10.1109/ICAASE56196.2022.9931576

Haleem, A., Javaid, M., Singh, R. P., & Suman, R. (2021). Telemedicine for healthcare: Capabilities, features, barriers, and applications. *Sensors International, 2*, 100117. doi:10.1016/j.sintl.2021.100117 PMID:34806053

Haleem, A., Javaid, M., Singh, R. P., & Suman, R. (2022). Medical 4.0 technologies for healthcare: Features, capabilities, and applications. *Internet of Things and Cyber-Physical Systems, 2*, 12–30. doi:10.1016/j.iotcps.2022.04.001

Haleem, A., Javaid, M., Singh, R. P., & Suman, R. (2023). Exploring the revolution in healthcare systems through the applications of digital twin technology. *Biomedical Technology, 4*, 28–38. doi:10.1016/j.bmt.2023.02.001

Halpern, C. B., & Antos, J. A. (2022). Burn severity and pre-fire seral state interact to shape vegetation responses to fire in a young, western Cascade Range Forest. *Forest Ecology and Management, 507*, 120028. doi:10.1016/j.foreco.2022.120028

Ham, Y., Han, K. K., Lin, J. J., & Golparvar-Fard, M. (2016). Visual monitoring of civil infrastructure systems via camera-equipped Unmanned Aerial Vehicles (UAVs): A review of related works. *Visualization in Engineering, 4*(1).

Han S, Shen W, & Liu Z. (2016). *Deep drone: object detection and tracking for smart drones on embedded system.* Stanford University.

Han, D., Mulyana, B., Stankovic, V., & Cheng, S. (2023). A Survey on Deep Reinforcement Learning Algorithms for Robotic Manipulation. *Sensors (Basel), 23*(7), 3762. doi:10.339023073762 PMID:37050822

Harik, E. H. C., Guerin, F., Guinand, F., Brethe, J.-F., & Pelvillain, H. (2016). Towards An Autonomous Warehouse Inventory Scheme. *2016 IEEE Symposium Series on Computational Intelligence (SSCI),* (pp. 1–8). IEEE. 10.1109/SSCI.2016.7850056

Hashem, I. A. T., Yaqoob, I., Anuar, N. B., Mokhtar, S., Gani, A., & Khan, S. U. (2015). The rise of "big data" on cloud computing: Review and open research issues. *Information Systems, 47*, 98–115. doi:10.1016/j.is.2014.07.006

Hashemi, A. M., Herbert, S. J., & Putnam, D. H. (2005). Yield response of corn to crowding stress. *Agronomy Journal, 97*(3), 839–846. doi:10.2134/agronj2003.0241

Hassan, M., Ali, E., & Nurelmadina, N. (2021). Artificial intelligence in IoT and its applications. Intelligent Wireless Communications. IET Digital Library. , doi:10.1049/PBTE094E_ch2

Hassan, A., Ahmad, R., Ahmed, W., Magarini, M., & Alam, M. M. (2020a). UAV and SWIPT assisted disaster aware clustering and association. *IEEE Access : Practical Innovations, Open Solutions, 8*, 204791–204803. doi:10.1109/ACCESS.2020.3035959

Hassan, M. B. (2022). Performance Evaluation of Uplink Shared Channel for Cooperative Relay based Narrow Band Internet of Things Network. *2022 International Conference on Business Analytics for Technology and Security (ICBATS)*, Dubai, United Arab Emirates. 10.1109/ICBATS54253.2022.9758935

Hassan, M.B., Alsharif, S., & Alhumyani, H. (2021). An Enhanced Cooperative Communication Scheme for Physical Uplink Shared Channel in NB-IoT. Wireless Pers Commun., 120, 2367–2386. https://doi.org/ doi:10.100711277-021-08067-1

Hassan, S. S., Park, Y. M., Tun, Y. K., Saad, W., Han, Z., & Hong, C. S. (2022). 3TO: THz-enabled throughput and trajectory optimization of UAVs in 6G networks by proximal policy optimization deep reinforcement learning. *ICC 2022-IEEE International Conference on Communications*. IEEE.

Hayward, M. W., Henschel, P., O'Brien, J., Hofmeyr, M., Balme, G., & Kerley, G. I. (2006). Prey preferences of the leopard (Panthera pardus). *Journal of Zoology (London, England)*, 270(2), 298–313. doi:10.1111/j.1469-7998.2006.00139.x

He, K., Gkioxari, G., Dollár, P., & Girshick, R. (2017). Mask r-cnn. In *Proceedings of the IEEE international conference on computer vision* (pp. 2961-2969). IEEE.

He, Z., Kays, R., Zhang, Z., Ning, G., Huang, C., Han, T. X., Millspaugh, J., Forrester, T., & McShea, W. (2016). Visual Informatics Tools for Supporting Large-Scale Collaborative Wildlife Monitoring with Citizen Scientists. *IEEE Circuits and Systems Magazine*, 16(1), 73–86. doi:10.1109/MCAS.2015.2510200

Hii, M. S. Y., Courtney, P., & Royall, P. G. (2019). An evaluation of the delivery of medicines using drones. Multidisciplinary Digital Publishing Institute, 3(3), 52. 226. doi:10.3390/drones3030052

Hobbs, F. R., & Erhardt, L. (2002). Acceptance of guideline recommendations and perceived implementation of coronary heart disease prevention among primary care physicians in five European countries: the Reassessing European Attitudes about Cardiovascular Treatment (REACT) survey. *Family practice*, 19(6), 596-604.

Hogan, S. D., Kelly, M., Stark, B., & Chen, Y. (2017). Unmanned Aerial Systems for Agriculture and Natural Resources. *California Agriculture*, 71(1), 5–14. doi:10.3733/ca.2017a0002

Hong, D., Gao, L., Yokoya, N., Yao, J., Chanussot, J., Du, Q., & Zhang, B. (2021). More diverse means better: Multimodal deep learning meets remote-sensing imagery classification. IEEE Trans. Geosci. Remote Sens., vol. 59, no. 5, pp. 4340–4354. *IEEE GRSM, 2021*, 19.

Hong, S. J., Han, Y., Kim, S. Y., Lee, A. Y., & Kim, G. (2019). Application of deep-learning methods to bird detection using unmanned aerial vehicle imagery. *Sensors (Basel)*, 19(7), 1651. doi:10.339019071651 PMID:30959913

Hong, T., Zhou, C., Kadoch, M., Tang, T., & Zuo, Z. (2022). Improvement of UAV tracking technology in future 6G complex environment based on GM-PHD filter. *Electronics*, 11(24), 4140. doi:10.3390/electronics11244140

Hoseini, S. A., Bokani, A., Hassan, J., Salehi, S., & Kanhere, S. S. (2021). Energy and Service-Priority aware Trajectory Design for UAV-BSs using Double Q-Learning, 2021 IEEE 18th Annual Consumer Communications & Networking Conference. CCNC. doi:10.1109/CCNC49032.2021.9369472

Hoseini, S. A., Bokani, A., Hassan, J., Salehi, S., & Kanhere, S. S. (2021). Energy and service-priority aware trajectory design for UAV-BSs using double Q-learning. *2021 IEEE 18th Annual Consumer Communications & Networking Conference (CCNC)*.

Hoseini, S. A., Bokani, A., Hassan, J., Salehi, S., & Kanhere, S. S. (2021). Energy and Service-Priority aware Trajectory Design for UAV-BSs using Double Q-Learning. *2021 IEEE 18th Annual Consumer Communications & Networking Conference. CCNC*. doi:10.1109/CCNC49032.2021.9369472

Hoseini, S. A., Hassan, J., Bokani, A., & Kanhere, S. S. (2020). *Trajectory Optimization of Flying Energy Sources using Q-Learning to Recharge Hotspot UAVs*. IEEE INFOCOM 2020 - IEEE Conference on Computer Communications Workshops (INFOCOM WKSHPS), Toronto, ON, Canada. 10.1109/INFOCOMWKSHPS50562.2020.9162834

Hossain, S., & Lee, D. (2019). Deep learning-based real-time multiple-object detection and tracking from aerial imagery via a flying robot with GPU-based embedded devices. *Sensors (Basel)*, *19*(15), 3371. doi:10.339019153371 PMID:31370336

Hsieh, M. R., Lin, Y. L., & Hsu, W. H. (2017). Drone-based object counting by spatially regularized regional proposal network. In *Proceedings of the 2017 IEEE International Conference on Computer Vision (ICCV)* (pp. 4165–4173). IEEE. 10.1109/ICCV.2017.446

Hsu, H. J., & Chen, K. T. (2017). Drone face: An open dataset for drone research. In *Proceedings of the 8th ACM on multimedia systems conference* (pp. 187–192). ACM. 10.1145/3083187.3083214

Huang, F., Chen, S., Wang, Q., Chen, Y., & Zhang, D. (2023). Using deep learning in an embedded system for real-time target detection based on images from an unmanned aerial vehicle: Vehicle detection as a case study. *International Journal of Digital Earth*, *16*(1), 910–936. doi:10.1080/17538947.2023.2187465

Huang, L., Wang, L., Hu, X., Chen, S., Tao, Y., Su, H., Yang, J., Xu, W., Vedarethinam, V., Wu, S., Liu, B., Wan, X., Lou, J., Wang, Q., & Qian, K. (2020). Machine learning of serum metabolic patterns encodes early-stage lung adenocarcinoma. *Nature Communications*, *11*(1), 3556. doi:10.103841467-020-17347-6 PMID:32678093

Huang, W., Zhou, X., Dong, M., & Xu, H. (2021). Multiple objects tracking in the UAV system based on hierarchical deep high-resolution network. *Multimedia Tools and Applications*, *80*(9), 13911–13929. doi:10.100711042-020-10427-1

Huang, Y.-Y., Li, Z.-W., Yang, C.-H., & Huang, Y.-M. (2023). Automatic Path Planning for Spraying Drones Based on Deep Q-Learning. *Wangji Wanglu Jishu Xuekan*, *24*(3), 565–575. doi:10.53106/160792642023052403001

Hughes, D., & Salathé, M. (2015). *An open access repository of images on plant health to enable the development of mobile disease diagnostics*. arXiv preprint arXiv:1511.08060.

Hu, J., Zhang, H., & Song, L. (2019). Reinforcement Learning for Decentralized Trajectory Design in Cellular UAV Networks With Sense-and-Send Protocol. *IEEE Internet of Things Journal*, *6*(4), 6177–6189. doi:10.1109/JIOT.2018.2876513

Hu, J., Zhang, H., Song, L., Schober, R., & Poor, H. V. (2020). Cooperative internet of UAVs: Distributed trajectory design by multi-agent deep reinforcement learning. *IEEE Transactions on Communications*, *68*(11), 6807–6821. doi:10.1109/TCOMM.2020.3013599

Hunter, S. B., Mathews, F., & Weeds, J. (2023). Using hierarchical text classification to investigate the utility of machine learning in automating online analyses of wildlife exploitation. *Ecological Informatics*, *75*, 102076. doi:10.1016/j.ecoinf.2023.102076

Hutcherson, Z. S. (2023). *A Literary Review on the Current State of Drone Technology in Regard to Conservation*.

Hwang, J., & Kim, H. (2019). Consequences of a green image of drone food delivery services: The moderating role of gender and age. *Business Strategy and the Environment*, *28*(5), 872–884. doi:10.1002/bse.2289

Hwang, J., Kim, J. J., & Lee, K. W. (2020). Investigating consumer innovativeness in the context of drone food delivery services: Its impact on attitude and behavioral intentions. Elsevier. *Article*, *120433*. doi:10.1016/j.techfore.2020.120433

Ihekoronye, V. U., Ajakwe, S. O., Kim, D. S., & Lee, J. M. (2021). UAV Assisted Real-Time Detection and Recognition of Citrus Disease in Smart Farm using Deep Learning. *In 2021 Korean Institute of Communication and Information Science*, (pp. 453-454). Research Gate.

Ihekoronye, V. U., Ajakwe, S. O., Kim, D. S., & Lee, J. M. (2022, February). Aerial supervision of drones and other flying objects using convolutional neural networks. In *2022 International Conference on Artificial Intelligence in Information and Communication (ICAIIC)* (pp. 069-074). IEEE. 10.1109/ICAIIC54071.2022.9722702

Ihekoronye, V. U., Ajakwe, S. O., Kim, D. S., & Lee, J. M. (2022a, November). Hierarchical intrusion detection system for secured military drone network: A perspicacious approach. In MILCOM 2022-2022 IEEE Military Communications Conference (MILCOM) (pp. 336-341). IEEE. doi:10.1109/MILCOM55135.2022.10017532

Imran, M., Zaman, U., Imran, Imtiaz, J., Fayaz, M., & Gwak, J. (2021). Comprehensive survey of iot, machine learning, and blockchain for health care applications: A topical assessment for pandemic preparedness, challenges, and solutions. *Electronics (Basel)*, *10*(20), 2501. doi:10.3390/electronics10202501

Ishengoma, F. S., Rai, I. A., & Said, R. N. (2021). Identification of maize leaves infected by fall armyworms using UAV-based imagery and convolutional neural networks. *Computers and Electronics in Agriculture*, *184*, 106124. doi:10.1016/j.compag.2021.106124

Islam, S., Huang, Q., Afghah, F., Fule, P., & Razi, A. (2019). Fire Frontline Monitoring by Enabling UAV-Based Virtual Reality with Adaptive Imaging Rate. In *2019 53rd Asilomar Conference on Signals, Systems, and Computers.*

Jacobson, A. P., Gerngross, P., Lemeris, J. R. Jr, Schoonover, R. F., Anco, C., Breitenmoser-Würsten, C., Durant, S. M., Farhadinia, M. S., Henschel, P., Kamler, J. F., Laguardia, A., Rostro-García, S., Stein, A. B., & Dollar, L. (2016). Leopard (Panthera pardus) status, distribution, and the research efforts across its range. *PeerJ*, *4*, e1974. doi:10.7717/peerj.1974 PMID:27168983

Jaiswal, R. K., Mukherjee, S., Raju, K. D., & Saxena, R. (2002). Forest fire risk zone mapping from satellite imagery and GIS. *International Journal of Applied Earth Observation and Geoinformation*, *4*(1), 1–10. doi:10.1016/S0303-2434(02)00006-5

Jamshidi, M., Lalbakhsh, A., Talla, J., Peroutka, Z., Hadjilooei, F., Lalbakhsh, P., Jamshidi, M., Spada, L. L., Mirmozafari, M., Dehghani, M., Sabet, A., Roshani, S., Roshani, S., Bayat-Makou, N., Mohamadzade, B., Malek, Z., Jamshidi, A., Kiani, S., Hashemi-Dezaki, H., & Mohyuddin, W. (2020). Artificial intelligence and COVID-19: Deep learning approaches for diagnosis and treatment. *IEEE Access : Practical Innovations, Open Solutions*, *8*, 109581–109595. doi:10.1109/ACCESS.2020.3001973 PMID:34192103

Janik, P., Zawistowski, M., Fellner, R., & Zawistowski, G. (2021). Unmanned aircraft systems risk assessment based on sora for first responders and disaster management. *Applied Sciences (Basel, Switzerland)*, *11*(12), 5364. doi:10.3390/app11125364

Jasim, M. A., Shakhatreh, H., Siasi, N., Sawalmeh, A. H., Aldalbahi, A., & Al-Fuqaha, A. (2022). A Survey on Spectrum Management for Unmanned Aerial Vehicles (UAVs). *IEEE Access : Practical Innovations, Open Solutions*, *10*, 11443–11499. doi:10.1109/ACCESS.2021.3138048

Javaid, M., Haleem, A., Singh, R. P., & Suman, R. (2022). Enhancing smart farming through the applications of Agriculture 4.0 technologies. *International Journal of Intelligent Networks*, *3*, 150–164. doi:10.1016/j.ijin.2022.09.004

Javaid, M., & Khan, I. H. (2021). Internet of Things (IoT) enabled healthcare helps to take the challenges of COVID-19 Pandemic. *Journal of Oral Biology and Craniofacial Research*, *11*(2), 209–214. doi:10.1016/j.jobcr.2021.01.015 PMID:33665069

Javed, S., Hassan, A., Ahmad, R., Ahmed, W., Alam, M. M., & Rodrigues, J. J. (2023). UAV trajectory planning for disaster scenarios. *Vehicular Communications*, *39*, 100568. doi:10.1016/j.vehcom.2022.100568

Jensen-Nau, K. R., Hermans, T., & Leang, K. K. (2021). Near-Optimal Area-Coverage Path Planning of Energy-Constrained Aerial Robots With Application in Autonomous Environmental Monitoring. *IEEE Transactions on Automation Science and Engineering*, *18*(3), 1453–1468. doi:10.1109/TASE.2020.3016276

Jiang, P., Ergu, D., Liu, F., Cai, Y., & Ma, B. (2022). A Review of Yolo algorithm developments. *Procedia Computer Science*, *199*, 1066–1073. doi:10.1016/j.procs.2022.01.135

Jiao, Z., Zhang, Y., Mu, L., Xin, J., Yi, Y., & Liu, D. (2019). A Deep Learning Based Forest Fire Detection Approach Using UAV and YOLOv3. In *2019 1st International Conference on Industrial Artificial Intelligence (IAI)*. IEEE. 10.1109/ICIAI.2019.8850815

Jiao, Z., Zhang, Y., Mu, L., Xin, J., Jiao, S., Liu, H., & Liu, D. (2020). A YOLOv3-based Learning Strategy for Real-time UAV-based Forest Fire Detection. In *2020 Chinese Control And Decision Conference (CCDC 2020)*. IEEE. 10.1109/CCDC49329.2020.9163816

Jin, B. (2023). A Mean-VaR Based Deep Reinforcement Learning Framework for Practical Algorithmic Trading. *IEEE Access : Practical Innovations, Open Solutions*, *11*, 28920–28933. doi:10.1109/ACCESS.2023.3259108

Jintasuttisak, T., Leonce, A., Sher Shah, M., Khafaga, T., Simkins, G., & Edirisinghe, E. (2022, March). Deep learning based animal detection and tracking in drone video footage. *In Proceedings of the 8th International Conference on Computing and Artificial Intelligence* (pp. 425-431). ACM. 10.1145/3532213.3532280

Juliani A. Berges V.-P. Teng E. Cohen A. Harper J. Elion C. Goy C. Gao Y. Henry H. Mattar M. Lange D. (2020). Unity: A General Platform for Intelligent Agents. *ArXiv:1809.02627 [Cs, Stat]*. https://arxiv.org/abs/1809.02627

Jung, S., Jo, Y., & Kim, Y.-J. (2019). Flight Time Estimation for Continuous Surveillance Missions Using a Multirotor UAV. *Energies*, *12*(5), 867. doi:10.3390/en12050867

Kaelbling, L. P., Littman, M. L., & Moore, A. W. (1996). Reinforcement Learning: A Survey. *Journal of Artificial Intelligence Research*, *4*, 237–285. doi:10.1613/jair.301

Kalantar, A., Edan, Y., Gur, A., & Klapp, I. (2020). A deep learning system for single and overall weight estimation of melons using unmanned aerial vehicle images. *Computers and Electronics in Agriculture*, *178*, 105748. doi:10.1016/j.compag.2020.105748

Kalathas, I., Papoutsidakis, M., Piromalis, D., & Katsinoulas, L. (2019). Machine Learning: Prospects, Opportunities and Benefits to the Greek Railways. *International Journal of Computer Applications*, *178*(24), 26–32. doi:10.5120/ijca2019919038

Kaleem, Z., Khalid, W., Muqaibel, A., Nasir, A. A., Yuen, C., & Karagiannidis, G. K. (2022). Learning-aided UAV 3D placement and power allocation for sum-capacity enhancement under varying altitudes. *IEEE Communications Letters*, *26*(7), 1633–1637. doi:10.1109/LCOMM.2022.3172171

Kalinov, I., Petrovsky, A., Ilin, V., Pristanskiy, E., Kurenkov, M., Ramzhaev, V., Idrisov, I., & Tsetserukou, D. (2020). WareVision: CNN Barcode Detection-Based UAV Trajectory Optimization for Autonomous Warehouse Stocktaking. *IEEE Robotics and Automation Letters*, *5*(4), 6647–6653. doi:10.1109/LRA.2020.3010733

Kalra, I., Singh, M., Nagpal, S., Singh, R., Vatsa, M., & Sujit, P. B. (2019). Drone SURF: Benchmark dataset for drone-based face recognition. In *Proceedings of the 2019 14th IEEE international conference on automatic face & gesture recognition (FG 2019)* (pp. 1–7). IEEE.

Kalyabina, V. P., Esimbekova, E. N., Kopylova, K. V., & Kratasyuk, V. A. (2021). Pesticides: Formulants, distribution pathways and effects on human health–a review. *Toxicology Reports*, 8, 1179–1192. doi:10.1016/j.toxrep.2021.06.004 PMID:34150527

Kanand, T., Kemper, G., König, R., & Kemper, H. (2020). Wildfire detection and disaster monitoring system using UAS and sensor fusion technologies. *The International Archives of the Photogrammetry, Remote Sensing and Spatial Information Sciences*, 43, 1671–1675. doi:10.5194/isprs-archives-XLIII-B3-2020-1671-2020

Karaboga, D., Gorkemli, B., Ozturk, C., & Karaboga, N. (2014). A comprehensive survey: Artificial bee colony (ABC) algorithm and applications. *Artificial Intelligence Review*, 42(1), 21–57. doi:10.100710462-012-9328-0

Karamitsos, G., Bechtsis, D., Tsolakis, N., & Vlachos, D. (2021). Unmanned aerial vehicles for inventory listing. *International Journal of Business and Systems Research*, 15(6), 748–756. doi:10.1504/IJBSR.2021.118776

Kashyap, B., & Kumar, R. J. I. (2021). Sensing methodologies in agriculture for monitoring biotic stress in plants due to pathogens and pests. *Inventions*, 6(2), 29. https://doi.org/10.3390/inventions6020029

Kauhanen, H., Rönnholm, P., Vaaja, M., & Hyyppä, H. (2020). Designing and building a cost-efficient survey drone. *The International Archives of the Photogrammetry, Remote Sensing and Spatial Information Sciences*, 43, 165–172. doi:10.5194/isprs-archives-XLIII-B1-2020-165-2020

Kellenberger, B., Veen, T., Folmer, E., & Tuia, D. (2021). 21 000 birds in 4.5 h: Efficient large-scale seabird detection with machine learning. *Remote Sensing in Ecology and Conservation*, 7(3), 445–460. doi:10.1002/rse2.200

Kerkech, M., Hafiane, A., & Canals, R. (2018). Deep leaning approach with colorimetric spaces and vegetation indices for vine diseases detection in UAV images. *Computers and Electronics in Agriculture*, 155, 237–243. doi:10.1016/j.compag.2018.10.006

Kerkech, M., Hafiane, A., & Canals, R. (2020). VddNet: Vine disease detection network based on multispectral images and depth map. *Remote Sensing (Basel)*, 12(20), 3305. doi:10.3390/rs12203305

Khalifa, O. O., Roubleh, A., Esgiar, A., Abdelhaq, M., Alsaqour, R., Abdalla, A., Ali, E. S., & Saeed, R. (2022). An IoT-Platform-Based Deep Learning System for Human Behavior Recognition in Smart City Monitoring Using the Berkeley MHAD Datasets. *Systems*, 2022(10), 177. doi:10.3390ystems10050177

Khalil, A. A., Byrne, A. J., Rahman, M. A., & Manshaei, M. H. (2021). Efficient UAV Trajectory-Planning using Economic Reinforcement Learning (arXiv:2103.02676). arXiv. https://arxiv.org/abs/2103.02676 doi:10.1109/SMART-COMP52413.2021.00041

Khan, I., Schommer-Aikins, M., & Saeed, N. (2021). Cognitive Flexibility, Procrastination, and Need for Closure Predict Online Self-Directed Learning Among Pakistani Virtual University Students. *International Journal of Distance Education and E-Learning*, 6(2), 31–41. doi:10.36261/ijdeel.v6i2.1860

Khan, M. G., Huda, N. U., & Zaman, U. K. U. (2022). Smart Warehouse Management System: Architecture, Real-Time Implementation and Prototype Design. *Machines*, 10(2), 150. doi:10.3390/machines10020150

Kharim, M. N. A., Wayayok, A., Abdullah, A. F., Shariff, A. R. M., Husin, E. M., & Mahadi, M. R. (2022). Predictive zoning of pest and disease infestations in rice field based on UAV aerial imagery. *The Egyptian Journal of Remote Sensing and Space Sciences*, 25(3), 831–840. doi:10.1016/j.ejrs.2022.08.001

Khattak, A., Asghar, M. U., Batool, U., Asghar, M. Z., Ullah, H., Al-Rakhami, M., & Gumaei, A. (2021). Automatic detection of citrus fruit and leaves diseases using deep neural network model. *IEEE Access : Practical Innovations, Open Solutions*, 9, 112942–112954. doi:10.1109/ACCESS.2021.3096895

Khurshid, T., Ahmed, W., Rehan, M., Ahmad, R., Alam, M. M., & Radwan, A. (2023). A DRL Strategy for Optimal Resource Allocation along with 3D Trajectory Dynamics in UAV-MEC Network. *IEEE Access*. IEEE.

Kiran, B. R., Sobh, I., Talpaert, V., Mannion, P., Al Sallab, A. A., Yogamani, S., & Pérez, P. (2021). Deep reinforcement learning for autonomous driving: A survey. *IEEE Transactions on Intelligent Transportation Systems*, 23(6), 4909–4926. doi:10.1109/TITS.2021.3054625

Kononenko, I. (2001). Machine learning for medical diagnosis: History, state of the art and perspective. *Artificial Intelligence in Medicine*, 23(1), 89–109. doi:10.1016/S0933-3657(01)00077-X PMID:11470218

Kouadio, L., El Jarroudi, M., Belabess, Z., Laasli, S.-E., Roni, M. Z. K., Amine, I. D. I., Mokhtari, N., Mokrini, F., Junk, J., & Lahlali, R. (2023). A Review on UAV-Based Applications for Plant Disease Detection and Monitoring. *Remote Sensing (Basel)*, 2023(15), 4273. doi:10.3390/rs15174273

Kraus, D., & Schmerbeck, J. (2021). Forest Fire Management Manual, India, Himalayas. In Indo-German Biodiversity Programme Conservation and Sustainable Use of Biodiversity in India. Himachal Pradesh Forest Ecosystem Services Project (HP-FES).

Krausman, P. R., & Johnsingh, A. J. T. (1990). Conservation and wildlife education in India. *Wildlife Society Bulletin (1973-2006)*, 18(3), 342-347

Krausman, P. R., & Cain, J. W. (Eds.). (2022). *Wildlife management and conservation: contemporary principles and practices*. JHU Press. doi:10.56021/9781421443973

Krestenitis, M., Raptis, E. K., Kapoutsis, A. C., Ioannidis, K., Kosmatopoulos, E. B., Vrochidis, S., & Kompatsiaris, I. (2022). CoFly-WeedDB: A UAV image dataset for weed detection and species identification. *Data in Brief*, 45, 108575. doi:10.1016/j.dib.2022.108575 PMID:36131952

Kreuzberger, D., Kuhl, N., & Hirschl, S. (2023). Machine Learning Operations (MLOps): Overview, Definition, and Architecture. *IEEE Access : Practical Innovations, Open Solutions*, 11, 31866–31879. doi:10.1109/ACCESS.2023.3262138

Krnjaic, A., Steleac, R. D., Thomas, J. D., Papoudakis, G., Schäfer, L., Andrew, W. K. T., Lao, K.-H., Cubuktepe, M., Haley, M., Börsting, P., & Albrecht, S. V. (2023). *Scalable Multi-Agent Reinforcement Learning for Warehouse Logistics with Robotic and Human Co-Workers*. ArXiv.

Ksibi, A., Ayadi, M., Soufiene, B. O., Jamjoom, M. M., & Ullah, Z. (2022). MobiRes-net: A hybrid deep learning model for detecting and classifying olive leaf diseases. *Applied Sciences (Basel, Switzerland)*, 12(20), 10278. doi:10.3390/app122010278

Kulkarni, O. (2018, August). Crop disease detection using deep learning. In 2018 Fourth international conference on computing communication control and automation (ICCUBEA) (pp. 1-4). IEEE. 10.1109/ICCUBEA.2018.8697390

Kulkarni, R., & Di Minin, E. (2023). Towards automatic detection of wildlife trade using machine vision models. *Biological Conservation*, 279, 109924. doi:10.1016/j.biocon.2023.109924

Kumar, A., Sharma, K., Singh, H., Srikanth, P., Krishnamurthi, R., & Nayyar, A. (2021). Drone-based social distancing, sanitization, inspection, monitoring, and control room for COVID-19. *artificial intelligence and machine learning for covid-19*, 153-173.

Kumar, R., Singh, M. P., Kumar, P., & Singh, J. P. (2015, May). Crop Selection Method to maximize crop yield rate using machine learning technique. In 2015 international conference on smart technologies and management for computing, communication, controls, energy and materials (ICSTM) (pp. 138-145). IEEE. doi:10.1109/ICSTM.2015.7225403

Kumar, R., Singh, L., & Tiwari, R. (2023). Novel Reinforcement Learning Guided Enhanced Variable Weight Grey Wolf Optimization (RLV-GWO) Algorithm for Multi-UAV Path Planning. *Wireless Personal Communications*, *131*(3), 1–31. doi:10.100711277-023-10534-w

Kuru, K., Clough, S., Ansell, D., McCarthy, J., & McGovern, S. (2023). WILDetect: An intelligent platform to perform airborne wildlife census automatically in the marine ecosystem using an ensemble of learning techniques and computer vision. *Expert Systems with Applications*, *231*, 120574. doi:10.1016/j.eswa.2023.120574

KurunathanH.HuangH.LiK.NiW.HossainE. (2022). Machine Learning-Aided Operations and Communications of Unmanned Aerial Vehicles: A Contemporary Survey. https://arxiv.org/abs/2211.04324

Kuswidiyanto, L. W., Noh, H. H., & Han, X. (2022). Plant Disease Diagnosis Using Deep Learning Based on Aerial Hyperspectral Images: A Review. *Remote Sensing (Basel)*, *14*(23), 6031. doi:10.3390/rs14236031

Kwak, J., Park, J. H., & Sung, Y. (2021). Emerging ICT UAV applications and services: Design of surveillance UAVs. *International Journal of Communication Systems*, *34*(2), e4023. doi:10.1002/dac.4023

Kwon, W., Park, J. H., Lee, M., Her, J., Kim, S. H., & Seo, J. W. (2020). Robust Autonomous Navigation of Unmanned Aerial Vehicles (UAVs) for Warehouses' Inventory Application. *IEEE Robotics and Automation Letters*, *5*(1), 243–249. doi:10.1109/LRA.2019.2955003

Kyrkou, C., & Theocharides, T. (2020). Emergency net: Efficient aerial image classification for drone-based emergency monitoring using atrous convolutional feature fusion. IEEE, 13, 1687–1699.

Lacotte, V., Peignier, S., Raynal, M., Demeaux, I., Delmotte, F., & da Silva, P. (2022). Spatial–spectral analysis of hyperspectral images reveals early detection of downy mildew on grapevine leaves. *International Journal of Molecular Sciences*, *23*(17), 10012. doi:10.3390/ijms231710012 PMID:36077411

Lamichhane, J. R., Barzman, M., Booij, K., Boonekamp, P., Desneux, N., Huber, L., & Ricci, P. (2015). Robust cropping systems to tackle pests under climate change. A review. *Agronomy for Sustainable Development*, *35*(2), 443–459. doi:10.100713593-014-0275-9

Lamini, C., Benhlima, S., & Elbekri, A. (2018). Genetic algorithm based approach for autonomous mobile robot path planning. *Procedia Computer Science*, *127*, 180–189. doi:10.1016/j.procs.2018.01.113

Lan, Y., Huang, Z., Deng, X., Zhu, Z., Huang, H., Zheng, Z., Lian, B., Zeng, G., & Tong, Z. (2020). Comparison of machine learning methods for citrus greening detection on UAV multispectral images. *Computers and Electronics in Agriculture*, *171*, 105234. doi:10.1016/j.compag.2020.105234

Lan, Y., & Wang, G. (2018). Development situation and prospects of China's crop protection UAV industry. *Nongye Gongcheng Jishu*, *38*, 17–27.

Lee, G., Wei, Q., & Zhu, Y. (2021). Emerging wearable sensors for plant health monitoring. *Advanced Functional Materials*, *31*(52), 2106475. doi:10.1002/adfm.202106475

Lee, J., Wang, J., Crandall, D., Sabanovic, S., & Fox, G. (2017). Real-time, cloud-based object detection for unmanned aerial vehicles. In *Proceedings of the 2017 first IEEE international conference on robotic computing (IRC)* (pp. 36–43). IEEE. 10.1109/IRC.2017.77

Lee, S., Song, Y., & Kil, S. H. (2021). Feasibility analyses of real-time detection of wildlife using UAV-derived thermal and RGB images. *Remote Sensing (Basel)*, *13*(11), 2169. doi:10.3390/rs13112169

Lee, W., Jeon, Y., Kim, T., & Kim, Y.-I. (2021). Deep Reinforcement Learning for UAV Trajectory Design Considering Mobile Ground Users. *Sensors (Basel)*, *21*(24), 8239. doi:10.339021248239 PMID:34960332

Leira, F. S., Helgesen, H. H., Johansen, T. A., & Fossen, T. I. (2021). Object detection, recognition, and tracking from UAVs using a thermal camera. *Journal of Field Robotics*, *38*(2), 242–267. doi:10.1002/rob.21985

Leiva, J. N., Robbins, J., Saraswat, D., She, Y., & Ehsani, R. (2016). Effect of plant canopy shape and flowers on plant count accuracy using remote sensing imagery. *Agricultural Engineering International: CIGR Journal*, *18*(2), 73–82.

Leong, W. H., Teh, S. Y., Hossain, M. M., Nadarajaw, T., Zabidi-Hussin, Z., Chin, S. Y., Lai, K.-S., & Lim, S. H. E. (2020). Application, monitoring and adverse effects in pesticide use: The importance of reinforcement of Good Agricultural Practices (GAPs). *Journal of Environmental Management*, *260*, 109987. doi:10.1016/j.jenvman.2019.109987 PMID:32090796

Leonid, T. T., & Kanna, H. (2023). *C. C., A S, H., & Lokesh, C* (Vol. J). Human Wildlife Conflict Mitigation Using YOLO Algorithm., doi:10.1109/ICONSTEM56934.2023.10142629

Li, W., Jin, B., Wang, X., Yan, J., & Zha, H. (2020). *F2A2: Flexible Fully-decentralized Approximate Actor-critic for Cooperative Multi-agent Reinforcement Learning.*

Liang, E., & Liaw, R. (2018). *Scaling Multi-Agent Reinforcement Learning.* Berkeley Artificial Intelligence Research. https://bair.berkeley.edu/blog/2018/12/12/rllib/

Liang, D., Liu, W., Zhao, L., Zong, S., & Luo, Y. (2022). An improved convolutional neural network for plant disease detection using unmanned aerial vehicle images. *Nature Environment and Pollution Technology*, *21*(2), 899–908. doi:10.46488/NEPT.2022.v21i02.053

Liang, J. H., & Lee, C. H. (2015). Efficient collision-free path-planning of multiple mobile robots system using efficient artificial bee colony algorithm. *Advances in Engineering Software*, *79*, 47–56. doi:10.1016/j.advengsoft.2014.09.006

Li, C., Tanghe, E., Suanet, P., Plets, D., Hoebeke, J., De Poorter, E., & Joseph, W. (2021). ReLoc 2.0: UHF-RFID Relative Localization for Drone-Based Inventory Management. *IEEE Transactions on Instrumentation and Measurement*, *70*, 1–13. doi:10.1109/TIM.2021.3069377

Li, D., Yin, W., Wong, W. E., Jian, M., & Chau, M. (2021). Quality-oriented hybrid path planning based on a* and q-learning for unmanned aerial vehicle. *IEEE Access : Practical Innovations, Open Solutions*, *10*, 7664–7674. doi:10.1109/ACCESS.2021.3139534

Li, F., Gnyp, M. L., Jia, L., Miao, Y., Yu, Z., Koppe, W., & Zhang, F. (2008). Estimating N status of winter wheat using a handheld spectrometer in the North China Plain. *Field Crops Research*, *106*(1), 77–85. doi:10.1016/j.fcr.2007.11.001

Li, H., Zhao, W., Zhang, Y., & Zio, E. (2020). Remaining useful life prediction using multi-scale deep convolutional neural network. *Applied Soft Computing*, *89*, 106113. doi:10.1016/j.asoc.2020.106113

Li, L., Huang, W., Gu, H., & Tian, Q. (2004). Statistical modeling of complex backgrounds for foreground object detection. *IEEE Transactions on Image Processing*, *13*(11), 1459–1472. doi:10.1109/TIP.2004.836169 PMID:15540455

Lim, S., & Lee, H. (2023). *Decentralized Q-learning based Optimal Placement and Transmit Power Control in Multi-TUAV Networks. 2023 IEEE 20th Consumer Communications & Networking Conference (CCNC).* IEEE.

Lin, J.-S., Chiu, H.-T., & Gau, R.-H. (2021). Decentralized planning-assisted deep reinforcement learning for collision and obstacle avoidance in uav networks. *2021 IEEE 93rd Vehicular Technology Conference (VTC2021-Spring).* IEEE.

Lina E. & Elmustafa, A. (2022). Deep and Reinforcement Learning Technologies on Internet of Vehicle (IoV) Applications: Current Issues and Future Trends. *Journal of Advanced Transportation.* doi:10.1155/2022/1947886

Linchant, J., Lejeune, P., Quevauvillers, S., Vermeulen, C., Brostaux, Y., Lhoest, S., & Michez, A. (2023). Evaluation of an Innovative Rosette Flight Plan Design for Wildlife Aerial Surveys with UAS. *Drones (Basel)*, *7*(3), 208. doi:10.3390/drones7030208

Linchant, J., Lisein, J., Semeki, J., Lejeune, P., & Vermeulen, C. (2015). Are unmanned aircraft systems (UAS s) the future of wildlife monitoring? A review of accomplishments and challenges. *Mammal Review*, *45*(4), 239–252. doi:10.1111/mam.12046

Li, S., Chen, X., Zhang, M., Jin, Q., Guo, Y., & Xing, S. (2022). A UAV coverage path planning algorithm based on double deep q-network. *Journal of Physics: Conference Series*. IEEE.

Liu, D., Dou, L., Zhang, R., Zhang, X., & Zong, Q. (2023). Multi-Agent Reinforcement Learning-Based Coordinated Dynamic Task Allocation for Heterogenous UAVs. *IEEE Transactions on Vehicular Technology*, *72*(4), 4372–4383. doi:10.1109/TVT.2022.3228198

Liu, H. (2023). A Novel Path Planning Method for Aerial UAV based on Improved Genetic Algorithm. *2023 Third International Conference on Artificial Intelligence and Smart Energy (ICAIS)*. IEEE.

Liu, H., Chen, Q., Pan, N., Sun, Y., An, Y., & Pan, D. (2022). UAV Stocktaking Task-Planning for Industrial Warehouses Based on the Improved Hybrid Differential Evolution Algorithm. *IEEE Transactions on Industrial Informatics*, *18*(1), 582–591. doi:10.1109/TII.2021.3054172

Liu, H., Ge, J., Wang, Y., Li, J., Ding, K., Zhang, Z., Guo, Z., Li, W., & Lan, J. (2021). Multi-UAV optimal mission assignment and path planning for disaster rescue using adaptive genetic algorithm and improved artificial bee colony method. *Actuators*.

Liu, Q., Shi, L., Sun, L., Li, J., Ding, M., & Shu, F. S. (2020). Path Planning for UAV-Mounted Mobile Edge Computing With Deep Reinforcement Learning. *IEEE Transactions on Vehicular Technology*, *69*(5), 5723–5728. doi:10.1109/TVT.2020.2982508

Liu, Q., Zhang, Y., Li, M., Zhang, Z., Cao, N., & Shang, J. (2021). Multi-UAV path planning based on fusion of sparrow search algorithm and improved bioinspired neural network. *IEEE Access : Practical Innovations, Open Solutions*, *9*, 124670–124681.

Liu, S. Y. (2020). Artificial intelligence (AI) in agriculture. *IT Professional*, *22*(3), 14–15. doi:10.1109/MITP.2020.2986121

Liu, S., Zhou, Y., Song, J., Zheng, T., Chen, K., Zhu, T., Feng, Z., & Song, M. (2023). Contrastive Identity-Aware Learning for Multi-Agent Value Decomposition. *Proceedings of the AAAI Conference on Artificial Intelligence*, (pp. 11595–11603). AAAI. 10.1609/aaai.v37i10.26370

Liu, X., Liu, Y., & Chen, Y. (2019). Reinforcement learning in multiple-UAV networks: Deployment and movement design. *IEEE Transactions on Vehicular Technology*, *68*(8), 8036–8049. doi:10.1109/TVT.2019.2922849

Liu, X., Wang, X., Huang, M., Jia, J., Bartolini, N., Li, Q., & Zhao, D. (2023). Deployment of UAV-BSs for on-demand full communication coverage. *Ad Hoc Networks*, *140*, 103047. doi:10.1016/j.adhoc.2022.103047

Liu, Y., Zhang, P., Ru, Y., Wu, D., Wang, S., Yin, N., Meng, F., & Liu, Z. (2022). A scheduling route planning algorithm based on the dynamic genetic algorithm with ant colony binary iterative optimization for unmanned aerial vehicle spraying in multiple tea fields. *Frontiers in Plant Science*, *13*, 998962. doi:10.3389/fpls.2022.998962 PMID:36186015

Liu, Y., Zheng, Z., Qin, F., Zhang, X., & Yao, H. (2022). A residual convolutional neural network based approach for real-time path planning. *Knowledge-Based Systems*, *242*, 108400. doi:10.1016/j.knosys.2022.108400

Li, X., Huang, X., Li, C., Yu, R., & Shu, L. (2019). EdgeCare: Leveraging edge computing for collaborative data management in mobile healthcare systems. *IEEE Access : Practical Innovations, Open Solutions*, 7, 22011–22025. doi:10.1109/ACCESS.2019.2898265

LiX.LiL.GaoJ.HeX.ChenJ.DengL.HeJ. (2015). *Recurrent Reinforcement Learning: A Hybrid Approach*. arXiv. https://arxiv.org/abs/1509.03044

Li, X., & Savkin, A. V. (2021). Networked unmanned aerial vehicles for surveillance and monitoring: A survey. *Future Internet*, 13(7), 174. doi:10.3390/fi13070174

Li, X., & Xing, L. (2019). Use of Unmanned Aerial Vehicles for Livestock Monitoring based on Streaming K-Means Clustering. *IFAC-PapersOnLine*, 52(30), 324–329. doi:10.1016/j.ifacol.2019.12.560

Li, Z., Liu, F., Yang, W., Peng, S., & Zhou, J. (2021). A survey of convolutional neural networks: Analysis, applications, and prospects. *IEEE Transactions on Neural Networks and Learning Systems*. PMID:34111009

Lo, L.-Y., Yiu, C. H., Tang, Y., Yang, A.-S., Li, B., & Wen, C.-Y. (2021). Dynamic Object Tracking on Autonomous UAV System for Surveillance Applications. *Sensors (Basel)*, 21(23), 7888. doi:10.339021237888 PMID:34883913

Long, Q., Zhou, Z., Gupta, A., Fang, F., Wu, Y., & Wang, X. (2020). *Evolutionary Population Curriculum for Scaling Multi-Agent Reinforcement Learning*.

Lowe, R., Wu, Y. I., Tamar, A., Harb, J., Pieter Abbeel, O., & Mordatch, I. (2017). Multi-Agent Actor-Critic for Mixed Cooperative-Competitive Environments. *Advances in Neural Information Processing Systems*, 30.

Lu, K., Hu, R., Yao, Z., & Wang, H. (2022). Onboard Distributed Trajectory Planning through Intelligent Search for Multi-UAV Cooperative Flight. *Drones (Basel)*, 7(1), 16. doi:10.3390/drones7010016

Lundin, O., Rundlöf, M., Jonsson, M., Bommarco, R., & Williams, N. M. (2021). Integrated pest and pollinator management–expanding the concept. *Frontiers in Ecology and the Environment*, 19(5), 283–291. doi:10.1002/fee.2325

Luo, J., Song, J., Zheng, F.-C., Gao, L., & Wang, T. (2022). User-centric UAV deployment and content placement in cache-enabled multi-UAV networks. *IEEE Transactions on Vehicular Technology*, 71(5), 5656–5660. doi:10.1109/TVT.2022.3152246

Lurie, N., Manolio, T., Patterson, A. P., Collins, F., & Frieden, T. (2013). Research as a part of public health emergency response. *The New England Journal of Medicine*, 368(13), 1251–1255. doi:10.1056/NEJMsb1209510 PMID:23534565

Lu, Y., Xiong, G., Zhang, X., Zhang, Z., Jia, T., & Xiong, K. (2022). Uplink Throughput Maximization in UAV-Aided Mobile Networks: A DQN-Based Trajectory Planning Method. *Drones (Basel)*, 6(12), 378. doi:10.3390/drones6120378

Luz-Ricca, E., Landolt, K., Pickens, B. A., & Koneff, M. (2023). Automating sandhill crane counts from nocturnal thermal aerial imagery using deep learning. *Remote Sensing in Ecology and Conservation*, 9(2), 182–194. doi:10.1002/rse2.301

Lygouras, E., Santavas, N., Taitzoglou, A., Tarchanidis, K., Mitropoulos, A., & Gasteratos, A. (2019). Unsupervised human detection with an embedded vision system on a fully autonomous UAV for search and rescue operations. *Sensors (Basel)*, 19(16), 3542. doi:10.339019163542 PMID:31416131

Lyu, J., & Zhang, R. (2019). Network-connected UAV: 3-D system modeling and coverage performance analysis. *IEEE Internet of Things Journal*, 6(4), 7048–7060. doi:10.1109/JIOT.2019.2913887

Lyu, Y., Vosselman, G., Xia, G. S., Yilmaz, A., & Yang, M. Y. (2020). UA Vid: A semantic segmentation dataset for UAV imagery. *ISPRS Journal of Photogrammetry and Remote Sensing*, 165, 108–119. doi:10.1016/j.isprsjprs.2020.05.009

Ma, B., Zhang, J., Zhang, Z., & Zhang, J. (2023). Time efficient joint UAV-BS deployment and user association based on machine learning. *IEEE Internet of Things Journal*, *10*(14), 13077–13094. doi:10.1109/JIOT.2023.3263208

Macrina, G., Pugliese, L. D. P., Guerriero, F., & Laporte, G. (2020). Drone-aided routing: A literature review. *Transportation Research Part C, Emerging Technologies*, *120*, 102762. doi:10.1016/j.trc.2020.102762

Magna, A. A. R., Allende-Cid, H., Taramasco, C., Becerra, C., & Figueroa, R. L. (2020). Application of machine learning and word embeddings in the classification of cancer diagnosis using patient anamnesis. *IEEE Access : Practical Innovations, Open Solutions*, *8*, 106198–106213. doi:10.1109/ACCESS.2020.3000075

Mahmood, M., Koc, A., & Le-Ngoc, T. (2022). PSO-Based Joint UAV Positioning and Hybrid Precoding in UAV-Assisted Massive MIMO Systems. *2022 IEEE 96th Vehicular Technology Conference (VTC2022-Fall)*. IEEE.

Maimaitiyiming, M., Ghulam, A., Bozzolo, A., Wilkins, J. L., & Kwasniewski, M. T. (2017). Early Detection of Plant Physiological Responses to Different Levels of Water Stress Using Reflectance Spectroscopy. *Remote Sensing (Basel)*, *9*(7), 745. doi:10.3390/rs9070745

Malang, C., Charoenkwan, P., & Wudhikarn, R. (2023). Implementation and Critical Factors of Unmanned Aerial Vehicle (UAV) in Warehouse Management: A Systematic Literature Review. *Drones (Basel)*, *7*(2), 80. doi:10.3390/drones7020080

Mamoon, S. M., Saeed, R. A., Gaid, A. S., Mokhtar, R. A., Khalifa, O. O., & Ahmed, Z. E. (2023, August). Attacks Detection in 6G Wireless Networks using Machine Learning. In *2023 9th International Conference on Computer and Communication Engineering (ICCCE)* (pp. 6-11). IEEE.

Mamoon, S. M., Ahmed, E. S. A., Saeed, R. A., & Azim, M. A. (2022). Green machine learning protocols for cellular communication. In *Green Machine Learning Protocols for Future Communication Networks* (pp. 15–62). CRC Press.

Mamoon, S. M., & Kamrul, H. (2022). Preserving Privacy of User Identity Based on Pseudonym Variable in 5G. *Computers, Materials & Continua*, *70*(3).

Mandloi, D., & Arya, R. (2023). Q-learning-based UAV-mounted base station positioning in a disaster scenario for connectivity to the users located at unknown positions. *The Journal of Supercomputing*, 1–32.

Mandloi, D., Arya, R., & Verma, A. K. (2021). Unmanned aerial vehicle path planning based on A* algorithm and its variants in 3d environment. *International Journal of System Assurance Engineering and Management*, *12*(5), 990–1000. doi:10.100713198-021-01186-9

Manici, L., Bregaglio, S., Fumagalli, D., & Donatelli, M. (2014). Modelling soil-borne fungal pathogens of arable crops under climate change. *International Journal of Biometeorology*, *58*(10), 2071–2083. doi:10.100700484-014-0808-6 PMID:24615638

Manogaran, G., Thota, C., Lopez, D., & Sundarasekar, R. (2017). Big data security intelligence for healthcare industry 4.0. *Cybersecurity for Industry 4.0: Analysis for Design and Manufacturing*, 103-126.

Mansour, R. F., Alfar, N. M., Abdel-Khalek, S., Abdelhaq, M., Saeed, R. A., & Alsaqour, R. (2022). Optimal deep learning based fusion model for biomedical image classification. *Expert Systems: International Journal of Knowledge Engineering and Neural Networks*, *39*(3), e12764. doi:10.1111/exsy.12764

Manullang, M. J. C., Priandana, K., & Hardhienata, M. K. D. (2023). Optimum trajectory of multi-UAV for fertilization of paddy fields using ant colony optimization (ACO) and 2-opt algorithms. AIP Conference Proceedings.

Mao, H., Liu, Y., Xiao, Z., Han, Z., & Xia, X.-G. (2023). Joint Resource Allocation and 3D Deployment for Multi-UAV Covert Communications. *IEEE Internet of Things Journal*. IEEE.

Marinescu, A., Dusparic, I., & Clarke, S. (2017). Prediction-Based Multi-Agent Reinforcement Learning in Inherently Non-Stationary Environments. *ACM Transactions on Autonomous and Adaptive Systems, 12*(2), 1–23. doi:10.1145/3070861

Markets and Markets. (2019). *Unmanned Aerial Vehicles (UAV) market.* Markets and Markets. https://www.marketsandmarkets.com/Market-Reports/unmanned-aerial-vehicles-uav-market

Markovchick-Nicholls, L., Regan, H. M., Deutschman, D. H., Widyanata, A., Martin, B., Noreke, L., & Ann Hunt, T. (2008). Relationships between Human Disturbance and Wildlife Land Use in Urban Habitat Fragments. *Conservation Biology, 22*(1), 99–109. doi:10.1111/j.1523-1739.2007.00846.x PMID:18254856

Markowitz, H., Aday, C., & Gavazzi, A. (1995). Effectiveness of acoustic "prey": Environmental enrichment for a captive African leopard (Panthera pardus). *Zoo Biology, 14*(4), 371–379. doi:10.1002/zoo.1430140408

Marsh, I. (2015). *Drones-a View into the Future for the Logistics Sector.*

Martini, B. F., & Miller, D. A. (2021). Using object-based image analysis to detect laughing gull nests. *GIScience & Remote Sensing, 58*(8), 1497–1517. doi:10.1080/15481603.2021.1999376

Marwah, N., Singh, V. K., Kashyap, G. S., & Wazir, S. (2023). An analysis of the robustness of UAV agriculture field coverage using multi-agent reinforcement learning. *International Journal of Information Technology : an Official Journal of Bharati Vidyapeeth's Institute of Computer Applications and Management, 15*(4), 1–11. doi:10.100741870-023-01264-0

Mason-D'Croz, D., Bogard, J. R., Herrero, M., Robinson, S., Sulser, T. B., Wiebe, K., Willenbockel, D., & Godfray, H. C. J. (2020). Modelling the global economic consequences of a major African swine fever outbreak in China. *Nature Food, 1*(4), 221–228. doi:10.103843016-020-0057-2 PMID:33634268

Matese, A., Baraldi, R., Berton, A., Cesaraccio, C., Di Gennaro, S. F., Duce, P., Facini, O., Mameli, M., Piga, A., & Zaldei, A. (2018). Estimation of water stress in grapevines using proximal and remote sensing methods. *Remote Sensing (Basel), 10*(1), 114. doi:10.3390/rs10010114

Mbunge, E., Muchemwa, B., & Batani, J. (2021). Sensors and healthcare 5.0: Transformative shift in virtual care through emerging digital health technologies. *Global Health Journal (Amsterdam, Netherlands), 5*(4), 169–177. doi:10.1016/j.glohj.2021.11.008

McComb, B. C. (2007). *Wildlife habitat management: concepts and applications in forestry.* CRC Press. doi:10.1201/9781420007633

McGuire, K., Coppola, M., De Wagter, C., & de Croon, G. 2017, September. Towards autonomous navigation of multiple pocket-drones in real-world environments. In *2017 IEEE/RSJ International Conference on Intelligent Robots and Systems (IROS)* (pp. 244-249). IEEE. 10.1109/IROS.2017.8202164

Megat Mohamed Nazir, M. N., Terhem, R., Norhisham, A. R., Mohd Razali, S., & Meder, R. (2021). Early monitoring of health status of plantation-grown eucalyptus pellita at large spatial scale via visible spectrum imaging of canopy foliage using unmanned aerial vehicles. *Forests, 12*(10), 1393. doi:10.3390/f12101393

Meng, W., Hu, Y., Lin, J., Lin, F., & Teo, R. (2015). ROS+unity: An efficient high-fidelity 3D multi-UAV navigation and control simulator in GPS-denied environments. *IECON 2015 - 41st Annual Conference of the IEEE Industrial Electronics Society.* IEEE. 10.1109/IECON.2015.7392488

Messina, G., & Modica, G. (2020). Applications of UAV thermal imagery in precision agriculture: State of the art and future research outlook. *Remote Sensing (Basel), 12*(9), 1491. doi:10.3390/rs12091491

Miao, Y., Hwang, K., Wu, D., Hao, Y., & Chen, M. (2023). Drone Swarm Path Planning for Mobile Edge Computing in Industrial Internet of Things. *IEEE Transactions on Industrial Informatics, 19*(5), 6836–6848. doi:10.1109/TII.2022.3196392

Micheal, A., Vani, K., Sanjeevi, S., & Lin, C.-H. (2020). Object Detection and Tracking with UAV Data Using Deep Learning. *Photonirvachak (Dehra Dun)*, *49*(3), 1–7. doi:10.100712524-020-01229-x

Mills, E. H. A., Aasbjerg, K., Hansen, S. M., Ringgren, K. B., Dahl, M., Rasmussen, B. S., Torp-Pedersen, C., Søgaard, P., & Kragholm, K. (2019). Prehospital time and mortality in patients requiring a highest priority emergency medical response: A Danish registry-based cohort study. *BMJ Open*, *9*(11), e023049. doi:10.1136/bmjopen-2018-023049 PMID:31753864

Minhas, H. I., Ahmad, R., Ahmed, W., Waheed, M., Alam, M. M., & Gul, S. T. (2021). A reinforcement learning routing protocol for UAV aided public safety networks. *Sensors (Basel)*, *21*(12), 4121. doi:10.339021124121 PMID:34203912

Misbah, M., Kaleem, Z., Khalid, W., Yuen, C., & Jamalipour, A. (2023). Phase and 3D Placement Optimization for Rate Enhancement in RIS-Assisted UAV Networks. *IEEE Wireless Communications Letters*. IEEE.

Mishra B, Garg D, Narang P, & Mishra V. (2020). *Drone-surveillance for search and rescue in natural disaster*. Elsevier. . doi:10.1016/j.comcom.2020.03.012

Mishra, A. R., Karimi, D., Ehsani, R., & Lee, W. S. (2012). Identification of Citrus Greening (HLB) Using a VIS-NIR Spectroscopy Technique. *Transactions of the ASABE*, *55*(2), 711–720. doi:10.13031/2013.41369

Mittal, P., Singh, R., & Sharma, A. (2020). Deep learning-based object detection in low-altitude UAV datasets: A survey. *Image and Vision Computing*, *104*, 104046. doi:10.1016/j.imavis.2020.104046

Mohammad, K., & Taher, M. (2022). A review on security threats, vulnerabilities, and counter measures of 5G enabled Internet-of-Medical-Things. *IET Communications*, *16*(5), 421–432. doi:10.1049/cmu2.12301

Mohammed S. M., Ali, E. S., & Saeed, R. A. (2023). Data-Driven Techniques and Security Issues in Wireless Networks. *Data-Driven Intelligence in Wireless Networks: Concepts, Solutions, and Applications*, 107.

Mohammed, S. M. (2023). Task Reverse Offloading with Deep Reinforcement Learning in Multi-Access Edge Computing. In *2023 9th International Conference on Computer and Communication Engineering (ICCCE)* (pp. 322-327). IEEE.

Mohammed, S. M., Saeed, R. A., Azim, M. A., Ali, E. S., Mokhtar, R. A., & Khalifa, O. (2022, May). Green Machine Learning Approach for QoS Improvement in Cellular Communications. In *2022 IEEE 2nd International Maghreb Meeting of the Conference on Sciences and Techniques of Automatic Control and Computer Engineering (MI-STA)* (pp. 523-528). IEEE.

Mohammed, F., Idries, A., Mohamed, N., Al-Jaroodi, J., & Jawhar, I. (2014). UAVs for smart cities: Opportunities and challenges. *2014 International Conference on Unmanned Aircraft Systems, ICUAS 2014 - Conference Proceedings*, (pp. 267–273). IEEE. 10.1109/ICUAS.2014.6842265

Mohan, M., Richardson, G., Gopan, G., Aghai, M. M., Bajaj, S., Galgamuwa, G. A. P., Vastaranta, M., Arachchige, P. S. P., Amorós, L., Corte, A. P. D., de-Miguel, S., Leite, R. V., Kganyago, M., Broadbent, E. N., Doaemo, W., Shorab, M. A. B., & Cardil, A. (2021). UAV-Supported Forest Regeneration: Current Trends, Challenges and Implications. *Remote Sensing (Basel)*, *13*(13), 13. Advance online publication. doi:10.3390/rs13132596

Mohanty, S. N., Ravindra, J. V. R., Narayana, G. S., Pattnaik, C. R., & Sirajudeen, Y. M. (Eds.). (2023). *Drone Technology: Future Trends and Practical Applications*. John Wiley & Sons. doi:10.1002/9781394168002

Mohsan, S. A. H., Khan, M. A., Noor, F., Ullah, I., & Alsharif, M. H. (2022). Towards the Unmanned Aerial Vehicles (UAVs): A Comprehensive Review. In Drones, 6(6). MDPI. doi:10.3390/drones6060147

Mohsan, S. A. H., Othman, N. Q. H., Li, Y., Alsharif, M. H., & Khan, M. A. (2023). Unmanned aerial vehicles (UAVs): Practical aspects, applications, open challenges, security issues, and future trends. *Intelligent Service Robotics*, *16*(1), 109–137. doi:10.100711370-022-00452-4 PMID:36687780

Mona, B., & Elmustafa, S. (2020). NB-IoT: Concepts, Applications, and Deployment Challenges. In B. Chaudhari & M. Zennaro (eds.) LPWAN Technologies for IoT and M2MApplications. Elsevier.

Moon, H., Martinez-Carranza, J., Cieslewski, T., Faessler, M., Falanga, D., Simovic, A., Scaramuzza, D., Li, S., Ozo, M., De Wagter, C., de Croon, G., Hwang, S., Jung, S., Shim, H., Kim, H., Park, M., Au, T.-C., & Kim, S. J. (2019). Challenges and implemented technologies used in autonomous drone racing. *Intelligent Service Robotics*, *12*(2), 137–148. doi:10.100711370-018-00271-6

Moon, J., Papaioannou, S., Laoudias, C., Kolios, P., & Kim, S. (2021). Deep Reinforcement Learning Multi-UAV Trajectory Control for Target Tracking. *IEEE Internet of Things Journal*, *8*(20), 15441–15455. doi:10.1109/JIOT.2021.3073973

Moradi, M. (2016). A centralized reinforcement learning method for multi-agent job scheduling in Grid. *2016 6th International Conference on Computer and Knowledge Engineering (ICCKE)*, (pp. 171–176). 10.1109/ICCKE.2016.7802135

Moradi, M., Bokani, A., & Hassan, J. (2020). *Energy-Efficient and QoS-aware UAV Communication using Reactive RF Band Allocation*. 2020 30th International Telecommunication Networks and Applications Conference (ITNAC), Melbourne, VIC, Australia. 10.1109/ITNAC50341.2020.9315157

Moradi, S., Bokani, A., & Hassan, J. (2022). *UAV-based Smart Agriculture: a Review of UAV Sensing and Applications*. 2022 32nd International Telecommunication Networks and Applications Conference (ITNAC), Wellington, New Zealand. 10.1109/ITNAC55475.2022.9998411

Moradi, S., Bokani, A., & Hassan, J. (2022, November). UAV-based Smart Agriculture: a Review of UAV Sensing and Applications. In *2022 32nd International Telecommunication Networks and Applications Conference (ITNAC)* (pp. 181-184). IEEE.

Mostafa, A. F., Abdel-Kader, M., Gadallah, Y., & Elayat, O. (2023). Machine Learning-Based Multi-UAVs Deployment for Uplink Traffic Sizing and Offloading in Cellular Networks. *IEEE Access : Practical Innovations, Open Solutions*, *11*, 71314–71325. doi:10.1109/ACCESS.2023.3293148

Mota-Rojas, D., Pereira, A. M., Martínez-Burnes, J., Domínguez-Oliva, A., Mora-Medina, P., Casas-Alvarado, A., Rios-Sandoval, J., de Mira Geraldo, A., & Wang, D. (2022). Thermal Imaging to Assess the Health Status in Wildlife Animals under Human Care: Limitations and Perspectives. *Animals (Basel)*, *12*(24), 3558. doi:10.3390/ani12243558 PMID:36552478

Motlagh, N. H., Kortoçi, P., Su, X., Lovén, L., Hoel, H. K., Haugsvær, S. B., Srivastava, V., Gulbrandsen, C. F., Nurmi, P., & Tarkoma, S. (2023). Unmanned Aerial Vehicles for Air Pollution Monitoring: A survey. *IEEE Internet of Things Journal*, 1. doi:10.1109/JIOT.2023.3290508

Moura, A., Antunes, J., Dias, A., Martins, A., & Almeida, J. (2021). Graph-SLAM Approach for Indoor UAV Localization in Warehouse Logistics Applications. *2021 IEEE International Conference on Autonomous Robot Systems and Competitions, ICARSC 2021*, (pp. 4–11). IEEE. 10.1109/ICARSC52212.2021.9429791

Mourtzis, D., Angelopoulos, J., & Panopoulos, N. (2021). Smart manufacturing and tactile internet based on 5G in industry 4.0: Challenges, applications and new trends. *Electronics (Basel)*, *10*(24), 3175. doi:10.3390/electronics10243175

Mozaffari, M., Saad, W., Bennis, M., & Debbah, M. (2016). Optimal transport theory for power-efficient deployment of unmanned aerial vehicles. *2016 IEEE international conference on communications (ICC)*. IEEE.

Mozaffari, M., Saad, W., Bennis, M., Nam, Y.-H., & Debbah, M. (2019). A tutorial on UAVs for wireless networks: Applications, challenges, and open problems. IEEE Communications Surveys and Tutorials, 21(3), 2334–2360. doi:10.1109/COMST.2019.2902862

Muehlematter, U. J., Daniore, P., & Vokinger, K. N. (2021). Approval of artificial intelligence and machine learning-based medical devices in the USA and Europe (2015–20): A comparative analysis. *The Lancet. Digital Health*, *3*(3), e195–e203. doi:10.1016/S2589-7500(20)30292-2 PMID:33478929

Muhammad, G., Alqahtani, S., & Alelaiwi, A. (2021). Pandemic management for diseases similar to COVID-19 using deep learning and 5G communications. *IEEE Network*, *35*(3), 21–26. doi:10.1109/MNET.011.2000739

Mukati, N., Namdev, N., Dilip, R., Hemalatha, N., Dhiman, V., & Sahu, B. (2023). Healthcare assistance to COVID-19 patient using internet of things (IoT) enabled technologies. *Materials Today: Proceedings*, *80*, 3777–3781. doi:10.1016/j.matpr.2021.07.379 PMID:34336599

Mulero-Pázmány, M., Stolper, R., Essen, L., Negro, J. J., & Sassen, T. (2014). Remotely Piloted Aircraft Systems as A Rhinoceros Anti-Poaching tool In Africa. *PLoS One*, *9*(1), e83873. doi:10.1371/journal.pone.0083873 PMID:24416177

Myanmar, W., & Lao, P. D. R. (2022). *Tiger IUCN Status Category: Endangered*. WCS.

Nabeel, M. M., & Al-Shammari, S. W. (2023). Fire Detection Using Unmanned Aerial Vehicle. *Al-Iraqia Journal for Scientific Engineering Research*, *2*(1), 47–56.

Nada, M., Mohammad, K., & Zeinab, K. (2021). Internet of vehicle's resource management in 5G networks using AI technologies: Current status and trends. *IET Communications*, *2021*, 1–21. doi:10.1049/cmu2.12315

Nahla, N., Mohammad, K., & Imran, M. (2021). A Systematic Review on Cognitive Radio in Low Power Wide Area Network for Industrial IoT Applications. *Sustainability (Basel)*, *2021*(1), 338. Advance online publication. doi:10.3390u13010338

Najafabadi, M. M., Villanustre, F., Khoshgoftaar, T. M., Seliya, N., Wald, R., & Muharemagic, E. (2015). Deep learning applications and challenges in big data analytics. *Journal of Big Data*, *2*(1), 1–21. doi:10.118640537-014-0007-7

Nayak, P., & Solanki, H. (2021). Pesticides and Indian agriculture—A review. *Int J Res Granthaalayah*, *9*(5), 250–263. doi:10.29121/granthaalayah.v9.i5.2021.3930

Nazarov, P. A., Baleev, D. N., Ivanova, M. I., Sokolova, L. M., & Karakozova, M. V. (2020). Infectious plant diseases: Etiology, current status, problems and prospects in plant protection. *Acta Naturae (English Ed.)*, *12*(3), 46–59. doi:10.32607/actanaturae.11026 PMID:33173596

Ndiaye, M., Salhi, S., & Madani, B. (2020). When green technology meets optimization modeling: the case of routing drones in logistics, agriculture, and healthcare. *Modeling and Optimization in Green Logistics*, 127-145.

Nebiker, S., Lack, N., Abächerli, M., & Läderach, S. (2016). Light-weight multispectral UAV sensors and their capabilities for predicting grain yield and detecting plant diseases. *The International Archives of the Photogrammetry, Remote Sensing and Spatial Information Sciences*, *41*(B1), 963–970. doi:10.5194/isprs-archives-XLI-B1-963-2016

Nedelea, P. L., Popa, T. O., Manolescu, E., Bouros, C., Grigorasi, G., Andritoi, D., Pascale, C., Andrei, A., & Cimpoesu, D. C. (2022). Telemedicine System Applicability Using Drones in Pandemic Emergency Medical Situations. *Electronics (Basel)*, *11*(14), 2160. doi:10.3390/electronics11142160

Neupane, S. B., Sato, K., & Gautam, B. P. (2022). A literature review of computer vision techniques in wildlife monitoring. *IJSRP*, *16*, 282–295.

Nex, F., Armenakis, C., Cramer, M., Cucci, D. A., Gerke, M., Honkavaara, E., & Skaloud, J. (2022). UAV in the advent of the twenties: Where we stand and what is next. *ISPRS Journal of Photogrammetry and Remote Sensing*, *184*, 215–242. doi:10.1016/j.isprsjprs.2021.12.006

Nguyen, A. Q., Nguyen, H. T., Tran, V. C., Pham, H. X., & Pestana, J. (2021). A Visual Real-time Fire Detection using Single Shot MultiBox Detector for UAV-based Fire Surveillance. In *2020 IEEE Eighth International Conference on Communications and Electronics (ICCE)*. IEEE. 10.1109/ICCE48956.2021.9352080

Nguyen, K. K., Duong, T. Q., Do-Duy, T., Claussen, H., & Hanzo, L. (2022). 3D UAV Trajectory and Data Collection Optimisation Via Deep Reinforcement Learning. *IEEE Transactions on Communications*, *70*(4), 2358–2371. doi:10.1109/TCOMM.2022.3148364

Nicheporchuk, V., Gryazin, I., & Favorskaya, M. N. (2020). *Framework for Intelligent Wildlife Monitoring.*, doi:10.1007/978-981-15-5925-9_14

Nikhat, A., & Yusuf, P. (2020). The internet of nano things (IoNT) existing state and future Prospects. *GSC Advanced Research and Reviews*, *5*(2), 131–150. doi:10.30574/gscarr.2020.5.2.0110

Nithya, P., Annamani, T., Kamble, V. S., Kumar, C. M. S., Karthikeyan, T., & Sujaritha, M. (2023). An Effective Transportation System Method for Optimal Path Planning Using Logistics UAVs Using Deep Q Networks. *International Journal of Intelligent Systems and Applications in Engineering*, *11*(9s), 424–428.

Norgeot, B., Glicksberg, B. S., & Butte, A. J. (2019). A call for deep-learning healthcare. *Nature Medicine*, *25*(1), 14–15. doi:10.103841591-018-0320-3 PMID:30617337

Ntakolia, C., & Lyridis, D. V. (2022). A comparative study on Ant Colony Optimization algorithm approaches for solving multi-objective path planning problems in case of unmanned surface vehicles. *Ocean Engineering*, *255*, 111418. doi:10.1016/j.oceaneng.2022.111418

Nuijten, R. J. G., Kooistra, L., & De Deyn, G. B. (2019). Using unmanned aerial systems (UAS) and object-based image analysis (OBIA) for measuring plant-soil feedback effects on crop productivity. *Drones (Basel)*, *3*(3), 54. doi:10.3390/drones3030054

Nyaaba, A. A., & Ayamga, M. (2021). Intricacies of medical drones in healthcare delivery: Implications for Africa. *Technology in Society*, *66*, 101624. doi:10.1016/j.techsoc.2021.101624

Ocana, C., Martin, J., Riccio, F., Capobianco, R., & Nardi, D. (2019). Cooperative Multi-Agent Deep Reinforcement Learning in Soccer Domains. *In Proceedings of the 18th International Conference on Autonomous Agents and MultiAgent Systems*. IEEE.

Oerke, E. C. (2006). Crop losses to pests. *Journal of Agricultural Science*, *144*(1), 31–43. doi:10.1017/S0021859605005708

Olatomiwa, L., Blanchard, R., Mekhilef, S., & Akinyele, D. (2018). Hybrid renewable energy supply for rural healthcare facilities: An approach to quality healthcare delivery. *Sustainable Energy Technologies and Assessments*, *30*, 121–138. doi:10.1016/j.seta.2018.09.007

Omran, O., & Ahmed, M. Z. (2022). A Stochastic Approach for Blockchain Internet of Things Integration. *2022 International Conference on Advanced Computer Science and Information Systems (ICACSIS)*, (pp. 219-224). IEEE. 10.1109/ICACSIS56558.2022.9923464

Ong, J. H., Sanchez, A., & Williams, J. (2007). Multi-UAV system for inventory automation. *2007 1st Annual RFID Eurasia*. IEEE. doi:10.1109/RFIDEURASIA.2007.4368142

Oroojlooy, A., & Hajinezhad, D. (2022). A review of cooperative multi-agent deep reinforcement learning. *Applied Intelligence*. doi:10.100710489-022-04105-y

Ortega, J. H. J. C., Resureccion, M. R., Natividad, L. R. Q., Bantug, E. T., Lagman, A. C., & Lopez, S. R. (2020). An analysis of classification of breast cancer dataset using J48 algorithm. *Int. J. Adv. Trends Comput. Sci. Eng, 9.*

Ortega, S., Halicek, M., Fabelo, H., Callico, G. M., & Fei, B. (2020). Hyperspectral and multispectral imaging in digital and computational pathology: A systematic review. *Biomedical Optics Express*, *11*(6), 3195–3233. doi:10.1364/BOE.386338 PMID:32637250

Othman, O., & Ahmed, M. Z. (2022). Blockchain Security for 5G Network using Internet of Things Devices. *2022 7th International Workshop on Big Data and Information Security (IWBIS)*. IEEE. 10.1109/IWBIS56557.2022.9924937

Othman, O. (2022). Vehicle Detection for Vision-Based Intelligent Transportation Systems Using Convolutional Neural Network Algorithm. *Journal of Advanced Transportation*, *2022*, 9189600. doi:10.1155/2022/9189600

Oubbati, O. S., Lakas, A., & Guizani, M. (2022). Multi-Agent Deep Reinforcement Learning for Wireless-Powered UAV Networks. *IEEE Internet of Things Journal*, *9*(17), 16044–16059. doi:10.1109/JIOT.2022.3150616

Oueida, S., Kotb, Y., Aloqaily, M., Jararweh, Y., & Baker, T. (2018). An edge computing based smart healthcare framework for resource management. *Sensors (Basel)*, *18*(12), 4307. doi:10.3390/s18124307 PMID:30563267

Outay, F., Mengash, H. A., & Adnan, M. (2020). Applications of unmanned aerial vehicle (UAV) in road safety, traffic and highway infrastructure management: Recent advances and challenges. *Transportation Research Part A, Policy and Practice*, *141*, 116–129. doi:10.1016/j.tra.2020.09.018 PMID:33024357

Öztürk, A. E., & Erçelebi, E. (2021). Real uav-bird image classification using cnn with a synthetic dataset. *Applied Sciences (Basel, Switzerland)*, *11*(9), 3863. doi:10.3390/app11093863

Ozturk, M., Nadas, J. P., Klaine, P. H., Hussain, S., & Imran, M. A. (2020). Clustering based UAV base station positioning for enhanced network capacity. *2019 International Conference on Advances in the Emerging Computing Technologies (AECT)*.

Palladino, N. (2023). A 'biased' emerging governance regime for artificial intelligence? How AI ethics get skewed moving from principles to practices. *Telecommunications Policy*, *47*(5), 102479. doi:10.1016/j.telpol.2022.102479

Panesar, A. (2019). *Machine learning and AI for healthcare*. Apress. doi:10.1007/978-1-4842-3799-1

Panetsos, F., Karras, G. C., & Kyriakopoulos, K. J. (2022). A Deep Reinforcement Learning Motion Control Strategy of a Multi-rotor UAV for Payload Transportation with Minimum Swing. *2022 30th Mediterranean Conference on Control and Automation (MED)*, 368–374. 10.1109/MED54222.2022.9837220

Panetto, H., Lezoche, M., Hormazabal, J. E. H., Diaz, M. D. M. E. A., & Kacprzyk, J. (2020). Special issue on Agri-Food 4.0 and digitalization in agriculture supply chains-New directions, challenges and applications. *Computers in Industry*, *116*, 103188. doi:10.1016/j.compind.2020.103188

Pang, M., Zhu, Q., Lin, Z., Bai, F., Tian, Y., Li, Z., & Chen, X. (2022). Machine learning based altitude-dependent empirical LoS probability model for air-to-ground communications. *Frontiers of Information Technology & Electronic Engineering*, *23*(9), 1378–1389.

Pan, Q., Gao, M., Wu, P., Yan, J., & Li, S. (2021). A deep-learning-based approach for wheat yellow rust disease recognition from unmanned aerial vehicle images. *Sensors (Basel)*, *21*(19), 6540. doi:10.3390/s21196540 PMID:34640873

Park, J. M., Lee, H., & Yu, H. (2023). *Optimal Power and Position Control for UAV-assisted JCR Networks: Multi-Agent Q-Learning Approach. 2023 IEEE 20th Consumer Communications & Networking Conference (CCNC)*. IEEE.

Pasandideh, F., & Rodriguez Cesen, E., F., Henrique Morgan Pereira, P., Esteve Rothenberg, C., & Pignaton de Freitas, E. (2023). An Improved Particle Swarm Optimization Algorithm for UAV Base Station Placement. *Wireless Personal Communications*, *130*(2), 1343–1370. doi:10.1007/s11277-023-10334-2

Paszke, A., Gross, S., Massa, F., Lerer, A., Bradbury, J., Chanan, G., Killeen, T., Lin, Z., Gimelshein, N., Antiga, L., Desmaison, A., Köpf, A., Yang, E., DeVito, Z., Raison, M., Tejani, A., Chilamkurthy, S., Steiner, B., Fang, L., & Bai, J. (2019). *PyTorch: An Imperative Style, High-Performance Deep Learning Library.* ArXiv.org. https://arxiv.org/abs/1912.01703

Patel, J. (2020). Unification of Machine Learning Features. *2020 IEEE 44th Annual Computers, Software, and Applications Conference (COMPSAC),* (pp. 1201–1205). IEEE. 10.1109/COMPSAC48688.2020.00-93

Pathak, P., Damle, M., Pal, P. R., & Yadav, V. (2019). Humanitarian impact of drones in healthcare and disaster management. *Int. J. Recent Technol. Eng, 7*(5), 201–205.

Pathak, V. M., Verma, V. K., Rawat, B. S., Kaur, B., Babu, N., Sharma, A., Dewali, S., Yadav, M., Kumari, R., Singh, S., Mohapatra, A., Pandey, V., Rana, N., & Cunill, J. M. (2022). Current status of pesticide effects on environment, human health and it's eco-friendly management as bioremediation: A comprehensive review. *Frontiers in Microbiology, 13,* 2833. doi:10.3389/fmicb.2022.962619 PMID:36060785

Patterson, L., Pigorovsky, D., Dempsey, B., Lazarev, N., Shah, A., Steinhoff, C., Bruno, A., Hu, J., & Delimitrou, C. (2022). HiveMind: A hardware-software system stack for serverless edge swarms. *Proceedings of the 49th Annual International Symposium on Computer Architecture,* (pp. 800–816). ACM. 10.1145/3470496.3527407

Pehlivanoglu, Y. V., & Pehlivanoglu, P. (2021). An enhanced genetic algorithm for path planning of autonomous UAV in target coverage problems. *Applied Soft Computing, 112,* 107796. doi:10.1016/j.asoc.2021.107796

Peng, H., & Shen, X. (2021). Multi-Agent Reinforcement Learning Based Resource Management in MEC- And UAV-Assisted Vehicular Networks. *IEEE Journal on Selected Areas in Communications, 39*(1), 131–141. doi:10.1109/JSAC.2020.3036962

Peng, Y., Liu, Y., Li, D., & Zhang, H. (2022). Deep reinforcement learning based freshness-aware path planning for UAV-assisted edge computing networks with device mobility. *Remote Sensing (Basel), 14*(16), 4016. doi:10.3390/rs14164016

Pérez-Gil, Ó., Barea, R., López-Guillén, E., Bergasa, L. M., Gómez-Huélamo, C., Gutiérrez, R., & Díaz-Díaz, A. (2022). Deep reinforcement learning based control for Autonomous Vehicles in CARLA. *Multimedia Tools and Applications, 81*(3), 3553–3576. doi:10.100711042-021-11437-3

Petso, T., Jamisola, R. S. Jr, Mpoeleng, D., Bennitt, E., & Mmereki, W. (2021). Automatic animal identification from drone camera based on point pattern analysis of herd behaviour. *Ecological Informatics, 66,* 101485. doi:10.1016/j.ecoinf.2021.101485

Pi Y, Nath N D, & Behzadan A H. (2020). *Convolutional neural networks for object detection in aerial imagery for disaster response and recovery.* Elsevier.

Pizetta, I. H. B., Brandao, A. S., & Sarcinelli-Filho, M. (2018). Control and Obstacle Avoidance for an UAV Carrying a Load in Forestal Environments. *2018 International Conference on Unmanned Aircraft Systems (ICUAS),* (pp. 62–67). IEEE. 10.1109/ICUAS.2018.8453399

Poljak, M., & Šterbenc, A. J. C. M. (2020). Use of drones in clinical microbiology and infectious diseases: Current status, challenges and barriers. *Clinical Microbiology and Infection, 26*(4), 425–430. doi:10.1016/j.cmi.2019.09.014 PMID:31574337

Pourdowlat, G., Panahi, P., Pooransari, P., & Ghorbani, F. (2020). Prophylactic recommendation for healthcare workers in COVID-19 pandemic. *Frontiers in Emergency Medicine, 4*(2s), e39–e39.

Prasad Tripathy, R., Ranjan Mishra, M., & Dash, S. R. (2020). Next Generation Warehouse through disruptive IoT Blockchain. *2020 International Conference on Computer Science, Engineering and Applications (ICCSEA)*, (pp. 1–6). IEEE. 10.1109/ICCSEA49143.2020.9132906

Prasad, A., Mehta, N., Horak, M., & Bae, W. D. (2022). A Two-Step Machine Learning Approach for Crop Disease Detection Using GAN and UAV Technology. *Remote Sensing (Basel)*, *14*(19), 4765. doi:10.3390/rs14194765

Puente-Castro, A., Rivero, D., Pazos, A., & Fernandez-Blanco, E. (2022). UAV swarm path planning with reinforcement learning for field prospecting. *Applied Intelligence*, *52*(12), 14101–14118. doi:10.100710489-022-03254-4

Pustokhina, I. V., Pustokhin, D. A., Gupta, D., Khanna, A., Shankar, K., & Nguyen, G. N. (2020). An effective training scheme for deep neural network in edge computing enabled Internet of medical things (IoMT) systems. *IEEE Access : Practical Innovations, Open Solutions*, *8*, 107112–107123. doi:10.1109/ACCESS.2020.3000322

Putra, H. M., Fikri, M. R., Riananda, D. P., Nugraha, G., Baidhowi, M. L., & Syah, R. A. 2020, April. Propulsion selection method using motor thrust table for optimum flight in multirotor aircraft. In AIP Conference Proceedings (Vol. 2226, No. 1, p. 060008). AIP Publishing LLC. doi:10.1063/5.0004809

Qie, H., Shi, D., Shen, T., Xu, X., Li, Y., & Wang, L. (2019). Joint optimization of multi-UAV target assignment and path planning based on multi-agent reinforcement learning. *IEEE Access : Practical Innovations, Open Solutions*, *7*, 146264–146272. doi:10.1109/ACCESS.2019.2943253

Qin, J., Chen, L., Liu, Y., Liu, C., Feng, C., & Chen, B. (2019). A machine learning methodology for diagnosing chronic kidney disease. *IEEE Access : Practical Innovations, Open Solutions*, *8*, 20991–21002. doi:10.1109/ACCESS.2019.2963053

Qin, P., Fu, Y., Xie, Y., Wu, K., Zhang, X., & Zhao, X. (2023). Multi-Agent Learning-Based Optimal Task Offloading and UAV Trajectory Planning for AGIN-Power IoT. *IEEE Transactions on Communications*, *71*(7), 4005–4017. doi:10.1109/TCOMM.2023.3274165

Qomariah, D. U. N., Tjandrasa, H., & Fatichah, C. (2019, July). Classification of diabetic retinopathy and normal retinal images using CNN and SVM. In *2019 12th International Conference on Information & Communication Technology and System (ICTS)* (pp. 152-157). IEEE. 10.1109/ICTS.2019.8850940

Qureshi, H. N., & Imran, A. (2019). On the Tradeoffs Between Coverage Radius, Altitude, and Beamwidth for Practical UAV Deployments. *IEEE Transactions on Aerospace and Electronic Systems*, *55*(6), 2805–2821. doi:10.1109/TAES.2019.2893082

Radoglou-Grammatikis, P., Sarigiannidis, P., Lagkas, T., & Moscholios, I. (2020). A Compilation of UAV Applications for Precision Agriculture. *Computer Networks*, *107148*, 107148. doi:10.1016/j.comnet.2020.107148

Raffo, G. V., & de Almeida, M. M. (2018). A Load Transportation Nonlinear Control Strategy Using a Tilt-Rotor UAV. *Journal of Advanced Transportation*, *2018*, 1–20. doi:10.1155/2018/1467040

Ragaveena, S., Shirly Edward, A., & Surendran, U. (2021). Smart controlled environment agriculture methods: A holistic review. *Reviews in Environmental Science and Biotechnology*, *20*(4), 887–913. doi:10.100711157-021-09591-z

Raj, P. A., & Srivani, M. (2018, December). Internet of robotic things based autonomous fire fighting mobile robot. In 2018 IEEE international conference on computational intelligence and computing research (ICCIC) (pp. 1-4). IEEE.

Raja, V., Gnanasekaran, R. K., Rajendran, P., Mohd Ali, A., Rasheed, R., AL-bonsrulah, H. A. Z., & Al-Bahrani, M. (2022). Asymmetrical damage aspects based investigations on the disc brake of long-range UAVs through verified computational coupled approaches. *Symmetry*, *14*(10), 2035. doi:10.3390ym14102035

Rakesh, D., Kumar, N. A., Sivaguru, M., Keerthivaasan, K. V. R., Janaki, B. R., & Raffik, R. (2021, October). Role of UAVs in innovating agriculture with future applications: A review. In *2021 International Conference on Advancements in Electrical, Electronics, Communication, Computing and Automation (ICAECA)* (pp. 1-6). IEEE. 10.1109/ICAECA52838.2021.9675612

Ramachandran, A., & Sangaiah, A. K. (2021). A review on object detection in unmanned aerial vehicle surveillance. *International Journal of Cognitive Computing in Engineering*, 2, 215–228. doi:10.1016/j.ijcce.2021.11.005

Ramli, M. R., Daely, P. T., Kim, D. S., & Lee, J. M. (2020). IoT-based adaptive network mechanism for reliable smart farm system. *Computers and Electronics in Agriculture*, 170, 105287. doi:10.1016/j.compag.2020.105287

Ramya, R., & Ramamoorthy, S. (2022). Analysis of machine learning algorithms for efficient cloud and edge computing in the IoT. Challenges and Risks Involved in Deploying 6G and NextGen Networks, (pp. 72–90). Elsevier.

Ramya, R., & Ramamoorthy, S. (2022). Development of a framework for adaptive productivity management for edge computing based IoT applications. *AIP Conference Proceedings*, *2519*, 030068. doi:10.1063/5.0111710

Ramya, R., & Ramamoorthy, S. (2022). Survey on Edge Intelligence in IoT-Based Computing Platform. *Lecture Notes in Networks and Systems*, *356*, 549–561. doi:10.1007/978-981-16-7952-0_52

Ramya, R., & Ramamoorthy, S. (2023). Hybrid Fog-Edge-IoT Architecture for Real-time Data Monitoring. *International Journal of Intelligent Engineering and Systems*, *17*(1), 2024. doi:10.22266/ijies2024.0229.22

Ramya, R., & Ramamoorthy, S. (2023). Lightweight Unified Collaborated Relinquish Edge Intelligent Gateway Architecture with Joint Optimization. *IEEE Access : Practical Innovations, Open Solutions*, *11*, 90396–90409. doi:10.1109/ACCESS.2023.3307808

Ramya, R., & Ramamoorthy, S. (2023). QoS in multimedia application for IoT devices through edge intelligence. *Multimedia Tools and Applications*. doi:10.100711042-023-15941-6

Rangarajan, A. K., Balu, E. J., Boligala, M. S., Jagannath, A., & Ranganathan, B. N. (2022). A low-cost UAV for detection of Cercospora leaf spot in okra using deep convolutional neural network. *Multimedia Tools and Applications*, *81*(15), 21565–21589. doi:10.100711042-022-12464-4

Rania, S., Sara, A., & Rania, A. (2020). *IoE Design Principles and Architecture; Book: Internet of Energy for Smart Cities: Machine Learning Models and Techniques*. CRC Press Publisher. doi:10.4018/978-1-7998-5101-1

Ranjith, C. P., Hardas, B. M., Mohideen, M. S. K., Raj, N. N., Robert, N. R., & Mohan, P. (2023). Robust Deep Learning Empowered Real Time Object Detection for Unmanned Aerial Vehicles based Surveillance Applications. *Journal of Mobile Multimedia*, (pp. 451–476). doi:10.13052/jmm1550-4646.1925

Räsänen, A., Elsakov, V., & Virtanen, T. (2019). Usability of one-class classification in mapping and detecting changes in bare peat surfaces in the tundra. *International Journal of Remote Sensing*, *40*(11), 4083–4103. doi:10.1080/0143116 1.2018.1558376

Rashid A. & Ahmed A. M. (2010). WiMAX, LTE and WiFi Interworking. *Journal of Computer Systems, Networks, and Communications, Hindawi Publishing Corporation.*

Rashid, A. S., Mohammed, A., & Rania, A. M. (2014). "Machine-to-Machine Communication", IGI Global, Encyclopedia of Information Science and Technology, Third Edition, , pp. 152-157). IEEE. 6195-6206. doi:10.4018/978-1-4666-5888-2

Rashid, T., Samvelyan, M., De Witt, C. S., Farquhar, G., Foerster, J., & Whiteson, S. (2020). Monotonic value function factorisation for deep multi-agent reinforcement learning. *Journal of Machine Learning Research*, 21.

Rauste, Y., Herland, E., Frelander, H., Soini, K., Kuoremaki, T., & Ruokari, A. (2010). Satellite-based forest fire detection for fire control in boreal forests. *International Journal of Remote Sensing*, *18*(12), 2641–2656. doi:10.1080/014311697217512

Ray, P. P., Dash, D., & De, D. (2019). Edge computing for Internet of Things: A survey, e-healthcare case study and future direction. *Journal of Network and Computer Applications*, *140*, 1–22. doi:10.1016/j.jnca.2019.05.005

Rezeck, P., Assuncao, R. M., & Chaimowicz, L. (2021). Cooperative Object Transportation using Gibbs Random Fields. *2021 IEEE/RSJ International Conference on Intelligent Robots and Systems (IROS)*, (pp. 9131–9138). IEEE. 10.1109/IROS51168.2021.9635928

Ricciardi, C., Ponsiglione, A. M., Scala, A., Borrelli, A., Misasi, M., Romano, G., Russo, G., Triassi, M., & Improta, G. (2022). Machine learning and regression analysis to model the length of hospital stay in patients with femur fracture. *Bioengineering (Basel, Switzerland)*, *9*(4), 172. doi:10.3390/bioengineering9040172 PMID:35447732

Richnák, P. (2022). Current Trend of Industry 4.0 in Logistics and Transformation of Logistics Processes Using Digital Technologies: An Empirical Study in the Slovak Republic. *Logistics*, *6*(4), 79. doi:10.3390/logistics6040079

Ristaino, J. B., Anderson, P. K., Bebber, D. P., Brauman, K. A., Cunniffe, N. J., Fedoroff, N. V., Finegold, C., Garrett, K. A., Gilligan, C. A., Jones, C. M., Martin, M. D., MacDonald, G. K., Neenan, P., Records, A., Schmale, D. G., Tateosian, L., & Wei, Q. (2021). The persistent threat of emerging plant disease pandemics to global food security. *Proceedings of the National Academy of Sciences of the United States of America*, *118*(23), e2022239118. doi:10.1073/pnas.2022239118 PMID:34021073

Riswantini, D., & Nugraheni, E. (2022). Machine learning in handling disease outbreaks: A comprehensive review. *Bulletin of Electrical Engineering and Informatics*, *11*(4), 2169–2186. doi:10.11591/eei.v11i4.3612

Rizk, H., & Habib, M. K. (2018). Robotized early plant health monitoring system. *IECON 2018-44th Annual Conference of the IEEE Industrial Electronics Society*. IEEE.10.1109/IECON.2018.8592833

Roca-Riu, M., & Monica Menendez. (2019). Logistic deliveries with drones: State of the art of practice and research. *19th Swiss Transport Research Conference (STRC 2019)*. IEEE.10.1145/3410404.3414235

Rofida, O. D., Rashid, A. S., Mohammad, K. H., & Musse, M. (2017). Persistent Overload Control for Backlogged Machine to Machine Communications in Long Term Evolution Advanced Networks [JTEC]. *Journal of Telecommunication, Electronic and Computer Engineering*, *9*(3).

Rogers, K., Karaosmanoglu, S., Altmeyer, M., Suarez, A., & Nacke, L. E. (2022). Much Realistic, Such Wow! A Systematic Literature Review of Realism in Digital Games. *CHI Conference on Human Factors in Computing Systems*. ACM. 10.1145/3491102.3501875

Rolly, R. M., Malarvezhi, P., & Lagkas, T. D. (2022). Unmanned aerial vehicles: Applications, techniques, and challenges as aerial base stations. International Journal of Distributed Sensor Networks, 18(9).

Roper, J. M., Garcia, J. F., & Tsutsui, H. (2021). Emerging technologies for monitoring plant health in vivo. *ACS Omega*, *6*(8), 5101–5107. doi:10.1021/acsomega.0c05850 PMID:33681550

Roy, A. M., Bhaduri, J., Kumar, T., & Raj, K. (2023). WilDect-YOLO: An efficient and robust computer vision-based accurate object localization model for automated endangered wildlife detection. *Ecological Informatics*, *75*, 101919. doi:10.1016/j.ecoinf.2022.101919

Rozenberg, G., Kent, R., & Blank, L. (2021). Consumer-grade UAV utilized for detecting and analyzing late-season weed spatial distribution patterns in commercial onion fields. *Precision Agriculture*, *22*(4), 1317–1332. doi:10.100711119-021-09786-y

Sacco, A., Esposito, F., Marchetto, G., & Montuschi, P. (2021). Sustainable Task Offloading in UAV Networks via Multi-Agent Reinforcement Learning. *IEEE Transactions on Vehicular Technology*, *70*(5), 5003–5015. doi:10.1109/TVT.2021.3074304

Saeed, M. M. (2022). *Green Machine Learning Approach for QoS Improvement in Cellular Communications*. 2022 IEEE 2nd International Maghreb Meeting of the Conference on Sciences and Techniques of Automatic Control and Computer Engineering (MI-STA), Sabratha, Libya. 10.1109/MI-STA54861.2022.9837585

Saeed, M. M. (2023). *Attacks Detection in 6G Wireless Networks using Machine Learning*. 2023 9th International Conference on Computer and Communication Engineering (ICCCE), Kuala Lumpur, Malaysia. 10.1109/ICCCE58854.2023.10246078

Saeed, M. M. (2023). *Machine Learning Techniques for Detecting DDOS Attacks*. 2023 3rd International Conference on Emerging Smart Technologies and Applications (eSmarTA), Taiz, Yemen. 10.1109/eSmarTA59349.2023.10293366

Saeed, F., Mehmood, A., Majeed, M. F., Maple, C., Saeed, K., Khattak, M. K., Wang, H., & Epiphaniou, G. (2021). Smart delivery and retrieval of swab collection kit for COVID-19 test using autonomous Unmanned Aerial Vehicles. *Physical Communication*, *48*, 101373. doi:10.1016/j.phycom.2021.101373

Saeed, M. M., Hasan, M. K., Obaid, A. J., Saeed, R. A., Mokhtar, R. A., Ali, E. S., Akhtaruzzaman, M., Amanlou, S., & Hossain, A. Z. (2022). A comprehensive review on the users' identity privacy for 5G networks. *IET Communications*, *16*(5), 384–399. doi:10.1049/cmu2.12327

Saeed, M. M., Saeed, R. A., Abdelhaq, M., Alsaqour, R., Hasan, M. K., & Mokhtar, R. A. (2023). Anomaly Detection in 6G Networks Using Machine Learning Methods. *Electronics (Basel)*, *12*(15), 3300. doi:10.3390/electronics12153300

Saeed, M. M., Saeed, R. A., Mokhtar, R. A., Alhumyani, H., & Ali, E. S. (2022). A novel variable pseudonym scheme for preserving privacy user location in 5G networks. *Security and Communication Networks*, *2022*, 2022. doi:10.1155/2022/7487600

Saeed, R. A., Saeed, M. M., Mokhtar, R. A., Alhumyani, H., & Abdel-Khalek, S. (2021). Pseudonym Mutable Based Privacy for 5G User Identity. *Computer Systems Science and Engineering*, *39*(1). Advance online publication. doi:10.32604/csse.2021.015593

Saffre, F., Hildmann, H., Karvonen, H., & Lind, T. (2022). Monitoring and Cordoning Wildfires with an Autonomous Swarm of Unmanned Aerial Vehicles. *Drones (Basel)*, *6*(10), 301. doi:10.3390/drones6100301

Salehi, S., Bokani, A., Hassan, J., & Kanhere, S. S. (2019). *AETD: An Application-Aware, Energy-Efficient Trajectory Design for Flying Base Stations*. 2019 IEEE 14th Malaysia International Conference on Communication (MICC), Selangor, Malaysia. 10.1109/MICC48337.2019.9037587

Salehi, S., Hassan, J., & Bokani, A. (2022) "An Optimal Multi-UAV Deployment Model for UAV-assisted Smart Farming," 2022 IEEE Region 10 Symposium (TENSYMP), Mumbai, India, pp. 1-6, 10.1109/TENSYMP54529.2022.9864512

Salehi, S., Hassan, J., Bokani, A., Hoseini, S. A., & Kanhere, S. S. (2020). Poster Abstract: A QoS-aware, Energy-efficient Trajectory Optimization for UAV Base Stations using Q-Learning. 2020 19th ACM/IEEE International Conference on Information Processing in Sensor Networks (IPSN), Sydney, NSW, Australia. 10.1109/IPSN48710.2020.00-22

Sami Oubbati, O., Atiquzzaman, M., Ahamed Ahanger, T., & Ibrahim, A. (2020). Softwarization of UAV Networks: A Survey of Applications and Future Trends. *IEEE Access : Practical Innovations, Open Solutions*, *8*, 98073–98125. doi:10.1109/ACCESS.2020.2994494

Sandom, C., Faurby, S., Sandel, B., & Svenning, J. C. (2014). Global late Quaternary megafauna extinctions linked to humans, not climate change. *Proceedings of the Royal Society B: Biological Sciences, 281*(1787), 20133254. 10.1098/rspb.2013.3254

Santoso, L. F., Baqai, F., Gwozdz, M., Lange, J., Rosenberger, M. G., Sulzer, J., & Paydarfar, D. (2019, July). Applying machine learning algorithms for automatic detection of swallowing from sound. In *2019 41st Annual International Conference of the IEEE Engineering in Medicine and Biology Society (EMBC)* (pp. 2584-2588). IEEE. 10.1109/EMBC.2019.8857937

Sartori, D., Zou, D., Pei, L., & Yu, W. (2023). Near-optimal 3D trajectory design in presence of obstacles: A convolutional neural network approach. *Robotics and Autonomous Systems, 167*, 104483. doi:10.1016/j.robot.2023.104483

Sayed, A., & Zahraa, T. (2021). Algorithms Optimization for Intelligent IoV Applications. In J. Zhao & V. Vinoth Kumar (Eds.), *Handbook of Research on Innovations and Applications of AI, IoT, and Cognitive Technologies* (pp. 1–25). IGI Global. doi:10.4018/978-1-7998-6870-5.ch001

Schaeffer, M., Hare, B., Rocha, M., & Rogelj, J. (2013). *Adequacy and feasibility of the 1.5 C long-term global limit.* Climate Action Network Europe.

Schneller, E., Abdulsalam, Y., Conway, K., & Eckler, J. (2023). *Strategic management of the health care supply chain.* John Wiley & Sons.

Schulman, J., Wolski, F., Dhariwal, P., Radford, A., & Openai, O. (2017). *Proximal Policy Optimization Algorithms.* arXiv. https://arxiv.org/pdf/1707.06347.pdf

Sejan, M. A. S., Rahman, M. H., Shin, B. S., Oh, J. H., You, Y. H., & Song, H. K. (2022). Machine Learning for Intelligent-Reflecting-Surface-Based Wireless Communication towards 6G: A Review. In Sensors, 22(14). MDPI. doi:10.339022145405

Senthilkumar, S., Anushree, G., Kumar, J. D., Vijayanandh, R., Raffik, R., Kesavan, K., & Prasanth, S. I. (2021, October). Design, dynamics, development and deployment of hexacopter for agricultural applications. In *2021 International Conference on Advancements in Electrical, Electronics, Communication, Computing and Automation (ICAECA)* (pp. 1-6). IEEE. 10.1109/ICAECA52838.2021.9675753

Şerban, O., Thapen, N., Maginnis, B., Hankin, C., & Foot, V. (2019). Real-time processing of social media with SENTINEL: A syndromic surveillance system incorporating deep learning for health classification. *Information Processing & Management, 56*(3), 1166–1184. doi:10.1016/j.ipm.2018.04.011

Shafiq, M., Ali, Z. A., Israr, A., Alkhammash, E. H., Hadjouni, M., & Jussila, J. J. (2022). Convergence analysis of path planning of multi-UAVs using max-min ant colony optimization approach. *Sensors (Basel), 22*(14), 5395. doi:10.339022145395 PMID:35891074

Shahi, T. B., Sitaula, C., Neupane, A., & Guo, W. (2022a). Fruit classification using attention-based MobileNetV2 for industrial applications. *PLoS One, 17*(2), e0264586. doi:10.1371/journal.pone.0264586 PMID:35213643

Shahi, T. B., Xu, C. Y., Neupane, A., & Guo, W. (2023). Recent Advances in Crop Disease Detection Using UAV and Deep Learning Techniques. *Remote Sensing (Basel), 15*(9), 2450. doi:10.3390/rs15092450

Shahi, T. B., Xu, C.-Y., Neupane, A., Fresser, D., O'Connor, D., Wright, G., & Guo, W. (2023a). A cooperative scheme for late leaf spot estimation in peanut using UAV multispectral images. *PLoS One, 18*(3), e0282486. doi:10.1371/journal.pone.0282486 PMID:36972266

Shahi, T. B., Xu, C.-Y., Neupane, A., & Guo, W. (2022b). Machine learning methods for precision agriculture with UAV imagery: A review. *Electronic Research Archive*, 30(12), 4277–4317. doi:10.3934/era.2022218

Shakhatreh, H., Sawalmeh, A. H., Al-Fuqaha, A., Dou, Z., Almaita, E., Khalil, I., Othman, N. S., Khreishah, A., & Guizani, M. (2019). Unmanned aerial vehicles (UAVs): A survey on civil applications and key research challenges. *IEEE Access : Practical Innovations, Open Solutions*, 7, 48572–48634. doi:10.1109/ACCESS.2019.2909530

Shakhatreh, M., Shakhatreh, H., & Ababneh, A. (2023). Efficient 3D Positioning of UAVs and User Association Based on Hybrid PSO-K-Means Clustering Algorithm in Future Wireless Networks. *Mobile Information Systems*, 2023, 2023. doi:10.1155/2023/6567897

Shamsoshoara, A., Khaledi, M., Afghah, F., Razi, A., & Ashdown, J. (2019). Distributed Cooperative Spectrum Sharing in UAV Networks Using Multi-Agent Reinforcement Learning. *2019 16th IEEE Annual Consumer Communications and Networking Conference, CCNC 2019*. IEEE. 10.1109/CCNC.2019.8651796

Shankar, K., Lakshmanaprabu, S. K., Gupta, D., Maseleno, A., & De Albuquerque, V. H. C. (2020). Optimal feature-based multi-kernel SVM approach for thyroid disease classification. *The Journal of Supercomputing*, 76(2), 1128–1143. doi:10.100711227-018-2469-4

Shan, T., Wang, Y., Zhao, C., Li, Y., Zhang, G., & Zhu, Q. (2023). Multi-UAV WRSN charging path planning based on improved heed and IA-DRL. *Computer Communications*, 203, 77–88. doi:10.1016/j.comcom.2023.02.021

Shao W, Kawakami R, Yoshihashi R, You S, Kawase H, & Naemura T. (2020). *Cattle detection and counting in UAV images based on convolutional neural networks*. Taylor & Francis. . doi:10.1080/01431161.2019.1624858

Sharifi, R., & Ryu, C. M. (2018). Biogenic volatile compounds for plant disease diagnosis and health improvement. *The Plant Pathology Journal*, 34(6), 459–469. doi:10.5423/PPJ.RW.06.2018.0118 PMID:30588219

Sharma, J., Granmo, O.-C., Goodwin, M., & Fidje, J. T. (2017). Deep convolutional neural networks for fire detection in images. In *International Conference on Engineering Applications of Neural Networks*. Springer. 10.1007/978-3-319-65172-9_16

Sharma, S., Sato, K., & Gautam, B. P. (2022). Bioacoustics Monitoring of Wildlife using Artificial Intelligence: A Methodological Literature Review. *Proceedings - 2022 International Conference on Networking and Network Applications*. IEEE. 10.1109/NaNA56854.2022.00063

Sharma, V., You, I., Pau, G., Collotta, M., Lim, J., & Kim, J. (2018). LoRaWAN-Based Energy-Efficient Surveillance by Drones for Intelligent Transportation Systems. *Energies*, 11(3), 573. doi:10.3390/en11030573

Shen, C. H., Albert, F. Y. C., Ang, C. K., Teck, D. J., & Chan, K. P. (2017, December). Theoretical development and study of takeoff constraint thrust equation for a drone. In *2017 IEEE 15th Student Conference on Research and Development (SCOReD)* (pp. 18-22). IEEE. 10.1109/SCORED.2017.8305428

Shen, H., Yang, X., Lin, D., Chai, J., Huo, J., Xing, X., & He, S. (2022). A Benchmark for Vision-based Multi-UAV Multi-object Tracking. *2022 IEEE International Conference on Multisensor Fusion and Integration for Intelligent Systems (MFI)*, (pp. 1–7). IEEE. 10.1109/MFI55806.2022.9913874

Shen, Y.-T., Lee, Y., Kwon, H., Conover, D. M., Bhattacharyya, S. S., Vale, N., Gray, J. D., Leong, G. J., Evensen, K., & Skirlo, F. (2023a). Archangel: A Hybrid UAV-based Human Detection Benchmark with Position and Pose Metadata. *IEEE Access : Practical Innovations, Open Solutions*, 11, 80958–80972. doi:10.1109/ACCESS.2023.3299235

Shin, J., & Piran, Md. J., Song, H.-K., & Moon, H. (2022). UAV-assisted and deep learning-driven object detection and tracking for autonomous driving. *Proceedings of the 5th International ACM Mobicom Workshop on Drone Assisted Wireless Communications for 5G and Beyond*, (pp. 7–12). ACM. 10.1145/3555661.3560856

Shirzadifar, A., Maharlooei, M., Bajwa, S. G., Oduor, P. G., & Nowatzki, J. F. (2020). Mapping crop stand count and planting uniformity using high resolution imagery in a maize crop. *Biosystems Engineering*, *200*, 377–390. doi:10.1016/j.biosystemseng.2020.10.013

Shivgan, R., & Dong, Z. (2020). Energy-efficient drone coverage path planning using genetic algorithm. *2020 IEEE 21st International Conference on High Performance Switching and Routing (HPSR)*. IEEE.

Shi, Y., Han, L., Kleerekoper, A., Chang, S., & Hu, T. (2022). Novel cropdocnet model for automated potato late blight disease detection from unmanned aerial vehicle-based hyperspectral imagery. *Remote Sensing (Basel)*, *14*(02), 396. doi:10.3390/rs14020396

Siemiątkowska, B. (2022). *Real-Time Object Detection and Classification by UAV Equipped With SAR. Sensors*. Academia. https://www.academia.edu/81075269/Real_Time_Object_Detection_and_Classification_by_UAV_Equipped_With_SAR

Šimek, P., Pavlík, J., Jarolímek, J., Oèenášek, V., & Stoèes, M. (2017, September). Use of unmanned aerial vehicles for wildlife monitoring. In *Proceedings of the 8th International Conference on Information and Communication Technologies in Agriculture, Food and Environment (HAICTA 2017)* (pp. 21-24). Semantic Scholar.

Singh, A. K., Ganapathysubramanian, B., Sarkar, S., & Singh, A. (2018). Deep learning for plant stress phenotyping: Trends and future perspectives. *Trends in Plant Science*, *23*(10), 883–898. doi:10.1016/j.tplants.2018.07.004 PMID:30104148

SinghT.GangloffH.PhamM.-T. (2023). Object counting from aerial remote sensing images: application to wildlife and marine mammals. https://arxiv.org/abs/2306.10439 doi:10.1109/IGARSS52108.2023.10282150

Singh, V., Sharma, N., & Singh, S. (2020). A review of imaging techniques for plant disease detection. *Artificial Intelligence in Agriculture*, *4*, 229–242. doi:10.1016/j.aiia.2020.10.002

Sisodia, S., Dhyani, S., Kathuria, S., Pandey, S., Chhabra, G., & Pandey, R. (2023). AI Technologies, Innovations and Possibilities in Wildlife Conservation. *International Conference on Innovative Data Communication Technologies and Application*. IEEE. 10.1109/ICIDCA56705.2023.10099721

Sivakami, K., & Saraswathi, N. (2015). Mining big data: Breast cancer prediction using DT-SVM hybrid model. [IJSEAS]. *International Journal of Scientific Engineering and Applied Science*, *1*(5), 418–429.

Sivakumar, V., Ruthramathi, R., & Leelapriyadharsini, S. (2020). Challenges of Cloud Computing in Warehousing Operations with Respect to Chennai Port Trust. *Proceedings of the 2020 the 3rd International Conference on Computers in Management and Business*, (pp. 162–165). IEEE. 10.1145/3383845.3383895

Skorput, P., Mandzuka, S., & Vojvodic, H. (2016). The use of Unmanned Aerial Vehicles for forest fire monitoring. *Proceedings Elmar - International Symposium Electronics in Marine*, *2016-Novem*, 93–96. 10.1109/ELMAR.2016.7731762

Škrinjar, J. P., Škorput, P., & Furdić, M. (2019). Application of Unmanned Aerial Vehicles in Logistic Processes. In Lecture Notes in Networks and Systems (Vol. 42, pp. 359–366). doi:10.1007/978-3-319-90893-9_43

Sobnath, D. D., Philip, N., Kayyali, R., Nabhani-Gebara, S., Pierscionek, B., Vaes, A. W., Spruit, M. A., & Kaimakamis, E. (2017). Features of a mobile support app for patients with chronic obstructive pulmonary disease: Literature review and current applications. *JMIR mHealth and uHealth*, *5*(2), e4951. doi:10.2196/mhealth.4951 PMID:28219878

Sodhro, A. H., Luo, Z., Sangaiah, A. K., & Baik, S. W. (2019). Mobile edge computing based QoS optimization in medical healthcare applications. *International Journal of Information Management*, *45*, 308–318. doi:10.1016/j.ijinfomgt.2018.08.004

So, H. (2023). Migratory Unmanned Aerial Vehicle System (MiUAV) for Automated Infrastructure Inspection. *IEEE Access : Practical Innovations, Open Solutions*, *11*, 56392–56399. doi:10.1109/ACCESS.2023.3282995

Solomon, S. (2007). *Climate change 2007-the physical science basis: Working group I contribution to the fourth assessment report of the IPCC* (Vol. 4). Cambridge University Press.

Son, K., Kim, D., Wan, J. K., Hostallero, D. E., & Yi, Y. (2019). Qtran: Learning to factorize with transformation for cooperative multi-agent reinforcement learning. *31st International Conference OnMachine Learning*. IEEE.

Souto, A., Alfaia, R., Cardoso, E., Araújo, J., & Francês, C. (2023). UAV Path Planning Optimization Strategy: Considerations of Urban Morphology, Microclimate, and Energy Efficiency Using Q-Learning Algorithm. *Drones (Basel)*, *7*(2), 123.

Stein, A. B., Athreya, V., Gerngross, P., Balme, G., Henschel, P., Karanth, U., & Ghoddousi, A. (2017). *Panthera pardus (amended version of 2019 assessment)*. WCS.

Stephenson, P. J. (2019). Integrating Remote Sensing into Wildlife Monitoring for Conservation. *Environmental Conservation*, *46*(3), 181–183. doi:10.1017/S0376892919000092

Stephens, S. L. (2005). Forest fire causes and extent on United States Forest Service lands. *International Journal of Wildland Fire*, *14*(3), 213–222. doi:10.1071/WF04006

Subha, R., Nayana, B. R., & Selvadass, M. (2022, December). Hybrid Machine Learning Model Using Particle Swarm Optimization for Effectual Diagnosis of Alzheimer's Disease from Handwriting. In *2022 4th International Conference on Circuits, Control, Communication and Computing (I4C)* (pp. 491-495). IEEE.

Sugiura, R., Noguchi, N., & Ishii, K. (2005). Remote-sensing technology for vegetation monitoring using an unmanned helicopter. *Biosystems Engineering*, *90*(4), 369–379. doi:10.1016/j.biosystemseng.2004.12.011

Su, J., Liu, C., Hu, X., Xu, X., Guo, L., & Chen, W. H. (2019). Spatio-temporal monitoring of wheat yellow rust using UAV multispectral imagery. *Computers and Electronics in Agriculture*, *167*, 105035. doi:10.1016/j.compag.2019.105035

Su, J., Yi, D., Su, B., Mi, Z., Liu, C., Hu, X., Xu, X., Guo, L., & Chen, W. H. (2020). Aerial visual perception in smart farming: Field study of wheat yellow rust monitoring. *IEEE Transactions on Industrial Informatics*, *17*(3), 2242–2249. doi:10.1109/TII.2020.2979237

Su, J., Zhu, X., Li, S., & Chen, W.-H. (2022). AI meets UAVs: A survey on AI empowered UAV perception systems for precision agriculture. *Neurocomputing*, *518*, 242–270. doi:10.1016/j.neucom.2022.11.020

Sunehag, P., Lever, G., Gruslys, A., Czarnecki, W. M., Zambaldi, V., Jaderberg, M., Lanctot, M., Sonnerat, N., Leibo, J. Z., Tuyls, K., & Graepel, T. (2018). Value-decomposition networks for cooperative multi-agent learning based on team reward. *Proceedings of the International Joint Conference on Autonomous Agents and Multiagent Systems, AAMAS, 3*, (pp. 2085–2087). AAMAS.

Sun, Y., Li, L., Cheng, Q., Wang, D., Liang, W., Li, X., & Han, Z. (2020). Joint trajectory and power optimization in multi-type UAVs network with mean field Q-learning. *2020 IEEE International Conference on Communications Workshops (ICC Workshops)*. IEEE.

Suo, J., Wang, T., Zhang, X., Chen, H., Zhou, W., & Shi, W. (2023). HIT-UAV: A high-altitude infrared thermal dataset for Unmanned Aerial Vehicle-based object detection. *Scientific Data*, *10*(1), 1. doi:10.103841597-023-02066-6 PMID:37080987

Sutton, R. S., & Barto, A. G. (2018). *Reinforcement Leaning*.

Sylvester, G. (2018). *E-Agriculture in Action: Drones for Agriculture*. Food and Agriculture Organization of the United Nations and International Telecommunication Union.

Symeonidis, C., Mademlis, I., Pitas, I., & Nikolaidis, N. (2022). Auth-Persons: A Dataset for Detecting Humans in Crowds from Aerial Views. *2022 IEEE International Conference on Image Processing (ICIP)*, (pp. 596–600). 10.1109/ICIP46576.2022.9897612

Szenicer, A., Reinwald, M., Moseley, B., Nissen-Meyer, T., Mutinda Muteti, Z., Oduor, S., McDermott-Roberts, A., Baydin, A. G., & Mortimer, B. (2022). Seismic savanna: Machine learning for classifying wildlife and behaviours using ground-based vibration field recordings. *Remote Sensing in Ecology and Conservation*, *8*(2), 236–250. doi:10.1002/rse2.242

Szokalski, M. S., Litchfield, C. A., & Foster, W. K. (2012). Enrichment for captive tigers (Panthera tigris): Current knowledge and future directions. *Applied Animal Behaviour Science*, *139*(1-2), 1–9. doi:10.1016/j.applanim.2012.02.021

Tadesse, E., & Seboko, B. (2013). *Forest/Wildland Fire Prevention and Control For Sustainable Forest Management. Manual*. Hawassa University, Wondo Genet College of Forestry and Natural Resources.

Tahir, M. N., Lan, Y., Zhang, Y., Wenjiang, H., Wang, Y., & Naqvi, S. M. Z. A. (2023). Application of unmanned aerial vehicles in precision agriculture. In *Precision Agriculture* (pp. 55–70). Academic Press. doi:10.1016/B978-0-443-18953-1.00001-5

Taiwo, O., & Ezugwu, A. E. (2020). Smart healthcare support for remote patient monitoring during covid-19 quarantine. *Informatics in Medicine Unlocked*, *20*, 100428. doi:10.1016/j.imu.2020.100428 PMID:32953970

Tang, C., Zhu, C., & Guizani, M. (2023). Coverage Optimization Based on Airborne Fog Computing for Internet of Medical Things. *IEEE Systems Journal*, *17*(3), 1–12. doi:10.1109/JSYST.2023.3244923

Tang, J., Duan, H., & Lao, S. (2023). Swarm intelligence algorithms for multiple unmanned aerial vehicles collaboration: A comprehensive review. *Artificial Intelligence Review*, *56*(5), 4295–4327. doi:10.100710462-022-10281-7

Tan, M., Xu, Y., Gao, Z., Yuan, T., Liu, Q., Yang, R., Zhang, B., & Peng, L. (2022). Recent advances in intelligent wearable medical devices integrating biosensing and drug delivery. *Advanced Materials*, *34*(27), 2108491. doi:10.1002/adma.202108491 PMID:35008128

Tan, Y. (2022). Artificial Bee Colony-Aided UAV Deployment and Relay Communications for Geological Disasters. *2022 8th Annual International Conference on Network and Information Systems for Computers (ICNISC)*. IEEE.

Tarekegn, G. B., Juang, R.-T., Lin, H.-P., Munaye, Y. Y., Wang, L.-C., & Bitew, M. A. (2022). Deep-reinforcement-learning-based drone base station deployment for wireless communication services. *IEEE Internet of Things Journal*, *9*(21), 21899–21915.

Tariq, M., Sadaat, A., Ahmad, R., Abaid, Z., & Rodrigues, J. J. P. C. (2023). Enhanced Border Surveillance through a Hybrid Swarm Optimization Algorithm. *IEEE Sensors Journal*, *23*(22), 28172–28181. doi:10.1109/JSEN.2023.3317531

Telli, K., Kraa, O., Himeur, Y., Ouamane, A., Boumehraz, M., Atalla, S., & Mansoor, W. (2023). A Comprehensive Review of Recent Research Trends on UAVs (arXiv:2307.13691). arXiv. https://arxiv.org/abs/2307.13691

Teo, C. P. J. (2018). *Persistent perimeter surveillance using multiple swapping multi-rotor uas*. [Ph. D. dissertation, the Naval Postgraduate School Monterey United States].

Terasawa, R., Ariki, Y., Narihira, T., Tsuboi, T., & Nagasaka, K. (2020). 3d-cnn based heuristic guided task-space planner for faster motion planning. *2020 IEEE International Conference on Robotics and Automation (ICRA)*. IEEE. 10.1109/ICRA40945.2020.9196883

Terry, J. K., Black, B., Grammel, N., Jayakumar, M., Hari, A., Sullivan, R., Santos, L., Perez, R., Horsch, C., Dieffendahl, C., Williams, N. L., Lokesh, Y., & Ravi, P. (2021, October 26). *PettingZoo: Gym for Multi-Agent Reinforcement Learning*. ArXiv.org. https://doi.org//arXiv.2009.14471 doi:10.48550

Thalor, M. A., Nagabhyrava, R., Rajkumar, K., Chakraborty, A., Singh, R., & Singh Aswal, U. (2023). Deep learning insights and methods for classifying wildlife. *2023 3rd International Conference on Advance Computing and Innovative Technologies in Engineering (ICACITE)*, (pp. 403–407). IEEE. 10.1109/ICACITE57410.2023.10183057

Thomas, S., Kuska, M. T., Bohnenkamp, D., Brugger, A., Alisaac, E., Wahabzada, M., & Mahlein, A.-K. (2018). Benefits of hyperspectral imaging for plant disease detection and plant protection: A technical perspective. *Journal of Plant Diseases and Protection*, *125*(1), 5–20. doi:10.100741348-017-0124-6

Tibbetts, J. H. (2017). Remote Sensors Bring Wildlife Tracking to New Level. *Bioscience*, *67*(5), 411–417. doi:10.1093/biosci/bix033

Tigga, N. P., & Garg, S. (2020). Prediction of type 2 diabetes using machine learning classification methods. *Procedia Computer Science*, *167*, 706–716. doi:10.1016/j.procs.2020.03.336

Tiwari, A. K., & Nadimpalli, S. V. (2019). Augmented random search for quadcopter control: An alternative to reinforcement learning. *arXiv preprint arXiv:1911.12553*.

Todorov, E., Erez, T., & Tassa, Y. (2012, October 1). *MuJoCo: A physics engine for model-based control*. IEEE Xplore. doi:10.1109/IROS.2012.6386109

Tokunaga, H., Anh, N. H., Dong, N. V., Ham, L. H., Hanh, N. T., Hung, N., Ishitani, M., Tuan, L. N., Utsumi, Y., Vu, N. A., & Seki, M. (2020). An efficient method of propagating cassava plants using aeroponic culture. *Journal of Crop Improvement*, *34*(1), 64–83. doi:10.1080/15427528.2019.1673271

Tolstaya, E., Paulos, J., Kumar, V., & Ribeiro, A. (2021). Multi-Robot Coverage and Exploration using Spatial Graph Neural Networks. *2021 IEEE/RSJ International Conference on Intelligent Robots and Systems (IROS)*, (pp. 8944–8950). IEEE. 10.1109/IROS51168.2021.9636675

Tran, T.-N., Nguyen, T.-L., & Voznak, M. (2022). Approaching K-Means for Multiantenna UAV Positioning in Combination With a Max-SIC-Min-Rate Framework to Enable Aerial IoT Networks. *IEEE Access : Practical Innovations, Open Solutions*, *10*, 115157–115178. doi:10.1109/ACCESS.2022.3218799

Tu, G.-T., & Juang, J.-G. (2023). UAV Path Planning and Obstacle Avoidance Based on Reinforcement Learning in 3D Environments. *Actuators*.

Tubis, A. A., & Rohman, J. (2023). Intelligent Warehouse in Industry 4.0—Systematic Literature Review. *Sensors (Basel)*, *23*(8), 4105. doi:10.339023084105 PMID:37112446

Tuia, D., Kellenberger, B., Beery, S., Costelloe, B. R., Zuffi, S., Risse, B., Mathis, A., Mathis, M. W., van Langevelde, F., Burghardt, T., Kays, R., Klinck, H., Wikelski, M., Couzin, I. D., van Horn, G., Crofoot, M. C., Stewart, C. V., & Berger-Wolf, T. (2022). Perspectives in machine learning for wildlife conservation. In Nature Communications, 13(1). Nature Research. doi:10.103841467-022-27980-y

Uddin, M. Z. (2019). A wearable sensor-based activity prediction system to facilitate edge computing in smart healthcare system. *Journal of Parallel and Distributed Computing*, *123*, 46–53. doi:10.1016/j.jpdc.2018.08.010

Ullah, Z., Al-Turjman, F., Mostarda, L., & Gagliardi, R. (2020). Applications of artificial intelligence and machine learning in smart cities. *Computer Communications*, *154*, 313–323. doi:10.1016/j.comcom.2020.02.069

Valavanis, K. P. (Ed.). (2008). *Advances in unmanned aerial vehicles: state of the art and the road to autonomy.*

Valente, J., Del Cerro, J., Barrientos, A., & Sanz, D. (2013). Aerial coverage optimization in precision agriculture management: A musical harmony inspired approach. *Computers and Electronics in Agriculture*, *99*, 153–159. doi:10.1016/j.compag.2013.09.008

Van De Vijver, R., Mertens, K., Heungens, K., Nuyttens, D., Wieme, J., Maes, W. H., Van Beek, J., Somers, B., & Saeys, W. (2022). Ultra-High-Resolution UAV-Based Detection of Alternaria solani Infections in Potato Fields. *Remote Sensing (Basel)*, *14*(24), 6232. doi:10.3390/rs14246232

van Lieshout, M., & Friedewald, M. (2018). Drones–dull, dirty or dangerous?: The social construction of privacy and security technologies. In *Socially Responsible Innovation in Security* (pp. 25–43). Routledge. doi:10.4324/9781351246903-3

Velusamy, P., Rajendran, S., Mahendran, R. K., Naseer, S., Shafiq, M., & Choi, J. G. (2022). Unmanned aerial vehicles (Uav) in precision agriculture: Applications and challenges. In Energies, 15. doi:10.3390/en15010217

Vembandasamy, K., Sasipriya, R., & Deepa, E. (2015). Heart diseases detection using Naive Bayes algorithm. *International Journal of Innovative Science. Engineering & Technology*, *2*(9), 441–444.

Venkatesan, E. V., & Velmurugan, T. (2015). Performance analysis of decision tree algorithms for breast cancer classification. *Indian Journal of Science and Technology*, *8*(29), 1–8. doi:10.17485/ijst/2015/v8i1/84646

Vong, C. N., Conway, L. S., Feng, A., Zhou, J., Kitchen, N. R., & Sudduth, K. A. (2022). Corn emergence uniformity estimation and mapping using UAV imagery and deep learning. *Computers and Electronics in Agriculture*, *198*, 107008. doi:10.1016/j.compag.2022.107008

Vroegindeweij, B. A., van Wijk, S. W., & van Henten, E. (2014). Autonomous unmanned aerial vehicles for agricultural applications. In: *Proceeding. International Conference of Agricultural Engineering (AgEng)*. Zurich, p. 8

Waheed, M., Ahmad, R., Ahmed, W., Mahtab Alam, M., & Magarini, M. (2023). On coverage of critical nodes in UAV-assisted emergency networks. *Sensors (Basel)*, *23*(3), 1586. doi:10.339023031586 PMID:36772624

Wall, J., Wittemyer, G., Klinkenberg, B., & Douglas-Hamilton, I. (2014). Novel opportunities for wildlife conservation and research with real-time monitoring. *Ecological Applications*, *24*(4), 593–601. doi:10.1890/13-1971.1 PMID:24988762

Wang S H, & Zhang Y D. (2020). Dense Net-201-based deep neural network with composite learning factor and precomputation for multiple sclerosis classification. *ACM Transactions on Multimedia Computing, Communications, and Applications (TOMM)*, *16*. ACM.

Wang, Y., Jiang, R., & Li, W. (2022). A Novel Hybrid Algorithm Based on Improved Particle Swarm Optimization Algorithm and Genetic Algorithm for Multi-UAV Path Planning with Time Windows. *2022 IEEE 5th Advanced Information Management, Communicates, Electronic and Automation Control Conference (IMCEC)*. IEEE.

Wang, Z., Han, K., & Tiwari, P. (2021). Digital Twin Simulation of Connected and Automated Vehicles with the Unity Game Engine. *2021 IEEE 1st International Conference on Digital Twins and Parallel Intelligence (DTPI)*. IEEE. 10.1109/DTPI52967.2021.9540074

Wang, Z., Li, D., Kuai, Y., & Sun, Y. (2023). A Model-Free Moving Object Detection and Tracking Framework Based on UAV Data. In W. Fu, M. Gu, & Y. Niu (Eds.), *Proceedings of 2022 International Conference on Autonomous Unmanned Systems (ICAUS 2022)* (pp. 3446–3456). Springer Nature. 10.1007/978-981-99-0479-2_318

Wang, H., Liu, N., Zhang, Y., Feng, D., Huang, F., Li, D., & Zhang, Y. (2020). Deep reinforcement learning: A survey. *Frontiers of Information Technology & Electronic Engineering*, *21*(12), 1726–1744. doi:10.1631/FITEE.1900533

Wang, H., Lu, B., Li, J., Liu, T., Xing, Y., Lv, C., Cao, D., Li, J., Zhang, J., & Hashemi, E. (2021). Risk assessment and mitigation in local path planning for autonomous vehicles with LSTM based predictive model. *IEEE Transactions on Automation Science and Engineering*, *19*(4), 2738–2749. doi:10.1109/TASE.2021.3075773

Wang, L., Huang, X., Li, W., Yan, K., Han, Y., Zhang, Y., Pawlowski, L., & Lan, Y. (2022). Progress in Agricultural Unmanned Aerial Vehicles (UAVs) Applied in China and Prospects for Poland. *Agriculture*, *2022*(12), 397. doi:10.3390/agriculture12030397

Wang, L., Wang, K., Pan, C., Xu, W., Aslam, N., & Hanzo, L. (2020). Multi-agent deep reinforcement learning-based trajectory planning for multi-UAV assisted mobile edge computing. *IEEE Transactions on Cognitive Communications and Networking*, *7*(1), 73–84. doi:10.1109/TCCN.2020.3027695

Wang, L., Zhang, H., Guo, S., & Yuan, D. (2022). Deployment and association of multiple UAVs in UAV-assisted cellular networks with the knowledge of statistical user position. *IEEE Transactions on Wireless Communications*, *21*(8), 6553–6567. doi:10.1109/TWC.2022.3150429

Wang, X., Gursoy, M. C., Erpek, T., & Sagduyu, Y. E. (2022). Learning-based UAV path planning for data collection with integrated collision avoidance. *IEEE Internet of Things Journal*, *9*(17), 16663–16676. doi:10.1109/JIOT.2022.3153585

Ward, S., Hensler, J., Alsalam, B., & Gonzalez, L. F. (2016, March). Autonomous UAVs wildlife detection using thermal imaging, predictive navigation and computer vision. In 2016 IEEE aerospace conference. IEEE.

Warrier, R., Noon, B. R., & Bailey, L. (2020). Agricultural lands offer seasonal habitats to tigers in a human-dominated and fragmented landscape in India. *Ecosphere*, *11*(7), e03080. doi:10.1002/ecs2.3080

Waseem, M., Liang, P., & Shahin, M. (2020). A Systematic Mapping Study on Microservices Architecture in DevOps. *Journal of Systems and Software*, *170*, 110798. doi:10.1016/j.jss.2020.110798

Watanabe, K., Agarie, H., Aparatana, K., Mitsuoka, M., Taira, E., Ueno, M., & Kawamitsu, Y. (2022). Fundamental Study on Water Stress Detection in Sugarcane Using Thermal Image Combined with Photosynthesis Measurement Under a Greenhouse Condition. *Sugar Tech*, *24*(5), 1382–1390. doi:10.100712355-021-01087-y

Wawrla, L., & Maghazei, O. (2019). Applications of drones in warehouse operations. *ETH Zurich*.

Weinblum, N., Cna'Ani, A., Yaakov, B., Sadeh, A., Avraham, L., Opatovsky, I., & Tzin, V. (2021). Tomato cultivars resistant or susceptible to spider mites differ in their biosynthesis and metabolic profile of the monoterpenoid pathway. *Frontiers in Plant Science*, *12*, 630155. doi:10.3389/fpls.2021.630155 PMID:33719301

Whitfield, S., Challinor, A. J., & Rees, R. M. (2018). Frontiers in climate smart food systems: Outlining the research space. *Frontiers in Sustainable Food Systems*, *2*, 2. doi:10.3389/fsufs.2018.00002

Wiens, J., Saria, S., Sendak, M., Ghassemi, M., Liu, V. X., Doshi-Velez, F., Jung, K., Heller, K., Kale, D., Saeed, M., Ossorio, P. N., Thadaney-Israni, S., & Goldenberg, A. (2019). Do no harm: A roadmap for responsible machine learning for health care. *Nature Medicine*, *25*(9), 1337–1340. doi:10.103841591-019-0548-6 PMID:31427808

Wilke, N., Siegmann, B., Postma, J. A., Muller, O., Krieger, V., Pude, R., & Rascher, U. (2021). Assessment of plant density for barley and wheat using UAV multispectral imagery for high-throughput field phenotyping. *Computers and Electronics in Agriculture*, *189*, 106380. doi:10.1016/j.compag.2021.106380

Witharana, C., & Lynch, H. J. (2016). An object-based image analysis approach for detecting penguin guano in very high spatial resolution satellite images. *Remote Sensing (Basel)*, *8*(5), 375. doi:10.3390/rs8050375

Wittstruck, L., Kühling, I., Trautz, D., Kohlbrecher, M., & Jarmer, T. (2020). UAV-based RGB imagery for Hokkaido pumpkin (Cucurbita max.) detection and yield estimation. *Sensors (Basel)*, *21*(1), 118. doi:10.339021010118 PMID:33375474

Wokorach, G., Edema, H., & Echodu, R. (2018). Sweet potato seed exchange systems and knowledge on sweetpotato viral diseases among local farmers in Acholi Sub Region-Northern Uganda. *African Journal of Agricultural Research*, *13*(45). PMID:33282145

Wootton, R. (2008). Telemedicine support for the developing world. *Journal of Telemedicine and Telecare*, *14*(3), 109–114. doi:10.1258/jtt.2008.003001 PMID:18430271

Wu, E., Wang, H., Lu, H., Zhu, W., Jia, Y., Wen, L., Choi, C.-Y., Guo, H., Li, B., Sun, L., Lei, G., Lei, J., & Jian, H. (2022). Unlocking the Potential of Deep Learning for Migratory Waterbirds Monitoring Using Surveillance Video. *Remote Sensing (Basel)*, *14*(3), 514. doi:10.3390/rs14030514

Wu, G., Fan, M., Shi, J., & Feng, Y. (2023). Reinforcement Learning Based Truck-and-Drone Coordinated Delivery. *IEEE Transactions on Artificial Intelligence*, *4*(4), 754–763. doi:10.1109/TAI.2021.3087666 PMID:37954545

Wu, J., Li, D., Shi, J., Li, X., Gao, L., Yu, L., Han, G., & Wu, J. (2023). *An Adaptive Conversion Speed Q-Learning Algorithm for Search and Rescue UAV Path Planning in Unknown Environments. IEEE Transactions on Vehicular Technology*. IEEE.

Wu, K., Wang, H., Esfahani, M. A., & Yuan, S. (2020). Achieving real-time path planning in unknown environments through deep neural networks. *IEEE Transactions on Intelligent Transportation Systems*, *23*(3), 2093–2102. doi:10.1109/TITS.2020.3031962

Wu, S., Xu, W., Wang, F., Li, G., & Pan, M. (2022). Distributed federated deep reinforcement learning based trajectory optimization for air-ground cooperative emergency networks. *IEEE Transactions on Vehicular Technology*, *71*(8), 9107–9112. doi:10.1109/TVT.2022.3175592

Wu, X., Li, W., Hong, D., Tao, R., & Du, Q. (2021). Deep Learning for UAV-based Object Detection and Tracking. *Survey (London, England)*.

Xiao-rui, T., Mcrae, D. J., Li-fu, S., Ming-yu, W., & Hong, L. (2005). Satellite remote-sensing technologies used in forest fire management. *Journal of Forestry Research*, *16*(1), 73–78. doi:10.1007/BF02856861

Xu, J., Solmaz, G., Rahmatizadeh, R., Turgut, D., & Boloni, L. (2016). Internet of things applications: Animal monitoring with unmanned aerial vehicle. arXiv preprint arXiv:1610.05287.

Xu, B., Wang, W., Falzon, G., Kwan, P., Guo, L., Sun, Z., & Li, C. (2020). Livestock classification and counting in quadcopter aerial images using Mask R-CNN. *International Journal of Remote Sensing*, *41*(21), 8121–8142. doi:10.1080/01431161.2020.1734245

Xue, Y., & Chen, W. (2023). Multi-Agent Deep Reinforcement Learning for UAVs Navigation in Unknown Complex Environment. *IEEE Transactions on Intelligent Vehicles*, 1–14. doi:10.1109/TIV.2023.3298292

Xu, J., Solmaz, G., Rahmatizadeh, R., Boloni, L., & Turgut, D. (2018). Providing Distribution Estimation for Animal Tracking with Unmanned Aerial Vehicles. *2018 IEEE Global Communications Conference (GLOBECOM)*, (pp. 1–6). IEEE. 10.1109/GLOCOM.2018.8647784

XuJ.SolmazG.RahmatizadehR.TurgutD.BoloniL. (2016). Internet of Things Applications: Animal Monitoring with Unmanned Aerial Vehicle. arXiv. https://arxiv.org/abs/1610.05287

Xu, L., Cao, X., Du, W., & Li, Y. (2023). Cooperative path planning optimization for multiple UAVs with communication constraints. *Knowledge-Based Systems*, *260*, 110164. doi:10.1016/j.knosys.2022.110164

Xu, L., Sanders, L., Li, K., & Chow, J. C. (2021). Chatbot for health care and oncology applications using artificial intelligence and machine learning: Systematic review. *JMIR Cancer*, *7*(4), e27850. doi:10.2196/27850 PMID:34847056

Xu, S., Zhang, X., Li, C., Wang, D., & Yang, L. (2022). Deep Reinforcement Learning Approach for Joint Trajectory Design in Multi-UAV IoT Networks. *IEEE Transactions on Vehicular Technology*, *71*(3), 3389–3394. doi:10.1109/TVT.2022.3144277

Xu, Y., Wei, Y., Wang, D., Jiang, K., & Deng, H. (2023). Multi-UAV Path Planning in GPS and Communication Denial Environment. *Sensors (Basel)*, *23*(6), 2997. doi:10.339023062997 PMID:36991708

Yagnasree, S., & Jain, A. (2022). A Comprehensive Review of Emerging Technologies: Machine Learning and UAV in Crop Management. *Journal of Physics: Conference Series*.

Yan, C., & Xiang, X. (2018). A path planning algorithm for uav based on improved q-learning. *2018 2nd international conference on robotics and automation sciences (ICRAS)*. IEEE.

Yan, C., Xiang, X., & Wang, C. (2019). Towards Real-Time Path Planning through Deep Reinforcement Learning for a UAV in Dynamic Environments. *Journal of Intelligent & Robotic Systems*. doi:10.100710846-019-01073-3

Yang, P., Tang, K., Lozano, J. A., & Cao, X. (2015). *Path Planning for Single Unmanned Aerial Vehicle by Separately Evolving Waypoints. IEEE Transactions on Robotics*. IEEE.

Yang, Q., Shi, L., Han, J., Yu, J., & Huang, K. (2020). A near real-time deep learning approach for detecting rice phenology based on UAV images. *Agricultural and Forest Meteorology*, *287*, 107938. doi:10.1016/j.agrformet.2020.107938

Yang, T., Li, Z., Zhang, F., Xie, B., Li, J., & Liu, L. (2019). Panoramic UAV Surveillance and Recycling System Based on Structure-Free Camera Array. *IEEE Access : Practical Innovations, Open Solutions*, *7*, 25763–25778. doi:10.1109/ACCESS.2019.2900167

Yang, X., Hua, Z., Zhang, L., Zhang, L., Fan, X., Zhang, L., Ye, Q., & Fu, L. (2023). *Preferred vector machine for forest fire detection*. Institute of Forest Resource Information Techniques, Chinese Academy of Forestry. doi:10.1016/j.patcog.2023.109722

Yan, L., Ahmad, M. W., Jawarneh, M., Shabaz, M., Raffik, R., & Kishore, K. H. (2022). Single-Input Single-Output System with Multiple Time Delay PID Control Methods for UAV Cluster Multiagent Systems. *Security and Communication Networks*, *2022*, 2022. doi:10.1155/2022/3935143

Yao, H., Liu, Y., & Zhang, X. (2020). Developing deep LSTM model for real-time path planning in unknown environments. *2020 7th International Conference on Dependable Systems and Their Applications (DSA)*. IEEE.

Yao, H., Qin, R., & Chen, X. (2019). Unmanned aerial vehicle for remote sensing applications—A review. *Remote Sensing (Basel)*, *11*(12), 1443. doi:10.3390/rs11121443

Yijing, Z., Zheng, Z., Xiaoyi, Z., & Yang, L. (2017). Q learning algorithm based UAV path learning and obstacle avoidence approach. *2017 36th Chinese control conference (CCC)*. IEEE.

Yin, S., & Yu, F. R. (2022). Resource Allocation and Trajectory Design in UAV-Aided Cellular Networks Based on Multiagent Reinforcement Learning. *IEEE Internet of Things Journal*, 9(4), 2933–2943. doi:10.1109/JIOT.2021.3094651

Yoo, W., Yu, E., & Jung, J. (2018). Drone delivery: Factors affecting the public's attitude and intention to adopt. *Telematics and Informatics*, 35(6), 1687–1700. doi:10.1016/j.tele.2018.04.014

Yousefi, D. B. M., Rafie, A. S. M., Al-Haddad, S. A. R., & Azrad, S. (2022). A Systematic Literature Review on the Use of Deep Learning in Precision Livestock Detection and Localization Using Unmanned Aerial Vehicles. Institute of Electrical and Electronics Engineers Inc. doi:10.1109/ACCESS.2022.3194507

Yuan, C., Liu, Z. X., & Zhang, Y. M. (2017). Aerial images-based forest fire detection for firefighting using optical remote sensing techniques and unmanned aerial vehicles. *Journal of Intelligent & Robotic Systems*, 88(2-4), 635–654. doi:10.100710846-016-0464-7

Yuan, C., Liu, Z. X., & Zhang, Y. M. (2019). Learning-based smoke detection for unmanned aerial vehicles applied to forest fire surveillance. *Journal of Intelligent & Robotic Systems*, 93(1-2), 337–349. doi:10.100710846-018-0803-y

Yuan, C., Zhang, Y. M., & Liu, Z. X. (2015). A survey on technologies for automatic forest fire monitoring, detection, and fighting using unmanned aerial vehicles and remote sensing techniques. *Canadian Journal of Forest Research*, 45(7), 783–792. doi:10.1139/cjfr-2014-0347

Yuan, J., Liu, Z., Lian, Y., Chen, L., An, Q., Wang, L., & Ma, B. (2022). Global optimization of UAV area coverage path planning based on good point set and genetic algorithm. *Aerospace (Basel, Switzerland)*, 9(2), 86. doi:10.3390/aerospace9020086

Yuan, W., & Choi, D. (2021). UAV-Based heating requirement determination for frost management in apple orchard. *Remote Sensing (Basel)*, 13(2), 273. doi:10.3390/rs13020273

Yu, K. D. S., & Aviso, K. B. (2020). Modelling the economic impact and ripple effects of disease outbreaks. *Process Integration and Optimization for Sustainability*, 4(2), 183–186. doi:10.100741660-020-00113-y

Yu, L., Song, J., & Ermon, S. (2019). Multi-Agent Adversarial Inverse Reinforcement Learning. *Proceedings of the 36th International Conference on Machine Learning*. IEEE.

Yu, M., & Leung, H. (2023). Small-Object Detection for UAV-Based Images. *2023 IEEE International Systems Conference (SysCon)*, (pp.1–6). IEEE. 10.1109/SysCon53073.2023.10131084

Yu, R., Huo, L., Huang, H., Yuan, Y., Gao, B., Liu, Y., Yu, L., Li, H., Yang, L., Ren, L., & Luo, Y. (2022). Early detection of pine wilt disease tree candidates using time-series of spectral signatures. *Frontiers in Plant Science*, 13, 1000093. doi:10.3389/fpls.2022.1000093 PMID:36311089

Yu, Z., Si, Z., Li, X., Wang, D., & Song, H. (2022). A novel hybrid particle swarm optimization algorithm for path planning of UAVs. *IEEE Internet of Things Journal*, 9(22), 22547–22558.

Zeinab, E., Hasan, K., & Rashid, A. (2020). Optimizing Energy Consumption for Cloud Internet of Things. *Frontiers in Physics (Lausanne)*, 8, 2020. doi:10.3389/fphy.2020.00358

Zema, N., Natalizio, E., & Yanmaz, E. (2017). *An Unmanned Aerial Vehicle Network for Sport Event Filming with Communication Constraints* (p. 1731379). https://hal.science/hal-01731379/document

Zeng, Y., Zhang, R., & Lim, T. J. (2016). *Wireless Communications with Unmanned Aerial Vehicles: Opportunities and Challenges*. IEEE. doi:10.1109/MCOM.2016.7470933

Zeng, Y., Xu, X., & Zhang, R. (2018). Trajectory Design for Completion Time Minimization in UAV-Enabled Multicasting. *IEEE Transactions on Wireless Communications*, *17*(4), 2233–2246. doi:10.1109/TWC.2018.2790401

Zhang, J., Luo, X., Chen, C., Liu, Z., & Cao, S. (2014). A Wildlife Monitoring System Based on Wireless Image Sensor Networks. In *Sensors & Transducers, 180*. http://www.sensorsportal.com

Zhang, K., Yang, Z., & Başar, T. (2021b). Multi-agent reinforcement learning: A selective overview of theories and algorithms. Handbook of reinforcement learning and control, (pp. 321-384). University of Illnois.

Zhang, Q. J., Xu, J. L., Xu, L., & Guo, H. F. (2016). Deep convolutional neural networks for forest fire detection. In *2016 International Forum on Management, Education and Information Technology Application*. Atlantis Press. 10.2991/ifmeita-16.2016.105

Zhan, G., Zhang, X., Li, Z., Xu, L., Zhou, D., & Yang, Z. (2022). Multiple-UAV Reinforcement Learning Algorithm Based on Improved PPO in Ray Framework. *Drones (Basel)*, *6*(7), 166. doi:10.3390/drones6070166

Zhang, H., Shao, F., He, X., Zhang, Z., Cai, Y., & Bi, S. (2023). Research on Object Detection and Recognition Method for UAV Aerial Images Based on Improved YOLOv5. *Drones (Basel)*, *7*(6), 6. doi:10.3390/drones7060402

Zhang, J., & Huang, H. (2021). Occlusion-Aware UAV Path Planning for Reconnaissance and Surveillance. *Drones (Basel)*, *5*(3), 98. doi:10.3390/drones5030098

Zhang, J., Zhang, J., Du, X., Kang, H., & Qiao, M. (2017). An overview of ecological monitoring based on geographic information system (GIS) and remote sensing (RS) technology in China. *IOP Conference Series. Earth and Environmental Science*, *94*, 012056. doi:10.1088/1755-1315/94/1/012056

Zhang, K., Yang, Z., & Başar, T. (2021). *Multi-Agent Reinforcement Learning: A Selective Overview of Theories and Algorithms.*, doi:10.1007/978-3-030-60990-0_12

Zhang, K., Yang, Z., & Başar, T. (2021a). Decentralized multi-agent reinforcement learning with networked agents: Recent advances. *Frontiers of Information Technology & Electronic Engineering*, *22*(6), 802–814. doi:10.1631/FITEE.1900661

Zhang, M., Xiong, Y., Ng, S. X., & El-Hajjar, M. (2023). Deployment of Energy-Efficient Aerial Communication Platforms With Low-Complexity Detection. *IEEE Transactions on Vehicular Technology*, *72*(9), 12016–12030. doi:10.1109/TVT.2023.3263275

Zhang, T., Yang, Z., Xu, Z., & Li, J. (2022). Wheat yellow rust severity detection by efficient DF-UNet and UAV multispectral imagery. *IEEE Sensors Journal*, *22*(9), 9057–9068. doi:10.1109/JSEN.2022.3156097

Zhang, X., Han, L., Dong, Y., Shi, Y., Huang, W., Han, L., González-Moreno, P., Ma, H., Ye, H., & Sobeih, T. (2019). A deep learning-based approach for automated yellow rust disease detection from high-resolution hyperspectral UAV images. *Remote Sensing (Basel)*, *11*(13), 1554. doi:10.3390/rs11131554

Zhang, Y., Song, C., & Zhang, D. (2020). Deep learning-based object detection improvement for tomato disease. *IEEE Access : Practical Innovations, Open Solutions*, *8*, 56607–56614. doi:10.1109/ACCESS.2020.2982456

Zhao, C., Liu, J., Sheng, M., Teng, W., Zheng, Y., & Li, J. (2021). Multi-UAV trajectory planning for energy-efficient content coverage: A decentralized learning-based approach. *IEEE Journal on Selected Areas in Communications*, *39*(10), 3193–3207. doi:10.1109/JSAC.2021.3088669

Zhao, H., Wang, H., Wu, W., & Wei, J. (2018). Deployment algorithms for UAV airborne networks toward on-demand coverage. *IEEE Journal on Selected Areas in Communications*, *36*(9), 2015–2031. doi:10.1109/JSAC.2018.2864376

Zhao, J., Zhang, J., Li, D., & Wang, D. (2022). Vision-Based Anti-UAV Detection and Tracking. *IEEE Transactions on Intelligent Transportation Systems*, *23*(12), 25323–25334. doi:10.1109/TITS.2022.3177627

Zhao, N., Liu, Z., & Cheng, Y. (2020). Multi-Agent Deep Reinforcement Learning for Trajectory Design and Power Allocation in Multi-UAV Networks. *IEEE Access : Practical Innovations, Open Solutions*, *8*, 139670–139679. doi:10.1109/ACCESS.2020.3012756

Zhao, S., Wang, W., Li, J., Huang, S., & Liu, S. (2023). Autonomous Navigation of the UAV through Deep Reinforcement Learning with Sensor Perception Enhancement. *Mathematical Problems in Engineering*, *2023*, e3837615. doi:10.1155/2023/3837615

Zhao, X. H., Zhang, J. C., Tang, A. L., Yu, Y. F., Yan, L. J., Chen, D. M., & Yuan, L. (2022). The stress detection and segmentation strategy in tea plant at canopy level. *Frontiers in Plant Science*, *13*, 9054. doi:10.3389/fpls.2022.949054 PMID:35873976

Zheng, H. (2022). Ant Colony Optimization Based UAV Path Planning for Autonomous Agricultural Spraying. *2022 IEEE 5th International Conference on Automation, Electronics and Electrical Engineering (AUTEEE)*. IEEE.

Zheng, H., Cheng, T., Li, D., Yao, X., Tian, Y., Cao, W., & Zhu, Y. (2018). Combining unmanned aerial vehicle (UAV)-based multispectral imagery and ground-based hyperspectral data for plant nitrogen concentration estimation in rice. *Frontiers in Plant Science*, *9*, 936. doi:10.3389/fpls.2018.00936 PMID:30034405

Zheng, J., Fu, H., Li, W., Wu, W., Yu, L., Yuan, S., Tao, W. Y. W., Pang, T. K., & Kanniah, K. D. (2021). Growing status observation for oil palm trees using unmanned aerial vehicle (UAV) images. *ISPRS Journal of Photogrammetry and Remote Sensing*, *173*, 95–121. doi:10.1016/j.isprsjprs.2021.01.008

Zhong, J., Li, M., Qin, J., Cui, Y., Yang, K., & Zhang, H. (2022). Real-time marine animal detection using yolo-based deep learning networks in the coral reef ecosystem. *International Archives of the Photogrammetry, Remote Sensing and Spatial Information Sciences - ISPRS Archives, 46*(3/W1-2022), 301–306. ISPRS. doi:10.5194/isprs-archives-XLVI-3-W1-2022-301-2022

Zhou, S., Cheng, Y., & Lei, X. (2022). Model-Based Machine Learning for Energy-Efficient UAV Placement. *2022 7th International Conference on Computer and Communication Systems (ICCCS)*. IEEE.

Zhou, Z., Diverres, G., Kang, C., Thapa, S., Karkee, M., Zhang, Q., & Keller, M. J. A. (2022). Ground-based thermal imaging for assessing crop water status in grapevines over a growing season. *Agronomy, 12*(2), 322. https://doi.org/10.3390/agronomy12020322

Zhu, C., Zheng, Y., Luu, K., & Savvides, M. (2017). CMS-RCNN: Contextual Multi-Scale Region-Based CNN for Unconstrained Face Detection. In B. Bhanu & A. Kumar (Eds.), *Deep Learning for Biometrics* (pp. 57–79). Springer International Publishing. doi:10.1007/978-3-319-61657-5_3

Zou, Y., Mason, M. G., & Botella, J. R. (2020). Evaluation and improvement of isothermal amplification methods for point-of-need plant disease diagnostics. *PLoS One, 15*(6), e0235216. doi:10.1371/journal.pone.0235216 PMID:32598374

Zviedris, R., Elsts, A., Strazdins, G., Mednis, A., & Selavo, L. (2010). LynxNet: Wild Animal Monitoring Using Sensor Networks, (pp. 170–173). Springer. doi:10.1007/978-3-642-17520-6_18

About the Contributors

Jahan Hassan is a Senior Lecturer at the School of Engineering and Technology, Central Queensland University, Australia. She earned her PhD from the University of New South Wales (Sydney, Australia), and her Bachelor degree from Monash University (Australia), both in Computer Science. Dr Hassan has dedicated her work to developing unmanned aerial vehicle (UAV) networks for various applications, with a focus on improving efficiency and effective communication among UAVs. Her work has utilized advanced machine learning algorithms to optimize UAV movement and energy usage based on experience. Additionally, she has explored in-flight UAV recharging methods, using energy sources in the air. She is an Area Editor for Elsevier Ad Hoc Networks journal. She has served as Guest Editor for IEEE Communications Magazine, IEEE Network, Elsevier Ad Hoc Networks, and MDPI Drones. Dr Hassan is a Senior Member of the IEEE.

Saeed Hamood Alsamhi received the B.Eng. degree from the Department of Electronic Engineering (Communication Division), IBB University, Yemen, in 2009, and the M.Tech. degree in communication systems and a Ph.D. degree from the Department of Electronics Engineering, Indian Institute of Technology (Banaras Hindu University), IIT (BHU), Varanasi, India, in 2012 and 2015. In 2009, he worked as a Lecturer Assistant in the Engineering faculty at IBB University. Afterwards, he held a postdoctoral position with the School of Aerospace Engineering, Tsinghua University, Beijing, China, in optimal and smart wireless network research and its applications to enhance robotics technologies. Since 2019, he has been an Assistant Professor at Shenzhen Institutes of Advanced Technology, Chinese Academy of Sciences, Shenzhen. In 2020, he worked as MSCA SMART 4.0 FELLOW at Athlone Institute of Technology, Athlone, Ireland. He is currently Senior Research Fellow at Insight Centre for Data Analytics, University of Galway, Ireland. He has published more than 160 articles in high-reputation journals in IEEE, Elsevier, Springer, Wiley, etc. publishers. His areas of interest include green and semantic communication, green Internet of Things, QoE, QoS, multi-robot collaboration, blockchain technology, federated learning, and space technologies (high altitude platforms, drones, and tethered balloon technologies).

***

Rizwan Ahmad is a Professor and Head of Research at the School of Electrical Engineering and Computer Science (SEECS), National University of Sciences and Technology (NUST), Islamabad - Pakistan. He earned his PhD from Victoria University, Australia in 2010 and his MS from the University of Stuttgart, Germany in 2004. From 2010 to 2012, he was a Postdoctoral Research Fellow at Qatar University, Doha, Qatar, on a QNRF Grant. His research interests include public safety networks, UAV-assisted networks, WBANs, medium access control protocols, spectrum and energy efficiency, energy harvesting, and performance analysis for wireless communication and networks.

Waqas Ahmed mad received the Ph.D. degree in electrical engineering from Victoria University, Melbourne, VIC, Australia, in 2012. He is currently a Professor with the Department of Electrical Engineering, Pakistan Institute of Engineering and Applied Sciences, Islamabad, Pakistan. His research interests include cognitive radios, cooperative communication, and physical layer aspects of wireless communication and networks.

Zeinab E. Ahmed received her Ph.D. in Computer Engineering and Networks from the University of Gezira, Sudan. Dr. Zeinab has been working as an assistant professor in the Department of Computer Engineering at the University of Gezira, Sudan since June 2020. Currently, she is working as a postdoc fellow at the Department of Electrical and Computer Engineering, International Islamic University Malaysia, Malaysia. I've been engaged in some projects related to the field of computer engineering and networks. She has published more than eight research papers and book chapters on networking in peer-reviewed academic venues. Her areas of research interest are wireless communication networks. An experienced lecturer with a demonstrated history of working in the higher education industry. She is skilled in research, e-learning, programming, and lecturing.

Ajakwe Ihunanya Udodiri received her Master of Science in Biochemistry from Federal University of Technology, Owerri, Nigeria in 2020. Prior to this, she obtained her Bachelor of Science Degree in Biochemistry from Imo State University, Owerri. She is a member of Nigerian Society of Biochemistry and Molecular Biology. Her research interest cuts across environmental toxicology, bioinformatics, environmental health, occupational health and safety, health education, etc.

Simeon Okechukwu Ajakwe received his Ph.D. degree in IT-Convergence Engineering from Kumoh National Institute of Technology (KIT), Gumi, South Korea in 2023. From 2020 to 2023, he worked as a scholar and full-time researcher at Networked System Laboratory (NSL), KIT, South Korea. Also, between 2019-2023, he worked as a lecturer with Federal University of Technology, Owerri, Nigeria in the Department of Software Engineering. Currently, he is a postdoctoral researcher with Wireless System Laboratory (WSL), Hanyang University, Seoul, South Korea. Simeon is a Chartered Information Technology Professional (Citp) with many years of IT-related industrial and academic experience. He is a member of IEEE, the Association of Computing Machinery (ACM), Computer Professionals of Nigeria (CPN), and the Nigeria Computer Society (NCS). Simeon is a reviewer of different reputable peer-reviewed journals, published several articles and conference papers, and has won different awards. His research interest cut across Anti-drone surveillance systems, drone technologies, Real-time and embedded systems, Artificial Intelligence, Deep Learning, Software Engineering, Information Systems, and Security.

Sumedha Arora is a highly accomplished professional with a Ph.D. in Computer Science and Engineering from Thapar University, Patiala, showcasing her dedication to advancing the field of technology. Her research interests encompass a broad spectrum, including cloud computing, energy efficiency, data centers, Big Data, Machine Learning, Internet of Things, and Data Analytics. Her exceptional academic journey was recognized with a Senior Research Fellowship (SRF) from the Council of Scientific and

Industrial Research (CSIR), Government of India. Dr. Sumedha holds an M.Tech degree in Big Data from Guru Nanak Dev University, Amritsar, and a B.Tech degree from PTU. Her contributions to the academic community extend beyond research, as she has also served as an Assistant Professor at Jaypee University of Information Technology, Waknaghat, and Chandigarh University. Currently, she is sharing her expertise as a visiting faculty member in Digital University Kerala, further enriching the field of computer science and engineering. Dr. Sumedha has also made significant contributions to the academic discourse with her published papers in prestigious journals and conferences.

Sanoufar Azeez is an accomplished MTech graduate with a diverse career spanning the globe. With extensive experience as a Product Manager and Research Scientist, Sanoufar has played pivotal roles in shaping digital transformation and consumer products in regions such as Asia Pacific, the Middle East, Europe, and North America.

Ram Bahadur Khadka received BS in agriculture in 2007 and MS in agriculture with Plant Pathology from Tribhuvan University, Institute of Agricultural and Animal Sciences, Rampur in 2009 and completed Ph.D. in Plant Pathology at The Ohio State University - Department of Plant Pathology under Dr. Sally Miller's supervision. Currently, he is working as a Scientist at Nepal Agricultural Research Council (NARC) – National Plant Pathology Research Center, Lalitpur, Nepal. His research programs include basic and applied aspects of plant pathology with the aim to improve national capacity in plant disease management. He uses various conventional omics, and machine learning tools to detect diseases, characterize pathogens, predict and forecast diseases; and develop strategies to manage them in a sustainable manner. His major specializations include soilborne diseases, diagnosing pathogens, and forecasting plant diseases. Ram will lead the overall implementation of the project in Nepal including supervision of MS and PhD students, run metagenomic study, organizing meetings, and workshops, and coordinating and collaborating with different stakeholders in project implementation

Opeyemi Deji-Oloruntoba received a Bachelor of Science in Biochemistry from the University of Ado-Ekiti Nigeria in 2003 and a Master of Technology from the Federal University of Technology Akure Nigeria with a distinction in Food Science and Technology, Akure Nigeria in 2012. She is currently pursuing a Ph.D. degree in Smart foods and Drug Biotechnology at Inje University, South Korea. She is a Part-time researcher with the Institute of Antioxidant and Antiaging. She is a member of the Nigerian Institute of Food Science and Technology (NIFST). Her research interests cut across Smart food solutions, Biotechnology, Antioxidants, and C.elegans models for biomedical research, and diabetic research. She is an ardent advocate for the sustainable development goals

Arefeh Esmaili is currently a PhD candidate in in Computer Engineering at Tarbiat Modares University. She is interested in using cooperative multi-agent reinforcement learning algorithms for addressing complex problems in real-world environments.

Nkechi Faustina Esomonu, a member of NCS and NIWIIT, attained her Bachelor's degree in Mathematics/Computer Science from the Federal University of Technology, Owerri, Nigeria, in 2004. She went on to achieve a Master of Science in Applied Mathematics from the same institution in 2012, followed by a Master of Science in Information Technology in 2015. Currently, she is actively pursuing a Ph.D. in Information Technology from the Federal University of Technology, Owerri, Nigeria. Nkechi serves as an Assistant Lecturer in the field of Information Technology at the Federal University of Technology, Owerri, Nigeria. She boasts extensive experience as a System Analyst/Programmer within the realm of Information and Communication Technology (ICTC) at the same institution. Her research pursuits encompass a wide array of topics including Artificial Intelligence, deep learning, machine learning, operations research, and data analysis.

Jaime Galán-Jiménez received his Ph.D. in Computer Science and Communications from the University of Extremadura (Spain) in 2014. He is currently working at the Department of Computer Systems and Telematics Engineering of the University of Extremadura (Spain) as an associate professor. During the past years, he has spent several research and teaching periods at University of Rome Tor Vergata (2018), and at University of Rome La Sapienza (2015), Italy. His main research interests are Software-Defined Networks, machine learning applied to networking, UAV-based 5G networks planning and design, 5G provisioning in rural and low-income areas and optimization of QoS in IoT Networks.

Santiago García Gil is a researcher currently working at University of Extremadura. He has a Bachelor's degree in Software Engineering and is currently pursuing a Master's degree in Computer Engineering, both at the University of Extremadura. His current line of research focuses on the development of mechanisms and systems that improve the feasibility of using UAVs and UAV swarms as network infrastructure by reducing latency.

José Antonio Gómez de la Hiz is a researcher currently working at University of Extremadura. He has a Bachelor's degree in Computer Engineering at University of Extremadura and is currently pursuing a Master's degree in Cybersecutiry Engineering at the International University of La Rioja. His current line of research focuses on the development of mechanisms and systems that improve the feasibility of using UAVs and UAV swarms as network infrastructure by maximizing throughput.

Aisha-Hassan is with the Department of Electrical and Computer Engineering, International Islamic University Malaysia, Kuala Lumpur, Malaysia.

Ali Hassan is currently doing PhD in Electrical Engineering from the National University of Sciences and Technology (NUST), Pakistan. He received a BSEE degree in telecommunication and electronics from The University of Lahore, Pakistan in 2018 and MS degree in Electrical Engineering from the National University of Sciences and Technology, Pakistan in 2018. He received a certificate of excellence for achieving academic excellence in Bachelor of Science in Electrical Engineering in the Session Fall 2014. His research interests include Software-defined networking, Blockchain, energy Harvesting, the Internet of Things, and public safety and critical networks.

Sadaf Javed received B.Sc. degree in Electrical Engineering from Mirpur University of Science & Technology (MUST), Azad Kashmir, Pakistan in 2018, MS in Electrical Engineering from National University of Science & Technology (NUST), Islamabad, Pakistan in 2021, and currently doing PhD in Electrical Engineering from National University of Science & Technology (NUST), Islamabad, Pakistan. Her research interests include UAVs, Block-chain, energy Harvesting, Internet of things, Security, public safety networks, cooperative communication networks.

Dong-Seong Kim received his Ph.D. degree in Electrical and Computer Engineering from the Seoul National University, Seoul, Korea, in 2003. From 1994 to 2003, he worked as a full-time researcher in ERC-ACI at Seoul National University, Seoul, Korea. From March 2003 to February 2005, he worked as a postdoctoral researcher at the Wireless Network Laboratory in the School of Electrical and Computer Engineering at Cornell University, NY. From 2007 to 2009, he was a visiting professor with the Department of Computer Science, University of California, Davis, CA. He is currently a director of KIT Convergence Research Institute and ICT Convergence Research Center (ITRC and NRF advanced research center program) supported by the Korean government at Kumoh National Institute of Technology. He is a senior member of IEEE and ACM. His current main research interests are real-time IoT and smart platforms, industrial wireless control networks, networked embedded systems and Fieldbus.

Jae-Min Lee received his Ph.D degree in electrical and computer engineering from the Seoul National University, Seoul, Korea, in 2005. From 2005 to 2014, he was a Senior Engineer with Samsung Electronics, Suwon, Korea. From 2015 to 2016, he was a Principal Engineer at Samsung Electronics, Suwon, Korea. Since 2017, he has been an assistant professor with the School of Electronic Engineering and Department of IT-Convergence Engineering, Kumoh National Institute of Technology, Gyeongbuk, Korea. He is a member of IEEE. His current main research interests are industrial wireless control networks, performance analysis of wireless networks, and TRIZ.

Anand M. is a Research Scholar at the Department of Computing Technologies, SRM Institute of Science and Technology, Kattankulathur, India. His research focuses on Machine Learning, Deep Learning, Image Processing, IOT, and Cloud Computing. He has completed his M.E Computer Science and Engineering from Anna University, Chennai, India. He has 6+ years of teaching and industry experience.

Arjun Neupane received the Bachelor of Computer Application degree from Pokhara University, MIT, Nepal, the Ph.D. degree in information systems from the University of Southern Queensland (UniSQ), Australia, the Graduate Certificate in higher education from Griffith University, and the Graduate Certificate in data science from the University of Queensland, Australia. He is currently a Lecturer with ICT, CQUniversity, Rockhampton, Australia. His main research interests include information systems, data science, machine learning, deep learning, AI, and image processing. He is interested in applying IT to solve real-world problems in different domains. He is a member and a Certified Professional of the Australian Computer Society

Nahla Nurelmadina holds an M.Sc. degree in Electronics Engineering with a specialization in Telecommunication, which she achieved in 2013, along with a B.Sc. (Honors) degree in Electronics Engineering with a similar specialization, which she completed in 2007. Her academic path is enriched by substantial professional experiences. Between 2013 and 2014, she took on the role of a lecturer at the Future University's Department of Telecommunications and Space Technology in Khartoum, Sudan. Afterward, she continued her teaching career at Taibah University's Department of Computer Science and Engineering, where she taught from 2014 until 2020, located in Saudi Arabia. As of 2023, she is actively engaged in part-time teaching at Safat College of Science and Technology within the Department of IT in Khartoum, Sudan. Furthermore, she is deeply involved in research and has made noteworthy contributions to peer-reviewed academic international journals, primarily through the publication of papers . Her research interests encompass a wide range of topics, including mobile wireless networks,

IoT (Internet of Things), and the intersection of machine learning with computer networks. Currently, she is pursuing her Ph.D. program at Alzaiem Alazhari University, specifically within the Faculty of Electrical Engineering's Department of Communications Engineering in Khartoum, Sudan.

Shams Qazi has more than 10 years of teaching and research experience in "Network and Computer Security" with Phd in the field of Wireless Network Security from University of Wollongong, Australia.

Diego Ramos Ramos is a researcher currently working at University of Extremadura. He has a Bachelor's degree in Software Engineering and is currently pursuing a Master's degree in Computer Engineering, both at the University of Extremadura. His current line of research focuses on the development of mechanisms and systems that improve the feasibility of using UAVs and UAV swarms as network infrastructure by improving energy efficiency.

Raffik Rasheed received his B.E. degree in Mechatronics Engineering from Kongu Engineering College, and his M.E. degree in Mechatronics Engineering from Anna University, Chennai. He is pursuing his doctoral research programme in Robotics field from 2019 at Anna University, Chennai. He is currently working as an Assistant Professor in the Department of Mechatronics Engineering, Kumaraguru College of Technology, Coimbatore. He has over 12 years of teaching experience and 4 years of research experience. He had published more than 50 papers in Scopus-indexed journals and WOS journals. He presented more than 15 papers at International and National conferences. His current research interests include Robotics, Industrial Automation, Applied Hydraulics and Pneumatics, Unmanned Aerial Vehicles and Machine Vision.

Mehdy Roayaei received his B.S., M.S., and Ph.D. in Computer Engineering from Amirkabir University of Technology (AUT) in 2008, 2010, 2016. He is currently an Assistant Professor of Computer Engineering at Tarbiat Modares University. He is interested in using reinforcement learning approaches for handling complex problems in real-world environments.

Ahsan Saadat is currently working as an assistant professor at the School of Electrical Engineering and Computer Science, NUST, Islamabad. Dr Ahsan completed his Ph.D. from Macquarie University Sydney, Australia, in 2017 and has worked in multiple Australian universities. Prior to Ph.D., he completed his MS in Electrical Engineering from NUST in 2013 and BS in Computer Engineering from COMSATS in 2009, where he secured two gold medals. His research interests include applied machine learning and game theory.

Mamoon Mohammed Ali Saeed is Deputy Dean of the College of Engineering and Information Technology, and Director of the University Branch, and a Lecturer at the Department of Communication and Electronics Engineering, UMS University, Yemen. received his Bachelor degree in Communication and Electronics Engineering from Sana'a University, Yemen 2005, the M.S. degree at department of Computer Networks and Information Security in Yemen Academy for Graduate Studies Yemen 2013. Recently, a Ph.D in Alzaiem Alazhari University, Faculty of Engineering, Electrical Engineering Department, Khartoum, Sudan 2021. His research areas include information security, communication security, and network security.

Rashid A. Saeed received his Ph.D. in Communications and Network Engineering, Universiti Putra Malaysia (UPM). Currently, he is a professor in Computer Engineering Department, Taif University. He was working in the Electronics Department, Sudan University of Science and Technology (SUST). He was a senior researcher in Telekom Malaysia™ Research and Development (TMRND) and MIMOS. Rashid published more than 150 research papers, books, and book chapters on wireless communications and networking in peer-reviewed academic journals and conferences. His areas of research interest include a computer network, cognitive computing, computer engineering, wireless broadband, WiMAX Femtocell. He is successfully awarded 3 U.S patents in these areas. He supervised more than 50 MSc/Ph.D. students. Rashid is a Senior Member of IEEE, Member in IEM (I.E.M), SigmaXi, and SEC.

Tej Bahadur Shah is an assistant professor, at Central Department of Computer Science and IT, Tribhuvan University (TU), Kathmandu Nepal and currently on study leave to pursue his PhD in computer science at CQ University, Australia. Prior to joining Tribhuvan University in 2017, he worked as a Computer Officer for Nepal Government from 2014 to 2017. He graduated with BSc and M.Sc. CSIT both with Gold Medals form TU in 2005 and 2012 respectively. He skilled in natural language processing for Nepali language, drone-based image processing and deep learning. His research interest includes application of machine learning for precision agriculture with a focus on drone-based remote sensing. He is a member of IEEE.

Index

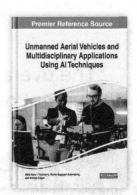

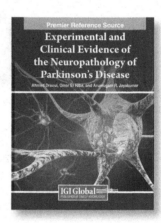
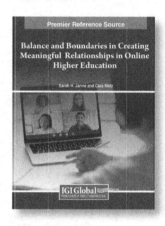

Submit an Open Access Book Proposal

Have Your Work Fully & Freely Available Worldwide After Publication

Seeking the Following Book Classification Types:

Authored & Edited Monographs • Casebooks • Encyclopedias • Handbooks of Research

Gold, Platinum, & Retrospective OA Opportunities to Choose From

Easily Track Your Work in Our Advanced Manuscript Submission System With **Rapid Turnaround Times**

Double-Blind Peer Review by Notable Editorial Boards (*Committee on Publication Ethics* (COPE) Certified

Publications Adhere to All **Current OA Mandates & Compliances**

Affordable APCs *(Often 50% Lower Than the Industry Average)* Including Robust Editorial Service Provisions

Direct Connections with **Prominent Research Funders** & OA Regulatory Groups

Institution Level OA Agreements Available (Recommend or Contact Your Librarian for Details)

Join a **Diverse Community of 150,000+ Researchers Worldwide** Publishing With IGI Global

Content Spread Widely to Leading Repositories (AGOSR, ResearchGate, CORE, & More)

? Retrospective Open Access Publishing

You Can Unlock Your Recently Published Work, Including Full Book & Individual Chapter Content to Enjoy All the Benefits of Open Access Publishing

Learn More

Printed in the United States
by Baker & Taylor Publisher Services